D1154022

CAMBRIDGE SOUTH ASIAN STUDIES

# THE HOLLOW CROWN

Engraving of Raja Ramachandra Tondaiman by F.C. Lewis 1853
**(British Library)**

# THE HOLLOW CROWN

## Ethnohistory of an Indian kingdom

### NICHOLAS B. DIRKS

The right of the
University of Cambridge
to print and sell
all manner of books
was granted by
Henry VIII in 1534.
The University has printed
and published continuously
since 1584.

## CAMBRIDGE UNIVERSITY PRESS

CAMBRIDGE

NEW YORK   NEW ROCHELLE

MELBOURNE   SYDNEY

Published by the Press Syndicate of the University of Cambridge
The Pitt Building, Trumpington Street, Cambridge CB2 1RP
32 East 57 Street, New York, NY 10022, USA
10 Stamford Road, Oakleigh, Melbourne 3166, Australia

First published 1987

Printed in Great Britain at the University Press, Cambridge

*British Library cataloguing in publication data*
Dirks, Nicholas B.
The hollow crown: ethnohistory of an Indian kingdom. –
(Cambridge South Asian studies)
1. Ethnology – India, South
2. India, South – Social life and customs
I. Title
306'.0954'8   GN635.I4

*Library of Congress cataloguing in publication data*
Dirks, Nicholas B., 1950–
The hollow crown.
(Cambridge South Asian Studies)
Bibliography.
Includes index.
1. Pudukkottai (Princely State) – History.
2. Ethnology – India – Pudukkottai (Princely State)
I. Title.  II. Series.
DS485.P83D57  1987  954'.82  86–24431

ISBN 0 521 32604 4

TM

For God's sake let us sit upon the ground
And tell sad stories of the death of kings:
How some have been deposed, some slain in war,
Some haunted by the ghosts they have deposed,
Some poisoned by their wives, some sleeping killed,
All murdered – for within the hollow crown
That rounds the mortal temples of a king
Keeps Death his court, and there the antic sits,
Scoffing his state and grinning at his pomp,
Allowing him a breath, a little scene,
To monarchize, be feared, and kill with looks,
Infusing him with self and vain conceit,
As if this flesh which walls about our life
Were brass impregnable; and, humoured thus,
Comes at the last, and with a little pin
Bores through his castle wall, and farewell king!

Shakespeare, *Richard II*

The heavens shower rain; the earth bears grain; why should I pay for my land?
Do you collect tax to command the elements? Does rain shower at your
command?

Tamil Folk Ballad, words spoken by Kattapomman to
British Collector shortly before Kattapomman's defeat and death

If one tries to erect a theory of power one will always be obliged to view it as
emerging at a given place and time and hence to deduce it, to reconstruct its
genesis. But if power is in reality an open, more or less coordinated (in the event,
no doubt, ill-coordinated) cluster of relations then the only problem is to provide
oneself with a grid of analysis which makes possible an analytic of relations of
power.

Michel Foucault

# Contents

## Contents

# Illustrations

## Figures

## Plates

# Maps

# Tables

# Preface

During my fieldwork in Pudukkottai, one of my principal teachers, informants, consultants, and friends was a Brahman who was the retired head clerk of the Settlement Office. Known by his acronym PMS, he was the descendant of a family of srotriya or learned Brahmans who had been settled on fertile lands in Pudukkottai state in the late eighteenth century by the Tondaiman Raja of the time. But PMS himself was a laukika or secular Brahman, educated in Shakespeare and British history at St Joseph's College, Trichy. He was initially employed by the Darbar of the Pudukkottai state, where for a long time his immediate boss was a mythic hero of late colonial times, a former ICS man named Alexander Tottenham who spent his retirement as head administrator of a state that until 1944 was ruled by a minor. After independence, or merger as it is called in Pudukkottai, PMS guided the completion of the Inam Settlement until his retirement from Government service in 1957. An honest bureaucrat and a true scholar, he was later helpful to academics and others who would come through Pudukkottai and stay for a time as guests of the royal family. He had helped me during my initial stay in the place years earlier, and he agreed to work with me again when I returned in 1981 for intensive fieldwork. But when I first arrived he was hard to track down; despite his poverty he refused to enter into any contractual arrangement, and aside from allowing me to pick up the tab for coffee, dosai, and bus trips, refused all payment. In the first few weeks he told me that he could not accept payment because he could not countenance being paid for simply sharing what he knew about the history, land system, and ethnology of Pudukkottai: after all, this was the love of his life, and to sell his knowledge would be to prostitute his most valued treasure. He secured my dependence on him, however, dragging me around as if I were a new and even more valued treasure to visit all of his relatives and friends, and resisting my attempts to find other learned citizens who might help me with old records and texts, even though his own eyes were failing and he was increasingly unable to read the eighteenth-century palm leafs I was myself often incapable of deciphering. He also disappeared periodically, making the point whenever I seemed to take him for granted that he was, still, a free agent.

But as time went on and he became a more regular, though I might add difficult and now virtually blind, companion, I was troubled by my growing sense of "debt" and so persisted in my attempt to work out an acceptable form of remuneration.

One day when we were stranded in my leaky Standard Herald on the side of the Tanjavur road during a particularly virulent outburst of the northeast monsoon, I handed him an envelope full of wads of rupees and told him this was a gift, a dana. He took it and told me the following story. Some years before the Maharaja (who ever since the amalgamation of the state has lived outside its former borders in the family's mock gothic palace in the Trichy cantonment, tinkering in a large machine shop with old engines) called PMS to attend upon him. There was a problem with some of the lands belonging to the royal family, and PMS was asked to find the relevant records and prepare a brief for the family lawyer, who was himself unable to use the old land records of the state. PMS happily did what he was asked, and when he had completed his services the Raja called him over and asked him to take a 100 rupee note. PMS refused to accept it, saying "O Maharaja, how can I accept payment from you when you are my king?" The Tondaiman prince, puzzled to see an obviously poor man refuse the money, asked him why he stood on ceremony since he himself was no longer a Maharaja and these were no longer the days of rajadharma. PMS replied first by quoting Shakespeare, "Not all the waters of the rough rude sea can wash away the balm from an anointed king" (thereby sanctioning in an indirect sense my taking the title of this book from *Richard II*) and then by telling the king what he meant to tell me by the recitation of the story: for services that involve my knowledge, I accept no payment. But of course this was not wholly true, for PMS had spent his life accepting payment for the exercise of his knowledge, and much of his earning life had been under the rajiyam of pre-colonial Pudukkottai. And, indeed, PMS ultimately accepted a gift of money from the king, as he accepted gifts of money from me. Labelled dana rather than campalam, or salary, gifts – whether in kind or cash – were okay. But I believe that it was in fact both more exalting and more difficult for PMS to accept gifts from the puzzled monarch than from me, and in turn more difficult to accept from me than from lawyers and local citizens when he helped them trace their land records as he often did. I was subsequently annoyed on more than one occasion to observe this, as for example when he held up the receipt from the BBC for 500 rupees which he had signed after spending three weeks doing all the work for a camera crew trying to film the construction and consecration of a clay horse made by local potters for the protection deity, Aiyanar. I might add that I was particularly annoyed because the AIIS refused to reimburse research expenses under the category of gift precisely because there were no signed receipts. To quote Rabelais, such is the nature of the gratuitous.

PMS would accept dana from the king rather than campalam because a dana is "freely given," without expectation of a return. It is not that he did not want to give a return – he offered it to begin with – but rather that he felt that the transaction of salary demeaned his offering, rendering it, too, less than freely given. PMS also meant to say that even a king could not control him by contract, and that in any case as a loyal subject he had no need to be controlled, thus recapitulating the conundrum of the Brahman's relation with the king. From this chance remark, indeed from my long relationship with PMS, I learned a great deal about the complexities of the gift in Indian society. But I also learned something about the debts that I have accumulated over what is now slightly more than a decade of work on this project. I will never be able to repay all those who have helped me. Some worked for nominal pay, some because of their institutional duties, some because it brought status to be associated with a foreign scholar who was clearly an honored guest of the Maharaja. But most have helped for no recompense at all. As for the many debts I have to academics around the world, I can invoke the old anthropological chestnut of generalized exchange to excuse the seeming asymmetry of the many gifts to me, and offer my book in return. But no length or eloquence of acknowledgement will in fact make a sufficient return to the many people and institutions who have been a part of this book. My only comfort is that while one of the lessons I have learned over the last decade has been precisely how laden all "knowledge" is with power, interest, and strategies of control, appropriation, and domination, I have in fact received many gifts that were freely given. No one can ask for more.

This project began as a dissertation based on research conducted in England and India between 1975 and 1977. The project was funded in that incarnation by the Social Science Research Council, the Fulbright-Hays Program, and the Danforth Foundation. A subsequent year's fieldwork in 1981–82 was supported by the American Institute of Indian Studies. The Division of the Humanities and Social Sciences at the California Institute of Technology provided me with time and resources for writing and delivering initial drafts as papers in a number of conferences. The staffs of the India Office Library, the Tamil Nadu Archives, the Government Oriental Manuscripts Library in Madras, and the Pudukkottai District Record Office all assisted me at various points in my research. The Universities of Madras and Madurai provided me with research affiliation, and the International Institute of Tamil Studies in Madras with Tamil language instruction.

Bernard Cohn not only advised me on my thesis but encouraged me at every stage of this study to pursue the special combination of history and anthropology that has made this book what it is. Ronald Inden encouraged me to extend my interest in modern Indian history as far back into history as epigraphical records would permit. The University of Chicago provided an ideal environment for graduate study. I was fortunate that while in Chicago I was free to study both history and anthropology, and was given the opportunity to meet and work with a number of people who have made the study of India an especially rewarding experience. In addition to my formal supervisors, Arjun Appadurai, Carol Breckenridge, Val Daniel, Mike Fisher, Jim Lindholm, Frank Presler, Kathy Rose, Lee Schlesinger, and Burton Stein all became friends and colleagues during this time. Burt Stein showed himself then, as he has continued to be since, an inspiration for those of us who study southern India, and as generous a teacher and colleague as any academic could hope to know. At Caltech Peter Fay and Robert Rosenstone worked hard to give me a secure academic base, and they and many others provided a true intellectual home. Milind Purohit wrote the graphics program I used to make the distribution maps. James Lee has been a valuable source of advice and encouragement. Linda Benjamin cheerfully typed and retyped many versions of the manuscript.

In Pudukkottai I was the guest of the royal family. The entire family did their best to make us feel at home and did all they could to facilitate my research. In particular, Rajkumari Rema Devi was a friend and support throughout my stay. P.M. Subramanian Iyer was but one of many people in Pudukkottai who gave unstintingly of their time and knowledge. I had a number of research assistants, but was aided far beyond the call of duty by Shyamala Venkataraman, Rama Raman, and P. Asai Thambi. Mrs Uma Iyer of Bombay and Professor Tirunavakkarasu of Madras were particularly helpful. And Ananda Wood was a constant support.

This book has been read in part and in whole by a great many people who deserve far more than the usual academic remark that they gave what is good and not what is bad. In particular I am grateful to Arjun Appadurai, Carol Breckenridge, Barney Cohn, Val Daniel, Peter Fay, Chris Fuller, Tony Good, Will Jones, Steve Lansing, Karen Leonard, David Ludden, Dennis McGilvray, Jerry McGann, Michael Moffatt,

Robert Rosenstone, Lee Schlesinger, Ted Scudder, Burton Stein, Mary Terrall, and David Washbrook.

Leela Wood has not only been through every word in this book, she has lived every word as well. I dedicate the book to her and to Sandhya, who spent the first eight years of her life with a father preoccupied by mounting piles of paper on which she was told not to draw.

# Glossary of terms

āgama: texts prescribing proper forms of worship.

agrahāram: Brahman settlement or hamlet.

ajnāpti: executor of grants in Pallava inscriptions.

Akampaṭiyār: caste group, third member along with Kallars and Maravars of the group of three families, or mukkulattar.

alaṅkāram: adornment of deity.

āḷ jīvitam: tax-free land given of sufficient amount to support one man (al) or family.

Āḷvār: Tamil Vaisnavite saints.

Amāṇi: share, often refers to a type of revenue collection calculated on the basis of shares of the harvest.

Amarakārar: soldiers and retainers, each given a land grant sufficient to support their family, divided into those who served Cervaikarars and those who were attached directly to the king.

Amaranāyaṅkāra: military/territorial chief under Vijayanagara.

ampalam: local big man, usually headman of caste, subcaste, lineage, and/or village.

ampaṭṭaṉ: barber.

Ampu Nāṭu: the royal subcaste, and the territory in which they lived.

aṇṇaṉ: elder brother.

antastu: royal status/privilege/honor.

apicēkam (Skt abhiṣēka): unction/bath/anointment.

aracu añcu: the group of five lineages, including the royal lineage, that made up the elite corps of the royal subcaste.

araiyar: chieftain or king.

arājika: lack of royal authority.

aśvamēdha: Vedic royal horse sacrifice, performed to confer kingship, to establish the area of dominion, and on occasion to declare universal sovereignty.

atikāram: authority.

aṭimai: serf, those low castes whose "rights" consisted of serving patron families.

aṭṭavaṉai: category of inam lands usually given for subsistence to chiefs or other great men.

ayan: non-inam, lands that were fully assessed.

Āyudha (Ta. āyuta) pūjā: ninth day of Dasara, the day all weapons, and implements, are worshipped.

batta: military "wages."

bhakti: devotional Hinduism.

bhandāravāṭa: crown land, term used in Vijayanagara inscriptions.

brahmadēya (brahmadēyam): royally instituted Brahman land grants.

Brihatampāḷ: tutelary goddess of the Tondaiman family.

cakti: the goddess, female power.

cāmaram: fly whisk, royal emblem.

camastānam: royal court, or kingdom.

cāmiyāṭi: one who is possessed by a deity.

campantam: marriage alliance.

camutāyam: sect, social group.

cantanam: sandalwood paste.

capā (Ta. Capai, Skt sabha): assembly.

carittiram: history.

cariyiruppu: rights to equal seating.

Carkar/Cirkar/Sarkar (Ta. Carkkar): the state, or Government.

carvamāniyam: tax-free lands given on extremely favorable terms to Brahmans.

cattiram: chatram, choultry; resting and/or feeding house for itinerant pilgrims, usually Brahmans.

cavari: chowry.

ceṅkōl: royal sceptre.

Cēra: one of three Cankam period Tamil dynasties, located in southwestern Tamil Nadu and parts of modern-day Kerala.

cēri: untouchable hamlet.

cērvai: diminutive form of Cervaikarar, referring to those Kallars who were settled with some lands throughout the state to keep watch on other groups and regions.

Cērvaikārar: The nobles of the Pudukkottai state, mostly affinal relatives of the royal family, all given large estates and numerous retainers (amarakarars) to serve and fight under them.

Ceṭṭiyār: a merchant caste, whose homeland was in the southern part of the Pudukkottai state.

Cētupati: the title of the line of Maravar kings who became known under the British as the Rajas of Ramnad (Ramanatapuram).

cēvakam: service.

cīmai: country.

cippanti ijāra: inams granted on various kinds of military tenures.

Cōla (Cōra): the great tenth to twelfth-century dynasty based in Tanjavur.

curōttiriyam (Skt śrōtriya): lands granted to Brahmans.

curutti: scroll with seal.

cuvēntiram: share, as in share of village harvest.


dakṣiṇā: ritual dues.

dāna: gift.

Dasarā: the festival otherwise known as Mahanavami, celebrated on the first nine nights and ten days of the month Asvina, first by the Vijayanaragar kings. Also known as Durgotsava, Navaratra, and Durgapuja.

desha cawel (Ta. tēcakkāval): rights to protect the countryside.

dēvadāna (Ta. tēvatāna): land grant for the support of temples.

dēvadāyam (Ta. tēvatāyam): lands that have been granted for the support of temples.

dēvasthanam: temple establishment.

dharma: the rightful order of things.

dharmadāyam: lands granted for feeding houses, i.e. for charitable (dharma) purposes.

Diwan (dewan): prime minister.

Diwan Peishkar: first assistant to Diwan, usually in charge of the treasury.


eccil: saliva.


Hāriyakārar: ritual preceptor of the king.

hiraṇyagarbha: one of mahadana rituals, depicting the birth from a golden embryo.


inām: tax-free lands given by kings as benefices.

inam: patrilineal relation.

ināmdār (Ta. ināmtār): holder of inam.

inavari: that subdivision of amarakarars attached to Cervaikarars.

Iṭaiyar: sheep herding caste.


jāgīr: estate, domain.

Jāgīrdār: a Persian/Mughal term, meaning noble or chief, used in Pudukkottai to apply to the two most important collaterals of the royal family.

jajmāni: a village system of customary payments, usually distributed at the time of harvest.

jīvitam: term meaning livelihood, used as a measure of land calculated to be sufficient to support a single family; often used in conjunction with term for person, al, as in *al jivitam*.

kālāñci: temple honors.

Kaḷḷar: The royal, and dominant, caste in Pudukkottai; they had a reputation as a warrior caste and were settled in parts of Madurai, Ramanatapuram, Tanjavur, Tiruccirappalli, and Pudukkottai.

kalveṭṭu: stone inscription.

Kampaḷattār: a Telegu-speaking caste, settled mostly in eastern Tirunelveli district.

Kanāṭu: the land of forest, referring to an area of land in Pudukkottai for the most part south of the river Vellar.

kāṇi: heritable entitlement.

kāṇiyāṭci: the possession of kani, the right of heritable entitlement.

kāṇiyāṭcikkārar: holder of kaniyatci.

karai: lineage, usually used in context of ranking.

karaikārar: head of lineage.

kāriyakārar: representative or agent.

kāriyam: an action performed for/on behalf of someone else, usually a superior.

Karttakkāḷ: title, meaning lord, and agent, used by the Nayakas of Madurai.

kaṭṭalai: endowment to a temple.

kaṭṭuppāṭu: code for conduct.

kāval: protection.

kāvalkārar: local person/chief who is empowered with rights of protection such as patikkaval.

kāval teyvam: protection deity.

kiḷai: branch, often used for lineage, as for example among certain groups of Maravars.

kirāmam: village.

kirāma teyvam: village deity.

kirāmavaṛi: that subdivision of amarakarars who were attached directly to the state, i.e. not to Cervaikarars.

kist: tax.

Kollaṉ: blacksmith.

kolu: assembly, court of the king, darbar.

Kōṉar: cow herding caste.

Kōnāṭu: the land of the king, referring to an area of land in Pudukkottai for the most part north of the river Vellar.

koṭi: flag, banner.

kōvil: temple.

kṣatra: lordly power, such as that held and exercised by kings in the exercise of territorial rule.

kuḷi: land measure, variably equal from 144 to 576 square feet.

kumāra: son.

kumāravarkkam: the special group of "adopted sons" attached to the Nayaka of Madurai: the elite corps of southern palaiyakkarars.

kuṅkum: vermilion.

kuppam: territorial subdivision within royal subcaste.

Kuṟikārar: lesser Kallar chiefs, given lands but only rarely retainers.

Kuṟumpar: caste group, considered to be aboriginal inhabitants of Karnataka, located in Pudukkottai and other areas of the Tamil country.

kuṭi: place of residence, residents of a place.

kuṭimakkaḷ: people of the village, the group of castes considered ideally to be necessary for the proper functioning of any village as a whole.

kuṭi umpaḷam: village service.

kūṭṭam: assembly.


lāvaṇam: list, often used for units of land as they were listed in registers.


mahādāna: great gift, particular rituals that were performed by kings from the eighth century on, involving massive gifting by kings, usually to Brahmans. The two most important of these "mahadanas" were the tulapurusadana or tulabhara, and the hiranyagarbha.

Mahāmaṇṭalēśvara: great chief, often kinsman of the royal family, used in Deccan regimes from Satavahanas and Rastrakutas up through Vijayanagara period.

Mahānāvami: the festival otherwise known as Dasara, celebrated on the first nine nights and ten days of the month Asvina, roughly the period from mid-September to mid-October.

māmaṉ: maternal uncle.

māmaṉ-maccaṉaṉ: lineage with whom women are exchanged as marriage partners.

māmūl (mamool): tradition, custom.

māṉiyakārar: holders of maniyam right or land, root for the anglicized term monigar referring to local headman.

māṉiyam: honor, often referring specifically to a grant of tax-free land and other associated privileges; derives from Sanskrit term manya, which means honor and privilege.

mantakappati: right to celebrate one day of the festival.

mantakappatitār: holder of the mantakappati right.

mantalam: country, as in Colamantalam, the central core region of the Cola empire.

māppillai: brother-in-law.

Maravar: a caste group found in Ramanatapuram, Tirunelveli, Madurai, and Pudukkottai; often grouped with Kallars because of their warrior reputation, and because the two castes, along with the Akampatiyars, together make up what is called the mukkulattar, the group of three families.

mariyātai: honor, often used for honors secured in temple worship.

matam: monastery.

Mēlakkārar: piper caste.

mēlvāram: the top or first cut or share of the crop, usually allocated to the crown.

mirāci: a general term originally signifying inheritance, from the late eighteenth century referring to rights of local landholding and, often, government service.

mirācidār (Ta. mirācitār): holder of miraci right, local big man, sometimes used interchangeably for the local ampalam(s), sometimes used specifically to designate a revenue agent appointed by the state.

Mukkulattār: the group of three families, or castes, specifically referring to Kallars, Maravars, and Akampatiyars.

Mutaliyār: a high peasant-agricultural caste of the Tamil country.

mūtatāyar: ancestor.


nagara (Ta. nakaram): city.

nagarattār (Ta. nakarattār): inhabitant of a city; specifically refers to merchants, and, in Pudukkottai, to Cettiyars.

nātalvān: ruler of a natu.

nāttampalam: headman of a natu.

Nattampati Kavuntār: agricultural caste living in the extreme western portion of Pudukkottai State.

nāttānmaikkārar: headman of a natu.

nāttār: lord or head of locality (natu).

nāttuppātal: folk ballad.

nāttu teyvam: subcaste/territory deity.

nātu: locality, or peasant micro region, also meaning subcaste among Pudukkottai Kallars, as well as locality assembly (as for example is found in Cola inscriptions).

Navarāttiri: festival of the nine nights, same as Dasara.

Nāyaka: general term meaning lord, or general; adopted by the ruling "viceroys" of the Vijayanagara empire who constituted the principal foci of political power in late medieval south India.

Nāyaṇār: Tamil Saivite saints.

nazr: Persian term for occasional presents given by an inferior to a superior.

nivētaṉam (Skt naivedya): offerings to deity.

oṛunku: order.

ottācai: military service, more properly translated as help such as that rendered to a kinsman.

pālai: wilderness, one of the five landscapes of classical Tamil poetic convention.

pāḷaiyakkārar: little king, or chief, corrupted by the British into poligar and polegar.

pāḷaiyam: literally armed camps, the domains over which the palaiyakkarars ruled.

pāḷaiyappaṭṭu: the title or right to a palaiyam.

Paḷḷar: one of the two major untouchable castes in the Tamil country.

Pallava: sixth- to tenth-century dynasty based in Tontaimantalam, the northern Tamil country, with Kancipuram as the center.

paṇi: to perform service, be humble, submissive, to worship.

pankāḷi: shareholder: refers to someone who holds a share of land or of other rights; the term also refers to those who are members of (have shares of membership in) a lineage.

panku: share.

paṇṇaiyāḷ: agricultural laborers hired on a year to year basis.

Pāṇṭiya: name of dynasty that ruled out of Madurai, both in Cankam period and later during the centuries before, during, and after Cola hegemony.

pantuttuvam: affinal tie.

pantuvam: affinal relative.

Paṛaiyar: one of the two major untouchable castes in the Tamil country.

parakuṭi: from outside, non-local, often referring to agricultural laborers from outside the village.

paramparai: family, generation.

parivaṭṭam: a temple honor consisting of the tying of the deity's vestment around the head of the worshipper.

paṭaipaṛṛu: military hamlet.

pāṭikkāval: protection over a place, usually a right conferred on a chief in return for certain shares of local produce.

paṭṭadār (Ta. paṭṭatār): landholder.

pattam: lease, deed, contract, receipt, land title.

pattapeyar: lineage, used among Kallars, literally meaning the name of a title.

pattāpicēkam (Skt pattābhisēkam): coronation, installation of king's title.

pattavan: ancestor deity.

pattayam: copper plate inscription.

patti: hamlet.

pattu: right, title.

periyanāttār: headman, lord, of periyanatu.

periyanātu: supra-local assemblies (collections of natu-s) characteristic of the twelfth and thirteenth centuries in areas of Cola rule.

Periyapurāṇam: the twelfth-century Tamil Puranic epic that tells the stories of the sixty-three Saivite Nayanar bhakti saints.

peshkash: tribute, tax.

piratāni: minister, emissary.

pirutu/virutu (Skt birudha): emblem, title, honor.

pitimān: handful of soil.

poṅkal: sweet rice prepared as offering to deity on special festival occasions.

pracātam (Ta. piracātam, Skt prasāda): transvalued substance, the leavings of the deity, what is returned in puja.

praśasti: the prefatory panegyric found in many inscriptions.

pulukkar: lower group of lineages, a term used by Maravars in Tirunelveli.

punyam: merit.

pūjā (Ta. pūcai): worship.

pūjāri (Ta. pūcāri): priest.

purāṇa: texts that post-date the Vedas and often consist of narratives of the exploits of gods and goddesses. The term applies both to a specific canon of texts and to a large body of texts that are modelled in some way or another on this canon.

purōhita (Ta. purōhitam): ritual preceptor.

pūti pattu: lower group of ten lineages in the royal kuppam.

rājadharma: the royal duty of protecting and maintaining the rightful order of things.

rājapantu: royal relations.

rājasūya: Vedic royal sacrifice, performed to confer kingship on the sacrificer.

rājiyam: kingship.

Rāyar: Telegu form of raja, meaning king.

rokkakuttikai: category of inam lands usually given to military persons.

ryotwari: the property settlement with individual cultivators that was first introduced in Madras Presidency.

Sardār (Ta. Cartār): Persian title for general that came to be used interchangeably with Cervaikarar.

Sirkele: Diwan, or prime minister; used in Pudukkottai until the late nineteenth century.

śrōtriya: learned, scholarly, referring to those Brahmans engaged in Vedic study and practice.

stānikar: temple manager.

taccan: carpenter.

tahsildar: local level revenue officer.

talaivar: head, headman.

talavāy: prime minister, or head official.

taluk: administrative subdivision of a district.

tampi: younger brother.

taricanam (Skt darśan): sight, vision.

teru: street, often used as a term for a subdivision of lineages.

Tēvar: title meaning godly, or godlike, often used by Maravars.

Tirukōkkarnam: the tutelary temple of the royal family, situated just to the northwest of Pudukkottai town.

tirupātam: the rite of worshipping the feet of the deity.

tiruppani: the giving of gifts to and renovation of a temple.

tiruvirā: festival.

ṭōpi: washerman (dhobi).

toril: service, particularly that of a menial description.

torilāli: village servants who perform menial tasks.

tulāpuruṣadāna: a mahadana, the gift to a Brahman of his weight in gold; same as tulabhara.

umpalam: tax-free land.

upacāram (Skt upacāra): rites of adoration to deity.

ūr: village.

ūrani: irrigational works.

uravumurai: affinal relations.

urimai: right.

urimai pen: the preferred female marriage partner.

Ūriyakārar: palace guards, all members of a special subcaste (named uriyakarar) of the akampatiyar caste.

ūṛiyam: service, particular kind of obligation to perform temple service in Pudukkottai.

vakuppu: class or group, and when used to modify Cervaikarar implied the small group of great chiefs who had vast numbers of retainers under them.

Valaiyar: caste group on the low end of the scale extensively settled in the more forested regions of Pudukkottai.

Vallampar: locally dominant caste settled in the southeastern part of Pudukkottai state.

vamcam: family.

vamcāvaḷi: family history.

vaṉam: forest.

varicai: order, group.

varipparikkam: highway robbery.

Vaṭuka: northerner, usually referring to a Telegu.

Vēdavirtti: teaching the Veda.

Veḷḷāḷar: the usually dominant peasant-agricultural caste of the Tamil country.

vettiyan: town crier, servant of village headman, usually from "untouchable" castes.

Vijayadaśami: the tenth day of the Dasara festival.

vipūti (Skt vibhuti): sacred ash.

virtti (Skt vritti): service, livelihood.

virutu (also pirutu; Skt birudha): emblem or title.

vīṭṭucāmi: household deity.

viṭuti: village, settlement.

yajamāna (Ta. ecamāṉ): patron, originally patron of Vedic sacrifice.

zamīndār: landlord.

*Note on transliteration scheme*

Like dictionaries and grammars, transliteration schemes tend to systematize languages in ways that misrepresent actual linguistic practice. I find transliteration schemes for Tamil problematic for two reasons. First, Tamil pronunciation and spelling vary greatly, particularly in spoken dialects and in the colloquial forms employed in eighteenth-century records and texts. Second, anglicized and/or sanskritized forms of words are often used and more readily recognized than accurate Tamil transcriptions. For example, few readers would recognize the word *agraharam* behind the Tamil *akkirakaram*, or *brahmadeya* behind *piramatayam*. Thus I have altered spellings where I thought strict transcription would cause difficulties for the reader, sometimes substituting g for k, d for t, or b for p (often a standard procedure in any case because the use of these letters can indicate when consonants in Tamil are voiced), and other times dropping a vowel as when I use *pracatam* (more recognizable if one knows the Sanskrit form *prasada*) for *piracatam*. My transcription scheme uses a dash over the vowel to indicate its lengthened form, a dash under the consonant to indicate its alveolar form, and a dot under the consonant to indicate its retroflex form. My transliteration scheme is consistent with that used in the Madras University Tamil lexicon with the single exception of the retroflex r/l which I transliterate as r̠ instead of as l̠ in spite of the fact that I adhere to convention with terms such as Tamil (Tamir) and Cola (Cora) in order to facilitate general recognition. In the text I italicize and use diacritics for Indian terms only on their first occurrence; and I provide definitions for most terms both in the text and in the glossary. In the glossary I indicate whether terms are Tamil (Ta.) or Sanskrit (Skt) when I use both; the first entry is the form I use in the text itself. I do not use diacritics for proper and place names.

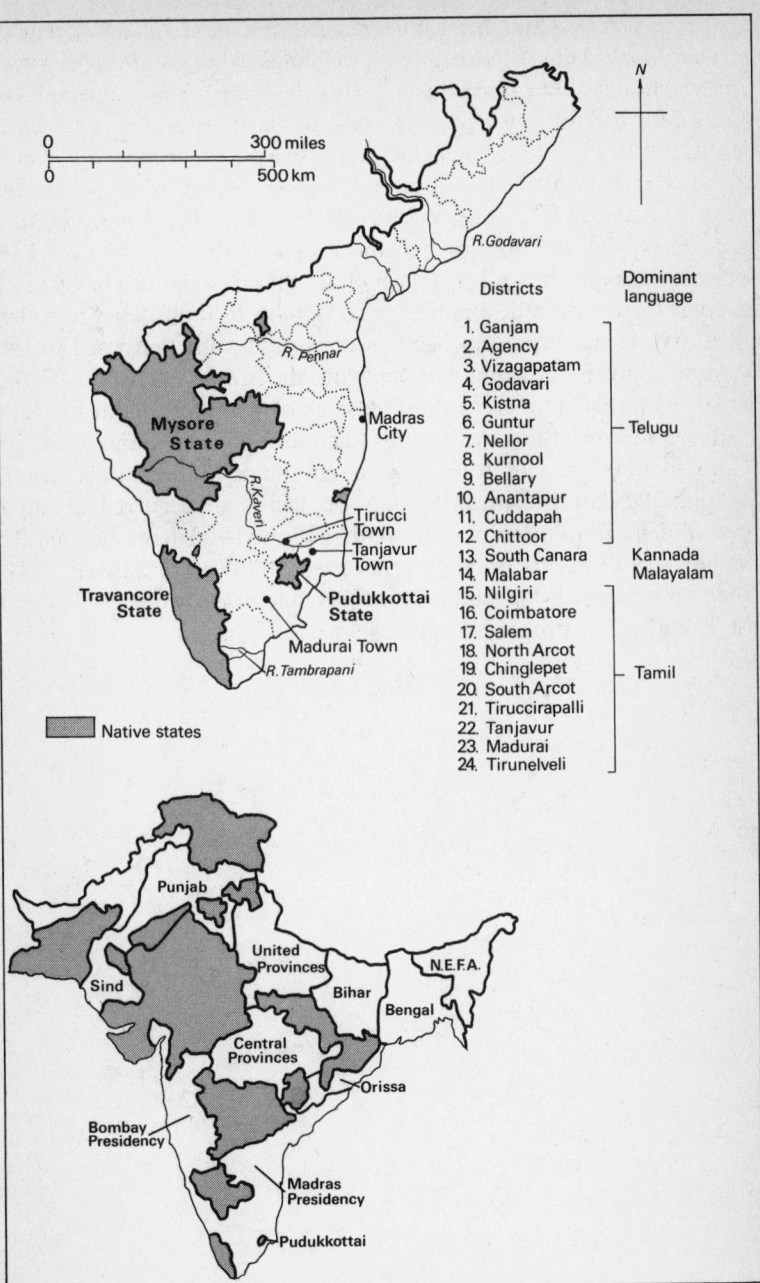

| Districts | Dominant language |
|-----------|-------------------|
| 1. Ganjam | |
| 2. Agency | |
| 3. Vizagapatam | |
| 4. Godavari | |
| 5. Kistna | |
| 6. Guntur | Telugu |
| 7. Nellor | |
| 8. Kurnool | |
| 9. Bellary | |
| 10. Anantapur | |
| 11. Cuddapah | |
| 12. Chittoor | |
| 13. South Canara | Kannada |
| 14. Malabar | Malayalam |
| 15. Nilgiri | |
| 16. Coimbatore | |
| 17. Salem | |
| 18. North Arcot | |
| 19. Chinglepet | |
| 20. South Arcot | Tamil |
| 21. Tiruccirapalli | |
| 22. Tanjavur | |
| 23. Madurai | |
| 24. Tirunelveli | |

Map 1 Madras Presidency, 1900

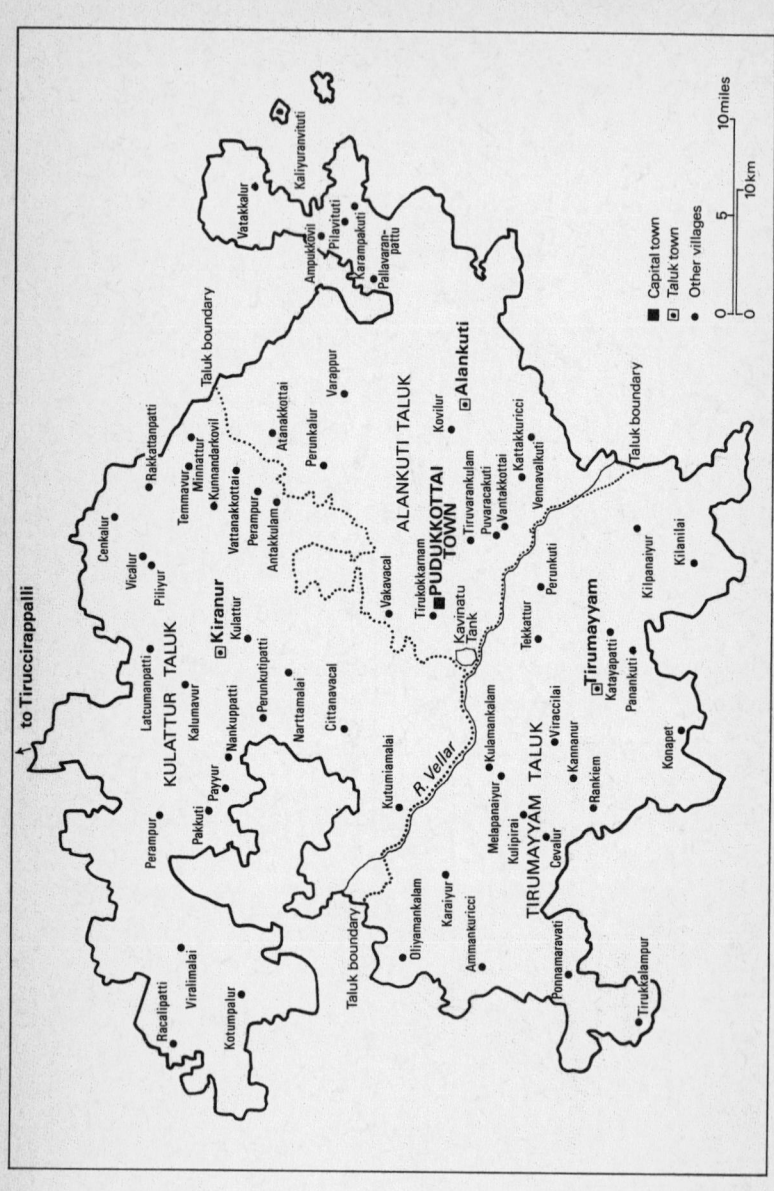

Map 2 Pudukkottai State

# THE TONDAIMAN LINE OF PUDUKKOTTAI

Avadai Raghunatha Tondaiman better known as Raja Tondaiman, died 1661.

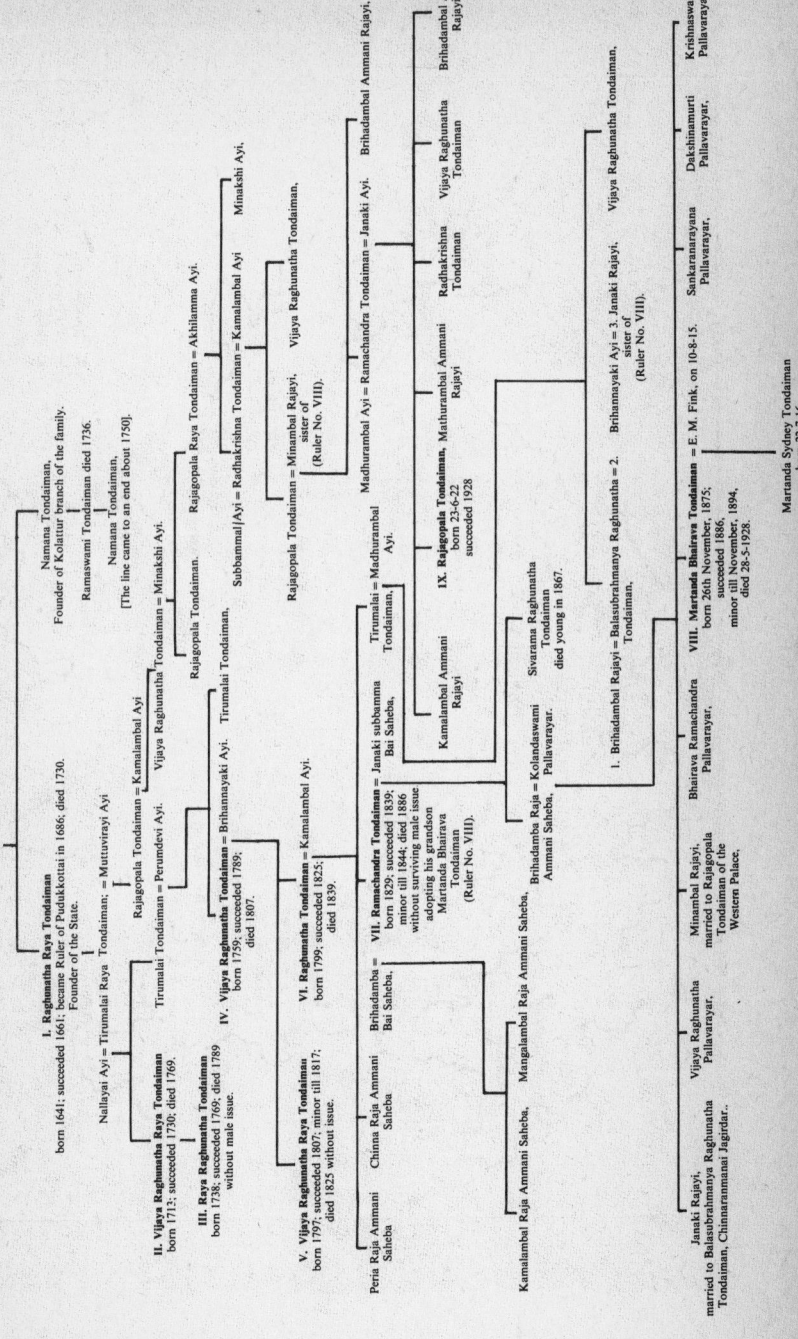

1 Raja Ramachandra Tondaiman

2 The Royal Darbar, 1858 (from L. Tripe, *Photographic Views of Poodoocottah*, Madras, 1858)

3 The Coronation of Raja Rajagopala Tondaiman, 1928 (courtesy of the Pudukkottai Royal Family)

4 The Royal Darbar, 1928

5 The Coronation procession from the Old Palace, 1928 (courtesy of the Pudukottai Royal Family)

6 The Old Palace, 1871. Photograph by Captain Lyons from *Archaeological Remains and Antiquities* Volume 30, No. 3031 (British Library)

7 The New Palace, opened in 1928 (photograph by Nicholas Dirks, 1976)

# PART 1

# Introduction

# 1

*The study of state and society in India*

### The legacy

The Indian state is barely visible to comparative sociology. When the state is evident at all it appears as a weak form of Oriental despotism, destined to disappear as suddenly, and as casually, as it emerged. It seldom possesses mechanisms – hydraulic or otherwise – that could enable it to sustain itself for long. It depends mostly on ruthless short-sighted taxation of the countryside, which eventually leads to such chaos that it dissolves on its own or is conquered by some new entrant on the political scene.

Weber, Marx, Maine, and more recently Dumont have all held that in India, in marked contrast to China, the state was epiphenomenal. Marx's view is typical: "Just as Italy has, from time to time, been compressed by the conqueror's sword into different national masses, so do we find Hindustan, when not under the pressure of the Mohammedan, or the Mogul, or the Briton, dissolved into as many independent and conflicting States as it numbered towns, or even villages" (1972, 35). Marx saw these village communities as the necessary complement of Oriental despotism: "these idyllic village communities, inoffensive though they may appear, had always been the solid foundation of Oriental despotism, that they restrained the human mind within the smallest possible compass, making it the unresisting tool of superstition, enslaving it beneath traditional rules, depriving it of all grandeur and historical energies" (p. 40). While states came and went, village communities endured.

For sociology, caste, not the state, held these village communities together. In a more general sense, caste is seen as the foundation and core of Indian civilization; it is responsible for the transmission and reproduction of society in India. Caste, like India itself, is represented as based on religious rather than political principles. The state is always about to dissolve into fragments made up of various "communal" elements. Modern day journalistic coverage of India has its roots in the early writings of British travelers and administrators, as well as in the more systematic work of such theorists as Weber. Weber writes that

"Caste, that is, the ritual rights and duties it gives and imposes, and the position of the Brahmans, is the fundamental institution of Hinduism. Before everything else, without caste there is no Hindu" (1958, 29). Weber goes on to say that the caste order is itself based on the greatest authority in the system, the sacerdotal Brahmans: "Caste is, and remains essentially social rank, and the central position of the Brahmans in Hinduism rests primarily upon the fact that social rank is determined with reference to Brahmans" (pp. 29–30). For Weber as for sociology in general, Indian society, headed by a Brahmanic elite,[1] is based on other-worldly and spiritual principles.

While Louis Dumont (1980) has rightly been hailed as one of the most important writers on India in recent years, he has in many ways only updated the view of India found in Marx and Weber. Dumont holds that the political and economic domains of social life are "encompassed" by the "religious." The religious principle becomes articulated in the Indian case in terms of the opposition of purity and impurity. For Dumont as for Weber the Brahman represents the religious principle, inasmuch as the Brahman represents the highest form of purity attainable by Hindus. The king, while important and powerful, represents the political domain, and is accordingly inferior to, and encompassed by, the Brahman. Caste is fundamentally a religious system.

Prevailing conceptions about Indian state and society reflect the larger history of Orientalism, in which the colonial and now post-colonial interest in controlling the East, an interest which entailed the delegitimization of pre- or postcolonial state forms, has merged with a nostalgia for spirituality and, more specifically, a religiously based society (Said 1979). India's represented past haunts not only studies of colonialism, but even the historical legacy handed down to modern India. India's need to invent the nation, the state, and to find the basis for a society which is neither narrowly religious nor ethnic is made far more difficult by prevailing forms of Orientalistic knowledge which have their immediate roots in representations of the old regime as despotic, decadent, and deformed by decontextualized versions of caste or the village community as the sole (and autonomous) basis of Indian society.

It is my contention in this book that until the emergence of British colonial rule in southern India the crown was not so hollow as it has generally been made out to be. Kings were not inferior to Brahmans; the political domain was not encompassed by a religious domain. State

---

[1] In a recent review of two books, one by a Sanskritist and the other by an anthropologist, Wendy D. O'Flaherty confirms this by writing that "In Indological Studies, it appears, all roads lead to the Brahman" (1984, 1357).

forms, while not fully assimilable to western categories of the state, were powerful components in Indian Civilization. Indian society, indeed caste itself, was shaped by political struggles and processes. In using the term "political" I am of course conscious of imposing an exogenous analytic term on to a situation in which, as I will argue, ritual and political forms were fundamentally the same. However, I must stress the political both to redress the previous emphasis on "religion" and to underscore the social fact that caste structure, ritual form, and political process were all dependent on relations of power. These relations were constituted in and through history; and these relations were culturally constructed. And it is on the cultural construction of power, in the final analysis, that I rest my case.

### The book

This book is about the relationship between the Indian state and Indian society in the old regime, and the transformation of this relationship under British colonialism, when the crown finally did become hollow. The particular focus for the study is a small region of southern India. This region was one of many similar political regions which constituted the lowest level of the late precolonial state, and is here called, borrowing a term from Bernard Cohn (1962), a little kingdom. While what I write about the Indian state must always be qualified by the fact that I am not looking at large transregional states, my perspective is one that will reveal the complex and integral interrelations of political processes which ultimately culminated in larger kingdoms with the social forms that are held to be autonomous and nonpolitical. By focusing on the cultural, political, social, economic and ritual basis of the little kingdom, I will show the inherent problems of these analytic categories and the distinctions they imply.

The little kingdom under scrutiny in the pages to follow is a place called Pudukkottai (Putukkōṭṭai), meaning "new fort." Pudukkottai, which at its most extensive did not exceed 1,200 square miles, was located in an exclusively rain-fed agricultural zone right in the middle of the Tamil speaking region of southern Indian, straddling the boundary between the two great medieval Tamil kingdoms. Ruled by *Kaḷḷar* kings from the end of the seventeenth century until 1947, it provides an excellent canvas for a study of the political history of Indian society, or, rather, a social history of the Indian state. Kallars were elsewhere thought to be highway robbers: the term itself is still used in Tamil for thief. Dumont, in his first work on India and his only ethnographic monograph (1957b), used Kallars as examples of a ritually marginal group that exemplified the Dravidian isolation of kinship from the influence of caste hierarchy. But in Pudukkottai Kallars were *kings*; they exercised every conceivable kind of dominance and their social organization reflects this fact.

I base my understanding of Pudukkottai on my reading of late medieval and early modern inscriptional and textual sources relating to local chiefs and kings, as well as on eighteenth- and nineteenth-century administrative and land records, colonial reports, and the results of my recent ethnographic fieldwork. Pudukkottai rose, as did other little kingdoms throughout southern India, within the context of a late medieval Hindu political order. In both its emergence to and its maintenance of power, it exemplified the social and military vitality of certain productively marginal areas in the seventeenth and eighteenth centuries before it began its long decline under a distinctive form of colonial hegemony engineered by the British.

Colonialism purposefully preserved many of the forms of the old regime, nowhere more conspicuously than in the indirectly ruled Princely State, of which Pudukkottai was the only one in the Tamil speaking region of India. But these forms were frozen, and only the appearances of the old regime – without its vitally connected political and social processes – were saved. The historical method in the book is thus both genealogical and archaeological; I trace connections but I also search for disjunctions in the historical, ethnographic, and textual shards I have found.

The book begins with one of the most momentous episodes in the British conquest of the south, the capture of the rebel chief Kattapomman in 1799, only to become an extended flashback to the old regime. In the first chapter I attempt to reconstruct the principal dynamics of the last millennium of south Indian history, exposing the changing political logic of social and ritual relations from medieval times to the old regime. I then turn my attention to the cultural construction of king and kingdom in the old regime. Using eighteenth-century texts – genealogies, chronicles, ballads – as cultural discourses,[2] I find persistent motifs, events, narrative forms, tropes, and images, and I read the parts they play in the poetics of power. This textualized discourse suggests the key elements to which I must attend in my historiographic inquiry: the core conceptions of sovereignty; the interpenetrating

---

[2] My use of the term discourse is influenced by Foucault's view of the structure and power of discourse, and of the practical nature of its formation and implementation: i.e., power and its technologies. For an anthropological reading of Foucault which I have found particularly helpful, see H. Dreyfus and P. Rabinow, 1983.

transactions in gifts, service, and kinship; the structure and form of hegemony.

I then close in on Pudukkottai, sketching in miniature my argument about the nature of the old regime political system and assembling inscriptional evidence to substantiate my sense of the rise of chiefs in areas like Pudukkottai in the period from the fourteenth century on. Building on my argument about the process of transformation implicit in the nature of south Indian little kingdoms, in brief the movement from bandit to little king through relations with higher kings, I show how textual readings are realized in historical processes. For I describe the political system of Pudukkottai in the old regime historically, as a dynamic system based on relations of service and protection, kinship and caste, lordship and gift, military might and discursive domination. In particular I show how rights to landholding were political rights, which reflected the structure of the little kingdom at the same time that they revealed the pervasive importance of royal honor.

But then, abandoning chronological consistency, I present my ethnographic evidence about the structure and ideology of social organization, both among Kallars and between them and other castes. Only through my fieldwork was I able to reconnect society and state; caste and kinship were profoundly political in their operation and their conceptualization. My conclusions directly oppose those of Dumont: thus I consider and often argue against his general writings about the nature of caste hierarchy, his technical writings about kinship, and his ethnographic conclusions about the nearby Pramalai Kallars of Madurai.

Specifically, I argue that caste was embedded in a political context of kingship. This meant among other things that the prevalent ideology had not to do, at least primarily, with purity and pollution, but rather with royal authority and honor, and associated notions of power, dominance, and order.[3] My analysis reintroduces this concern with power and dominance into studies of culturally determined structures of thought. It is a mistake to try to separate a materialist *etic* from a culturalist *emic*: even the domain of ritual action and language is permeated with the complex foundations and lived experience of hierarchical relations. At least this is true for the Kallars of Pudukkottai,

---

[3] This is not a totally new proposal. Arjun Appadurai (1981), Carol Breckenridge (1976), Valentine Daniel (1984), Dennis McGilvray (1982), and others have raised various aspects of this agenda in important ways. I hope, however, that this book will provide the ethnohistorical evidence to give still greater credibility and sharper clarity to this alternative to the dominant theory of caste.

less affected perhaps than most other groups by colonialism and the demise of the old regime in the nineteenth century. The concerns of comparative sociology are not only the products of a nineteenth-century Orientalism, but also of the colonial intervention that removed the politics from colonial societies. It was not merely convenient for the British to detach caste from politics; it was necessary to do so in order to rule an immensely complex society by a variety of indirect means. Colonial sociology was an outgrowth of letters and reports which represented the eighteenth century as decadent and all legitimate Indian politics as past (Cohn 1983). But caste – now disembodied from its political contexts – lived on. In this dissociated form it was appropriated, and reconstructed, by the British. Paradoxically, they were able to change caste only because caste in fact continued to be permeable to political influence. Ethnohistorical reconstruction is thus important not only for historians confronting new problems of data and analysis, but for anthropologists who confront in their fieldwork a social system that was decapitated by colonial rule.

The final section of the book concerns the impact of colonialism and the "modern state" on south Indian society, closing the flashback historically and historiographically. It is meant both as contribution to colonial history and as a way of critiquing colonial historiography, in which little kings were at worst rebels and at best landlords, and in which the Indian state was deconstructed and the nature of Indian society misconstrued. Colonialism changed things both more and less than has commonly been thought. While introducing new forms of civil society and separating these forms off from the colonial state, colonialism also arrested some of the immediate disruptions of change by preserving many elements of the old regime. But by freezing the wolf in sheep's clothing, it changed things fundamentally. Paradoxically, colonialism seems to have created much of what is now accepted as Indian "tradition," including an autonomous caste structure with the Brahman clearly at the head, village based systems of exchange, the ceremonial residues of the old regime state, and fetishistic competition for ritual goods that no longer play a vital role in the political system. The book ends with a picture of the Princely State as the "theatre state" (Geertz 1980), the final and only realization in the south Indian context of a state where ritual has been set apart on a stage with dramatic but ultimately only fictional power for the anonymous audience.

My work on Pudukkottai and other little kingdoms in the south has led me to the realization that the history of these little kings (called "poligars" by the British) has been substantially based on the writings of colonial administrators who had developed a systematic view of old regime state and society in order to justify and facilitate their own land settlements, including the Permanent Settlement, the subsequent *ryot-wari* settlement, and finally the settlement of *inams* (tax-free lands) in the late nineteenth century. The land settlements were predicated on the dual aim of securing order and extracting revenue, the cornerstones of colonial policy. Taxonomies of land type and use, caste constituency and status, and political relations under the Raj became first fixed and then reified through the colonial institutions that promulgated and implemented this colonial sociology. This process of the reification of new forms took place against the background of the old regime. Whether we are concerned with the changing nature of the state, the implementation of new forms of private property and revenue collection, the creation of new forms of social relations and communal tensions, or the formalization of a colonial sociology in which the immediate past of India was represented for the purpose of controlling and appropriating the political dynamics of Indian society, the old regime must be studied.[4]

If it be argued that my interpretation, though perhaps true for marginal regions like Pudukkottai, can hardly apply generally to south India, let alone to the subcontinent as a whole, I reply that it is precisely the marginality of Pudukkottai that makes it possible to detect there the forces that were at work elsewhere. Because Pudukkottai was not brought under patrimonial control – neither that of the Islamic rulers in the south nor later that of the British – caste was never set completely loose from kingship. Many current theories of caste, particularly those emphasizing Brahmanic obsessions concerning purity and impurity, or the proper and improper mixing of substances, are in large parts artifacts of colonialism, referring to a situation in which the position of the king has been displaced, and sometimes destroyed. However much Dumont's theory is predicated on an a priori separation of what he describes as the domains of religion and politics, Dumont was also almost certainly influenced by an ethnographic reality in which kingship played only a very small, residual role. As for the ethnosociological theories that compete with Dumont for credibility in the contemporary marketplace of cultural theories of caste, Inden has himself recently noted that his early work is largely derived from texts which were generated only after the demise of kingship as a powerful cultural

---

[4] This period, sometimes labeled the "old regime," sometimes late pre-colonial India, and sometimes not labeled at all, has recently received some important, if as yet only preliminary, attention. See Barnett 1980; C. Bayly 1983; S. Bayly 1984; Dirks 1979; Gordon 1977, 1978; Leonard 1979; Perlin 1978, 1983; Richards 1976; Stein 1984; and Washbrook 1984.

institution (Inden 1983). The texts, he now says, reflected new traditions which attempted to deal with the problem of regulating caste interaction in an environment in which there was no longer a king.

To resolve in such a clear-cut historical manner the "great conundrum of Indian social thought" – whether the Brahman or the king had precedence (Trautmann 1981; Heesterman 1978) – is perhaps to do injustice to the complexity of the issue. However, the historical case of Pudukkottai strongly suggests that the caste system, and its attendant hierarchical forms, reached a particular stage of development and articulation under a social formation in which the king was supreme. The demise of kingship, in some areas as early as the twelfth and thirteenth centuries, progressively later in southern India, and perhaps last of all in Sri Lanka, led to major changes in the caste system. The demise of kingship was accompanied by the steady ascendancy of the Brahman, as the maintainer of social order and the codes of caste. Brahmans reached a new high under British colonialism both in their participation in the development of Hindu Law and in their preponderance in colonial administration (Dirks 1974). Even in the realm of the ideological basis of the caste system, the role of Brahmans, not as honored and valued members of kingdoms, but as the colonially constituted arbiters of caste order, has changed in major ways in the last two centuries.

The importance and reference of a study of a region such as Pudukkottai should now be clear. Kings in Pudukkottai continued to rule until very recently. And Brahmans were heavily patronized by these kings. The ethnohistorical case before us facilitates rather than obstructs the reconstruction of a caste system that was profoundly political.

## History and anthropology

In this book I propose new methods and new possibilities in the emerging collaboration of "history" and "anthropology," what is here and elsewhere called ethnohistory. Ethnohistory has many meanings (Cohn 1968). It can mean the reconstruction of the history of an area and people who have no written history. As such, it has been used to denote the field of studies concerning the past of American Indians, or of other "primitive" or pre-literate societies. Ethnohistory can also mean the use of anthropological theory and methods in historical practice; we sometimes call this historical anthropology. As such, ethnohistory unites a concern for the social and cultural forms studied by anthropologists with the multiple contexts and temporal dimensions invoked and identified by historians. Like all hybrid labels, whether in history or in anthropology, it is most useful when it points us to the possibility of a collaborative enterprise which is both open-ended and more than simply the sum of its parts.

Unfortunately, however, such hybrids often serve to do little more than lend mystique and legitimacy to traditional practices. It is not enough to borrow some terms, and perhaps even some theories, from another discipline. What we get then is too often nothing more than the reproduction of the attenuated and decontextualized notions of Malinowski, Turner, or Geertz; or a preliminary chapter in an ethnography based on brief archival forays. Instead, ethnohistory must operate as a reflexive critical technique, challenging our basic presuppositions at every point. It must push us to revise our standard historiographical methods and theories, or to "explode the concept of history by the anthropological experience of culture" (Sahlins 1985, 72). It must also identify the limitations of anthropological practice and theory, investing time, process, contingency, discontinuity, and agency into functional, structuralist, or semiotic models. In all of these respects, I believe that ethnohistory has the potential to rework basic parameters in the study of society, culture, and the past.

I am, of course, alone neither in believing this nor in attempting to practice it. The book that results in this case, however, is long and in some ways unwieldy precisely because it seeks to reconstruct the basis for the interdisciplinary study of Indian society. I do not want to finesse fundamental problems. I want to engage the inherited legacies of political history, caste and kinship studies, textual hermeneutics, and colonial historiography. So the book tacks back and forth between a new set of methods and the recognition that it is difficult to engage these methods in scholarly contexts where many discourses have remained unexamined for far too long. Historians will recognize some ground as familiar, some as less so; anthropologists will recognize some of the debates, and perhaps be bored by details on landholding; textualists will find texts but then lose them when they are resituated in their referential worlds. My hope is that my challenge to conventional strategy and taxonomy will indeed result in a kind of culture shock, but one that will be welcomed as the necessary accompaniment to deeper understanding, not disparaged as an annoying and unsettling experience.

There is, nonetheless, precedent for my approach. Historians as various as Robert Darnton, Natalie Davis, William Sewell, Hans Medick, Emmanuel Le Roy Ladurie, Jacques Le Goff, and Keith Thomas – to name only a few – have advocated new ways to anthropologize history. As one of the most sophisticated consumers of anthropology, Sewell (1981, 10) has written that the "deepest and most powerful message of cultural anthropology" is that it reveals "not only that certain kinds of activities can be analyzed to reveal popular beliefs and preconceptions but that the whole of social life, from such symbolically elaborate practices as religious festivals to such seemingly matter-of-fact activities as building houses or raising crops, is culturally shaped. 'Ideas' or 'beliefs' are not limited to certain classes of activities or to certain classes of people." Natalie Davis has observed in a similar vein that "Anthropology can widen the possibilities, can help us take off our blinders, and give us a new place from which to view the past and discover the strange and surprising in the familiar landscape of historical texts" (1981, 275). But it is not just that anthropology has a message, or that "it" can simply widen possibilities; it must be reconstituted even as it is received. Historians, specifically ethnohistorians, must not leave anthropology untouched. Historical anthropology must involve a full scale reevaluation of its constituent disciplinary bases.

Anthropologists, meanwhile, have been exhibiting increasing interest in historical approaches, and have called for more attention to everyday practices. As Sahlins writes: "there is no phenomenal ground – let alone any heuristic advantage – for considering history and structure as exclusive alternatives. Hawaiian history is throughout grounded in structure, the systematic ordering of contingent circumstances, even as the Hawaiian structure proved itself historical" (1985, 144). Sherry Ortner, in chronicling developments in anthropology since the sixties, observes that "practice" is now the buzz word of record (1984). Attending to practice is part of a move away from standard subjects such as kinship or ritual, and certainly away from standard approaches to these subjects; it is also part of a reaction against abstracted idealist and/or normative approaches to the study of society (Bourdieu 1982). History – viewed more as process than as chronology – is fundamental to this concern with practice.

Fieldwork is of course the *sine qua non* in anthropology, though fieldwork as an activity and as a ritual has been recently examined through a number of critical lenses (Rabinow 1977; Clifford 1983; Stocking 1983). Fieldwork traditionally served to privilege certain kinds of research activities and foci, justifying small scale units and synchronic questions. These apparent difficulties have not stood up well under scrutiny; as Geertz has said, anthropologists do not study villages, they merely study in them. Lévi-Strauss (1967) has himself written that the critical fact about social structure is that it must be produced and reproduced. And the recent study by Renato Rosaldo (1980) brilliantly reveals that fieldwork can itself lead the fieldworker, sometimes in spite of himself, to appreciate the centrality of history.

But what is ethnohistorical fieldwork? While historians such as Marc

Bloch and R. H. Tawney did fieldwork of a sort, and both advocated that rural historians put on their boots and experience life in the country, neither of them had any feeling that fieldwork in an anthropological sense was either essential or possible. Historians mainly concern themselves with change; can fieldwork do anything more than reveal the extent of change, or worse, blind one to the extent of change by the temptation to extrapolate directly back from the present? And in what would fieldwork consist?

In my study fieldwork was not only possible, it was necessary. From the start I intended my study to be ethnohistorical. I began with a concern about social structure and the insufficient role accorded by South Asian anthropology to the interpenetration of politics, the state, and the development of social forms (Dirks 1981). However, when I first went to the "field" between 1975 and 1977, I spent most of my time in archives, libraries, and government offices. Though I spent some time in the little kingdom, interviewing important citizens and living in the guest annex of the royal residence, I did not do the kind of fieldwork that could teach me what I needed to know about the social structure of the little kingdom. Nor could I frame in any serious contextual way the material garnered from interviews, which for the most part were held on the verandah of my annex room. As I became increasingly aware of the continuing cultural salience of royal forms of power and authority, as well as of the intricate segmental structure of royal Kallar subcastes, I realized that if any of my speculations about kingship and society were to amount to much I had to return to what was left of the little kingdom. I had to do *fieldwork*.

My conviction that I had to do fieldwork was motivated both by the gleanings of my first research stint and by my interest in stretching the methodology of ethnohistory, or historical anthropology, to the limits. I felt this need in spite of the obvious and compelling doubts I had about the relevance of any kind of ethnographic fieldwork in a region which had undergone major changes since the eighteenth century, the period on which my interest focused. How, I asked myself, can serious ethnographic fieldwork done in the late twentieth century be relevant to the reconstruction of old regime forms of society, polity, and mentality? Was I not engaging in the very colonial and comparative sociology from which I wished to break free? Was I not myself becoming a victim of what I had come to recognize as the old cliché about the timelessness of India's past?

In the course of my fieldwork, I realized even more vividly than I had in archival work that historical anthropology was not always a straightforward affair: it involved, and was often about, contradiction and struggle. The big struggle took place over meaning, not only out there between historical objects, but between me as subject and "others" as objects; between my attempt to appropriate some other past for my own uses and my recognition of a past that I knew must be approached in terms of its otherness and its silences; between me as a fieldworker who rendered confusion and disorder into significance and my "informants" who resisted my constant quest for meaning. When I returned to the field I went with the idea that I could do ethnographic work that would shed light both on the old regime and on changes that had taken place during the colonial regime as well as later in the postcolonial period. Accordingly, I held everything I learned up against the mirror of the historical shards that claim a certain chronological, if not always epistemological, priority. But I also learned that the more I learned the more confused I really was, the more I doubted my data, the more I wondered about the retrievability of any past. And I learned that fieldwork, perhaps at its best, is allegory.

While in the field during my second research stint between September 1981 and August 1982 I continued to work in the local record office with land records and new files that I found only after long months of searching. But I also played the part of the anthropologist, spending extended periods of time in a series of villages which I selected to satisfy my own research requirements. I did not look for isolated communities miles from market towns, railheads, and metalled roads, though I found myself in these on many occasions. Rather, I selected villages that had clearly had an important role in the social organization of first the royal Kallar caste and then of other castes that I selected for my study. For example, each Kallar subcaste had a central village where the head of the subcaste had lived and where the principal temple in which the members of the subcaste had their major festivals and assemblies was located. I began by visiting these communities, and then followed leads and contacts, sometimes doing intensive fieldwork with a community or set of informants, sometimes simply collecting survey information before moving on to the next village down the road or track. I attended festivals when invited, as I often was. I watched village dramas and goat sacrifices in the early hours of the morning, attended weddings at dawn, rested on the verandahs of village, lineage, or subcaste headmen during the heat of the day, chased down names and events long into the dark and mysterious evenings of the rural landscape, and pestered patient folk for meanings and memories more often than I care to remember. I recorded many conversations in their entirety, which were then transcribed by research assistants. I kept diaries. I felt myself becoming, in the sense that I too was going through that sacred rite of passage called fieldwork, an anthropologist.

But in spite of my own distance from conventional anthropological procedures and preparations, for a long time I took it for granted that my "real" fieldwork took place only in villages after I had left my home base of Pudukkottai town, where I lived first as a guest of the royal household and later as the occupant with my family, research staff, occasional informants, and servants of the second, modern, palace of the town: Sivagangai House. Then gradually I became aware that, as important as my village work was, real field work also took place in the town: in the palace, the record offices, the homes of people who became both friends and informants, and most of all in my own palace where I presided over a floating population of eight to eleven members and received countless visitors. I discovered that I had become an ethno-historical fact. People who had not thought about the old "state days" for years found a new reason and audience for their nostalgia. Other people who felt that my proximity to the royal family constituted a special form of power sought proximity to me. Still others used me as a surrogate to express their fears, ambitions, and dissatisfactions about things as they used to be and still were. Finally, I realized that I was a little – a very little – king, with my own position constituted by my relations with a larger king, and my own person surrounded by a ramified and complex social world, full of status aspirations, jealousies, intrigues, and relations of power and sometimes powerful emotion. But I also learned that I was a little king of a very particular colonial stamp. For I had no local, no horizontal, position, no kinship network that could sustain me beyond the fragile vertical relations that were clearly temporary and artifactitious. Indeed, when all was said and done I was another colonial hanger on of the princely state, there not for shikari but for business, with what seemed immense financial resources deriving from distant shores.

In my fieldwork, I not only acquired much new information, I also learned new ways of evaluating old information. Fieldwork is the production of new texts and the construction of related contexts: contexts of power, interest, motivation, intention, meaning, and action. As James Clifford has succinctly, if rather critically, put it, this process can be called "textualization" (1983).

It is the process through which unwritten behavior, speech, beliefs, oral tradition or ritual, come to be marked as a corpus, a potentially meaningful ensemble separated out from an immediate discursive or performative situation ... textualization generates sense through a circular movement which isolates and then contextualizes a fact or event in its englobing reality. (p. 130)

But fieldwork is also, as Clifford goes on to propose, the generation of discrete contexts of discourse, in which the dialogical process of field interpretation is itself the subject of critical study. The situating and resituating of texts into contexts – contexts often unspecified in "historical records" – provides not only the possibility for a critical anthropology but also for developing a more critical historical method, a method that should operate between textualization and detextualization, between construction and deconstruction.

The contexts discovered in fieldwork can lead to more general insights as well. Through context we learn that all knowledge, all meanings, are used. As Sidney Mintz writes, "I don't think meanings inhere in substances naturally or inevitably. Rather, I believe that meanings arise out of use, as people use substances in social relationships" (1985, 17). Fieldwork, particularly ethnohistorical fieldwork, reveals just how true this is. For one of the principal activities of ethnohistorical fieldwork is the "collection" of texts: ballads, folklore, family histories, temple puranas, genealogies, land records, even locally held copper plate inscriptions. As soon as the ethnohistorian becomes interested in these texts, they become valuable in new ways; we can infer the significance of these texts in part from our sense of context, and in part from reflecting about our own experience of creating new meanings for texts.

Even when using what would seem to an historian to be neutral texts, for example the eighteenth-century family histories collected by Mackenzie and his men (see Chapter 3), we must be aware that we are confronting meanings and texts that have been used and contested. Returning from my first stint of fieldwork by way of the India Office Library in London, I was stunned to discover a letter written by one Nitala Naina about his difficulties in procuring the Tondaiman Vamcavali (the family history of the Tondaiman kings of Pudukkottai) in 1804. The letter reveals that as soon as it became known that an agent of a Company servant was seeking to collect the palm leaf manuscript, the royal court became worried and protective; the king and his ministers no doubt wondered why the British sought information about the royal family. At the same time, incentives were created for the production and delivery of the text; many court retainers represented themselves as capable of procuring it, hoping all the while to gain influence if not employment with the Company Master. It took Nitala several months of wrong leads and frantic misunderstandings finally to procure a copy of the text.[5] Thus the text Nitala sought, like all texts everywhere, was not neutral: as soon as he began seeking it, he produced new contexts and meanings. Knowledge is never neutral, and the stakes are no less important today.

[5] "Letters and Reports from Native Agents Employed to Collect Books, Traditions, etc., in the Various Parts of the Peninsula," India Office Library Records, Mackenzie Collections, unbound Translations, Class XII, vol. 1, no. 3.

# PART 2
# History and ethnohistory

# 2

# *The historical context of the old regime*

## The end of the old regime: the Poligar Wars

Be it known to all the Tinnevelly Polegars, and all the inhabitants of the Pollams, that Major Bannerman is commissioned by the Honourable Company to make inquiry into misconduct of the Tinnevelly Polegars in communications with the Collector, and to punish such as may be found deserving thereof. And having, on full inquiry into the conduct of the several Polegars of Yalarampanna, Naglepore, Colarpettah, Cadulgoody, and Kolattoor, discovered that they were leagued with PanjalumCourchy in the late levying of war against the Polegar of Shevagherry, who is under the Company's protection; and that the conduct of all these Polegars has been alike disobedient and rebellious to the Government of the Company, in disregarding the authority of the Collector, refusing to pay Company's kists, committing depredations, disturbing the peace of the country, and oppressing and murdering its inhabitants; he has deemed it expedient, by virtue of his instructions, and the powers with which he is invested from the Company, to mark in the strongest manner their displeasure against such criminal proceedings; and therefore proclaims, that the Polegars of Panjalum-Courchy, Naglepore, Yalarampanna, Colarpettah, Cadulgoody, and Kolat-toor, are dispossessed of their Pollams.

*Translation of a Proclamation from Major John Bannerman Commanding Detachment on Service, to the several Polegars of the Tinnevelly Province, on the 18th Day of September, 1799*

This proclamation was issued at the commencement of a major military campaign, one of the last of the "Poligar Wars." The usual concerns of colonial conquest frame the discourse of this proclamation. The "polegars" (more frequently spelled by the British as poligars) were in fact *pāḷaiyakkārar-s* (chieftains, lords), here called "little kings" over domains (*pāḷaiyam-s*, literally armed camps) that varied greatly in size and description. According to the British, who by this time were dealing directly with these rural chiefs, some of these "poligars" had proved themselves treasonous by levying war against a protectorate of the East India Company; they had been disobedient and rebellious in not paying their taxes and engaging in murder and depredation. For these reasons, enunciated by the colonial power which redefined resistance as criminality, the poligars were declared dispossessed of their chiefly domains.

The proclamation was directed principally at the leader of the above-mentioned rebel confederacy: the "Polegar" of "PanjalumCourchy." Bannerman penned these words after two years of attempts by the British to persuade this notorious poligar, Kattapomman Nayakar, to accept Company rule, stop fighting against neighboring poligars, and start paying his tribute on a regular basis. Attempts at persuasion began in earnest in 1797 when a Mr Jackson, Collector of Poligar Peshkash [tribute] between 1797 and 1799, summoned Kattapomman to his headquarters in Ramnad (Ramanatapuram). According to British accounts, the poligar evaded the Collector for four months, and when he finally came to Ramnad attempted to escape halfway through the interview (Kearns 1873). According to the account in a Tamil ballad memorializing this encounter, the reason Kattapomman tried to escape was that he had been put in detention with the understanding that he would only be released when the tribute, or ransom, was paid (Vanamamalai 1971; Chandrasekharan 1954). Both accounts agree that when challenged, Kattapomman drew his sword and killed a young British Adjutant. In the scuffle that followed two sepoys and several of the palaiyakkarar's retainers were slain or wounded. Kattapomman escaped and joined the five palaiyakkarars mentioned above, forming the conspiratorial league which occasioned Bannerman's proclamation of 1799. Kattapomman was captured shortly thereafter by one of the military chiefs of a loyal ally of the British, the Tondaiman (Toṇṭaimāṉ) of Pudukkottai. He was hung on October 16 that year in Kayattar, a small town in Tirunelveli District.

The resistance of the palaiyakkarars did not end abruptly with the death of Kattapomman, neither had it begun only two years before. The Poligar Wars, which dragged on until 1801, might be seen as having begun in the 1740s when two campaigns were waged against these recalcitrant chieftains by the then Nawab of Arcot, Muhammed Ali, a Subahdar of the Mughal Emperor. The British joined these efforts when the Nawab, financially in a bad way after the "Second Carnatic War" (of 1749–1755) in which he defeated Chanda Sahib, his principal contestant for the Nawabship and ally of the French and the Mysoreans, commissioned the East India Company to assist him in an attempt to raise money from the southern palaiyakkarars. In early 1755 the Nawab sent Maphuz Khan with his troops and Colonel Heron with Company sepoys south to fulfill this objective. After several months of fighting the two managed to collect only 40,000 rupees more than they had spent on their expedition, a total which was less than twenty-five per cent of the settlements they had demanded. They retreated in such disarray that the brass icons from local temples, the only booty they had been able to extract from the Kallars around Madurai (Maturai) on the way south, were recovered by the Kallars along with livestock and other provisions on the return march home (MMC 17 Sept. 1755, 4:159). In late 1755 the Nawab sent Maphuz Khan to be governor of Madurai. This led to renewed outbreaks of violence when, unable to pay the annual revenue required of the governor, he joined with groups of palaiyakkarars against the Nawab and his newly deputed agent, Khan Sahib, who was posted in charge of Madurai in 1759. A year later Khan Sahib in turn joined the local palaiyakkarars in rebellion against the Nawab. Thereafter Company forces supported the Nawab in 1765 and 1767. In 1783, again under the framework of their alliance with the Nawab, the Madras Council commissioned Colonel William Fullerton to lead an expedition against Civakiri and Pancalankuricci. These expeditions were hardly more successful than that of 1755. However, the percentage of years when "poligar peshcash" was successfully collected rose with steadily increasing regularity after 1761, the decade before which it was collected in full only forty per cent of the time, to the high point of eighty per cent during the 1780s (TCR 1808, 3583:309–311).

In 1792, at the end of the Third Mysore War, a treaty was concluded between the Nawab and the Company in which the powers of administration, in particular the right to collect tribute from the palaiyakkarars in recompense for the Company's military services to the Nawab, were handed over to the Company. The treaty clearly stipulated that the Company was "desirous of preserving the rights of sovereignty over the said polygars to the said Nawab," and furthermore that the Company would "engage to the utmost of their power, and consistent with the realization of the tributes or peshcush from them, to enforce the allegiance and submission of the polygars to the said Nawab, in customary ceremonies..." (Aitchison 1930, 10:65). Under the terms of this treaty the Company pursued with increasing vigor a policy of ensuring order among and extracting revenue from the southern palaiyakkarars. In the 1790s the revenue was collected ninety per cent of the time and the average yearly collection rose from 2,560 chakrams for the 1780s to 5,300 chakrams (TCR). This decade also saw a series of intense military encounters, leading to the apprehension and execution of Kattapomman in 1799 (Rajayyan 1974).

The stage was set for the final encounters in the colonial war against the chieftains of the southern countryside. After Kattapomman was caught and put to death, his younger brother, a deaf mute by the name of Umaitturai, remained at large. Others among the rebel palaiyakkarars also continued to resist Company rule. Military activity reached a high point again in 1801, when Panjalankuricci fort was besieged for two months in April and May. The "war" finally concluded in October when

Umaitturai was captured together with the Marutu brothers of Civakankai who had joined forces with him and the other rebels. Like Kattapomman, the principal offenders were hung. In addition, "The Panjalankurichi fort was razed to the ground; the site was ploughed over and sown with castor seed, and the name of the place was expunged from all the registers of the district" (Pate 1917, 85). In 1801, on the grounds that the Nawab had violated the terms of the 1792 treaty by conspiring with Tipu Sultan against the British, a new treaty was drawn up in which the Nawab's successor became in effect a pensioner of the Company.

Thus began, in the full sense of the term, the colonial regime in south India. While the productive centers of the south had already been subjected to the patrimonial rule of the Nawab, a peculiar form of intensive but individualized administration which was heavily dependent on "tax-farmers" who were awarded contracts by the Nawab for the collection of revenue, those areas of the south outside economic and political centers had continued to be ruled by local chiefs, usually the dominant heads of the dominant castes. The local control of some of these chiefs, particularly in the northwestern areas of the Tamil country, southwestern Andhra, and southern Mysore, had already been challenged by Haidar Ali and Tipu Sultan of southern Mysore, who set out to establish highly extractive and interventionist systems of revenue collection and administration wherever they could in the late eighteenth century. But throughout the dry and mixed economy zones of Tirunelveli, Madurai, Ramanatapuram, Pudukkottai, Tiruccirappalli, Konku (Coimbatore) and to a lesser extent in northern Tamil Nadu, as well as throughout vast portions of the Andhra country, little kings continued to rule with power and authority throughout the eighteenth century. Until the turn of the century, most of these chiefs resisted attempts to incorporate them fully into the new political economy, which whether it was pushed forward by the Mysoreans or the East India Company was based on the steady collection of revenue by their local contractors or agents. Only after 1801, with the defeat of the palaiyakkarars and the new treaty with the Nawab, was the East India Company in a position to begin designing a revenue system that could be systematically implemented with a high degree of political and military control.

Still, it is an indication of the continued strength of these local lords that in the areas which had been ruled by them the British did not hasten to make revenue settlements either with individual cultivators or, given their experience in the eighteenth century under their treaty with the Nawab, the intermediary revenue contractors. Under the terms of a Permanent Settlement which was in all important respects modeled on the Cornwallis Settlement of Bengal (Guha 1963; Stokes 1978; Dirks 1986), some old regime chiefs were given the "opportunity" to become *zamindars*, the Persian term for landlord adopted by the British. A number of chiefs lost their lands for being rebellious. Those who survived the eighteenth century and were not deemed subversive by the British were "permanently" settled as zamindars on proprietary estates. Political relations were rechanneled into the new domain of proprietary law. If the zamindar defaulted on his fixed yearly payment, the estate would be put up for auction. As long as the terms of the settlement were upheld, the zamindar's position was secure. Whoever held the title, by virtue of transfer – whether by heredity, sale, or gift – was the zamindar.

The drafters of the Permanent Settlement were convinced that a series of favorable consequences would flow from this single transformation. The principal change, they thought, would be the redirection of the interests and energies of the little kings from local warfare and intrigue to agrarian management and investment. The zamindars would become the rural gentry, sources both of local stability and a steady flow of revenue. That events did not turn out this way had to do with the fact that colonial institutions only encouraged a transformation to agrarian capitalism in limited respects (Washbrook 1981). There were many contradictions in early colonial rule, which though it dismantled the old regime political system continued to maintain certain aspects of the cultural logic that had been part of that older system.

A large area of southern India was, until the late eighteenth century, still under the rule of powerful chiefs and kings. It was in large part the resistance of the little kingdoms and the obvious persistence of the local social structures they represented which led the British to make permanent revenue settlements with local kings in approximately one-third of the area demarcated as Madras Presidency, the very area which is associated in the minds of all Indian historians with the rise of the ryotwari revenue settlement. By 1829–30 there were 49,607 square miles under zamindars in Madras Presidency, about thirty-five per cent of its total area (Kumar 1965, 10–11). And these figures do not include the princely states of Mysore, Travancore, Cochin, and Pudukkottai (as well as two smaller states, Banganapalle and Sandur, located in the northern section of the Presidency) which taken together constituted about the same area as that under zamindari (not including the vast territory of the Nizam of Hyderabad).[1]

[1] Figures available in C. U. Aitchison 1930.

| | |
|---|---|
| Cochin: | 1,417 sq. miles |
| Pudukkottai: | 1,179 sq. miles |
| Banganapalle: | 275 sq. miles |
| Sandur: | 161 sq. miles |
| Travancore: | 7,625 sq. miles |
| Mysore: | 29,475 sq. miles |

Although the British officers involved in the formulation and implementation of the Permanent Settlement held low opinions of these chiefs, the settlement had few critics until some years later, when Thomas Munro and his group introduced and implemented the "ryotwari" settlement, whereby the Company contracted with individual cultivators (Beaglehole 1966; Mukherjee 1972; Stein 1981). While the initial success of the Permanent Settlement in the south had in part to do with the continued political ascendancy of a group of Company officials which saw its pathway to success in the implementation of the Cornwallis settlement, sixty years of poligar wars had persuaded many in Madras that there was no other alternative.

Stephen R. Lushington, Collector of Poligar Peshkash during the crucial years of the formulation of the Permanent Settlement from 1799 to 1803, was one of the severest critics of the palaiyakkarars, and yet he never gave public expression to any doubts about the wisdom of the settlement. His note on the "Origins of the Poliagars"[2] was one of the principal texts of the settlement. In this note Lushington advanced the following conclusions about their origins:

First, that the pretension which the Poligars advance to their present lands, on the ground of ancient immemorial possession, have little foundation. Secondly, that they were created about 300 years ago, by the policy of the hindoo Government, for the protection of the country and the support of the Sovereign; and that in the time of Tirumala Naicke, 160 years ago, they had not degenerated from the original purpose of the institution.

He saw their existence as totally contingent on an arrangement with a sovereign ruler, and that therefore they had neither political nor proprietary rights. He thereby accorded full authority to the Company to develop an appropriate policy for them. Moreover, his characterization of the palaiyakkarars was hardly flattering:

Their insolent tyranny in the absence of authority is as proverbial as their treacherous intrigue in the presence of it, and ... your records teem with relations of their delight in times of tumult and disorder, when all their favorite passions of tyrannising over the country and of contempt of their rulers may with impunity be indulged ....

Political history was little more than convenient political theory. The subordination of the poligars to the authority of the Nayakas in the sixteenth and seventeenth centuries was proof of their dependence; the insubordination of the poligars in the eighteenth century, that regret-

---

[2] Reprinted in *Collector's Report Regarding the Tinnevelly Poligars and Sequestered Pollams, 1799–1801.* Madras: At the Government Press, Tamil Nadu Archives.

table historical interlude characterized only by the absence of central authority, was proof of their insolence and their tyranny.

Lushington explained the tyranny of the palaiyakkarars by two principal factors. First,

The *assumed* power and state set up by these people is most attended to, and we believe will be found the principal cause for their turbulence. It misleads the most powerful to uphold themselves against the Circar and it stimulates the rest to rivalry and insolence. This propensity is to be seen in the six principal Poligars... These men have indulged themselves and we have no doubt still rest their ideal consequence upon their Forts, a few old guns, and a wretched equipment of stores ... by which they overawe their weaker neighbors. *The false pride derived from thence demands attention as the source of a spirit of insolence and aggression in the Poligar that is fatal to all order, obedience, and security of property* [my italics].

That obedience was owed to the British, who were busy redefining the meaning of order, and that "property" – in the sense in which the British employed the term – be secure even though it had not yet been "created" by them, were but a few of the assumptions of British conquest. The second source for the palaiyakkarars' actions rested, according to Lushington, in their illegal appropriation of "desha cawel" (*tēcakkāval*), or rights to protect the countryside which justified collecting various fees and "taxes." He saw these "rights" as one of their most invidious means of oppression:

The Collection of it was made in the most oppressive manner, by parties of armed peons, whom the Poligar detaches from his fort *as suits his convenience*, and who receives payments in money or in grain, cattle, etc., *according to circumstances*; the payment of the tax being often disputed and becoming the cause of many quarrels and the armed peons employed on these occasions frequently compelling the inhabitants to allow them batta, betel, etc., and putting them to considerable inconvenience besides extra expence [my italics].

One of Lushington's first recommendations was that the "desha cawel" right, something which he felt the palaiyakkarars as political subordinates should never have claimed in the first place, should be abolished as soon as possible. He further recommended that the palaiyakkarars' forts be demolished, their firearms appropriated, and their tribute increased. Without firearms they would not be able to collect the "desha cawel" fees, and with a higher tribute they would have fewer resources to justify their arrogance or to support their military and political establishment. Ironically, the higher tribute was explained as a commutation of "desha cawel," in what the British did not see as an implicit admission of the legitimacy of the otherwise pernicious institution.

All of these recommendations, of course, added up to nothing other than a continuation of eighteenth-century policies (i.e., of the Nawab, Tipu, and the East India Company),[3] with the new advantage of nineteenth-century colonial command. Unsurprisingly the Company followed Lushington's proposals. A report of 1803 from the Special Commission to the Governor in Council, Ft St George, explained the adoption of such a policy in terms which congratulated the Company's enlightened attitude and "progressive approach":

The Honorable Court have uniformly insisted on the absolute suppression of the military power of the poligars; and on the substitution of a pecuniary tribute more proportionate than the ordinary peishcush, to the resources of the poligar countries, and more adequate to the public demand, for defraying the expenses of general protection and government. The circumstances connected with the rebellion of the poligar (Kattaboma Nayaka) of Panjalamcourchy; the general commotion excited in the southern provinces, subsequently to the defection of that chieftain; the punishment of the rebellious chiefs, by the confiscation of their lands; the demolition of the poligar forts; the discontinuance of their military retinues; the consequent augmentation of the public revenue, and the several proclamations published by the authority of your Lordship in Council; are events which serve to mark the progressive approach in the administration of poligar affairs, inculcated by the Court of Directors, and enforced by necessity of providing for the internal tranquillity, and for the efficient exercise of the authority of government over that part of the British territories. (Mudaliyar 1940)

But why stop here? If the palaiyakkarars were such a scourge, why not make settlements with the principal peasants, as was done later in the nineteenth century in many parts of Madras Presidency?

The reason why not was succinctly stated in a Minute of the Board of Revenue, dated January 5, 1818:

The ancient zamindars and polygars were in fact the nobility of the country, and though the origin of their tenures would not bear too minute a scrutiny, they were connected with the people by ties which it was more politic, more liberal,

---

[3] Tipu Sultan in particular seems to have provided the British with a convincing role model. In the last years of the eighteenth century, Tipu commenced what appeared to be a systematic attempt to remove the local palaiyakkarars and replace them with revenue officials called *amildārs*. Often, rather than risking local revolt by directly attacking the palaiyak-karars, he would invite them to Srirankapattinam, his capital, give them honorary posts, such as that of *buksi*, and settle their families there as well with armed guards to make them in essence captives. Tipu even resumed many of the local inams in the Baramahal and had brahmadeyam lands assessed in 1784. See Firminger 1918, vol. 3; and *Baramahal Records* 1906–1920.

and more just to strengthen, than to dissolve ... when the attachment of the people to their native chieftains and the local situation of many zamindaries are considered, it may be greatly doubted whether such a policy [of reducing them to pensioners] would not have been as unwise as it would have been ungenerous, and at the time perhaps impracticable. (Mudaliyar 1940, para. 369)

The question as to whether their decision had more to do with "wisdom" than "generosity" notwithstanding, it never seems really to have occurred to officials such as Lushington, who worked in the palaiyakkarar's areas, that settlements should not be made with the local chiefs. When opposition to the Permanent Settlement mounted in the years subsequent to its enactment in 1803, the principal opponents were men who worked in areas, such as the Baramahal, where the traditional structure of political authority had already been significantly eroded by the revenue and political policies of Haidar Ali and Tipu Sultan of Srirankapattinam. Furthermore, a major impetus behind the ryotwari settlement came not from actual experience in India, but from the changing intellectual and political climate of Britain in the early nineteenth century (Stein 1981). The continued power and position of the old regime through the eighteenth century in south India was, therefore, attested to by the very institutional arrangements designed by the British to dismantle it.

Indeed, the anarchy and decay "found" by the British in south India, in addition to providing a convenient excuse for their own rule, was one way of saying that the position of the palaiyakkarars had in fact expanded during the seventeenth and eighteenth centuries. As Caldwell wrote in his history: "A very considerable portion of Southern India, south of Trichinopoly, had passed into the hands of the Poligars. In Madura and Dindigul hardly anything remained in the sovereign's possession; and in Tinnevelly the greater part of the country north of the Tāmraparnī river was in the possession of the Poligars" (Caldwell 1881, 102). The encroachment of the "periphery" over the "center" was one of the major developments of the old regime, reversing, if only partially and temporarily, the medieval balance between dynamic centers and encompassed peripheries. For the British, of course, the demise of "sovereign" rule was lamentable, and palaiyak-karar rule corrupt in the extreme:

When the English first made their acquaintance with Tinnevelly they found the whole country, whether in the hands of the Poligars or nominally in the hands of the central government, in a state of anarchy and misery, of which it is scarcely possible in these times to form any conception. This lamentable condition of things was partly owing to the feebleness and corruption of the Nawab's Government, and partly to the chronic lawlessness and incessant wars and rebellions of the Poligars. At the time referred to, when the Nawab at last determined to call in the help of the English, there were thirty-two of these hereditary chieftains in Tinnevelly, each of whom had entrenched himself in a fort and surrounded himself with a large body of armed retainers. The constant endeavour of each was to encroach on the domains of his neighbours, and especially to swallow up any villages, revenues, or rights that still remained in the possession of the central government. (Caldwell 1881, 102–103)

What the British saw as corrupt can now be read as vital and therefore threatening to the success of British conquest and control over the south.

In spite of the obvious importance of the palaiyakkarars, both because they represent the last and most vigorous survival of older social and political forms and because of their importance in the study of early British colonialism, they have been neglected by most historians. The few existing studies go little further than quoting from Lushington's much-quoted report and the military records of the time, reconstructing in considerable detail the dates and sequences of battles, seen by some as evidence of a southern precursor to the Indian war of Independence of 1857 (Rajayyan 1974; Kadhirvel 1977). Indeed, not only is there no systematic historical study of palaiyakkarar rule, there is little basis for even a preliminary conceptualization of an old regime in south Indian history. Before proceeding further with my own attempt to remedy this situation I must go briefly back in time to provide some sense of the sources of structure and ideology for old regime polity and society in southern India.

## The rise of ritual kingship in south India

The development of overarching ritual kingship in south India underwent its initial and perhaps most influential phases under the Pallava kings of the sixth through ninth centuries.[4] During this period many of the mechanisms by which hierarchical order was displayed and ritual incorporation effected first came into being. Most importantly, under the Pallavas sacrificial kingship, i.e., the notion that kings were constituted in the sacrificial arena by Vedic sacrifices such as the *rājasūya* and *aśvamedha*, was supplanted by a larger conception of the ritual domain of kingship in which the king was seen as descended from one of the two great gods of the *purāṇic* traditions, Visnu or Siva. Royal beneficence played a major role in this enlarged conception of kingly authority. Great gifts were no longer tied specifically to the sacrifice in the form of ritual dues (*dakṣiṇā*) to Brahman sacrificers. Rather, great

[4] See Dirks 1976. The next six paragraphs summarize the arguments of that paper.

gifts, in the form of large endowments of land and wealth to learned (*śrōtriya*) Brahmans and temples, became both the major ritual institution of puranic kingship and the *sine qua non* of kingly activity. Under the Pallavas, the vast proliferation of royally instituted Brahman settlements (*brahmadēyas*) and gifts which supported the construction and maintenance of temple complexes gave concrete manifestation to this royal beneficence.

Equal in importance to this development was the parallel expression of relations of hierarchical solidarity between chiefs and kings, an expression often achieved within the very context of royal gift giving. Besides the king the dominant figure in inscriptional records of grants to Brahmans and temples prior to Nandivarman II (*c.* A.D. 731-796) was the simple executor of the grant, the *ajnāpti*. In grants made during Nandivarman II's time and later the dominant figure became the petitioner, the *vijnāpti*, who petitioned that the grant be made by the king and who was presented as a powerful local chieftain in his own right. The inscriptional hymns of praise to these personages, which followed directly upon the praises to the Pallava kings themselves, suggest that these chiefs represented an order of magnitude previously embodied only in the king and his family. The expansion of the political system was such that the king was now able to establish hierarchical relations with individuals who had previously been either rivals or allies. In the inscriptions these chiefs are said to be independently virtuous and deserving of honor. They received honor by participating in the granting of royal gifts (*dānas*). In so doing they entered into a relationship with the Pallava king predicated on the sharing of the king's sovereignty. That is, they became active and necessary participants in the central royal ritual; the sovereignty of the Pallavas which was predicated on their divine origin was shared with the chieftains who embodied similar virtues on a lesser scale. In this capacity the ritual of the royal gift proclaimed the basis of sovereignty and then, by sharing the royal perquisites of that sovereignty, established authoritative relations with loyal subordinates. In pre-Pallavan periods these relations, and their perquisites, had been restricted to members of the royal family.

The development of overarching ritual kingship and the growing centrality of the royal gift during the Pallava period took place along with substantial structural changes in Tamil society. Settlement in the Tamil country appears to have accelerated during this period with the conversion of many forest tracts to settled agriculture, the inclusion of nomadic pastoralism in the context of more settled patterns of agrarian life, the growth of important mercantile towns such as Kanchipuram, the building of irrigational tanks and canals, and the rapid proliferation of royally endowed Brahmanical settlements and temples both great and small. Pallava rule was still associated with towns and settled agricultural tracts in the most productive areas, the deltaic and riverine lands where rice was the main crop. But in the eighth century Pallava rule spread further than ever before, so that rock cut temples and even some irrigational works were constructed in areas as dry as Pudukkottai (S.R. Aiyar, 1916, 44). The inclusion of both a new level in the political system and new modalities of relations between the chiefs and the king provided the mechanisms for the expansion of a regional system into a transregional system. The new ideology of sovereignty, associated as it was with the universalism of Visnu and the primordiality of the royal family's own sovereign constituents, was well suited to accommodate the larger political and economic system.

As more and more networks of chieftains and their subjects became allied to the Pallava king, the particular institutions that were proliferating as a result of the royal gifts also added to the depth and scale of the central polity. Temples became increasingly important, both as institutions with constituencies and organizational capacities and as symbolic centers in which the growth of new forms of worship was responsible for transmitting new ritual and mythological formulations to larger and more diverse groups of people. Temple worship was overshadowing Vedic practices, replacing them with the new *āgamic* codifications of rules for worship. Honors garnered in temple worship were becoming more important than those which had previously been gained in sacrificial contexts. They became constitutive of membership in social (lineage, subcaste, caste) units as well as of authority with respect to these groups, up to the level of the king. The growing importance of temples can be seen as a reflection of and a stimulus to the elaboration and consolidation of local communities, making their rulers sufficiently honorable (or powerful) to make possible (or necessitate) their incorporation into royal relationships in hitherto unprecedented ways.

This was also a period when brahmadeyas (land grants to Brahman communities) increased and grew in importance. In later Pallava times brahmadeya settlements began to develop the social infrastructures and the cultural centrality that characterized them later during Cola rule. In addition to praying for the prosperity of the kingdom and continuing to act as domestic ritual preceptors, Brahmans now took an active interest in agrarian institutions. It has been suggested that Brahmans developed a series of alliances with dominant agrarian groups during this period (Stein 1968), and their early and marked participation in locality assemblies suggests the extent of their influence in agrarian politics. The gift of a brahmadeya was the gift *par excellence* of the Pallava kings. The usual procedure for endowing a brahmadeya consisted of the redirection (*parihara*) of royal cesses (the royal share of the crop, the *mēlvāram*, and the allotment of services that were owed to the king) and the allocation of a plot of land.

The expansion of the political system developed in concert with a transactional network that extended the province of the gift as a mode of statecraft beyond the borders of single localities. Very few of the royal cesses mentioned in the inscriptions actually found their way to the central court of the king. The proliferation throughout Pallava territory of tax exempt Brahman land settlements, temples and temple land, and their accompanying corporate institutions as well as the seemingly great number of personages referred to as *bhoga gramyakas* (in the enjoyment of villages) all suggest the above conclusion. Records of local provision for other "intermediary" recipients, such as warriors, local chiefs, village headmen, as well as village servants and artisans, further confirm the vast number of short circuits in the transactional system. In addition, this system of redistribution is confirmed by the emphasis on revenue attained from plunder and the booty of war rather than from a bureaucratic system of taxation. The kingdom was, in a sense, the jajmani system writ large, if by jajmani we mean nothing more than the exchange and redistribution of goods and services in the context of a hierarchical system of social relations. The king and his intermediaries (i.e., those sanctioned and given gifts by the king), like high-caste landowning families in modern Indian villages, were provided goods and services by the various lower castes such as carpenters, potters, blacksmiths, watercarriers, sweepers, and laundrymen. This system also included relations of protection and worship.[5]

Since the ideological coherence of the king's centrality was maintained by the subordination of these various units to the Pallava dynasty, the inscriptional rhetoric which posited a royal claim on all these goods and services was in no sense vitiated by the decentralized functioning of the system. However, the initiative for the reallocation of certain resources to recipients such as Brahmans and temples became diffused throughout the higher levels of the system over time. This appears to have been a constant feature of imperial systems in the south, where the expansion of the kingly jajmani system seemed to necessitate

---

[5] Hocart (1968, 68) was perhaps the first to note, though with respect to material on the Kandyan state of Sri Lanka, the structural homology of the royal state and jajmani relations. Jajmani itself was less a colonial invention, as Perlin has suggested (1983), than it was the truncated residue of colonial intervention, a system of exchange localized solely within villages. See Fuller's (1977) discussion of this.

this devolution of kingly activity and agency. More and more intermediaries – persons who had local constituencies and control over local institutions such as temples and locality assemblies – arose in the system. Under the Pallavas, the mechanism of shared sovereignty relations made it possible for the political system to expand as a single cultural entity, at least for some time.

While the Pallava empire soon grew weak under the repeated onslaughts of the Rastrakutas from the northwestern Deccan, the importance of the local chiefs did not diminish. Their importance continued throughout the succeeding centuries under an even greater dynastic system. The magnificent Cola empire, based in Tanjavur and thus centered in the fertile basin of the Kaveri river (a much larger and more fertile area than that around the Palar river in the Pallava's home base of Tontaimantalam), ruled at its height from A.D. 1000 to 1200. Burton Stein, in his careful and highly suggestive work on the Colas, convincingly demonstrates that the most significant units of social structure and agrarian organization under the Colas were not villages, as important as their constituent assemblies were, but rather "peasant micro-regions," or *nāṭus*: "the enduring and basic units of south Indian peasant society" (Stein 1980, 13).

These natus were of a variety of kinds, mostly depending on whether or not they were in the Cola macro region and on their placement either within or outside of this region near central, intermediate, or peripheral ecological zones. But in all natus, albeit in varying degrees depending on the above-mentioned coordinates, multi-village assemblies which represented each natu orchestrated the principal affairs having to do with agrarian decision making over cultivation rights, the management and allocation of usufructuary rights to irrigation sources, and the particular organization and disposition of local systems of redistribution. In addition, these natus, even when as in many central areas their caste composition was especially heterogeneous, were characterized by a sense of "shared ethnicity." Stein's thesis, developed largely on the basis of his analysis of the rhetoric of Cola inscriptions, seems all the more convincing in the light of ample modern-day ethnographic evidence that territorial association has played a strong role in defining social groups in south India, a tendency accentuated by cross-cousin types of marriage systems as well as locally elaborate and culturally distinct systems of ranking and caste interaction (Inden and Marriott 1974; Daniel 1984).

Two major structural developments took place in the twelfth and thirteenth centuries. First, supra-local assemblies called the *periyanāṭu* emerged. Acting over congeries of localities, the periyanatu signalled the diminished isolation and autonomy of the discrete natu units, and increased the authority of certain supra-local leaders, or *Periyanāṭṭār* (Stein 1980, 216). Second, the process of settlement proceeded more quickly than ever before. *Veḷḷāḷars*, the highest non-Brahman caste, continued to expand their control over riverine and deltaic areas in the south, and also moved into new areas such as the upland plain of the Konku country.

In addition, prefiguring the important changes of the Vijayanagara period, throughout much of the Tamil country new groups such as Kallars and *Maṟavars* progressively converted uncultivated lands which were often just outside the major areas of settlement to peasant agriculture. This settlement probably occurred first, during Cola times, in the Ramnad, Madurai and Pudukkottai areas, and later in portions of Tirunelveli and Tanjavur. Stein notes that in these areas "the relationships between a particular ethnic group and the territory were perhaps stronger than in the older peasant core areas" (Stein 1980, 109). These areas for the most part correspond with the mixed economy zones of Ludden's description in which local territorial forms of dominance were most highly developed (Ludden 1978a). Both Maravars and Kallars have been divided into endogamous sub-divisions which correspond with territorial sub-divisions. For the most part (except for Tanjavur), both Maravars and Kallars settled in areas left unoccupied by the earlier high caste settlers of the Tamil country (mostly Vellalars and Brahmans) or in areas where they ousted these other caste groups from positions of dominance. In addition, both Kallars and Maravars settled in ways designed to facilitate single caste, and at a local level single subcaste, dominance. Although both groups often settled in areas contiguous to each other, Kallars and Maravars rarely settled together in the same locality. The areas of Kallar and Maravar settlement were not unoccupied by lower caste or tribal groups. In many forest tracts, the earliest settlers seem to have been *Kuṟumpars*, *Vetars*, and *Valaiyars*, all of whom are associated with the forest. These groups soon became subordinated to the new dominant agrarian groups.

Strong locality institutions such as the natu were not incompatible with the existence of strong chiefs in the countryside, since these chiefs were the authoritative representatives of their locality and social formations (which were often in essence territorially segmented and politically shaped subcaste and lineage systems of dominant caste groups). On the contrary, these chiefs were of crucial importance during the Cola period, particularly after the rise of the periyanatus. Stein suggests that these chiefs were none other than the myriad "officials" and "bureaucrats" of traditional south Indian historiography. According to many south Indian historians, personages who held titles such as *uṭaiyār, aracar, mummaṭi, mūventavēḷār, atikāri*, etc., were the officials in what Nilakanta Sastri labels a "byzantine monarchy" (1955, 447). In Stein's more general critique of this conception of the Cola state, he argues that these figures were not officials of a centralized state but rather locality chieftains who were incorporated into a segmentary state in different degrees over time and space. Stein claims that these chieftains and their natus were incorporated into the ritual order of the Cola state both through the imitation by these local chiefs of the "dharmic" activities of the Cola kings and the acceptance by these chiefs of the latters' ritual hegemony (Stein 1975, 1980).

In the period following the demise of the Cola empire in the thirteenth and fourteenth centuries, the locality assemblies which figured so prominently under first the Pallavas and later the Colas declined steadily in importance. The ascendancy of the Deccan over the Tamil country played an important role in this. Initiated by the Hoysala kingdom of the late thirteenth and early fourteenth centuries, this ascendancy was an indisputable fact after the rise of Vijayanagara a century later. Under this new "warrior regime" (Stein 1969, 192), the chiefs (*araiyars*) of the more marginal areas of the Tamil country thrived. These chiefs included the chiefs of Tamil castes with strong subcaste and lineage organization such as the Kallars and Maravars who had earlier settled in marginal areas and the new Telegu migrant chiefs who moved south along with the influence of Vijayanagara. The vast migration of Telegu warriors and castes into the Tamil country made visible one of the major transformations of the Vijayanagara period – the breakdown of traditional geographical and ethnic boundaries and the corollary reconstitution of political centers and peripheries, both between the Tamil country and greater south India and within the Tamil country itself.

The Vellalar chiefs of the riverine and deltaic regions came under increasing pressure and control from these smaller chiefs, a significant part of whose livelihood came from predatory raids on the granaries and villages of the productive centers. They also came under pressure from within their own areas by new Telegu overlords, or Nayakas. Three major Nayakas ruled as the representatives of Vijayanagara and as the successors of the ancient Tamil kings in Gingee (Pallavas), Tanjavur (Colas), and Madurai (Pantiyas). These Nayakas dominated the periyanatu assemblies and ultimately replaced leaders of the periyanatus with their own agents, many of whom were the chiefs of previously marginal areas. The Vellalars thus lost their ability to control natu localities through the combination of ideological solidarity (called "ethnicity" by Stein) and institutional management (viz. the periyanatu assemblies) which had characterized the Cola heartlands in the Cola period. The palaiyakkarars were instrumental to the success of Nayaka rule because of their strong military capabilities which in turn derived from their kin based control over the peripheral domains over which they gained increasing control during this period. In conjunction with the Nayakas, the palaiyakkarars consolidated their own forms of locality control over areas that had only recently undergone substantial settlement and asserted increasing forms of pressure on the central regions, ultimately reducing the regional social and political forms of the core areas to village level forms.

Because of the establishment of close political relations between the peripheral palaiyakkarars and the Nayakas, the former group became linked to the great imperial political system known by the name of its capital city, Vijayanagara. The Vijayanagara sovereigns provided a center which oriented all political activity and which was emulated – even after its demise – by all the kings, big and little, of the south (Dirks 1982). We must therefore take a brief look at the crystallization of kingship under Vijayanagara in late medieval south India.

## Vijayanagara: the city of victory

When the first of four successive Vijayanagara dynasties was established in the early fourteenth century, the regional base of the kingdom was in the western Deccan, north of the base of the preceding Hoysala dynasty, and south of the centers of the still earlier Chalukyas and Rastrakutas. The city of Vijayanagara, literally meaning the city (*nagara*) of victory (*vijaya*), was established along the banks of the river Tungabhadra, a tributary of the river Krishna, in and around what is today called the village of Hampi. This city, continually extended and fortified by its kings, served as the capital of the empire until 1565, when it was sacked by the combined Muslim forces of Bijapur, Golkanda, and Ahmednagar (and some say Bedar as well) in the battle of Talikota.

Vijayanagara's rise to supra-regional power departs from earlier dynastic patterns in several major respects. Most historians have emphasized the "martial" character or aggressively "Hindu" ideology of Vijayanagara in relation to earlier states such as the Colas and the Pallavas, but while the military apparatus of the kingdom was indeed highly developed the ideological attribution of "Hindu" bears far more relation to late colonial notions of the term and concept than to anything found in contemporaneous political discourse. Two other changes stand out as being of far greater importance. First, Vijayanagara added the southern Tamil country to the same power base as earlier

Deccani regimes. Though the Rashtrakutas succeeded in humbling the Pallavas, they were never able to establish hegemony over the Tamil region for any extended period of time. Secondly, the growth of Vijayanagara power was coincident with, and in many important respects vital to, the process by which the authority of centrally placed natus and their "peasant chiefs" was replaced by that of warrior chiefs and clans who came from both Telegu and previously marginal Tamil areas.

Whether in relation to Telegus or Tamils, or big Nayakas or small palaiyakkarars, Vijayanagara clearly provided the locus of political authority throughout a large area for several centuries. However, there are no grounds for proposing that the Vijayanagara state was any more "bureaucratic" than previous states, and only minor grounds for proposing that it had a higher degree of centralization than earlier political systems. Ritual forms continued to constitute and express relations between lesser and greater kings in the political system, though often in new ways. We will now look briefly at state ceremonial under Vijayanagara and its relation to the ideological construction of sovereignty in the new regime.

The prefatory panegyric (*praśasti*) of the Nallur grant of Harihara II (EI, 3:113–126), the third Vijayanagara king who ruled in the last quarter of the fourteenth century, aptly prefaces not only the grant itself but this discussion of Vijayanagara sovereignty as well. First, it tells us that the Vijayanagara kings were of the lunar race. Most medieval Indian kings were thought to have a special connection with either the sun or the moon. As Inden explains, "To have the substances of the sun and moon in their bodies meant that kings too were powerful deities transcending the earth and were, like the sun and the moon themselves, intimately involved in the regulation of the day, the month, and the year" (Inden 1978a, 35). Harihara II's divine nature is made additionally clear by his title of *Maheśvara*, which in general means a great lord and specifically refers to Siva. The panegyric compares their attributes. It identifies them even more directly asserting that Harihara is an incarnation of Skanda, the son of Siva. It adds that this great lord, Harihara, whose name identifies him with Visnu (*hari*) as well, is renowned in particular for his power (*sakti*). This is both explained and exemplified by his substantial and metaphorical likeness to the two great gods of the medieval Indian pantheon. The panegyric specifies that Harihara protects the earth according to *dharma* (the rightful order of things; *rājadharma*, the duty of the king, is the protection of this order) and presides over a prosperous realm, where the people, "unafflicted by calamities, were continually enjoying festivals." As further aspects of the Vijayanagara king's performance of rajadharma, Harihara upheld "the observances of all the castes and orders [*varnashramadharma*]" and by so doing made the earth (up to the four oceans) "the celestial cow itself in fulfilling all desires."

The inscription goes on to state that King Harihara, "having taken away the wealth of rival kings (as suddenly) as a falling thunderbolt, performed the sixteen great gifts, viz. the gift of his weight in gold (tulāpurushadāna), etc....".

An important general source of income, plunder provided for the "great gifts," *mahādānas*. These gifting ceremonies, performed earlier by the Rastrakutas and the Colas (Sastri 1955, 135, 186, 451–452), became central to the constitution of Vijayanagara sovereignty. Other inscriptions confirm that the reign of Harihara was particularly well known for his performance of these great gifts. They point to these ritual actions as of special importance for the representation of Vijayanagara's supreme sovereign status. In an inscription of Harihara's son in 1405, the opening genealogy includes the statement that "His [Bukkaraja's] son is King Harihara, who equals Sutrâman [Indra] in power [and] who, being devoted to [the performance of] the sixteen great gifts, has destroyed [the sins of] the Kali (age)" (EI, 3:224–230).

The two most often cited great gifts were the *tulāpurusadāna* (or *tulabhāra*), the weighing of the king against gold, and the *hiraṇyagarbha*, or the birth from a golden embryo. Inden notes that in the puranic sources for the mahadana these are the two most important, and that "the Hindu *mahādāna* was first performed as a replacement for it (the *srauta* sacrifice) by Dantidurga, the first imperial Rastrakutas around 753" (Inden 1977, 11). This is especially pertinent for two reasons. First, the Rastrakutas were based in the western Deccan, not far from the subsequent seat of Vijayanagara rule. Second, the Rastrakutas loomed large for the Colas, who were able to attain their imperial position in large part because of the Rastrakuta's success in humbling their powerful northern neighbors, the Pallavas. Situating Rastrakuta and Cola ritual discourse in a larger context, Inden writes that "By the eleventh century, founders (or restorers) of imperial kingdoms in all quarters but the western declared their independence by performing a Hindu 'great gift' ceremony" (Inden 1977, 11). In other words, by the time of the great Colas the performance of the great gift ceremony became the principal ritual modality of kingly beneficence as well as the particular sign of overlordship and independence.

Vijayanagara exemplifies this pattern. The inscriptional announcement of the performance of great gifts by the early Vijayanagara kings proclaimed their beneficence as well as the independence of their new empire. The same had been true of inscriptional references to performances of Vedic sacrifice by the early Pallava kings. The initial performances of sacrifices such as the rajasuya were adequate for the whole dynasty. Thereafter direct descent from the line of kings who had performed the sacrifice was sufficient. Not so with great gifts, references to the performance of which continued throughout the corpus of Vijayanagara inscriptions. As late as 1634 an inscription of Venkata III claimed that the "learned Brahmans were anointed (or abundantly presented) with gold" by Venkata himself (EI, 3:236–258).

The shift from the Vedic sacrifice to the great gift as the central constituent action of ritual kingship was part of a more general transition from the ritual worship practiced in the sacrifice to the devotional worship, or *pūjā*, of puranic Hinduism. The building of temples and their steadily increasing importance in Tamil society was predicated on the formulation and practice of this new conception of worship. Puja involves the honoring of the deity by the offering of garlands of flowers, clothing, hymns and mantras, as well as other sanctified things or actions. The most central offering is food, more often uncooked items such as plantains and coconuts but also cooked food such as sweet rice. The fundamental actions of puja attend "to the bodily needs of a deity placed in an enlivened image or emblem – bathing, oiling, dressing, fanning, perfuming, waving lights, doing obeisance, holding an umbrella and making offerings of food to the deity ... [in short] the rendering of hospitality or service to the deity" (Inden 1978a, 36–37). The highlight of puja is feeding the god and then returning some portion of the offerings used in worship as *pracātam* (transvalued substance). Pracatam typically consists of the leavings (*ucchiṣṭa*) of the food which was first tasted by the deity and then returned to the devotees for their consumption. Other privileges concerning "physical contact" are also part of the performance of puja.[6]

Complicated procedures for puja, particularly in temples, but also in domestic shrines, were codified in the *āgamas*, texts which became as important procedurally for the conduct of puja as the Vedas had been for the sacrifice, though the Vedas were still considered preeminent and Vedic mantras (sounds, chants, verses) still played a major role in the new forms of worship. Most ritual activity thus became a puja.

If the mahadana became the principal ritual performance of Vijayanagara polity, the principal ritual occasion for this and other

---

[6] Inden 1978a, 37. For other accounts of puja see Babb 1975; and Breckenridge 1976.

gifting activity became the *Mahānāvami*, otherwise called *Dasarā*, *Durgôtsava*, or *Navarātra* (in Tamil, Navarāttiri, meaning nine nights). The festival, in all of its many forms, was celebrated on the first nine nights and ten days of the lunar month *Aśvina*, roughly the period from mid September to mid October. As yet another name of the festival, *Durgāpūjā*, readily suggests, the ritual occasion consisted basically of the worship of the goddess Durga, although in later and variant forms the worship of other goddesses, often tutelary, also took place.

According to the *Devipurāṇa*, the purposes and objects of this festival were all-encompassing:

> This is a great and holy *vrata* conferring great *siddhis*, vanquishing all enemies, conferring benefits on all people, especially in great floods; this should be performed by Brahmanas for solemn sacrifices and by ksatriyas for the protection of the people, by vaiśyas for cattle wealth, by Sūdras desirous of sons and happiness, by women for blessed wifehood and by rich men who hanker for more wealth. (Kane 1974, 5:156)

But, as Kane notes, these objects were scaled down in the *Devīmāh-ātmya*, which simply states that, "by listening with devotion to my greatness in the great annual puja performed in autumn, a man becomes free from all troubles and becomes endowed with wealth and agricultural produce by my favour" (Kane 1974, 5:156–157).

A great variety of puja rites characterized the performance of the Durgôtsava. The texts prescribed the sacrifice of animals, particularly goats and buffaloes. In addition, animals figured in the ritual in that kings and others who kept horses were advised to honor horses from the second to the ninth days, in way reminiscent of all but the culminating features of the Vedic horse sacrifice, the asvamedha. In addition to the particular rites associated with each day, there were certain ubiquitous daily features such as the worship of Durga (the goddess) and extravagant gifts to Brahmans and others. The ninth day became known as Ayudha puja, when, in conjunction with the worship of the goddess Sarasvati, one worshipped the implements of one's profession – horses and weapons for warriors, tools for workmen, ploughs for cultivators, books for scholars. *Āyudha* means weapon or arms, thus suggesting the possible military etymology of this rite, an etymology all the more convincing because of the specific associations of the next and final day with Ksatriyas and military victory.

As the kings of Vijayanagara performed it, Durgôtsava culminated on *Vijayadāsami*, the tenth day, the day of victory. According to Kane (p. 190), Vijayadasami, or Dasara, though a great day for people of all castes, was especially so for ksatriyas, nobles, and kings. There was a major procession to a place of worship. The royal priest (*purōhita*) accompanied the king, ceaselessly reciting verses about the victory of the king in the four quarters. The king honored worthy Brahmans, the astrologer, and the purohita, and "arrange[d] sports of elephants, horses, and footsoldiers" (p. 191). After the puja of the goddess, arrows were shot in the presence of the king signifying the victory of the gods over the asuras and, more specifically, Durga's defeat of the buffalo demon, Mahisasura. When the king reentered his palace his entire retinue shouted "jaya," meaning victory, while courtesans waved lights before him. The king who performed this auspicious ceremony every year would gain long life, health, prosperity, and victory. A king who did not celebrate Vijayadasami could not anticipate victory within the year.

The great importance of this ceremony for Vijayanagara is shown by the massive architectural presence of the Mahanavami Dibba (platform) that still dominates the ruins of the old city and the elaborate if culturally problematic accounts of the festival in the contemporaneous reports of two Portuguese observers. The narratives of Domingos Paes, probably written between 1520 and 1522, and Fernao Nuniz, composed between 1535 and 1537, provide historians with most of their information about Vijayanagara society and polity.[7] These accounts, at the very least, reveal a splendor for which even these world-wide travelers were unprepared. Their observations and descriptions provide a general sense – however flawed in its particulars – that the ritual activity of the Mahanavami was central to the Vijayanagara state.

These Portuguese sources confirm, for example, that the main action of the ritual was the worship of the goddess by the king, the principal devotee. While the king performed his puja, he underwent his yearly coronation, the *paṭṭābhiṣēka* (ritual unction). This ritual commenced the king's rule. It was repeated at least once a year to renew the king's sovereignty (Inden 1978b, 20). To further effect the infusion of cosmic power into the king, the king's sceptre (*ceṅkōl*), his principal emblem, was entrusted to the goddess during most of the festival. The king sat before the deity, who occupied the royal throne. "Many Brahmans stand round the throne on which rests the idol, fanning it with horsetail plumes, colored, the handles of which are all overlaid with gold; these plumes are tokens of the highest dignity; they also fan the king with

[7] See accounts in Sewell 1970, 228–376. As valuable as the accounts are, they must be read very carefully, for they reveal preconceptions about everything from feudal political structures to religious beliefs. For example, a Portuguese observer once speculated that the reason Navaratt-iri consisted of nine nights was to represent the nine months of the gestation of Christ in the virgin's womb.

them" (Sewell 1970, 260). The king is depicted as the principal devotee of the deity with whom he is simultaneously identified. The emblems of both are conspicuously mixed together, though the king has relinquished his throne to the deity.

The honoring of the deity and of the king are ritually homologous. The king is given offerings by his nobles at the same time, and in the same ways, as the king himself gives offerings to the deity. As Nuniz writes,

The greatest mark of honour that this King of Bisnaga confers on a noble consists of two fans ornamented with gold and precious stones, made of the white tails of certain cows, he gives them bracelets also. Everything which the noble receives is placed on the ground. The King confers very high honours, too, if he permits a certain one to kiss his feet, for he never gives his hands to be kissed by anyone. When he wishes to receive good service, he gives them scarves of honour for their personal use, which is a great honour; and this he does each year to the captains at the time that they pay him their land-rents. (Sewell 1970, 356–357)

These honors thus included emblems which were part of the king's person and which the king had used in his worship of the deity. In addition, the king dispensed honors such as the privilege of kissing his feet, replicating the *tirupātam* rite, literally the worship of the feet of the deity. The various emblems and privileges given in this context – like the returned portion of the pracatam – all "symbolized the incorporation of the recipient into his [the king's] person as his subordinate, to act in future as an extension of himself" (Inden 1978a, 56).

On the tenth day, according to Paes, a tent was pitched a league from the city. On the processional route from the palace to the tent, "the captains range themselves with their troops and array, each one in his place according to his rank in the king's household" (Sewell 1970, 264). Then, after a long description of the impressive spectacle of these soldiers lining the route, concentrating in particular on their costumes, decorations, and heraldic emblems, Paes describes the progress of deity and king:

The king leaves his palace riding on the horse of which I have already told you, clothed in the many rich white cloths I have mentioned, with two umbrellas of State all gilded and covered with crimson velvet, and with the jewels and adornments which they keep for the purposes of wearing at such times: he who ever wears such jewels can understand the sort of things so great a lord would wear... There went in front of the king many elephants with their coverings and ornaments, as I have said; the king had before him some twenty horses fully caparisoned and saddled, with embroideries of gold and precious stones, that showed off well the grandeur and state of their lord. Close to the king went a cage such as is seen at Lisbon on the day of the Corpo de Dios festival, and it was gilded and very large; it seemed to me to be made of copper or silver; it was carried by sixteen men, eight on each side, besides others who took their turns, and in it is carried the idol ... Thus accompanied the king passed along gazing at his soldiers, who gave great shouts and cries and struck their shields; the horses neighed, the elephants screamed, so that it seemed as if the city would be overturned, the hills and valleys and all the ground trembled with the discharge of arms and musquets; and to see the bombs and fire-missiles over the plains, this was indeed wonderful. Truly it seemed as if the whole world was collected there. (ibid., pp. 267–268)

In a sense, of course, the whole world was there, and certainly the scale of ceremony was such to render the concept of ritual microcosm virtually meaningless.

The first nine days of the festival can thus in retrospect be viewed as preparation for the tenth, the day on which the king's procession and his glorious worship of the deity regenerates the cosmos with the king at its manifest center. During each part of the festival victory is achieved: through the ritual unction and installation (or reinstallation) of the king, through the king's magnificent pujas to the deity, and through the homologous offerings made to the king by the chieftains of the realm, what Nuniz calls land rents. Puja was conducted through the medium of emblems, the emblems with which the king worshipped the deity – central to which were his throne and sceptre – and which thereupon represented the newly charged sovereignty of the king. The sharing of the king's sovereignty through the transactions of the festival had the effect of incorporating the disparate elements of the kingdom into his sovereign being and rendering them all parts – metonyms – of himself, even as the emblems were themselves metonyms of his sovereignty.

This ritual splendor, however theatrical (Geertz 1980), was not mere entertainment. It was simultaneously based on cosmology and command. The Vijayanagara sovereign derived authority through the significant displays of ritual kingship, which itself depended by then on arms and muskets to make the earth tremble. He then differentially distributed that authority among those chiefs who sought a place under (and often a piece of) the imperial umbrella. But in order to garner the wealth necessary for these displays, indeed to make possible the creation of the great city which was the stage for the ritual, and to provide the protective shelter implied by the largess and largeness of the umbrella, cosmology was in turn dependent on command. Command, after all, made victory possible.

Command was exercised over many subordinate kings, who in turn commanded "chiefs," and so on down the line to the predominantly peasant base of southern society. The loyalty of kings and chiefs made possible the military supremacy of Vijayanagara, largely unassailed until the fateful battle of Talikota in 1565. The maintenance of Vijayanagara's military supremacy, however, increasingly required new and more diverse arenas of command and control, such as the monopoly over the import and trade of horses from Arabia. Nuniz came to south India for three years as a trader in horses. The use of muskets and artillery was also a crucial determinant in Vijayanagara's success against the great Muslim powers north of the Tungabhadra river. Great fortresses were built to enclose the cities of the Nayakas. The temples of the period were constructed as much like forts as like places of worship (Stein 1980, 400–404). Ritual and military technologies symbiotically sustained the wonder of Vijayanagara through "warrior rule."

### Warrior rule and the Tamil country

But what exactly was "warrior rule"? This convenient phrase masks the historiographical problem of determining who these warriors were, what this rule consisted of, and how polity and society changed – and continued to change – as a result of the set of interconnected transformations which began in the fourteenth century.

The greatest of the subordinate warrior lords of the Vijayanagara empire, prime candidates for any examination of "warrior rule," were the *Nāyakas*. According to Nuniz, some 200 Nayakas held land rights from the Vijayanagara king who "owned" all the land (Sewell 1970, 379).[8] Vijayanagara inscriptions often use the term *amaranāyaṅ-*

---

[8]  This assumption has been cited by at least one scholar as a justification for applying the term "feudal" to what virtually all scholars have called the Vijayanagara "Nayaka system" (Krishnaswami 1964, p. 179; see Stein 1975). Sathyanatha Aiyar writes about the establishment of the Madurai "Nayakship" (R. S. Aiyar 1924). D. C. Sircar in his epigraphical glossary accepts Mahalingam's view that a Nayaka was "one who held lands from the Vijayanagara kings on the condition of offering military service" (Sircar 1966, 214). Nilakanta Sastri writes that "military fiefs studded the whole length and breadth of the empire, each under a *Nāyak* or military leader authorized to collect revenue and to administer a specified area provided he maintained an agreed number of elephants, horses, and troops ever ready to join the imperial forces in war" (Sastri 1966, 307). In common with most other historians of this period, Sastri cites as principal evidence for this notion the writings of the Portuguese observers whose perceptions of Vijayanagara we have already seen to be determined by their experience of Christian Europe.

*'kara* for the rights over land held by these Nayaka lords.[9] Aside from the Portuguese accounts and subsequent historiographical systematization of the "tenures" of these chiefs, there is no evidence supporting the claim that the Nayakas held their lands in a tenurial system in which feudal obligations were contractually specified. Political relations were contingent on kinship and other social and strategic considerations and were dependent on the continuance of the offerings and gifts which constituted them in the first place. They were therefore necessarily always in flux. In fundamental contrast to the western European world of feudalism, the order, and therefore the relational significance, of land and service was reversed. In Europe lands were held by vassals on the condition of service. In south India, however, service was offered first, with the hope/expectation that gifts (of land, titles, emblems, honors, privileges, etc.) would follow, in turn leading to new opportunities to offer service.

Rights to land under Vijayanagara rule were distributed widely throughout polity and society. According to some estimates, seventy-five per cent of all land was not crown (*bhandāravāṭa*) but controlled by amaranayankaras. Inscriptions offer evidence that many villages were endowed to support Brahmans, temples, monasteries, and other such charities. Within villages, many shares of village income were directed to various village "servants" or *āyakārs*.[10] The twelve ayakars identified by Krishnaswami include the village headman, accountant, watchman, priest, goldsmith, waterman, blacksmith, carpenter, potter, washerman, barber, and cobbler. These persons were granted tax-free lands and were allocated a specified share of the harvest (pp. 104–105).

The title Nayaka was used by a great variety of chiefly personages, ranging widely in position and power. If there was a Nayaka system, feudal or otherwise, it was not very systematic. Nonetheless, there was an upper tier of Nayakas who were powerful chiefs in their own right as well as being powerfully connected to the Vijayanagara kings. According to Krishnaswami, the prototype of the great Nayakas were the *Mahāmaṇṭaleśvaras*, most of whom were kinsmen of the royal family in the early stage of Vijayanagara rule. Later Nayakas (particularly those who settled in the Tamil country) were not actually royal relatives, but saw themselves as closer than kin because of the acceptance of gifts from

---

[9] The term means the person (*kara*) holding the title of chief (Nayaka) who is in command (*amara*) of a body of troops. The term *amar* itself means war, battle, fighting, battlefield, among other things.

[10] Krishnaswami suggests that the demise of the old village institutions made necessary the formalization of certain village "offices" and procedures for remunerating village level services.

the hands of the Vijayanagara kings. These Nayakas never assumed the titles of great kings or universal overlords even though they became increasingly "independent" as time went on. This process accelerated after the great defeat at Talikota in 1565, but did not have major implications for the foundations of Vijayanagara rule until the "civil war" of Topur in 1616, when the Nayakas battled among themselves on the occasion of a succession dispute in the Vijayanagara royal family. While the reflected glory of Vijayanagara continued to be an important component of the representation of the authority of these Nayakas, there are numerous indications that they operated more as kings in their own right than as agents for their superior overlords.

Madurai in particular was a political liability and a drain on the empire because of its geographical position at the southern end of the empire and because of the relatively recent and powerful rule of the Pantiyas. From the campaign of Madurai's first "viceroy" Kumara Kampana against the Muslim sultanate in the late fourteenth century (or even from the beginning of Cola decline which dates back to a twelfth-century Pantiyan uprising) to the British experience in the late eighteenth century, Madurai unfailingly provided ample ground for imperial anxiety. In the early sixteenth century, when Madurai was being more troublesome than usual, Nagama Nayaka, a major figure in the imperial court, was despatched to Madurai (Taylor 1835, 2:11). Despite the difficulties of commanding the allegiance and the tribute of the many local chiefs, including descendants of the Pantiyan rulers who had been most recently ruling in western Tirunelveli and other Maravars and Kallars, Nagama's son, Visvanatha, regained control of Madurai for Vijayanagara. Yet the rule of Visvanatha is seen by most historians not as the end but as the beginning of the quasi-independent rule of the Madurai Nayakas (R. S. Aiyar 1924).

The Madurai Nayakas ruled from at least the early sixteenth century until 1736, the year the last Nayaka queen, Minaksi, committed suicide after she was imprisoned by the Nawab of Arcot. Contemporary Jesuit observers and most historians refer to the Madurai Nayakas as "viceroys" of Vijayanagara, while conceding the increasing independence of the Madurai dynasty from their overlords during the seventeenth century. Dating this "independence" is the major focus of contentious debate among historians of the period. The cultural form and meaning of political relationships has been more assumed than examined in this debate, with "independence" a simple gloss for not paying tribute or, in an even more extreme form, active rebellion.

Early inscriptions of the Madurai Nayakas refer to them as "agents" (the word is usually some form of *kāriyam* or *kāriyakārar*, or *karttākkaḷ*) of the Vijayanagara kings. In an inscription of 1546, Visvanatha Nayaka is said to be the agent (*kāriyattukku kattarāṉ*) of Devamaharaja Sadasivamaharaja (Burgess 1886, 108–109). An inscription of 1550 records a gift of *dēvadāṉa* (gift to god) land, by Visvanatha the *agent* of Mahamandalesvara Ramaraja Vittalayyadeva-Maharaja, for the latter's merit (R. S. Aiyar 1924, no. 33, 337). An inscription of 1558 contains a similar formulation (no. 48, pp. 339–340). An inscription of 1570 records a grant by Ariyanata Mutaliyar and two others, all agents of Visvanatha, Krisnappa, and Virappa, who were themselves agents of the Mahamandalesvara Ramaraja Tirumalai Raja (no. 65, p. 342).

At about this time a shift takes place in the rhetorical style of these inscriptions, especially in those post-Visvanatha inscriptions in which there are no references to him. For the first time grants were made by the Vijayanagara sovereign at the request of the Madurai Nayaka. An inscription of 1566 records a grant of a number of villages to the Tiruvenkatanata temple made by Sadasiva at the behest of Krisnappa Nayaka (who is said to know the truth about duty) (EI, 9:328–342); an inscription of 1586 records a grant of the Vijayanagara king, Venkatapati I, made at the request of Virappa Nayaka (EI, 12:159–187); and a similar inscription of 1634 records a grant by Vira Venkatipati Maharaja (EI, 3:236–258). On the one hand, these grants suggest a renewed solidarity in the relations between subordinate kings and their overlords, or at least a new mode of relations to replace the more personal tie between Visvanatha and Vijayanagara; on the other hand, as had been the case with relations between Pallava kings and their subordinate chiefs in the eighth century, these imperial inscriptions (the earlier inscriptions we cited were issued locally) now had to incorporate the praiseworthy nature of these lesser kings. These lesser kings have moved from being passive reflections of the great and undisputed overlordship of the Vijayanagara kings to acting in more innovative ways.

During the reign of Tirumalai Nayaka (1623–1659), the best known and most dynamic ruler of the Nayaka line, references to Vijayanagara in Nayaka inscriptions recede to the position of regnal dating. In most of the inscriptions which record grants made by the Nayakas after 1634, the year of the grant is identified in terms of the year in the reign of a particular Vijayanagara sovereign without making any explicit connection between Vijayanagara and the Nayakas (R. S. Aiyar 1924, 353–372). Nevertheless, as late as 1729 a long panegyric on the Vijayanagara kings accompanies the regnal dating. But no specific connection between the two dynasties is made aside from the bare statement that while the Vijayanagara kings ruled in the north the Madurai Nayakas ruled in the south (Burgess 1886, 118).

The conventional historical emphasis on the growing "independence" of the Nayakas in general, and the Madurai Nayakas in particular, is inadequate to explain the continued references to Vijayanagara rule and greatness long after tribute stopped flowing to the north. It is far more useful to think about political (and social) relations in terms of a logic in which there is a continuum between such poles as dependence and independence, inclusion and separation. The continuum is made up of a set of points which must necessarily be positioned in specific space and time. Tensions of varying types and degrees always exist between these poles, but the nature and degree of tension are as subject to contextualization as the points and poles of the continuum itself. Neither pole is ever realized exclusively. Not only do the two poles define each other relationally but they cannot exist in total independence or separation from the other.

Like the relations of worship established in puja, the root political metaphor, political relations commence when a lesser king or noble offers service to a greater lord or king. They are "established" once the service is recognized in the form of gifts made by the superior to the inferior. The gifts include titles, emblems and honors, rights to enjoy the usufruct of particular lands, and/or the privilege to rule on behalf of the superior over a particular area. They are thus gifts of limited sovereignty. Sovereignty which is gifted, or shared, is always partial, and always represented as a part (not the whole) of the specific sovereignty of the overlord. Gifted titles, for example, are often one, or several, of the titles possessed by the overlord himself, or they describe the heroic actions performed by the lesser lord on behalf of the greater lord. Gifted emblems are usually one or more of the emblems held by the overlord. Even when a subordinate captures emblems from an enemy king he must first present them to the overlord who then gifts him the right to appropriate them for himself.

The sovereignty of a subordinate lord, thus, is always dependent on, indeed part of, the sovereignty of the greater lord. However, the king's gift is at once binding and potentially divisive. The more gifts of honors and rights the overlord makes to his subordinate, and – in what is a logical and political consequence of this – the more the subordinate participates in the sovereignty of his overlord, the more the subordinate is represented as sovereign in his own right. While gift giving articulates relations both of solidarity and hierarchy, simultaneously creating by its own internal dynamic the transactional poles of center and periphery,

47

the possibility implicit in every gift is the cessation of the gift relationship. This possibility is made real by the very substance of the gift: authority itself.

If the emblems of sovereignty are not gifted by an overlord somewhere higher in the political system, they are worth less, thereby providing the basis for a lesser claim to local sovereignty. Viewed from below, that is from the perspective of those who have dealings not with the overlord but rather with his "agent," the greater the power and significance of the emblems the greater the subordinate whose persona is defined by this very same power and significance. However, the better and more powerful an "agent," the more likely he is to start acting on his own, and to begin claiming praise for himself as well as for his overlord. These claims need not be interpreted as signs of disloyalty; the agent can claim he is enhancing his position only to enhance that of the overlord. Yet there is an inexorable movement towards the increasing separation of the representative from the overlord represented, of the signifier from the signified. This separation, or growing independence, may inherently lead to conflict, as it often did in the case of Madurai. On the other hand, as a process it possesses the multidimensional character alluded to above. At the moments of greatest separation, or independence, the continued maintenance of certain forms of connection is not a contradiction. Inscriptions and chronicles reflect the changing forms of connection in various rhetorical ways. Inscriptions move from emphasizing different forms of agency and gifting relationships to regnal dating and distanced panegyrics of praise. Chronicles depict subordinate lords as looking and acting downwards in the system rather than upwards.

The necessary response of any superordinate lord or king to the logic of political relations is to keep escalating his command over the symbolic and material capital of his rule, simultaneously getting and giving more. The gift as a mode of statecraft compelled the king to engage in expansive and incorporative activity. Plunder and warfare were far better suited to this political modality than revenue "systems" and bureaucratic rule. Little kingdoms, themselves often perched on precarious agrarian bases and therefore dependent on a political economy that could usually generate wealth by plunder more readily than by production, were well suited to this kind of activity. Caldwell's pejorative characterization of a palaiyakkarar as one who had "grown rich by easy plunder" (Caldwell 1881, 120) conveys an important element of truth. Expansion, incorporation, plunder, battle and gifts all made the state inherently dynamic.

The Nayakas of Madurai exemplify many of the general points made above. They increasingly separated themselves from Vijayanagara, differentiating their own inscriptional identities from that of the Vijayanagara kings, reducing the flow of tribute to the capital city, ultimately engaging in warfare against the neighboring Nayakas of Tanjavur and irrevocably undermining the power of the Vijayanagara center. But the Madurai Nayakas never yielded their position as representatives of Vijayanagara. They never proclaimed themselves to be fully independent kings. At the same time, the Nayakas did not base their sovereignty solely on their relationship with the great imperial center, but also on their capacity to set themselves up as the successors of the Pantiyans, the proper rulers of Madurai.[11] Madurai's reputation as a difficult province had to do with the continuing presence of the Pantiyans as a source of local sovereignty and, not unrelatedly, with the even more pervasive presence of the local palaiyakkarars. The latter's forces had by now been augmented by the immigrant northerners, mostly Telegus, who had moved south with the Nayakas before establishing themselves and their kinsmen in localities on the periphery of the riverine centers of the Madurai area.

It was to these palaiyakkarars that the Madurai Nayakas increasingly looked down in order to sustain the changed preoccupations of their ascendant kingly position. The conventional dating of the quasi-independence of the Nayakas of Madurai coincides with what has been called the organization of the "*pāḷaiyam* system," though in fact what is at issue is as much the directional stress of these chronicles as any objectively certifiable political event. According to Sathyanatha Aiyar, the palaiyams (domains of the palaiyakkarars) were organized into a "system of government, which would conduce to the peace and prosperity of the country" (p. 58). The bureaucratic interpretation (based on the same chronicles which inform my own rather different sense of the logic of political relations) misconstrues what was a fundamental shift in the political preoccupations of the Nayakas (Taylor 1835, 2:3–146). Visvanatha invited each of the seventy-two palaiyakkarars – which is to say that he "invented" and canonized a group of seventy-two chiefs of differing size and complexion – to assume the guardianship of one of the seventy-two bastions of the Madurai fort in a classic rhetorical formulation of political-symbolic incorporation. Although there is no firm evidence, it is probable that the importance of the term palaiyakkarar in the southern Tamil country dates from this moment. Each bastion of the fort became a metonym of the protective

---

[11] Nayaka Krishnappa is seen as the reestablisher of the Pantiyan throne. See R. S. Aiyar 1924, 94:346.

sovereignty of the Madurai Nayaka, and thus the basis for the reconstitution of the old regime Tamil political order in the Madurai area. The family histories of the Nayakas and many of the family histories of these palaiyakkarars identify the key moment when the latter shift their political allegiance from the Pantiyans to the Madurai Nayakas as the gifting of the privilege of guarding the bastion allotted to them. The family histories of these palaiyakkarars make use of this incident to represent the attainment of a particular form of political recognition, one in which those selected in the group of seventy-two saw themselves as superior to those not selected. In many of these texts the actual number of the bastion is cited, suggesting that even among the inclusive unity of the seventy-two there was a hierarchical order.[12]

Despite the inclusion of only *Vaṭuka* (Telegu) palaiyakkarars among the seventy-two in some lists and traditions, many Maravar and Kallars were also allocated bastions as palaiyakkarars in the fort (Taylor 1835, 2:161–167). At the top of the regional political system, an especially privileged inner circle of superior palaiyakkarars was signified by the term *kumāra varkkam*, which literally meant those who were counted among the sons of the Madurai Nayaka. This inner group of "adopted sons" of the great king included the Kallar Tondaiman of Pudukkottai and the Maravar rulers of Ramanatapuram and Civakankai. The highest of the local kings were not Telegus at all.[13]

In the chronicles[14] of the Madurai Nayakas the establishment of the great Madurai fort is not so much herald of the "independence" of the Nayakas as it is a clear sign that the regional context in which authority had to be asserted over the local little kings was to be privileged over the context in which sovereignty was displayed by the enunciation of the close relation between the Nayaka and the Vijayanagara king. The latter concern did not cease to be important, but the beginnings of a process of "separation" are now unmistakable. The very last reference to Vijayanagara in the Madurai Nayaka chronicles occurs just before the episode including seventy-two palaiyakkarars in the Madurai fort. The chronicle reflects a change in the political system which closed in upon itself more and more during this period.

[12] In addition to the text printed in Taylor 1835, see the Mackenzie Manuscripts, the Tamil texts of which are in the Government Oriental Manuscripts Library. See Chapter 3.

[13] See Taylor 1836, 2:160–167 for two lists of the kumaravarkkam and the seventy-two palaiyakkarars. Both lists include palaiyams that would today be in Tirunelveli, Ramanatapuram, Madurai, Tiruccirappalli, Coimbatore, and Salem Districts.

[14] For an examination of one of these chronicles see the next chapter.

Vijayanagara authority declined during the seventeenth century. The warfare which increasingly broke out in the south among the Nayakas of Madurai, Gingee, Tanjavur, and the Wodiyars of Mysore was fueled by competition for relative positions with respect to a center on the wane. In the seventeenth century, the regional states which grew up under Vijayanagara and the little kingdoms which grew up under them replicated within themselves a political structure which no longer had any pan-regional realization.

The Nayakas had to assert control over a ramifying social and economic base largely through political relations with these little kings as well as to respond to other complicating factors. Chief among these were the declining military strength of the Vijayanagara overlord, the associated rise of Muslim powers in the Deccan, and the growing penetration of European commercial interests (Stein 1982). The Nayakas responded by appropriating Vijayanagara sovereignty without defending the Vijayanagara sovereign; by engaging in continuous warfare with other Tamil political centers; by building and endowing temples and sectarian institutions on a scale never before achieved; by supporting and encouraging the literary arts and constructing libraries; by building, perhaps for the first time, places that were distinct from temples and other "sacred" buildings; and finally by taxing European trade and concerning themselves with coastal commerce. The Nayaka period thus had many integrating facets which served to make new linkages at the same time that old ones were being eroded.

The conclusion of one Madurai Nayaka chronicle, while painting this picture for south India as a whole and, writ small, for Madurai's own fortunes, also clearly reveals the Nayakas' continued belief that their sovereignty was still dependent on Vijayanagara. As the chronicle enters the eighteenth century, the two principal factions at the court of the last Madurai Nayaka become fractious and begin fighting in the open. Much slaughter and chaos ensues. The Raja, Vijaya Kumara Muttu Tirumalai Nayaka, announces to both sides:

Why does this disturbance and loss arise between you; another day better times will befall us (the king), and then equitable rulers will come from the north: these, inquiring into the ancient rule and claims of right, will crown us; and when such persons do this, our rule will be stable; but as you cannot do this for us, we no longer consent to remain here. Fight not between yourselves on our account. (Taylor 1835, 2:49)

Thus ends the chronicle, enunciating again the importance of an overlord such as Vijayanagara, whose demise brings about that of the Madurai Nayakas themselves. Without a great overlord to maintain order, the Nayakas retire in hopes that one day soon, a great king will arise again.

## The palaiyakkarars

The recontextualization of Tamil regional politics in the late sixteenth and seventeenth centuries both reflected and responded to a set of major transformations in the local Tamil social and political order. The relevant locality unit important for decision making at the level of agricultural production and social reproduction changed from the natu to the periyanatu during the late Cola period, and then from the periyanatu to the palaiyam during the Vijayanagara period between the thirteenth and the late sixteenth century. As the social base of warrior rule, the palaiyam had severe implications for locality social forms in the older core regions, where under sustained pressures from palaiyakkarars the village became far more important than any larger territorial unit. The peripheral zones of the Tamil country, and the little kings who ruled over the clans and subcastes of these zones – their position infused with new life from the Telegu castes who settled, under Vijayanagara and Nayaka patronage, in areas adjacent to the Maravars and the Kallars – ascended to a role of key importance. By providing protection (*pāṭikkāval*) to local communities and institutions, often from their own predatory raids, and by consolidating their local authority by extending their own subcaste dominance and wielding ritual and military mechanisms which could be used to forge new forms of political relationship and command, the palaiyakkarars steadily displaced the Vellalar chiefs of the riverine and deltaic centers who had been dominant as *nāṭṭārs* (locality – natu – headmen) in the Cola and Pantiyan periods.

Little kings began to participate in a larger social, cultural, and political universe when, according to their own cultural accounts, certain families underwent a set of transformations from tribal hunters, to devotional saints, to chiefly dependants, and finally to little kings. The principal mechanism which effected these transformations, as in the Madurai Nayaka chronicle, was the gift: of emblems, titles, and land. Though heroic action was a necessary prerequisite, genuine transformations only took place when the chief developed a relationship with a greater king who endowed him with these gifts. The chiefs became little kings when, emulating the actions of kingly overlords, they gave gifts to temples and to Brahmans. Structural and cultural replication was the final realization of a complexly gradated series of relationships between large kings and small, ultimately preserving, in spite of the force of the periphery, a sense of the traditional center's hegemony.

These gifts linked individuals and corporate groups symbolically, morally, and politically with the sovereignty of the king, great or little. They created a moral unity and a political hierarchy. The redistributional system of resource allocation within little kingdoms served both to identify and strengthen the center and to articulate the relations of the periphery to each other and to the center. These gifts, of "real" and "symbolic" resources, were neither mere tokens nor signs of political weakness. In many of the smaller states in eighteenth-century Tamil Nadu between sixty and eighty per cent of all cultivable land was given away to military chiefs, retainers, temples, Brahmans, village officers, priests, servants and artisans. Lands were given away in central and peripheral areas of the state. When insufficient cultivable land was available for such grants, the king gave grants of forest land to be brought under cultivation or embarked upon predatory warfare for honor, fame, booty, and new lands.

Aside from Brahmans and temples, to whom palaiyakkarars gave gifts to attain kingly status, the greatest beneficiaries of land and honors from the rise of any given palaiyakkarar were the members of the royal caste. These benefits had progressively greater impact at each further segmental specification of royal identity, from the royal subcaste to the royal lineage. The palaiyams were primarily realizations of subcaste dominance over their own territories. The rule of the palaiyakkarars was based on strong corporate lineage organization and territorially dominant and segmented subcastes. Political control at the locality level represented the extension of the dominance of these powerful constellations of Maravars, Kallars, and Vatukas beyond their own territorial strongholds into adjacent areas, sometimes, as in the case of the Kontaiyankottai Maravars, fundamentally changing the territorial distribution of a subcaste group.

My contention that palaiyakkarars were the key political actors of the old regime in south India does not assume that a study of them will tell us everything we need to know to understand the old regime. This study deals with areas that were very different from the key riverine areas which from the late seventeenth century were more fully incorporated into the patrimonial rule of the new entrants in the political scene. The little kingdoms were little monetized though highly militarized, their armies supported by land grants rather than cash payments. Despite their incorporation into larger systems of political and economic relationship they were still organized in more profoundly local ways than any of the central areas. As vestigial polities, the little kingdoms reveal as much about the formative basis of early old regime polity as about the structural transformations already seen to be fundamental to the final two centuries of the old regime. The transformations identified with proto-capitalism were less in evidence in these areas than in those where there were high levels of revenue extraction under various tax farmers and where initial European penetration was greatest.

However, if there were structural contradictions between the old regime of the palaiyakkarars and the newer regimes of the Nawab of Arcot and Tipu Sultan (inter alia), they led neither to total transformations nor to a breakdown of the vitality and buoyancy of society and economy in the eighteenth century. Recently, scholars have been suggesting that the seventeenth and eighteenth centuries, seen as so decadent by colonial observers, were anything but decadent, let alone stagnant (Bayly 1983; Perlin 1983; Stein 1984; Washbrook 1984). The growing position of the palaiyakkarars was neither a symptom nor a cause of decadence. Their localistic, collegial, and redistributional polities continued to constitute an important part of the old regime right up until the end of the eighteenth century. They were finally defeated only by the extraordinary efforts and resources of British conquest. The British themselves realized the extraordinary vitality of these local rulers, preserving them in many areas while carefully demilitarizing and delegitimizing their local authority. The institutional and ideological means whereby this was done will be explored at the end of this study.

The old regime society of the little kingdoms did not disappear immediately upon the assumption of colonial power by the British. It lingered on in part because of its peculiar cultural character, and in part because of the contradictions of British colonial rule in India, contradictions which displayed themselves most forcefully perhaps in Britain's relations with the rural and often kingly vestiges of the old regime. However truncated by colonial intervention, the old regime continued in many ways to dominate rural society in south India until well into the nineteenth century. To this day it continues to exert its powerful force on modern Indian society and polity in curious ways.

As generalizable as many of my conclusions seem to me to be, about the palaiyakkarars as a class and about the old regime as a historical formation, my argument proceeds chiefly through a detailed examination of one particular little kingdom: Pudukkottai. But before launching into this examination, I will turn to a set of eighteenth-century texts in order to identify and analyze the discourse of Tamil kingship in the old regime.

# 3

# *The discourse of kingship: representations of authority in the old regime*

From the little attention given by the natives of India to History, or tradition, historical subjects are generally involved in dark obscurity or embellished with unintelligible fables.

*S. R. Lushington, Collector of Poligar Peshkash*
*Southern Pollams, December 24, 1800*

## History and ethnohistory

That Hindu India has had a severely underdeveloped sense of history is a commonplace assumption. Unfavorable contrasts are made not only with the West, but with that most historical of Asian civilizations, China, and with the Islamic world. Traditional Indian "historiography," when it is referred to at all, is most often characterized as fabulous legend and religious myth, bearing no relation to the past succession of real events. Not only is there thought to be a paucity of chronicles providing the political historian with definite dynastic details and other political facts, there is no philosophy or philosopher of history to allow one even to identify an intellectual domain, let alone to compare with something like Ibn Khaldun's sage and still much cited *Muqaddimah*. But is it true that India had no sense of history until the British introduced it? If not, why has this assumption borne so little critical scrutiny?

For the past 200 years historians of India have remained unquestioning in their assurance that they are the first practitioners of the art of Clio. They have only recently begun to use any indigenous "histories" at all. This has often been because of a continued acceptance of Lushington's view of Hindu history, a view that dismisses local histories as interesting myths at best. Fortunately, the preoccupation with caste in the study of India has also meant that some caste and family histories have been collected for scholarly purposes. Though a number of recent studies have forcefully demonstrated the potential range of uses to which these sources can be put (Hardgrave 1969; Conlon 1977; Leonard 1978; Inden 1976), most discussions of this kind of material have viewed these "histories" only as social charters directed toward the census, where the decennial designation of caste status became a major focus for contests over rank between 1870 and 1930. While it is true that caste histories were written, published, and submitted as petitions for census recognition, the study of caste histories from this single perspective has obscured the persistence of a cultural genre as well as the significance of this genre in a much wider social and historical context. Among other things, the so-called mythical components of these histories are considered in such analyses as nothing more than rhetorical fictions generated for a real political arena, rather than as important clues toward understanding indigenous social and historical thought. (A significant departure from this approach is found in Inden's 1976 book on the caste histories of Kayasthas and Brahmans in Bengal. Although he recognized that some of the caste histories he used were clearly propagandistic and that many others produced in the late nineteenth century owed their form to the census, Inden used the "cultural categories" in these histories and genealogies as the "categories of social historical analysis" [p. 1].)

Those who are interested in discovering the structure and content of indigenous "historical" thought are not the only students of indigenous histories; nor do I mean to suggest that this is the only legitimate use of these histories. Jan Vansina has done brilliant work on oral traditions in Africa, and, by demonstrating the potential accuracy and usefulness of oral tradition, he has immeasurably broadened the scope of African historiography (1961). The importance of the Malay *Hikayat*, or the traditional chronicle, for Southeast Asian history has been increasingly accepted by scholars of differing backgrounds, interests, and disciplinary persuasions. (See Errington's 1979 review of the historiographical literature.) But, as Shelly Errington has pointed out, the exogenously conceived classification of hikayat into "histories" and "romances" exemplifies the common underlying assumption that Western notions about history should be used exclusively to define the proper domain of historical thought (Errington 1979; Winstedt 1969). Writing about Sumatra, James Siegal has noted that early Dutch historical writing was characterized by a special vigor deriving from the Dutch scholars' belief that they were "establishing a realm of 'fact' in the face of a tradition which seemed practically to lack it or at best to accord it with little importance" (Errington 1979, 16). Even in more recent and far more sophisticated scholarship where the boundary of the realm of fact has been expanding, the central intent behind the treatment of indigenous texts has continued to be much the same (1979, 232).

Both Errington and Siegal make the point that underlies my approach here: indigenous texts and traditions that concern the "past" must be classified and analyzed in terms and categories that are consonant with the particular modes of "historical" understanding posited by the texts and traditions themselves. When this is not done, what usually results is the denial of the possibility that there is a legitimate and integral historical sensibility expressed in the texts, and, more concretely, a distortion of the intended meanings of the texts. As Errington says about the question of the hikayat's relation with the past:

The form in which that question is posed intrudes into any possible direct answer, for when those with a historical consciousness ask such a question, we imagine "the past" as a structured and sequential whole. If *hikayat* in general had a relationship to the past, thus conceived, then we would expect that the genre *hikayat* would present us with a consistent "way of viewing the past." Such is not the case. (1979, 242)

Errington's critique is made all the more searching by her contrasting the structure of time, the organization and evaluation of past events, and the status and meaning of language in the post-Renaissance political rhetoric of the West with those in the Malay hikayat. The most important consequence of this kind of critique is that it frees us to examine any given text (or tradition) in its own terms before we ask (or simply classify) in what sense it is or is not "historical."

The way in which this problem has usually been treated has been to distinguish between history, which is how we in the West understand the past, and myth, which is how "primitives" understand it. In disciplinary terms, historians have been those who set out to "discover" the past of those areas where there was no prior history, using fragmentary records from fossils to inscriptions to establish a chronological record of actual past events, empirical if sometimes meager. Anthropologists have collected myths and native legends, seeing them as vital superstructural components of a synchronic social structure. The full strength of this disciplinary caricature has been waning for years, but in genealogical terms it explains why historians and anthropologists have often talked past each other, the one analyzing myths irrelevant to the other translating epigraphy or ruminating over remains. While historians and anthropologists now share many of the same sources and concerns about the nature of social structure in a diachronic dimension, there is still a fairly sharp demarcation between those who study myth and those who study history.

As this demarcation fades, the irony is that we are only just beginning to realize what the ancient Greeks took for granted: that history by itself is simply speech about the particular, but that this record of particulars has no meaning or form until it is "configured" in some narrative (or theoretical) structure, which for the Greeks was, appropriately enough, epic poetry and tragedy (Finley 1965, 282). Without myth such configurement would have been impossible. Prior to the question of narrative configuration, myth worked to select the very particulars that would be configured. As M. I. Finley remarks:

The atmosphere in which the Fathers of History set to work was saturated with myth. Without myth, indeed, they could never have begun their work. The past is an intractable, incomprehensible mass of uncounted and uncountable data. It can be rendered intelligible only if some selection is made, around some focus or foci. In all the endless debate that has been generated by Ranke's *wie es eigentlich gewesen* ("how things really were"), a first question is often neglected: what "things" merit or require consideration in order to establish how they "really were"? Long before anyone dreamed of history, myth gave an answer. That was its function, or rather one of its functions; to make the past intelligible and meaningful by selection, by focussing on a few bits of the past which thereby acquired permanence, relevance, universal significance. (1965, 283)

Myth did not simply record a part of the past: it created the whole of it.

If myth is seen as an integral historiographic possibility, a distinctive way of establishing sequence and relevance in the understanding and representation of the past, then the separate analytic treatment of myth and history becomes problematic. Anthropologists must realize that myths have histories, and that they are histories. Historians must accept, as Bernard Cohn has written, that they must read texts and codified oral traditions not simply "to establish chronologies, or to sift historical fact from mythic fancy, but to try to grasp the meanings of the forms and contents of these texts in their own cultural terms" (Cohn 1980, 59).

In this chapter I will present and analyze portions of several texts which represent, in different contexts and genres, the structures and meanings of authority in the old regime. I will report what is said about the past and analyze in what sense the past exists for the text. Taking seriously Finley's comment that the function of myth is "to make the past intelligible and meaningful by selection, by focussing on a few bits of the past which thereby acquired permanence, relevance, and universal significance," I will identify the relevant events selected for narrative employment and establish how these events are talked about and the key symbols through which they are expressed. I will then discuss the significance of these patterns of selection for the general structure of historical representation and for the variable meanings and constructions of authority.

As I wrote in the first chapter, ethnohistory is the reconstruction of an indigenous discourse about the past. However, such representation cannot be seen as an end in itself. Discourse must be applied outside of its own domain. Indeed, it is only by operationalizing discourse that we can represent it, for it is never self-enclosed in some artificial container set apart from its own external referents, however much it constitutes those referents in the first place. It is therefore discourse-for-itself rather than discourse-in-itself which is the subject of this book. I wish not merely to show how these texts created ideas of the past for certain Tamilians of the eighteenth century, but to suggest how this past engaged these ideas. At the level of textual analysis, this past is the referential world of the text, encoded in narrative forms and enshrined in symbolic motifs. But the past is also more than that. Often, it is unknown, however much we can sense it through its necessary relation to the known. To approach both the known and the unknown, I will use the past of the texts to enable us – the external others of the twentieth century – better to create and configure our own analytic consideration of their past, to help us select relevant events, and then to interpret these events in our reconstruction of kingship and the nature of local-level political authority in the little kingdoms of southern India. In so doing, discourse will speak for itself, both in constituting some of the referents of the historical discourse, and in engaging its referential world.

But let us be clear. It is at this latter point that "ethno" and "history" oppose each other again, with the history of the analyst encompassing the history of the ethno-ized subject. For while I intend to use this "ethnohistory" to shape my own "historical" investigation, it is also at this point that I introduce perspectives and ask questions that do not derive from the texts themselves. One of the consequences of this analytic intervention is that I suggest interpretations that, in the form in which I have put them, would not occur to the participants. This is the sense in which cultural analysis creates an episteme that is different from the episteme of the cultural form itself. Although this shift is always problematic, it is not only inevitable, but necessary. We should neither forget nor trivialize our intrusion, but we must be aware both of our theory and of what occurs when that theory constitutes an exogenous framework of historical explication, however much our theory seeks to deconstruct itself.[1]

---

[1] My sense of the problematic here was influenced by the work of Siegal, who says about his own study of Sumatran historical thought:

> My analysis of the texts is an attempt to shift the concerns of the text into a vocabulary familiar to readers of English. I do not, however, claim either to have succeeded in freeing myself of a metalanguage or to say that my interest stops here. For it is also my wish to point out the Atjehnese interest in literature, to align myself with the Dutch, however narrowly. (Siegal 1979, 17)

I will consider three texts in this chapter. First, we will look at the ballad (*nāṭṭuppāṭal*) of Kattapomman, the palaiyakkarar whose defeat and death prefaced the discussion of the old regime in the last chapter. Second, we will look at the family history (*vamcāvaḷi*) of one of the Maravar palaiyakkarars of Uttumalai, a text similar in many ways to the vamcavali of our principal family, the Tondaimans of Pudukkottai. Finally, we will look at the chronicle of the Nayakas of Madurai, already discussed in the previous chapter. Each of these texts provides a slightly different perspective on the question of authority in the old regime in south India. The ballad vividly describes the highest moment of the career of the rebel palaiyakkarar, just before his defeat at the hands of the British. The family history depicts the past of the chiefly family, tracing their rise from forest chiefs to little kings largely in terms of their relations with greater kings in the south Indian political landscape. The chronicle narrates the initial relations between the Nayakas and the greatest overlord of all, the king of Vijayanagara, and then traces the establishment of Nayaka authority in Madurai and the gradual shift in perspective from a peripheral viceroy looking up at his central overlord to a regional king looking downwards at the chiefs whose loyalty and support he must secure.

## The poetics of power: the ballad of Kattapomman

The palaiyakkarar Kattapomman, based in Panjalankuricci in eastern Tirunelveli, was one of the last and most renowned of the southern rebels against British rule. A Vatuka, Kattapomman belonged to one of the two most important chiefly caste groups in Tirunelveli. Vatuka is a general term meaning "northerner." In this particular area it refers to the three major Telegu-speaking castes (*Kampaḷattārs*, *Kammavārs*, and *Reddis*), each of which settled in contiguous areas of eastern Tirunelveli, the driest part of the district (Pate 1917, 373). According to the family histories of certain Vatuka little kings (Pillai 1890), these groups first came to prominence far to the north in the Vijayanagara court and then migrated south after the defeat of Vijayanagara at the hands of the Muslims in 1565. The Vatukas settled predominantly in the black soil tracts of northeastern Tirunelveli, perhaps because they were already skilled in farming such soil, and perhaps because they had little choice. The Maravars, the other major caste group in Tirunelveli, had already established control over the tank-irrigable red soil land of the western part of the district (Ludden 1978a, 66).

As we saw in the last chapter, Kattapomman became for the British the symbol of palaiyakkarar resistance, and at the end of the poligar wars was hung as an example to all the other palaiyakkarars. In addition, his fort was razed to the ground, and "the name of the place was expunged from all the registers of the district" (Pate 1917, 85). But Panjalankuricci and its heroes were not forgotten. They lived on in legend, in particular in a series of epics, or ballads, called nattuppatal. A number of different versions of this epic have been collected, though only after the passage of more than half a century. No copy of this text made its way into the Mackenzie MS collection of the late eighteenth and early nineteenth century, which provides all the other texts under discussion. This may be because none of its versions were composed until well into the nineteenth century, rendering these texts as retrospectives on the old regime. A similar epic which was written about the Marudu brothers of Civakankai was not actually composed until 1840 (Chandrasekharan 1954). However, even if versions of the text were available, they would no doubt have been withheld from Mackenzie or his men because the epic was so clearly anti-British. The first Englishman to comment on the text noted in the late nineteenth century that, "The Poem is not easily procurable, being on cadjans, and those who possess it are not easily induced to lend it, from an idea that, as it contains many statements disparaging to the English, it might cause trouble" (Kearns 1873, Appendix 1). Indeed, even when vamcavalis concerning families which participated in the "poligar wars" surface in the Mackenzie collection, they contain within them long justifications for the action of the palaiyakkarar, usually hinging on the claim that they were forced into cooperating with the rebellion because of threats issued by Kattapomman and his group.[2] The earliest printed version of the Kattapomman ballad I know about was reported on and summarized by a Rev. J. F. Kearns in a book published in 1873 (Kearns 1873).

Kearns makes the usual British comments about Indian notions of history. As he says,

no reliable account of the Polegar war can be obtained from the Epic. Like all Indian Epics, it deals largely in the marvellous, and in the absurd; impossible men performing impossible feats, meet us at every turn, and few Europeans would care to read it a second time, and yet, that which renders it distasteful to European ears, is the very thing which gives it charm for the Natives.

Kearns records for us the way an epic such as this was transmitted and appreciated. "It abounds in the most palpable misstatements, and the most absurd exaggerations, yet the Natives, especially the peasantry,

---

[2]  For example, *Erāyiram Paṇṇai Citampara Vaṉṉiyaṉ Vamcāvaḷi*, Madras, GOML, D. 3577.

will sit the entire night, listening to some strolling bard, singing it, and will wait upon his lips, with the eagerness and simplicity of children" (also see Beck 1982). The Kattapomman story is still told by bards, though the best-known version today is the one enshrined in the film starring Sivaji Ganesan, one of Tamil Nadu's most popular film stars.

The version of the Kattapomman story I will use here was published in 1971 (Vanamamalai), but probably composed sometime in the mid nineteenth century. It is similar to but not the same as the text summarized by Kearns.[3] Beginning with an invocation to the gods on behalf of the poet and the poem, the ballad then proceeds to a lengthy panegyric on Kattapomman and his capital city, Panjalankuricci, both portrayed rather differently than in the British records. The panegyric expounds upon the prosperity of that beautiful place, attributing perfection and prosperity to the presence of the generous and brave king, Kattapomman. The action of the text begins when Major Jackson summons Kattapomman in 1797. The following excerpt provides an explicit and eloquent statement of the ideal moral order of a little kingdom, as well as a critical, and dramatic, view of the colonial encounter.

### *The text I: The kingdom of Kattapommu*[4]

#### INVOCATION

As we sing the Tamil song in praise of the king of Pancai city, renowned round the world, may we be assured the protection of the armed son[5] of Sampuva,[6] who wears the garland crown of *konrai* flowers and whose forehead has the crescent moon and the flowing Ganges; in the movement of his anklets may we be protected. Virapantiya Kattapommu, owner of every title and master of the perfect city, has shown his manhood by conquering the eight directions, and has cut down the neighboring mischief-makers so that their crowned heads rattled on the ground, their blood flowing.

The darshan[7] of Kattapommu is like the darshan of Cupramaniyar.[8] Half the months of the year it rains, and for the other half it is summer and the world is dry; but at the beautiful red hands of the Virapantiya gold is showered in Pancai for all the twelve months of the year to those who merely come and ask.

---

[3] Unless otherwise noted, the translation is mine.
[4] This is the Telegu spelling; in Tamil the name is usually rendered as *Kattapomman*.
[5] Ganapati.
[6] Another name for Siva.
[7] The Tamil word is *taricanam*; the Sanskrit word has been incorporated into Indian English, and literally means vision.
[8] Commonly spelled Subramaniyam, one of the two sons of Siva.

O – elephant-faced one, who is dark as a rain-cloud;[9] O Kanta; we entreat protection at your feet, so we may recite the pure Tamil Kummi in praise of excellent Kattapommu.

We ask for protection at the feet of the white lotused one – the patron of learning[10] so that we may recite the pure Tamil kummi in praise of the hero who brought prosperity to the city of Pancai.

Oh Manonmani,[11] protect us too at your lotus feet, that we may say the pure Tamil kummi in praise of the world renowned Kattapommu.

May the golden feet of Pancai's elephant-god protect us, so we may sing the Tamil kummi joyfully in praise of Kattapommu, who brings merit to world-famed Pancai.

The goddess Cakkatevi[12] will bestow her grace so we may passionately sing the Tamil kummi in praise of the great king Virapantiya Kattapommu, who flourishes in Pancai city.

O Cakkatevi, at whose feet one may attain the four states of bliss,[13] protect us that we may sing the Tamil kummi in praise of the great Pantiyan, Kattapommu.

O Cakkatevi, goddess of the six-syllable mantra, may your feet protect the clan of the brave Pommu.

### THE PROSPERITY OF PANCAI

I will tell of the abundance of Pancai, where shines the true and great hero, Kattapommu. I will tell of the country's fertility: O listen to the excellence of the Pancai fort: The fort, its strong walls and bastions – what good solid jobs they are! Jewel-bedecked platforms high atop the houses, and houses with many storeys, surrounded by a great moat. Look, large and many are the fine locked doors of the treasury house, and beautiful – the gateway to the goddess's shrine at Cakkatevi's temple, the long avenues and the great expanse of the Assembly Hall,[14] spacious sleeping platforms, picture galleries, sandalwood groves, canopies of flowers, straight and symmetrical entrance ways. The decoration of these avenues and gateways are the ornaments of the king.

The smell of flowers, fame's fragrance, the scent of gold, and rosewater's perfume waft everywhere. O the beauty of the banks of the pond, the groves and the pleasure gardens. Banana and jack-fruit trees shower down their ripe fruit; good mango and areca nut trees grow high. Fragrant screwpine pour forth their petals, and the river blossoms with glorious water lilies. Along the marvelous avenues there are expansive shop-fronts. Flower gardens, sandalwood groves, rivers, red paddy, and areca nuts; armories on one side, stables where horses are

9  Vinayaka.
10  Saraswati.
11  Parvati.
12  The tutelary goddess of Kattapomman's ancestral family, brought with them when they migrated from Andhra under the Nayakas; in Telegu the pronunciation is Jakkadevi.
13  Namely: *cālōka, cāmīpa, cārūpa, cāyucya.*
14  The *kolu* hall – where the king sits in state, conducts his public business, and gives his darshan to the people.

raised on the other. To one side festooned platforms, to the other streets checquered like game-boards. In the groves, the mango-cuckoo calls, and peacocks play, signaling prosperity. By the mercy of the maiden, Cakkatevi, milk and honey abound. Listen: I will tell of wonders in the Pancala country, where love thrives.

In the southern Pancai country, it is the hare that turns round to chase away the hounds. Yes, in the courageous Pancala country the hares chase away the hounds. Cows and tigers come together to the ghat to drink water and nurse their young. Crows will not drink the milk which has been freshly milked. If one says the name of Kattapommu, Cakkatevi will give boons, Cakkatevi will bestow the grace of her holy word.

### THE ASSEMBLY OF THE KING

In front of the Pommakkal shrine, graceful Kattapommu sits in state, and the different castes – Kammalas, Kampalattars, Tottiyas[15] – gather round. A chair, embedded with the nine precious stones, set down on the ever-beautiful platform; a lovely wide bolster spread out; the large half-circled pillow put down; the arrangement of the jasmine bouquet, the proper fragrance for the great king Kattapommu who sits exultantly in state. The various "officials" – Umaitturai,[16] Civattaya, Muttaiya, Vimankaruttayya, and Vetappattitturai Turaiccami – all have come to the assembly. The little talavay[17] and the big talavay, King Pulikutti Nayakkar, and good Mappillai Nayakkar,[18] whose beautiful work shines, have also come.

The great and wealthy king, Cekavirapantiyan Kattapommu, who is praised throughout the land. Good Civa Cupramaniyapillai, who is guardian of the entrance ways. As the celebrated one, Chief of the Ganges clan,[19] wields his authority;[20] the musical ensemble, in the beautiful Pancala land, is ready to play; the drum begins to sound; the voice of the conch is heard; officials and supervisors, good Kampalars[21] and Ceruvaikkarars[22] assemble most majestically; the cock-fight is set up, and they play; the bejeweled women sing a kummi for victory; and young princes play; Pantiyan Umaitturaiccami, who is mute, listens to the investigations of justice; the Lords of Pancai country, marching in procession so gracefully, make a fine sight indeed; the great king,[23] putting on

[15] Different caste groups said to have migrated from Telegu speaking regions of South India.
[16] Umaitturai was Kattapomman's mute younger brother, reputedly very popular.
[17] Talavay has variably been translated as minister, or chief official.
[18] *Māppillai* means brother-in-law, or son-in-law.
[19] In Tamil, *kankai kulam*.
[20] Semi-colon used to denote simultaneity.
[21] The Vatuka caste of which Kattapomman was the leading member.
[22] A general term for chieftain or general, which has been taken as a subcaste name for groups of Maravars in the Ramanatapuram region, as well as by the royal Kallars of Pudukkottai.
[23] *Rāca pōca makārācan.*

his white silk shawl, is being attended to: One puts on the round forehead mark,[24] another paints his eyes with collyrium, and the archers bring him his bow, all properly done, in good order.

Oh, Good People, listen to the conduct of King Kattapommu. Coming like a son-in-law, a mattress unrolled on the bed; doing daily puja to Manonmani Cakkatevi, goddess of the Pommus; listening to the investigation of justice, and closing the cases with despatch; giving food to orphans, Indra-like he sits in state; Kattapommu, the great King Virapantiya of the Pancai country, in the presence of his palaiyakkarars and other dignitaries, went on giving gifts and doing charities in this manner.

### The moral order of a little kingdom

Kattapomman is the owner of every title (*virutu*) and the master of the perfect city (*nagara atipati*). We saw above that one of the features which distinguished great kings from little kings was that little kings were given some, but not all, of the titles of the great king, whom we can now see as a king who possesses all titles. Throughout this text Kattapomman is presented as totally self-sufficient in his kingship. Not needing to look up in the political universe, he will soon be shown to be contemptuous of Major Jackson, who makes demands on him as if from above. Kattapomman is specifically compared to Cupramaniyar, the eldest of Civa's two sons. In excellent Kattapomman's kingdom it rains for half the year, suggesting a tremendously prosperous agricultural region. This directly contradicts what we "know" about eastern Tirunelveli, one of the driest regions of southern India. More important than the six months of rain, for all twelve months of the year Kattapomman showers gold on all those who merely come and ask. No wonder Pancai is famous throughout the world.

The excellence of the king and his capital city are related both instrumentally and metaphorically. Kattapomman's adherence to and performance of rajadharma are responsible for the excellence of the city, which is a direct extension of Kattapomman. As the text says, "The decoration of these avenues and gateways are the ornaments of the king." The city is beautiful as much because it exudes prosperity in every corner as because it is beautifully decorated and symmetrical in its design. The poem's extravagantly described moral/cultural order has indeed appropriated a brute and often ungenerous natural order, re-working and refining it, and sometimes specifically reversing it: "In the southern Pancai country, it is the hare that turns round to chase away the hounds. Yes, in the courageous Pancala country the hares chase

[24] *Pottu.*

away the hounds. Cows and tigers come together to the ghat to drink water and nurse their young. Crows will not drink the milk which has been freshly milked."

Presiding over this order is Kattapomman, who sits in state in front of the Pommakal shrine which houses the goddess Cakkatevi. Kattapomman's power has much to do with his relationship to his tutelary goddess. Milk and honey abound through the mercy (*kirupai*) of Cakkatevi, who grants boons if the petitioner merely utters the name of Kattapomman. In the Dasara festival the Vijayanagara king sat in front of the throne on which the deity, Durga, was placed during the ten days of the festival. Here, on every day of the year the throne of Kattapomman is placed before the shrine of the goddess. The poem proceeds to tell us that Kattapomman does daily puja to Cakkatevi. The throne on which he sits is embedded with the nine precious stones (*navaratna*), which represent great wealth, and a totalization evoking the mastery of all titles mentioned earlier. Nine is a particulary important number as there are nine planets in the universe, nine orifices in the body, and nine boundary markers corresponding to nine major points of entry to south Indian villages. The king sits in splendid state, with jewels and flowers supplying the proper ambience.

The king who is praised throughout the land presides over the kingdom in general and the court in particular. In his assembly (*kolu*), his nobles and officials gather round him as he wields his authority (*atikāram*). All visitors who come to this magnificent court attend musical performances, athletic contests, cock fights, and other gala events, where the great king and the great lords of the Pancai country sit in state as at a great festival or wedding. Kattapomman, who performs daily puja to the goddess Cakkatevi, listens to disputes and other matters concerning "the investigation of justice." His justice is swift and sure. This section of the text concludes with the statement that this magnificent king feeds orphans, gives gifts, and performs acts of charity in the presence of his assembly.

Kattapomman is thus a great king in all respects. He has a splendid court, he gathers around himself all the great men of the country, he patronizes the arts and performs festivals, he worships his tutelary goddess regularly, he adjudicates disputes and upholds justice, and he is generous with his gifts and charities. In Geertzian terms, this is indeed an exemplary center, a theatre state. But it is also a state in which the center serves as a magnet through both its pomp and its circumstance, for the military displays, the quick and fair despatch of justice, and the continual beneficence are all vital to the political structure of the little kingdom. However idealized the account, the integration of ceremony and command are fundamental. But the kingdom is about to come under attack. The British want revenue.

## The text II

Listen to the way destruction was visited upon the harmonious city of Pancai. I will tell of the fateful things which came; O good people, listen to the way it happened.

Major Jackson,[25] the collector, over the eight districts[26] ruled by the foreigners, who were tricky; O listen, good people, to the power and strength of this English gentleman, Major Jackson, how he came to Ramanatapuram, according to the orders given by the Chief of the Madras Town Government. His mind joyful, Major Jackson wielded Europe's authority. The minister (*piratāṇi*) of Ettayapuram came; what complaint did he bring to the Englishman?

So skillfully he spoke; O good gentlemen listen!

"He has plundered a thousand well-guarded grain heaps of millet, he has wantonly set great fires to the mounds of straw, he has made unnecessary trouble, forever entering into our very houses for pillage; in the town of Kattu Nayakkanpatti he drove away thirty, forty milch cows, as well as the cattle which are grazed in the border areas, and robbed three hundred bullocks; in Tuttukkuti he took ninety sacks of gold coins from the houses of white people. Do you see any justice in this? He has set a conflagration downwind of the strong Ati gales.[27] The entire country-side has fallen as his prey, he has plundered the barns of their grain. This wicked man, Kattapommuturai, is very good indeed at breaking in and thieving. Since we are so robbed, how are we to survive? If the Turai[28] does not summon him here now and investigate this case, where will we find homes to live in? Great suffering will be wrought by him. If the Turai does not open an investigation, summoning him to come here now, look, in a moment I will go to Madras Town to make my complaint." Look, look; all this the minister said. Hearing this news, this superintending Governor, Collector of the land, understood all. After undertaking the various customary proceedings, he angrily spoke of the situation.

### JACKSON'S ANGER

"Having now summoned this excellent Kattapommu, I will suppress his wickedness, properly despatching justice. I will stop the mischief of this great hero, Kattapommu. For seven years, in his pride, ruling over his land, he has gone without sending me tribute; and for that he is a wicked man. In comfortable

---

[25] In Tamil, *Cāhishan Mēshar*.

[26] The southern palaiyams.

[27] The fourth Tamil month, roughly equivalent to July, when a strong west wind blows across the Tamil plain.

[28] *Turai* is the Telegu word for gentleman. In addition to being an honorific title, it is often used more specifically for a European.

Pancai country, he has ruled the land as if independent. We must summon this robber, Kattapommu, who puts up forts and does charities."[29] Jackson thought all these things, that having summoned him, he must speak justice. Through deliberations with his high committee, he commenced police proceedings in the Magistrate's Office.

### JACKSON'S LETTER

He wrote the sharp Company letter in haste, though in the proper way, informing the ungovernable Kattapommu that he must come and meet them, in a friendly manner. Straightaway he wrote the letter, insisting that patrols of the seventy-two palaiyams[30] should now come. He put on his seal, folded the letter in the form of a moon in the third quarter, and sent that elaborate letter speedily by post. That letter was delivered to the minister of the chief of Pancai, Kattapommu.

### THE LETTER'S ARRIVAL IN PANCAI

The letter came as if by magic, and was then read by the Pillai. Having read it, this trusted man took the letter's news to Kattapommu, the king. In a minute, he carefully explained it all... Umaitturai asked about the situation. The Pillai told him, using hand signals. While the Pillai spoke those truthful words, Umaitturai bit his hands, and slapped his thigh in challenge; and both his eyes grew red with anger: "Let it be, we must be ready to leave tomorrow. What does my older brother think?" "Yes, we must go on this outing; as for this evil, we must face it without fear," he said.

### SETTING OUT FOR THE INTERVIEW

"If Major Jackson is to give us an occasion for a meeting, let us go to the Assembly and meet him. If they should deceive us, we shall break open and scatter their skulls." Thus, Kattapommu and Umaitturai got together and conferred. Umaitturai said, "We'll go and meet him properly; our regiments must be ready in an hour's time." After he said this, the Pillai arose. What nice proper words did Kattapommu say? He said that he had to see this strong Company man, Major Jackson, with his own eyes, that he must see the Company troops; he wished to make the journey in a majestic manner, and go to meet this Major Jackson in a way befitting himself, with all customary demeanor. He told his minister to go and quickly gather the armies.

(After this they collected their army and went to Ramnad to meet Major Jackson, who interrogated Kattapommu in an exchange which is perhaps the best known of the entire ballad:)[31]

---

[29] To do charities, by giving gifts, is a conspicuous act of sovereignty.

[30] Mirroring the system of the Madurai Nayakas, the Ramnad Chieftain was said to have maintained a relationship with seventy-two subordinate chiefs.

[31] This particular passage is taken from the most dramatic version in Vanamamalai 1971.

Jackson: Who gave Arumukamankalam to you?
Kattapommu: I gave it to myself. Why should anyone else give it?
Jackson: And why did you seize five hundred sheafs of grains in Arunkulam?
Kattapommu: I took it to feed the birds. Is that so treacherous?
Jackson: Why did you steal the cattle of the Ettaiyapuram Zamindari?
Kattapommu: I drove them home to give milk to my children.
Jackson: And why have you not payed the *kist* (tax) for the last seven years?
Kattapommu: The heavens shower rain; the earth bears grain; why should I pay for my land? Do you collect tax to command the elements? Does rain shower at your command?

(The ballad goes on from here to narrate the courageous, though ultimately unsuccessful resistance of Kattapommu and his younger mute brother, Umaitturai, against the British troops.)

## The destruction of the old regime

In this second section, the text introduces the way in which destruction is to be visited upon the harmonious city of Pancai, or, rather, the way its moral order is challenged and then extinguished. The primary complaint of the British is that Kattapomman has plundered the neighboring countryside, stealing grain and cattle and even gold currency from the houses of white people: "The entire countryside has fallen as his prey . . ." We have already seen that plunder had the legitimacy in the old regime that tax systems came to have under the colonial regime. Kings of old garnered many of their resources from plunder, often doing so as an act of war. In British eyes, however, Kattapomman is not a legitimate king but a wicked man and a thief. The complaints which brought Kattapomman's "iniquities" to British attention come from the minister of a neighboring palaiyakkarar, of Ettaiyapuram, who has consistently been an enemy of Pancalankuricci, though he is of the same region and the same caste. When Major Jackson hears these complaints, his British sense of justice is aroused and he announces that he will stop the mischief of this wicked man, adding the Ettaiyapuram minister's complaints to his own concern that Kattapomman did not pay his tribute, acting as if he were independent: "For seven years, in his pride, ruling over his land, he has gone without sending me tribute; and for that he is a wicked man. In comfortable Pancai country, he has ruled the land as if independent. We must summon this robber, Kattapomman, who puts up forts and does charities." The rhetorical structure of the text renders the fact that Kattapomman behaves like a true king as the most salient complaint of the British.

The dramatic confrontation of the text is thus set up. Though it manifests itself in and is ultimately decided by military action, this confrontation is in the final analysis not between armies but between two conceptions of the world, as the rhetorical encounter between Kattapomman and Major Jackson so clearly articulates. By his own right Kattapomman possesses the countries which the British accuse him of stealing. In this light, Kattapomman's helping himself to grain and cattle to provide sustenance for the people of his kingdom, far from being treacherous acts, are part of his kingly duties. Since the heavens shower rain, and the earth bears grain, why indeed should Kattapomman pay for his lands? In asking the British Collector whether he collected tax to command the elements, Kattapomman echoes the fundamental conception about royal authority in the text, and invokes his own capacity to command the elements and maintain a kingly order that is at once moral and natural. Since the British did not have any control over nature, neither did they, Kattapomman and this text assert, have any moral right to collect tax and subordinate this great king to a new political order which appeared to be based solely on revenue. As we know, and as this text narrates in tragic detail, the British did make good this revenue demand, and later established a system of political rule in which revenue played a major role by upending the old natural order on the battlefield of might, where all the courage of our hero and all the grace of Cupramaniyar and Cakkatevi combined could not in the end prevail.

The text presents us with a portrait, albeit idealized and possibly retrospective, of the moral order of the old regime in which the palaiyakkarar has become as close to being like a universal king as possible. No other king is represented as above Kattapomman, who himself asks nothing less than to be left alone, untaxed by the British and unattacked by any force greater than his own in retaliation for what, clearly, was an active plunder economy. Exemplifying an important aspect of palaiyakkarar polities, Kattapomman gives expression here to the pride and independence that caused one political superior after another to find himself unable to balance his commitments above to exigencies below. The representation of the palaiyakkarar's political landscape as uninhabited by superiors is the exception rather than the rule in texts of the eighteenth century. In many texts, even the British manage to succeed to the rightful position of overlord in a political world that is represented as having changed only in subtle ways. In all the family histories of palaiyakkarars, it is recognized that little kingship could not be attained without great kings. In the next text we will see that authority was acknowledged as relative and relational. I turn now to an extensive analysis of the family history of one Maravar palaiyakkarar from Tirunelveli.

### From tribal chiefs to little kings: the ethnohistory of the Uttumalai Maravars

The Maravars seem to have migrated into western Tirunelveli somewhat earlier than the Vatukas, in all probability coming from no further than contiguous Ramnad (Stein 1980, 109). Sometime during Pantiyan rule, perhaps around the thirteenth century, they settled in the dry but fertile red soil areas along the foothills of the western Ghats which were unoccupied by the earlier settlers in south India (Vellalars and Brahmans). Where Maravars settled they did so with sufficient density to assure their dominance over their new areas (Ludden 1978a). This pattern is geographically and demographically consistent with the distribution of Maravar settlement in the early nineteenth century, when they were found in dense pockets of different Maravar subcastes stretching from Civakiri and Cettur in the north, on the border between Tirunelveli and Madurai districts, to Kalakatu and Valliyur in the south, only twenty-five miles north of the Indian Ocean.[32] Geographically, the areas of Maravar settlement were, like those of the Kallars, dry, at best only partially irrigated by small rivers and rain-fed tanks.

The Maravar subcaste (i.e., the endogamous group, often called the *utpirivu*) that produced the greatest number of palaiyakkarars and lesser chiefs called *kāvalkārars* (those who engaged in protection, *kāval*)[33] was the Kontaiyankottai group. The Uttumalai kings were prominent members of this group. Of the fourteen Maravar palaiyakkarars in Tirunelveli, eight belonged to this subcaste.[34] These palaiyakkarars had an entire Maravar subcaste, called *Cērvais* and sometimes *Puḷuk-*

---

[32] *Census and Dehazada of the Province of Tirunelvelie*, Revenue Department Sundrie, no. 39, Tamil Nadu Archives.

[33] Kavalkarars were usually chiefs of collections of hamlets or villages who in exchange for protection received a specified share of village produce and certain other perquisites, including emblems and honors. Although there were kavalkarars throughout the Tamil countryside, the best-known and most prominent kavalkarars were those of the southern Tirunelveli region around Nankuneri where, interestingly, there were no major palaiyak-karars in the late eighteenth century. These kavalkarars were also of the Kontaiyankottai subcaste.

[34] The eight Kontaiyankottai palaiyakkarars were located in Uttumalai, Maniyacci, Katampur, Curantai, Talaivankottai, Avutaiyarpuram (Nel-katanceval), Cokkampatti, and Natuvakuricci.

*kamaṟavar*, devoted to their service.[35] Within the Maravar caste as a whole this subcaste was second in importance only to the Cempunattu group, to which the Ramanatapuram and Civakankai rulers belonged.[36] Within the Kontaiyankottai subcaste, as was true of all Maravar subcastes, there were considerable differences of status among the different exogamous lineages (called *kiḻai* or branch). The royal lineage was at the top. The other lineages were ranked downward in large part according to the nature of affinal and service relations between them and the royal group. The subcaste unit as a whole seems to have been less relevant for defining the organization of its constituent lineages than it was for defining the organization of its little kingdom. Each kingdom had its own royal lineage and its own particular interlineage hierarchy.

The Maravars, as well as the Kallars, with whom they have a traditional bond (the two castes, along with the *Akampaṭiyārs*, are often called the *Mukkulattār*, the three tribes), have always had the reputation of being a fierce group renowned for its great military prowess and, later on, for its considerable "criminal" proclivities. Two passages from the ancient Tamil poem, the *Kalittokai*, depict the Maravars of old:

the wrathful and furious Maravar, whose curled beards resemble the twisted horns of the stag, the loud twang of whose powerful bowstrings, and the stirring sound of whose double-headed drums, compel even kings at the head of large armies to turn their backs and fly.

Of strong limbs and hardy frames and fierce-lookings as tigers, wearing long

[35] Cervai, short for Cervaikarar, is a title that usually means some kind of military commander, although the title has great contextual range and variance. In western Tirunelveli the Cervais seem to be a distinct subcaste, which functions as the hereditary service group for the palaiyakkarars. Pate noted that the "servants of marava zamindars forming another subdivision are known as Pulukka Maravans, or Parivārams, and usually bear the title Sērvaikāran" (Pate 1917, 132–133), and Dumont has written that the "servais" are of "slightly inferior status" and "appear to be associated with them [the zamindars] in most places (Uttumalai, etc.)" (Dumont 1964, 299). More ethnographic work must be done on this group to establish their status as a subcaste and the nature of their relations with the Kontaiyankottais, although we have before us Dumont's more general suggestion that all groups called "*pulukkar*," as the Cervais seem to be from the information given above, are the descendants of irregular unions (Dumont 1957a, 8). Thus, for example, the Cervais who are hereditary servants of the Kontaiyankottai Maravars may be the offspring of junior wife marriages, especially since polygamy was frequently practiced by the Maravar palaiyakkarars.

[36] According to the *Maṟavar Cāti Viḷakkam*, filed under R. 370a, GOML, Madras.

and curled locks of hair, the blood-thirsty Maravar, armed with the bow bound with leather, ever ready to injure others, shoot their arrows at poor and helpless travellers, from whom they can rob nothing, only to feast their eyes on the quivering limbs of their victims. (Kanakasabhai 1965, 42–43)

Thus, the Maravars are represented as fierce warriors and merciless robbers as early as the first few centuries of the Christian era. This same poetical corpus characterizes Maravars as inhabitants of the most marginal landscape of all, the wilderness (*pālai* – see Shulman 1980, 289). This early reputation, which was exaggerated by such poetical flourishes while the reality was diminished by their progressive conversion to settled agriculture, is not inconsistent with their position in later years as warriors, protectors, and chiefs and with their settlement in areas on the periphery of the settled centers of Tamil civilization.[37]

The historiographical problem we confront when looking at the Maravars (and the same is true for the Kallars) is that, although this group has been widely portrayed as consisting of "outsiders" who fiercely preyed on the respectable Tamilians of South Indian history, within their own areas they did in fact develop positions of dominance and traditions of kingship. Maravars and other similar groups do not fit neatly into conventional South Indian notions of caste hierarchy. Many of my informants (Brahmans as well as Maravars and Kallars) have told me that the Mukkulattar are really the Ksatriyas (the noble warrior and kingly caste) of southern India; other informants (usually from wet-land regions) have ranked them quite low in the social hierarchy. Such

---

[37] Their proclivity to violence was not unnoticed, and not uninterpreted, by the British. Throughout the nineteenth century, the Maravars (though never to such an extent as the Kallars) were seen as positively dangerous to the rural social order, and some groups of Maravars were classified as criminal tribes or castes. In a letter dated July 15, 1824, written to the Collector of Tinnevelly District, the British judge of that district noted that the Maravars are

at best a lawless people, and robbers by profession ... Almost in every part of the District you see this caste; idling about, and they can give no satisfactory explanation as to their means of livelihood; they represent themselves as the adherents of the Chokkampatty zamindar or other neighbouring ones of the same caste [such as Uttumalai], these persons are generally very well dressed though they receive no pay. The conclusion therefore, must be, that they live by unlawful means, under the cloak of being the Zamindar's followers, and Guards of the Estates. (Quoted in PRPW, TNA, ASO(D)–338)

Although the Maravars could make kings fly in terror, they had to establish a legitimate claim to kingly status. Subsequently, in the face of British classificational notions, which in their own peculiar way were more prone to hyperbole than the Cankam poems of old, they had to worry about being branded as a "criminal caste."

ranking is often the result of unwarranted generalization. These groups have always been associated with dry and hilly landscapes and cannot accurately be placed in hierarchical comparison with groups such as Vellalars who dominate the wet-land areas.[38]

But to defend the Maravars (as Blackburne has recently done with the Kallars [1978]) as yeoman agriculturalists of the same stripe as Vellalars equally misses the point. Control over land (and thus the right to cultivate it) has always been achieved through means that link the positions of bandit and king – violent conquest. While according to many myths of settlement the Vellalars moved into regions already protected by kings (Mahalingam 1972, 94–96), Maravars and Kallars became kings by virtue of their settlement. More specifically, these two groups often gained their political authority as well as their right to shares of the harvest – and eventually their direct control over land – by providing protection as local chiefs. To be entrusted with this position, they had to possess the means (and these means entailed violence) to defend villages and temples and enact revenge. Shulman has correctly commented on the close symbolic affinity of bandit and king, noting that the opposition between the two is most often complementary (Shulman 1980, 300–306). This complementary opposition becomes a curious form of identification in the case of the Maravars and the Kallars. This paradox is best explored by looking at the self-perception of a group of Maravar kings who record their own past as bandits. The ambivalence of their position is neatly encapsulated in their view of the past.

The text of the Uttumalai Maravars is a particularly interesting source for such an inquiry as it is a compelling account of becoming a little king – of intermediate size and significance – in the Tamil country during the old regime. The Uttumalai kings ruled over the largest (in area though not in population) of the Maravar little kingdoms in Tirunelveli, which were all far smaller than Ramanatapuram, Civakankai, and Pudukkottai.[39]

[38] In any case, "the relatively small spread of each caste leaves it available to be ranked consistently by its members' exchanges with other castes in just a few nearby localities" (Inden and Marriott 1974).

[39] In 1823, twenty years after the boundaries of the permanently settled zamindari estates were drawn, the total population of Uttumalai was 14,612, and its area was about 123 square miles. Adjacent on its northwestern side to the Cokkampatti Zamindari, the second largest of the Maravar estates, it was situated just to the north of the river Cittar, near the early Pantiyan stronghold of Ukkirankottai (see SII 1962; EI 1936, 283–288; and Pantarattar 1966, 50–53, 76–77. I am grateful to David Ludden for providing these references) and only ten miles to the east of Tenkaci, the seat of Pantiyan rule in its last phase during the late fourteenth and fifteenth centuries.

## Vamcavali: genealogy as ethnohistory

The Uttumalai Maravar text is basically a genealogy; vamcavali literally means the line of a family (*vamcam*). Every palaiyakkarar family has at least one vamcavali that recounts the "history" of the family. Each vamcavali consists of a succession of episodes concerning selected ancestral heads of the family. Episodes are linked by successional lists of from one to ten generations, consisting only of the names of the intervening family heads. The vamcavalis are genealogies both in that they list the entire line of the family and in that genealogy acts as the narrative frame of the text. What chronology is to narrative history in the West, genealogy is to the vamcavali: it provides sequence, relevance, and structure. It also provides the principal purpose of the vamcavali, which is to narrate the origins of the present palaiyakkarar and his family. The events included are chosen on two bases: those considered necessary to establish the present and those that represent the record of the past. This text covers thirty-six generations, probably (to be momentarily chronological) seven to eight hundred years, and contains thirteen episodes.

Typically, each episode consists of some action performed by a hero-ancestor, which is then followed by gifts made by a great king to that ancestor. For example, the hero may kill a tiger that has been plaguing villagers in the king's domain or set off to do battle against some enemy of the king's. The king then calls the palaiyakkarar to court where he presents him with gifts consisting of titles, emblems, and rights over land (sometimes over the very land of the enemy who has been conquered). As a result of this basic structure the texts often seem repetitive. Each episode is about the establishment of a relationship. It soon becomes clear that no relationship can be fixed and enduring; relationships must be constantly reestablished. This text[40] not only provides an example of the basic structure of this genre, it also reveals a narrative logic, which, though always present, is not usually so easily discernible. In all these texts the episodes are put together in such a way as to accomplish a series of transformations; the repetitiveness of the episodes does not simply reproduce the status quo but keeps changing it. However much we may

[40]  This text is somewhat less repetitive than others, mostly because traditions connected with both early medieval Tamil bhakti groups of saints, the Vaisnavite *Ālvārs* and the Saivite Nayanars, are extensively incorporated in the early portions of the text. This is not the only vamcavali in which well-known legends and traditions are incorporated. For example, stories from the Madurai *Tiruvilaiyātal* are included in the vamcavalis of the palaiyakkarars of Alakapuri and Elayirampannai (Vanniya Maravars of Tirunelveli). However, the Uttumalai text is the only one in which I have come across the use of two such disparate traditions.

experience repetition, there is nothing static about the sense of the past expressed by these texts.

In these respects, the text of the Maravars and the Vatukas of the southern area are similar both in form and content. However, the Maravar texts incorporate well-known Tamil traditions to a much greater degree. Aside from this, the principal difference between vamcavalis of the Maravars and Vatukas of Tirunelveli is that the former begin with the establishment of political relations with the Pantiyans, and the latter begin with the establishment of relations with either the Nayakas of Madurai or the kings of Vijayanagara. These relations are by no means mutually exclusive, for after the eclipse of the Pantiyans the Maravars seek recognition from the new overlords, even as both the Maravars and certain of the Vatukas are quick to declare their loyalty to the Nawab and then to the East India Company in the eighteenth century. The Uttumalai family history begins before the Maravars have established any proper political relations. We can therefore survey the dynamics of the political and cultural transformation of this Maravar family in particularly bold relief.

All the vamcavalis which I have read, this text included, were collected in the late eighteenth and early nineteenth centuries under the direction of Colonel Colin Mackenzie. Some of the texts in Mackenzie's vast collection[41] are difficult to use in cultural analysis as they suffer from the effects of dubious compilation by Mackenzie's assistants.[42] Clearly, the

[41] Mackenzie, the first Surveyor General of India, collected local histories of kingly dynasties, chiefly families, castes, villages, temples, monasteries, as well as other local traditions and religious and philosophical texts in Sanskrit, Persian, Arabic, Tamil, Telegu, Kanarese, Malayalam, and Hindi. He also took rubbings of stone and copper plate inscriptions, collected coins, images, and antiquities, and made plans and drawings. When Mackenzie died in 1821, the extent of his collection was: 3,000 inscriptions from stone and copper, 1,568 literary MSS, 2,070 local tracts (many of which were vamcavalis), 8,076 other inscriptions, 2,630 drawings, 79 plans, 6,218 coins, 106 images, and 40 antiquities (Wilson 1828, 14–15). What remains of this collection today, along with other related materials, is housed in the India Office Library, London, and the Government Oriental Manuscripts Library, Madras.

[42] Some of the manuscripts, for example, were compilations by Mackenzie's assistants, who clearly had an agenda of their own. Most problematic of all are the texts that were translated into English (IOLR). One, perhaps extreme, instance, "Mootiah's Chronological and Historical Accounts of the Modern Kings of Madura," begins with the following preface:

I turned my thoughts towards the Chronological and Historical Accounts of the Gentoo Kings of Madura written upon Palmyra leaves in a vulgar style of the Tamil language which I found to be satisfactory but the same being in a confused order

numerous texts that were not compiled but merely collected are the most useful of the Mackenzie collection, although we know far less than we would like about the circumstances of their collection.[43] Fortunately, the vamcavalis were composed well before Mackenzie and his men came around searching for historical documents. Many of the vamcavalis seem, however, to have undergone last-minute accretions. In their new forms, they appear at the end to be petitions to the East India Company for favorable consideration. They petition the Company to permanently settle their kingdom as a zamindari estate, or to reduce their tribute, or, in some cases, even to release the descendant of the kingly line from prison, where he was languishing for participating in the poligar wars of the late eighteenth century.[44]

The Uttumalai vamcavali expresses loyalty to the British in the last paragraphs, but the earlier parts of the text were clearly not composed with the British in mind. The last paragraph alone is written in the first person, and, although the original palm-leaf manuscript is signed by the Uttumalai Palaiyakkarar, it is doubtful that the text was composed by the little king himself. Most of the little kingdoms had court poets who composed both vamcavalis and panegyrics in praise of their patrons. (Even today, Uttumalai has a court poet who also plays the parts of jester and sycophant. Unfortunately, we know the names of only a few of the eighteenth-century court poets, for example Venkannan of Pudukkottai, who wrote the Tondaiman Vamcavali.) This text was probably composed by such a court poet, while the last paragraph was merely tacked on at the end by the Palaiyakkarar when he presented the manuscript to Mackenzie's men.

Given all the historiographical problems of using texts of this genre,

> and full of tautologies and repetitions which, if I proceed to translate literally into the English, it would prove absurd in the sight of the learned, I have therefore, in my following version of the said account, omitted the tautological and repeated expressions and set aside prolixity but following laconism, digested the Chronicles into eleven chapters and a preamble prefixed thereto, to which I added the characters of the Madurean kings as I learnt them from the above mendicant. (IOLR, Mackenzie Manuscripts, General, vol. 4)

It takes little imagination to realize the consequences of this kind of tampering with both content and form for a cultural analysis of a text.

[43] Some imprecise insights can be garnered from the "Letters and Reports from Native Agents Employed to Collect Books, Traditions, etc., in the various Parts of the Peninsula," IOLR, Mackenzie Collections, Unbound Translation, Class XII.

[44] See, e.g., the *Emakkalāpuram Zamīntārutaiya Vamcāvalikkanakku* and the *Āvutaiyārpuram Pālaiyakkārar Mallarāca Vamcāvali*, both in the GOML, Madras.

the manuscript collection of Colonel Colin Mackenzie stands (and has stood for over a century and a half) as a great potential mine of source material for scholars interested in the late medieval and early modern period of South Indian history. Yet the collection has been virtually ignored in the scholarly literature, for reasons that are certainly not peculiar to the state of south Indian studies. On the rare occasions these texts are referred to, the references are scant and limited to attempts to date or eulogize the battles of the little kings against the British in the late eighteenth century (e.g., Rajayyan 1974). In recent years these texts have been used in efforts to trace settlement patterns in the south (Ludden 1978a; Stein 1980, 108), but their existence as important ethnohistorical accounts has been totally ignored.

This neglect stands in marked contrast to the overwhelming importance granted to inscriptions, which are often used in a way, for example, by dating them and working them into chronological order, that correlates with Western notions of time. Historians treat local histories as relatively unimportant because they exist only as single moments in our terms, and so are timeless. We would do better if we could view these texts as the evidential base for understanding indigenous conceptions not only of time, but also of what a historical "moment" was and how these moments were classified, interpreted, and represented by the real subjects of our history. In our enthusiasm for reconstructing the history of an area that appears to have had no prior history, we are often far too unaware of the fundamental question behind our stated objectives: Whose history are we really constructing?

## The family history of the Uttumalai kings

As in the other vamcavalis, the central events of this text (*Ūttumalai Pāḷaiyapaṭṭu Vamcāvaḷi*, filed under D. 3583, Government Oriental Manuscripts Library, Madras) consist of gifts of honors, titles, emblems, land, and other privileges and of the actions that lead up to these gifts. The narrative presents what we need to know to understand these exchanges: what the little king does to merit the attention of the great king, and what the latter gives the former in appreciation and recognition of his merit. These gifts are linked together by a narrative frame that traces a series of transformations in the kingly line. The Uttumalai Maravars who begin as devout but unlettered saints of the forest and as highway bandits end up as cultured kings who have not only become aware of, but have extensively endowed, the persons and institutions of Sanskritic culture. Nonetheless, the little kings never become great kings. Their being and the significance of their actions are always constituted in reference (and in direct relationship) to one of a series of superior kings, their transactions with whom form the key events of the narrative.

Although many of the episodes in this and other vamcavalis seem repetitive, structural analysis reveals that each episode is part of a narrative flow that advances the story in discrete and ordered sequences. On one level there are oppositions within each episode between order and disorder, field and forest, ritual and nonritual, and center and periphery. These oppositions are then mediated by devotion and service, that is, by actions that merit the recognition of the king (and in two cases the God) and then result in the central transformative events of the texts – the gifts. On another level, across episodes, the transformations of each episode provide the coordinates, if not always the starting point, for subsequent transformations. So, for example, we do not witness the steady transition of a tribal chief into a dharmic king but a series of transitions each of which are relevant to one aspect of the more general transformational process. To see this more concretely let us turn to the text. Afterwards I will diagram this two-tiered narrative structure.

The text opens with the creation/generation of the Uttumalai kingly family (vamcam). Interestingly, the first cause of creation invokes a theme that occurs often in the vamcavalis, namely, the failure to produce male progeny and hence a potential crisis of succession, a crisis both personal and political. The creation of the Maravar clan (*kulam*) is the result of two integrally linked events: first, the worship of Parvati, and second, the decision of the Pantiyan king to go on a *Digvijayam* (conquest of the quarters). Both these actions are undertaken in order to beget a son. An army is needed for the Digvijayam. In fulfillment of this need, Parvati appears before the king, and an army emerges from her right side. These soldiers are Maravars, born of divine substance, born of *cakti* (the goddess, and the female principle of power), born of the right side.[45] Because of their origin, Parvati calls the Maravars gods, *Tēvars*. As we shall see, naming constitutes an important part of the structure of exchange; one must be named by a superior, unless one is a god or a universal king. The first act of these Tevars is to perform service (*paṇi*, which also means to be humble, submissive, and to worship) to the king. These few opening lines, therefore, establish the relational axes that will determine subsequent action in the narrative. The Maravars

[45] It may not be far-fetched to conclude that one of the reasons why the Maravars were said to have been born out of Parvati's right side was to associate them with the right-handed castes, who in turn were usually associated with landed rights and rural dominance (Appadurai 1974; Beck 1972; Stein 1980).

begin with parental relations with a deity and service relations with a king. From the start, these relations are profoundly interdependent, the creation of the Tevars by the deity being for the service of the king.

Given this auspicious beginning, the next episode proves rather surprising. There, the royal Tevar soldiers of the previous story are suddenly presented as uncultivated hunters roaming about in the hills. As the vamcavali tells us:

A descendant of this great Maravar caste was King Tinnan. Tinnan was off in the forest hunting with his clan but, as at one point he went off alone, he became lost. He continued, however, to hunt alone. Roaming about, he came upon a temple to Siva. Tinnan was thereupon overcome by the serene beauty of the idol and of the sacred place, and he then and there dedicated himself to the worship of the god. He went out and killed animals which provided tender meat, cooked the meat in fire, and tasted each piece before offering it to the god. He chose only those tender morsels that were properly cooked. For his offerings, this Maravar king carried the pre-tasted meat in his hands, the water for the ritual unction in his mouth, and the garlands of flowers and the vermillion in his hair. He approached the idol and removed the flowers and other offerings with the help of his feet and slippers, washed the idol with the water that he carried in his mouth, adorned the god with the flowers from his hair, and finally offered the pieces of cooked meat that he had already tasted and judged to be fine. The priest of the temple noticed that someone had been coming to the temple every day, and, after removing the flowers the priest had placed there, had polluted the temple with common flowers, meat, etc. The priest became very upset, but one day in his dream Lord Siva appeared to him and told him about King Tinnan and his complete devotion and told the priest to hide and observe this for himself. Siva added that he would put Tinnan's devotion (*bhakti*) and determination to the test. The next morning the priest came and performed worship (puja) and then hid himself nearby. Shortly thereafter Tinnan came and performed his own worship and proceeded to pray to Siva. As he was praying, blood began to ooze from one eye of the idol. Tinnan saw this and offered his own eye to the deity; when he took out his eye and placed it on the idol's eye the bleeding stopped. Then the other eye of the idol started to bleed. Seeing this, Tinnan felt that he must offer his second eye, as that alone would be the proper remedy. In order to locate the bleeding eye after completely blinding himself, he placed his foot (on which he still wore his slippers) on the idol's eye and removed his second eye and placed it on the idol. At this moment Siva appeared and embraced Tinnan and blessed him with the name Kannapan, "he who applied his own eye." With this blessing, Kannapan attained release.

The story of Kannapan is well known throughout Tamil Nadu, being one of the most popular of the legends in the *Periyapurāṇam*, the twelfth-century Tamil puranic epic that tells the stories of the lives of the sixty-three Saivite *Nāyaṇār* bhakti saints. The above adaptation has no major alterations, although it is shortened and as colloquial in tone as the rest of the vamcavali. No caste is ascribed to Kannapan in the Periyapuranam, but he is clearly the chief of a tribe of hunters who live somewhere in the remote forests of the hills. In the vamcavali, Tinnan is the chief of the Maravars, in what seems a self-conscious acceptance of the usual assumption that the Maravars were originally a hunting and gathering (and warring) group which did not occupy the mainstream areas of early Tamil civilization. Tinnan becomes separated from his group while on a hunting expedition, and as he roams about on his own he comes across a temple dedicated to Siva. The text clearly shows that, although Tinnan is a man of great devotion, who recognizes the sacred significance of this shrine to Siva, he is totally ignorant of the textual (agamic) forms of worship.

The detailed description of Tinnan's worship makes explicit a set of oppositions. Tinnan's actions are consistent with a hunter's mentality and are specifically opposed to textual prescriptions for worship. As we saw in the last chapter, worship involves the honoring of the deity by the offering of garlands of flowers, clothing, hymns and mantras, as well as other sanctified things or actions, and perhaps most importantly by the offer of some kind of food, most often uncooked items, such as plantains and coconuts, but also cooked food, such as sweet rice prepared by Brahmans, to the deity. The usual order for the conduct of worship in a temple would be, first, the unction/bath (*apicēkam*) of the deity with consecrated water (*tīrttam*), second, the adornment (*alankāram*) of the deity with flowers (*tirupūkaḷ*), vermillion (*kuṅkum*), and perhaps sandalwood paste (*cantanam*) and certain vestments – the number and actual composition of the rites of adoration (*upācāram*) are somewhat variable – and finally, and invariably, the deity would be presented with food. All of these presentations honor the deity, and all of the substances presented to the deity are transvalued by their contact with the deity. Tinnan performs his worship in exact contravention of the actions and principles underlying puja. For his offerings (*nivētanam*), he carries the water for the ritual unction in his mouth, which of course means that the water becomes thoroughly mixed with his saliva (*eccil*); he carries the garlands of flowers in his hair, which is defiling to the deity who will be adorned with these flowers; worse, given the explicit body imagery that casts the feet as the lowest and most polluting part of the body, he touches all of his offerings with his feet and his slippers; and, worst of all, not only does he give meat to the deity, he tastes it first to find the tastiest morsels. In short, Tinnan not only debases the deity, he structurally reverses the worship, performing actions that make it seem as if the deity is worshipping him.

This story comes from the traditions of devotional Hinduism (bhakti), and Tinnan's actions, far from intending such debasement and insult, are based on his devotion, which turns out to be pure and extreme. The image is clearly imprinted at the end of the episode; while Tinnan's feet (with, as the text insists, his slippers still on) rest on the head of the deity, a picture that not only would revolt the proper Hindu, but that represents the reversal of the rite of tirupatam (the worship of the feet of the deity), he plucks out his second eye because of his intense love of God. Indeed, the major focus of and selection of detail in the vamcavali version concerns Tinnan's thorough violation of worship, a violation that in the end is balanced by his great sacrifice. However much ritual is undervalued in favor of devotion, the extreme degree of devotion demanded does not so much dispense with ritual as demonstrate the latter's importance. Certainly, there would be little power in this story if the reader were not convinced of the value and truth of the rituals of worship. In this variant of bhakti, ritual is not denounced and deliberately defied as it was in certain other forms of bhakti, for example, Viraśaivism (see Ramanujan 1973). Rather, we see here the way in which devotion can compensate for the lack of ritual knowledge, and, in a corollary sense, the use of this tradition to explain the incorporation of new groups into the increasingly heterogeneous fold of the Hindu community.

The inclusion of an episode from the Periyapuranam in a local text suggests that the Uttumalai palaiyakkarars sought to lend weight to their family's past by including a legend from one of the great Tamil traditions. Further, the use of this particular episode at this point in the narrative suggests that the purpose of the tale is to explain how a family which was once a tribal group of hunters and gatherers came to be associated with, and became appropriate for, the worship of Siva and the traditions of kingship. Birth from Parvati, the consort of Siva, might seem enough, but it is not. The set of transformations that contribute to this basic development will orient the narrative format of the entire text. The progression from episode to episode is characterized less by the sequential development of an historical relationship than by a structurally ordered accumulation of differently contextualized relationships that establish this fundamental transformation. The interrelation of episodes is not immediately apparent and is only revealed as the structures of internal relations and patterns of mediation within a series of episodes are established. Within this particular episode, the opposition is between the violation and proper performance of ritual norms, a structurally ordered opposition, which is then mediated by devotion. Devotion transforms a hunter into a saint, a saint who attains release (*cuvarkkam*) and who is clearly identified with one of the principal canonized saints of a great tradition text who is worshipped and praised in temples throughout Tamil Nadu. But the incipient nature of this transformation is only revealed by reading on in the text.

Yet another descendant of the Maravar clan was named Kaliyan. He desired to perform *tiruppani* (the giving of gifts to and renovation of a temple) to the Srirankam temple. Kaliyan spent all the money from his treasury and prepared the offerings. These offerings suddenly disappeared, as a result of which Kaliyan sold his kingdom and, still short of money, resorted to highway robbery with his affines. When they collected sufficient treasure by this means, they were able to perform the tiruppani. They went on worshipping Sri Renkanatar Cuvami (a form of Visnu) of Srirankam, but the source of income for this worship continued to be highway robbery. They then stole a golden image of the Buddha hidden in a cave in Nakapattinam. When it became increasingly difficult to rob they prayed to Sri Renkanatar to help them. Then they went out on another mission. Sri Renkanatar himself dressed in fineries, adorned himself with many valuable jewels, and mounted a horse and came near them. When they attacked the Lord he pretended to be overpowered by them and allowed himself to be robbed of everything he had including the horse on which he rode. But one ornament on the Lord's foot could not be removed. So, Kaliyan used his teeth to try and pry it off. As soon as Kaliyan's tongue touched Renkanatar's foot he realized who He was and began to pray and sang a hymn of praise to the deity. Having revealed himself, Renkanatar blessed Kaliyan with the name Kalla Mankai Alvar, and thus he became a saint.

The story of Kaliyan rendered here is a modified version of the story of Tirumankai Alvar, one of the best-known and most prolific of medieval Tamil Vaisnavite bhakti saints and poets. The legendary account of his life (Bharati 1942; Zvelebil 1975, 159-160) is very colorful, and of great interest in calculating the ethical content of bhakti. He was born a Kallar (though many Maravars claim him as one of their own – see Pate 1917, 134), and a Saivite, and was called Nilan. He was given lands and was made a commander in the army by the Cola king. He then fell in love with the maiden Kumutavalli, who was a great devotee of Visnu. To win her hand he also became a devotee of Visnu and pledged to feed 1,008 Vaisnavite devotees every day. To fulfill his pledge he stole from the king, who imprisoned him, although he was subsequently saved from prison by Visnu. Nilan then turned to highway robbery, which enabled him to enlarge the Srirankam temple in addition to feeding the devotees. He was even said to have stolen the large golden image of the Buddha in Nakapattinam. Finally, he set upon and robbed a wealthy Brahman, who turned out to be Visnu himself. Visnu then taught him the all powerful mantra that led to his enlightenment.

The vamcavali omits the earlier events of this legend. Its version begins with Kaliyan's desire to renovate the Srirankam temple. The inclusion of this bhakti story connects the mediational and incorporative effects of bhakti, already established in the previous episode, with temple worship, something the Maravar family has yet to demonstrate its adeptness at and fitness for. So, for example, the presentation of gifts to temples rather than the feeding of devotees figures in its version of the story, thus contributing to the general emphasis in the episode on the mastery of prescribed ritual codes for conduct by this Maravar group. Not unnaturally, the vamcavali departs from the traditional texts in not designating the hero as a Kallar, although the choice of the story suggests (at least at this point in the narrative) little embarrassment about one of the Kallars' traditional occupations, highway robbery (*varipparikkam*). Here, the purpose of highway robbery is the exalted one of renovating the temple (tiruppani). And Visnu does not seem to disapprove, for he takes on a disguise and becomes the robber's victim in order to engineer the enlightenment of his great devotee. Interestingly, in the Uttumalai text the mode of enlightenment is not the mantra of the traditional accounts but the contact of Kaliyan's tongue with Visnu's holy feet (tirupatam); the motif – in sharp and direct contrast to the previous episode – is again one in which the relation between deity and devotee is depicted by the contact of head and foot. While Tinnan's devotion offsets the literal subordination of the deity's head to his shod foot, here the final action is the literal touching of Kaliyan's tongue to the deity's foot, an image that neatly encapsulates the movement toward the increased ritualism of temple worship in the earlier part of this second story. Both stories stress devotion, but the contrast between them is striking, especially in their final images.

Although this second episode recapitulates certain basic components of the first – there is yet another incorporative use of well-known Tamil bhakti traditions and another demonstration of the religious devotion of these illustrious Maravar forebears – two transformations occur. First, the Uttumalai Maravars become Vaisnavites, which marks them off from most other Maravars who are Saivites. Second, and more important for the narrative, we move from a scene in which the ancestor devotee is completely unaware of the textual forms of worship to one in which his descendants are now patrons, massively endowing one of the most important Tamil Vaisnavite temples. The complexity of this transformation is underscored, however, by the means used to procure resources for this temple endowment, namely, highway robbery, at best unorthodox behavior. The text will soon show highway robbery to be highly destructive of the social order. In the previous episode, the structural opposition was between socially and ritually sanctioned behavior and Tinnan's peculiar worship; in this episode, the opposition is between the exalted end of renovating a temple and the dubious and dangerous means of highway robbery. The coordinates of these transformations thus establish baselines for subsequent transformations: whereas the procedures for worship are violated in one episode, in the next they are not only upheld but endowed; whereas highway robbery is the means of this endowment in one episode, in the next it will take on another important, although quite different, role. For both of the episodes we have examined so far, borrowed as they are from great bhakti traditions, devotion is the mechanism of transformation. In the story of Kaliyan, however, the end-point of transformation is not simply a jungly saint, but a saint whose devotion leads him to make extensive gifts to a major temple and who achieves enlightenment through a metaphorized enactment of puja (the worship of Visnu's feet at the end). As such, the Maravar is simultaneously associated with the great tradition of a major temple center and with kingship, for the granting of great gifts to temples is something done by kings.

In the next episode, the highway robbers are no longer the heroes but the enemies of the heroes. In this role they provide the occasion for another key transformation. In the previous episode, the Maravars made the transition from jungly saints to kingly saints who also happened to be robbers; now they become chieftains who enter into a series of relations with great kings – a pattern that will hold for the rest of the text – by virtue of their subduing a band of country robbers (*cīmaikkaḷḷars*) who were terrorizing the countryside. It is noteworthy that in this episode the Maravars are said to be living in Srivaikontai-yankottai, the latter part of which is the name of the subcaste itself. In other words, the first specified space inhabited by the Maravars other than the forests and roadsides is the place that provides the basic identity of the entire subcaste. Nevertheless, they seem to move away from their ancestral place almost immediately. The reason for this has to do with their establishment of relations with the Pantiyan king.

At this point in the text, the Maravars take on a political identity which supersedes their territorial identity in importance. Simultaneously we as readers and outsiders sense a movement "into" history, or at least "our" history. This sense derives from our own reading of history and not from any narrative clues in the text. Even so, we cannot correlate this moment in the text with any particular period of Pantiyan history, as the name of the Pantiyan king given in the text does not appear in the standard successional lists of the dynasty. If we calculate from the number of generations of Maravars listed in our text, the year would be about A.D. 1100, a time when the Pantiyans were still subordinate to the reigning Colas.

The Maravar hero of the third episode is summoned to the court of the Pantiyan king because of his heroic actions in subduing the country robbers. At this Pantiyan court, where (as we might remember from the first episode) the Maravars made their first appearance, the Maravar chief is congratulated for bringing peace to the countryside and given titles, emblems, and rights over land. The title is the Pantiyan's own name, Vijayakunarama Pantiya, and thus represents the establishment of a special bond as well as the grant by the king of part of his own substance, or persona, to the Maravar. As emblems, the Pantiyan gives the Maravar a pair of fly whisks (*cāmaram*) – general symbols of kingship – and three banners with the emblems of Indra (*valārikkoṭi*), king of the Gods, and of the Cola (*pulikkoṭi*) and Pantiya (*makarakkoṭi*) dynasties. Thus, the Maravars are literally presented with the substance of kingship and those emblems of kingly authority bearing the greatest significance in the medieval Tamil context. The land the Maravar is given is the very land where the highway robbers who had been subdued had lived. It is presented as a *pāḷaiyappaṭṭu*. Palaiyappattu means the title or right (*paṭṭu*) to a palaiyam. As mentioned earlier, palaiyam is the base from which we get palaiyakkarar, one who rules over a palaiyam.

We have seen that the principal symbolic mechanism for the establishment of "political" relations is the gift of titles and emblems, as well as land. The word in Tamil that signifies both title and emblem is virutu (otherwise spelled *pirutu*). Virutu also means banner, trophy, badge of victory, pedigree, genealogy. Other Dravidian cognates include additional glosses such as panegyric, praise, power, and valor.[46] The king's emblems not only signify his own sovereignty, but their present-ation to lesser kings and nobles marks and establishes a special relationship, a substantial bond. The bestowal of emblems and titles, titles that sometimes describe the heroic action performed in the service of the king and that are often one or more of the king's own titles, has the symbolic effect of sharing part of the sovereignty of the king with one of his subjects. The subsequent acceptance of these emblems completes the act of service/worship and serves to acknowledge that it is a great honor for the recipient to share, as a subordinate, part of the king's own royalty. Through this transaction the king not only shares part of his sovereign substance, but incorporates the "servant" into his own sovereignty, or lordship.

[46] See the *Tamil Lexicon* (1900, p. 2638) and Burrow and Emeneau (1961, 372). For the borrowing of this into Sanskrit, see Monier-Williams (1979, 536).

The emblems, the title, and the rulership over the palaiyam, all given by the Pantiyan king, represent both the newly constituted kingship of the Uttumalai Maravar and the fact that this kingship is something constituted by and in relation to the Pantiyan king. All vamcavalis make it clear that honors and emblems are only meaningful when given by a superior, a king or a deity. Honors must not only be identified in relational terms, but these relations are necessarily hierarchical. Similarly, the heroic action of the palaiyakkarars must be symbolically encoded in this hierarchical world; the subduing of a wild elephant or of highway robbers takes on special meaning in these texts only when honors are conferred by superior kings as a result of these actions. The relationship is always one of periphery to center, and of part to whole; the periphery (palaiyakkarars) is always oriented to the center (great kings), even as the metonymic part (emblems) only derives meaning from its relation to the whole (the sovereignty, and the full set of emblems, of a great king).

Having witnessed the initial structuring of hierarchical relations, we find the next and fourth episode somewhat curious, for the Maravar kings refuse a marriage alliance both with a series of unnamed kings (all of whom waged war and were defeated, with their elephants, horses, weapons, titles, banners, and crowns all seized) and with the Pantiyan kings themselves. Contradictory as this may seem, particularly in light of the Maravars' subsequent reestablishment of subordinate relations with the Pantiyans, the compelling logic of the text at this point shows that the Maravars have become little kings who can not only accept royal gifts but refuse them as well. This episode demonstrates the hierarchical and metonymic nature of honors and emblems and the symbolic politics of marriage in a particularly vivid passage. The request of the Pantiyan king for the hand of a Maravar girl renowned for her beauty receives this bold saying (cribbed, it turns out, from Tamil literary sources. See *Maturaikkalampakam* [1968]; and *Tiravankakalampakam* [1957].)

The fates of other kings who have made such an offer are well known. If you do not know this, you can see that we Maravars have captured their weapons and keep them on the outskirts of our country, their crowns are being looked after, their possessions are used as borders in decorating the roofs of our houses, and their umbrellas are folded and kept aside. Do you really hope to get a girl from such a Maravar family for the royal wedding?

Hierarchical relations are established and represented symbolically through these emblems; thus the way of saying that one king has subdued another is to say that he has captured his emblems, not his lands, and that this conquest is boldly displayed. Indeed, the victor uses the emblems to embellish his own kingship, even as they are degraded and made to represent the loss of another's power. This form of symbolic conquest and metonymic domination has occurred repeatedly in South Indian history. When Maravarman Sundara Pantiyan I (1216-1268) defeated the Cola king, he "seized his crown of fine gold, and was pleased to give it to the Bana" (Sastri 1975, 394), thus displaying not only his conquest of the Cola throne, but metonymically appropriating it by using the crown as one emblem among others that he could present to a subordinate king.

The refusal of a marriage alliance with the series of unnamed kings serves as a symbolic expression of the Maravar's refusal to admit inferiority to – and perhaps even equality with – these kings. More curious is the Maravar's refusal of a marriage alliance with the Pantiyans, whose gifts the text has just proclaimed as constituting the former's new position of authority. The particular reason given in the text for the refusal is that the Pantiyans are of the solar race and are therefore not suitable marriage partners for the Maravar girls, who belong to the lunar race (*cantira kula*). Some of the other family histories from the Tirunelveli region contain similar disputes between the palaiyakkarars and the Pantiyans though these are over the honors granted by the Pantiyans to the little kings and not refusals of marriage. For example, in the vamcavalis of the Alakapuri and Elayirampannai families[47] the dispute has to do with the demand for equal seating rights (*cariyiruppu*) with the Pantiyans; in both cases this demand is tested by ordeal. The palaiyakkarars are asked to mount copper horses that have been heated till they are red hot; fortunately, the goddess intervenes in both cases, transforming the copper horses into living ones as soon as they are mounted. As in the Uttumalai text, these disputes confirm the claimed status of the palaiyakkarars without leading to disharmony. In respect of the specific nature of the dispute, the Uttumalai text bears more resemblance to the texts of many of the Vatuka little kings, which often begin with the refusal of a marriage proposal from the kings of Delhi as a result of which the Vatukas migrate to the southern country (Mahalingam 1972). In all these cases the purpose of these stories is to demonstrate the enhanced royal authority of the palaiyakkarars as well as sometimes to explain the migration of the group. Similar motifs figure in many modern caste histories (see Daniel 1984).

The Uttumalai vamcavali proceeds at this point to the next and fifth

---

[47] Both Vanniya Maravars from Tirunelveli. See the *Alakāpuri Zamintār Vamcāvali* and the *Ēlayiram Paṇṇai Citampara Vanniyaṉ Vamcāvaḷī*, in the GOML, Madras.

episode in which the Maravars subdue a group of forest (*vanam*) dwellers who have been causing trouble along the roads of the northern land to which the Maravars have retreated, following their dispute with the Pantiyans.[48] In recognition of their actions, the Maravars are summoned to court by the "*camastānam*," which although unidentified must refer to Vijayanagara, and presented with emblems, land as a palaiyapattu, and a title. This short episode, largely repetitive but suggestive of the establishment of royal relations with Vijayanagara, also renders the move to the north meaningful in terms other than retreat. By the fifteenth century the Vijayanagara court had become by far the most powerful political and cultural center of southern India, not merely dwarfing the Pantiyans but also providing an imperial umbrella for the subsequent establishment of a series of Nayaka kingdoms. Thus, the move to the north ends up serving an even grander purpose than the dispute with the Pantiyans.

In the sixth episode the genealogical succession is threatened by a king who has no issue. This predicament is solved through the intercession of Venkateswarar, a form of Visnu around whom one of the grandest Vaisnavite temple traditions in all of South India, that of Tirupati, was established largely under the patronage of Vijayanagara. This intercession establishes a second relationship for the Maravars in the northern country, thus providing a dual axis of the sort that had initially been set up with the goddess Parvati and with the Pantiyans in the far south at the beginning of the text. These relations established, however, the Maravars then move back to the south. On their way they kill a group of "country Kallars" (*nāṭṭukkaḷḷars*) who attack them. This encounter serves to reestablish a relationship with the Pantiyans, for the Maravars are invited to the Pantiyan court in recognition of their feat, the former problems between them apparently totally forgotten. At this point in the text, the Pantiyan court is no longer in Madurai but in Ukkirankottai, an important Pantiyan stronghold in the Tirunelveli region located on the banks of the river Cittar about twenty miles to the east of Tenkaci. We can thus assume that this was the period of the last phase of Pantiyan rule sometime after the late fourteenth century.

On this visit to court, the Uttumalai Maravar is given no honors;

---

[48] When this story is repeated in the vamcavali of the Natuvakkuricci Maravar palaiyakkarars, who at this point claim not to have been divided from the Uttumalai branch, the Pantiyan's request is likewise refused. But it is specifically stated that the Maravars feel it would not be right (or just – *niyāyamalla*) to fight against the Pantiyans. So they leave the country before any battle can take place (see the *Natuvakkuricci Pālaiyakkāran Vamcāvaḷi*, GOML, Madras).

rather, he is told that, if he can subdue the troublesome Kurumpars of the countryside around Ukkirankottai, he will be given their country as his own domain. The Kurumpars were early inhabitants of southern India; according to some accounts they came from Karnataka and settled in Tamil areas in the first millennium A.D. (See "Account of Tondamantalam and its ancient inhabitants, Baders and Kurumbars, their customs, etc." in Wilson [1828, 423] and in Mahalingam [1972, 96].) They were a group known for their military power who were credited with building many sturdy forts. The Kurumpars settled initially in Tontaimantalam (the northern part of the Tamil country), where they set up the twenty-four forts and domains that traditionally constituted and divided that country. There they were subdued by Atontai Cola, a legendary king designated as progenitor of the Pallava dynasty who vanquished the forest-dwelling Kurumpars and subsequently settled the area with Vellalars. (See "Account of Kandava Rayan and Setu Rayam who ruled from the Fort of Tiruvitaiccuram in the Arcot Forest," in Mahalingam [1972, 49].) In most accounts, the Kurumpars are also said to have been longstanding enemies of the Colas and the Pantiyans, as well as caste enemies of the *Mutaliyars* and Vellalars, castes associated with agricultural settlement in the major cultural centers of Tamil Nadu (Mahalingam 1972, 96; Taylor 1835, 420).

Whether or not these accounts provided a direct model for this section of our vamcavali, the Pantiyan king's request that the Maravars defeat the Kurumpars reassociates the Maravars with the Pantiyans. It also establishes a basis for their acquisition of settled land rights in southern Tamil Nadu in a clear parallel to the origin myths of the most conspicuous Tamil cultivating castes and of the kings with whom these castes were aligned. Indeed, as soon as the Maravars defeat the Kurumpars, they take possession of the kingdom that they have won by conquering it for the Pantiyan king who grants it to them together with great honors and many other gifts. This new domain is Uttumalai, and here they clear the jungles and build a fort.

In the next and seventh episode, five generations later, the Uttumalai Maravar goes to the Navarattiri festival hosted by Sri Vallapa Maharaja. To calculate backward through the number of generations mentioned in the text, this was probably the Pantiyan king Jatavarman Srivallapa, who ruled in Tenkaci from approximately A.D. 1534 to 1543. By the time of Vijayanagara rule, Navarattiri or Mahanavami had become the most important festival for kings in southern India.[49] At this

---

[49] The political and cosmo-moral centrality of Vijayanagara for late

point in the text the palaiyakkarars do not claim to have performed this festival themselves; rather, they are still attending the courts of greater kings in hopes of further recognition and gifts. The text characterizes the Maharaja's festival as renowned for its athletic and agonistic events, in particular its wrestling matches and animal fights, thus conjuring up the kind of scene so eloquently described in the ballad on Kattapomman. The contest of royal elephants provides the occasion for the Maravar hero to display his bravery and skill:

One day two intoxicated elephants were brought and were let loose to fight. But one elephant ran amuck and escaped from the arena and threatened the lives of many who had come for the festival, and no one was able to tame the elephant. Hearing this, the Maravar king came outside and went to confront the beast. He caught hold of the elephant's tail and twisted it until the animal was tamed. Then the mahout came and took the elephant away. The Maharaja was very pleased, and mounted him on the same tamed elephant which was duly decorated with many emblems, flags, and banners, including the howdah, a pair of fly whisks, the five-colored shawl, the tiger flag, and he was sent off to the accompaniment of drums and musical instruments, after having been given the title: "He who caught and subdued the royal elephant."

Not only is this particular elephant the royal elephant, elephants in general are symbols of royalty, and the vehicles of kings. Thus, in this metonymic victory, which occasions the same kinds of gifts of emblems, honors, and titles discussed earlier, we see a further progression in the Maravar's attainment of kingly appropriateness and power.

Unsurprisingly, therefore, one of the first acts of the successor of the Maravar who subdued the royal elephant is to establish a landed settlement for Brahmans (agraharam) and to build a temple for these Brahmans. But the Uttumalai palaiyakkarars are still not universal

medieval south India led to the proliferation of performance of Maha-navami in the larger little kingdoms. The Nayakas performed it in Madurai, the Cetupatis in Ramanatapuram, claiming that this mandate of sovereignty had been awarded them by the Madurai Nayakas. Somewhat later the Tondaimans performed it in Pudukkottai. Interestingly enough, it was never performed on a grand scale in Uttumalai, where Pan-kunipramodsa was the principal state festival. The occurrence of Pan-kunipramodsa on the first ten days of the month of Pankuni (roughly equivalent to March/April) soon after the northeast monsoon makes it a more appropriate harvest festival for Tamil Nadu than Dasara. Most significant, however, the deity worshipped in Navarattiri or Dasara in southern India was Durga, or some other, usually Saivite, form of the goddess, whereas the tutelary deity of the Uttumalai family was Navanit-takirusna, the child Krishna who is the most often worshipped incarnation of Visnu.

kings. Embedded within this narrative is the relatively brief comment that power in Madurai passed from the Pantiyans to the Nayakas, who summon the Maravar to assist them in the protection of their fort in Madurai. (This is consistent with my earlier chronological assumption, because the Nayakas assumed power in Madurai around A.D. 1530.) This event, given scant notice here, takes on greater significance in the vamcavalis of Vatuka rulers and in the chronicles of the Nayakas, where the incorporation of the southern palaiyakkarars as protectors of the seventy-two bastions of the Nayaka fort is a major event and becomes the central metaphor for the reconstitution of the late medieval southern Tamil political order.

The next and eighth episode in the text demonstrates even more clearly the continued participation of the Maravars in a hierarchical system of relations, one in which they still look up:

In those days the Karttakkals [the Nayakas] established a Brahman settlement (agraharam) in the southern country. Some criminals came and set fire to the settlement and destroyed it. The Karttakkals, wishing to avenge this terrible act, commanded Sri Vallapa Marutappattevar [the Maravar, who now carries the title of the Pantiyan king who hosted the Navarattiri] to apprehend the criminals, though in the fight he lost many men. Because of this he was honored (*apimānam*) and was given gifts of land on half-assessment (*arttakkānikkai*) and was given a palanquin, banners with the emblems of Hanuman and the Brahminy kite, a copper umbrella, some musical instruments, a tiger skin, and a horse. These sixty-four criminals were taken to the agraharam where they committed their crime and one by one their heads were severed.

Interestingly, much greater emphasis is given to this episode in the narrative than to the Maravar's own establishment of a Brahman settlement; protecting the royal agraharam has far greater political significance than establishing such an institution oneself.

After this, ten generations (and, the historian adds, about two hundred years, correlating well with the standard assumption of twenty years per generation) after the Nayakas assumed their prominence in the text, the Muslim rulers take over the southern Tamil country. The Maravars are as helpful and submissive to them as they had been to previous kings, and they are awarded emblems and honors by Muhammed Yusuf Khan, an agent of the Nawab of Arcot who, I might add, brought independent palaiyakkarars under control before he too was declared rebellious by the Nawab in 1763. Among other things, the Maravar helps the Muslim ruler bring under control those who are causing trouble (*tuṣattanam*), those who are not submissive (*kiṛppaṭintu naṭavāmal*), and those who do not pay their tribute (*tōppāvuṅkoṭāmal*). At that time, the text tells us,

92

anarchy (*arājika*, i.e., no kingly authority) prevails in the Tirunelveli country, and Muhammed calls the Uttumalai Maravar and gives him 2,000 men and asks him to restore order in the area. On doing so, the Maravar is congratulated and told that he should continue to perform carefully "the work of the palace" and do what is asked. This passage suggests far more concern than before with specified and regularized forms of command.

The final changeover in overlordship occurs when the British supplant the Muslims as the regional rulers. Even here, there is no break in the fundamental forms and content of the narrative. Again, the Maravars are of service to the ruling kings, who again give them gifts and honors. One significant shift, however, began under the Muslims and receives even more emphasis now; this is the new concern of the ruling powers with taxes. One of the ways in which the Palaiyakkarar assists the Muslim ruler is to bring under control those who do not pay taxes. Under the British the Maravars are engaged in collecting taxes from recalcitrant palaiyakkarars. The sudden emphasis on taxes signals a reorientation of priorities in the political system. Yet the arrival of taxes in their new form is not associated in the text with the disappearance of honor and gifts, for the Maravars' political relations with the Muslims and the British continue to be defined by services performed for their sovereign overlords and by the recognition of these deeds in the form of the presentation of honors and privileges. The Honorable Company awards the Maravar Palaiyakkarar a palanquin, a horse, and a green umbrella. Well they should have, for, as the vamcavali announces, "we have severed the heads of bulls belonging to our neighboring enemies and thus shown our devotion to the Company."

To recapitulate, gifts of various privileges – emblems, titles, honors, and land – are not only the central points of each narrative episode, they are central events in that they constitute the relationship of the chief and the king, and in that they transform the chief into a little king by adding to his persona those rights and privileges that are fundamental to the cultural definition of authority. But however "freely given" these gifts are, they always follow some kind of "service," which really means (as, e.g., in the case of the word pani) worshipful action performed both to demonstrate submission to the authority of the great king and to display this submission in the form of some heroic action in honor of the great king. The concepts of loyalty and service are thus subsumed under this more general notion of worshipful submission, which in the form of some act, gesture, or statement always regenerates the kinds of "political" relationships (in turn constituted by gifts) we observe in these texts.

## Narrative structure, ethnohistory, and little kingship

Several major contiguous oppositions are established at the beginning of our text. They serve to orient much of the action and supply much of the structure of the narrative format. These oppositions might be diagrammed as:

Forest/Field
Disorder/Order
Nonritual/Ritual
Periphery/Center

In the story of Kannapan, the forest is the Maravar chief's habitat, whereas later in the text the forest is claimed and cleared by the same Maravars. Similarly, the movement from disorder to order is signified by robbery and lawlessness, which the Maravars initially engage in themselves but which their descendants later subdue when practiced by others. In addition, the Maravars begin by being totally ignorant of ritual forms of worship and behavior and end up by performing such ritually mandated activities as making gifts to temples and setting up and protecting Brahman settlements. Finally, in the one opposition that is never completely mediated, the Maravars move throughout the entire text from the periphery toward the center, although they never become the center themselves.

These oppositions set up the basic structure for the particular transformations that occur in the text. A diagram of these transformations would look like this:

| | | |
|---|---|---|
| 1 From: tribal chief | Through: devotion; grace | To: jungly saint |
| 2 From: highway robber | Through: devotion; grace | To: kingly saint |
| 3 From: subduer of highway robbers; vanquisher of forest tribes; and settler/cultivator/ruler | Through: service to king; gifts from king | To: chieftain |
| 4 From: chieftain | Through: service to king; refusal of marriage; emulation of dharmic kingship in gifts to temples and Brahmans | To: little king |
| 5 From: little king | Through: transfer of loyalty to Muslims and British; payment of tax | To: zamindar |

At the risk of oversimplification, this diagram collapses the episodic structure of the text into five major transformations. It can now readily be observed that these transformations are not always perfectly linear. We noted earlier that the first two episodes use the traditions of bhakti to explain, first, the origins of the Maravars as tribal chiefs and, second, their traditional reputation as thieves and marauders. Both episodes then have different starting points but use stories of devotion to propel their heroes into sainthood, albeit of different types and qualities. But in the third episode the saintly heroes are forgotton while their original forms are not so much transformed as directly opposed and reversed; now the Maravars are vanquishing tribal chiefs such as the Kurumpars, subduing highway robbers such as the Kallars, and clearing forests and bringing under cultivation lands given them by great kings. As these activities are performed as services to these kings, the Maravars at this point have become chieftains in direct relationship with one of the major Tamil dynasties. However, not until the next few episodes do these chieftains become, in the full sense of the term as I employ it here, little kings, differing from chieftains in that they now are emulating dharmic kingship in their gifts to temples and Brahmans. Although the term palaiyakkarar is used for all of these stages, the Uttumalai text reveals the expansion of the significance of this term over time. The final transition is of course from little king to zamindar, the full implications of which were hardly understood at the time by the newly christened "landlords" of the southern Tamil country.[50]

One of the consequences of the simplification of this diagram is the danger of overlooking the serious tension in the predicament of little kings who on the one hand refuse a marriage alliance with the Pantiyan kings and on the other hand give more weight in their own history to the protection of some great king's dharmic gifts than to the establishment of their own kingly institutions. This tension is the result of the incomplete mediation of the opposition between periphery and center. Much as these little kings might like to occupy the center, they cannot. First, their social base is in areas that, for irreversible ecological reasons, can never be central. Second, the very nature of little kingship as depicted in vamcavalis derives from the recognition and grace of the overlords whom the little kings serve and worship and from whom they

---

[50] The estate had a checkered career during the nineteenth century. There were frequent succession disputes while mounting arrears of tribute occasioned the repeated attachment of the estate by the government (Pate 1917, 469–71). Nonetheless, in spite of the ill feeling of certain British officials toward them (see letter from R. Eden to Board of Revenue, October 14, 1836, in India, Government of [SORBS 1934, 8]), the zamindars were important patrons of Tamil arts and culture in the nineteenth and twentieth centuries (communication from David Ludden).

accept gifts. And yet, even where the texts sing the praises of overlords, the principal motive is to proclaim the greatness of the honors that the little kings receive from their overlords. Thus, the texts enhance the prestige of the little king, for the greater the overlord the greater the little king under him.

The principal merit of this analysis is that it allows us to see that the text is not broken up into "fanciful" and "historical" sections, even though we can determine from external evidence what seems to be an increasing degree of historicity as the text progresses. The first episodes set up the coordinates for all the transformations in the text and are as integral to the text as any of the other episodes. By identifying the narrative logic of a text in this manner, we realize that the text does indeed have an integrity of its own. Further, we can begin to discern the indigenously conceived units, events, and diachronic structures of a particular tradition: the discourse of the past. But this kind of ethnohistorical investigation must not stop here. As I stated earlier, this reconstructed discourse can provide a culturally sensitive analytic framework for our own "outside" study of the history of south Indian little kingdoms.

The Maravar kings of Uttumalai are as aware of the paradox of their "little kingship" as I was earlier; in this text we see how they use their origins as tribal chiefs and highway robbers to provide the structure for their subsequent refinement and their attainment of many of the qualities of dharmic kings. The oppositions in the text are indeed complementary: the disorder that the Uttumalai kings represent in the beginning becomes the disorder that they subdue and incorporate at the end. But as we have seen, while the Maravars are proud to boast of their achievements, they are also aware of their limitations: unlike Kattapom-man, they know they can never become universal kings. Rather, they remain little kings who, inasmuch as they emulate dharmic kings, continue to seek gifts and derive consequence from them. They also continue to excell in agonistic feats – on the battlefield, in the overlord's court, and finally in the notorious guise of tax collector – which preserve the original base of their powerful position (and the original source for their "martial" reputation). And, again unlike Kattapomman, they survive into the colonial regime, becoming Zamindars under the Permanent Settlement of 1803.

### Regional politics from the top down: the Nayakas of Madurai

The orientation of the little kings of Uttumalai up toward larger kings, first the Pantiyans and then the Nayakas of Madurai, was basic to the representation of their sovereignty. For example, we learned that the protection of the royal agraharam was, initially at least, an act of greater political significance than the establishment of their own. Clearly, the development of Maravar sovereignty was constantly and consistently dependent on their relations and transactions with greater kings. In this final section of the chapter, we will look at a text which narrates the history of the Nayakas of Madurai. Like the Uttumalai vamcavali, this narrative recounts the history of a dynastic family focusing on heroic acts and political relations. It begins with the Nayakas looking up from an inferior position, recounting the way in which the founder of the family receives the authority to rule in Madurai from the kings of Vijayanagara. However, the gaze of the Nayakas soon turns downwards. We will examine the internal dimensions of this transformation of perspective as well as the relational components of the south Indian political landscape using this and other texts as our guide.

The historical chronicle of the Madurai Nayakas[51] shares a basic generational structure with the vamcavali of the Uttumalai family, especially its second half, where episodes are no longer separated by long lists of unnoteworthy kings, and no Tamil puranic tales are incorporated. Still, the performance of heroic feats and the intervention of gods and goddesses do figure importantly at various points in the Nayaka chronicle. Like the vamcavalis, the Tamil is colloquial rather than formal and poetic. On the other hand, the chronicle is significantly longer, more discursive, and more systematic in its coverage of a progression of events and a succession of rulers than any of the palaiyakkarar vamcavalis I have read. The chronicle traces the history of the family beginning with Visvanatha down through each generation to descendants quietly living out their exile from power in the early 1750s in the village of Vellaikurricci, near Madurai. Thus we know that the text was written some time after 1752. However, we have no other

---

[51] This manuscript is printed in Tamil with a translation in Taylor (1835, "History of the Carnataca Governors who Ruled over the Pandiya Mandalam," vol. 2, pp. 3–49). My summaries and translations are based on my own reading of the Tamil text.

They [the three basic manuscripts used by Taylor to reconstruct the history of the Madurai country, including the present one] were first procured by Mr W. C. Wheatley, a confidential employee of our late Governor Lushington, at the time when he was Collector of the District of Ramnad, Tinnevelly, and Madura [from 1792 to 1801]. Mr Wheatley was a singularly mild, able, and well-informed man; and, as such, duties of very great importance and responsibility were often confided to him ... at the time when Colonel Mackenzie was making his very extensive inquiries after manuscripts and inscriptions throughout the Peninsula, Mr Wheatley was pointed out to him as a suitable person to help forward the work. (p. xvii.)

The manuscript thus became a part of the Mackenzie collection around 1800.

information to pinpoint when in the second half of the eighteenth century the manuscript was written, or by whom.

The chronicle begins with Nagama Nayakar, a chief general of the armies of the Vijayanagara *Rāyar* (Telegu form of Raja), who is said to be the overlord of the fifty-six kingdoms. Nagama Nayakar was the ruler of Madurai from *c.* 1533 to 1542. What follows here is a (slightly) paraphrased translation of the beginning of the Tamil text.

All the revenue of the country from Arcot to Travancore was assigned to Nagama Nayakar for the support of his own retinue of six thousand cavalry and twenty thousand infantry. Nagama's only problem was that he had no issue, but after many prayers and much devotion and penitence he was blessed by God (*cuvāmi*) with a son, whom he named Vicuvanata (Visvanatha) Nayakar.

Shortly after this youth turned sixteen, the Navarattiri festival took place in the capital city. A crisis developed when the buffalo which had been caught for the sacrifice to Durga on Vijayadasami day was thought to be too large to permit the severing of its head in one blow, a necessary feat for the ritual to be a success. Visvanatha Nayakar was visited in a dream by the goddess [Durga], who informed him that he would be able to perform this feat with a special sword she would provide for him, and so he offered his services to the Rayar. As he was indeed successful, the Rayar was most pleased, and embraced him (*āliṅkanam*), and further presented him with all the valuable jewels and clothes which he had on his person, and said to him: "Since you were born by the special favor (*varappiracātam*) of god you were able to do this work (*kariyam*). You are worthy to rule on a throne even as we do."

Shortly after this Visvanatha Nayakar was sent off to subdue some rebellious kings in the north, and having done so with success he was awarded by the Rayar with some of the Rayar's own emblems (virutu) as well as all the banners and emblems which he had captured from the rebel kings.

At this time the Raja of Tanjavur was Vira Cekara Coran (Cola) and the Raja of Madurai was Cantira Cekara Pantiyan. The former conquered the latter, who managed to escape and fled to the Rayar for protection. Upon hearing the Pantiyan's report, the Rayar called Nagama Nayakar to his presence and told him to assemble an army in order to restore the Pantiyan king on his throne. Nagama Nayakar thereupon went south and conquered the Cola but did not restore (did not crown him: *pattaṅkaṭṭāmal*) the Pantiyan; rather, he kept the kingdom for himself. When the Vijayanagara Rayar learned of this he became very angry and assembled all the chief men of his kingdom to ask which of his agents/servants (kariyakkarar) would go and bring him the head of Nagama Nayakar. Then, Visvanatha Nayakar, Nagama Nayakar's son, rose and said that with the Rayar's permission he would go. The Rayar turned to him and asked if he planned to go and join his father in rebellion. To this charge, Visvanatha Nayakar replied: "As I have eaten your food (*annam*), my lord's (*ecamān*, same as *yajamana* in Sanskrit) service/duty (kariyam) comes before that of my father. As you command, so shall I act." On receiving the Rayar's permission,

Visvanatha went to Madurai, conquered his father, and reinstated the Pantiyan king. As it turned out, one of the boons awarded by the Rayar to Visvanatha Nayakar was that his father be spared; so he did not need to cut off his father's head after all.

After some time, the Pantiyan dynasty, for want of issue, became extinct. The Vijayanagara Rayar called Visvanatha Nayakar to his court, and on reciting all these previous events he anointed Visvanatha as the Raja of Madurai, installed him on the Pantiyan throne and bestowed this kingdom upon him and his successors for as long as the sun and the moon would endure. Indeed, the Rayar even granted Visvanatha's request that he be allowed to take the image of the goddess Durga with him to Madurai, against the warnings of the Rayar's attendants. Arriving in Maduarai, Visvanatha then received the sceptre (cenkol) in the presence (*canniti*) of goddess Minatci, the tutelary goddess of Madurai.

We learn here how the Nayakas become the legitimate kings of Madurai. The story begins when Visvanatha Nayakar distinguishes himself in the eyes of the Vijayanagara Rayar in the Navarattiri/Mahanavami festival. The crucial importance of this festival for the maintenance, indeed the regeneration and prosperity, of the sovereignty and kingdom of the Rayar was discussed earlier. In this episode the successful performance of the entire festival is threatened by the possibility that the sacrifice of the buffalo will be improperly performed. Visvanatha Nayakar, though a youth, heroically performs the sacrifice and thus ensures the success of the festival. Of course, the reason for his success is the favor of the goddess, who chooses Visvanatha as her vehicle and provides him with the means to attain success. The Vijayanagara Rayar is not aware of this, yet when he grants the young Nayakar various gifts he notes that the reason for his success was his special birth as a favor of god to Visvanatha's father. The gifts, or favors, which the Rayar bestows upon the young man are his embrace and all the jewels and clothes he was wearing, and finally the pronouncement that he is worthy to rule even as the Rayar himself does.

The transactions between the Rayar and the Nayakar closely parallel the transactions of puja, or worship. First, Visvanatha offers his service, at the risk of his life, to his lord, the Rayar. The word for the task he performs for the Rayar is kariyam. Kariyam derives from the Sanskrit *kārya*, which means "to be made or done or practised or performed; proper to be done, fit, right; a religious action or performance."[52] If dharma can be interpreted to mean the set of moral norms and codes which underpin and sustain the universe, karya refers to that particular action which in any one context should be performed as well as the norms and codes that would orient any such action. This term has been

[52] Monier-Williams 1979, 276.

seen to have particular significance in its Sinhala form in the Kandyan kingdom. In a fascinating article,[53] Alex Gunasekara has discussed the multiple meanings of the term *rājakāriya*, literally duty to the king, including the implicit notion that any enjoyment (*bhukti*) of land or rights to land entailed rajakariya, a set of variably formalized obligations to the king, usually actualized in the form of service. While in the Tamil country kariyam never became highly formalized, we have seen that it is nonetheless the word most often used in texts and inscriptions of the late medieval period to suggest service to, the business of and action as the agent of, the king.

Upon the successful performance by Visvanatha of his kariyam, the Rayar favors him by sharing part of his person/substance with him. He embraces Visvanatha, and then presents him with all the jewels and clothes he has on his person. These honors are similiar to honors procured in puja such as the right to tie the vestment (*parivaṭṭam*) of the deity around one's head. This honor is usually bestowed in a context in which the deity's own emblems – banners, flags, umbrellas, temple elephants, etc.–are used to receive the devotee, who in the case of this type of temple honor is usually a distinguished personage. According to the Madras Lexicon,[54] the term parivattam means both the "vestment of a deity tied around the head of a devotee as a mark of honor" and the "robes given by a king to a minister upon appointment to office." The symbolic parallel is thus both behavioral and lexical. Emblems take on the same transactional significance whether in the temple in exchanges between deity and devotee or in the court in exchanges between great and little kings.

The appropriation of the emblems of rival chiefs is the object of a king who must, to preserve his power and centrality, be the source of all honor. In this instance, Visvanatha Nayakar subdues some rebellious chief on behalf of the Rayar (as his agent: kariyakarar) and among other things captures the banners and emblems (virutu) of the rebels. In recognition of this service, the Rayar, having just accepted these emblems as tokens of his subject's service, bestows them upon Visvanatha. What is significant here is that Visvanatha does not simply take the emblems himself, but that he presents them to the Rayar, who, having taken possession of them then returns them to Visvanatha. The Rayar thus becomes (makes himself) the sovereign source of the royal symbols, the center of the transactional system.

The next episode reveals even more dramatically the way in which

---

[53] Gunasekara 1978, 119–143.
[54] TL 1936, 2518.

"political" relationships are modeled on worship. At the very moment when the Vijayanagara Rayar calls together his principal nobles to inform them of Nagama Nayakar's defiance of his rule, and to ask for a volunteer to journey south and bring him the head of this notorious rebel, who should rise to the challenge but Nagama's own son, Visvanatha? And, when Visvanatha is asked whether his real plan is to join his father's rebellion – the first presumption of both the Rayar and the reader – he responds by saying that as he has eaten the Rayar's food (annam, meaning rice, but used synecdochally for food), the service (kariyam) due to his lord (ecaman) comes before that due to his own father.

The taking and eating of food given by the deity (who is often also called yajaman) in the form of pracatam is as we have seen the key action of puja. In its most general meaning, pracatam means favor, kindness, gift, and grace.[55] In a more marked sense, it refers to boiled rice, or anything offered to an idol and then redistributed by priests to the people. Today, in general parlance, pracatam is used for various substances associated with temple worship, in particular the transvalued substances which, after being given to and enjoyed by the deity, are returned to the devotees as the favor of the god. Even in common lexical usage, pracatam can also refer to the grace and favor of a king. What is particularly interesting in the passage in our text concerning Visvanatha is that the literal consumption of food, rice, given by the king creates a substantial bond which outweighs in significance the kinship bond between father and son. The favor of the king is presented in precisely the same form as puja itself.

The significance of this passage can be further elucidated by turning for a moment to a similar passage in a text called *Maṟavar Cāti Viḷakkam* (literally: light on the Maravar caste)[56]. This text claims that the Ramanatapuram *Cētupati* (the title of the line of Maravar kings who became known under the British as the Rajas of Ramnad, the largest zamindari estate in the Tamil country) was worshipped with reverence by a number of important kings in the area. The reason for their worship was that "Tirumalai Nayakkar, the Raja of Madurai and Tiric-cirapuram, bestowed upon him the title of Tirumalai Cetupati, as well as the requisite royal insignia, presented him with a lion-headed palanquin, made him one of the Kumaravarkkam (group of sons), and fed him with the rice which he himself had taken first."

[55] TL 1936, 2670.
[56] This was collected by Mackenzie as well. I consulted it in the GOML, Madras (R. 370a); it was subtitled by Mackenzie's assistant, "A History of the Maravars in Ramanatapuram and Civakankai Countries."

As in all the texts we have examined, the principal gifts made by the king to a subject are of titles (in this case the king's own title) and emblems (both virutus). But here the conjunction of two other gifts with these sheds light on the cultural significance of the transaction both in this particular instance and for the story of Visvanatha. Tirumalai Nayakar is said to have made the Cetupati one of his own sons (*kumāra*) and one of the mechanisms by which this was accomplished was by feeding him with rice which he had himself already tasted. This action is clearly equivalent to the central action of puja. To eat food which has already been mixed with the saliva (eccil) of another is to demonstrate great inferiority. Yet it can be, under certain circumstances, an act which establishes a close substantial bond. The logic here is the same as that which underlies the strong rules and strict proscriptions regarding commensality; and yet this same logic sanctifies the eating by a wife of food taken first by her husband, and indeed the devotee's eating of pracatam, food presented to and tasted by the deity. To eat food already consumed by another is to partake of their "coded substance,"[57] one of the substantial benefits of puja. Here, the lordship of the king is vividly demonstrated by the use of this same transactional logic to establish a special relationship between a king and his subordinate chieftain.

But the invocation of the logic in conjunction with the incorporation of the Cetupati into the kumaravarkkam in the Maravar Cati Vilakkam, and the privileging of this kind of ritual relationship over that between a father and his son in the Nayaka chronicle, suggest even more strongly the substantial nature of political relations. As we have already noted, both the Vijayanagara Rayar and the Madurai Nayaka marked special political relationships by this privileged category of kumaravarkkam. This category has usually been interpreted to mean the establishment of a royal connubium, a set of marriage ties. While this must often have been the case, to insist on such a literal reading may well be an artifact of Western kinship theory. For in both of the texts under discussion, the establishment of a kumara relationship, whether metaphorically as in the Ramnad case or literally as in the Nayaka instance, is accomplished by the eating of food offered by the lord. Thus, puja becomes more than a simple root metaphor for political relations. It is a cultural mechanism for the establishment of a privileged form of substantial relationship which can take precedence not merely over more mundane types of political relations but over "bio-genetic" social relations as well.

---

[57] The phrase, and indeed the theoretical basis for much of the argument, comes from the work of R. Inden and M. Marriott. For a succinct summary of their position see Marriott and Inden 1977, 227–238.

The significance of this transformational process is further under-scored and elucidated by the pervasiveness of the terms kariyam and kariyakarar to signify the action and personage of a political subordi-nate. We noted earlier that kariyam means everything from business and action, to duty and obligation, to service. However, the common semantic identity of these glosses is revealed both in the above texts and in the epigraphical sources which we consulted in the last chapter. To do kariyam for/to someone else is in part to act, to do business, on their behalf. Thus the noble warrior who sets off for Madurai to subdue Nagama Nayakar acts as the representative of the Vijayanagara Rayar in gaining victory. The transformational process we have identified makes manifest and immediate the nature of this representation; for the warrior in this case embodies within himself the sovereignty of his lord. Acting on behalf of one's lord thus does not constitute the realization of a relationship rationally structured by bureaucratic form and normative prescription. Rather, it is a relationship established by the actual, though always partial, sharing of the substance[58] of sovereignty by the sovereign lord: substance which comes in the form of titles, emblems, land, and sometimes even pre-eaten rice. All these gifts partake of the same transactional logic.

Returning to the chronicle of the Madurai Nayakas, the Rayar anoints (apicekam) Visvanatha as the Raja of the Pantiyan throne shortly after the dynastic line of Pantiyas becomes extinct. Thus Visvanatha goes to Madurai, taking with him, by the special dispens-ation of the Rayar, the goddess Durga, chief deity of Mahanavami, as his own tutelary deity. Visvanatha then receives the sceptre (cenkol) in the presence of the goddess Minatci, Madurai's tutelary goddess. He thus establishes his kingship in relation to the Rayar and the Rayar's deity as well as to the deity of Madurai. His first acts of kingship are to build a large new fort, construct temples and endow them with great munificence, establish many Brahman settlements, cause extensive irrigation canals to be built, create new villages, peopling them with new inhabitants, and in general increase the welfare, prosperity, and population of his new kingdom. This is what rajadharma is all about.

But let us reflect upon the structure of this transformation. The appropriation of first the emblems and privileges and then the actions of kingship is prefigured in the initial transactions of the text. After the initial heroic feat that displays Visvanatha's fitness, and his special

---

[58] The concept of substance in this sense was first formulated by Inden and Marriott. Here, I draw particularly on the recent work of E. V. Daniel for the use of this concept in the Tamil country (1984).

relation to the goddess, he is told that he is worthy to rule on a throne even as the Vijayanagara Rayars themselves do. He then acts in such a way to display his worthiness, by defeating northern kings and subduing his own rebellious father in the south. He is anointed and installed on the Pantiyan throne–the Nayakas portray themselves as successors of the Madurai Pantiyan dynasty even as they are agents of the Vijayanagara Rayars – and permitted to take with him the image of the goddess who has been responsible for his special powers, and by implication for his appropriateness for kingly status. In short, at the very moment he acts out his service to the Vijayanagara king and comes closest to the overlord in whose name he acts, he becomes increasingly "independent." As we saw in the previous chapter, the independence and dependence of the subordinate ruler were not opposed or mutually exclusive but, as it were, dependent on each other.

As we noted before, the incorporation of the southern palaiyakkarars as protectors of the seventy-two bastions of the Nayaka fort is a major event both in the historiographical construction of the "palaiyam system" and in the vamcavali accounts of political relations between palaiyakkarars and the Nayakas. The central historiographical source and the Nayaka's own representations of this "event" are found here in our chronicle. According to the text:

As many of the chiefs of the Tottiyar castes who had earlier served in battle under Nagama Nayakar had done the same under Visvanatha, the latter divided his country into seventy-two palaiyams and then allocated one each to the chiefs, and then the king built seventy-two bastions on his fort in Madurai and allocated one each as well to the chieftains with the charge that they should defend the same with their soldiers against all attack.

This event, recapitulated in almost all the family histories of the southern palaiyakkarars, thus establishes for the Nayaka relations of service as well as of symbolic incorporation with the principal chiefs of the countryside. The palaiyakkarars all become responsible for the protection of a specified part of the kingdom (metonymized in the bastion of the fort) at the same time becoming part of the central symbolic and political structure of the kingdom: the central fort. This event symbolizes the establishment of central and incorporative sovereign relations with the Nayakas in the newly constituted political universe of the southern Tamil country.

At the very point at which the kingship of the Madurai Nayakars is firmly established under Visvanatha, we find no further references in the chronicle to the Vijayanagara Rayar. From now on the Madurai Nayakas shift their perspective and look downward in the system. The last mention of Vijayanagara occurs before the episode about the inclusion of the seventy-two palaiyakkarars in the central fort. The chronicle says little more about the palaiyakkarars, but the establishment of relations between the Nayakas of Madurai and the Cetupatis of Ramanatapuram is treated at some length. This is of special interest to us since we have already looked at a manuscript describing the special nature of this relationship. This dramatic narrative shift alerts us to changes in political preoccupations. The Nayakas may not declare themselves as fully independent, but they conspicuously ignore their nominal overlords. According to the chronicle,

during the reign of Muttu Krisnappa Nayakar, third in succession after Visvanatha, the chief guru [spiritual preceptor] of the Nayaka went to the temple of Ramesvaram on a pilgrimage. His pilgrimage was conducted under the protection of Utaiyan Cetupati, and thankful for this protection the guru introduced the Cetupati to the king and bestowed manifold praises upon him. Grateful for the protection of his guru, the king gave Utaiyan a grant of certain lands and villages, an honorary dress, and many jewels. Utaiyan then returned to his own country, built a fort, and created order by subduing rebellious chiefs. He also collected money from the inhabitants of the country and took the surplus/remainder (*mattappanam*) to the king [who is here called by the title most often used by the Nayakas: karttakkal, meaning lord-cum-agent]. The king was very pleased, and gave him the title of Cetupati, elephants and horses, vestments and jewels, banners and emblems, and anointed him in his position (pattapicekam) as ruler of the country. The Cetupati then went and ruled as a king, and built a mud fort in Ramanatapuram.

Under the reign of a subsequent, and the most celebrated, Nayaka, Tirumalai, the Cetupati distinguished himself by responding to a call for help by the king by raising sixty thousand troops and vanquishing the army of the Mysoreans. After this great conquest, he returned to the Nayaka king, who was immensely pleased. The king put on a feast for him at the place, and gave him horses, elephants, and many beautiful garments; he also gave him the title of Tirumalai Cetupati (i.e., a title incorporating his own name); and in addition gave him his own lion-faced palanquin, along with many banners and emblems and a canopy; he made him a member of the kumaravarkkam; and gave him his lands as *carvamāniyam* (literally meaning with full honors, which meant that he could hold his lands without paying any tax or tribute). From that time onward the Cetupati ruled over his kingdom without paying any tribute, and he built himself a fort made of stone in Ramanatapuram, his capital town.

The transformation in the career of the Ramnad Cetupati in this text reveals a great deal about the nature of political relations and the process by which kingship is seen to develop, this time from above rather than below. Here, at the very moment when the subordinate chief is most identified with the king, he becomes most like a king himself. He distinguishes himself first by protecting the royal guru, one of the most significant components of the Nayaka's sovereignty, second by subduing rebellious chiefs, and finally by raising troops for a decisive battle against the Mysoreans. In turn, he is given substantial parts of the Madurai Nayaka's sovereignty – first, lands, villages, jewels, and dresses, then, the title of Tirumalai Cetupati, elephants, and horses – and is finally anointed as the king over his land. Note the hierarchy of gifts. The most important gifts are given last and consist of the Nayaka's own name (Tirumalai, the greatest of the Nayaka kings who ruled in the mid-seventeenth century) and emblems (his own lion-faced palanquin), inclusion within the kumaravarkkam (that highly privileged, perhaps connubial, circle of the king's sons), and the exemption from the payment of tribute, an exemption prefaced by the definition of tribute as an offering of worship made to the overlord. The new solid foundation upon which the Cetupati's own lordship is finally based is concretely symbolized by his building a stone fort in place of the mud fort which had initially marked the Cetupati's entry on to the political map of southern India some generations before.

While there is no further mention of the Vijayanagara Rayars, we might remember from the previous chapter that the text ends by invoking their perpetual presence through their final absence. For at the conclusion of the Nayaka chronicle the absence of equitable rulers from the north who can adjudicate disputes and crown kings is lamented by the last (for this text) of the Nayaka kings as the reason for his own eclipse. In the end, the independence of the Nayakas is seen to be hollow when it ceases to be complemented by a hierarchical relationship in which the great overlord can create and sustain the very basis of conflict and dissolution in the political system. However precarious and shifting absolute political power is, it is far less so than its opposite. The king is dead. Long live the king.

## Conclusion

Our consideration of "fanciful" texts enables us to identify the key elements of political action and the significant moments in indigenous thought about the past. We see that service and worship are indissolubly combined in political relationships, that gifts of "symbols" can determine political and economic relations, and that service/worship only takes on meaning through the gifts that follow and encode its meaning into the substance of a political relationship. More generally, we realize that the realms of the "religious" and the "political" cannot be separated. Worship as a form of transaction and a mode of relationship pervades the political process, rendering the service of killing Kallars or subduing elephants an offering, and making the gifts of emblems, land, and office/position into pracatam, the transubstantiated return of the offering from the lord to the devotee. These texts present us with representations of the idealized moral order of the little kingdom, which constitutes an exemplary center through display, redistribution, and command not only over a military force but over an entire social order which has its fundamental hierarchical relations articulated and ordered by the king. We can identify the seemingly contradictory logic whereby relational interdependence is one side of a coin whose other side depicts the basis for the independence of either a Kattapomman or a Kartakkal (the Nayaka as "viceroy"). The political landscape, with its trajectories and orientations, is made palpable in each of these stories, with their memorable encounters, their structural parallels, and their inescapable narrative movements and transformations.

In our present study, these lessons are all the more interesting because we learn them through the particular histories of persons and dynasties which we can locate on the historical map of the old regime in southern Tamil Nadu at the very moment that we use these histories to constitute the very contours and lines of the map itself. These ethnohistorical texts can thus be used to select and interpret the relevant "bits of the past" in the "incomprehensible mass" of data about the history of south Indian kingship. In this way, ethnohistory can, indeed must, inform history. As we now turn to the history of the little kingdom of Pudukkottai, we will attempt to apply this recommendation, situating the discourse of these texts within a set of particular contexts which are themselves interpreted, and constructed, by this discourse.

# PART 3

# A little kingdom in the old regime

# 4

## *Pudukkottai and the old regime: gift, order, and authority in a south Indian little kingdom*

### Mise en scène

The Tondaiman kings of Pudukkottai were ranked as the third highest of the Tamil kings among the "seventy-five" who participated in the protection of the Madurai fort under the rule of Tirumalai Nayakar in the mid seventeenth century (Taylor 1835). Together with the Rajas of Ramanatapuram and Civakankai, the Tondaimans of Pudukkottai were part of the kumaravarkkam, the group of sons, the elite corps of the Nayaka's supporters. According to all accounts, the Tondaimans were among the most important of the Tamil little kings from the late seventeenth through the eighteenth century. By the nineteenth century, Pudukkottai, which had played a crucial role in the political and military fortunes of the East India Company, had not merely survived the turmoil of the last years unscathed, but had achieved an even more distinguished status. It became the only Princely State in the Tamil region of Madras Presidency under British rule.

Pudukkottai means "new fort" and seems to refer to a fort that was built in the early eighteenth century in what became the capital town of the little kingdom. It did not have fixed geographical boundaries, but was the area over which the Tondaiman kings had political control at any given time. Until the end of the eighteenth century the region was simply called the "Tondiman's country" (see Orme 1803). The general area over which this political control was exercised was the historically and geographically crucial interstitial area between the traditional domains of Pantiya and Cola authority. The river Vellar, which flows through the center of the state from northwest to southeast, was the proverbial dividing line between the Pantiya and Cola countries. Before Tondaiman rule, the area's political fortunes were alternately dominated by ruling powers based in these great countries. During the medieval period, Pudukkottai was never the seat of any major or lasting political system, though some middle level dynasties such as the Mutturaiyars were closely associated with the history of the area.

With the reconstitution of the Tamil political order under the Nayakas in the mid sixteenth century, previously marginal areas and groups rose to new prominence. In particular, serious rivalry between Madurai and Tanjavur developed in the early seventeenth century, and the Pudukkottai region took on enhanced significance. As important as the palaiyakkarars to the south of Madurai were for the Nayakas, they were geographically safe, hemmed in by mountains and seashore, unlike Madurai's troubled borders to the north. Far less isolated than its southern counterparts, Pudukkottai – like its neighbors and rivals in size and power, Ramanatapuram and Civakankai – was well situated to take an active role in the political history of the seventeenth and eighteenth centuries. From being an area that was constantly fought over by the Colas and the Pantiyas, it became a region that, increasingly, spawned its own kings and kingmakers.

When its boundaries were finally fixed in the early nineteenth century, Pudukkottai was about 1,130 square miles in size (see maps 1 and 2). In 1826, it had a population of 211,742.[1] Pudukkottai town, situated roughly in the center of the state, was fifty-five kilometers south of Tanjavur, fifty kilometers southeast of Tiruccirappalli, and roughly one hundred kilometers north (and a bit to the east) of Madurai. The region as a whole was most heavily populated by low caste *Valaiyars* and *Pallars*, most of whom were agricultural laborers and marginal producers. However, the northern two-thirds of the state was dominated by Kallars, who could claim dominance because of their generalized control of local agrarian and symbolic resources and because they numbered among themselves the kingly family of the state, the Tondaimans. Although far less numerous, the Maravars were the second most powerful caste in the state, at least until the mid nineteenth century when the *Cettiyārs*, a merchant caste, began their meteoric economic rise under the Pax Britannica. Most of the Maravars in Pudukkottai had migrated to the region south of the river Vellar from the Maravar kingdoms of Ramanatapuram and Civakankai which bordered Pudukkottai on the south. There were also a significant number of Brahmans in the state who had been invited to settle on land grants (brahmadeyams) by the Tondaiman kings in the seventeenth and eighteenth centuries. Brahmans later provided the vast majority of civil servants under the Tondaiman Raj.

Pudukkottai was a relatively arid region. The Vellar, its major river, was dry for all but a few months of the year when it became a catchment

---

1 Most of the statistics given in the following chapter are taken from the following sources: MPGO, 15 October 1875, no. 703; see also Ad. Rep. PDRO, and The Census of India, 1913, Pudukkottai State, Report by Rao Sahib S. Dandapani Ayyar, B.A., Superintendent of Census Operations (Pudukkottai: Printed at the Sri Brihadambal State Press, 1933).

canal for the monsoon rains. The lack of any permanent source of water and the associated absence of alluvial agriculture dominated the ecological regime of the entire area. As a result, Pudukkottai was an area of periodic scarcity and therefore of considerable risk and uncertainty. Frequent drought and occasional flooding because of the variable and cyclonic nature of the northeast monsoon meant that a secure livelihood was far less certain there than along the great rivers.

One of the severest famines in Pudukkottai's history took place in 1708–1709, when according to an inscription many lands were wasted and villages abandoned. Letters of the Madura Mission describe the famine as "the like the oldest among the living have never witnessed ... and everywhere along the roads and in the fields heaped up corpses or rather bleached bones are left unburied, amidst a people amongst whom funeral ceremonies could never be considered dispensable" (Ayyar 1938, 19). Between 1858 and 1895, there were twelve years of drought and four years when unseasonable or cyclonic rains caused serious damage to crops and irrigational infrastructures. To give some idea of the fluctuation of paddy cultivation in Pudukkottai, it is worth noting that in the decade between 1925 and 1935 there were six years when more than one hundred thousand acres of paddy were under cultivation, but four years when drought conditions dictated that a far smaller amount of paddy could be sown, ranging from 91,000 acres in 1926 to 37,000 in 1927. Although I could not find such precise figures for the nineteenth century, we know that the area of cultivated land also fluctuated widely then. According to a record dated 1840, "About $\frac{1}{4}$ of the country consists of villages, jungles, rocks, and other uncultivated land – of the remaining $\frac{3}{4}$, about 18% is waste [which should leave 61.5% open for cultivation]."[2] From the few years for which figures are available in the mid nineteenth century, between forty-eight and sixty per cent of the land was cultivated on average, though no doubt there were years of drought when this percentage must have dipped even lower. To return to the early nineteenth century, the first known Gazetteer of the State records that in 1813 there were 1,301 inhabited villages, 1,288 uninhabited villages, and 249 deserted villages. Unfortunately we are given no information as to why the villages were uninhabited, or for how long. Since we know that drought and famine were often extremely localized, some migration was periodic because of empty tanks in one region and full tanks somewhere else within state boundaries. Long before the Ceylonese tea estates lured Tamil workers there was a great deal of migration and territorial mobility. Nonetheless,

[2]  Parker's Report, Consultation no. 22 and 24, MPP dt. 17 October 1854.

when conditions back home improved many people returned to their native villages, as they did over the longer terms and far greater distances involved in the jobs in Ceylon, where approximately half of the emigration did not result in permanent settlement. (To give some idea of the extent of migration from Pudukkottai to Ceylon, during the decade of 1921–1931, when there were serious crop shortages, 75,000 people out of a total population of 400,000 migrated there.)

When population statistics began to be kept more systematically and precisely with the first British census of 1871, population density was about a third of what it was in areas such as Tanjavur which supported multiple paddy crops. The total population of Pudukkottai had risen to 316,695, averaging 229 people per square mile. There were 1,580 villages (uninhabited, and therefore untaxable, villages, were no longer counted) in a state of 1,130 square miles, though it shoud be noted that when revenue villages were counted rather than "hamlets" in 1881 there were just 597 villages.[3] In 1871 the average number of houses in each village was less than sixty-one, showing a greater proportion of small villages than any other district in the Tamil region of Madras Presidency except Chingleput (for example, in Tanjavur the average was 96). There were very few large villages and only one town, the capital. Despite the below average population density, the villages were closer together than in most of the Madras Presidency, with 56.2 houses per square mile against 45 Presidency-wide. The average number of persons per house was 4.07 as against 7.67 for South Arcot district, itself a dry district compared to Tanjavur (in 1881, the average number of persons per house in Pudukkottai was 5.17; in 1891, 5.35).

Nevertheless, Pudukkottai's location provided it with a strategic and symbolic importance not shared by other dry lands in the south. Further, while rainfall was unpredictable and often highly concentrated, the region averaged close to 35 inches of rain a year. When it came on time – i.e., half in the three months of October, November, and December and the rest fairly evenly over the other nine months – this amount was enough to irrigate substantial areas of paddy for one crop a year. The steady development of complex networks of rain-fed irrigation tanks and associated systems for the control and distribution of water, including large stone wells dating back to the first millennium A.D., permitted a mixed pattern of agriculture in which up to one-third of the cultivated land could produce paddy in years of normal rainfall. By the early nineteenth century, there were almost four thousand tanks

[3]  MPGO, 15 October 1875, no. 703.

in Pudukkottai connected together by canals forming 146 interlocking systems (Ayyar 1938, 171–188). In addition to paddy, other crops requiring far less water such as ground nuts, pulses, gram, ragi cholam, and cumbu were grown with little year-to-year fluctuation, for, except during the worst drought years, the best fields near tanks could be converted to dry crop production when there was insufficient water for paddy. In addition to sustaining settled agrarian communities, agricultural production in Pudukkottai provided a surplus sufficient to support, albeit later and to a lesser degree, the same complex of temples, land-grant communities, and other local institutions so characteristic of the richer riverine and deltaic areas of south India.

Pudukkottai, to use the three-part scheme which David Ludden has developed to typologize the ecological zones of Tirunelveli district, was neither a wet nor a dry zone, but a "mixed economy zone" (Ludden 1978a). Dry zones, using this scheme, had little if any irrigation. In these areas family labor was sufficient to provide subsistence but little more. In addition, population density was low and village communities never became highly articulated cultural institutions. Brahmans and Brahmanic institutions were scarce. In wet zones irrigational facilities were well developed and were usually maintained and controlled by Brahmans and Vellalars, who in alliance with each other elevated temples and brahmadeyas to key institutional and cultural positions. They also usually controlled various groups such as landless laborers in subordinate tenancy relations. The mixed economy zones had some irrigation which was not river-based, thus combining some of the features of wet and dry zones. In Tirunelveli these were the places where Maravars and some of the Vatukas gained control, establishing clan-based dominance over areas that extended beyond village communities. As we have dealt with some of the historical reasons for the different social formation of central and peripheral areas, it is important to remember that many of the key peripheral areas in the old regime period were mixed economy rather than dry zones. The latter acquired major economic significance only after certain strains of cotton were introduced and/or expanded as cash crops in the nineteenth century and when population pressures led to their increased settlement and cultivation. Pudukkottai shared many geographical features with other mixed economy zones. However, its central position between the Pantiya and Cola heartlands and the extensive nature of Kallar dominance in the region gave it a far more important role in political history than any of the palaiyams in Tirunelveli. Further, Pudukkottai was significantly larger than any of the Tirunelveli palaiyams, and only slightly smaller in size than either

Ramanatapuram or Civakankai.[4] There was tremendous range in the size of these little kingdoms. My particular concentration will be on a state at the larger end of a spectrum in which there was a large gap between the cluster at the bottom and the few at the top.

Chiefs of a Kallar subcaste, who, according to their family history, moved south from the Tirupati hills in the service of the Vijayanagara rulers, the Tondaimans emerged in Pudukkottai as two collateral ruling houses in the late seventeenth century. The state took its modern form when the two families, one in Pudukkottai and the other in the northern village of Kulattur, merged in the middle of the eighteenth century, only fifty years before the British consolidated their control over southern India. Because of the military aid the Tondaimans gave to the British and the Nawab of Arcot in the 1752 siege of Trichinopoly, in the wars against Haidar Ali and Tipu Sultan, and finally in the operations against rebel palaiyakkarars at the turn of the nineteenth century, the British exempted the Tondaimans from the Permanent Settlement of 1803, which converted such large kingdoms as Ramnad and Civakankai to zamindari status. Instead, Pudukkottai was allowed to continue in an ambiguous privileged status, being later classified, according to the self-fulfilling principle of precedent, as a native or princely state.

As a privileged state Pudukkottai was exempted from paying any tax or tribute to the British government. When in 1803 a tract of land was finally granted to Pudukkottai after a long dispute with Tanjavur, the agreement stipulated the yearly tribute of an elephant. This tribute was never paid and was objected to on the grounds that it compromised Pudukkottai's special tribute-free status. In 1836 it was formally excused. Thereafter, the British did not interfere with the revenue structure of the state until the late nineteenth century so that till then revenue procedures and tenurial arrangements within the state hardly changed. Most important for understanding old order political relations, the inams – the tax-free lands granted by kings to their subjects – remained under the control of the princely state, whereas in the zamindari estates the British government assumed all inams at the

[4] In 1800 there were thirty-one southern palaiyakkarar estates in the districts of Tirunelveli, Madurai, and Ramnad, not including the six estates that had been "sequestered" in 1799 after the defeat of Kattapomman. There were numerous palaiyams as well in areas further to the north, particularly to the north-west, in what became Coimbatore District. The largest of the southern palaiyams, Ramnad and Civakankai, had within them 2,152 villages and 1,937 villages respectively (these were revenue villages, or kiraman). The other twenty-nine palaiyams had 814/2 villages in toto. As we have seen, in the nineteenth century Pudukkottai State, by way of comparison, had approximately 1,580 villages.

time of the Permanent Settlement. Thanks to the comprehensive records kept in the state during the Pudukkottai Inam Settlement of 1888, we have access to a picture of the structure of "landholding" which reveals in considerable detail the fundamental forms and features of the pre-nineteenth-century social and political system. This picture holds valid despite changes in the content of many relationships and in the distributional structure of inams after the Pax Britannica and the demilitarization of kingly polity.

## Land and the political order

In my research on Pudukkottai, it took little study of local land records to uncover the most surprising fact about this south Indian little kingdom: how little of the land was taxed. In mid-nineteenth-century Pudukkottai, less than 30 per cent of the cultivated land was either taxed (9 per cent) or given out from year to year on a share (*amāni*) system (18 per cent), in which one-ninth of the produce was accorded to village servants and four-ninths each to the cultivator and the government. Seventy per cent of the cultivated land was inam, or tax-free. This mid-nineteenth-century statistic was if anything far higher in the eighteenth century, when there were at the very least another five thousand military inams (MPC, May 23, 1864, no. 14). Roughly 30 per cent of the inams (i.e., numbers of inam units) were for military retainers and their chiefs, and for palace guards and servants; 25 per cent were for village officers, artisans, and servants; and the remaining 45 per cent were for the support of temples, monasteries, rest and feeding houses for Brahman priests and pilgrims, and land grants to Brahman communities. In terms of acreage, roughly 19 per cent of the alienated land was for military retainers *et al.*, 7 per cent for village officers, artisans, and servants, 51 per cent for temples, monasteries, and charities, and 22 per cent for Brahmans (for an extensive discussion of the structure of inam holdings, see Appendix).

This structure of privileged landholding reflects the structure of political power and socio-cultural participation within state and village institutions. The chief landholders were the great Kallar *Jagirdars* and *Cērvaikārars*. The former were collateral relations of the Raja. Jagir estates were created for the two brothers of the Raja after a succession dispute in 1730 severely threatened the stability of the state. These collateral families kept these estates intact until their settlement in the late nineteenth and early twentieth centuries. The Jagirs were, in effect, mini kingdoms in their own right, each containing a small court and a full set of inam grants, including "military ones." Importantly, however, the jagirs were not made up of contiguous villages and were therefore never geographically isolable units.

Just below the Jagirdars came the Cervaikarars. All but one of the Cervaikarars were of the same subcaste as the Raja, and most had one or more affinal ties with the royal family. The Cervaikarars were given large grants of land, titles, honors, and emblems. Each of the Cervaikarars was awarded a specified number of retainers, or *amarakārars*, to serve them at home, to go to battle with them abroad, and to carry their honors and emblems to ritual occasions in the royal court and in temples. Lesser chiefs, called *Kuṟikārars*, came from Kallar subcastes other than royal Ampu Natu. Lands and privileges throughout the state were also given to other Kallars, called in diminutive form *Cērvais*, to keep watch over villages and localities not dominated by loyal Kallars (i.e., all groups other than the Vicenki Nattu Kallars who were only finally brought under control in a series of wars in the late eighteenth century). The Cervais were mostly members of the royal Ampu Natu subcaste who had no affinal ties with the royal family.

The royal family and court was itself protected by *Ūṟiyakārars*, all of whom were members of the *Akampaṭiyār* caste, aligned with the Kallars and the Maravars, through membership in the classificatory group of the three "families," or mukkulattar. These Uriyakarars had become a separate subcaste by virtue of their connection with and service to the Raja. A number of Uriyakarar chiefs had a prominent role in the kingdom. Like most of the Kurikarars, these chiefs were given extensive lands but no formal group of amarakarar retainers under them (see Chapter 6).

In addition, within each village the state headmen were given lands in recognition of their rights to local authority as well as to render this authority representative of the state's power at large. These headmen came from the locally dominant castes. Kallars were dominant in the northern and eastern parts of the state. Maravars had a significant presence in the south. Other caste groups such as the *Nattampaṭi Kavuṇṭārs* and the *Vallampars* were dominant in some of the peripheral portions of the state. *Ampalams* – the title for headman (literally meaning the central common ground of the village) used by most of the castes in Pudukkottai – were also called *mirācidārs*[5] after the mid

---

[5] *Mirāci* was a general term which originally signified inheritance. In the early nineteenth century, British officials took miraci to mean a variety of rights "all more or less connected with the proprietary possession, or usufruct, of the soil, or of its produce," and which were often held jointly (Ellis 1814). Baden-Powell wrote that miraci villages were jointly held

eighteenth century, when their local positions of power were formalized through bureaucratic incorporation. This new label, borrowed from Persian revenue terminology, was used in an attempt to render local authority as dependent as possible on recognition by the "bureaucratic" state. Nonetheless, well into the twentieth century these local headmen were often as powerful as small palaiyakkarars and kavalkarars elsewhere, with retinues and legends sufficient to cause their power to be felt over significant areas of the countryside.

In Pudukkottai, miraci service principally entailed the collection of government taxes and acting as government agent for all village concerns. In some villages miraci duties included the protection of the village temple and the maintenance of irrigational facilities (R. 2986/c – 1915, 2 December 1915, PDRO). In one village for which we have detailed records there were ten miracidars, who held their land severally but had held it jointly not long before (PFR, no. 3755). Each of the miracidars shared their holding with their own *paṅkāli* group, though miraci services did not rotate within those groups. At least two of the miracidars also held other inams besides miraci, which itself had a high proportion of wet land. One of the inamdars held a *ūraṇi māṇiyam*, an inam for the maintenance of some irrigational structure, in addition to his miraci inam. The ten miracidars and their coparceners constituted a dominant group in the community. All ten of the miracidars were Kallars.

The prestige of the position of miracidar came from its direct link with the king made manifest through key responsibilities and valued perquisites. The perquisites included both land and honors. These honors (specific emblems and privileges) were viewed as crucial components of the authority of office, and were often fought over far more bitterly than the "material" privileges attached to village office. Take, for example, the following dispute between brothers over miraci respects (R. 2986/c – 1915, 2 December 1915, PDRO). The complaining miracidar said that although he performed all the duties of the position, he willingly shared the usufruct of the inam lands with his brother "just as any natural brother does of common family property." But honors ("respects") were another matter altogether. As he wrote in his petition:

> villages found principally in Chingleput, North and South Arcot, Tanjavur, and Tirunelveli Districts. He attributed their origin to the special colonization by the state of noble families (Baden-Powell 1892, 3:109–127). Miracidars held shares (panku) of rights over village land and production, the control over which was vested in the body of shareholders in a variety of ways (Murton 1973).

(1) I am the elderly: I should enjoy the respects.
(2) I am the Pattadar: He may be my equal but I am the first or foremost among equals. In my absence he may take my place, but when I am present, I am entitled to respects and not he.
(3) For not one day in his life has the said Muthupalani enjoyed any respects whatever. I have been enjoying it throughout and adversely too to him.
(4) As a rule, and as is the practice obtaining among other mirasdars, the Pattadar alone is entitled to respects.

First among equals meant that the coparceners shared everything but respects, which were allocated only to the titleholder of the inam. As this inamdar tersely said, he had been enjoying the respects, "and adversely too to him." Respects, in short, could not be shared. The honors served to maintain the indivisibility of a title within the tradition of shared rights among shareholders (pankalis). Thus, honors or respects were seen as more fundamental to the office than land or its usufruct; hence, the frequency of the quarrels. We will examine a number of other such disputes in the penultimate chapter of the book.

Various village officials, artisans, and servants were also given inam – more properly *māṇiyam* – lands by the state. In addition to this land, each village servant was also rewarded with shares of the village grain heap. Since the one-ninth share of the harvest that was owed to village servants was taken from the grain heap before its division into the Raja's and the village's share, this classic jajmani-like payment was borne equally by the village and the Raja. Thus, the sets of relations usually characterized as "jajmani," that is as an institution of the village community alone, were sanctioned and underwritten not only by the community but also by the king both through inams and the share system.

Maniyam, the term used for many village grants, meant land that was held free of tax. In a more general sense it also meant privilege. Maniyam derives from the Sanskrit *māṇya*, which means honor and privilege. Many of the land grants to Brahmans were called carvamaniyam, meaning completely tax free and honorable. However, the term maniyam was not reserved for Brahmans, as British categories which separated "religious" from "nonreligious" grants implied. Indeed, in its most unmarked form maniyam was sometimes used for inams in general. Maniyam was also used in a more marked sense for land grants given to village servants whose task was to maintain and operate irrigational facilities, to village officers or headmen, to the priests of small village temples or shrines, and to inamdars (holders of inams) who had such variable responsibilities as blowing the conch for a village festival or tending a flower garden which produced garlands for the village deities. These maniyams reveal that royal grants sustained the entire structure of local village ritual.

Even small locality temples were linked to the king through the inam. These local temples organized the ritual systems of villages, often constituting some of its fundamental cultural coordinates as well: they demarcated boundaries, centers, the relationships of social groups within the village, defining and internally ranking lineages, subcastes, and castes. Service to the temple was in many respects structurally equivalent to service to the village community, even as most village service inams specified services to both temples and the village. A. M. Hocart pointed out the myriad interconnections which linked the constituent parts of the village community together and which in turn linked the village to the state. Seeing each village service group as a priesthood, Hocart also saw the link between the mundane services of barbers and washermen and the ritual performances of priests: "the barber and the washermen, like the drummers are not so much technicians as priests of low grade [Hocart 1950, 11], . . . potters sometimes officiate as priests in temples of village goddesses and of the god Aiyanar [ibid., 13], . . . carpenters make the temple car in return for grants of land" (ibid., 14). Hence Hocart's emphasis on service and lordship as the articulating principles of Indian political-ritual communities. The relation of the village to the state was based on the development of kingship, which played an important role in organizing the complex of ritual and social services.

In addition to many inams granted to village and local temples in the form of maniyams to local priests and village servants, many inam grants were also made to Brahmans, temples, and charities of various sorts. Indeed, the principal sources for south Indian historiography are epigraphical records of such grants, publicly proclaimed because of the merit which accrued to the donors from them and because of the centrality of these gifts to the ideology of kingship. One of the fundamental requirements of Indic kingship was that the king be a munificent provider of fertile lands for Brahmans who would study and chant the Vedas, perform sacrifices and provide ritual services for the king so as to ensure and protect his prosperity and that of his kingdom; for temples, which were the centers of worship; for festivals such as Dasara which renewed the sovereignty of the king and regenerated the kingdom, and which together with temples were central to the constitution and maintenance of the social collectivities of localities, villages, castes, and subcastes; and for *cattirams* (chatrams, also called choultries, which were feeding, sometimes lodging, houses for pilgrims), which provided sustenance and shelter for itinerant Brahmans and pilgrims. The merit (*puṇyam*) of a king who made a grant could be shared by all those who protected the gift, a duty enjoined upon all subsequent kings. This belief was articulated in a Pudukkottai copper plate inscribing a gift of land to a group of learned Brahmans:

Those who respect the above rights and see that they are continued properly will be blessed with the merit of bathing in the Ganges, of feeding many thousands of Brahmans, and of pleasing God. He who makes a grant will find a place in the world of the stars. He who continues it will find a place near God who is above the world of the stars. He who continues a grant will be blessed thrice as much as he who makes a grant. But he who destroys one of the grants will not be blessed even for the grants which he might make. (*Ammacattiram Copper Plate*, Brahmadeya Volume, PSO)

It is small wonder then that kings, and others too, took special care to preserve and protect gifts of this sort. As the copper plate put it: "Poison is not poison but a Brahman's property is. For poison will take the life only of him who drinks it. But a Brahman's property will take the life of one's descendants for three generations" (ibid.).

The prevailing force of royal ideology ensured that Pudukkottai was well endowed with temples and brahmanic institutions in spite of its marginal social and political position. In the mid nineteenth century fifty-six whole villages covering about 44,899 acres were classified as Brahmadeyam, meaning lands granted tax-free to Brahmans. Lands granted to Brahmans were likely to be closer to the state's only major river and to the center of villages, to be better watered by tanks, of higher classification in terms of the quality of the soil, and relatively secure and productive. Learned Brahmans, usually highly distinguished Vedic scholars, were enticed to Pudukkottai by an initial royal gift of between twenty and forty acres per family, especially attractive because they were beginning to suffer the effects of increasing population and the fragmentation of landholdings further north on their wetland holdings along the river Kaveri. Furthermore, 136 villages in the state were set apart for the support of temples. In addition, there were ten major, and quite a few minor, feeding houses at the end of the nineteenth century (see Appendix).

Some of the lands for temples, Brahmans, and charitable institutions were granted before the Tondaimans became rulers of Pudukkottai. In these cases the Tondaimans simply obeyed the injunctions and the inscriptions recording these grants: protect them. Many others were newly created by the Tondaimans. Even though a cursory study of south Indian history prepares us for this general pattern of endowment, we cannot but be impressed by the extent to which Pudukkottai's resources were alienated for the support of these institutions. Grants of this nature and extent were not just made to legitimize kingship. They underpin a world view which insists on the centrality of brahmanical learning, of ritual performance, and of royal support for the worship of temples.

The underlying political base of any little kingdom in the old regime was, nonetheless, its military capacity. This capacity was in turn based on structures of alliance and command, articulated by gifts, privileges, and kinship. No little kingdom could survive if it did not have an efficient system of military mobilization. These systems were organized around subordinate chieftains, connubial connections, and privileged landholding rather than centralized or bureaucratically organized revenue collection and military rule. Royal grants helped to sustain military organization as well as local village ritual and an impressive complex of larger temples and brahmanic settlements. The political economy – by which I mean here the institution of kingship, the distribution of authority, and the nature and structure of resource allocation – of the state was based on a logic of redistribution that penetrated far and wide.[6]

The gift of land exempt from onerous burdens of taxation, the occasional participation in wars in which honor and booty could be won, and the organization of land and military rights in relations of ritual clientage to chiefly and kingly patrons resulted in a political system of great fluidity and dynamism. Individuals could vie for relative distinction in a social system where honor was intimately tied up with rank through interpenetrating forms of political and ritual action. The extensive grants of land that established authoritative relations also meant for their numerous recipients a life of relative security given the tremendous uncertainties of agricultural production. A large percentage of the peasants in the little kingdom (though by no means all) lived in a "moral" economy in which risk and uncertainty were controlled and reduced by their political privilege, and in a morally constituted hierarchical social and political system in which the valued constituents

---

[6] Even at this level, the redistributive model (itself a Western theory to be discussed later in the chapter) could hardly be used without realizing that what is being redistributed here is the culturally stipulated share (the melvaram: the first or top share) of the produce of the land. Much of the grain that is called the king's share never actually traveled to the king's granaries before being returned to the subjects who are in "real material" terms therefore hardly "sustained" by gifts that come from the king. While the land over which the king demands the first share must, indeed, have been conquered by the king, and the loyalty of the cultivators who produce the harvest on these lands be maintained, the material forms of redistribution are themselves culturally defined.

of sovereign authority were differentially and partially shared through the redistributive mechanisms of the gift. Service was offered as a way of entering this redistributive system. Kinship – a relatively open and inflected system – became the basis for and expression of social and political relations. Honor – in particular the emblems and privileges that were given with each grant (itself a privilege), but also the honors in temples that were procured through puja and were ordered in relation to local and royal prerogatives – was both the mediation and the mechanism by and through which relations were established.

In 1888 there were more than thirteen thousand entries for holders of inams.[7] The number of inams had been far higher before; there were at least another 5,000 amaram tenures in the last decade of the eighteenth century. Because the proceeds of each inam were shared among families and sometimes patrilineages this meant that a large percentage of the total population was supported at least in part by inam land. According to my calculations, at the very least thirty per cent, and quite possibly sixty per cent of the population would have been direct or indirect beneficiaries of inam privileges. For these speculative calculations I have taken into account three factors: first, a population of 200,000; second, the existence of approximately 18,000 inams; and third, an average family size of four, calculated on the probability that at least a third or so of the inams were shared among lineages of ten members or more.[8]

We have seen that the inam was the most common "tenurial" arrangement within the state, and that a conservative estimate suggests that perhaps one-half of the population were beneficiaries of the king's gift. At a more general level, however, all land, while not the "property" of the king in a Western sense, was implicated in a structure of political authority.[9] Between the old regime and the colonial one the meaning of

[7] These are in handwritten records in the Pudukkottai Settlement Office, called Faisal Registers.

[8] In 1871 it was only slightly higher, though in the more precise census of 1881 it was 5.17: keep in mind that even if the number was less in the earlier nineteenth century, with possibly a higher rate of mortality and a smaller rate of fertility – though these are unknown – the tendency was always for the wealthy to have larger families, thus creating the possibility of a major discrepancy between mean family size over all and the mean size of "privileged" families.

[9] The very term inam, itself Persian rather than Tamil, is part of a late patrimonial and early colonial formalization of land rights which disguises the meanings and structure of the old order political system. The currency of inam as a revenue term has in large part to do with the fact that the British saw themselves inheriting a mantle of sovereign authority from the Mughals rather than from any of the Hindu kings. Persian revenue terminology seemed naturally to lend itself to colonial objectives of

land underwent a fundamental change. Land, as something which was "owned," "possessed," or even "controlled," meant something very different before and after the British arrived on Indian soil and set out to determine "property" rights in order to assess and collect revenue.[10] The British were concerned about property because it was the basis of their own social and political system. They also regarded it as the fundamental means for ordering Indian agrarian society, an ideologically coherent and functionally systematic basis for revenue collection. British concerns have been reproduced in most recent agrarian historiography of India, where revenue has been seen both as the principal modality of agrarian relations within villages and as the basic function, and agrarian concern, of the state.

The problem with this preoccupation with revenue, let alone with the question of who owned the land, is that in the old regime property existed only in the context of social and political relations. At the risk of some simplification, the two terms used for property in Tamil – *paṅku* and *kāṇi* – suggest the different but interdependent nature of these social and political relations (Ludden 1978a, 171–174). Panku means "share" and was often used to characterize the shares of rights to the usufruct of land. It is fundamentally a horizontal term. Shares of land were shares among a group of family or lineage members, and sometimes among the dominant caste (or castes) of an entire village (or locality). These pankus were sometimes related to specific plots of land and sometimes to a specified proportion of a larger unit of land, proportions which would be redistributed and reallocated periodically (Bayley and Hudleston 1862; Murton 1973, 169–179). Pankus in land were related to pankus in a variety of other contexts, including shares in local temple festivals, and shares in kinship units (in which, for example, members of the same lineage were called pankalis).

The complementary term kani means a heritable entitlement. It implies a vertical relation, since entitlement to a share was usually granted by a superior agent. This agent was ideally a king, or the agent of

bureaucratic systematization and revenue extraction. Most of the relevant terms related to "landholding" used by the British after the late eighteenth century were Persian in origin and Mughal in application. See Chapter 11 for a discussion of the history of the term.

[10] As Marx aptly wrote, "In Bengal they [the British] created a caricature of large-scale English landed estates; in south-eastern India a caricature of small parcelled property; in the northwest they did all they could to transform the Indian economic community with common ownership of land into a caricature of itself" (Marx 1974, 3:334). For more recent views, see Neale 1969; Kessinger 1974; Obeyesekere 1967; Stein 1980.

a king, although in certain cases it could have been the chief of a dominant caste group. To possess this entitlement, or kani, was to have *kāṇiyāṭci*, which meant that one had control over land and could participate in the village/lineage assembly. As with panku, it included the right to a share in the local temple, which in turn entailed both rights to receive honors and also responsibilities to invest in the temple. Indeed, shares (panku) were themselves shares in this general entitlement (kaniyatci). The holders of this entitlement in any given village or locality formed a corporate group which in the drier areas of the south – not yet brought under patrimonial forms of rule and revenue collection – was hierarchically situated within the larger structure of subcaste and caste dominance at the level of the little kingdom.

These corporate groups could not possess or control these rights without the sanction – and this meant active participation – of the king. The king who gives land is the overlord of all the land in his kingdom. The term which suggests the nature of the king's mastery over land perhaps better than any other is *kṣatra*. According to Robert Lingat:

Kṣatra ... is a power of a territorial character, exercised within a given territory and stopping at the frontier of the realm ... Of the same nature as property, it implies a direct power over the soil. That is why the king is also called svāmin, a word which can be applied equally to a proprietor as to a husband or a chief, and which denotes an immediate power over a thing or over a person. (Lingat 1973, 212)

The king's mastery of the land, far from being opposed to the panku and kani rights in land held by peasant cultivators, complemented those rights, entitlement to land always being the gift of a higher agency, preferably a king. The British, with a very different view of property rights, misunderstood all this. When they attempted to sort out who owned the land, they assumed opposition, not complementarity: the owner, they thought, must be either the cultivator or the king, thus creating many of the classificatory problematics of the land systems debates in the late eighteenth and early nineteenth centuries.

To sum up, in precolonial south India most land rights were seen as having been granted in one form or another by a king. All land was therefore a royal privilege. However, the inam – in its precolonial unmarked maniyam form – was a particular privilege, and entitlement to a special status, a royal relationship. The rights and privileges of inamdars included rights to titles, offices, and honors; rights to command groups of people; as well as the right to offer particular services to an overlord in a hierarchical political and social system. In other words, the inam, as both gift and entitlement, was a basic ingredient of the social and political relations of the little kingdom, in which it became one of the principal means for the creation and maintenance of the local structure of privilege.

And it was a structure of privilege. Even though it is in part a colonial anachronism to link great warriors (Cervaikarars) and village *veṭṭiyans* (town criers and servants of village headmen who often were from "untouchable" castes), the rights constituted through royal grants and allowances were – each in their own particular context – rights indicating, indeed creating, privilege. The king did not grant these special rights directly to subordinate groups such as the vettiyans; their membership in the village community was mediated and determined by local dominant groups. While "essential" village services (including those performed by local priests, vettiyans, smiths, carpenters, potters, etc.) were provided for by a combination of *cuvēntiram* (share of village harvest) and maniyam, most subordinate groups only received shares of or rights to village resources, either as local *aṭimai* (serfs) or as "nonlocal" *parakuṭi* (those who came from outside the community) laborers, through the dominant groups and their own, sometimes desperate, devices.

The atimai laborers, whose frequent classification as serfs overlooks their status as laborers with hereditary rights of service and to subsistence, were for the most part "untouchable" Pallar and *Paṟaiyar* groups whose most important social units were constituted not in terms of the relations within a group but rather in terms of their relations to another dominant group. They were often organized according to which lineages of the dominant caste they worked for. These atimai workers did not have "rights" to land, but to service, to work for people. Though not direct beneficiaries of the structure of privilege, they were attached to it. When labor was scarce this attachment was no doubt onerous, though it was relatively advantageous when resources were scarce, for unless patron–client ties were pushed to the extreme limit by drought and famine the atimai clients were always provided with subsistence.

The other major group not significantly integrated into the structure of privilege through gift relations with the kings were the Valaiyars, a caste group which lived near the many forests of the state and apparently worked as agricultural laborers. The Valaiyars maintained a precarious balance between engaging in cultivation as outside labor and following their traditional hunting and gathering activities in forests, which provided their sole sustenance during the periodic famines. While the Valaiyars never had to suffer the caste humiliations of untouchables, their integration within the settled agrarian economy was always partial and provisional. Despite this, many Valaiyars held inam grants for beating the forest for the Raja's hunt and for guarding the royal forests.

Sheep and cattle herders (*Iṭaiyars* and *Kōnars*) made up a third group which was even less significant a part of the structure of landed privilege. Their itinerant life style rendered them marginal to a land based political economy, even though their trade in bullocks and their provision of herds for soil fertilization played an important role in agrarian life.

Of these three groups, only the atimai laborers appear to have had any genuine entitlement to subsistence, and that too through the privileged elite and not directly through their relations with the king. When I refer to the moral community of the little kingdom, I do not mean that all inhabitants of the state were full members of this community. Furthermore, there is no firm evidence indicating that the boundaries of inclusion within the relevant moral communities were not open to redefinition and considerable constriction during times of greatest scarcity (Greenough 1982). But the 50 per cent or so of the population which had some form of political relations with the king can be said to have been members of the privileged moral community of the little kingdom. These were the subjects of the king who participated – however hierarchical, differentiated, and mediated this participation was – in the structure of political privilege.

## The gift: resources and authority in the little kingdom

The royal gift was basic to statecraft in all the kingdoms of the old order in southern India. However, all gifts were not the same. Gifts to Brahmans and temples were made to fulfill kingly dharma, to sustain the dharma of Brahmans, to earn merit, and to bring prosperity to the kingdom.[11] Gifts made to other institutions and persons were different and followed other logics. Yet there is only a murky distinction between gifts to temples and many other kingly grants, since most grants to village officers, servants, and artisans were concerned with the maintenance of the structure of village ritual. And while grants to local chieftains and warriors were the furthest removed from grants to temples and Brahmans, chiefs and warriors did play key roles in village ritual. Though it is necessary to make careful distinctions between different kinds of gifts – especially since the colonial use of the term inam deliberately obscures these fundamental differences – we must also

---

[11] I am not including here gifts/endowments made to temples by individuals and groups who are not kings, for these gifts are more like offers of service to kings than royal gifts, however much they may be part of a strategy to become royal. In a later chapter on the temple I will contrast different kinds of gifts made in relation to temples and discuss the nuances of these gifts.

accept the lack of any clear distinction between ritual and nonritual domains of action, and the political implications inherent in all gifts made by kings. Gifts were public acts of kingship and established relations, however variable, between the grantor and the grantee. On the one hand, ritual was a pervasive political fact; on the other, politics was permeated by ritual forms.

The substance of the gift – the land rights, the titles, emblems, honors, and privileges of service, usufruct, and command – was the partial sovereign substance of the king. All those who were given (and who accepted) gifts became parts of the whole king, and by implication of the king's realm, the kingdom. Participation in the whole was not, however, unranked, for the differential nature and contingent character of all these entitlements provided the basis for the creation of a political hierarchy. Entitlements implied service, stipulated command, and were often contingent upon (and determinative of) kinship forms. Entitlements further expressed hierarchy, involving as they did both the ranking and mediation of individuals and of categories, as well as the (implicitly ranked) degree of inclusion within or exclusion from ranked categories. Ultimately, entitlements by their very nature constituted hierarchy through a logic of variable proximity to the king, to sovereignty itself. Within Pudukkottai, this same logic applied to the construction of caste unities and caste ranking. Castes were not ordered by an autonomous logic based on oppositions of purity and pollution. They were inherently political and politicized. The political process contained within itself a logic which pervaded other nominally nonpolitical forms as well.

The gift cannot therefore be disentangled from its political and social context. The gift was often initiated by offers of service, perhaps the performance of some heroic deed on behalf of the king. Gifts were also given to those whose close relationship to the king was based on factors other than service, the most important of which were consanguinity and affinity, relations which themselves were transformed by gifting activity. No gift was given without reason, intention, and interest. The reasons could be as variable as rewarding the subduing of rural bandits or the scholarly attainments of a learned Brahman, or providing a village with a blacksmith, or assuring the necessary ritual services in the village temple. The intentions and interests caught up in the web of gift transactions and relationships could be equally diverse. To privilege the gift as a principal medium of rule is not to elevate it as the sole basis of rule. Rather, my aim here is to focus on gifts because of their unique symbolic provenance with respect to the political process of the old order in south India.

A Brahman in a village near Pudukkottai told an anthropologist that the soil of that village was not appropriate, not well matched, for him as a Brahman (Daniel 1984). The problem was that the land was not given as inam by a true Ksatriya king. Instead, the land had been acquired in quite ordinary fashion. It had been purchased by the ancestors of this Brahman family, who continued to live in this village with a sense of being in but not of the territory. The value of the land, in other words, was initially identified not in market terms but in terms of the kinds of socio-political relations and cultural meanings I am writing about here. In Pudukkottai, all the Brahmans I met had been granted lands by the Tondaiman kings, who, in spite of their Kallar caste and therefore non-Ksatriya status, were said to be true kings – and gods – by these Brahmans. Similarly, the Vellalars who managed the main temple of the royal Kallar subcaste demonstrated their authoritative rights and position by displaying a sword and other emblems that they told me had been granted them by the Tondaiman kings. Village headmen could not conduct their ritual duties in village festivals without worshipping and prominently displaying the emblems that had been granted by kings. Even the great Kallar Cervaikarar warriors, who attained their high positions by being Kallars, providing crucial assistance at one time or another to the Tondaimans, and establishing affinal ties with the royal family, despite all this had to appeal to the emblems and privileges of their authority which, likewise, had been granted by the Tondaiman kings.

The gift was thus a principal element of statecraft. The chief means for the formation and articulation of a "political community" was the kings' gifts of rights to land and of various honors, emblems, titles, and privileges which symbolically and morally linked individuals with the sovereignty of the king. The political economy was thereby predicated on a set of moral principles and understandings. Resources were exchanged, transacted, used, and generally valued in terms of moral conceptions of the social universe in which the development of relationships with the king was of central importance. What Geertz has written about Bali is true of the old order in south India. "The whole of the negara [state] – court life, the traditions that organized it, the extractions that supported it, the privileges that accompanied it – was essentially directed toward defining what power was; and what power was was what kings were" (Geertz 1980, 124). Power was attained by proximity to the king. In the political world, therefore, royal gifts were particularly significant because they provided the basis for a relationship with the king, the gifts themselves representing a part (differentially coded and ranked depending on the gift) of the king.

Marcel Mauss, under whose authority the gift has attained the status of a major sociological category, convincingly argued that the gift was of dominant significance in "primitive" societies. A gift established a relation which was not only created but continually recreated by exchange. The first gift established obligation and dependence, a debt which could only be erased by a return gift, which in turn established dependence and obligation. Mauss summarized his major argument early in his book, *Essai sur le don*:

In the systems of the past we do not find simple exchange of goods, wealth and produce through markets established among individuals. For it is groups, and not individuals, which carry on exchange, make contracts, and are bound by obligations; the persons represented in the contracts are moral persons – clans, tribes, and families; the groups, or the chiefs as intermediaries for the groups, confront and oppose each other. Further, what they exchange is not exclusively goods and wealth, real and personal property and things of economic value. They exchange rather courtesies, entertainments, ritual, military assistance, women, children, dances, and feasts; and fairs in which the market is but one element and the circulation of wealth but one part of a wide and enduring contract. Finally, although the prestations and counter-prestations take place under a voluntary guise they are in essence strictly obligatory, and their sanction is private or open warfare. We propose to call this the system of *total prestations*. (Mauss 1967, 3)

In other words, the gift was part of a system of exchanges which included both "economic" and "ritual" goods (and made no distinction between them), thereby instituting relations not between individuals, but between moral persons, or individuals who represented groups. The gift constituted groups and their relations, and as such formed the very basis of society.

Marshall Sahlins has suggested that a Hobbesian logic informs Mauss's conception of the gift. For Mauss, the gift provided the integration, solidarity, and peace which Hobbes could attribute only to the state. Without the gift, in other words, society could not exist. As Mauss noted, the cessation of the gift (i.e., of the gift relationship) was tantamount to a declaration of war; as with Hobbes, the underlying nature of society – mediated in Mauss's version not by tyranny but by the gift – was "warre" (Sahlins 1972, 174).

But Mauss restricted his conception of the gift to primitive societies in which incipient structural forms based on fundamental equality endow the gift with a preeminent role in determining rank, precedence, and the nature of segmentary interdependence. Sahlins has gone beyond Mauss in attempting to delineate the political logic of the gift and to argue that it is relevant to an understanding of early state forms, namely, chiefly polity. The gift, he argues, forms the basis for a structural transformation from exchange to redistribution. Redistribution, or pooling, is based on many of the same principles as reciprocity, but the nature and structure of relations is fundamentally different. Sahlins writes that:

Pooling is socially a *within* relation, the collective action of a group. Reciprocity is a *between* relation, the action and reaction of two parties. Thus pooling is the complement of social unity and, in Polanyi's term, "centricity"; whereas reciprocity is social duality and "symmetry." Pooling stipulates a social centre where goods meet and thence flow outwards, and a social boundary too, within which persons (or subgroups) are cooperatively related. Reciprocity can establish solidary relation, insofar as the material flow suggests assistance or mutual benefit, yet the social fact of sides is inescapable. (Sahlins 1972, 173)

According to Sahlins, redistribution or pooling can have two functions, one practical and logistic, the other instrumental. The first sustains the community in a material sense. In the second, redistribution "sustains the corporate structure itself" by serving as a "ritual of communion and of subordination to central authority ... chiefly pooling generates the spirit of unity and centricity, codifies the structure, stipulates the centralized organization of social order and social action" (Sahlins 1972, 188–189). In other words, both the social itself, and the political order which is structurally posited as the center of and basis for the social in a chiefly form of polity, are created and maintained by the gift.

To engage in such structural-functional reasoning in the Indian context is dangerous for several reasons. Perhaps most importantly, there are explicit textual statements about the significance of both kings and gifts, and the clear formulation of a world view which is hardly dependent on our functional explanations. Furthermore, the different types, contexts, grantors, and recipients of gifts are sufficiently complex to warrant concern about grouping all these things together under a single rubric. To begin with, there were major changes in the textual formulations concerning gifts after the Vedic period. While the Vedic gifts to gods were made in a ritual context in which notions of mutual obligation if not of symmetrical reciprocity permit reference to Mauss, the gifts given to deities and favors bestowed by them on devotees in the post-Vedic period did not entail instrumental logics of dependency and obligation. Thus, there is all the more danger in reproducing, along with Mauss, the concerns of Hobbes, Rousseau, and other classical European political theorists.

Sahlins' characterization of the structural properties of gifts suggests an iron-clad functionalism, and can distract us from the particular cultural as well as the strategic character of gifting activity. Pierre

Bourdieu warns of the consequences of focusing only on the rule or the structure in this context.

> To stop short at the "objective" truth of the gift, i.e. the model, is to set aside the question of the relationship between so-called objective truth, i.e. that of the observer, and the truth that can be scarcely called subjective, since it represents the official definition of the subjective experience of the exchange; it is to ignore the fact that the agents practise as irreversible a sequence of actions that the observer constitutes as reversible. The observer's totalizing apprehension substitutes an objective structure fundamentally defined by its *reversibility* for an equally objectively *irreversible* succession of gifts which are not mechanically linked to the gifts they respond to or insistently call for: any really objective analysis of the exchange of gifts, words, challenges, or even women must allow for the fact that each of these inaugural acts may misfire, and that it receives its meaning in any case, from the response it triggers off, even if the response is a failure to reply that retrospectively removes its intended meaning ... It is all a question of style, which means in this case timing and choice of occasion, for the same act – giving, giving in return, offering one's services, paying a visit, etc. – can have completely different meanings at different times .... (Bourdieu 1982, 4)

Thus Bourdieu cautions against a formalization of gift giving activity into systems of rules, and proposes instead the need to analyze gifts as symbolic actions that take place in particular contexts and in reference to the strategic considerations of individuals in action.

That the political world is a morally cohesive system does not mean either that actors do not act to maximize their position and resources or that the system itself is homeostatic and highly ordered. Bourdieu is correct to caution us against functionalist or normative readings of gifts. All gifts are potentially strategic, and all gifts are particular. However, all gifts also take on meaning in reference to more general codes and contexts, and all gifts have structural consequences. Bourdieu's strictures need not blind us to the integrity of the moral universe or to the fact that we can identify a structural logic in political action.

If we are careful not to conflate structural reasoning with intentional meanings, and if we propose a contextual reading of the "gift," grounding it in culture and history, we need not abandon it as a key element of the political order in old regime south India. Land as a material resource takes on special value by virtue of its being given by a king. The value of land is thus in part culturally determined, and is inseparable from the value of the emblems, honors, and perquisites that are given along with it. Public goods in this system attain value not in the market but through social relations. As Mauss writes in his analysis of Maori exchange, all articles that are part of the prestational system take on the life-force (*hau*) of the persons who produce and exchange them. Our examination reveals that gifts given by kings all continued to have the "hau" of the king within them.

The "hau" of the king, like the pracatam of the deity, is highly valued. Gifts do not, as an extreme reading of Sahlins might lead us to believe, gain significance simply through the fact that they are given, but also, and more importantly, through the identity of the giver. The king's ritual centrality is not predicated solely on his beneficence. Gifts are as much a sign of sovereignty as they are a contributing factor to it. As we saw in the ballad on Kattapomman, gift-giving is just one aspect of the excellence of the king. A great king reigns with justice and charity, and when he does so prosperity necessarily ensues. The political economy of the south Indian kingdom was therefore "moral" in the sense that access to power and resources was predicated on a set of culturally specific meanings regarding kingship.

All political action was therefore predicated on understandings and assumptions about the meaning of gifts, honors and emblems, agnatic and affinal ties, offers of service, and various codes for conduct. These meanings were simultaneously practical, instrumental, and cultural. In our attempt to discover typologies, rules, and structural logics, we cannot assume that brute power took the forms we might assume from the standpoint of another political culture. But in our attempt to establish culturally pervasive discourses, frames of reference, and forms of action, we must also be careful to consider each event as unique, and each context as differentially constructed in time and space.

The political world is very like the world of the temple, so well described by Appadurai and Breckenridge (1976), where the deity gives honors and favors, thereby ensuring prosperity and creating society, with its differential groups, ranks, and identities. But, while puja operates as a root metaphor for political relations, there are important differences in the codes and contexts of the two worlds, differences which particularize the strategies and consequences within them. For example, the kingdom and the temple diverge as soon as we start to contrast the structural logics of royal gifts and divine favors. Since the deity could not arbitrate disputes within the temple, requiring thereby the periodic intervention of the king, transactions within temples often led to conflict. The royal gift could also lead to conflict, but this eventuality was destabilizing in a very different way and for different reasons. It sowed the seeds of disorder through its very authoritative and kingly substance, not because the king was unable to act as arbitrator of conflict, one of his central roles. In making a gift the king shared with his subjects the very substances that rendered him powerful. The king therefore could only share *parts* of his sovereign power, expanding it all the while to maintain his distinctive centrality. Actions such as service, marriage, heroism, banditry, and devotion all had important strategic implications not simply because they could alter proximity to the king and lead therefore to alterations in status, but also because the recipients of royal gifts could potentially replace the king. This was never the object of action within the temple, for the recipients of temple honors could struggle for first honors but never become the deity itself.

Nonetheless, because of the moral and ritual position of the king, and because the king was well situated to maintain and augment his monopoly over public goods in his kingdom, the royal gift only had a latent tendency to work towards devolution. Far more saliently, royal gifts did create, to use Sahlins's words again, a "spirit of unity and centricity, codif[y] ... the structure, [and] stipulate ... the centralized organization of social order and social action." The king not only signified and displayed his authority but achieved it through activity which could be interpreted from the standpoint of different political assumptions as signs of weakness and decay.

When Western notions of command and domination are imputed to the operation of this political system and the structural consequences of gifting activity are ignored or misconstrued, analyses of the relation of landholding and politics in India take the form of Eric Stokes's important but flawed essay on inams. Stokes looks at inams as functions of differing administrative systems (Stokes 1978). Legitimate inams, Stokes suggests, should best be seen as salary for service. The problem was that "by the beginning of the nineteenth-century a long period of disturbed political conditions and unstable central authority had swelled inam to an *unnatural* extent" (italics mine; ibid., 60). But Stokes makes nineteenth-century assumptions about what is natural and unnatural. Building on these assumptions he sees the proliferation of inams as a sign of political weakness and decay. Stokes's analysis of inams is thus conditioned by his revenue-centered view of the Indian state: "Even so," he writes, the proliferation of inams "provided no permanent defence against a rapacious revenue demand since this merely pitched up the rates on revenue-bearing land to extreme levels" (ibid., 60). This zero-sum view of revenue accepts the nineteenth-century British colonial belief that the state was first and foremost an institution concerned with the extraction of revenue. It even neglects the well-known fact that in Indian political systems control over land, and revenue, was secondary to control over men. Stokes's notion of the state, and particularly his assumptions about what constitutes its strengths and weaknesses, is appropriate to British colonial government in India, but is largely irrelevant to pre-British state systems.

The gifts kings gave to their subjects were often the means by which the latter became, in a special sense, not just subjects of but subject to their kings. While the gifts did not specify service in a contractual form, they were often given after services were performed and/or with the expectation that future services would be performed. Even Brahmans who were granted lands simply for their scholarly attainments signified their participation in the rule of particular kings and dynasties by accepting land grants. When persons were incorporated into the kingdom – into the sovereignty of the king – through gifts, they became, in a relational sense, obligated to the king.[12] These obligations were clearly moral obligations, and our analysis of this political system depends upon an understanding of the moral as well as the institutional structures which gave politics its particular meanings and forms. While, as Geertz has written, in most European views and theoretical frameworks, "Political symbology, from myth, insignia, and etiquette to palaces, titles, and ceremonies, is but the instrument of purposes concealed beneath it or towering over it" (Geertz 1980, 122), the case in Bali and in south India would be misunderstood, even granting the importance of coercion, violence, and domination, if we simply carried forward the assumptions of Western political theory. It is not that "political symbology" of the above sort is any more, or less, symbolic (which is often taken to mean not real) than the "brute" facts of power. Rather, the facts of power in old regime south India were themselves different, if not unique.

If inams represented royal weakness, we would expect that inams would only be "given" in the border areas where the king would have had less control over the countryside and its inhabitants. In Pudukkottai, this expected pattern is reversed. Only the Cervaikarars were uniformly situated near the borders of the state, though this was for obvious strategic reasons. If we take them all together (Map 3), inams were more heavily concentrated in the central portions of the state than at the periphery.

From the perspective of Stokes's argument, it would seem natural that the strength of the state would fall off increasingly towards the

[12] Brahmans were, curiously, among the first to speak of their loyalty and obligation. The royal gift of land, rather than creating danger and dependence per se, preserved the relative autonomy of the Brahman at the same time that it displayed the moral excellence of the king. For the Brahman, the king's gift was the best possible kind of gift.

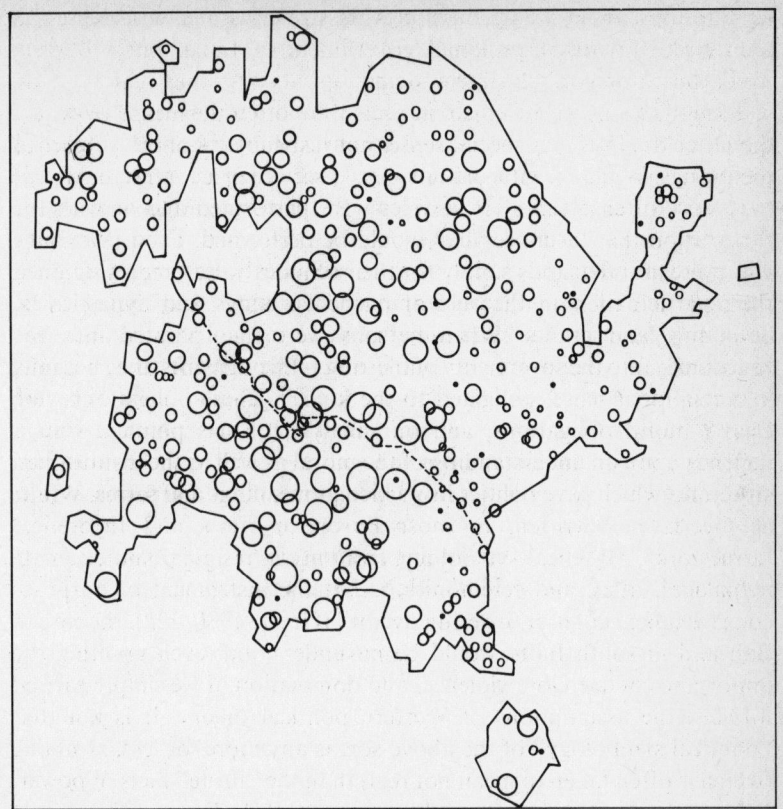

Map 3 All inams

peripheries. It would also seem natural that, given collections in kind, the king should hold on to rights to the royal share near the center of the state and give away lands at the periphery, minimizing, all other things being equal, substantial transportation costs. But we can see here conclusively that more units of inams were given away in the center than in the periphery.[13] Clearly the simple economic rationality proclaimed by neo-classical economics must yield to other explanations. Giving land away was not really giving it away as much as it was incorporating new people into a moral-political economy in which the king was at the center. Protecting the state and provisioning its villages with basic infrastructures and services, ritual forms being as "basic" as irrigational

---

[13] For want of sufficient data, I have not been able to demonstrate this conclusively in terms of acreage.

facilities, was not wasting resources but signifying and sustaining the social fact of royal authority.

While land rights in the form of inam grants were thus central to the institutionalization of kingship in the old order, we have also seen that these rights cannot be analyzed apart from other coordinates of political relations – kinship, honor, and service. Each of these categories was at once a cultural category of entitlement, filiation, and power, and a rhetorical trope which provided the terms of discourse about authority and political relations. All of these coordinates were predicated on a common matrix which gave origin and form to their possibilities, ultimately enclosing them. This matrix was kingship; and the lines that connected the points were drawn through the gifts of these various interrelated rights. This kingship was neither Oriental Despotism nor some organic extension of a segmentary kinship system: comparative sociology and colonial history have together obscured the powerful, if semi-autonomous, political forms which were so fundamental in the old regime.

We will now examine the origins of kingship as a socio-cultural and political institution in the little kingdom of Pudukkottai.

# 5

# *The early history of the Pudukkottai region*

### The settlement of Pudukkottai

Settlement in the Pudukkottai area was relatively sparse until the early Cola period, that is the ninth and tenth centuries. However, the construction of a number of early rock cut temples of the Pallava style, the occupation of the area's numerous natural caves by wandering hunters and herders, Jaina ascetics, and early settlers, occasional *Caṅkam* literary references to chieftains in the area, and a few lithic inscriptions detailing such events as the feeding of Brahmans, the construction of a sluice, and the provision of arrangements for sacrifice and puja worship suggest that the area had been by no means unoccupied (Ayyar 1940, 526–527, 542, 546; IPS nos. 1–19; CLIPS). With the coming of the Cola era there is strong evidence of increasing agrarian settlement, the growth of locality institutions such as community, village, and town assemblies, and the construction and expansion of temples. During the ninth to the fourteenth centuries, which included periods of both Cola and Pantiya hegemony over the region, many of the local level social and political institutions which remain important in Pudukkottai through to the nineteenth century are already identifiable.

Oral traditions and palm leaf manuscripts provide accounts of settlement in Pudukkottai which express certain fundamental features of social and political relations in the early medieval period. Perhaps the most cited version is found in the Tekkattur palm leaf manuscript:

Ādoṇḍaicakravarti brought these Vellālars with him (from Conjeevaram) into the Cōla territory, and Ugra Peru Valudi, the Pāndya king, selected 48,000 good families and imported them from east Conjeevaram and settled them in Pandya land. The Cōlanādu territory occupied by the Vellālars was called Kōnādu or the land of the king, and the Pāndya territory, Kānādu or forest land. (Ayyar 1940, 547–548)

The role of the king in initiating and sponsoring settlement is central in this settlement story as in many others, such as the "Story of the brothers" which recounts the settlement of the Kavuntars in Konku Natu (Beck 1972, 1982) and the accounts of the settlement of Vellalars in Tontaimantalam (Mahalingam 1972, 93–98). The king is explicitly credited with constituting the new community. The stories all make reference to the need for the initial conquest over and subsequent protection from the much-feared Kurumpars and Vetars who are thought to have traversed these regions before their settlement by higher castes. After this conventional opening, the stories describe the structure of the caste. The Tekkattur Manuscript concerns the Karala Vellalars, and the settlement story accounts for the basic division of the caste into *Kanāṭṭars* and *Kōnāṭṭars*, each of which in turn have many exogamous sub-divisions. *Kōnāṭu* was for the most part north of the river Vellar, though it extended south of the river in the western part of the state; *Kanāṭu* was situated in the southeastern part of the state. Konatu, literally meaning land of the king, was usually thought to be in Cola Natu, Kanatu, literally the land of forests, was included in Pantiya Natu (see Map 13). The manuscript proceeds to eulogize the agricultural skills of the Vellalar community and describe the clearing of the land, the first use of the plough, the building and digging of dams, anicuts, tanks, channels, and wells. We are also told that when the Vellalars settled in the Pudukkottai region, they brought the eighteen castes with them. These included barbers, potters, washermen, scribes and accountants, blacksmiths, goldsmiths, braziers, carpenters, masons, oil pressers, betel leaf growers, flower sellers, garland makers, tailors, Valaiyars, shepherds, bards, and Pallis (Ayyar 1940, 549).[1]

The Tekkattur manuscript then explains the decline in the position of Vellalars in Pudukkottai after their initial golden age. Disputes and quarrels arose between the two major branches over land, temples, tanks, rights to the water of the river Vellar, and temple honors (ibid., 548).[2] The fighting that resulted weakened the Vellalars, leading to the settlement and eventual dominance of Maravars in the country. The Konatu Vellalars imported five hundred families of Maravars from Rajendramankala Natu, in Ramnad to the south, and gave them rights of protection. The Vellalars of Kanatu also invited Maravars, from eastern Ramnad, to protect them. The fighting was fierce, and Konatu was victorious.

---

[1] Conspicuously, this group does not include the atimai group, the servants who performed domestic services and agricultural labor.

[2] Interestingly, in the most recent oral traditions that I collected while in the field in 1982 temple honors were singled out as the major, sometimes even sole, cause of this rivalry. An important example is the dispute over honor in Malaiyakovil, a temple which marks one of the most important boundary sites between Konatu and Kanatu. As I will suggest later, this may be because of the peculiar fetishization of honors in the late nineteenth and twentieth centuries.

According to copper plate inscriptions that can be found with virtually every Maravar community in Konatu, the Konatu Vellalars were confirmed as the victors by none other than the Pantiyan kings, who ironically had earlier been responsible for the settlement of their chief rivals. According to one such inscription, which begins with a long eulogy to the Vijayanagara kings: "The Maniya Turai, King Cuntara Pantiyan, came to the place and saw the copper plates and stone inscriptions and they decided that the place was for the Konattu Vellalars ... The seven lineages of Karukatta are the overlords of the Perunallur Kaniyatci in Ponnamaravati, having 756 villages, 1,511 hamlets, 21 brahmadeyams, 212 devadayams, and 64 natus ..." (Melapanaiyur copper plate no. 1). In similar inscriptions the Konatu Vellalars were referred to as the Karkatta Vellalars (Kulamankalam copper plate no. 2).

Nonetheless, the copper plates held by the Konatu Maravars reflect less the victory of the Vellalars than the cost of that victory. All of them treat the war as the turning point not for Konatu Vellalar hegemony, but rather for the establishment of the local rights of the Konatu Maravars. Because of their important role during the war, the Maravars were given rights to lands (kaniyatci) in the Konatu villages where they were settled by the Konatu Vellalars (the Karkatta Vellalar was said to be owner of the kaniyatci right). One plate avers that "the wetlands ... are given to [the Maravars] in exchange for 350 Madurai gold coins and as reimbursement of the expenses incurred during the Konattu border war" (Kulamankalam copper plate no. 1). In another plate, "He and eight lineage headmen were given kaniyatci in Perunallur Nacai Puva tank and Putuvettu Manal tank in Mankurucci Vayal for their army expenses in the great Konatu–Kanatu border fight" (Kulamankalam copper plate no. 2); and in yet another plate, "the chiefs from Uraiyur kurram to Oliyur kurram gave kaniyatci to the people who migrated first to Panaiyur-Kulamankalam" (Melapanaiyur copper plate). Not only were the Maravars given kaniyatci rights to enjoy the land and fields, they were also given rights to "the temple and tank, ampalam [headmanship over village] and umpalam [tax free lands], the services of Valaiyar and Itaiyar ["hunter" and "herdsman" castes], and the services of the Pallan and the Paraiyan [the two untouchable castes which performed agricultural and domestic labor on a hereditary or atimai basis]" (Kulamankalam copper plate no. 1). After this point the history of Pudukkottai is characterized by the rise to chiefly status and finally kingship of the Maravars in the south and the Kallars in the north, both of whom first acquired kaniyatci rights and then protection responsibilities and privileges as a result of the great war.

Other manuscripts concerning the migration of Maravars into the area (Ayyar 1940, 548) confirm their early connection with the ruling Vellalars. They specify that Vellalars invited large groups of Maravars to settle in the southern and western parts of the state to protect them. Other traditions suggest that the Kallars arrived under similar conditions, or at least that those Kallars already settled in proximity to the Vellalars were accorded rights of protection by local Vellalar groups. According to these traditions Kallars lived in the forest tracts of Kanatu where were employed by Vanatiraiyar, a Vellalar chief of Kanatu, to fight against the Vellalars of Konatu. While the Kallar traditions provide much less detail than the Maravar accounts, they do make it clear that a number of villages and many lands were granted to Kallars because of their participation in one or another of the wars between Konatu and Kanatu.

Certain basic structural features which emerge from these variable traditions correspond with other evidence about the history of the area. Old copper plates found in the state mention a number of settlements of Karalar Vellalars. Traces of forts built by Vellalars are still to be found in Kotumpalur and elsewhere in the state. A number of wells built by Karalar Vellalars as early as the tenth century remain in use in the southern part of Pudukkottai state (Ayyar 1940, 548). Vellalars were certainly among the earliest agricultural settlers in Pudukkottai, but either they never settled in great numbers, or a considerable portion of their population migrated elsewhere before the eighteenth century. Vellalars who continue to live in Konatu trace their ancestry to these early Vellalar settlers. The single remaining family of Kanatu Vellalars claims that the entire group left Pudukkottai shortly after the Konatu–Kanatu war, with the exception of one family, enjoined to stay by the god so that the entire group would not vanish (interview with Tekkattur Vellalar).

All the Maravar groups trace their settlement in Pudukkottai to the great war between Konatu and Kanatu. Though this event figures in some Kallar histories, it is far less central for them than for the Maravars. The Maravars became the dominant caste throughout much of the southern part of the state, restricting their settlement to the eastern portion of Kanatu and that portion of Konatu south of the river Vellar. The already established presence of Kallars north of the river Vellar was most probably the reason why the Maravars restricted their settlement in such a way. It is therefore reasonable to assume that the Kallars have been the dominant caste in the northern part of the state from perhaps as early as the tenth century, although pinpointing an exact date may never be possible. The Kallars seem to have come in a number of different waves. In all likelihood the earliest Kallar settlers were those of Vicenki Natu, in the north-central part of the state. Early on this group of Kallars was associated with violent and predatory behavior; if there were many Vellalars settled in this region they did not stay long. From the Kallar traditions already referred to, other Kallar groups which settled in the area now known as Alankuti taluk might well have arrived before the last of the Konatu–Kanatu wars, since the names of the areas from which Kallars were said to have been recruited by the Kanatu chiefs are the same as the natus which still organize Kallar settlement in these regions. Nonetheless, the vagueness and paucity of Kallar accounts lend little credibility to the venerability of their settlement in regions which might simply have provided them with territorial labels and boundaries for their own lineage or subcaste organizations.

We are on somewhat surer ground with respect to the final migration of Kallars, which took place later and further to the north. Certain areas of northern Pudukkottai, particularly the northeastern region of Ampu Natu (the area around Karampakuti), were settled by Vellalars before the arrival of the Kallars. According to some Kallar informants in this region as well as the descendants of Vellalars still living there, the Vellalars settled there at the invitation of the Cola kings. In a by now familiar pattern, they lost their dominant position sometime thereafter, possibly as late as the fifteenth century, to the Kallars, who settled in the region as local chiefs and protectors, and later spawned the royal subcaste of Pudukkottai state. Nonetheless, these Vellalars were never totally ousted from their earlier position of authority in the region, as shown by their inclusion in Ampu Natu, where they still accept honors along with Kallars in the local subcaste temple. Even today Vellalars act as headmen in the royal Kallar subcaste, maintaining the honor roll calls, convening and adjudicating subcaste assemblies, and managing the subcaste temple (see Chapter 7).

As is evident from these stories about the settlement of Kallars and Maravars in Pudukkottai, the dominant position of both these castes is in large measure a result of their military prowess and strong territorial clan organization, which enabled them to establish and maintain rights of protection and local adjudication over the communities where they settled. The martial traditions of these two castes made them appropriate candidates for the awarding of protection rights. Since Kallars and Maravars effectively controlled the means of coercion in these areas, they were well suited to provide protection, as well as occasional though ample demonstration of the need for their protection. As we will now see, the development of rights of protection was perhaps the key to the rise not only of the Kallars and the Maravars but of chiefs, and then kings, in the Pudukkottai area.

## The rise of kingship in Pudukkottai

The inscriptions of Pudukkottai State indicate that chieftains (araiyars) appeared at about the same time as locality (natu) assemblies. The araiyars are shown to have played an important role in the decision making of the assemblies (Ayyar 1940, 653; IPS no. 198). They are most conspicuous in the inscriptions first as major donors to temples (IPS nos. 107, 119, 139, 141, 146, 159, 169, 295, 304, 313, 314), and later as chiefs providing protection (patikkaval) at the village and locality level. Endowing gifts to temples fulfilled textual prescriptions of kingly beneficence; more particularly the araiyars reenacted models of kingly behavior which had become well established in south India under the Pallavas, Colas, and Pantiyas. These gifts further demonstrated the early relation between temple honors and kingly authority, since an endowment to a temple brought about increased participation in the distribution of honors in the temple even as in more general terms it underscored the importance of kingly patronage for temple development. The chieftains' participation in a larger political universe was also manifested by the occasional designation of merit accruing from a gift by a chieftain to a larger king (IPS no. 169).

While Pudukkottai inscriptions of the period from 1350 to 1600 offer a great many examples of common religious donations, they seem to Peter Granda, who has compared them with the wider corpus of south Indian inscriptions for this period, to be "both less detailed and less significant than the inscriptions which provide copious illustrations of frequent social upheavals in this region" (Granda 1984; see also Ayyar 1940, 290). The Puddukkottai inscriptions contain many references to disputes and conflicts (often leading to violence), to demands for arbitration by village level organizations and local chiefs, to inabilities and refusals to pay taxes, and to migration (S. R. Aiyar 1916, 110–112). The inscriptions also enumerate a large number of chiefs and their military retainers and settlements. The term for relations of protection, patikkaval, is found almost exclusively in Pudukkottai; it appears in fourteen inscriptions in Pudukkottai, and in only three others in the Tamil area (Granda 1984). The term for military hamlet, *pataiparru*, is found exclusively in Pudukkottai. Pudukkottai was clearly an active area for chiefs and for the development of institutional forms of political-cum-military relations with local dominant social groups.

Given the correspondence between more modern forms of territorial and hierarchical organization among the dominant castes of Puduk-kottai and the structure and operation of locality assemblies in the medieval period, we might infer that these little kings had their origins in positions of authority in both the locality assemblies (as nattars or *nāṭāḷvāns* – see IPS no. 124) and in their local lineages and subcastes. Indeed (to use later ethnography as our guide) locality assemblies were nothing more than an extension of lineage and subcaste assemblies, which, as the assemblages and representative bodies of the constituent segmentary units of the dominant caste group, provided authoritative leadership for the entire territorial constellation of social groups. As indicated in palm leaf manuscripts and copper plates, the grant of kaniyatci to a particular territory included not only rights to land and temple honors, but also rights to the service of the eighteen castes together with the Pallar and Paraiyan. That the early villages which made up the constituencies of these assemblies had strong caste bases is suggested by the frequent mention in the inscriptions of single caste villages, such as *akaraparru* (Brahman villages), *kaḷḷaparru* (Kallar villages), and *veḷḷanparru* (Vellalar villages).

The settlement of villages, the endowments of gifts to temples, the exchange of protection rights between villagers and chiefs for shares of the produce, and the particular types of relations that existed between chiefs and their military retainers were all articulated in terms of more general Tamil ideas concerning rights to and shares of the produce of the land. In particular, the melvaram, the top or first cut that was thought to be the right of the king or landlord, was shared with, or rather redirected to, many individuals and institutions represented in the inscriptions, from chiefs to temples to tanks and their keepers. For example, one araiyar remitted (*iraiyoli*) the melvaram share owed by a particular landholder ordering him to make in its place certain contributions both in kind and coin to the temple at Nelvayil (IPS no. 277; also see nos. 305, 321, 328, 329, 424). All inscriptional grants in the Tamil country from the Pallavas on follow this basic form.

What makes the Pudukkottai inscriptions particularly interesting is that in addition to this classic sharing of the king's right, we also see the appropriation of kingly rights through the assumption of patikkaval, or protection rights, by araiyars, and even on some occasions by temples, on whose behalf a chief would carry out the required protection as a form of devotion while directing the perquisites of the rights to the temple (see IPS no. 799). Patikkaval means the protection (kaval) of a place (pati). In the fourteenth century and after, the position of the araiyars as chief donors was complemented by the accordance of patikkaval rights to them over villages and localities (IPS nos. 439, 440, 454). The perquisites of the patikkaval right usually included particular lands which were set aside and specified shares of the total produce of the area. For example in one inscription of A.D. 1380, patikkaval rights included (Ayyar 1938, 328–329):

1. For lands growing paddy, a head load of sheaves per *tati* of land (tati means a measuring rod, or stick, but the unit of land apparently varied over time and space).
2. For lands growing sugar-cane, twenty palams (an Indian ounce, twelve of which make an English pound) of sugar per tati.
3. For lands growing turmeric, ginger, karanai, and betel, he is to receive his share.
4. Of cocoanuts, jackfruit trees, plantains, and mangoes growing in the village, he is to receive his due.
5. For cotton growing on dry land, ten pods of cotton for each unit of land.

Other rights were also included. Further, a plot of land was purchased for the private use of this chieftain. The araiyars often made an initial payment of coin to obtain the patikkaval, but the significance of this is unclear. The payment could have been for a private plot of land as in the above case, but it was far more likely made as a combination of prestation and security, or potential collateral. While there was no open market in protection rights, there was occasionally considerable competition between competing warrior groups for rights to protect certain prosperous communities or prestigious temples. The right might have been auctioned off with the intention not only of securing protection but also cash. The shares of village produce awarded for patikkaval were initially labelled *pāṭikkāval cuvēntiram*. During the fifteenth and sixteenth centuries, this share gradually became known as *aracu cuventiram*, or the kingly share. The appropriation of protection rights seems to have been the major means by which local chiefs attained local sovereignty, an important social fact reflected in the history of inscriptional terminology.

The provision of protection was, as the name suggests, basic to the patikkaval agreement. An inscription from Tiruppuvalaikkuti narrates a case in which one village attacked another. A small raiding party killed many of the men and plundered the village, leaving it in ruins. The survivors of the devastated village convened an assembly of eight neighboring villages and offered to grant local chiefs temple land and patikkaval fees for undertaking the protection of the village (S. R. Aiyar 1916, 110). Initially, protection was provided by local groups, but from the fourteenth century on local araiyars began to monopolize patikkaval agreements.

Given the vital importance of protection for cultivation and the livelihood of any village, no araiyar would have been accorded the right of patikkaval, however much he could pay for it, if he lacked the ability to muster powerful forces. All araiyars appear to have had command over a group of military retainers as well as the lands to support them. In addition, every expansion of patikkaval responsibilities was accompanied by the allocation of increased shares of produce to the araiyar to support his retainers, thus illustrating both the means by which araiyars could gain in strength and power and the reasons behind competition for patikkaval rights among them. The granting of lands by araiyars for the support of their military retainers is confirmed by the existence of a number of pataiparrus, or hamlets of military holdings (IPS nos. 354, 364, 403, 421, 439, 453, 455, 462, 583, 596, 648, 708, 711, 744, 792). Pataiparru denotes land rights accorded to local chieftains in association with their maintenance of a specified number of troops, much like the conditions under which Cervaikarars later held land and other rights under the Tondaimans in the eighteenth century. Like patikkaval, the term has a special (and in this case unique) association with Pudukkottai. There were seven named pataiparrus in Pudukkottai: Kiranur, Viraiyaccilai, Karkuricciparru, Kuruntanparai, Pulivalam, Kottiyur-Ilambalakkuti, and Ilancarppuram (IPS nos. 690, 706, 711, 727, 731, 743, 744, 745, 759, 792, 800, 829, 838). Five of these villages continued into the eighteenth century as important Kallar and Maravar strongholds. Araiyars themselves are often identified as belonging to a particular pataiparru (IPS nos. 403, 439, 462) but the exact nature of the relation between the chief and his soldiers, and of both with the residents of the hamlets, is unclear. One inscription records that a number of pataiparrus regularly paid fees to a particular araiyar, who ordered a substantial reduction in those fees in recognition of service and for help rendered when one Valuttur Pallavarayar invaded the territory of the chief (IPS no. 462). It seems likely that while each araiyar had his own military base, he was able to secure the loyalty and service of other military camps on the basis of kin ties and political alliances.

In addition, the araiyars played an important role in the settlement of new villages and in developing and maintaining infrastructures necessary for agricultural production, most centrally, facilities for irrigation. In an early twelfth century inscription one natalvar (who is also called an *aracan*, or ruler) was responsible for building a sluice (*kalinku*) for the Kavinatu tank, located just to the southwest of present-day Pudukkottai town (IPS no. 123). In the mid thirteenth century the village of Vicalur, left uncultivated for years, was resettled by one Vippurutaiyan who is said to have conquered the surrounding natu. This chief contributed directly to the resettlement of the area by digging tanks and diverting water from the river Vellar into them (IPS no. 375). In another record (IPS no. 477), the araiyars joined with the residents of the village Cempattur in making a gift of land for the maintenance of a tank. In yet another village the residents granted certain patikkaval rights to their fellow villager, Kannan, for the excavation of the Umayanti tank (IPS no. 478). In addition, inscriptions from the next few centuries amply document the role of araiyars in arbitrating disputes connected with the utilization of irrigational facilities (IPS nos. 512, 513). In Kiranur, the people agreed that any damage to wells, tanks, or dams would result in the forfeiting of a specified amount of land to the local temple by the araiyars who had the relevant patikkaval right (S. R. Aiyar 1916, 110–111). Even gifts (or forfeitures) from araiyars to temples contributed to the development of agrarian infrastructures as a consequence of the multifaceted activities of the temple (Stein 1960). Temples controlled many irrigational infrastructures and temple treasuries often served as rural banks (IPS no. 379).

The role played by araiyars in developing and maintaining irrigation was significant for many reasons. Without providing support for the notion of a "hydraulic state," the araiyars operated supra-village mechanisms for the construction, maintenance, and integration of the large and inter-locking tanks and sluices of Pudukkottai. Warrior rule, far from dismantling the agrarian institutions of the earlier medieval period, permitted – indeed encouraged – the extension of cultivation and the growth of a productive agrarian system. Not only did araiyars actively involve themselves in the productive base of society, they did so through the patikkaval agreement. For example, in one inscription the temple trustees and villagers of Tiruvenkaivacal granted patikkaval rights to the villagers of Irumbali in return not for cash but for the repair of breaches in the tank and the restoration of all lost water (IPS no. 681). Through these kinds of agreements and relations warrior rule thus facilitated rather than retarded the integration of village communities and the increase of agricultural production.

To return to our earlier examination of manuscripts concerning the early settlement of the state first by Vellalars and later by Kallars and Maravars, it seems plausible to assume that chiefs of the latter two castes were particularly successful in developing the resources and leadership capabilities which led, firstly, to their being accorded patikkaval rights, and secondly, to their becoming the araiyars of the inscriptions, especially from the fourteenth century on, when protection became both the means of securing sovereign rights and of procuring the resources for substantial donorship. Unfortunately, given the variable nature of the titles accorded members of these castes, it is usually impossible to verify this assumption from inscriptional evidence alone. However, local oral, inscriptional, and manuscript traditions are all clear about the growing dominance of Kallars and Maravars over Vellalars and the importance of the provision of protection rights for the changing balance of power. Furthermore, the subsequent history of political relations in Pudukkottai reveals the appropriation of local-level military control and caste dominance by Kallars in the north and Maravars in the south so dramatically that it is difficult to doubt a correlation. Nonetheless, there might still have been some Vellalar chiefs in the area through parts of the seventeenth century.[3]

The increasing importance of araiyars from the fifteenth century on and their transformation into "little kings" of the old regime type can further be seen (IPS nos. 693, 696, 704) in the new privileges accorded them and in the increased formalization of the transfer of patikkaval rights in the *āciriyapiramāṇam*, a deed of *āciriyam* (from *āśraya*, meaning seeking refuge from, Monier-Williams 1979, 158), a term which suggests a more wide ranging "submission" on the part of the residents of the localities to the authority of the araiyar than might have been the case before. Further, at this point the share accorded to the araiyar began to be called the aracu cuventiram rather than patikkaval

---

[3] One of the most important chiefly allies of the Colas in the eighth through tenth centuries had been the Irukkuvels of Kotumpalur, the site of an important Cola temple on the banks of the river Vellar in the northwestern part of modern Pudukkottai state. Stein (1980) disputes Arokiaswami's claims that the Irukkuvels were Vellalars on the basis of the later dominance of Kallars and Maravars in the whole area, but the congruence of Irukkuvel titles (velir, velar, muventavelar) with titles used by Vellalars of the area today and the coincidence of the dates of Irukkuvel dominance with the time sequences implied in the many origin stories, copper plates, and palm leaf manuscripts all of which attribute initial settlement and leadership in Konatu to Vellalars may suggest otherwise. Certainly, the Irukkuvels were emulating conceptions of local kingship established in core areas of Vellalar and Brahman dominance. These ideas were impressively realized in the building of major temples and the establishment of Brahman settlements (brahmadeyas). Nevertheless, whoever the Irukkuvels were, and whatever their relationship to Karalar and/or Karkatta Vellalars referred to in local sources, the distinctive development of Kallar and Maravar kingship in this region seems a result both of trends established by the local araiyars who secured patikkaval rights in the period after the thirteenth and fourteenth centuries and of the earlier forms of chiefship so central to the Pallava and Cola periods which seem to have been examplified by dynasties such as the Irukkuvels.

cuventiram, marking the transition from a terminological stress on the right itself to the royal status of the person holding the right.

The new and broader nature of the privileges accorded to patikkaval araiyars can be seen in an inscription of 1477 (IPS no. 715). For assuming the patikkaval of a cluster of villages, the araiyar was entitled to receive twelve *ari* (a handful) and one *patakku* (as with all measures they vary, but this usually means 200 cubic inches) of paddy for every *mā* (approximately one-third of an acre), a share in the fees leviable by temples, special rights over tanks, one cage of hares from the Valaiyars (hunters) during the months of Ati and Kartikkai (roughly, July and November), milk and ghee from the shepherds, and two fowl from the Pallars and Paraiyars during the same two months. In addition, various food offerings to the deity were made, and lamps in the temple lit, in his name. When he went on procession, flags and torches were to be carried in front of the araiyar during the day and conches to be blown as he mounted or dismounted from his horse or vehicle. Finally, he was entitled to append a long series of titles (*virutāvalli*) to his name. In other words, the honors of kingly authority were now being added to the shares of produce. The araiyar had become a little king of the sort we read about in the vamcavalis. It was through the protection right, itself a royal perquisite, that kings emerged in Pudukkottai.

The history of the Curaikkuti chiefs of Atalaiyur Natu in south-western Pudukkottai exemplifies the general picture already presented. The first inscriptional reference to chiefs of this area occurs in the eighth century (IPS no. 238) when the headman (natalvan) of this natu gave a gold offering for the maintenance of a lamp to one Tirumulattanattu-matever who belonged to a certain devadana (a land grant for the support of temples and temple personnel). This gift was placed under the protection of the residents (*ūrom*) of Punnankuti, suggesting that the rights of and the capacity for protection at that time rested with locality assemblies. In the early twelfth century (IPS no. 124) another Atalaiyur Natalvan made a gift, this time in conjunction with the local natu assembly, of tax free land to support offerings to a Visnu temple in Irumpunatu. Although the gift was given jointly by the chief and the assembly, the offering was consecrated in the chief's name.

In the early thirteenth century (IPS no. 263) the Atalaiyur Natalvan, acting alone, assigned the cesses from a particular village for daily offerings in a temple. This inscription, especially in so far as it contrasts with those before it, suggests the increased concentration of rights to the melvaram (or structural equivalent) of the village produce in the hands of the chief and the associated decline in the power and position of the local assembly. This trend is further advanced in a grant of the early fourteenth century (IPS no. 438) in which the local chief, no longer called the natalvan but now entitled Ponnan Alakiya Perumal, again acting alone, assigned the melvaram of a particular piece of land to support some temple offerings. In the mid fourteenth century (IPS no. 440) an inscription registers the grant of patikkaval lands and rights by the residents of Melur to the Curaikkuti chief. Forty years later (IPS no. 454) the residents of nearby Atanur followed suit and also granted their patikkaval rights to the Curaikkuti chief. In a grant of 1421 (IPS no. 622) the subordinate position of the local assembly is again suggested by its perfunctory acceptance of alienations made by the chief. Other grants of the same period show the chief patronizing priests and monasteries (*matam*) in addition to making the usual temple offerings in his own name (IPS nos. 707, 783, 786, 792). In 1449 (IPS no. 462) a chieftain in this line reduced the cesses owed him by members of a number of pataiparrus in recognition of their military services, thereby demonstrating the royal nature of the rights over military hamlets as well. In the sixteenth century, a chief of Curaikkuti granted land and shares of produce (cuventirams) to military commanders (*pataittalaivari*) serving under him (IPS nos. 743, 758.). The mention here of military commanders rather than military hamlets suggests the increased number of levels in the chain of command and perhaps the enhanced power of the Curaikkuti rulers over a group of subordinate chiefs.

Beginning with a grant of 1498 (IPS nos. 463, 464), the inscriptions of this line of chiefs were routinely prefaced by eulogies listing their glorious titles. The earliest title in these grants referred to their fame as protectors: "He who preserved those who sought protection," a clear reference to their ability to fulfill all the terms of the patikkaval right. A title used twice in the sixteenth century claimed their lordship over the Pantiyas: "He who mounted his horse while the Pantiyan was holding the stirrup" (IPS nos. 734, 758). In one of the two inscriptions containing this epithet the Curaikkuti chiefs included among their own titles a laudatory address (prasasti) to the Vijayanagara king: "The establisher of the Pantiya and the Cola dominions, the conqueror of Iram [Sri Lanka], Kampalam, and Yatpanam, the victor over the army of the Muslims and the subduer of their pride." Thus the Curaikkuti rulers represented their victorious achievements first in terms of their local exploits and then by their metonymic identification with the great overlord of Vijayanagara. These prasastis succinctly record the history of the chiefly line. Starting as local protectors these chiefs rose in power at the time of Pantiyan decline and proudly proclaimed a symbolic victory over a once powerful and still culturally pervasive dynasty. This victory was accomplished under the aegis of the new supreme overlord of Vijayanagara.

Other local dynasties which exercised intermittent control over various regions in Pudukkottai during this period followed similar paths. The Pallavaraiyar line (not the same Pallavaraiyars who immediately preceded the Tondaimans in the late seventeenth century) first appeared in Perunkalur and Vaittur (in the north-central part of the state) in early-fourteenth-century inscriptions as araiyars (IPS nos. 462, 476, 711, 713, 714, 726, 752, 864, 866, 945, 968). By the mid fifteenth century they were appending illustrious epithets to their names such as "those who protected the crown of the Pantiya and the dignity of the Caluva" (IPS no. 752). They claimed that one Ramappa Nayakar, the representative of Visvanatha Nayakar of Madurai granted them land (IPS no. 752). The last two rulers of this line assumed the title of *Rājyampaṇṇi Aruḷukaiyil*, or those who performed the act of ruling with grace (Ayyar 1940, 735). The Vanataraiyars, or Banas, another translocal dynasty of the same period, ruled over a region in western Pudukkottai contiguous to and in parts overlapping those areas "ruled" by the Pallavaraiyars. They made their first inscriptional appearance as cattle raiders in 1274 (IPS no. 380) and by the late fifteenth century had become quite powerful. One of their inscriptions announced that when the banner of the Banas was unfurled, the tiger of the Cola, the carp of the Pantiya, and the bow of the Cera all disappeared (IPS no. 674). Although it is not clear to which caste the Banas belonged, the Tekkattur Manuscript mentions that they enrolled Kallar chieftains to assist them in fighting against the Konatu Vellalars (Ayyar 1940, 728). Other similar local chiefly families in Pudukkottai were the Kankaraiyars, the Dharmaraiyars, the Tondaimans of Arantanki, and the chiefs of Perampur and Kuttalur, of Iluppur, Kumaravati, and Marunkapuri.

Thus we see the political dynamic of little kingship operating at the level of the araiyars who then developed into little kings of the type seen above. The inscriptional record closely parallels the vamcavali stories depicting the palaiyakkarars' rise to little kingship. In the vamcavalis the little kings began their "political" careers by subduing (sometimes rival) bandits in the service of a chief or king. In the inscriptions, the araiyars similarly began their ascent to kingship by subduing bandits, or rather by providing villages and local institutions with protection from the exploits of bandits. In both the vamcavalis and the inscriptions the road to little kingship led from protection to forms of royal beneficence and behavior. The warrior kings who began by offering their military services for the purpose of protection proceeded to grant lands to temples and Brahmans and to receive grants of various royal honors and privileges from higher kings to mark and signify their transformation. These greater kings provided not only honors but also models for kingly behavior that were rigidly adhered to all over the Tamil countryside.

What about the social base of these little kings? Did they abandon the local level and tightly knit social and political groups which provided the initial base for their emergent political activity? As noted above, inscriptional evidence for the period after the fifteenth century suggests that in Pudukkottai (and elsewhere) there was a marked decline in the functional importance of the village (*ūr*) and locality (natu) assemblies. Later inscriptions of the sixteenth century (e.g., IPS nos. 818, 833, 834, 898, 972) refer to meetings of temple authorities, leaders of various castes and communities, and representatives of villages, without using the old assembly names of the ur, *capā*, or natu. When villagers met together it was often to sell or grant patikkaval rights to a chieftain (IPS nos. 681, 703, 715, 751, 799, 821, 843, 898).

However, this conventional interpretation based on how and when certain terms appear in a terminological study of the inscriptional record may miss the actual structural dynamic. Village and locality assemblies did not so much decline as become increasingly encompassed by leaders who represented them and assembled them in new hierarchical forms. These hierarchical forms, because of the congruence seen earlier between kin-based and territory-based assemblies, inevitably entailed newly formulated relationships over time between different groups and different territories as well as changes in the structures of lineages and subcastes. As I will argue throughout this book, the political development of regional hegemony led to the development and elaboration of particular forms of subcaste organization which can be seen very clearly among the dominant Kallars of Pudukkottai. In Pudukkottai local Kallar chiefs and headmen extended their social relations well beyond the village community and strengthened Kallar locality control and regional integration through their political success. I believe that this process is representative of many similar changes in other parts of South Asia during the old regime.

In order to explore the development of Kallar kingship we must strive, often without much help from the inscriptional record, to understand the developing structures of local level Kallar society. Similarly, we will not be able to understand Kallar social organization unless we study it in the light of its political history. In a larger sense, my argument is that neither society nor polity can be understood when looked at as separate domains or entities, and that Stein's proposal of a segmentary argument (1980) can be most usefully employed in this kind of inquiry, where we can see direct links (as well as instructively inexact fits) between the segmentary structure of lineages, subcastes, and castes on the one hand and the emerging structure, at the regional level, of the pre-colonial old regime state on the other.

### Conclusion

The vast expansion of the political and geographical universe in the Tamil country under Vijayanagara provided unprecedented opportunities for mobility and migration especially since it also removed the Pantiyas, the last of the great Tamil kingdoms, from serious contention for overlordship. As a corollary to this expansion, the political geography of Tamil Nadu became more subject to frequent alteration and adjustment, depending on the military skills and political ambitions of the araiyars and their capacity to make lasting local alliances and institutional relationships. As we noted earlier, this was particularly true in the "mixed economy" zones where agrarian settlement was still at an early stage, and where mobility, for reasons of political and ecological instability, was most pronounced. These developments were encouraged by forces above and outside the locality as well as being outgrowths of local political developments. Chiefly groups and individuals emerged out of a context in which local authority and decision making were vested in locality assemblies first by mobilizing their local resources to secure protection rights and then by being conspicuous donors to temples, charities, and Brahman communities. Their control over the resources necessary for such beneficent activity was steadily intensified by the transfer of protection rights from locality assemblies to these chiefs. The chiefs gradually acquired more generalized rights than had initially been awarded to them in their position as patikkaval chiefs. Some of these additional rights had to do with the honors accorded the chiefs; others had to do with their control over military followers and their communities. The chiefs continued to be active donors, and they garnered increasing shares of local and temple honors and of local production, as well as greater responsibilities to provide protection to all the villages and temples under their general dominion.

It was through this process that palaiyakkarars began to dominate south Indian society and polity at the local level. Local conditions varied considerably throughout southern India as did the positions of local palaiyakkarars. This is amply demonstrated by the spectrum of political authority in the south, which – below the regional kings of the three great mantalams – ranged from Ramanatapuram and Pudukkottai on the one hand to the tiny estates of certain Tirunelveli palaiyakkarars on the other. At an even lower level, the developmental process of becoming a little king probably includes certain kavalkarars (protection chiefs) as well, for example the Maravar kavalkarars of the Kalakkatu and Nankuneri regions of Tirunelveli. Local big men took on rights of kaval not only in this region, but in much of southern Tamil Nadu. In exchange for their service of protecting the grain, cattle, and other domestic property of village inhabitants they were accorded a share of village production in arrangements similar to those made for patikkaval cuventiram as outlined above (Kadhirvel 1970). Whether these kaval chiefs represented one stage in a developmental cycle of political authority or whether they belonged to a different category altogether, the institutional processes by which protection rights were exchanged for shares of production remained similar and were at the base of local political systems.

We will now look at the particular process by which the Tondaimans acquired local authority in Pudukkottai, first as local heroes, araiyars, and hangers-on of regional courts, and then as little kings who attained the distinction of becoming the grandest and most important Tamil dynasty of the eighteenth century.

# 6

## Tondaiman Raj: 1686–1801

### From ethnohistory to history:
### the Family History of the Tondaimans

The family history of the Tondaimans begins with Indra, king of heaven. When Indra was touring the earth he met a maiden whom he married and who bore him many children.[1] They grew up to be skilled warriors, and one became a king who was the ancestor of the Tondaiman's line. This is a variant of the origin story of the Tondaiman's caste group, the Kallars, which traces the origin of the Kallars as a whole to Indra's seduction of Ahalya, the wife of the sage Gautama (Thurston 1909, 3:62–63). According to traditions recorded in the state Manual, the

[1] There are at least two major sources for my reconstruction of the vamcavali. I have only indirect access to both of them. One is the *Tontaimān Vamcāvali* which was apparently written in Telegu by a court poet named Venkannan about 1750. Radhakrishna Aiyar, who was Principal of H. H. the Raja's College in Pudukkottai in the early twentieth century, used it, in places summarizing it, in his excellent history of Pudukkottai state, as much a tribute to the long and wonderful relations between Britain and Pudukkottai as to "history" itself. I have not been able to find the actual text. However, as Aiyar represents it, it has a great deal in common with (indeed may even be a variant of) the other major source, another Telegu manuscript written by Nayana – or possibly by one Rakunata Pupalan who has compiled a text by Nayana – at an unknown time (Mackenzie MSS, GOML, R. C. no. 483/B/77). This second text was collected in 1805 by Nitala in Tanjore for Colonel Colin Mackenzie's collection of native manuscripts and traditions (see the "Letters and Reports from Native Agents Employed to Collect Books, Traditions, etc. in the various parts of the Peninsula," India Office Library Records, Mackenzie Collections, unbound translations, Class XII). Although I do not read Telegu, I have access to this text through a summary in Mahalingam's index (presuming this to be the same manuscript; see Mahalingam 1976, 334–352) and through a Tamil translation of the Mackenzie text made for me by Professor Sharma of Madurai Kamaraj University. Unlike the text used by Aiyar, the Mackenzie text is not called a vamcavali. It is labelled, perhaps by Mackenzie's men though possibly by the poet, as poems (*ceyyutkal*) about the family (paramparai), the deeds (*natattai*), and the emblems (*virutukal*) of the Tondaiman palaiyakkarar.

Tondaimans were one of many groups of Kallars who lived in the Tirupati hills as skillful hunters and catchers of elephants, skills which they subsequently put to good political use (Ayyar 1940, 755). Though the choice of Indra as chief ancestor was in large part just a reflex of the larger Kallar tradition, a royal line could have no better ancestor than the king of the gods himself.

Sixteen generations later Raya Tondaiman was born. As a palaiyak-karar his domain was one of the seventy-two palaiyapattus of the Madurai Nayaka. He was ranked below Madurai, Tiruccirappalli, and Karunatakam and on a level with other kingdoms such as the Malaiyalam. The family history continues with another list of twelve names, adding the comment that these twelve Tondaimans were the protectors (kavalkarars) of Ampu(l) Natu.[2] After a third list of names, the text again notes that all twelve of these groups (*varicai*) resided together in Karampakuti to defend the Ampu Natu. Karampakuti is the main town of the Kallars of Ampu Natu, the region in the northeastern part of the state which defines and gives the Pudukkottai royal subcaste its name. Thus, from an early period, the royal subcaste was thought to have been divided up into separate groups, each charged with the protection of the entire natu.

This ethnohistorical background is congruent with evidence from various stone and copper plate inscriptions (Ayyar 1940, 756–757). Certain inscriptions refer to the Tondaimans as chiefs (araiyars) who exercised their rights in Ampu Natu. Each of these inscriptions has a slightly different preface. I give here the text of a typical copper plate inscription which prefaces the grant of lands, vessels, cows, sheep, the services of oil pressers, and the right of collecting cesses for the creation of a cattiram by the wife of the king's elder brother. The king was

Raja Sri Raja Vijaya Rakunata Raya Badar [Raja Bahadur] Tondaiman, son of Tirumalaiappa Raya Tondaiman, son of Srimad Tirumalai Raya Tondaman of Kasyapa gotra and Indra kulam, the *aracumakkal* [also called *araiyanmakkal* in other similar copper plates, meaning in both cases the members of a kingly dynasty and therefore kings by inheritance], possessing kani rights in Terkalur in Ampil in Panrisulanatu of Rajendra Cola Valanatu in Raja Raja Valanatu, the lord of Ampilnatu, the lord of the southern cape, the tiger of the tract on the northern bank whose shoulders were adorned by the vagai garland. (Copper plate no. 26, PSM)

The Tondaimans appear here as local araiyars who were given rights of protection (patikkaval) in this region of the south. The protection

---

[2] Ampul Natu is also called Ampil Natu and Alumbil Natu in various sources. Today it is called Ampu Natu.

(kaval) rights first acquired by the araiyars are here represented as kani rights. The right to protect is thus transmuted into the right to use, control, and inherit land and other local productive and symbolic resources. According to other inscriptional sources, the Tondaimans ruled as one of the "five *kuṭi* araiyars" (S. R. Iyer 1916, 118), the chiefs of the five communities. The five "kutis" must refer to the five chief lineages of the Tondaiman's own territorial cluster (*kuppam*) of Ampu Natu Kallars. These five araiyars joined together, creating a dense network of privileged affinal alliance. They ruled over a large and territorially subdivided subcaste. The Tondaimans, referred to in many other inscriptions as the chiefs (araiyars) of Karampakuti, emerged from this early base to become the chiefs of the entire group.

To return to the family history, Paccaiya Tondaiman of the twelfth territorial group (consisting of those settled in Karampakuti) was the father of a boy who was very gifted and became the lord over all of Ampu Natu. When he was ruling.

Sriranka Rayar [the Vijayanaragara king, most likely Sriranka Raya III who ruled from 1639 to 1668] came to Srirankam [the great temple town close to Tiruccirapalli] as a pilgrim. At that time, his elephant ran amuck and ran into the south. The elephant caused great trouble for the people and then went off roaming about in the forest. Paccaiya Tondaiman's son, the head (*talaivar*) of the people of that region, found the elephant coming across his territory. He made an attempt to subdue it. The servants of the king who were in search of the elephant met him and told him that if he could bring the elephant back to its stable the king would receive him. The Tondaiman subdued the elephant and arrived in Srirankam for an audience with the king. The king, Sriranka Raya, was very pleased with the story of the Tondaiman's exploits, and questioned him about his family history. The Tondaiman told him about his family (*paramparai*) and about his rule in Ampu Natu. The Rayar was most pleased. He told the Tondaiman to ask for whatever he wanted. The Tondaiman said that by the Rayar's grace he would like to be given the *kittāp* (honor). The Rayar conferred the honor of using his own title on the Tondaiman, henceforth known as "Raya Tondaiman." He also presented him with many other emblems (virutus), such as a silver lion-faced palanquin, decorated umbrellas, a horse, a drum carried by an elephant, conches, flags marked with the emblems of the Garuda, the lion, and Hanuman, various musical instruments, the use of an incense burner and rosewater sprinkler, gold and silver torches, and finally the *praudha-satkavikriti*, or the privilege of having a book dedicated to him and composed in his praise.

As in the other family histories we have examined, the establishment of an appropriately royal (and divine) genealogy prefaces a story in which the performance of some brave deed on behalf of an overlord leads to the acquisition of great honors. These honors include a variety of royal paraphernalia and privileges as well as a mark of the overlord's own sovereign identity: his title. In this family history, as if to prefigure the possibility of the poem itself, the very right to be textualized in a family history is added to the list of honors. In passages that echo this primordial event, the descendants of this Tondaiman continue to distinguish themselves by performing heroic actions on behalf of the Nayakas of Tanjavur, Madurai, and the Cetupatis of Ramanatapuram, receiving in turn special honors which progressively mark and establish their particular sovereignty. The importance of the primordial transaction is further reflected in the panegyrics of inscriptions which begin with praises of the Vijayanagara kings and then refer to this first Tondaiman not by name but as "Raya Tondaiman, who got the name of Raya from Sriranka Rayar."[3]

Raya Tondaiman had two sons (one version says four, and another adds a daughter named Kattali), the elder of whom was born in 1641 as a result of a boon from Lord Atmanata, after whom he was named. Vijayarakava Nayakar, king of Tanjavur, hearing of the physical strength and courage of these two boys, invited them to come to his court. According to the Mackenzie text, the Nayaka requested them to take seats on a par with him in court, and awarded them honors for their valor in hunting. They were given, among other things, a sword called the *Ramapānam*, dresses, jewels, elephants, and horses. This happy relationship came to an abrupt end when the Nayaka, a Vaisnavite, insisted that the Saivite Tondaimans join him in embracing the Vaisnava sect. The boy left the palace in a hurry. In similar texts, a motif of this sort customarily provides the excuse for a parting of the ways. Usually, however, the conflict develops from an unwanted marriage proposal, though conversion of some sort is often implicit.

The Tondaiman brothers (only the elder one in one version) were then sent gifts and betel leaves from the Cetupati of Ramanatapuram, who

---

[3] See the inscriptions in the Pudukkottai Museum. The inscriptions eulogized the Vijayanagara Rayar as the

owner of vast lands, the conqueror of the Ariyas, he who cannot be described by words, who conquered all lands he saw and did not part with the lands which he conquered, the ruler of the Pantiya territory, he who reestablished the Cola kingdom, the hero of Tontaimantalam, warrior of the Caluva dynasty of Vijayanagara, on whose appearance enemies fled and the captured paid homage, the conqueror of Ceylon, Jaffna, and Kerala, an ardent lover of music, the king of kings, the terror of other kings, the victorious, the most proud, the king who was handsome and pleasant and a devotee of Lord Mallikarajuna, the king who was great and strong, who was a warrior and victorious, the ruler of Anai konti, the king who was like a father to his subjects, the overlord of Kurumpars, the owner of many horses and elephants, the possessor of infantry, the king who was the overlord of the south.

invited them to his court in the south. One text has an intervening episode in which the brothers are appointed the royal protectors (aracukavalkarars) of Tiruccirapalli by the Nayaka kings of Madurai who had by that time moved north to the rock fort at Tiruccirapalli (Ayyar 1940, 759). While in Ramanatapuram, the Tondaimans subdued some rebellious Maravars and a number of neighboring palaiyakkarars, including the Ettaiyapuram chief in Tirunelveli. They also distinguished themselves by taming another elephant which had run amuck, in an episode that distinctly recalls the earlier relation with Vijayanagara. In gratitude, the Cetupati awarded them many honors, including a golden chain. He gave the privilege of using his own name to the elder brother, Rakunata. The name of this Tondaiman, Rakunata Raya, thus inscribed the significant political relations of his past and furnished him with a large part of his own sovereign claim and position.

The Cetupati thereupon took the sister of the Tondaiman, Kattali, as his second wife.[4] The Cetupati had to take a Maravar woman as his first wife, but was then free to marry women from other castes, usually Akampatiyars. Kattali thus could attain no higher position in Ramnad than to be the king's second wife. According to a Jesuit account, she committed sati upon the funeral pyre of the Cetupati after his death in 1710.[5]

Whether as the brideprice, or as a further gift to reward the Tondaiman for his bravery in subduing Maravars, palaiyakkarars, and elephants, the Cetupati presented the Tondaiman with a domain of his own. The Cetupati chose the domain of the Pallavaraiyar, who ruled over a tract of land south of the river Vellar in the southern portion of present day Pudukkottai state. He sent for the Pallavaraiyar to attend him. The Pallavaraiyar who was in worship replied that he could come only after the completion of his worship. Immensely provoked, the Cetupati abused the Pallavaraiyar for thinking more of his devotions than his lord (i.e., himself). Giving his son the state elephant he directed

[4] According to Nelson (1868) and the family traditions of Ilantari Ampalakarar.

[5] According to Nelson, whose account appears to be based on the Jesuit letters of Father Martin of the Madurai Mission:

The second widow was a kalla woman, the sister of the Tondiman Raja of Puthu Kottei, who as has been shown above was appointed by the Kilavan soon after the commencement of his reign. He was present on this occasion, and had to take from his sister the jewels with which she was adorned; and whilst so doing he could not restrain his tears. Throwing himself upon her bosom he embraced her with the tenderest affection; but the unhappy woman appeared to be all unmoved; and after looking for a few moments now at the pile now at the attendants, and crying out now and again O Siva, threw herself on the burning mass with the same boldness as the first (Nelson 1868, 245).

him to go and slay the impious chief. Remembering the way in which puja provided the root metaphor for political relations in the texts we examined earlier, we can see that the proper relationship between chief and king has been reversed. It was therefore terminated. After the Pallavaraiyar was deposed and killed, the Cetupati sent the Tondaiman in a golden palanquin accompanied by one of the former's chiefs to take possession of his new domain. The Cetupati also gave the Tondaiman a sword of honor, again called the Ramapanam, thereby replicating the earlier action of the Tanjavur Nayaka when he gave a sword of the same name to the Tondaiman and his brother. Replication, as we also saw in our analysis of the Uttumalai text, suggests both similarity and difference. A new political relationship has been established, but the symbolic forms parallel precisely those that had previously character-ized earlier political relations. Importantly, however, the new emblem does not supplant the old; to this day both swords are kept in the private puja room of the Tondaiman kings.

The inclusion of the younger brother of Rakunata Tondaiman in some of the texts reflects the separate identity of his collateral line. While Rakunata, already the ruler of northeastern Pudukkottai, established himself in the southern part of the state in the 1680s, his younger brother, Namana Tondaiman, set himself up as a lesser Raja in the northwestern region of the state very soon thereafter. The career of the younger brother was predicated on the absence of primogeniture and the potential divisibility of sovereignty, of which there are a number of examples in south Indian history. Despite the cultural legitimacy of divided rule, collateral relations are almost always fraught with tension, particularly when the stakes are greater than local property-holding rights. At one extreme the triumphant brother avoids such conflict by executing all of his unlucky rivals. Far more often various forms of conciliation create accord, however provisional. In Pudukkottai, where the lineage system has provided many examples of hierarchically shared authority (for example of lineage and subcaste heads) a distinctive form of dual kingship characterized the first half century of sovereignty.

At about the time his elder brother was given the Pallavaraiyar's kingdom Namana Tondaiman (S. R. Aiyar 1916) went off to serve the Nayaka of Madurai by subduing the Nagalapuram palaiyakkarar. The Nayaka rewarded him by publicly gifting him the horse, elephants, and other objects he had captured from the enemy. The Nayaka also granted him the land around Kulattur as a domain. From this time on, Namana called himself Ranka Krishna Muttu Virappa Nayakar after the Nayaka. In the letters of the Madurai Mission of 1690 Namana was referred to as the "little Tondaiman." He was said to maintain a close relationship with the Nayaka of Madurai (S. R. Aiyar 1916, 137). In Mackenzie's list of the seventy-two palaiyakkarars under the Nayaka of Madurai, the chief Tondaiman is mentioned as one of the kumaravar-kkam, and the little Tondaiman of Kulattur is listed as one of the seventy-two chiefs (Taylor 1835).

Relations between the Tondaiman and his young brother appear to have been cordial. The establishment of parallel if asymmetrical rule in two adjacent regions in the late seventeenth century allowed for some division of labor in the process of state formation. During the years in which both collateral branches ruled with some degree of independence, they each increased the areas under their rule. For example, *circa* 1711 Namana defeated a number of local chiefs and annexed their lands, thereby extending his rule to the borders of Tirucci and as far south as Viralimalai. The two Cervaikarars of Antakkulam and Nankupatti and a few other neighboring chiefs were his chief support. Together they continued to expand the area over which they had control. They also brought many of the rough and rebellious Vicenki Nattu Kallars under their rule. In 1713 Namana was succeeded by his son, Ramacami, who was in turn succeeded by his son Namana II in 1736. Although there is some suggestion that Ramacami contested the succession to the main Tondaiman throne in 1730 when Rakunata died, there is no firm evidence that, even if he did so, this action adversely affected relations between the big and little Tondaimans over the long term. After 1750 there is no further mention of the Kulattur branch in our sources. One traditional account claims that in 1750 Namana II attempted to install a son he had through a concubine as his heir. The Cervaikarars under him rebelled, finally marching to Pudukkottai, where they requested the chief Tondaiman to annex the state (S. R. Aiyar 1916, 143–144).

Rakunata Tondaiman, the elder brother and the "big" Tondaiman, assumed rule in Pudukkottai *circa* 1686. He was the builder of a city called Navasalapuram (Mahalingam 1976, 344–352); his first act as ruler was to give large grants of land to his chief supporters. He gave lands to Ilantari Ampalakarar, the Cervaikarar whom the Cetupati had sent to accompany the Tondaiman, and to Nallakutti Valankontan, a supporter who had been faithful servitor from the beginning, following the Tondaiman from Karampakuti to Ramanatapuram.[6] These two

---

[6] My information about Ilantari Ampalkarar comes from two sources: a manuscript prepared by the descendant of the Cervaikarar and put in the hands of Radhakrishna Aiyar, and a statement found in the Inam Settlement Records. According to the latter Tamil text (PFR 1701):

My ancestor was originally a military Sardar under the Cetupati of Ramanata-puram. At that time this kingdom was under the rule of Civanterunta Pallavaraiyar.

men and their descendants remained two of the most important military chieftains, Cervaikarars, of the kingdom. We know from later records that they were given extensive lands in the southern part of the state.[7] Of all the chief Cervaikarars, only Ilantari Ampalakarar never had an affinal alliance with the royal family, by reason of the peculiar circumstances of his recruitment, and the related fact that although he was a Kallar, he belonged to a different subcaste than the Tondaimans.

The name of Pudukkottai for the capital city of the Tondaimans first appeared on a map of 1700 drawn by Bouchet, the Jesuit Missionary of nearby Avur. Pudukkottai means new fort, and although the site had been important in previous times, the town must have been newly fortified in the first ten years or so of Rakunata's reign. The fort walls were later destroyed either by Chanda Sahib, the French backed contender for the Nawabship of Arcot, or by Ananda Rao, the general of Tanjavur, when they captured the town in 1734. From a letter of 1754 written by the Company's agent in Tanjavur, we learn that "Puducota is the principal town. Tondaman resides in it as well as myself. There is neither stone nor mud wall. The place is surrounded by woods and secured by inclosures" (S. R. Aiyar 1916, 145). Through most of the eighteenth century the Tondaimans were referred to in British records by their family name and not by the name of the country. The earliest record I have found which refers to the ruler as the Raja of Pudukkottai dates from 1754.[8] In a Tamil Geography composed in 1740, the town is called the town of the Tondaimans, and is said to be one of the four principal towns of the Pantiyan country, the others being Madurai, Tirunelveli, and Ramanatapuram (*Tēsanirnayam*, GOML).

Despite the obvious neologism of its name, the town had a history of urban settlement and a number of compelling advantages as a capital. Although it lacked a large stone hillock, such as the one which provided the base for the large and formidable fort-town of Tirumayyam sixteen

But when it was annexed to the Cetupati's empire it existed as a small state. In reward for the fine help provided by the ruler of Karampakuti, Rekunata Tondaiman, and his two brothers, the said state was granted to the Tondaiman and he was crowned (pattapicekam). The Sardar was from then on in the service of the Tondaiman. His forefathers participated in several wars and won many battles.

[7] Ilantari Ampalakarar was given lands in Munacantai, near Perunkuti, about six miles due south of the town and about six miles to the northeast of Tirumayyam. Nallakutti Valankontan was given lands in and around Kannanur, located in the southwestern part of the state about five miles due west of Tirumayyam.

[8] Records of Fort St George. Country Correspondence: Public Department, 1754 (Madras: Printed at the Government Press, 1912).

miles to the south, Pudukkottai was located near both the river Vellar and the large Kavinatu tank. Therefore it was close to the areas of greatest local agricultural production. In addition, there was an important rock cut temple, dating back to the seventh century, in Tirukokarnam, just outside Pudukkottai town. This temple was dedicated to Kokarnesa. Some time in the late seventeenth century a shrine to Brihatampal, tutelary goddess of the Tondaimans and subsequently the principal consort of Kokarnesa, was added to the temple, presumably at the behest of the Tondaimans (Ayyar 1944, 981). The town had the advantage of being centrally located, given the ruling family's base in Karampakuti and their new acquisitions in Kulattur to the north and near Tirumayyam to the south. Early on it developed what is to this day one of the most important periodic markets in central Tamil Nadu, providing wholesale bulking facilities, ready transport because of good roads (much better than in the Tanjavur delta), and opportunities for the exchange of foodgrains for locally produced textiles and locally grazed cattle (Gough 1981). The provisioning capacity of the Pudukkottai area, based both on local production and on its regional marketing networks, was one of the most important reasons why this little kingdom became crucial to the military successes of the British in their southern battles throughout the eighteenth century.

Rakunata married at least six wives, all from prominent Ampu Natu families within his own territorial kuppam, thus fortifying his kinship ties with the prominent families among the top five lineages in the Ampu Natu Kallars, and assuring himself of a loyal home base. He and his chiefs and soldiers attained visibility in the late seventeenth century by defeating the Travancore army on behalf of the Madurai Nayakas and joining the Nayaka in campaigns against Mysore, Tanjavur, and Ramanatapuram. The Tondaiman became so powerful that, according to letters from the Madura Jesuit Mission to Rome, "by 1711 the Tondaiman Raja had made himself formidable to the king of Madura himself" (S. R. Aiyar 1916, 151). The military and diplomatic history of this period makes for confusing reading, as the alliances between the principal powers of the Tamil country were temporary and perpetually shifting. The political logic proclaimed by the *Artha Sastra* was prevalent, the enemy of an enemy being an ally. At one time or another, the Tondaimans fought against all of their neighbors, though they remained on good terms with the Madurai Nayakas, and, as the century progressed and the Nayakas suffered eclipse, with the Nawab and the East India Company. The reasons for war ranged from aiding an ally to disputing boundary villages and fields. The family history ends with the Tondaiman being granted an audience by the Nawab. "With kettle drums sounding loudly, he was received by the Nawab, and in his court all the titles won by his forefathers were fully confirmed."

Penetrating behind the confusion of these shifting and frequent military engagements, we can see that during this entire period the Tondaiman was expanding his territory by performing and providing military services for which he was rewarded with villages and land. In addition, the Nayaka permitted him to chip away at the possessions of lesser chiefs on the periphery of his own domain. As the century unfolded so did a steadily escalating process of gift, plunder, and annexation, revealing the historical dynamics of the transition from royal protector (aracu kavalkarar) to little king. During this time the Tondaiman expanded his area of authority well beyond the country of the territorially segmented Kallar clans under his direct control from whence came the nobility and military of his early state. In the first third of the eighteenth century the Tondaiman expanded his rule by conquering lands in the now southwestern portion of the state (around Ponnamaravati, Viraccilai, and Oliyamankalam); by extending his rule to the southeast by building a fort in Mirattunilai in 1710; and by seizing extensive tracts of land around Viralimalai in what is now the northwestern part of the state from a number of small palaiyakkarars. In one case, the inhabitants of a village, half of which belonged to the palaiyakkarar of Marunkapuri and the other to the Tondaiman, wished to be united under one king. The Tondaiman persuaded them to opt for him by giving them substantial concessions in their tax payments (S. R. Aiyar 1916, 155). Other groups on the boundary were persuaded by a mixture of good rhetoric, tempting promises, and mischievous action that the Tondaiman could offer them the best protection. By 1735 the state had essentially expanded to its 1800 boundaries, the only exception being a small parcel of land in the southeastern part of the state. This was gifted later, first by Tanjavur and then, after they rescinded their present, by the British in 1803.

As soon as an area was "conquered," the Tondaiman settled it with his men to provide the protection he promised and collect the dues he demanded. In many cases these protectors were members of the royal subcaste and were called Cervais, a diminutive form of the title of the great Kallar chiefs, or Cervaikarars. On certain occasions these protectors were amarakarars from different Kallar subcastes than the Raja's. While the Raja gave these loyal protectors local lands, rights, and privileges, he also granted large amounts of land to Brahmans whom he invited from the more crowded Kaveri river banks and deltas further north. In addition to granting tax-free brahmadeyams, some to learned Brahmans who distinguished themselves in royal courts during scholastic competitions held on the occasion of the Dasara festival, the Raja endowed temples and feeding houses, or cattirams, throughout the state.

Rakunata Raya Tondaiman died in 1730. He was succeeded by his chosen heir, his eldest grandson Vijaya Rakunata Raya Tondaiman, though not without a bloody succession dispute. The two Cervaikarars whose lands were among the earliest granted by the first Tondaiman Raja were responsible for assuring the succession. One of them, Ilantari, was entitled "Aracu Nilainiruttina Avutaiyappa Cervaikarar," or the Avutaiyappa Cervaikarar who established the Raj. The experience of the succession dispute was probably responsible for one of the first acts of the new Raja, the granting of estates to his two younger brothers, Rajakopala Tondaiman and Tirumalai Tondaiman. A third Kallar chief, Ramacami Rankia Tevar, served with distinction during the succession dispute. Henceforth he too was included in the inner circle of powerful nobles.

The new Raja, like his predecessor, gave large grants of land not only to his brothers, but also to his affines, assorted chiefs, and to Brahmans, temples, and charities. He endowed temples in Viralur, Nankupatti, Vaittikovil (the latter two in places where important Cervaikarars lived and received honors), and built feeding houses in Ammacattiram, Tirukokkarnam (the site of the Raja's tutelary temple), and Pilavituti (the ancestral village of the Tondaiman Rajas) (S. R. Aiyar 1916, 175–179). He also made endowments outside the state, for instance to a monastery in Tirucci and a feeding house in Varanasi. In 1738, the Raja acquired his own guru, or spiritual preceptor.

According to the palace *Hāriyakārar* (the Brahman who works in the palace as the "ritual coordinator" for the Raja and his family), the Tondaiman initially sought instruction from the sage Brahmentira Cataciva because he had no sons. Having taken a vow of silence, the sage instructed the Raja by writing on some sand with a stick. He instructed the Raja to feed one hundred thousand Brahmans and their wives morning and evening for the ten days of Navarattiri, to give each of them four *amman kācu* (coins minted in the state with the image of the goddess Brihatampal, the royal tutelary deity who is worshipped during Navarattiri), and to repeat this every year. As long as his family did this they would flourish and reproduce. The holy sand (*mān piṭi*) on which the saint wrote his words has been preserved. Each year thereafter it was wrapped in a silk towel and taken in procession with full palace honors to the temple along with the Raja.

Navarattiri or Dasara was established as Pudukkottai's central state ritual to emulate Vijayanagara. The performance of Dasara, like the great gift ceremonies earlier, signaled a new form of sovereign achievement and "independence" (however qualified that independence was by the fact that the privilege of performing the ceremony often had to be granted by an overlord). When palaiyakkarar chiefs reached a certain status they sought to perform their own Dasara festival rather than attend the ceremony of an overlord, as we saw in the family history of the Uttumalai Maravar. When Nayakas of Madurai granted the privilege of performing the Navarattiri to the Cetupatis of Ramnad, they gave them one of the greatest gifts in their power. The instructions of a great sage instituted the Navarattiri festival in Pudukkottai, with the blessing that the unbroken performance of the festival would assure the continuation of the royal family. The acquisition of a Brahman spiritual preceptor was in itself a replication of Vijayanagara (and Nayaka) kingship. The performance of the Dasara festival gave kings an opportunity to invite learned Brahman scholars from all over the south to compete for great prizes, and perhaps the chance of being given vast new tax-free lands on which to settle.

The Raja and the kingdom worshipped the tutelary deity of the royal family, Brihatampal, at the Dasara festival, the central events of which were the processions and devotions of the king. The great military chiefs marched behind the Raja displaying their honors and their retinues. Generous gifts were given to learned Brahmans who came from far and near to contest their learning and accept prizes and general largess. Great ritual displays, from buffalo sacrifices to temple dancing, also took place during the course of the festival.[9]

By the middle of the eighteenth century the Kallar Tondaiman chiefs had made the full transition from local chiefs to important regional kings. Though the British still called them "poligars," they had identified themselves in key cultural ways with the codified forms of kingship that they borrowed from Vijayanagara. The Tondaimans had consolidated their rule over an area which extended far beyond their lineage and subcaste base, had acted as one of the chief supporters of the Madura Nayaka, and fought on equal terms with the Rajas of Tanjavur and Ramanatapuram (*inter alia*), had given extensive land rights and political privileges to their own subordinate chiefs, had made gifts to Brahmans, temples, monasteries, and feeding houses, and had taken on a Brahmanic guru at the same time as they had begun to host their own Dasara celebration in an ancient rock cut temple which from this time

---

[9] In the nineteenth and twentieth centuries the festival became highly bureaucratized and increasingly modernized. Detailed schedules for its performance were released each year by the Diwan Peishkar's office.

forward became known by the name of their tutelary goddess, Brihatampal. While they never attained the status of the Madurai Nayakas, by the late 1730s when Queen Minaksi hanged herself leaving local Muslim, Mysorean, and Maratha (and to a far lesser extent European) competitors holding the rope as the only potential trans-regional powers, the Tondaimans were one of the most important of the local "country powers" (as the British called them) in the Tamil region.

All this happened in less than a century on an ecological base that was fragile at best to a caste group whose name was (and continues to be) synonymous with the term "thief" all over the Tamil country. This was no mean accomplishment. The success of the Tondaimans had much to do with their military organization. I will now reconstruct the structure of this organization.

## The structure of the military

Pudukkottai's extraordinary military system made it possible for the Tondaiman to mobilize large numbers of brave Kallar warriors at short notice. At least 8,000 amarakarars, or military retainers, had inam lands in the late eighteenth century. They served under the Jagirdars, Cervaikarars, and other chiefs and generals who were often recruited from outside the state. All of these generals, whether Kallar Cervaikarars or recruited Rajputs, were called, in addition to their other titles, *Sardars*, from the Persian military term for commander then in vogue. Since many of the records for the early eighteenth century have not survived, it is difficult to construct a chronological sense of the operation and makeup of the military system, yet one fact is clear. The number, kind, and background of military generals expanded and diversified as the century progressed.

The great Cervaikarars resided alternately in the fort town of Pudukkottai and on their country estates. On all public occasions – on the battlefield, in court, and in the temple – they were flanked by their retainers and their emblems, all given by the Tondaiman Raja, and all signs of their political position and relations. The number of Cervaikarars varied over time between eight and eighteen. We have already seen how some of the Cervaikarars entered the service of the Tondaiman, providing major military and political assistance at crucial moments in the history of the state. All Kallars, and all but one of the same Kallar subcaste as the Tondaimans, the Cervaikarars often developed or consolidated affinal kinship ties with the Raja after their elevation to this special status.

The Sardars who were not Cervaikarars were also given large grants of land, though the records make it clear that they were not granted the same kinds of privileges and emblems as were the Cervaikarars. Some of the generals, following a Vijayanagara tradition, were Brahmans, for example Annaiyan and Atinarayana Aiyar. Others came from the Maratha army in Tanjavur. Among the most important non-Kallar Sardars were the Lalas (P.F.R. nos. 2589, 2590, 2591) and the Rajput Singhs (no. 3803) from north India, and the Rowths from Andhra (no. 2884), all of whom commanded retinues of soldiers and trained troops in the use of new weapons and techniques. They also arranged for the personal security of the Raja. The single most important non-Kallar family invited to settle in the state was the Owk family from Anagundi (1546). Descendants of the Vijayanagara royal family, they were well versed in the arts of war. Among the contemporary weapons of war were the pike (long hard sticks), the bow and arrow, the sling and the boomarang, bow and clay pellets, swords, spears, daggers, and increasing numbers of matchlocks. Pikes and bow and arrows were used to storm forts; slings and boomerangs to engage the enemy in the thick scrub jungles of the countryside. Some Sardars organized their men into groups which specialized in the use of different weapons. Given the simplicity of most of these weapons, the value of the Kallar soldiers had more to do with their bravery and stealth than their knowledge and use of the most modern military hardware.

The soldiers, or "peons" as they were dubbed in British records, were called amarakarars. Under Vijayanagara, the word *amaram* (which like amarakarar derives from the root amar, meaning war or field of battle) meant (1) land which was granted to military chieftains, and (2) the command of different units, sometimes consisting of one thousand foot soldiers. Some centuries earlier therefore amarakarar meant military chieftain, one whose titles were more usually conjoined with the term nayaka, meaning lord, as in amaranayaka or amaranayankarar. In eighteenth-century Pudukkottai, the amarakarars were not military chieftains at the top of the military structure, but the soldiers at the base of the system.

In a letter written in 1807 to the Governor-General, the British Resident William Blackburne described the military system as he thought it operated in Pudukkottai; in fact, he mistook how amarakarars held land under Cervaikarars for the entire system of military tenure.

The largest portion of the [alienated] land was held by individuals on the condition of leading into the field when called upon a certain number of peons and supporting all their expenses during their service, excepting a very small allowance from the Government as Batta. The advantageous nature of this tenure to the tenants is proved by the punctuality and readiness with which they have fulfilled the conditions of it, even when required to march with their quotas to distant provinces and to serve for many months there at considerable expense. (MPC, 17 October 1854, no. 199)

The land held by the "peons" was land that had initially been granted by the Raja to the Cervaikarars who then gave it to the amarakarars. Blackburne reported that the number of peons in the state was 7,983 in 1807.[10] As many as 8,000 amarakarars were sent off in battle under the Tondaiman or his generals in the second half of the eighteenth century. In 1854 the number of "peons" was estimated at 3,375, and by 1888 there were still 2,635 amarakarars in the state. Although they no longer performed military duties in the nineteenth century, they had been both soldiers and cultivators in the centuries before.

The amount of land given amarakarars, whether by Cervaikarars or directly by the Raja, was usually one *āḷ jīvitam*, which literally means the livelihood (*jīvitam*) of a person (*āḷ*). One al jivitam was 800 *kuḷies* of wet land, or 3,000 kulies of dry land, which is roughly equal to 2.6 acres of wet or 10 acres of dry. According to the records of the Inam Settlement, the amarakarars were given lands for "war service," not as contracts for service but rather as rewards after service in battles.[11] In addition to being granted jivitam lands for subsistence, when the amarakarars actually went to battle they were given batta, a combination of payments in kind (there are some grounds for supposing a relation between the term paddy and batta) and shares of the spoils of victory.

Amarakarars were cosharers (pankali) in patrilineages. Though an inam granted to an amarakarar could only be registered in one name, usually, though not always, that of the eldest son of the previous inamdar, it was "enjoyed" (i.e., its usufruct was shared) by the group of coparceners. For instance, a particular amaram inam entered in one man's name was shared by nine pankalis, all the live males in a patrilineage four generations deep (CFR, no. 122). Sometimes the pankalis divided the inam among themselves; in one case two brothers had divided an original inam of three al jivitams into two separate inams of 1.5 al jivitams each (PFR, no. 1719). Unfortunately, we are not told whether the original inam of three al jivitams had meant that three

---

[10] MPC, 17 October 1854, no. 199 (enclosed letter written on August 21, 1807).

[11] By the nineteenth century at the latest, succession to these jivitam lands, usually by the eldest or most competent (or most influential) son, was predicated on assumptions of service, as fitness for service and loyalty were adduced as important criteria for securing the title. (See Amara Lavana Pativus, in PSO; though some of the original sanads of grants were presented to the Inam Settlement Officers, none of them are extant.)

individuals had to report for military service or not. When the inam was divided the heads of each family or lineage were responsible for providing some service. Although in theory each inam was one al jivitam, in fact there was considerable variation, ranging on the average from a half to five al jivitams. Again, we do not know whether the number of al jivitams indicated the different numbers of pankalis who had to serve the Raja as amarakarars or whether the varying amounts of land represented status differences among amarakarars. These discrepancies in the size of inams could also be caused by the division that inams underwent in the nineteenth century, the bureaucratic handling of these inams after the demise of the military system, and the probability that succession disputes were more difficult to resolve when the military system was replaced by the policing of an unwieldy revenue system.

There were three basic types of amarakarars: *inavari amarakārars*, or amarakarars attached to the Cervaikarars; *jagirdari amarakārars*, or amarakarars attached to one of the two Jagirdars; and *kirāmavari amarakārars*, or amarakarars appointed directly by the Rajas, and usually commanded either by a member of the royal family or a general (Sardar or *Jemadar*). In the Palace lists of 1802, there were 867.12.0[12] al jivitams attached to the Cinnaranmanai Jagir, 2,914.3.2 al jivitams granted through Cervaikarars as inavari, and 3,562 al jivitams granted in villages by the Rajas directly as kiramavari. At the time of the Inam Settlement of 1888, there were 1,373 amarams under Cervaikarars and Jagirdars, and 1,262 amarams under the direct control of the Raja. According to the list in the War Accounts dated 1802, there were 1,017 amarakarars under Jagirdars, 2,914 amarakarars under Cervaikarars, and 3,562 amarakarars under the Raja, totalling 7,693 amarakarars in the state.[13]

### *The Jagirdars*

The two Jagirdars, descendants of the two younger brothers of the second Tondaiman Raja, controlled a large number of amarakarars. Unlike the Cervaikarars, however, they were not allocated a certain number of al jivitams, but were given extensive estates within the little kingdom. Unfortunately, we know little about the early history of the jagirs, aside from their creation in the mid eighteenth century after the succession dispute involving a collateral member of the royal family.

---

[12] The numeration system for the last digits is on a base of 16.
[13] MPC, 17 October 1854, no. 199 (enclosed letter written on August 21, 1807).

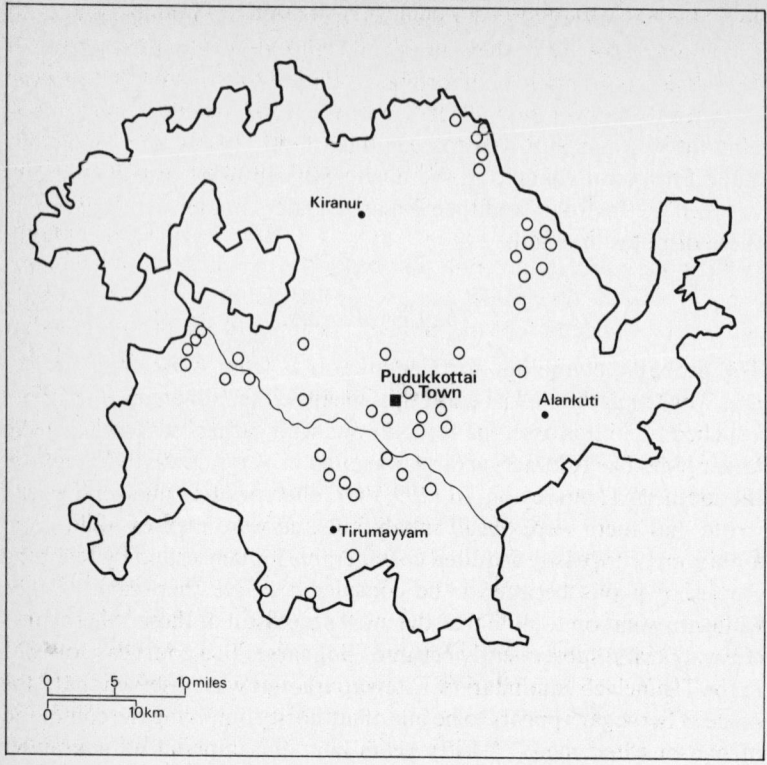

Map 4 Villages of the Cinnaranmanai Jagir, *c.* 1800

For example, it is not clear whether the Jagirdars simply took over control of amarakarars who had previously been under the control of the Raja or whether they started anew by giving grants in their own name to the amarakarars.

The extensive Jagir lands were not concentrated, but widely scattered throughout the state. They consisted of separate and non contiguous villages controlled by the Jagirdar. Map 4 shows the distribution of lands belonging to the Cinnaranmanai Jagir, the only one of the two jagirs to survive until the Inam Settlement of 1888. The Jagirdars themselves did not live on their estates, but in Pudukkottai town in palaces just outside the central fort which enclosed the palace of the Tondaiman Raja. The *Mēlaranmanai* (meaning western palace) Jagir acquired its name because its palace was built just to the west of the main palace; the *Cinnaranmanai* (meaning small palace) because it was smaller than the palace. Thus the Jagirdars maintained, in spite of the

172

considerable resources under their control, both a symbolic and spatial proximity to the Raja, their kinship position reified by other powerful factors determining their subordinate relation to the Raja. All this was intended to support the Jagirdars in considerable style, in some ways as diminutive Rajas, but also to keep them firmly below the Tondaiman Raja. Structural changes in the nineteenth century led to new strains between the Jagirdars and their Raja; in a later chapter we will consider these disputes in detail.

## The Cervaikarars

The probable etymology for Cervaikarar is from *Cēru*, the verb "to join," or "to gather." The word thus means either adherent, one who is attached to, in this case, the Raja, or one who gathers together a group under him. The title Cervaikarar was used in varying ways throughout the southern Tamil region. In 1799, the Collector of Tirunelveli District wrote that there were "head inhabitants, as were men of ability and ambition, [who] easily acquired considerable influence, and by retaining parties of peons became to be considered active sherogars."[14] The Collector went on to note that the most successful of these "sherogars" (Cervaikarars) subsequently became "poligars." In a court case of 1861 in the Tirunelveli zamindari of Ettaiyapuram, it was observed that "the office of Servagar appears to be one of authority, implying the command of one hundred men."[15] Fifty years later the imperial ethnographer Thurston wrote that "Servaikkaran" was the usual caste title for Akampatiyars (Thurston 1909, 3:91). Thurston seems to have acquired this information from Ramnad, where many of the chieftains holding command in the Cetupati's army belonged to this caste. Since Thurston, this title, or its shortened form Cervai, has been treated as a caste title by most observers, the particular caste changes depending on the area under consideration. In Tanjavur the title was predominantly used by Kallars, though several other groups adopted the title as well (Beteille 1971, 80); in Tirunelveli it was used by certain sub-groups of Maravars, in particular the servants of Maravar zamindars;[16] in Ramnad the Akampatiyars have carried the title, though some Maravars also used it (Ramasamy 1972, 142). In South Arcot District the *Pallis* often used it; and in Pudukkottai the title was used mostly though not exclusively by

[14] *Collector's Report Regarding the Tinnevelly Poligars.*

[15] *Vencata Swara Yettiapah Naicker vs. Alagoo Mootoo Servagarer*, Tinnevelly Court Records, Bundle 62, TNA.

[16] Pate (1917), 132–133. Also based on fieldwork conducted in Tirunelveli in 1976.

Kallars, with some Maravars, Akampatiyars, and Valaiyars using it more recently (Ayyar 1938, 106). In the Kattapomman Ballad the title of Cervaikarar was even adopted by a number of Kampalattars, the Telegu, or Vatuka, caste to which Kattapomman belonged.[17]

In late-eighteenth-century Pudukkottai there were between ten and fifteen Vakuppu Cervaikarars, or chieftains.[18] The adoption of the title Cervai by other Kallars could not include the term *vakuppu*, meaning

[17] These examples suggest that titles were used in a number of ways to specify position and to express identity. The twentieth-century understanding of caste titles is based on special conditions in operation in this century, when the nature of the political superstructure has undergone immense change. The relation of caste to politics in the modern world has been articulated by the objectification of the census (Cohn 1970) and by the political mobilization of caste associations (Rudolph and Rudolph 1967, 17–154). The relationship of the political order to the social world was a far more integral one in the eighteenth century; chieftains had titles which simultaneously expressed their relation to the king and their identity with particular groups. Mobility within society was linked to mobility within the political order, with titles expressing relations that were as fluid as the nature of local politics. With the breakdown of this old political order titles have become substantialized in much the same way Dumont has argued has happened to caste groups themselves.

In his work on caste Hocart noticed the fine line between proper names and titles; he gives many examples of the incorporation of titles into personal names and even proposes that perhaps personal names as such cannot be said to have existed until relatively recently (Hocart 1950, 61). Hocart further notices a tendency for a headman's titles to spread to the whole caste (ibid., 59). Tracing this back to the classical period, he writes that, "Not only the king, but members of the royal caste are there called Rajahs" (ibid.). Following Hocart, Dumont notes the replication of titles by the western branch of Kallars, the Pramalai Kallar, who settled to the west of Madurai. According to Dumont, the caste title of Tevar has three usages: first, it refers generally to all the Pramalai Kallars; second, it refers to lineage chiefs; and third, in its most restricted usage, it refers to the headman or chief of the caste (Dumont 1957b, 136–137). Similarly, the title of Cervaikarar seems clearly to have been a political title, variably meaning chief or commander, which spread through the general process of emulation, finally becoming fixed as a caste title for different warrior castes in different regions of southern India.

[18] According to the *Yuttakurippu* (PSO). Unfortunately, none of the records are as clear on this question as one would like. To complicate the matter further, there was only an uncertain fit between the use of titles as political and social indicators. Only one of the Vakappu Cervaikarars actually used Cervaikarar as a title, whereas three of the six Kurikarars did. In addition, many of the amarakarars and uriyakarars used the title Cervaikarar or Cervai. While titles do tend to spread down in the system, as suggested by Dumont and Hocart, they are not always kept as personal titles by those at the top of the relevant unit, suggesting the inexorable tendency of status differentiation.

class or group, since unlike the great chiefs they did not have a group of amarakarars allocated to them. The numerical variation of these Vakuppu Cervaikarars in the palm leaf lists of the eighteenth century may represent actual fluctuations over time; a more probable explanation is the separate listing at different times of certain collateral lines within Cervaikarar families. Little is known about the Cervaikarars whose lines disappeared before the mid nineteenth century, when detailed records about the Cervaikarar families began to be preserved.

Those Cervaikarars whose lines did survive were all Kallars. With one exception they all belonged to the same endogamous subcaste, Ampu Natu, as the Tondaiman family, each having one or more affinal ties (*pantuttuvam*) with the royal family as well. Even the single exception of the Cervaikarar whose service the Ramnad Cetupati had granted to the Tondaiman in the late seventeenth century can be seen as an expression of alliance, both political and social, the first Tondaiman's sister having been given in marriage to the Ramnad Cetupati some years before.

Like Cervaikarars in some respects, the Kurikarars were in fact of far inferior status. The probable etymology of the title was from *kuri*, to aim, the title meaning "marksman." In the late nineteenth century there were six of them. Only a few amarakarars were posted under these Kurikarars, who were all Kallars who did not belong to the royal subcaste. They could not, therefore, establish a marriage alliance with the royal family. The most important of the Kurikarars were the Anjunilaiparru group, who had served the little Tondaiman (of Kulattur) in the early eighteenth century (Ayyar 1944, 1067). All members of the same Unjanai Natu subcaste, the four Anjunilaiparru chiefs had by the time of the Inam Settlement been separate entities for at least fifty to eighty years but might earlier have split off from a single family. After the amalgamation of the Kulattur family in the early eighteenth century these chiefs declined in status from Sardars to Kurikarars. This suggests a combination of social and political reasons for their slide from the highest category of state noble. Importantly, the one Ampu Natu Cervaikarar who had been a chief supporter of the Kulattur family did not slip in status to Kurikarar, but became the third highest among Cervaikarars under the big Tondaiman.[19]

---

[19] However, the possibility that even an Ampu Natu Cervaikarar could decline to the position of Kurikarar was demonstrated again in the final years of the nineteenth century. The first Cervaikarar to support the Pudukkottai Tondaiman in his bid for political authority over an area larger than that of Ampu Natu was the Cervaikarar of Kannanur. But in the late nineteenth century the family had no heirs. A junior branch of the family was allowed to bear this lesser classification and keep some of the family emblems though none of the amarakarars and few of the lands.

The inam lands given to the Cervaikarars consisted of a certain number of al jivitams, which they used to support themselves, their families, and their amarakarars, and retainers who maintained the emblems, honors, and perquisites granted to them by the Tondaiman Raja. The number of al jivitams as well as the number and nature of the honors granted by the Raja provided the basis for ranking the Cervaikarars, a ranking made manifest in public processions such as Dasara. Among the honors were insignias or pirutus which became essential components of the structure of privilege for chiefs. These pirutus were displayed during battles, on ritual occasions, and in public processions such as when the Cervaikarars came to the palace for state occasions like Dasara, the coronation, the Raja's birthday, or the visit of a neighboring Raja or representative of a sovereign overlord. Examples of pirutus were horses, umbrellas, torches, palanquins, drums, swords, spears, shields, and fly whisks. In addition to the honors that were part of the infrastructure of the grants to Cervaikarars, the Raja customarily

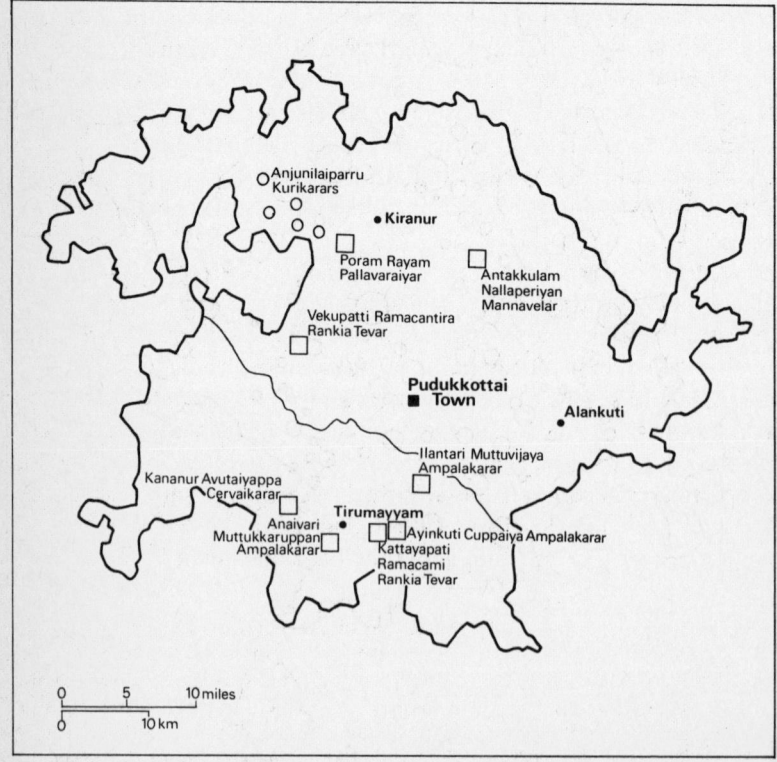

Map 5  Vakuppu Cervaikarars (□) and kurikarars (○), *c.* 1800

176

sent special honors to these chiefs on occasions such as marriages in the family and local ritual performances. For example, Antakkulam Utaiyappa Mannavelar Cervaikarar was sent the following honors from the palace when there were marriages in his family: (1) an elephant with a silver howdah; (2) a horse; (3) a palanquin; (4) a small drum; (5) a big drum; (6) cloth from the palace; (7) a carriage; (8) a carpet; and (9) lustres and gloves (R. 1219/c – 1902, 22 September 1902, PDRO).

The inam lands given to the Cervaikarars lay in peripheral portions of the state which confronted its chief neighboring rivals to the south and northwest. Most of the important Cervaikarars were based in the southern part of the state, where the local population was non-Kallar and where the leading nattars belonged to the same Maravar caste as the rulers of Ramanatapuram and Civakankai, just to the south of Pudukkottai. (Map 5 shows the distribution of Cervaikarars in the nineteenth century. Also see Map 6, which shows the distribution of

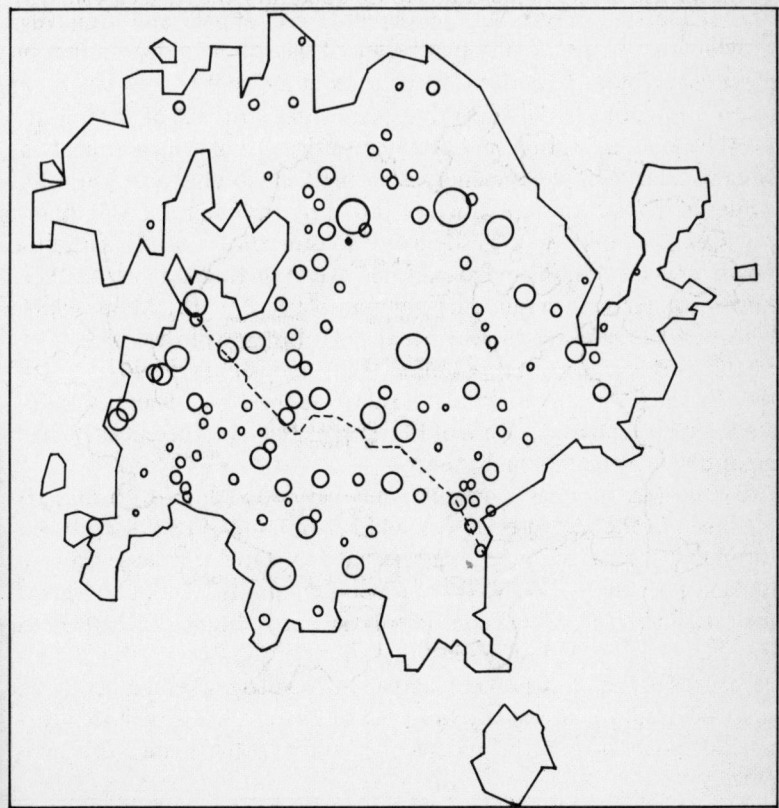

Map 6  Attavanai inams

lands granted as attavanai, a category which includes lands given to Cervaikarars as well as land given to ministers of state and other prominent persons.) All of the major Cervaikarars were placed outside of their own subcaste territories. Among them, only the Antakkulam Cervaikarar was given lands within a Kallar natu, though not his own.

The distribution of Cervaikarars, and Kurikarars, illustrates the political geography and the strategic borders of eighteenth-century Pudukkottai. The four Anjunilaiparru Kurikarars were located in the northwestern part of Kulattur Taluk near the border with Tiruccirappalli, one of the major centers of Nayaka rule. They were flanked by the Pallavarayars. The Antakkulam Cervaikarars were situated northeast of Pudukkottai, toward Tanjavur. Five Cervaikarars were placed in Tirumayyam Taluk near the southern border with Ramnad, with whom Pudukkottai was not always allied despite Ramnad's early role in the formation of the state. The Kallar Natus were distributed relatively evenly through Kulattur and Alankuti Taluks in the northern half of the state where they bordered Tiruccirappalli and Tanjavur, providing a band of loyalty that balanced the southern distribution of most of the more powerful Cervaikarars in the south.

The geography of the state presents us with a structure of "conquest" overlaying the territorially segmented settlement of Kallar subcastes. But this was no simple segmentary state in the classical African sense, for while the Kallar kinship structure provided an important base many political mechanisms were established to centralize control, neutralize possible segmentation, and extend rule over non-Kallar areas. Neither, however, are the Cervaikarars comparable to Mughal Mansabdars, whose territories were frequently changed in order to prevent them from establishing local bases of opposition. The Cervaikarars ruled as chiefs of the royal subcaste, but they did not rule from their own subcaste base of strength, particularly in areas of Maravar settlement where Kallars had great difficulty maintaining control.

By the late nineteenth century only seven Vakuppu Cervaikarars remained in the record books. A number of families had disappeared through lack of heirs; others had declined in status. Of the seven who remained, two were brothers who constantly quarreled about which of their families should be considered the main branch. Katayapatti Ramacami Tevar had the undisputed status of top Cervaikarar. As his name tells us, he was based in Katayapatti, a village several miles to the east of Tirumayyam. Exactly when the lands were given to his family is unclear; according to the statement he gave to the Inam Settlement officers:

the present inamdar says that six persons of the name Ramacami Rankia Tevar enjoyed the inam in succession before him, and that they had participated in and won many battles against the enemies of the state and the Nawab. One of his forefathers, Ramacami Rankia Tevar, served as the chief commander (*piratāna cēnātipati*) in the Vallam war and the Kilanilai war. In reward for these military services (*ottācai*) rendered by his forefathers and on account of his pantuttuvam between the royal family and the inamdar's family the inam lands were liberally granted to them with honors (*mariyātai*) second only to the royal family. (PFR, no. 823)

The Vallam War, fought against the Raja of Tanjavur, took place in 1771; the capture of Kilanilai in 1781. The first Cervaikarar of this line was active from the 1760s at the latest.[20]

The Katayapatti Cervaikarar's contention that he was ranked first among all the Cervaikarars is borne out by other evidence. In the 1888 Settlement registry his emblems were listed as the horse, an umbrella, torches, a palanquin, a chowrie (*cavari*), a white cloth, a wind instrument (*ūtari*), and a scroll with a seal (*curuṭṭi*); his weapons were the spear and a fan made out of an elephant's tail (*tālavattam*). In a protocol list of 1934 prepared by the Pudukkottai Darbar Office (R. Dis. no. 375, 1934, PDRO) he was listed first among Sardars and was said to have the following emblems: horse, umbrella, double torch, palanquin, drum, page boy, elephant seat (*howdah*), a scroll with a seal, a cloth or shawl, and a chowrie.

The Cervaikarar stressed in the Inam records that the Tondaiman Rajas gave his ancestors these emblems and honors together with the inam. These emblems were inherited along with the inam lands and the amarakarars attached to the Cervaikarar from generation to gener-ation. The "land records" faithfully preserved the list of emblems with the same care and specificity as they recorded the amount and kind of land held by the chiefs.

The Inam Settlement officers used either *cēvakam* or *ūṛiyam* as terms for "service"; the Cervaikarar used ottacai. According to the Madras Lexicon, ottacai means aid, help, or assistance. Ottacai does not mean service as much as it means favors, lending a hand, and even companionship. Ottacai also means attendance, as at the wedding of a kinsman. By using this word, the Cervaikarar claimed that his relationship to the Raja was defined both by kinship and by the actions performed by the Cervaikarar's family on behalf of the Raja's ancestors on the battlefields of old. Service was not an isolated fact, or an obligation, but rather an implicit aspect of a relationship. In a later

---

[20] This entry is typical of the statements made by Cervaikarars in the Inam Settlement Records.

chapter we will explore the important contrast between terms and meanings as employed by the chiefs and the settlement officers, as well as the need to interpret all lexical choices in the context of the discursive framework of the settlement itself.

Second in rank (according to the 1934 protocol list) among the Cervaikarars was Ilantari Muttuvijaya Ampalakarar. The lands granted this Cervaikarar were in Munacantai, near Perunkuti, six miles due south of Pudukkottai town and the same distance to the northeast of Tirumayyam. The Ampalakarar was the only Cervaikarar not of the Ampu Natu subcaste. He was the one whose ancestor was "granted" to the Tondaiman by the Cetupati of Ramnad. The Inam Registry (PFR no. 1701) provides detailed information about the disposition of al jivitams and amarakarars under this Cervaikarar.

There are one hundred and thirty-two amarakarars under him, who hold jivitams at Vattakkottai and at Potiyam Vayal and Putu Vayal located next to Munacantai; of these one hundred and thirty-two amarakarars, one-third render personal service to him (or, do his own work, *tan conta vēlai*) and the other two-thirds render service (cevakam) to the Government (*Carkar*). The amarakarars in his personal service include six attendants (*jokkalum*), two umbrella holders, two torch bearers, two stable boys, one drummer, and other holders of pirutus. His forefathers were granted pirutus such as a palanquin, an umbrella, double torches, a drum, a sword, a spear, a shield, a chowrie, and an elephant seat, as well as other musical instruments; of these, the spear, the sword, the shield, and the drum were won by his forefathers in the Kiranilai war, and these have continued to be enjoyed by them as allowed by the Government. Whenever the above weapons had to be used some of his amarakarars were employed for this service.

In 1888 there were one hundred and thirty-two amarakarars under this Cervaikarar. One-third of them were assigned to the personal service of the Cervaikarar, among whom were the bearers and maintainers of his pirutus, or his emblems and appurtenances: stable boys to tend the processional horse, a drummer to herald the march of the chief, torch bearers, umbrella holders, and so on. The pirutus themselves were listed in detail and were included in all the previous records as well as the present one. They were as important a part of the inheritance of the inam as the land itself. The pirutus were emblems of royalty and worship, as well as actual weapons used in battle. Once again the entry notes specifically that these emblems were granted to the ancestors of the Cervaikarar by the Raja; certain of the emblems were said to be won in the Kilanilai war, which means either that they were appropriated from the enemy as a part of the victory, or that they were granted to the Cervaikarar after the war to commemorate his heroic actions in the war, or both. In addition, the Cervaikarar stated that "one umpalam of fifty al jivitams has been enjoyed by every inamdar of his family in reward for their acts done on behalf of the Raja. It was registered in the diary as a palanquin umpalam and it was granted as such." The palanquin *umpalam* (a sub-category of inam land) was land that was specifically granted for the support of the Cervaikarar's rank and honor.

Antakkulam Nallaperiyan Manna Velar was third among the Sardars. This Cervaikarar stated that his forefathers had been given pirutus such as a palanquin, umbrella, double torches, chowrie, rights to keep various palace attendants including *aṭappakārars* (a server of betel nut) and uriyakarars, and that he continued to enjoy them. He claimed that he was one of the specially honored (*kavuravam*) Vakuppu Cervaikarars to whom the Raja had given special honors. He had seventy amarakarars in his group who served under him and under the Cirkar. The word the Cervaikarar used for this service was cevakam, not ottacai, thus clearly differentiating his own relationship to the Raja from that of his amarakarars to him.

The entry (PFR no. 691) regarding another Cervaikarar (of Kannanur) gives us further information about the way in which the "honors establishment" of a Cervaikarar was organized. The Cervaikarar's request of twenty-five al jivitams for the support of his personal attendants was considered extravagant by the settlement officers. They did not include a breakdown of this request in the registry, listing instead the compromise they allowed. However, to give some idea of how al jivitams were allocated for the amarakarars who were part of the honors establishment of the Cervaikarars, I reproduce this list here.

| | |
|---|---|
| 10 palanquin bearers | 10 al jivitams |
| 1 horse man | 1 |
| 2 torch bearers | 2 |
| 1 umbrella bearer | 1 |
| 2 chowrie bearers | 2 |
| 1 elephant keeper | 1 |
| 1 drummer | 1 |
| 2 pages | 2 |
| Total | 20 |

Again we see that emblems were supported by al jivitam lands. Half the total number of retainers and by far the largest single group were the ten bearers of the palanquin in which the Cervaikarar and members of his family were taken to the central palace and on procession. The other half were responsible for embellishing the procession by leading a horse and an elephant, holding an umbrella, waving flywhisks, and beating a drum. These were all symbols of royalty, metonymic of the royalty of the Pudukkottai Tondaiman in that they were given to the Cervaikarar by the Raja and in that they represented part of the totality of the emblems which the Raja himself possessed. The Cervaikarars could not attend the palace without their pirutus.

The position of Cervaikarar was in theory impartible, though as we have already noted this was often contested. The position of the Cervaikarar, like that of the king, was sufficiently important that the title and the inam could (or rather should) not be divided. Cervaikarar lines were not always kept from dividing; in one case the division of an inam led to two brothers both becoming Vakuppu Cervaikarars, though the nature of their relationship and "independent status" never became fully unambiguous. However, succession was usually unilineal, going to the eldest son, though there was no absolute rule of primogeniture. If there was no suitable heir, succession went to a collateral member of the patrilineage, often through adoption.[21]

[21]  Even when impartibility of the "office" (i.e., its responsibilities and basic perquisites, including the al jivitams for inavari amarakarars and for personal maintenance and honors) was rigorously maintained, there was still the problem of looking after the other members of the family, in particular the sons who were excluded from office. In addition to explaining how this particular family failed to keep the Cervai inam through the failure to have heirs, this record (PFR, 691) shows that there were subsidiary inams specifically for the support of collateral branches of the Cervaikarar's family. A portion of the Cervaikarar's estate, called the *ulkatai lāvanam*, was set apart for the maintenance of the second son, when there was one, and sometimes for other collateral kin as well. Succession to the ulkatai lavanam, at least in the initial stages of its transfer, was determined by relation to the incumbent Cervaikarar rather than by descent; when there were two potential heirs for Cervaikarar the unsuccessful one was accorded the ulkatai lavanam over the claims of the descendant of the previous holder. In this particular case the successors of the third son split off completely from the Cervaikarar's family after two generations, in large part because of the limits imposed on the stirpital sharing of the perquisites of the Cervaikarar estate. There was no hard and fast rule that only one collateral relation could be supported by the Cervai lavanam itself – and some Cervaikarar families supported a very wide range of relations – but the institutionalization of collateral support (at least up to certain limits) reveals the tension between the state's political imperative to maintain single and therefore powerful Cervaikarar lines and the socially customary sharing of property rights within the patri-lineage. Among families holding amaram inams, it was customary for pankalis to share rights to land for an average of three to four generations.

In some other entries we learn a little more about the relations between the Cervaikarars and the amarakarars under them. One Inam registry reveals that the Cervaikarar transferred some of his amarakarars from his lands in one area to those in another. This was common practice in the nineteenth century, and if anything was more common in the preceding centuries.[22] As a local official wrote in another context,

the other Vakuppu Cervaikarars have been allotted lands on the basis of the relationship with the amarakarars. The Cervaikarars are empowered to appoint, dismiss, or to transfer the amarakarars under them and to get the services of these amarakarars included in their vakuppu. So what the Cervaikarars do can be considered as the final action in the matter.

This is the clearest statement I found about the rights of Cervaikarars with respect to the amarakarars under them.

Although the inavari amarakarars were appointed and controlled by the Vakuppu Cervaikarars, the ultimate authority for all amarakarars was the Raja. Whether or not this authority was actively exercised in the eighteenth century, in the nineteenth century the Raja did exert his control. Evidence for this comes from the nineteenth-century amaram

---

[22] That the settlement officers disallowed and reversed his actions does not indicate that the Cervaikarars did not have a major voice in deciding what particular lands would be held by individual amarakarars, whose rights were not to fixed land parcels but rather to a share of land that was the equivalent of the amount fixed for the subsistence of one family.

A similar case involved the Cervaikarar Poram Pallavaraiyar. Years before, citing his desire to consolidate his holdings, the Cervaikarar had transferred some of his amarakarars to lands closer to his holdings than those on which they had initially been settled. I suspect that the reason for the initial transfer was to gain further control over the amarakarars, far more important than the land itself. By the end of the nineteenth century, the Cervaikarar wished to reclaim his lands, his prime consideration now being their newly created "market value." So he requested that the amarakarars be moved back to their original lands during the settlement on the pretext that some of their present lands were unfit for cultivation because of river erosion.

The Cervaikarar's request was denied by the settlement officers, who cited as precedent the case of the Ilantari Cervaikarar, in which the amarakarars had been favored in a similar dispute. Nonetheless, records which came to light during the course of this latter dispute suggest strongly that in all previous cases the wishes and rights of the Cervaikarars had been sustained. For example, in one case during the settlement when a group of amarakarars demanded the right of occupancy over a particular piece of land (*kutikāni*) the Cirkar clearly conferred this right on the Cervaikarar, not on the amarakarars. And in most cases in the nineteenth century, amarakarars were simply converted into the tenants of the Cervaikarars.

succession registers, called *Amara Lavana Pativu*, which had been kept for many years independently of the Inam Settlement. These registers, maintained by the Raja's officers, recorded the procedures followed and the decisions made concerning the succession of amaram inams. On the death of an amarakarar, the jivitams enjoyed by him were placed under "attachment" by the state until a suitable heir was found. A typical entry goes as follows:

One Ataikkan Kalati, son of Pocala Ataikkan, belonging to the Ponnamaravati Amaram of Vellaiyan Kalati, son of Rakkan, is reported to have died on the 5th of Tai and that he has been enjoying 1.0.0 al jivitams and that the lavana diary has to be transferred in the name of Pocalan, the elder of the two sons. It is also reported that the diary has been transferred in the name of Pocalan on the 10th of Pankuni. The lands may be placed under attachment. It should also be reported with proofs, to show that he is the son of the deceased inamdar. The date of the death of the inamdar should also be reported after proper inquiry. (Entry of 27 March 1860)

After a proper investigation, this inam was transferred as requested. I have found another case where an inavari amarakarar who held 2.8.0 al jivitams under Kannanur Cervaikarar was dismissed by the Cervaikarar on the grounds that he participated in a conspiracy, apparently the rebellion of 1854. The amarakarar petitioned the Raja that his case be reconsidered, and was subsequently reinstated by the king's officers. The record entry reads:

But there are no records to prove that he was a participant of the said conspiracy. The appellant has presented a petition in the year Ananta (1854) to the Cirkar (Government) but it has not been considered until now (1861). There are no records to show that the appellant was involved in the conspiracy. It is therefore believed that the Cervaikarar dismissed him out of ill feeling and assumed his jivitams. Hence the Cervaikarar's case is dismissed and the jivitams are hereby restored to the petitioner – signed, the Cirkele (Diwan), and the Karbar, dated 12 August 1861.

Unfortunately, it is impossible to know whether or not such an action would have been taken in the eighteenth century. By the nineteenth century the centralization of the state's bureaucratic organization had advanced to a point that the Raja (and as the century elapsed increasingly the Diwan, who was appointed as chief administrator by the Raja and the British together) regularly made these kinds of decisions. Whether this case reveals more about the old or the colonial regime, note that the grounds for dismissal by the Cervaikarar were not the nonperformance of service, but participation in a rebellion, in which the Kannanur Cervaikarar himself was, after initially joining in the chorus of complaints that constituted the beginning of the rebellion, one of the staunchest supporters of the Raja. I have found no instances where an amarakarar was dismissed by the Raja against the wishes of the Cervaikarar.

### The Amarakarars

Inavari amarakarars were those commanded by the Cervaikarars, strictly speaking the only amarakarars who had their "beneficial tenure" constituted in the way described above by Blackburne. The word inavari means patrilineage, *inam* (not to be confused with *inām*) meaning kinship in general and agnatic kinship in a more marked sense, and *vari* meaning line. The use of the term inavari thus suggests an agnatic kinship tie between the retainers and the particular chieftains under whom they served. Unfortunately the records do not provide sufficient information to determine whether or not this was the case. However, I discovered from interviews that members of the royal Kallar subcaste were rarely engaged as amarakarars because of the tremendous status differential between Cervaikarars and their amarakarars. Members of the royal subcaste attained their position in the little kingdom just by being associated with the Raja as *rājapantus* (royal relations). Other Kallars, including many from the lowest subcaste, comprised the bulk of the amarakarar group, and there were non-Kallars as well, including some Valaiyars.

How, then, can we account for the term inavari? What seems most likely is that the relationship between the Cervaikarar and his attendant amarakarars was so close, despite its hierarchical nature, and involved such a high degree of mutual responsibility and obligation, that this term was used to express the vertical kinship quality of the relationship. As we saw with the term kumaravarakam, the "group of sons" of the Madurai Nayaka who may or may not have had affinal ties with the Nayaka, "kinship" terms play an important role in "political" relations. Kinship terms not only specify varying genealogical relations, but signify and constitute domains of powerful intimacy and connection. In this particular context, it is possible that inavari amarakarars were recruited by lineage, but it is doubtful that this, as also the patrilineal nature of amaram holding, would have differentiated inavari from other types of amarakarars.[23] Rather, inavari amarakarars were particularly closely connected to their Cervaikarar chiefs, whom they served in war and at

[23] Succession registers called *Amara Lavana Pativu* were kept in the PSO, and I used these records to formulate this interpretation.

home, in domestic services, public rituals, periodic darbars, and processions.

Aside from the Jagirdari amarakarars, about whom we know very little, the other category of amarakarars was kiramavari. These were amarakarars who lived in villages (kiramam) throughout the state and who were appointed and controlled by the Raja and his officers, and by chieftains and generals who were not Vakuppu Cervaikarars. In 1802 there were 3,562 such amarakarars listed, located in twenty-five major areas in the state. These areas correspond closely to the areas in which there were amarakarars still on inam land in the late nineteenth century when the Inam Settlement was undertaken, at which time there were 2,635 amarakarars in all. Map 7 shows the location of kiramavari amarakarars in the state in 1802.

On the basis of surviving records it is impossible to break the 1888

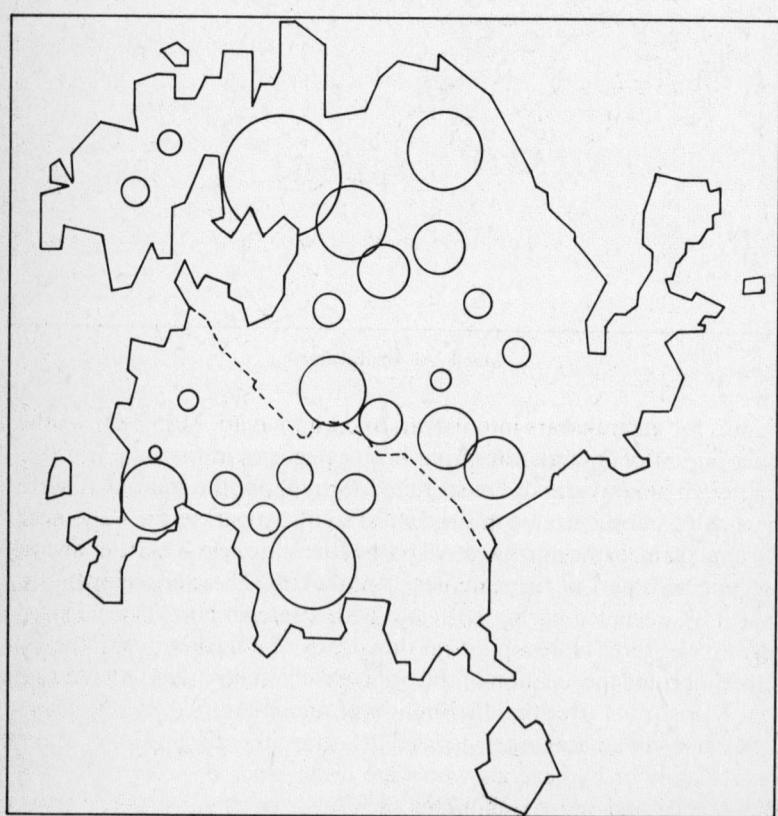

Map 7 Kiramavari amarakarars

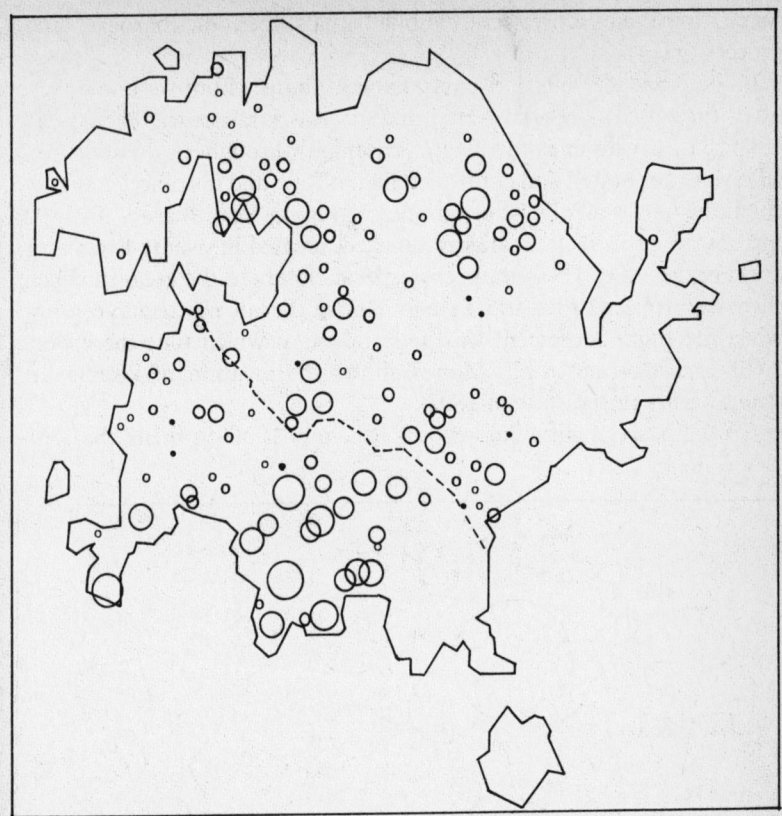

Map 8 All amarakarars

figures for amarakarars into inavari and kiramavari. Map 8 shows the distribution of amarakarars from both categories in the state in 1888. Although amarakarars were scattered throughout the state, they were particularly concentrated in the central southern part of the state, near Tirumayyam, in the northwestern part of the state near Kolattur, and in the northern part of the state near Antakulam. These concentrations, which as we noted earlier correlate with strategic borders defending against the three closest political threats, can be further illustrated by superimposing the location of the principal chieftains, the Cervaikarars and Kurikarars, over the distribution of amarakarars (see Map 9).

Kiramavari amarakarars were led in battle either by a member of the royal family or by generals who were given lands only for their own subsistence and not to maintain their own potential armies. These "officers" were granted inam lands under either the *attavanai* or

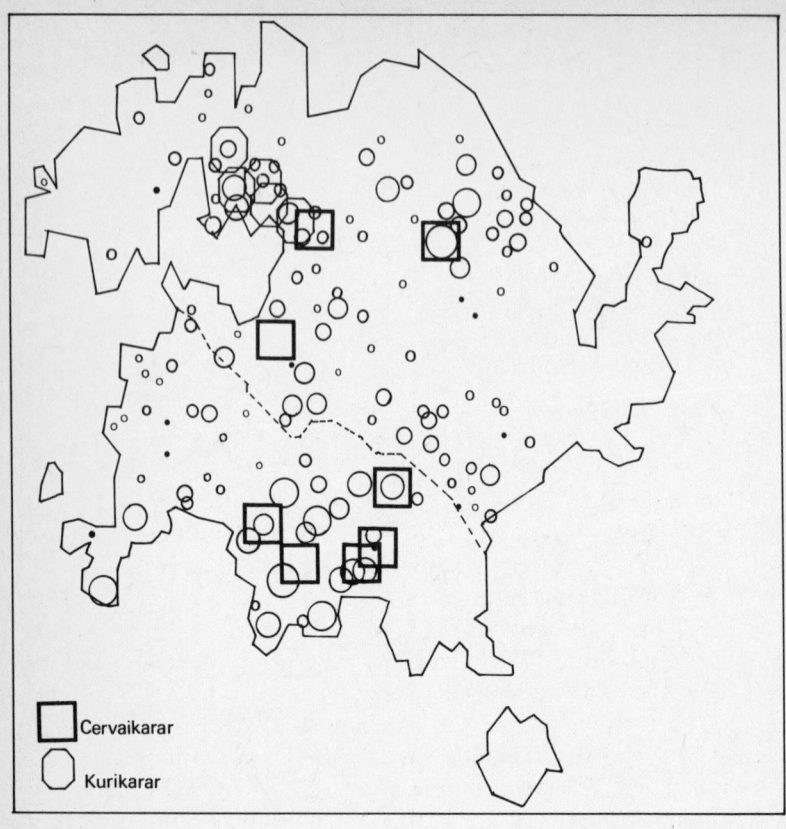

Map 9 Cervaikarars, Kurikarars, and amarakarars

*rokkakuttikai* headings (also known as *cippanti ijāra*). The distribution of this type of inam, which includes grants to other military personnel, and to certain members of the Rajakkal, Nayakkar, and Muslim communities who served in the palace, is shown in Map 10. A relatively large number of these particular inams are in Ampu Natu. In addition to the Vakuppu Cervaikarars perhaps lesser relations of the royal sub-caste were made generals and were thus supported. The largest number of inams in this category are in and around Tirumayyam, the site of the largest fort in the state.

The maniyam grants given to many Ampu Natu Kallars to settle in various parts of the state were also listed in the Settlement records under the heading amaram. However, these members of the royal subcaste were not in any formal sense amarakarars, nor were they called such, adopting instead the title of Cervaikarar, or Cervai. Unlike the Vakuppu

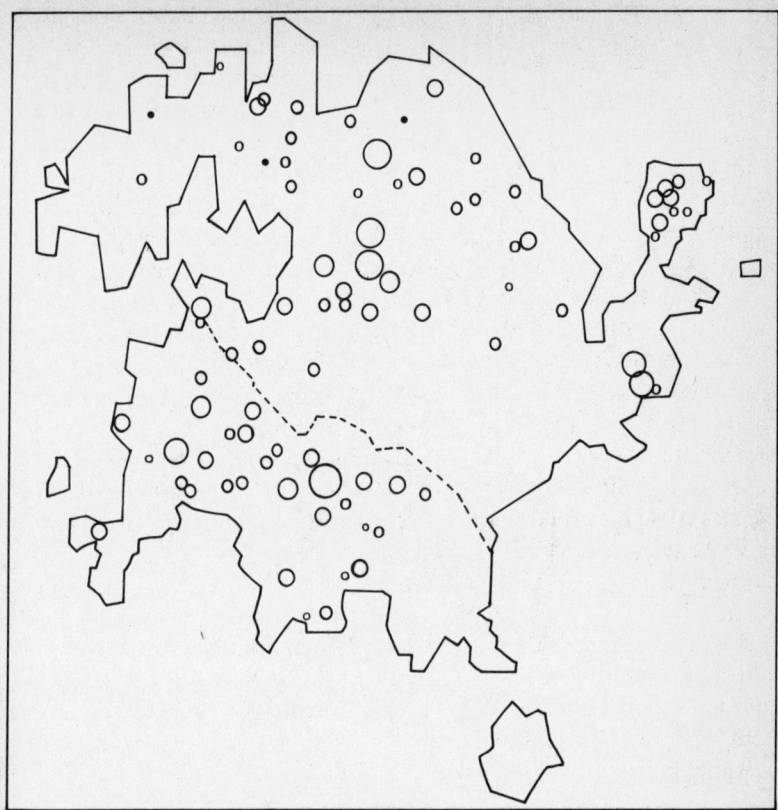

Map 10 Rokkakuttikai inams

Cervaikarars, however, their inams did not include al jivitams for amarakarar retainers under them. Nor is there any clear record of their participating in any important way either in state festivals or in battles outside the state, though such participation was certainly possible, and at times probable. The inams of these Cervais were spread throughout the state, particularly in areas outside of Kallar settlement, for these AN Kallars were originally resettled to keep a watch on troublespots and provide a constant royal presence all over the state. This royal presence was most forcefully dramatized during village festivals when the Cervais ritually enacted the king's role by accepting temple honors on his behalf.

### The Uriyakarars

In addition to the retainers and nobles mentioned above there were the palace guards, or uriyakarars. Although they could be mobilized for

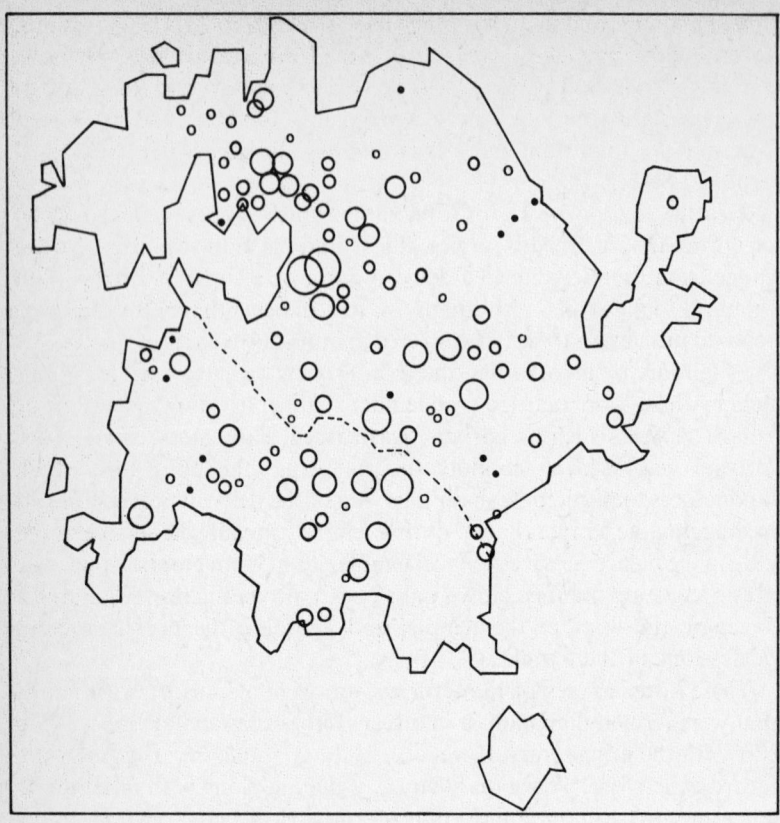

Map 11 Uriyakarars

battle, for the most part they stayed in the capital protecting the Raja and his palace. In 1802 there were 1,518 uriyakarars under twenty-eight uriyakarar commanders who directly served the Raja, and another 174 uriyakarars under the Cinnaranmanai Jagirdar. Map 11 shows the distribution of uriyakarar landholdings throughout the state.

Besides guarding the palace, uriyakarars escorted the Raja and the royal family when on tour, carried their palanquins, held their umbrellas and royal emblems, served betel nut to the Raja and to his guests, performed sundry services in the palace, and beat the forests for the Raja's hunt. There was considerable range in status among uriyakarars, from head palace guards to palace servants. Of the twenty-eight uriyakarar chiefs listed in the 1802 palace list, Uriyan Murukaiyan Cervaikaran held 477 al jivitams, Venkannan Cervai held 254 al jivitams, Arumukam Cervai held 119, the next eight held between 35 and

100 al jivitams, and the remaining sixteen held from 2 to 17 al jivitams. Interestingly, only the three above-named uriyakarars had the suffix Cervaikarar or Cervai. Some of the lesser uriyakarars had titles such as *Aṭappaṇ*, signifying that they served betel to the Raja and his guests. This was an important duty as it involved being in effect a kind of protocol officer.

Uriyam, the root word for uriyakarar (which simply means one who performs uriyam), means service; the definitions in the Madras Lexicon range from "service due to a deity, a guru, or a superior by birth" to "natural obligation." Although in the nineteenth century uriyam referred principally to service rendered in or for the palaces of the Raja or the Jagirdars by uriyakarars, the term uriyam was also used for inams held by those who guarded crops under share cultivation, as well as by village servants such as barbers, washermen, carpenters, and smiths. Uriyam was used to connote the following: the obligation of all landholders to participate in the carrying of the deity in procession and in dragging the temple chariot during temple festivals; the service of the king in the palace; services to local temples, as in inam grants for playing music, enacting dramas, blowing the conch, providing flower garlands, sweeping the floor of the temple, and guarding the provisions and possessions of the temple.

These latter usages of the term uriyam were associated with inams that were termed umpalam or maniyam rather than jivitam, as was the case with the uriyakarars. If we look at the conjunction of terms in the records, therefore, we see that the use of jivitam along with other terms connotes service in the context of protection. Even here, however, terms overlap in confusing ways. Some of the Cervaikarars and Sardars were given lands called attavanai umpalam, even though the units of land granted were specified in al jivitams. Terms cannot be taken to signify fixed meanings, but must be seen both in relation to other terms as well as other contextual features. While uriyam was a term of general application, the units in which land was measured and specified (jivitam, umpalam, maniyam, etc.) provided a classificatory taxonomy of sorts to separate the personal retainers and nobles of the kingdom engaged in various forms of protection from other kinds of state and village servants.

To write about all these groups under the simple rubric of a "military system" is, of course, to do violence to the complexity and cultural constructions of the system. As we have seen, political relations involved kinship relations and kinship tropes, emblems, and honors, titles and status categories, and variable forms of control over land, labor, loyalty, largess and symbolic capital that are difficult to separate. But the capacity of these diffuse relations to produce military success was consistently impressive, and explains much about why Pudukkottai continued to thrive in the late eighteenth century, when, if anything, the stakes were even higher than they had been before.

For, as successful as the Tondaimans had been in the early eighteenth century, they went on to outdo themselves in the second half of the century. All around them their rival "country powers" dropped out of the limelight one by one because of political ambition and intrigue that miscued. The Tondaimans survived as the only non-tribute paying local kings in the Tamil country, becoming the only Tamil princes of the colonial Raj.

## Country powers in the Carnatic, 1750-1801

From the beginning you have been faithful and attached to the English and have supported the interests of the Nabob [Nawab]. The engagement of cowle is therefore given to you. From henceforth you and we are firmly united and we will support and protect you in all time to come. Your aid also must be given to us whenever we require it. Your people shall receive batta [military pay]. If any enemy should attempt to molest you we will immediately send troops and arms and ammunition to your assistance. In the event of any great reverse, you shall always find a secure refuge in Devanampattam or Madras. The titles of honors and the Jageers which may be conferred on you by the Nabob shall be confirmed and secured to you.
letter from George Pigot, Governor of Ft St George, to the Zemindar of Trichinopoly (the Tondaiman), September 28, 1755.

The mid eighteenth century saw the escalation of the terms and framework of conflict in the Carnatic, reaching a new peak of activity in the war of Carnatic succession. The great Nizam-ul-mulk of Hyderabad, Subahdar of the Mughals and the undisputed Muslim sovereign of the south, appointed a new Nawab in Arcot in 1744, continuing to claim the undivided loyalty of his southern viceroy until his death in 1748. Upon the Nizam's death there was a succession dispute between Nazir Jung, the Nizam's son, and Muzaffar Jung, the son of a deceased elder brother, As we have seen, succession often proved the weak point of dynastic rule, Hindu or Muslim. Disputes over succession were often moments for the forging of new alliances and the making of extravagant promises. But now for the first time the English and the French, bitter rivals in trade as well as in the war of Austrian Succession, became involved in the bidding war. Rival contenders fought first for the position of Nizam, then for the position of Nawab, with the English and the French on opposing sides, and the Mysoreans and the Marathas occasionally entering the fray.

The Tondaimans were active participants in these struggles, aiding both the Nawab (Muhammed Ali) and the English by sending troops and a regular stream of provisions. The importance of the fort at Trichinopoly (Tiruccirapalli) and its proximity to Pudukkottai made the Tondaiman's support both possible and necessary. The Tondaiman consistently offered support during the second half of the century, unlike Tanjavur, which was only an intermittent ally though it had far more in the way of provisions. In 1751 the Tondaiman sent a force of 400 cavalry and 3,000 Kallar infantry to Trichinopoly. Hardly a year went by over the next half-century when the Tondaiman did not send at least one similar contingent in support of one of his allies. A combination of British records and the palm leaf manuscript "War accounts" (*yuttakurippu*) which I found in the Palace Records reveal a sense of the amazing frequency and large numbers involved. Perhaps the largest number of soldiers ever sent by the Tondaiman was in 1762, when 8,000 Kallars and 300 horse were sent under Sardar Cataciva Rao to aid the Nawab and the British in a series of battles commanded by Major Preston against the rebel Yusuf Khan (Hill). An equally large contingent was sent in 1773 against Tanjavur under the above mentioned Sardar and the crown prince Rajakopala Tondaiman. The next years saw similiar contingents setting out to help fight against Ramanatapuram, Civakankai, the Dutch at Nakapattinam, Haidar Ali and Tipu Sultan. In the last years of the eighteenth century they fought against the rebel palaiyakkarars of Ariyalur, Utaiyarpalaiyam and Turaiyur. The final military engagements in which troops from Pudukkottai participated were the third and fourth Anglo Mysore Wars, and the last phases of the "poligar wars" against Kattapomman and the Marutu brothers of Civakankai between 1799 and 1801.

According to the military historian Orme, "These Colleries were chiefly used for cutting off small parties, surprising convoys or stealing or disabling horses or cattle, at which they were most expert" (Orme, 1:208). The Kallars, called colleries, were valued highly for their bravery and their evident mastery of guerrilla tactics in everything from major battles to border raids. Throughout the records of the seventeenth and eighteenth centuries, the Kallars inspired fear and terror among all who faced them. According to the Annual Letter of the Madura Mission for 1759, "it is well known to every one that the mussulman besiegers of Trichinopoly dreaded much more the sudden night attacks of the Kallars than the broad daylight sorties of the garrison" (S. R. Iyer 1916, 107). All the armies that fought and marched through the central Tamil countryside were given strict orders against straggling behind and leaving artillery, cattle, and provisions defenceless, all for fear of the Kallars. It is no wonder that the provision of Kallar soldiers, especially in regularly organized and well trained groups, was well appreciated.

While the Tondaimans proved themselves to be indispensable allies by sending Kallar troops, the Nawab and the English placed even more importance on their dependable delivery of provisions for the latter's armies. Orme wrote that the Tondaiman's "attachment to the English alone enable them to stand their ground at Tritchinopoly" (Orme 1803, 357). William Fullerton, who led many a campaign through the Tamil south, wrote in 1787 that the "Tondaiman is less uncultivated than his neighbours and has at all times proved himself the most faithful adherent of the Nabob and the Company. The father of the present chief, by his firmness and attachment in the days of General Lawrence, supplied the force at Trichinopoly with provisions at a time when their cause seemed desperate" (Fullerton 1787, 86-87). The provisions included food grains, hay, sheep and cattle. Since the transport of provisions to the armies was fraught with danger from local bandits and enemy troops, they had to be sent under heavy guard, sometimes via circuitous routes, usually at night. Because the Tondaiman was known as a constant supplier of the Nawab and the English, his territory, particularly in the northwest, was often raided by enemy troops. Wilks records one such incident in which the inhabitants, apparently well prepared, "quitting their villages and driving off their cattle to the depths of the woods, left the roofs of their houses, composed of bamboo and dry grass, to be burned by the enemy, the only injury (easily replaced in a single day) which they effected in this expedition. . . " (Wilks 1810, 204). The area in the northwest (like much of the Tondaiman's country) abounded with thick scrub forests. On British maps of the late eighteenth century it was labelled as the "Tondiman's Woods" (Orme 1803).

Some documents make it clear that the provisions were paid for, and the soldiers remunerated. There are indications that the prices were set at a concessional rate and the supplies given on long term credit, but the provisions were not free. In one letter from a Company agent to the Tondaiman, the Raja was told that he should instruct his men to collect rice, sheep, fowls, and other provisions for agents of the Company to purchase "for the actual cost" (PPC, 10). In another letter the Nawab thanked the Tondaiman for the "constant supply of provisions" and requested him to send more: "The men and the sepoys in the Fort should not suffer and the things should be cheap" (PPC, 12). Other letters also make it clear that the availability of provisions for purchase was greatly appreciated, particularly because of the unpredictability of the markets of Tanjavur, the rice bowl of the south. On at least one occasion the

Raja of Tanjavur instructed his merchants to stop making supplies available for purchase outside (Orme 1803, 1: 346). Even where a surplus of provisions clearly existed kings often instructed merchants as to whom they could and could not sell them. Often, there was no surplus of readily available grain and livestock in any one given area of the Tamil country, and thus local rulers had to arrange to procure, organize, and transport grain for military operations, especially for pitched battles and long-term sieges. In particular the transport and storing of the supplies required sustained protection. In short, even though the provisions had to be paid for, anyone who could arrange for and ensure their regular supply provided an indispensable service, in some ways even greater than the provision of troops. Markets alone could not and did not provide this service.

Some of the letters reveal frequent requests for money along with provisions (whether as loan or as contribution is not made clear, though certain letters suggest that the money was formally sent as loan, even though it might not be repaid). Despite this, the provision of supplies for the armies of allies, however much embedded within a structure of political alliance and exchange, was neither a simple market transaction nor a form of indirect taxation. This point is particularly important in the case of the Tondaiman since a number of different sources assert that the Nawab granted the Tondaiman a tribute-free status. Fullerton wrote that "the Nabob, sensible of the obligation [incurred from the sending of provisions], ever afterwards exempted him from tribute" (Fullerton 1787, 87). The Tondaiman asserted this himself when in 1803 the British requested the nominal tribute of an elephant a year, a request the Tondaimans ignored until the British rescinded it some years later.

What this tribute-free status meant was that no specified amount of tribute (peshkash) was required from the Tondaiman every year. According to one source which confirms this reading, we see that Pudukkottai was not alone in this respect. "Upon inquiry it appeared that neither Marawar (Ramnad) or Nalcooty (Civakankai) ever paid any regular or yearly tribute to the government of Trichinopoly, which, according to the power and opportunity they met with, received sums of money from them by way of Nazirs or presents: with regard to Tondiman they did the same."[24] Instead, the Tondaiman made occasional presents (*nazr*) to the Nawab, the most significant of which were made on the occasion of a succession. When Vijaya Rakunata Tondaiman succeeded to the throne in 1789, he paid fifty thousand

[24] Anonymous author, *An Inquiry into the Policy of making Conquests for the Mahometans in India with the British Arms*, 1779.

"pagodas" (a gold coin, worth about three and one half rupees in 1818) to the Nawab, Muhammed Ali, who refused to confirm his succession until the money was received. Some years later, in 1796, this Nawab conferred on the Tondaiman the title of Raja Bahadur, upon the reception of which the latter sent the former a nazr of 25,000 pagodas:[25]

As a reward for the faithful services rendered by you and your ancestors, the title of "Raja Bahadur" is bestowed upon you and a mansab; you can keep a force of 1,500 cavalry; a flag, a naggara [kettle drum], a turband, a Jaga [a jewel for the head inlaid with precious stones], an elephant and a khillat [are sent] and you are elevated thereby. Regarding these as marks of good will, you should be solicitous of obtaining more. You should follow the footsteps of your ancestors in rendering service and carrying out instructions without any objection. This should be regarded as a mark of good fortune.

The language of this letter, or sanad, is significantly different from that employed in the vamcavalis. Although the gifts of titles, emblems, and privileges are much the same as those in the vamcavalis (with the obvious addition of the title Bahadur, a Mughal title of honor), the sanad is more explicit about the importance of performing services in the future and "carrying out instructions without objection." This is the first instance of such an explicit statement of political obligation, clearly modelled on Mughal forms of entitlement and political relationship. Further, the use of money in late-eighteenth-century Pudukkottai seems more conspicuous at these ceremonial moments than in transactions concerning land revenue and military payment. Far from facilitating regularized taxation, money provided the medium for hierarchically oriented presentations, the object being political recognition and the creation of closer ties. In a dramatic reversal of the usual assumptions about the process of monetization, money and ceremony complemented rather than opposed each other.

During the second half of the eighteenth century, gifts to Brahmans, temples, and charities increased in number and in scale. The most generous giver was Raja Vijaya Rakunata Tondaiman Bahadur (1789–1807). In addition to the usual endowments of land to temples within the state, he established a number of Tondaiman *Kaṭṭaḷais* (permanent endowment funds) in great temples outside the kingdom (viz. Ramesvaram, Madurai Minaksi, and Srirankam). He gave extensive endowments to learned Brahmans and made arrangements for Vedic instruction (*vēdavirtti*) to ensure the continuity of Vedic studies within the Brahman communities. He gave Brahmans land in the central areas of the state, and fifty plots of forest land to encourage their settlement

[25] Quoted in Naidoo.

196

and cultivation as well as to promote the wider impact of brahmanic learning throughout the kingdom (S. R. Iyer 1916, 327–329).

As the eighteenth century ended, the Nawab's political position was eclipsed by that of the British. The Tondaimans, with their title of Raja Bahadur now firmly imprinted on the flags that heralded their march, helped the British to capture the notorious rebel Kattapomman, and sent 2,147 men and 19 horse against the Marutu brothers of Civakankai who resisted British rule into the first year of the next century. S. R. Lushington, Collector of Poligar Peshkash, wrote to the Madras Government that "indeed in whatever point of view it was considered, the service which the Tondaiman had performed was of the highest importance" (MPP, July 1803). As we shall see in more detail in the final chapter, the British distinguished the Tondaiman as the most loyal of all Tamil palaiyakkarars because of these final services. They presented him with the area around the fort of Kilanilai which had been in the control of the Raja of Tanjavur, as well as with two gold chobdar sticks as marks of honor. Most importantly, they excluded Pudukkottai from the Permanent Settlement of 1803 and allowed it to become a Princely State.

### Palaiyakkarar politics: the old regime in Pudukkottai

The Tondaimans emerged out of a medieval context as the lineage heads of a Kallar subcaste who became araiyars due to their capacity to provide protection in the region which now constitutes the northeastern portion of Pudukkottai state. We saw in the previous chapter how araiyars generally began as protectors, both of village communities and temples. They soon expanded their position of local authority by claiming rights to shares in local production as well as to honors in local temples. Thereafter, successful araiyars were granted titles, honors, and further rights to shares of local material and symbolic production by local communities and regional kings. Some araiyars made the further transition from local chief to regional king, as did the Kallar Tondaimans in the seventeenth century. During that century the Tondaimans established relations with the Nayakas of Madurai and Tanjavur as well as with the Cetupati of Ramanatapuram. They turned these contacts into the relational bases of an authority which – stretching in ideological terms all the way up to the retreating Vijayanagara kings of the northern Deccan – extended well beyond the boundaries of their local subcaste dominance.

The eighteenth century was a period of continued and continuous state formation in Pudukkottai, its boundaries expanding constantly through conquest, negotiation, and gift. The military "system" was crucial to this set of developments, and it is no surprise that the Tondaiman made many gifts to his supporting Kallar chiefs and retainers, giving honors, which implicated the followers all the more firmly into the structure of Tondaiman sovereignty, and lands, which positioned the followers all the closer to the strategic borders requiring active vigilance. It is also not surprising that military specialists – Rajputs, Muslims, and Marathas – were recruited to live in Pudukkottai and support the local fighting apparatus. In addition, local markets were linked up to the larger world of political alliance and conflict. Relations of production, distribution, and consumption were increasingly inflected by the larger context of demand and supervision that developed as a result.

In spite of these gestures in the direction of the larger changes overtaking the Tamil country in the eighteenth century, the palaiyak-karar polity continued to display many traces of its late Vijayanagara formation. Honors continued to herald and demarcate status and political relations at the same time that they were inseparable from other "material" resources, especially land. The use of money increased, but in such a way as to permit the continuance of ceremonial political forms rather than to break down the old regime reliance on social relations as determinants of social transactions. Merchants still served kings instead of challenging them. Land continued to be held and given without reference to what were elsewhere new forms of systematic assessment and taxation. The military system itself continued to be constituted by relations of gift and kinship. And the cultural imperatives of Hindu kingship continued to be followed, with the result that many of the material resources not swallowed up by the demands of political alliances were consumed to benefit the temples that organized worship and the Brahmans who chanted the Vedas.

The old regime therefore permitted and continued the transformation of peripheral zones in the Tamil country into small replicas of the great Vijayanagara kingdom. The great gifts of the Vijayanagara kings were replicated in the Tondaiman grants to Kallar supporters. From the early eighteenth century most of these gifts were made during the Dasara festival, performed in mimesis of Vijayanagara. Gifts provided the infrastructural circuitry which connected ritual and politics, for re-lations of worship and loyalty were articulated through this single process.

Until their final demise, the palaiyakkarar domains preserved the strong social bases – their lineage and subcaste formations – which had permitted their rise to power in the first place. Having seen this in general terms, we must now turn from the historical trajectory of our study to

198

delve into the problematical nature of the relation between politics and society in the little kingdoms of the south. If we have moved from ethnohistory to history in this chapter, we must now move from history to ethnography. In the next three chapters I will present ethnographic data in order to arrive at a better understanding of the historical formation and cultural character of caste relations in Pudukkottai.

# PART 4

# Social relations of a little kingdom

# 7

## Royal Kallars

### The past: from bandits to kings

The Kallars, like the Maravars, settled in mixed economy zones such as Pudukkottai on the borders of the central political and economic regions of the south. They quickly attained dominance in these areas by exercising rights of protection over local communities and institutions. The Kallars were chosen for this role because their strongly kin and territory based social structure and cultural valuation of heroism and honor were highly conducive to the corporate control of the means of violence and coercion. It was no accident that Kallars, like Maravars, were often, when not granted rights of protection, the very groups from which others sought protection.

The martial and predatory traditions of Kallars and Maravars were commented on very early in Tamil history. The *Caṅkam* classic *Akanāṉūru* refers to the Kallars as a fearless and uncultured people who lived originally in the mountains about Tirupati, capturing elephants and exchanging their tusks indirectly through other mountain people for grain. Their leader is said to have been one Pulli, highly skilled in taming violent and uncontrollable elephants. The correspondence of these traditions with those recorded in the vamcavalis of Maravar and Kallar kingly families suggests the integrity and venerability of the tradition concerning the early martial and heroic character of these groups, as well as their position on the periphery of Tamil culture and kingly civilization. Both the vamcavalis and the history of the Kallars of Pudukkottai attest to a remarkable transformation of at least some of these groups over time (poems no. 62, 83, 209, 311, 359, 393, 342).

In spite of the transformation of some Kallars into kings, the last chapter revealed that as recently as the eighteenth century certain groups of Kallars were reputed to inspire more terror in their predatory raiding than the enemies of opposing armies in open and declared warfare. Further, Kallars were usually seen as independent chiefs only by virtue of their undisputed control of certain highly forested areas in zones between major towns such as Tiruccirappalli and Madurai (S. R Aiyar 1916, 107). In a description of 1709, one European wrote that "These colleries are the absolute masters of all the country. They pay neither tax nor tribute to the king [evidently of Madura]. They issue from their woods every night, sometimes five or six hundred in number, and go to plunder the territories under the king's dependence. In vain till now has he tried to reduce them" (ibid.).

The word Kallar also means thief in Tamil. As noted by Turnbull (1817):

The word Culler is used to express a thief of any caste, sect or country, but it will be necessary to trace their progress to that characteristic distinction by which this race is designated both a thief, and an inhabitant of a certain naud [natu], which was not altogether exempted from paying tribute to the sovereign of Madura. This race appears to have become hereditary occupiers, and appropriated to themselves various nauds in different parts of the southern countries; in each of these territories they have a chief among them, whose orders and directions they all must obey. They still possess one common character, and in general are such thieves that the name is very justly applied to them, for they seldom allow any merchandize to pass through their hands without extorting something from the owners, if they do not rob them altogether, and in fact travellers, pilgrims, and Brahmans are attacked and stript of everything they possess, and they even make no scruple to kill any caste of people, save only the latter.

While this account is obviously pejorative, we saw earlier that the family histories of some palaiyakkarar families often accept their early associations with banditry, however much it is glossed in terms of religious devotion.

In these same family histories one of the ways these emergent palaiyakkarars distinguished themselves in the service of greater kings was by vanquishing other groups of bandits and predators. In most of the texts, these other groups are labelled as Kurumpars, a caste group which migrated from the Karnataka country at a very early time, and Kallars. These claims are made mostly by Maravars, and sometimes by Telegu Vatuka castes, but it is clear that the Kallars have been seen, and not only by the British, as a group given to banditry. In both Kallar and Maravar family histories the first movement of these groups towards some appropriation of local level political authority was accomplished by taking on rights of protection, an entitlement provided both by the local community and by higher kings. It is clear that the special qualifications of Kallars and Maravars to receive this entitlement had to do both with their connection to the problems necessitating protection and with their capacity to enforce the rule of law by means little different from those exercised against it.

While there was therefore a continuity (and as we saw earlier an important structural relationship between banditry and kingship), British commentators from later periods saw no distinction at all between "legitimate" rights of protection and less legitimate forms of expropriation and terror. Any kings other than their own were seen as bandits. This colonial political theory, or doctrine, was part of a generalized attempt to discredit all forms of political authority as they existed under an old regime in which the British had no place. For the British in south India, the Vellalars were the caste which best met their expectation of potentially loyal and productive supporters of the Raj. Many Kallars and Maravars were classified as "criminal" under the Criminal Tribes Act. The Kallars of Tanjavur, on the other hand, were seen as agriculturalists of a type one notch below the respectable Vellalars because they had abandoned the criminal activities of their southern brethren and imitated the local Vellalars instead.

While some Kallars were branded as congenital criminals, and others were lauded for imitating Vellalars, the Kallars of Pudukkottai were clearly exempted from this mode of colonial classification because they had been set apart by the special status of the Princely state. However, the position attained by the Kallars of Pudukkottai was not substantively different from that attained by many of the Maravars of Ramanatapuram and Tirunelveli, where these politically dominant castes were organized under kingships which sustained, and in some vital respects transformed, their social organization. In examining the social structure of Pudukkottai, we will be viewing the royal attainments of the Kallars as representative of a particular kind of social formation typical of the mixed economy zones of Tamil Nadu in the late medieval and early modern period of south Indian history.

## The general structure of Kallar society

However one defines "dominance," the Kallars have been the dominant caste throughout Pudukkottai state, though their dominance (at the village and locality levels) applies particularly to the northern and eastern portions of the state, roughly demarcated by Kolattur and Alankuti taluks. The only group with a higher statewide population is the Valaiyars, whose caste rank and economic position has been only slightly above the untouchables and certainly below all the other major caste groups. In the 1931 census the Valaiyars numbered 56,607, the Kallars, 46,743. In Kolattur taluk, Kallars held an absolute majority. Even in Alankuti taluk, where the two groups have roughly equal populations, if one discounts Pudukkottai town – a defendable procedure given our central interest in agrarian dominance – there were more

Kallars than Valaiyars. In Tirumayyam, where Kallars settled only at the specific invitation of the Tondaiman kings, there were fewer Kallars than Valaiyars, or Cettiyars, or for that matter Pallans.

Dominance need not correlate with population, though it is important to note the preponderance of Kallars in absolute numbers in major portions of the state. Far more importantly, Kallars owned the greatest amount of land, occupied the greatest number of authoritative positions, particularly as village and locality headmen and as miracidars, and controlled the most important temples as trustees. These temples were often their lineage, village, or locality temples, in which they received honors only after the king and Brahmans. In short, Kallars were dominant not only in terms of their number, but for economic, political, and ritual reasons. While Kallars in other regions have been considered to be relatively low among non-Brahman castes, this is not true in Pudukkottai. Some Brahman informants told me that they were the local representatives of Ksatriyas. All informants agreed that the Kallars of Pudukkottai had been transformed by the kingship of the Tondaiman family.

In Pudukkottai the Kallars are organized into exogamous patrilineal lineages called, among other terms, *paṭṭapeyars* (literally meaning the name of a title – lineages are also called karais, particularly when referred to in the context of temple honors of wherever rank might be invoked). These are grouped into territorially based endogamous subcastes called natu, a word which means social group in a marked sense but in an unmarked sense means territory or country (as in Tamil Nadu). Each lineage within the natu, with a few stated exceptions, can marry in any other lineage within the natu, but in no lineages outside of the natu. In Pudukkottai there are at least thirty-four Kallar natus, each of which represent discrete territorial groupings that are often contiguous but not overlapping, except where natus have split. The natus vary in size. Most natus average between twelve and eighteen villages. Some are even smaller. The largest natu is Vicinki Natu (hereafter VN). It is followed by Ampu Natu (hereafter AN), the royal subcaste, which has internal territorial subdivisions called kuppams. VN constitutes an exception to the rule of natu endogamy, in that it is divided into a number of territorial subdivisions which, unlike those in AN, are of roughly equivalent size and are called natus as well. These internal VN natus, while important for ritual and juridical reasons, define neither endogamy nor exogamy, unlike the other natus which represent endogamous social boundaries. The Kallar natus are fairly evenly distributed across that part of the state which is north of the river, and which is today represented by the two taluks of Kolattur and

Alankuti (see Map 12). More than half of the natus I have mapped correspond to, and nearly as many take their names from, natus that existed in the Cola and Pantiya periods. Those natus that do so correspond tend to be situated along or near the river Vellar (see Map 13). Each natu has one central town where the subcaste temple is located. The town is usually located in the center of the natu. However, there are a number of natus which have apparently split into northern and southern or eastern and western divisions and which continue to share the same subcaste temple and deity.

Each Kallar lineage, village, and subcaste has some sort of headman, and a tutelary deity, although in some cases individual lineages do not have a formal headman but belong to a group of lineages or a village which does. Often the lineage and the village are coterminous.

The usual term for headman is ampalam, which means more generally the central square and/or meeting place of the village. This central square is sometimes more specifically marked by a raised stone platform, and in some villages a stone pillar represents the village ampalam. The ampalam of the subcaste is usually called the *nāṭṭampalam*. In some villages which constitute the centers of their natus the raised stone platform might have as many stone pillars as there are village ampalams with one larger pillar representing the nattampalam. In some parts of Pudukkottai, and also elsewhere, Kallars are referred to as *ampalakkārars*, people of the ampalam; in this instance this title has been generalized in exactly the same manner as the title Tevar for Madurai Kallars (Dumont 1957b).

The subcaste as a whole and its two most important (and variably interrelated) constituent units of villages and lineages are represented not only by ampalams but also by deities. There are lineage deities, village deities (sometimes the same as the lineage deity of the highest lineage but often separate), and subcaste deities. Sometimes the lineage deities (*kula teyvam*) are housed in formal, though small, temples. On other occasions the lineage deities are more simply household deities (*vīṭṭucāmi*) and are housed under trees or behind houses in simple shrines, sometimes to ancestors (*paṭṭavaṉs, mūtatāyars*; among the royal subcaste it is also the custom to worship female *satis* in the family). Village deities (*kirāma teyvam*) may be the same as the lineage deity if it is a single lineage village. In some cases even when the village has more than one lineage the deity of the head lineage is the same as the village deity. Whether this is the case or not, deities classed as village deities are often protection deities (*kāval teyvam*) such as Aiyanar and Karuppar, though sometimes a goddess such as Maryamman will serve in this role instead. The choice of one or the other reflects the particular inflection of

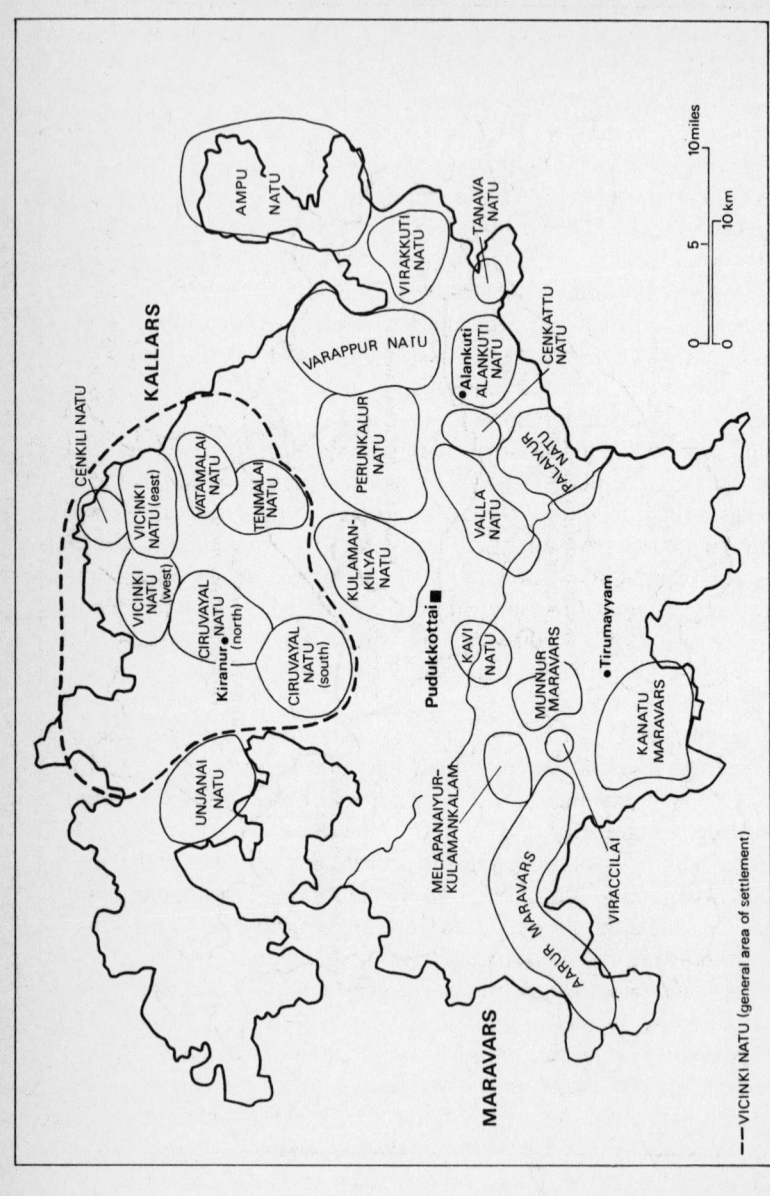

Map 12 Kallar and Maravar subcaste settlement in Pudukkottai

Labels on map:

KALLARS

MARAVARS

AMPU NATU

VIRAKKUTI NATU

TANAVA NATU

VARAPPUR NATU

CENKILI NATU

PERUNKALUR NATU

•Alankuti ALANKUTI NATU

CENKATTU NATU

VATAMALAI NATU

VICINKI NATU (east)

TENMALAI NATU

VICINKI NATU (west)

CIRUVAYAL NATU (north)

Kiranur•

KULAMAN-KILYA NATU

PALAIYUR NATU

VALLA NATU

Pudukkottai■

CIRUVAYAL NATU (south)

KAVI NATU

MUNNUR MARAVARS

•Tirumayyam

UNJANAI NATU

KANATU MARAVARS

MELAPANAIYUR-KULAMANKALAM

AARUR MARAVARS

VIRACCILAI

——VICINKI NATU (general area of settlement)

0   5   10 km
0       10 miles

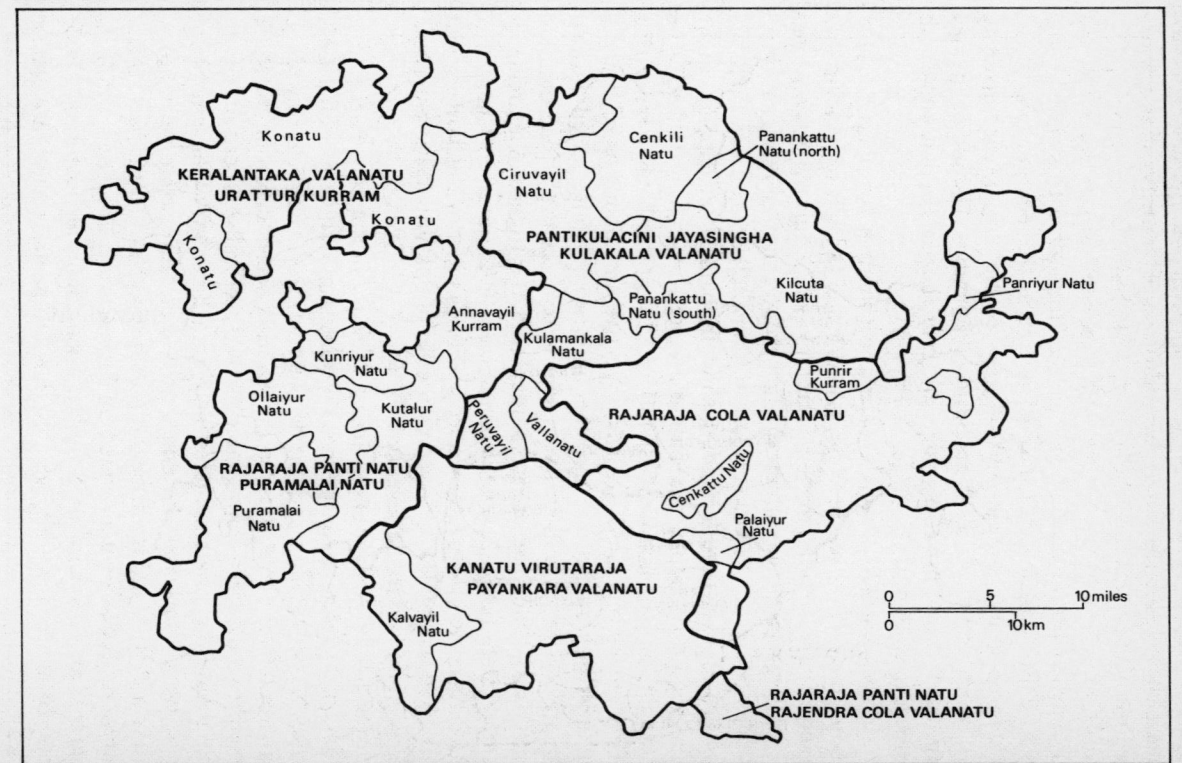

Map 13 Map of Pudukkottai State showing territorial subdivisions as described in inscriptions from the ninth through twelfth centuries

the common stock of village deities by local social concerns and orientations. Most villages have temples both to goddesses and to protection deities. The subcaste deity (*nāṭṭu teyvam*) is often a goddess, though here again there is much variation, since this deity can sometimes be Siva or even Aiyanar. The subcaste deity is housed in a temple (*nāṭṭu kōvil*) which serves as a locus for subcaste festivals (*tiruviṟā*) and meetings (*nāṭṭu kūṭṭam*). These temples thus serve to symbolize the hierarchical supremacy of the natu as well as the incorporation of the two lower units – lineages and villages – within a single encompassing entity, with ritual, political, and juridical functions. They do not merely represent a whole but also gradate and rank the parts of that whole with respect to each other.

Membership in a village, a lineage, and a subcaste is ultimately talked about in terms of whether one has kaniyatci (a right to worship and receive temple honors) in the relevant temples. Kaniyatci was acquired by settling in a village with the original group and by grants from kings. While all *kāṇiyaṭcikārars* (holders of kaniyatci) are equal in that they hold an equal right to (*urimai*) or share in (panku) participation in the affairs of the temple, the nature of participation is ranked. The nattampalams are honored first, followed in order either by a ranked list of villages (represented by their respective ampalams) or of lineages (likewise represented). Thus, the units are hierarchialized in two major ways: each unit in the system is represented by one or more persons, and each unit at each particular level is ranked. Hierarchialization extends beyond even the boundaries of the subcaste. The natu of the Pudukkottai king, AN, was recognized as superior to all others, and in each local temple a local representative of this natu, if present, could receive first honors on behalf of the Raja.

The term for lineage is pattapeyar. This is not the only, or the most frequently used, term for lineage. The other important term for lineage is *karai*. Karai literally means border, or boundary, often referring to the bank of a river or the shore of the sea. It is a term depicting the space where two different things meet: more specifically, where these two things are differentiated. Interestingly, karai has many of the same literal meanings as mariyatai, the term which is generally used to mean honor but in a more literal sense means boundary as well. This is particularly important because karai is used for lineage when lineages are ranked, and they are most commonly ranked when honors are involved in some form or another. Karais, whether they are named or not, are almost always talked about in numerical rank order: as in first karai (*mutal karai*), second karai (*irēṇṭam karai*), and so on down the line. In this context, karais usually refer to lineages, but karai can also mean village.

This in itself is not so extraordinary, since there is a markedly strong correlation between particular villages and particular lineages. But the term karai, though less commonly, can mean other things as well, such as family, or even subcaste or caste, depending upon context. The use of this term is not specific to Kallars. It is used among most other castes even when the term pattapeyar is not used. Not only are karais always ranked, this ranking usually has something to do with honor(s) in the specific context of temple festivals. The term pattapeyar is usually used in talking about kinship, which seems to privilege sentiments of equality rather than rank, even though this equality is often mitigated by asymmetrical alliances and ranked marriage circles. This difference will be seen as crucial in considering the way in which kinship can be variably inflected by political and territorial concerns.

I have noted that Kallar social forms are defined by the authority of the ampalam and the deity. These summary statements rest on a thick ethnographic base. At one point when I asked a group of Kallars about the meaning of kuppam (the territorial subdivision within the royal subcaste), I was told: "By kuppam we mean the assemblage of Kallars in a group having a common temple and headed by an ampalam of their own. This group discusses the issues in the common temple under the leadership of the ampalam. They also discuss the festival at these times. We settle our issues and our disputes within the kuppam." It is in these terms that the kuppam, like the natu, is a political, ritual, and juridical group. That it is a social group as well is assumed because of marriage rules, which are talked about by informants in any conversation concerning social units from that of the lineage to that of the subcaste.

I have also suggested that temples and worship were of especially critical importance for the development of social forms in Pudukkottai. Let me quote again from a different interview. I asked about the origin of the AN Kallars, and was told: "You see, in the beginning temples were formed. Each temple was constituted by a social group (*camutāyam* – the term for group that is also often used for sect) which worshipped in common. The people of this camutayam – all who came to worship – became relatives (*oru murai*). The people worshipping in Ampu temple are AN Kallars. We are so called because of the God we worship, our temple, our customs, etc." This statement is extraordinary because it expresses the cultural fact that membership in a temple is seen as historically prior to the formation of kinship units, groups of relatives. The usual assumption that kinship is primeval, the original and unmediated basis of group formation, is here turned upside down. The temple is the original group, the first focus of group identity, and the institution around which kinship relations subsequently develop. Historical sequence here reveals ontological priority. I take this remark seriously, and allow it to guide my understanding of the significance of temples and honors and their relationship to kinship, which I view as inherently, because perceptually, permeable, constituted as it is here first around the community of worship rather than the community of "kin."

Such a statement does not relate only to our interpretation of kinship, but also to our view of the temple. As noted earlier, most of my informants noted that the most important right in society was kaniyatci, the right to worship in a particular temple at a particular time and in a special way, for this right was fundamental to all other social, political, economic, and of course religious rights.[1] Within the context of my fieldwork in Pudukkottai, the temple is clearly synonymous with community, both as a domain of discourse and a field of action. The temple is (*inter alia*) about social identities; worship is (*inter alia*) about social relations. In the context of the little kingdom, however, even the temple cannot be abstracted as primary, since it is more a locus of social formation and political inflection than an autonomous institution.

My suggestions about the relation of kinship (social relations), and politics (relations with/and constituted by kings), to worship (activities that go on in and around temples) are derived from many similar statements – the long conversation – elicited in the field, as well as from explicit statements written in court cases and petitions to the king and his officers. For example, disputes over temple management often led to explicit statements, as in the following petition to the Darbar:

In the village of Themmavoor there is a Mariammankovil endowed with manyam lands by Sircar and with other property and income by the petitioner and others of the village. The social unit of the village consists of six karais and other laboring classes. One of the karais represents the chief of the six karais and is served as the Ampalakarar. All the social and religious functions common to the residents of the village are performed by the said social unit and the duties, respects, and responsibilities are shared by the various groups in the social unit. So to say, the diversions of the social unit form a component part for all the common affairs of the village, and no individual can have his own way of doing things in respect of the common affairs ... (R–3292 1934 dt. 28–9–35)

This English document, however much its discourse was constructed in relation to the bureaucratic adjudication in the state durbar of a dispute between lineages over management of a temple, is surprisingly

---

[1] Appadurai and Breckenridge have charted the central importance of the temple in south Indian culture and society, identifying the domain of temple honors as constitutive of authority and fundamental to kingship (Appadurai and Breckenridge 1976). See Chapter 9, where I discuss the temple in more detail.

congruent with fragments of speech directed at me as an ethnographer many years later. The village is conceived of as a whole, divided into ranked parts with one part the metonymical representation of the entire village. Karais, also incidentally lineages, were formed with the aim of ordering the affairs of the village and of the village temple. Here, then, kinship units are organized and ordered for the purpose of maintaining the institutions of local village life.

Let us now examine the data in context. Although no subcastes are alike, there are three general types. First, the royal subcaste is of crucial and unique ethnographic importance, for we observe here a subcaste which has been inflected at its core by "politics," and which, through its political and cultural hegemony, took an active role in inflecting other social groups. Second, VN, the most extensive of all natus, was subdivided in turn by (sub)natus, and was the least inflected of all natus in Pudukkottai by the political order. Third, most other subcastes fall under the common type of natu, middling in status, smaller in size.[2]

Briefly, the social organization of Kallar groups in the third category is relatively standard. Each natu is comprised of a group of exogamous lineages, settled in twelve, eighteen, or thirty-two villages (or hamlets). The natu is the unit of endogamy. It has neither internal natus nor other supra-village territorial units. As elsewhere, the lineages are distinguished by titles, or pattapeyars, and are ranked as karais. In one exceptional case, lineages are not named, and marriages are simply contracted with families known not to be agnates. Most of the natus have one headman, the nattampalam, who is the ampalam of the lineage ranked first for the receipt of temple honors at the annual festival of the natu temple. However, the singling out of one lineage headman from the others never prevents the category from proliferating into a gradation, usually of three ranks. Curiously, the tendency for royal authority to fission into *two*, whether because of the breakdown of patrilateral succession or the simple division of the kingdom, does not occur at the level of subcaste leadership, which instead divides into three positions.

For example, Varappur Natu is made up of six chief villages and eighteen *pattis*, or hamlets. There are twelve lineages, some of which live in villages named after the lineage. Three such villages are named after the three chief lineages of the natu. These lineages spawned the three nattampalams of the natu. The original lineages which settled in the natu

---

[2] There was one other group of Kallars as well. These were the Terketti Kallars, the most recent immigrants in the state. They migrated to Pudukkottai from Ramanatapuram in the south (as their name implies) in the eighteenth century when a major chief of this subcaste, Ilantari Cervaikarar, recruited them for the service of the Pudukkottai king.

did so in discrete villages. Later migrant lineages settled in a less clearly differentiated manner, though a few of them are associated with particular villages. I was told that the ancestors of the three nattampalams were the first settlers of the natu. These were the only families to have true kaniyatci in the natu. In the main natu temple, dedicated to Aiyanar, there is a small shrine to the ancestor of the head nattampalam. Puja is offered to him every day by his descendants; the entire Kallar subcaste offers him puja at the big annual festival.

The preferred marriage partners in Varappur Natu are the same as for other Kallars: the mother's brother's daughter, the father's sister's daughter, and the sister's daughter. As is also true for other Kallars, the maternal uncle (the *maman*) has to give his permission, and (as Dumont has demonstrated) in representing the "bride's family" in any given marriage decision, mitigates the dominance of the descent group at the most significant moments of its own reproduction. But the key role of the maman is not correlated, as it can be elsewhere, with an exclusive preference for matrilateral cross cousin marriage partners. In contrast to what Dumont reports for other Kallars, it does not stand in the way of sister's daughter's marriage. Only in two exceptional subcastes, one recent migrants from Ramnad where the Maravars had been organized in matrilineal *kilais*, the other a group with a strong residual matrilineal component, was there a prohibition of sister's daughter's marriage. In the latter subcaste, Palaiyur Natu, I was told that: "We cannot marry sister's daughter because it is the same blood – irattam." The children take the *tiral* – the blood line – of the mother, through today this line is said to hold only for one generation. They say that they can marry the sister's granddaughter because the blood gets diluted. In other respects, these groups are like other Kallars, with the same terms for patri-lineages, i.e., pattapeyar, karai.

Marriages are bilateral in theory and practice. Lineages that are called maman-maccanan are lineages with which affinal ties have been established. In the majority of cases I asked about these include both wife-giving and wife-taking families. The only restriction, and this is also true for Dumont's Pramalai Kallars, is that it was thought unwise to exchange wives in the same families, for if one of the marriages did not work out it was thought likely that the other marriage would then break up as well.

With the exception of the AN Kallars, who maintained their strong ties with their original natu group even though they had settled all over the state, any Kallar who lived in a particular territorial natu was also a social member of that natu. Territory, as Dumont has noted, cannot be dissociated from its social content. At the same time, territory itself has exercised a strong influence on the social organization of Kallars. The territorial natus of Pudukkottai for the most part predate actual Kallar settlement. Many of the names of these territories appear in early Cola inscriptions with boundaries that are largely congruent with their later social realization in Kallar society. While it is impossible to know the historical dynamic by which territorial divisions might have exercised some influence on the way in which lineages settled and established affinal networks, we must accept that historically mandated territorial boundaries could have had cultural significance prior to the full working out of Kallar social forms. Dumont has perhaps underemphasized the importance of territory in his study of the Pramalai Kallars who settled in regions to the west of Madurai. It is possible that in Dumont's area there were no natus prior to Kallar settlement, for reasons that have to do with the more marginal nature of the lands where the Pramalai Kallars settled. Other differences of a more systematic nature between the Pramalai and the Pudukkottai Kallars will be considered in the next chapter.

The remainder of this chapter will concern the royal subcaste. The next chapter will examine the other major Kallar group and contrast it not only with other Kallar groups in Pudukkottai but also with Dumont's depiction of the Pramalai Kallar. We will then use these comparisons as a way to begin considering other castes in Pudukkottai, indeed to construct a sense of the historical formation of caste relations in different parts of the Tamil country.

### The royal subcaste: Ampu Natu

The royal natu is located in the far northeastern part of Pudukkottai state, extending beyond the boundaries of the state. The natu is divided into nine kuppams, clusters or groups, which are territorial divisions named in all but two cases after villages. These divisions are not found anywhere else in Pudukkottai. Kuppam has a strong territorial connotation (keeping in mind that territory does not exist independently of the social groups it defines and demarcates). On several occasions my informants used kuppam interchangeably with natu.

Kuppam derives from the term *kumpam*, meaning "a village of small houses or huts" (Winslow 1862, 134). The term kuppam is used among no other groups within Pudukkottai for any kind of territorial unit. I have found no reference to it in the ethnographic literature concerning Tamil Nadu. As we noted above, kuppam here seems to mean natu, or rather a sub-natu of the type found among the VN Kallar. However, the kuppam is sometimes a single village, more commonly several villages, and never more than fifteen villages. The list of the nine kuppams is a list of villages and subdivisions thereof which provides the particular rank order of kuppams, reflecting the order in which the kuppams receive honors in the natu temple. Each kuppam is said to contain a specified group of lineages. Sometimes these are settled in a number of villages each taking its name from its dominant lineage; others are mixed together in a single town or set of villages.

There are a number of instances where people of one lineage migrate to and settle in another kuppam. The interesting question then becomes: did they join another kuppam or did they continue to be acknowledged as migrants, who moved for various reasons (often because they were the second or third sons who came to live with their affinal relatives)? I asked this question many times. In no response did migration change the specific kinship rule among pankalis. Marriages could never be contracted within the exogamous group, which continued to be the same. But I was struck by what at first appeared to be a contradiction. Some families or sets of families continued to have rights (kaniyatci) to honors (mariyatai) in their original temple after they had migrated from their native village. Other groups had lost the right to receive their traditional honors. They could only receive honors, usually at a lower rank, in the temple in the village (or kuppam) where they made their new home. My informants felt no compulsion to explain what to me seemed contradictory.

This seeming contradiction can be resolved by taking three interrelated factors into account: the reasons for resettlement, the status of the migrant group within the new settlement, and the duration of time since the migration. Families which were resettled by the king maintained their local status in their original village and kuppam, while in their new places they did not merge with any new group but rather became the *in loco* representatives of the Raja. Families which moved for economic reasons, often moving to the village of the wife's family, clearly moved with less status and reversed the usual patrilocal pattern of marriage residence. Status within the new community was also determined in part by how large, and subsequently how wealthy and powerful the migrant lineage became. The length of stay within the new village explains why certain groups increasingly merged with their new kuppams: the powerful assertion over time of the territorial factor, part of the original dynamic involved in the creation and ordering of the kuppams. As we recall, the first karai to settle in any given village (or kuppam) tended to be the dominant karai and to maintain its position of firstness when subsequently joined by other groups. It was far easier, and part of general discourse, to change kuppams than it was to change natus. Very few informants in any natu talked about processes which involved the transfer by any family from membership in one natu to another, although as we will see there were traditions which involved the incorporation of new groups into natus at the time of territorial migration.

One of the nine kuppams had been produced entirely by migration from other kuppams in the remembered past. Pantuvakkottai, ranked eighth, was made up of settlers from Vata Teru and Ten Teru, the two top kuppams of the subcaste. Since the kuppam was not one of the original group, it was originally, as I was told by the headman of Pantuvakkottai kuppam, given the value of only half a kuppam, sharing its honors with Kallakottai. But, perhaps because the kuppam is made up of what have become some of the most distinguished lineages in the subcaste, it is now seen by most informants as a separate kuppam. The head lineage of this kuppam is one of the higher, though not the highest, lineages of Ten Teru, the Tevars. This is the only instance of a kuppam in which the head lineage is also a major lineage in another kuppam. It is impossible, from fragments such as this, to reconstruct the historical dynamic by which a single subcaste became divided into nine distinct territorial units (or vice versa). Nonetheless, it seems clear that the process took place over a long period of time, during which the migration of groups was a constant occurrence. We will see that the migration of groups from outside and the subdivision of groups within the subcaste were in all probability the principal dynamic factors behind the formation of subcastes themselves as well as the development of kuppams into multi-lineage territorial groups.

The two kuppams not named after villages (given sometimes as the first and second kuppams and other times as the two halves of the first kuppam) are named after streets, a commonly used way of subdividing villages. In both of these cases, *Vata Teru* (VT) and *Ten Teru* (TT) (northern street and southern street), the kuppams now occupy more than one village, though each group has a head village. Since these two groups occupy the first, or first and second, kuppams, the particular names suggest an early division within the first and most important lineage (TT is the Raja's kuppam) at a time before the subsequent diversity of settlement developed, and perhaps even before the other kuppams had joined the natu. It would not initially have been necessary to specify the village because in the beginning the village in which the two streets were located was probably the only village in the group, the initial point of settlement by the first settlers to identify themselves as AN Kallars.

Although it is not clear how many lineages were initially members of the two streets, it is likely – particularly given the apparent limitation in the number of lineages which would settle in any given village – that as time went on other lineages joined, perhaps leading to the division of the two streets into two separate kuppams. I speculate here without the help of a specific oral tradition about this group – although it is widely held that the streets did divide from one village and one kuppam – but rather on the basis of comments made by a number of informants that all natus began with an initial primordial lineage. Other lineages joined the "subcaste" later in time. The order of joining is reflected in the order in which temple honors are given at the annual natu festival. As I will show later, informants noted both in particular statements and in general formulations that subcastes developed from the settlement and assimilation of other groups that were accepted as affines by the primordial, and ruling, lineage of any given natu. Not only does this formulation express the powerful structural role of territorial association, as well as the historical basis for karai ranking within subcastes, it also provides a logic for the exogamous nature of lineages (which is in marked contrast to the non-exogamous lineages of the Pramalai Kallars). There are, as we shall see, certain lineages that do not intermarry, but these are few and always specified. Sometimes there is a prohibition of marriage with a particular lineage because it has been excommunicated for one reason or another. Other times the specification of a particular relationship between lineages means they cannot intermarry, as for example in the rare cases when lineages may start with divisions of brothers of the same father but of different mothers.

Although all my informants agreed that there were nine kuppams, the exact list varied in a number of renditions, according to whether certain groups were said to be half kuppams or full (see Table 1).

The subcaste temple, Ampu Kovil, while located relatively centrally for the natu as a whole, was not situated in the middle of a central village for the natu. Today no Kallars live in the village that takes its name from the temple, an old Siva temple built most probably in early Cola times, perhaps in the tenth century. The nattu teyvam is a goddess, Vira Makali Amman, housed in a separate shrine outside the wall (*prakara*) of the main Siva temple. This suggests that the goddess's shrine was added considerably later. The temple's connection to the Colas also figures in the origin myth stated by some of the AN informants. According to these informants, the AN Kallars were brought to AN by the Colas to secure their borders and protect their temples.

The AN Kallars are the only Kallar group to have well-developed conceptions of their settlement in Pudukkottai (with the single exception of the Terketti Kallars, who migrated to the state in the eighteenth century). Those AN Kallars of the Raja's kuppam (and here I refer both

# Table 1 Ampu Natu: the royal subcaste

The nine kuppams and their constituent lineages in ranked order

A   Vata Teru
    1.  Manikka Rayar
    2.  Panikontar
    3.  Racaliyar
    4.  Arccuttiyar
    5.  Toppayar
    6.  Katu Vettiyar
    7.  Vellattevan Vituti Tevar
    8.  Onciya Vituti Zamintar
    9.  Kaliran Vituti Zamintar
    10. Akkara Vattam Maniyam
B   Ten Teru
    1.  Pallavaraiyar
    2.  Tondaiman          the royal lineage
    3.  Rankiyar           aracu ancu (5)
    4.  Kaliyarayar        (the group of five)
    5.  Tevar              the upper strata
    1.  Terancirar
    2.  Kurantai Rayar
    3.  Valankontar
    4.  Arar
    5.  Vettuvar           puti pattu (10)
    6.  Cammattiyar        (the group of ten)
    7.  Ceppalar           the lower strata
    8.  Makali
    9.  Maravarayar
    10. Narankiyar/Narankiyapattu
C   Vatakkalur
    1.  Cammattiyar
D   Kallakottai
    1.  Cinkaputaiyar
E   Karampakkuti
    1.  Tennatirayar
    2.  Maravarayar
    3.  Valankontar
    4.  Narankiyar
F.  Neiveli
    1.  Mannavelar
    2.  Kaliyarayar
    3.  Maravarayar
    4.  Matiyappiliyar
G   Ammanipattu
    1.  Kalinkarayar
    2.  Cukkirar
H   Pantuvakkottai
    1.  Tevar
    2.  Kalinkarayar
    3.  Cukkirar
    4.  Maravarayar
I.  Vellalavituti
    1.  Cinkappuliyar
    2.  Arccuttiyar
    3.  Muttuppillai

to VT and TT) share their origin story with the Tondaiman Rajas. They came from the north, from the forests and hills around Tirupati, which is on the northern border of the Tamil country where it becomes increasingly inhabited by Telegu speakers. Tirupati is one of the most sacred sites in the south, a rough outcrop of the Eastern Ghats which was of special importance during Vijayanagara times because of the major temple center there. From Tirupati they went a little further south to Kancheepuram, the ancient capital of the Pallava dynasty and the Tontaimantalam country, from which the royal family took its title, and from which the first group in TT, the Pallavaraiyars, also took theirs. During Cola times they moved to Ampil, near Lalkuti, on the northern banks of the Kaveri river midway between Tiruccirappalli and Tanjavur (this explains one folk etymology for AN, which derives Ampu from Ampil). Finally, according to Pallavaraiyar informants, the Cola kings brought the AN Kallars from Ampil and settled them in AN, a southern outpost of the Cola kingdom (just to the south of the plain irrigated by the Kaveri). This would suggest a time period roughly between the tenth and late twelfth centuries. According to the Pallavaraiyars, the nine kuppams then dispersed from Ampu Kovil to their different respective places within the natu.

Origin accounts from other AN kuppams provide a different story of settlement. Informants from Karampakuti and Neiveli kuppams both said that they came from Manapparai, located about thirty miles southwest of Tiruccirappalli. I was told by the nattampalam of Karampakuti kuppam that:

Our kula teyvam was originally at Manapparai and still there is a temple in Manapparai called Antavar Kovil. This Manapparai temple is like the "head of the department" [spoken in English, using a familiar bureaucratic metaphor]. We took the swami from Manapparai to Vatavalam and from there to Karampakuti, where we finally settled down. The Sri Karuppar Muttaiya in Karampakuti, our family deity [for all members of his pattapeyar, Tennatirai-yar] here, is the same god as the ones in Vatavalam and Manapparai.

This statement, in conjunction with the other stories, suggests that AN is an amalgamation of at least two different migrations of Kallars who, when they settled down in the same area, formed a social basis (the natu grouping) for their territorial proximity. While we noted above that such a process was in all likelihood responsible for the development of all subcastes, in this case the remembered incidence of two separate migrations might be responsible for the special category of kuppam. In other words, the particular hierarchies of different groups which initially settled in different villages that were only subsequently joined together in a single subcaste were encoded in this unique improvisation on a basic theme. Once again, whatever merit there might be to our speculation, we see the central importance of territorial association.

In both the statements of my informants and in various texts dating from the eighteenth century, we see many cases of groups, sometimes fractions of larger groups which divided because of a quarrel, migrating and settling down together in a new area. Migration was obviously a constant feature of life, even as the association of a group with its own territory was highly pronounced. This potential contradiction was resolved in part through the important role played by family deities in migration. All of these groups established their family deity in the new places to which they migrated. The AN Kallars followed the same method of transferring their deity as that described for the Pramalai Kallar by Dumont and elucidated by Daniel. They took a handful of soil – *pitimān* – from the site of the original shrine and used it to install their deity in a new shrine in their new place of settlement. Given the strong territorial associations of Kallars, we might assume that migration was not undertaken lightly. And yet this technique of migration, as Daniel writes, provides a means for the mixing of the old soil which was appropriate to the particular group (indeed part of their substance) with the new soil, making it, too, appropriate. The establishment of the deity is of course crucial since the social group is defined largely in terms of its common worship of tutelary deity.[3]

An informant from the Neiveli kuppam also said that his family migrated from Manapparai. He told me that when his forefathers came from Manapparai, the headman of their group walked with an arrow which he used like a walking stick. The group stopped walking when the arrow became stuck in the ground in Ampu Kovil. According to him, there is still an arrow there which is worshipped along with Siva and the goddess. Thus he explained to me how Ampu Kovil got its name, since ampu means arrow. This kind of etymological explanation is an important component of folk discourse about origins. Interestingly, both the Pallavaraiyars and the latter informant invoke etymology as proof of the veracity of their tales, however much they differ. In this last story, we also see that migration is guided by the deity, which resides within the arrow. A family deity often has no iconic form other than a spear or sword. The arrow, guided by the deity, finds the soil which is appropriate for it, and therefore for the group at large. In other family

---

[3] E. V. Daniel has demonstrated the salience of these kinds of territorial traditions and technologies in his rich ethnographic study of a region less than 100 kilometers away from Pudukkottai (Daniel 1984).

histories from other areas, a deity will often appear before the headman in the chosen place and instruct the headman to terminate his migration there. The first action signifying the end of migration is the building of a temple to the family deity.

I found out little more about the formation of AN. I was consistently told that the reason that one lineage was ranked first and received first honors was that it was the first to settle in a particular place. Other groups that migrated later on were incorporated as affines but could never be accorded first rank. This might also explain why it is that in some cases the family deity of the head lineage is also the deity of the natu, although even in these cases the head lineage may have two different family deities, hereby suggesting the possibility of the appropriation of first honors in an earlier "territorial" temple by the first family. While we can only form sketchy notions of the settlement of any of the Kallar natus, we can say that territorial association is not the product of affinal alliance, but rather that it helps to create an imperative for the development of territorially bounded and internally ranked affinal networks.

In order both to understand the structure of the subcaste and the curious position of the Raja within it, we will now proceed to analyze the first kuppam – or rather the first two kuppams – of the subcaste in particular detail.

## The royal kuppams

The royal kuppam of TT was most commonly spoken of as the second kuppam, after VT. Although they are sometimes called half kuppams, they are more often thought to have become separate groups. Whether or not at some early point VT was clearly superior to TT, as certain structural sediments suggest, the rise to kingship of the Tondaiman family, paradoxically a lineage that was ranked second in the second kuppam, changed the position of TT vis-à-vis both VT and the rest of the subcaste. VT, which consists of ten villages, was left completely outside the boundaries of the eighteenth-century state; far from being in command, it became politically, socially, and territorially marginal to the rest of the subcaste.

VT consists of ten villages and ten lineages. The villages take their names from the lineages that settled in them. Each village is the territorial realization of a single lineage structure. The first lineage (see Table 1) is the Manikkarayar karai; they live in Manikkarayarvituti. *Vituti* is a common term for settlement or village.

The common temple of the VT kuppam is a Mariyamman temple in

222

Tiruvonam, a small town located just two miles north of Manikkarayar-vituti, more or less in the center of the kuppam. This town does not belong to any one of the lineages. Larger than any of the vitutis, it is a multi-caste marketing and temple center for the entire area covered by the kuppam. The Mariyamman temple serves as a locus for the annual kuppam festival and all assemblies of the whole kuppam. On the next level are the village temples. Because of the direct correspondence between lineage and village, the village temple is the same as the lineage temple. These temples are for the most part dedicated to Aiyanar, as is often the case when the kuppam, or natu, temple is dedicated to a goddess.

The Karpaka Pillaiyar temple in a village called Cervaipatti is also important for VT, though not for it alone like the Tiruvonam Mariyamman temple. According to the Pallavaraiyar chief, headman of the TT kuppam and one of my principal informants, VT and TT share it "equally." The boundary stone of VT and TT (as also the boundary between Tanjavur and Pudukkottai Districts) lies near the ample navel of Pillaiyar (Ganesha), indicating that the god himself was to be shared equally by both groups. Perhaps this temple marks the spot of the original settlement of the two kuppams.

Like other temples, it defines a social community. As the Pallavarai-yar chief said: "If one could not find a place to prepare *ponkal* during the festival in this Pillaiyar temple, then one is considered to be an alien to AN, or as unfit to be an AN Kallar. The VT and TT Kallars are the shareholders who have original rights in this temple." Since the temple is located in the middle of Cervaipatti village, one-half of the village comes under the authority of VT and one-half comes under TT. Interestingly, the Pallavaraiyars represent their teru by preparing ponkal at this temple, while a group of Vellalars, who as we shall soon see have an important priestly role in AN, represent VT. After worship, the leaders of these two groups receive the temple honors and then distribute them to the other karais in their respective terus.

The logic of division in Cervaipatti village is so absolute that all the people and resources of the village are divided equally. Even the Vellalars are part of the divided resources of the village. "During the partition (of VT and TT), a complete bifurcation was made between brothers. In Cervaipatti, half of the Vellalars belong to VT and the other half belong to TT. All honors must be shared by both terus. Even if a fish is caught in the village tank, the two groups should divide it equally." This is yet another sign of dominance, where the clients of the dominant group divide at the instance and according to the structure of divisions within that group. However, we usually see this happening not with

Vellalars, but with subordinate castes such as Valaiyars, Pallars, and Paraiyars.

This kind of division is also in evidence in TT, though interestingly not in VT. It seems likely that when TT split off from VT, it did not break all of its connections. The Aiyanar temple in Pilavituti, the head village of TT, is divided between the two terus. When TT celebrates its own festivals in this temple it gets the first respects. But during the one festival that is still jointly celebrated here VT receives the first respect. In spite of TT's association with the Pudukkottai kings, at this structural level its subordinate position continues to be expressed.

I asked the Pallavaraiyar chief why the two kuppams divided. He said that:

Actually, there were only eight kuppams in the beginning. At that time, VT and TT were united and observed as a single kuppam. The population of the kuppam became too dense and it resulted in a partition between VT and TT. The Manikkarayar (first lineage of VT) is the *annan* (elder brother) and the Pallavaraiyar (first lineage of TT) is the *tampi* (younger brother). The VT Manikkarayar, the TT Pallavaraiyar, and the Narankiyapattu Conaiyar (chief lineage of another TT kuppam) are brothers, pankalis, and so there is no marriage (*kolvinai kotuppinai* – exchange of women) among them. These three rank first in their respective kuppams.

Thus the first karais of the two kuppams were the descendants of two brothers. The hierarchical relationship between the two kuppams is that of older and younger brother as well as that of north and south (north is usually seen as superior to south). Even though the first karais of each teru are related as pankalis, and therefore do not exchange women, other karais in the two terus are not agnatic relatives.

However, what is most striking here is that the Pallavaraiyar chief does not mention what would seem to be the obvious cause of the division between the two terus. While it is possible that population pressures and the organizational constraints of size and geographical spread led to division, it is more likely that the two divided when the Tondaimans became chiefs. But, while he later attributes the reversal of status between the two terus to the rise of the Tondaimans, he never assigns this as a possible cause for the unique division of a kuppam.

There is also a third brother, the Narankiapattu Conaiyar, head of the first karai of the sixth kuppam. This suggests another and perhaps earlier division. When pressed, the Pallavaraiyar suggested that this story of the brothers was probably metaphorical rather than literal. In contrast, the Conaiyar himself claimed historical truth for the story. He explained that the three were brothers from the same father but from different mothers. Thus he implied that the hierarchical gradations among the brothers were due to the relative seniority of their mothers as wives and not so much to their relative ages. Given the fact that Narankiyapattu kuppam is ranked sixth and not third, it may be that the first two brothers were born of the same mother, while the third brother was born of a junior wife. The Pallavaraiyar chief admitted that the ranked position of the Narankiyapattu kuppam was anomalous but had no explanation of his own to offer.

Another of the nine kuppams has a close, though different, relationship with the Pallavaraiyars of TT. Ammanipattu, usually ranked seventh, is located close to the head village of the Pallavaraiyars, Pilavituti. In the kuppam temple of Ammanipattu, the first honors are given to the Pallavaraiyars. The headman of Ammanipattu explained that the Pallavaraiyars were their affinal relatives. "Once, when they came to our temple, we gave the first honors as they were our brothers-in-law (mappillai) and the same practice still occurs as tradition (*māmūl*)." The usual honors accorded to the brother-in-law, however, are not reciprocated. The reverse privileges are not given to Ammanipattu when they go to worship in the Pallavaraiyar's temple.

To return to the curious relations between TT and VT, though the latter is structurally superior to the former, the former nevertheless became superior to VT by virtue of its connection to the Tondaiman Rajas. In the words of the Pallavaraiyar chief:

when we assumed our royal status (*antastu*) we became, as it were, a royal family. Hence we, the five *karaikārkaḷ* (the five top lineages of TT) began to have affinal relations (*uṟavus*) with the royal families. So we became more dignified than the other kuppams. In the course of time, financial conditions might change; but we five karaikararkal maintain our antastu. We have *Raja antastu* and we sit in the king's assembly (*Raja capai*). While the influence and glory of the Raja was high, the influence of those of us living in TT also went up accordingly. Others who do not have marriage ties with the five chief lineages also reside here [in TT] but we classify them at a lower level (*kuṟainta taram*).

Here is a clear statement about the inflection of kinship by politics. All AN Kallars were loosely called Rajapantu, which means those who had a connection with the Raja. Nonetheless, not all AN Kallars had actual affinal ties with the Raja. As we shall shortly see, even the royal kuppam was divided into two parts, one with (potential) affinal ties to the Raja and the other (generally speaking) without such ties. However, because of the diffuse connection of all AN Kallars with the Raja, they were entitled to accept honors on behalf of the king if the king was absent when the palace honors (aranmanai mariyatai) were announced. The palace honors were called first in all temples in the state. While all AN Kallars were elevated to the status of Rajapantu, the elevation was more or less pronounced at each further segmental specification of the social structure. If one member of each segment was present when the royal honors were given, the segment with the highest royal marking would "represent" the Raja. The TT, variably classified as the second kuppam or as the second half of the first kuppam, became in effect the chief kuppam of the subcaste. Its members became the highest nobility of the land, as the Pallavaraiyar chief makes clear. Within this kuppam, those Kallars with direct affinal ties to the Raja found their status even more greatly elevated. They often contested that they alone had the right to call themselves Rajapantu. Even among these the Cervaikarars formed a specially marked group. Finally, the greatest impact of this extended sovereignty was felt within the Raja's lineage itself, the Tondaimans. The chief agnates of the Raja became Jagirdars, the chief nobles of the kingdom.

TT is not only unique in that the royal nobility of the little kingdom comes from its ranks, but it is the only kuppam to have two levels within it, two groups of lineages. The higher group, *aracu ancu*, contains five lineages; the lower group, *pūti pattu*, ten. Aracu is the Tamil word for kingship. Ancu (aintu) means five. Thus the top five lineages are the royal five. They share the sovereignty of the Raja more than the group of ten. The aracu ancu is the group from which, for the most part, the Rajas take their wives. It is in effect the royal connubium. With certain key exceptions, for instance the Kannanur Cervaikarars, the Rajas did not marry within the group of ten.[4]

Within the royal five, the lineages are ranked. The Pallavaraiyars (whose headman was my principal informant) are the first lineage. The Tondaiman lineage comes second, thereby posing structural problems for the kuppam. The other three lineages in this group are the Rankiars, the Kaliyaraiyars, and the Tevars. This hierarchy is reflected in the affinal choices made by the royal family over the last hundred years. By far the greatest number of royal marriages have been contracted with members of the Pallavaraiyar lineage. Indeed, when Ramachandra Raja, ruler of the state for much of the nineteenth century, had no issue, he was succeeded by his adopted son-in-law, the son of a Pallavaraiyar. Other royal marriages have been contracted with the

---

[4] Only in very recent times have marriage alliances occurred regularly between the aracu ancu and the puti pattu. This is because since "merger" the royalty of the king has become less important than the rising wealth of some of the puti pattu, who trade their economic position for the status of the aracu ancu.

other lineages of the aracu ancu, the frequency of the ties with each lineage descending in rank order. As important as inclusion in the aracu ancu *per se* is the political position of the family. For example, the Rajas had marriage ties with their military chiefs, or Cervaikarars. Because of the multiple criteria influencing the choice of marriage partners, there were also ties between particular families in the lower group of ten lineages (puti pattu) and the royal family. It should also be noted that many of the earliest affinal ties of the Tondaimans were not with fellow members of TT, but with lineages in VT. The first wife of the son of the first Raja of Pudukkottai came from the Pannikontar family, the second lineage in VT, one branch of which continues to be very closely related to the Rajas. This branch was granted extensive lands in Kattakurricci, close to the center of the state. It was from this line that the Pudukkottai kings, all the way down to Ramachandra who ruled until 1886, had descended. The son of the first marriage also had a second marriage, conducted in a ceremony in which he was emblematically represented by a sword, with a member of the Maravaraiyar lineage of the puti pattu. The present line of Pudukkottai kings descends from this union.[5]

That there is not an absolute correspondence between the royal connubium and the division of the kuppam into two groups does not vitiate the general assumption that this division was prompted at least in part by the setting off of lineages with royal affinal ties from those without such ties. The sub-division of subcastes according to a hierarchical principle in which affinal ties with chiefs form the major basis for membership in the highest tier has been noted by Louis Dumont for many other subcastes in the southern Tamil country. What is different in Pudukkottai from the areas studied by Dumont, however, is that the tiers are not explicable in relation to the offspring of senior and junior sons, but only in terms of the creation of loose affinal circles such as I have described. Furthermore, in Pudukkottai there is only a very loosely stated preference for marriage with the matrilateral cross cousin, which has to do with the centrality of the mother's brother in the marriage ceremony. When I asked about marriage preferences, I was told that the rightful girl (*urimai peṇ*) was the mother's brother's daughter, the father's sister's daughter, or the sister's daughter. (Dumont found no instances where sister's daughter's marriages occurred with Kallars and Maravars in Madurai and Tirunelveli.) If the marriage partner was not the matrilateral cross cousin, the mother's

---

[5] One of the difficulties in tracing royal kinship ties in the nineteenth century was caused by the break in succession in 1886, when the royal successor was the daughter's son, a Tondaiman by adoption though a Pallavaraiyar by birth.

brother had to give his assent, but I was given every indication that this assent was merely formal. However, if the marriage were to be conducted with a non-preferential partner then the assent was of more crucial, and possibly disruptive, significance. When I took genealogies, I soon realized that the qualified bilateral theory expressed by my informants was supported by practice, and that marriages did in fact take place with all three preferential categories in roughly equal proportion, with perhaps a slight edge for the matrilateral cross cousin. Although I will consider the implications of this bilateral marriage system more fully later in the study, it is important to note here that no systematic hypergamy operated in royal marriages. Where the royal family took brides they usually gave them as well. When any AN family talked about another lineage with which they had an affinal alliance, they would call it their *māman-maccanan* karai, which implied that they both gave and took wives from this allied lineage. (The very term maman-maccanan was used with this intent, to say that they had both mother's brothers, i.e., potential wife givers, and brothers-in-law, i.e., potential wife takers, in a single lineage.) Bilateral marriage exchange thus permitted the creation of ranked circles of affinal alliance without the asymmetrical effects of hypergamous relations, which constantly tended to threaten any status-based unit of endogamy within a larger endogamous structure. Even when kinship was significantly affected by political concerns, the ideology of marriage still privileged equality over hierarchy, at least within certain boundaries.

The operation of the kinship system thus mitigated rank within circles of affinal alliance (though at the same time it created new ranks between such circles). Nonetheless, it is still peculiar that the royal lineage was not ranked as the highest within the royal five. Paralleling the position of TT vis-à-vis VT, the Tondaimans were structurally below the Pallavaraiyars. As we shall see, the separation between royal honor and caste honor rendered this disorder unproblematic. That is to say, whenever kinship as a quasi-autonomous form became a problem, kinship forms were encompassed by the political (the honors accruing to the Raja as Raja and not as Tondaiman). Even so, given the system's responsiveness to political changes, it is indeed curious that certain adjustments remained unmade.

The Pallavaraiyar chief classifies the puti pattu as *taram kuraintatu*. Taram means quality. It is used in land records to refer to the classification of land according to its quality, i.e., sandy, loamy, irrigated, etc. Kurai means lower. Therefore the use of taram kuraintatu suggests that the puti pattu are lower in quality even though they are within the same classificatory group as the other lineages in TT. This is further evidenced by the name puti pattu itself. *Pūti* probably derives from *pū*, meaning earth. Earth is lower than the sky which is the domain of the king, who enjoys the fruits of the earth. *Pattu* means ten. Like ancu, it merely specifies the number of lineages within the group.

To remind us of the total structure of the kuppam, I reproduce the list of lineages within TT kuppam once again:

Ten Teru

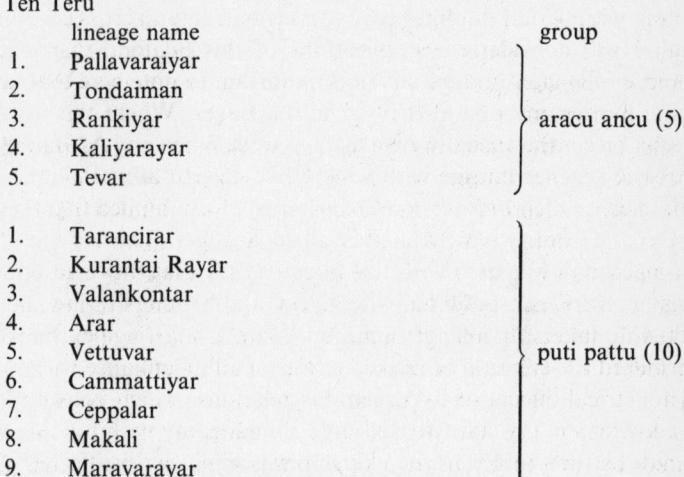

|  | lineage name | group |
|---|---|---|
| 1. | Pallavaraiyar | |
| 2. | Tondaiman | |
| 3. | Rankiyar | aracu ancu (5) |
| 4. | Kaliyarayar | |
| 5. | Tevar | |
| | | |
| 1. | Tarancirar | |
| 2. | Kurantai Rayar | |
| 3. | Valankontar | |
| 4. | Arar | |
| 5. | Vettuvar | puti pattu (10) |
| 6. | Cammattiyar | |
| 7. | Ceppalar | |
| 8. | Makali | |
| 9. | Maravarayar | |
| 10. | Narankiyar/Narankiyapattu | |

According to the Pallavaraiyar chief, these groups initially had their own settlements. These are still maintained to some extent, though today most of the members of TT live in or near Pilavituti. The Pallavaraiyars initially settled in Pallavaranpattu Putupatti. Long ago a majority of this group migrated to Pilavituti. The Tondaimans probably settled initially in Tondaiman Vituti. The Tevars live in Korantaranpattu and Tirttan Vituti. The Kaliyarayars live in Kaliyarayar Vituti and a nearby hamlet called Kattali. Makalis, though they seem not to have had an original place of their own, live in a hamlet called Makali Teru near Pilavituti. There is also a Rankiyan Vituti for Rankiyars, most of whom have also shifted to Pilavituti, important because it is the residence of the first karai.

TT is unique in another respect. Though all of its lineages have their own temples, TT as a whole has no single kuppam temple. The border temple in Cervaipatti that TT shares with VT is a Pillaiyar temple. It is therefore unsuitable as a kuppam temple, which is usually dedicated to village goddesses such as Mariyamman or to village protection deities such as Aiyanar. According to the Pallavaraiyar chief, TT has many

229

temples: "We constructed temples wherever we settled." The only Mariyamman temple in Pilavituti is now in ruins. Its idol was taken to Karampakuti, where a temple was built for it twelve years ago (1970). However, no major festival is held in the new temple, reportedly because then the Karampakuti kuppam would claim honors for themselves during the festival. No one knew if this temple had served as a central kuppam temple in the past, which suggests that if this had been its function earlier, it could not have been for at least sixty years. Another common temple is located in nearby Mullankuricci. It is also a Mariyamman temple. All those who are entitled to a share in honors in TT can get honors there as well.

The lack of a central kuppam temple suggests that TT never achieved full structural differentiation apart from VT, unlike VT and the other kuppams. A major reason for this probably lies in the fact that TT split off from VT. TT could hardly have kept the Mariyamman temple in Tiruvonam as its kuppam temple, both because VT would not have permitted it and because TT had no access to it. It was located well outside the limits of TT and of Pudukkottai state, with which TT so strongly identified. With the attainment of royal status by the Tondaimans, TT was no longer a mere kuppam but a royal elite. The need for a kuppam temple to provide the basis of kuppam identity has been supplanted by the more important identification of the kuppam members with the Raja and with his temples. The most important of these is the goddess temple in Pudukkottai, in which Brihatampal was established by the Raja as the Tondaimans' central tutelary deity. Further, the disjunction between the position of the Raja as Raja and the Raja as head of the secondary lineage in TT was highly problematic. Who would receive first honors in the kuppam temple? Finally the internal differentiation of the kuppam into two strata suggests that relations with and identification with the Raja have become more important than the solidarity of the kuppam.

### Authority within the subcaste

Largely because of these potentially anomalous conditions no one particular lineage has special rights in the management and organization of the central natu temple. Instead, these rights, while belonging in a sense to the entire subcaste, are vested in a small group of Vellalars who act as "trustees." Indeed, by virtue of these rights of management, this group of Vellalars is structurally included as a section of the AN Kallars. We know nothing about the past associations of the goddess Vira Makali Amman with any particular group within AN. What seems likely is that the Siva temple to which this goddess shrine is now attached was under the management of Vellalars who were settled in the area by Cola kings sometime in the tenth or eleventh centuries. As in southern Pudukkottai, Vellalars were the chief previous residents of the area.

Two branches of Vellalars live in AN. The subcaste temple is managed by a small group of Coriya Vellalars (Vellalars who come from the Cola country) variably called *Āṇṭipiḷḷai* (*āṇṭi* means those who render service in temples; *piḷḷai* is a common Vellalar surname), *Kāṇṭiyār* (the village from which these Vellalars claim originally to have come), and *Stāṇikar* (a term often used for those who manage the internal affairs of the temple). The principal duty of the Kantiyar Vellalars is to supervise the honors (mariyatai, or *kālāṉci*; mariyatai is the general term meaning honor or respect, and kalanci are the actual items given as honors, such as sandalwood paste, holy ash, betel nut, and the pracatam, or returned food, of rice, plantains, and coconuts) in the temple, and make sure that every one gets their due honor in the proper order. The Kantiyars also oversee the major festivals in the temple, and have been allocated important *maṇṭakappatis* during the major festivals (mantakappati means the right to host and conduct a day of worship and receive first honors on that day).

The Kantiyars claimed that they were the *talaimai* (headmen) of the AN Kallars, on whose behalf they did this service and to whom they gave honors. They said that they were given this duty by the Raja. Furthermore, it is generally acknowledged that they have the privilege of calling the natu assembly (or *kūṭṭam*) within which they oversee the arbitration of disputes. This is unusual, as in every other subcaste the nattampalams themselves call the assembly and settle the disputes. However, since one of the major causes of dispute these assemblies are called to resolve has to do with honors, the adjudicative function of these Vellalars is a natural extension of their role as the guardians of honor in the natu.

How long the Kantiyars have acted in this role is unclear. It could be a longstanding traditional arrangement. It could be that because the head of VT lived outside of Pudukkottai state when the boundaries were drawn in the late seventeenth century it was thought inappropriate to have him fulfill it. Perhaps since the Raja was obviously the *de facto* and *de jure* head of the natu, and the person from whom the peculiar status of the natu is derived, this would ordinarily be his role. But the Raja did not perform this role, either because of a potential structural conflict between him and the classificatory head of the natu (the head of the first VT lineage) or because he had no time for or did not want to associate himself so closely with the adjudication of affairs in his particular community. He was the ultimate court of appeal for all Kallars and all communities in the whole state. And yet, no other Kallar leader had the *locus standi* to fill in for the Raja in this role. Thus, the Vellalars performed their duties as much by default as by virtue of their original settlement in the region, and by extension of their early relationship to the temple.

According to a Kallar informant from the Narankyapattu lineage: "It was the Vellalars who were living here originally. We were brought here by them. Even now, they have the first mariyatai." In the words of another Kallar informant from the Ammanipattu lineage: "Ampu Kovil is the *talaimai iṭam* (the head place) for AN. No AN Kallars live there. The Raja placed a Kantiyar there to protect (do the *paripālaṇam* of) the temple. He gives honors in the temple." The head of the Pallavaraiyar lineage told me that: "The natu kuttam for AN should be convened only by the Piccar and Kantiyar, i.e., the AN Vellalars. For the services of being the stanikar of AN, they were given a tax-free maniyam grant of eighty acres of land. These stanikars have to meet the expenses for arranging the natu kuttam such as providing meals for the participants from their maniyam lands. They do not only organize the kuttam but also function as arbitrators." Another Pallavaraiyar continued to explain: "The nine ampalams guided by the Stanikar pass the judgement. Though the Raja does not come, on the final day, they place lime, betel nut, etc., on a chair to represent the Raja. The others sit on a mat spread on the ground." Thus the claims made by the Kantiyars are borne out by the Kallars.[6] This last statement is striking in that it suggests that the Vellalars do in a curious way represent the authority of the Raja himself. They constitute the symbolic presence of the king by setting up a chair (perhaps a symbol of the throne – in other traditional assemblies the nattampalams were distinguished either by sitting on the only mat, or by sitting on a raised stone platform) with honors to represent the Raja. As the guardians of honor they are uniquely empowered to handle and invoke kingly honors. Indeed, the Kantiyars were occasionally called the *kāṇṭirājas*, thereby expressing the perception that they were, in some sense, kings. As the greatest honor of all, they alone were allowed to sit on a platform equal with that of the Raja during palace functions.

[6] A similar situation exists within one of the AN kuppams, that of Karampakuti. In this kuppam, and particularly in their kuppam temple – to Aiyanar – a stanikar was appointed for similar reasons. As I was told, "In spite of the pujas performed by the Brahman Gurukkal, other duties such as breaking the coconut, sacrificing the goats, distributing the viputi to the Kallars, etc., were done by the local group of stanikars, also Cola Vellalars."

In their capacity as guardians of honor the Vellalars received first honors. This means that they received honors before the nine kuppams, but, importantly, not before the Raja, whose claim to first honors in all the temples in Pudukkottai precedes that even of learned Brahmans. In addition, the Vellalars had certain emblems which they were entitled (and indeed enjoined) to use in temple rituals and on state occasions. As the Kantiyars told me, "If there was any function in the Palace, we used to go with all of our emblems and honors, with music, etc., taking us in procession, taking the mariyatai. Palace functions could only take place with our presence." Certain of the honors were privileges rather than emblems *per se*. For example, the Raja used to provide a vehicle to bring them to palace functions. As mentioned above, the Kantiyars alone were allowed to sit on an equal platform with the Raja.[7] Among the specific emblems used by the Kantiyars were the *paṭṭā katti* (a sword of honor), betel, garlands, and sandalwood. "The sword is a *perumai* (mark of honor)." I asked for whom the sword was an honor, for him or for the Raja. He answered by saying that it was an honor for both: "For us because we serve the Raja, for the Raja because we show respect to him."

Thus we see again the importance of honors and emblems for constituting and representing social relationships and political authority. The honors given by the Raja to the Vellalars contain, especially in the case of the Kantiyars, some of the sovereign honor of the Raja himself. Here, as elsewhere, honors not only depict hierarchical forms, but express the worship and service components of hierarchical relationships. All honors have the dual role of marking a particular group within the total structure and marking them in such a way as to display the preeminence of the king. In the particular ethnohistory of Pudukkottai, we realize that the special position of Vellalars is as precursors as well as emblems of Kallar kingship. Insofar as they possess residual authority from being the previous "honorable" settlers of the Pudukkottai country, they are best qualified to represent the new kingly authority of the Kallars.

The position of the other group of Vellalars in AN is also somewhat special. These other Vellalars live in Vellalavituti, which forms one of the AN kuppams. They receive a full share of honors as one half of a kuppam; another share for the other half being given to the Kallars in nearby Kallakottai. The Vellalars told me that whereas all other kuppams were given only one honor, which could be shared, this

---

[7] The importance of equal seating (cariyiruppu) is made clear in a number of the vamcavalis.

233

kuppam was specifically given two. These Vellalars, who do not have affinal relations with the Cola Vellalars of AN, call themselves Karukatta Vellalars. This is the title used by the early Vellalar inhabitants of southern Pudukkottai. According to the chief of the Pallavaraiyar lineage:

For a long time, the Vellalars were ruling the areas around Vellalavituti as *kurunilamannars* (little kings). They were ruling the palaiyapattus. When the Kallars migrated from Anpil to this area, they destroyed the dominance of the Vellalars. When the Vellalars lost their hold and leadership, they retreated to the single settlement of Vellalavituti. They requested that we include them as the rightful shareholders (*urimaikārars* and *paṅkukārars*) of the temples and families of this kuppam, since they were the ruling family of this area. So we gave them the position of a half kuppam and they receive the honor for this half kuppam only from us.

This serves as an explanation for this anomaly within AN: that a Vellalar group receives honors as Kallars, at least in a structural sense. This is the only instance in which a separate caste group receives honors along with the dominant caste. In all other cases within AN and in other natus the representatives of other castes are given honors after those of the individual lineages of the dominant caste. Dominance is signified not only by the fact that the lineages of the dominant group precede other castes in receiving honors but that in structural terms individual lineages in the dominant caste are given equivalence to other entire caste groups.

These Vellalars also provided me with a possible reason for the continued significance of this non-Kallar group in AN. As we have seen, the position of the Raja is anomalous because while he is head of the natu (and of his entire kingdom) by virtue of being the king, he, in his kinship position, is not entitled to first respects. The Vellalars told me that

The Raja, as ruler of the state, is given the first honor. He represents the kingship (*rājiyam*) and so he gets this privilege. But the Raja as an AN Kallar cannot claim the first honor (mutal mariyatai) and he will not be given it by the temple on these grounds. When the Stanikar of Ampu temple calls the kuppams during the distribution of honor, the persons representing the concerned kuppam only can get the honors. The Raja cannot go and get respects by means of representing any kuppam. The *Rāja mariyātai* is different from *ina mariyātai* (ina(m) means caste, community, patrilineage).

Thus the continued centrality of Vellalars in AN, as managers of the subcaste temple, arbiters of honor, adjudicators of the assembly, and members of the royal subcaste, works to resolve the potentially anomalous situation in which the head of the royal subcaste would be some Kallar other than the king himself.

So we see the partial sedimentation of historical process in the structure of categories and groups. A segmentary logic renders unnecessary certain rearrangements of categories and groups such as the elevation of the Tondaimans over the Pallavaraiyars, or of TT over VT. The fact that the Tondaimans became kings made it rapidly irrelevant within the context of the little kingdom that they were not the first lineage. Any inhabitant of Pudukkottai state or member of the subcaste has only to hear the term Tondaiman to know that one is talking of the royal family. The natural consequence of this politically generated cultural grammar is that certain types of rearrangements within encompassed segments need never be made in structural terms, particularly given the lack of a kuppam temple. The Tondaimans would never appear to receive honor in the local temple as Tondaimans (ina mariyatai) but only as Rajas (Raja mariyatai). The honors given to a king because of his position as a king are different from the honors given to individuals on the basis of their position in their caste or social group. Thus apparent contradictions are immediately resolved by resort to a higher domain (that of kingship over kinship) as well as to the higher segment (that of kingdom over kuppam). This process is not just convenient but necessary, though it remains a puzzle.

There are many other empirical complexities which should but perhaps never can be fully explained. Like all complexities, they push us further in our search for order and make our acceptance of received structures more difficult. While in a general sense we can explain the subversion and transformation of a presumed original structure by reference to the peculiar historical processes affecting this kuppam and the central identification of the kuppam with the Raja, there are many details about the particularities of the kuppam which, partly because certain structures became sedimented at different though unknown times, and partly because other changes seem to be taking place all the time, we cannot begin to explain.

As in all other social groups in Pudukkottai state assemblies (kuttams) were held to decide various issues and questions relating to the festival and to arbitrate disputes and settle problems as they came up within the community. Such assemblies took place in villages. The village ampalam would act as officiant and judge. In all the natus, the highest court of appeal for village assemblies was the natu assembly. This was also the body which would judge all issues whose significance extended beyond the boundaries of a single village. It would be headed by the nattampalam(s), sometimes one, sometimes three persons who were ranked. The AN assembly was not led by the nattampalam but rather by the Vellalar Kantiyars. There were also kuppam assemblies, which were officiated by the head ampalam of the kuppam. Like the natu assemblies, they were held at that temple which constituted and defined the relevant social and territorial unit. TT is again exceptional. No one was designated as the ampalam of the kuppam. Again this is no doubt because of the inherent contradiction that the king was not the senior member of his kuppam. The head of the Pallavaraiyar lineage was in effect the ampalam. Issues which concerned members of the teru were first brought to him. He was simply called *Ayyā*, a term of respect meaning lord. The assemblies were held at his house, called the *Ayyāviṭu*. When asked why the meetings did not take place in a temple, the Pallavaraiyar chief was unable to provide an answer. The lack of any temple which served as the single focus for the identity of the group was obviously the reason for this departure from the normal structure. The political anomalies of this royal kuppam led to significant modifications at every level of its structure.

The special position and particular dominance of the TT kuppam were displayed not only within AN but throughout the entire kingdom. During the eighteenth and nineteenth centuries Pudukkottai kings had settled AN Kallars in villages throughout Pudukkottai. One or two and sometimes more AN families were given inam lands and certain special privileges in virtually every village in Kolattur Taluk and many villages in Alankuti and Tirumayyam taluks. Their privileges included being allowed to accept temple honors on behalf of the Raja. These palace honors came before all other honors. Many of these AN Kallars took the name or suffix Cervai or Cervaikarar, deliberately modelling themselves on the great chiefs, the Vakuppu Cervaikarars, with whom they are not to be confused. In a structural sense these Kallars were like the Cervaikarars. Their dispersed settlement, their exalted local position, their relationship to the royal family through their maniyam lands and their kinship ties to the Raja (whether actual or potential, mostly the latter) suggest a structural replication of the Cervaikarars at a lower level. They were settled for the same reasons as the Vakuppu Cervaikarars: to secure Tondaiman rule and protect its institutions. They were settled to provide a local presence throughout the little kingdom of the royal subcaste and to be the spies and informants of the little kings. Most of the Vakuppu Cervaikarars and the local Cervais were from the TT Kuppam of AN. Even though I was able to secure a partial list of these AN Kallars, it is impossible to say more than this since the addition of the surname Cervai often substituted for the pattapeyar, the lineage title which indicates kuppam membership. All other AN Kallars, even the Vakuppu Cervaikarars, use their lineage title in their name. But outside AN, membership in the kuppam became less important for establishing identity than relationship to the Raja and so the title was dropped. Many of these local Cervais, while from TT, were from the lower ten lineages. This may further help to explain why these Cervais let their lineage title drop while the Vakuppu Cervaikarars did not.

As we have seen, the great Cervaikarars were not only all Kallars, but with one exception were all AN Kallars. The exception was the one who was "gifted" to the Pudukkottai Raja by the neighboring Cetupati of Ramnad, with whom the Tondaimans had contracted an affinal tie when the Cetupati married the Raja's sister in the late seventeenth century. All but one of the AN Cervaikarars were from the TT kuppam. Again, there is the ubiquitous exception. As noted throughout this study, there is never a perfect correspondence between the so-called political and so-called kinship structures, however much they seem to determine each other. We would predict that the Cervaikarar who did not come from TT, however unimportant a Cervaikarar he may be, would at least come from a similarly high kuppam. Instead he came from Neiveli, one of the lowest kuppams, so low that some informants claimed that it did not even receive honors at Ampu temple. The Neiveli Cervaikarar was, however, one of the most important nobles in the land. Further, another great Cervaikarar, the Kannanur Valankontar, came from one of the ten lower lineages of TT. In the late seventeenth century the Kannanur chiefs had been instrumental in making the kingship of the Tondaimans secure. Thus their special position has a very particular historical cause. The other great Vakuppu Cervaikarars come from the most important of the TT karais, the Pallavaraiyars and the Rankiyars. They have many marriage alliances with the royal family.

This pattern holds all the way down the political hierarchy. The Kurikarars occupy the next level below the Cervaikarars and above the Cervais. Some of the Kurikarars were from the Kaliyarayar lineage of TT, members of the aracu ancu. Others were members of the Terketti Kallars, the same group to which Ilantari Ampalakarar belonged. Because of their relationship to Ilantari Ampalakarar their status, like his, was that of honored guest within the little kingdom. Through him they too were connected to the Cetupati of Ramnad, who was an affine of the Raja. As outsiders, they were not likely to provide the basis for any kind of internal threat.

As we have also seen, at the highest level in the political hierarchy were the two Jagirdars, whose status in the little kingdom was second only to the Raja. They represented the collateral members of the royal lineage.

These Jagirdars were given extensive lands, which were less like the jivitam lands given to Cervaikarars than they were discrete parcels of the little kingdom. Not all Tondaimans were Jagirdars. Many of them appear simply to have hung about one or another of the royal houses. Another group of Tondaimans which was settled near Taccanpatti had the dubious honor of taking on the pollution of the royal family and conducting their funerals. They also represented them on other ritual occasions when it was unsuitable or impossible for the Raja to attend.

In thinking about the set of issues involved in the structuring of identity within the royal subcaste, it is necessary to return briefly to the question of what happens to members of lineages when they migrate outside their original place of settlement. We saw that families which were resettled by the king maintained their local status in their original village and territorial kuppam, while in their new places they did not merge with any new group but rather became the *in loco* representatives of the Raja. Other families, not settled at the specific instance of the Raja, tended over time to lose contact with their original kuppams and to accept honors from the new kuppam temple. The families which were settled by the king were usually from TT. Once again, the position of TT is distinctive because the Raja, and relations with the Raja, provided the principal context for the formation and expression of identity not merely within the kuppam but outside it as well.

The privileged position of the TT kuppam among the AN Kallars was also exemplified by the special "privileges" accorded to women of the aracu ancu as well as the families of Cervaikarars and other important nobles. They were virtually kept in purdah. The customary freedom and boldness of Kallar women was not in evidence among them. They rarely left their domestic compounds. Visitors did not come inside their houses but were entertained in a separate house or mantapam constructed some distance from the domestic hearth. When these Kallar women did leave their houses, they did so in royal style, in covered palanquins. They also covered their bodies from head to foot when they went out. The only Kallar women allowed to wear blouses (*ravikkai*), they also wore special earrings (*mēmēlaṭu*), a necklace of black glass beads (*karukamaṇi*), and green and black glass bangles (*paccai* and *karuvaḷaivi*).

We have thus seen the many ways in which the royal kuppam was set off from and placed above the rest of AN society, and the specific political and cultural dynamics of this hierarchical marking. We will conclude this chapter with an analysis of some remarks by the Pallavaraiyar chief about the nature of hierarchy and status, and analyze them in terms of what we know about the socio-political structure of the royal caste.

### Hierarchy and kingship: royal honor and royal order

I had many discussions with the Pallavaraiyar chief about what he meant by hierarchy and status, and how he could explain the way in which the AN subcaste was structured. In the early days, he told me, his forefathers had instituted the laws of society. He was not absolutely sure why the VT and TT had been at the top of the subcaste. Nor did he know why these two chieftains, who were brothers, had maintained power while the third brother, the head of the Narankiyapattu kuppam, had fallen in stature. Each kuppam has its own merit and only by merit, status, and dignity was each kuppam classified. The Pallavaraiyar chief used the English word "merit." Merit was determined by four things. First, merit was thought about in terms of *antastu*, which means status or dignity, and refers particularly to a royal model for what would constitute dignity. It also suggests proximity to royalty. Second, merit was measured by the temple in which one had kaniyatci or rights to receive honors. Third, merit was determined by one's life style, one's code for conduct (*kaṭṭuppāṭu*) and how strictly this code was enforced and followed. Finally, merit had to do with a group's scrupulous concern with social relations and in particular marriage ties (*uṟavumuraikaḷ*).

I quote from one discussion at length:

One has to maintain one's family status, one's temple, one's karai, and royal blood. Antastu can take its meaning from one's village, or kuppam, or natu. By dignity and status we do not mean money, but rather having alliances through marriage. To maintain and establish good alliances, one must maintain one's dignity and status. Even the poor of TT are regarded as having higher status and members of other kuppams would desire to have an alliance with a poor Pilavituti Kallar. They feel that if they have an alliance (*campantam*) with us, their status among Kallars will go up. We have this belief. Why are we superior to others? Because we maintain the *camutāya kaṭṭuppāṭu*. We do not allow widow remarriage and we abide by the moral codes of our society strictly. Other Kallars may say that all Kallars are the same. It is popularly assumed that all Kallars were thieves (*kalavānis*). But we are not thieves. How can the ruling Kallars steal from others? Our Kallars are Panchayattars, Zamindars, Kurikarars, Cervaikarars, and Miracidars. We have to maintain law and order. How can we go off thieving? We decided that we should lead a life of kattuppatu and *orunku* (restriction and order). Others are not like us. We lead a life for mariyatai and antastu (honor and status). Our Kallars base their lives on the temple and on our marriage alliances (uravumuraikal). Therefore, when we go out to seek an alliance, we ask the following questions: what is your lineage? What is your temple? What is your kuppam? Only if these questions are answered satisfactorily will we have an alliance (campantam). Otherwise, we judge the other party as inappropriate, less dignifying, as if judging the quality of gold by the number of carats. Our honors are usually measured [by the nature of the honors we get] in temples and [the kind of] marriages [we contract] or when we convene the assembly (capai). When we measure honor in those places, will we like less dignified lineages to take seats on a par with us? We say that their status is such that they are not fit to sit with us.

There is much that seems circular in this statement. Definitions often appear tautological. But there is a cultural logic which is at the base of these assumptions, apparent tautologies, and assertions. The AN Kallars are superior because they are royal, and because they are ordered. Because they are royal, they have control not only of the order of things but also over the enunciation of order. Indeed, they define what order is in the social world of Pudukkottai. What is important is that the AN Kallars are leaders of society: rulers rather than thieves, kings rather than bandits. As kings they are the fount of honor. As the nobility they are the honored (and honorable) people of the little kingdom.

The first and fundamental element of this world view is the possession by these AN Kallars of royalty and honor. Royalty is implied by the term antastu; the particular honor (mariyatai) of these Kallars is dependent on their participation in the royalty of the Tondaiman king. The status of royalty is achieved through proximity to the king: kinship networks with the royal family, more generalized membership in the royal subcaste, and the privilege of performing services on behalf of the king. The preeminent position of the king in the kingdom has had the effect of making the royal subcaste the preeminent community in the kingdom as well, and every conception of social reality held by AN Kallars is colored by this basic social fact. As we have seen, the AN Kallars are entitled to accept honors in the place of the king; they are endowed with their political importance throughout the little kingdom because of their capacity to represent the king. Political, social, economic, and ritual hierarchy, at least among Kallars, is explicable only in the context of the historical accident that the king was an AN Kallar. The locus of enunciation in kingship was not arbitrary, but the particular forms of order that then became enunciated were dependent on the particular history of the ascendance of a single subcaste and their particular constructions of their authority.

The preeminence of the AN Kallars is explained not only by reference to the fact that the king hailed from this subcaste, but by noting that this subcaste has the most rigidly defined and maintained code for conduct of all subcastes. These Kallars have the most order (orunku); and they enforce this order through the set of restrictions which are implied by the term kattuppatu. Kattuppatu, which can be taken to mean code for conduct and discipline, literally means something more like restriction, or even constriction. It derives from the root *kaṭṭu*, which means tied or knotted or restricted. The code for conduct includes rigid kinship behaviors. Concern about social relationships is part of a general conception of status. One must, for example, avoid widow remarriages. The Vatakkalur kuppam had made the grievous mistake of allowing widow remarriage and now most of the AN Kallars with whom I spoke said that they would not contract a marriage with this kuppam. The Neiveli kuppam had not allowed any remarriages, but had spoken up in the subcaste assembly in favor of Vatakkalur. For this reason alone it was held to be lower than most other kuppams. Kattuppatu involved other dictates such as marrying according to the wishes of the maternal uncle. But kattuppatu is not simply a code for conduct, but also a set of authoritative procedures which renders this code enforceable within the community. Kattuppatu thus has to do with a special order which is rigidly defined and maintained by authoritative figures who represent and command the total social group.

Concern with royalty, honor, order, and codes for conduct entails concern with the position of one's own lineage and the kind of alliances one contracts through marriage. Marriage with the Raja is best. Failing that comes marriage with a Cervaikarar; failing that, with a Pallavarai-yar, or a member of Pilavituti, or a member of the royal five karais, and so on down the line. Complicated marriage strategies and transactions reveal the highly complex structure of social relations, demonstrating both the functioning of social units such as karais and kuppams and the definition of units such as the aracu ancu. We also realize here the incapacity of any reified conception or representation of the kinship system to encapsulate the full range of potential strategies and the full political context within which kinship operates. For example, a Kurikarar from the TT kuppam contracted a marriage tie with a Cervaikarar of a lower kuppam (Neiveli), thereby "trading" "social" for "political" status. And marriage has implications for more than the individual families involved in the affinal alliance. If, for example, one marries a girl from Pilavituti, one becomes the son-in-law – mappillai – of the entire village.

In all discussions of marriage, no expression of hierarchical differenti-ation between wife givers and wife takers was ever made. However, establishing marriage relations with a family of higher status was clearly the aim of all AN Kallar families. These kinds of alliances were sought after because, as we have seen, they could result in the inclusion of one's lineage in a connubial circle which would have the effect of raising that lineage's status, as occurred with the four lineages that had established affinal ties with the Tondaiman lineage. In a structural context in which hypergamy was not part of the kinship system *per se*, status elevation was still very much a part of the set of concerns influencing marriage strategies.

In choosing alliances the initial questions were basic: what is your lineage (karai), your temple (*kōvil*), your territorial unit (kuppam or natu)? The resolution of any given affinal decisions was far more difficult. Temples defined membership in social groups and also provided contexts in which these social groups were more finely gradated and ranked. Ultimately, social relations and the set of units, conceptions, rules, and strategies concerning them were organized in relation to a complex conception of status in its two interrelated senses: antastu and mariyatai. Antastu was measured in the king's court; mariyatai was measured in the temple, in the subcaste assembly, and in marriages. These primary concepts, therefore, take on their relevant meanings only in these specified institutional contexts.

The Pallavaraiyar's statements, and indeed the general ideological orientation they reflect, reveal the continuation of concerns about the past reputation of Kallars as thieves, bandits, outlaws. The ethnographic discourse here shares much in common with the eighteenth-century family histories, in which this acknowledged past becomes totally transformed. Again, there is an implicit opposition between the activities of thieves and the activities of kings. In this case, the royal duty of protecting and subduing disorder is combined with an ideology of order and restriction which organizes the social relations of the subcaste.

As we noted at the beginning of this chapter, the very word Kallar means thief in Tamil, and no one, certainly not the Pallavaraiyar, disputes the fact that at certain places and times particular groups of Kallars engaged in predatory activity. The Kallars initially attained their position of political authority in the Pudukkottai country by providing protection to local communities and institutions, often necessary because of their own presence. Kallars were given rights of protection because of their capacity to control and to a very large extent monopolize the means of violence. But however close the position and activities of bandit and king, the nature of violence and coercion effected by the two differs fundamentally. The violence of the bandit is illegitimate; it represents and causes disorder. Banditry is defined as such because it is exercised from outside the central institutions of rule and the culturally mandated positions of authority.

Kingship, of course, is just the opposite. Kings are not only legitimate, they define the realm of the legitimate. The discourse of the Pallavaraiyar chief reveals this rather vividly. The way in which the royal subcaste organizes its social relations makes it impossible that they could be thieves, or indeed affected in any way by this general reputation. Not only is the royal subcaste headed by a king, it provides almost all the royal nobles of the kingdom. The fundamental duty of these members of the elite is to subdue disorder, destroy lawlessness, and enforce law and order, both within the kingdom at large and within the subcaste itself. In this context, we can better understand the Pallavaraiyar's subsequent statement: "most important of all is the kattuppatu, the fact that our society [i.e., the AN Kallars] only exists as such because our group [corporately] set and then enforced a comprehensive code for conduct. It is no accident of history that we are the ones who belong to the royal family, since we have all the virtues and qualities of a royal and noble group." Here we see why notions of order and restriction exist in such a vitally complementary way within the context of the centrality of the king. It is no accident, after all, that the king is an AN Kallar. The identity of the group in relation to the king and in opposition to the conventional category of bandit is the subtext of its social and ideological organization.

The maintenance of social order and restriction was not achieved without cost. As the Pallavaraiyar chief said, "We have so many things to do, so many responsibilities. We have to conduct festivals. We have to feed people. Even if we have to starve ourselves we have to do these things. We have to follow our codes so rigidly that it is not uncommon for men, and even women, to marry very late in life. Thus our population has been declining for many years." This culturally specific statement of noblesse oblige, whether accepted generally or not, still communicates the sense of duty which accompanies the understanding of political, or royal authority in Tamil India.

However much the capacity for appropriate behavior was encoded by birth, the actual behavior of any individual was what ultimately mattered. The Pallavaraiyar chief told me that "if someone else is able to follow all of our restrictions and codes we welcome them. They too can become AN Kallars." This statement not only confirms the interdependency between substance and code insisted upon by Inden and Marriott (1974), it also emphasizes the cultural appropriateness of Kallar kingship. The AN Kallars are defined as much by their birth into a given family as they are by their behavior, specifically their adherence to a royal code for conduct. Social and political position are not independent variables, but are vitally connected. Kinship is part of a wider domain of social recruitment. We see here the cultural basis for the historical significance of migration. New groups could be accepted not only as territorial neighbors, but as potential affines, if they proved themselves worthy.

The importance of deeds is also noted in relation to the recruitment of the political elite. The Pallavaraiyar explained that: "The titles have not just been given away like that. There must be deeds attached to them. Rankiyar Tevar [perhaps the most powerful of the Cervaikarars] does not, for example, just go and solicit titles. Rather, the titles and privileges will be given to him in recognition of his service to the community and his heroic deeds, which are first class (*mutal taram*)." Status thus has to do with both action and recognition, the two being indissolubly combined.

Given a cultural logic in which kinship (specifically birth and marriage and the set of constructions which orient the meanings of these categories) and politics (the exigencies of action being such that great deeds can create the basis for closer relations with kings, and therefore greater honors and more important positions in kingdoms) are seen as so mutually interdependent, we must still seek to explain why there are a great number of systematic irregularities, or structural anomalies, in the way in which the organization of the Kallars of Pudukkottai has been inflected by the political history of the region. Let us recapitulate some of these anomalies. The royal subcaste is distinct from all other subcastes in several respects. It is the only Kallar subcaste which has its disputes adjudicated by non-Kallars, in this case Vellalars. The royal subcaste is also unique in that it is subdivided into kuppams. Kuppams are ordered in much the same way as are the karais in other subcastes, with the exception of the curious relation of VT and TT. While VT has structural precedence over TT, TT has, over time, become the chief kuppam of the natu. Within TT, there is a further, and also unique, subdivision into two tiers. And, in the top tier, the Pallavaraiyars have precedence over the Tondaimans even though the latter constitute the royal lineage. This problem is resolved by the dual form honors can take, as royal honor and as caste honor, itself a distinction relevant only in this particular social unit. TT is the only kuppam not to have a single kuppam temple. Further irregularities occur when one attempts to order positions within the little kingdom in terms of these kinship divisions. Most of the Cervaikarars are from the top tier of TT, but not all. Most of the Cervais are from the lower tier of TT, but, again, not all. Even the term Rajapantu, meaning relative of the king, is a term that has only contextual significance, as it is used by some to mean all AN Kallars and by others to mean a set of further specifications of internal kinship divisions all the way to actual affinal relations.

Anomalies are, paradoxically, a problem of order, and yet order (in the kattuppatu sense) is what the system is all about. What is significant here is that it is the Raja who defines order and disorder. Kattuppatu is a construction of order which correlates with the particular practices of the royal subcaste. The Raja, in fact, has the enunciatory function, in Foucault's terms, with respect to what order and disorder will be said to be, both generally and in any particular case. Since this is so, what seems paradoxical is that all the anomalies occur at the level where the king "intervenes" in the system: in the royal subcaste, the royal kuppam, and the royal lineage. The Raja defines disorder at the same time as he seems to create it. The Raja creates order in a dynamic sense, and it seems that in the very same sense in which he directly imposes new ordering principles he must change the given order. The political inflection of the kinship system, thus, occurs principally through the intervention of the Raja, whose transformational effects on the system do not become destabilizing precisely because the king is at the center of the new disorder. In a peculiar sense, the disorder creates the need for kings, even as disorder is caused by them. Perhaps this last observation provides part of the explanation for why the anomalies are not smoothed over as quickly as possible.

The king who creates disorder also adjudicates it. As Lingat makes clear (Lingat 1973), and as Appadurai (1981) has subsequently argued, the king negotiates problems of disorder case by case, so as not to set up precedents which could make the system self-regulating in a diffuse and rationalized way. The system is, therefore, inherently anomalous. The structural whole is full of rifts and potential contradictions that are not perceived as problems because of the central role of the king in mediating all contradiction and controlling all disorder. The king has the enunciatory function over the discursive formation of order itself. No king would be able or would wish to put together a permanent and self-ordering structure of communities. If he had, his own role would become, strangely, superfluous. Indeed, the king must maintain the enunciatory function. It is for this reason that the anomalous structure of the social system coincides with the level of the greatest political inflection of kinship and social relations.

The disorder that I have identified here through a structural examination of anomalies is not perceived as disorder. The contradictions that I identified from my analytical perspective were not granted the status of contradictions by any of my informants. The king not only defined order, but he himself was so much at the center of order that it was impossible to conceive of him apart from order. The king had full powers to construct the sets of relations and categories that made up the social and political system. In a peculiar (and circular) way his hegemony was sustained by the ideological fact of his role as the creator, definer, and protector of "culture." That I – an outsider – could come along and say that the process of ordering makes certain of these relations seem asymmetrical or disharmonious is an artifact not of disorder, but of the extreme embodiment of order represented by the king.

# 8

# *Political hegemony and social relations: caste in Pudukkottai*

## Vellalars, Brahmans and the social formation

One of the most glaring ethnographic peculiarities of the Pudukkottai region is that it was not dominated by Vellalars. Tamil culture has frequently been assumed to be synonymous with the Vellalars, the highest ranking Sudras in a caste system in which there were neither Ksatriyas nor Vaisyas. Most historical and anthropological studies of the Tamil area consider Vellalars to be the most important community (Barnett 1970; Beck 1972; Ludden 1985; Stein 1980). Vellalars have been seen as the carriers of high caste culture in the Tamil country, adapting Sanskritic traditions (Daniel 1984) while preserving important Tamil ones. They provided the crucial node for the entry of Brahmans into Tamil society (Stein 1968). They were the chief agriculturalists of the central wet land areas of the south, growing rice and managing irrigation with great facility through their social networks and managerial skills (Stein 1980). Given the importance of Vellalars, is it possible to suggest the wider relevance of conceptions of caste, kinship, and politics garnered from an area such as Pudukkottai where Vellalars were, in recent times, virtually absent?

Indeed, Vellalars were different from Kallars, and Pudukkottai was a different kind of region than, say, Tanjavur. Castes such as the Kallars and Maravars proved themselves able to rule over areas such as Pudukkottai and not areas such as Tanjavur. However, this does not render Pudukkottai irrelevant or anomalous. Extensive areas of the Tamil countryside were mixed economy zones like Pudukkottai. More importantly, during much of the old regime period these areas were crucial for the structure of rule and society throughout much of southern India. The prevalence of warrior rule had profound though varied repercussions for all areas of the Tamil countryside. In addition, Vellalars had been kings (e.g., the Irukkuvels in Kotumpalur), and, like all other south Indians, had been ruled by kings. Vellalars and Kallars were, despite their differences, both implicated in social forms that had a great deal to do with the institution of kingship.[1]

Furthermore, Vellalars once had a strong presence in Pudukkottai. As we have seen, they settled in the Pudukkottai region in the Cola and Pantiyan periods (roughly the ninth through the thirteenth centuries), clearing forests and cultivating land, granting land rights and other privileges to their dependants, in particular to the Maravars and Kallars, whom they invited to the region to protect them. The Vellalars were said to have been kings during this period. But they did not maintain their position of dominance and many left the area. Their emigration began with the defeat of the Kanatu Vellalars in the great wars when all but one family of this vanquished group vacated the Pudukkottai region. Some of the Konatu Vellalars stayed on, mainly in twelve villages clustered near the river Vellar in the western part of Pudukkottai state, but most of them also migrated elsewhere. In the areas of Vellalar settlement in Pudukkottai today, Vellalars are known as good and industrious agriculturalists, as they are throughout Tamil Nadu. But unlike their counterparts elsewhere, they neither exercise any important dominance nor provide a cultural model for emulation. In many areas of Tamil Nadu the addition of the title Pillai to one's name is a commonly used form of status mobility, reflecting the tremendous cultural dominance exerted by Vellalars over lower, upwardly mobile, castes. In Pudukkottai, on the other hand, Kallar titles such as ampalakarar and Cervaikarar have played the same role. There is a well known Tamil saying concerning the three castes of the Mukkulattar: Kallars, Maravars, Akampataiyars, by slow degrees become Vellalars (Kaḷḷan, Maṛavan, Akampaṭaiyan, mella mella vaṇṭu Veḷḷāḷar āvāṉ). Interestingly, this saying is not common and has little cultural resonance in Pudukkottai. If an equivalent saying could be found, it would no doubt consist of gradations of castes and Kallar subcastes and position the AN Kallars in the highest rank.

While Vellalars did not have a major presence in Pudukkottai, Brahmans played an important role in the region from the earliest period of Vellalar dominance through Tondaiman rule. Under the

---

[1]  The marginality of Vellalars in Pudukkottai may be said by some to explain the curious forms of social organization and caste ideology prevalent there. Nonetheless, the recent work of D. McGilvray (1982) on the eastern coast of Sri Lanka demonstrates that the social formation of Pudukkottai is not too different from that where the Mukkuvar chiefs provided the fundamental forms of ideology and organization so powerfully that the local Vellalars were subsumed as well. Vellalars followed Mukkuvar norms of dominance as much as possible. Like Mukkuvars they stressed royal honors, shares and rights in local temples.

Karukatta Vellalars there had been twenty-one brahmadeyas. Under the Tondaiman Rajas, fifty-six whole villages were granted as brahmadeya land, totalling almost forty-five thousand acres. These lands were given to learned Brahmans to entice them away from the overcrowded brahmadeyas along the river Kaveri. In Pudukkottai, Brahmans settled on large plots of land and were promised a role in a growing state which supported and celebrated brahmanic institutions.

At one level, the most important contribution of Brahmans to Pudukkottai was to augment the honor of the Raja. The acceptance by learned Brahmans of grants of land from the Tondaiman Rajas signified that these Kallar chiefs were now true Ksatriya kings. The Brahmans themselves became emblems of the king's sovereignty and honor. Further, many of the Brahmans were given lands with the specific injunction to pray for the prosperity of the king and his kingdom. The very presence of learned Brahmans in the state was thought to transform its character, making the soil sweet and fertile, and the kingdom as a whole prosperous.

Brahmans exerted other forms of influence as well on social customs and norms. For example, the fact that the AN Kallars were the only Kallars to prohibit the remarriage of widows (an important feature of their kattuppatu) can no doubt be correlated with Brahmanic influence. Whether as scholars and teachers or as bureaucrats and generals, Brahmans have played a major role in the history of Pudukkottai. If Pudukkottai is seen by some as irrelevant to the larger history of Tamil society, it is not because Brahmans have been absent. But in the old regime period the significance of Brahmanic values and institutions was always mediated through the king, whose kingship was in turn made all the more powerful because of the presence of the Brahmans. Brahmans did not displace the ideological ascendency of royal honor; they added to it.

In the previous chapter we established the basic features of the ideological and social structure of the royal Kallars of Pudukkottai. Having addressed the question of the general relevance of our findings, we will now examine a different group of Kallars in Pudukkottai, and then move on to look at the social system as a whole.

### The Kallars of Vicinki Natu

The royal subcaste, which attained the highest level of refinement among Kallars in Pudukkottai, defined the constituent features of social order (orunku, kattuppatu), basing the authority of its members on their proximity to the king. Furthest from the ordered center, the least refined

Kallar subcaste was the Vicinki Natu Kallars. The VN Kallars were the last of the Kallars to throw in their lot with the Tondaiman kings. As late as the end of the eighteenth century, they provided a steady source of resistance and rebellion throughout the state.

Probably the earliest Kallar settlers in the region (whose own traditions of migration to Pudukkottai are at best vague), they settled first in the northern part of the state.[2] While some groups stayed on, others moved to the west. There they were joined by other waves of migrating Kallars who entered into affinal relations with them, becoming members of the subcaste. Over time, the subcaste came to dominate a large swath of territory in the northern and western parts of Pudukkottai.

Local traditions and some early inscriptions emphasize the fact that the VN Kallars could be disruptive and violent. Many stories told both by Kallars and non-Kallars concern the resistance of VN Kallars to any outside authority. Whenever a revenue official went to VN to demand the payment of revenue, the VN Kallars would cut off his head and send it back (S. R. Aiyar 1916, 137; field interviews). A number of campaigns were fought against the VN Kallars in the eighteenth century to bring them under the control of the state. The first of these was conducted by Namana Tondaiman sometime around 1700. He encountered the VN Kallars in Puliyur, where they had assembled for a great subcaste festival, and executed the leading rebels. The last of these campaigns was in 1797, when the Tondaiman Raja sent a force of 700 men under a Pallavaraiyar general to punish the VN Kallars. Upon the success of his mission, the Pallavaraiyar was made into one of the grandest of the Vakuppu Cervaikarars, and was endowed with extensive lands in an area adjacent to the territory of the VN Kallars. The intention was that he, and his vast array of retainers, should keep a close watch over the unruly Kallars to the north. This campaign is referred to in a local folk ballad: "The Tondaiman made the Kallars of Cenkalur and Rakkattan-patti who did not join him tremble with his chained dogs (in pursuit of them). In the central Kallar country of Nallur and Puliyur, the Tondaiman had the heads of the Kallars cut off and sent to him in bundles. The Tondaiman subdued the recalcitrant Kallars of VN and lived prosperously without foes like Visnu" (S. R. Aiyar 1916, 297 n).

Though after this campaign the VN Kallars became nominal subjects of the Tondaiman rulers, they were never fully reconciled to Tondaiman sovereignty. They held aloof from the solidarity of the other Kallar natus in Pudukkottai. During the late eighteenth and nineteenth

[2] Inscriptions and palm leaf manuscripts suggest that these Kallars settled first in villages near the temple of Kunnandarkovil.

centuries the Tondaimans found it necessary to settle families of Cervaikarars and AN Kallars in many areas of VN habitation. This was not done in other Kallar areas. In addition to the Pallavaraiyar Cervaikarar, a second Cervaikarar, Ilantari Ampalakarar, was given lands in Vattanakkottai (in addition to those he already had in Munacantai in the south). Vattanakkottai was the head village of one of the VN natus. The Mannavelar Cervaikarars were settled in Antakkulam, a town just to the south of another of the VN natus. There was a major concentration of Kurikarars in areas just to the west of VN settlement, around Perampur and Nankupatti. The settlement of these chiefs was supplemented by the settlement of families of AN Kallars called Cervais in many VN Kallar villages. These Cervais here, as elsewhere, provided local security, kept the court informed about the activities of the local population, aided local officials in the collection of revenue, and accepted honors on behalf of the Raja in the local temples.

Although VN was often a troubled area for the Tondaimans, many VN Kallars were recruited into the Tondaiman's armies where they served as warriors (amarakarars) with the same distinction as when they fought on their own behalf. There was an unusually high incidence of "military" jivitam tenures in the area of VN settlement, although many local amarakarars belonged to other Kallar subcastes than VN. VN amarakarars were usually settled outside of their own natu. In the most conspicuous example of this, about three hundred families of VN Kallars were settled in villages in the southwestern area of the state near Tirukkalampur to provide protection against the even more feared Kallars of Madurai, who constantly raided villages just across the border. These VN Kallars were given jivitam and maniyam lands and local privileges, under which circumstances they proved loyal subjects of the Raja (PFR).

VN Kallars are found throughout the area of northern Pudukkottai between Kiranur on the west and Perunkalur on the east and from ten miles north of Pudukkottai town to as far north as Vallam and Cenkipattu, just beyond the northern borders of the state. According to most informants, VN itself consists of five smaller natus, though the list of five varies. Part of the reason for this variance has to do with the fact that a number of the natus are further divided into southern and northern or eastern and western natus, and these are sometimes included in a list which for formal reasons can never contain more than five natus. The area covered by VN settlement is far more extensive and less centralized than that of any other Kallar subcaste.

The five basic natus are Vicenki Natu, Tulacima Natu, Cenkali Natu, Vatamalai Natu, and Tenmalai Natu. The first, VN proper, has been subdivided into eastern and western portions. Many informants told me that VN proper was the head natu of the entire subcaste. I was told, for example, that Vicilikovil, the Siva temple which serves as the natu temple for the subdivided natu, also serves as the head temple for the entire natu. In addition, I was told that the three nattampalams of VN proper likewise could adjudicate disputes for the whole subcaste, and that subcaste assemblies under their leadership were and would be held at Vicilikovil. However, when pressed, no informant could remember such a gathering. Furthermore, I was never able to confirm the report that honors were available in Vicilikovil's annual festival for ampalams of all the natus. Quarrels over the precedence of natus, caused by a general decline of centralized leadership within VN after its absorption into the Tondaiman state, have rendered such gatherings, as well as subcaste festivals, things of the past. At times when the subcaste was sovereign and engaged in warfare beyond its own boundaries it might have been fully realized as a total hierarchical order. Today only traces of this order remain.

Like the kuppams of AN and unlike all the other social units called natus in Pudukkottai, none of the smaller natus were endogamous. VN marriage circles were apparently less exclusive than for any other group of Kallars. All VN informants insisted that their lineages had marriage ties with lineages of other natus, though not with any outside of greater VN. Whenever I asked questions about natu temples, ampalams, and the social relations of the subcaste, I was invariably told about the smaller natus. Clearly, these units circumscribed most ritual and social interaction within the community. In some cases the responses concerned pairs of small natus which had originally been one natu, but never VN in its entirety.

While few origin myths exist for the VN Kallars as a whole, each lineage has its own story. These stories often take the form of etymologies of the titles of particular lineages. For example, the Colatirayars were warriors, who helped in the Cola army. Panturars were those who fought and won in Pantur. The Tennatirayars were those who received tribute (*tirai*) from the rulers of the south (*tennatu*). The Munaitiraiyars were those who faced their enemies, fighting bravely against them. The Colatirayars and Tattuvantars, the two head lineages of western VN, said that they had been given umpalams for supplying *kalāpam* to Rajas. Kalapam means an umbrella made of peacock feathers, which is a royal honor when used by the Raja. Thus, their special position was constituted in terms of their relations with kings. I was told here that umpalam (the tax-free lands given to them for this service) means "raja mariyatai," or royal honors. Umpalams, then, were royal honors given in exchange for the provision of royal honors. These honors provided the basis for their own preeminence within the local subcaste group. Umpalams were also seen, here and elsewhere, as necessary in order to have the kaniyatci right. In this particular tradition, the privileges granted by kings constituted the basis for a lineage's claim to positions of authority within the community.

Whenever two natus divided and maintained some kind of formal relationship with each other, the two natus together always consisted of thirty-six villages, with eighteen in each. This was held to be true even when an actual list with that number of villages could not be verified or recited. Clearly, both of these numbers are auspicious and express wholes. Eighteen is a number that ethnographers and historians frequently encounter. For example, every time the Vellalars settled in a new region they were accompanied by members of the "eighteen castes."

VN proper fits this general pattern; it had divided into a western and an eastern half. The three nattampalams of greater VN were also the heads of VN proper. Two of these headmen came from lineages in the western half; the other came from the eastern portion. While I was told that all three of the nattampalams had to agree if their decisions about major disputes or temple matters were to hold, there was a hierarchy among them, with the highest ranking headman being the nattampalam from the eastern side (Nacciappatti Tankavelu Tattuvantar), the second and third both coming from the head village of the western side, Piliyur. All three of these nattampalams were enjoined not to marry within their natu, i.e., VN proper. This restriction was observed, I was told, because they should not be biased in the natu assemblies in favor of their close affinal relations. Perhaps also it was considered to be a mark of higher status to restrict the affinal network in some way. The set of marriage alliances among these three nattampalams created a kind of privileged connubium at the highest level of the natu as a whole, a visible marker of a higher status group and one of the few residual reminders of the authority of the three ampalams throughout the greater Natu.

Vicilikovil was the head temple of the eastern and western halves. At the annual festival there honors were given to the three nattampalams as well as to ampalams of each of the thirty-six villages. This meant that the Colatiraiyars, the head ampalams of Piliyur, received honors twice, first in their capacity as representatives of the natu and later on behalf of their village. The natu assembly met on the temple compound of a small outdoor shrine which included icons of Karuppar, Aiyanar, and Cuppramaniya. This compound, surrounded by tall trees, is within 100 yards of the entrance of the larger Vicilikovil. According to a number of informants: "Once, one person challenged the greatness of Karuppar and placed a pole in the middle of the tank. The tree lizard, which was on the banyan tree, jumped into the river, swam across to the pole, climbed up on it and began to chirp. That was how it demonstrated the existence of Karuppar's power." People from all of the thirty-six villages were said to attend the natu assembly, where they tried to solve their disputes without going to the court. Today, the natu assembly is only held to decide about the festival.

The head village of the eastern half was Vicalur (from which Vicilikovil took its name), that of the western half was Piliyur. Piliyur was divided into two moieties classified under the cardinal directions of north and south. The north had three karais, the south, five. There was no ampalam for each karai, only one for each division, the head of the first karai in each division filling this role. The ampalam for the whole village was the ampalam of the northern moiety.

North
1. Colatirayar
2. Palantar
3. Matiyani
South
1. Vatakki Valavu Panturar
2. Terku Valavu Panturar
3. Kolar
4. Karukkar
5. Rankiyar

The original settlers in Piliyur (*pūrvīka kuṭikaḷ*) are said to be Panturars and Colatirayars. They have original kaniyatci rights in the VN proper. The village temple was a goddess temple, with the Karuppar-Aiyanar shrine serving as a subsidiary village temple with special associations for particular lineages.

The division of eastern and western VN proper was less complete and less formalized than the division between Vatamalai Natu and Tenmalai Natu, each of which had one headman. Though these two natus together had no single leader, they shared a joint temple in Kunnandarkovil. They each had their own natu temple as well. In Kunnandarkovil there has been a longstanding dispute between the two natus over precedence. The only way the festival there can be conducted today is for the chief priest to give the honors to the two headmen simultaneously, with his hands crossed to blur any possible precedence accruing to the receipt of honors from the right hand as opposed to the left. Recently, the dispute over precedence took the form of quarreling about which hand would be crossed over or under. Disputes over precedence and honor seem to be interminable, no cases being more difficult to resolve than those in which some form of equality is insisted upon. Equality in a situation involving honor is a virtual impossibility.

Here, precedence was once again defined in terms of who was the original settler. Kaniyatci, I was told, meant original right (*pūrvīka urimai*). Kaniyatci is often correlated with landholding, because the original settlers hold the greatest amount of land, and because these rights usually entail some grant of inam land by the Raja. However, kaniyatci is used most frequently, and most importantly, with respect to temples, concerning one's right to worship in the local temple and one's precedence in that worship.

Disputes with respect to precedence occur within these two sub-natus as well as between them. For example, the headman of Tenmalai Natu told me that there had been a major dispute between his village, Vattanakkottai, and nearby Perampur. Long ago, he said, the people of these two villages had been dacoits. On one occasion they had captured a tremendous booty of goats, cows, treasure, and idols of Siva and Parvati. They stopped in the forest on their way home to divide the booty. The Vattanakkottai people asked for the goats, cows, and treasure, and the people of Perampur got the idols. However, as time went on the people of Vattanakkottai were denied rights in the temple in which these idols were housed. During the festival, when they went to touch the rope (*vaṭam*) used to pull the chariot which carries the processional deity they were not allowed to do so. A fight ensued. The Raja resolved the dispute by saying that the people of Perampur should touch the rope first, followed by the people of Vattanakkottai. Then, after the distribution of honors, in which the nattampalam receives first honors (he is from Vattanakkottai), the people of the two villages should drag the chariot together around the temple. This story, which involves a self-conscious admission of the thieving past of these Kallars, again reiterates the ubiquity of disputes over honors. Touching the chariot rope, a symbol of devotion to the deity and usually a royal perquisite when a king is present, connects the problem of precedence to the structure of worship: the chief devotee is the head of the congregation. In this particular story, the past of the Kallars is especially interesting, since the deity being worshipped is part of the booty procured in one of the group's early raiding parties.

The difficulty in systematically diagramming the cultural order of VN attests to the fluidity in the structure of the subcaste. Though this fluidity is found elsewhere in Kallar society, there is here no discernible presence of anomalous features correlating with any single mode of inflection, as is the case in AN. Territorial principles have played a dominant role in the social organization of the VN Kallars. VN lineages migrated more widely than those of other Kallar natus. As they moved into new areas previously uninhabited by Kallars, they reorganized themselves and set themselves off with separate temples and headmen but without constituting new endogamous social units. The group as a whole was symbolized by a temple and three nattampalams, but this whole was too infrequently invoked to maintain the clear dominance of the whole over the parts. Partly because of the usual importance of honor in Kallar society, but also perhaps because of the lack of any clear leadership and the uncertain relationships of the parts to each other or to the whole, quarrels over precedence occurred even more frequently in VN than in other Kallar natus.

The pattern of settlement was more dispersed in VN than in AN. Further, VN has no single lineage villages, and it is difficult to trace historically the origins of lineage hierarchy within its villages. The same lineage is often found in more than one of the sub-natus, but members of these lineages claim no relationship with their counterparts, even though to be safe they will not exchange wives. Here, the pull of territory seems even stronger than in AN, where territorial pulls were mediated and mitigated in increasing proportion to the connection of any given lineage with the Raja.

VN provides a marked contrast with AN. Territorial divisions remained unranked, and hierarchical forms largely undeveloped. The fissiparous tendencies of greater VN reflect the lack of centralized leadership, and the related absence of any strong political motivation for centralization, at least after the Tondaiman conquest. In part as a result of these factors, there are many interesting correlations between VN and the Kallars studied by Dumont, the Pramalai Kallars of the Madurai region.

### Interpreting Kallar society

Among the Pramalai Kallars, lineages, though exogamous, are not the units of exogamy, as they are in Pudukkottai with only a few exceptions. Again unlike Pudukkottai, natus are not endogamous. Dumont has written that "The patrilineal, patrilocal, exogamous lineage is the basic grouping of Kallar society. It groups the paternal descendants of a common ancestor around a headman who bears his name. It is the only group which has unity of this kind" (Dumont 1986, 184). If anything, this statement is more applicable to the Pudukkottai Kallars, for whom the lineage represents the basic exogamous group. But Dumont also writes: "Only lineage agnates constitute a genuine community. The unity of a more extended group can be defined only by identifying it with one of its lineages taken as pre-eminent" (Dumont 1986, 161). While it is true that the unity of the natu is in part defined by the pre-eminence of a single lineage, represented by one or more natu headmen, it can hardly be said that this is the only basis for the constitution of a community. For Dumont, "Alliance does not unite lineages. The real situation is more complex" (Dumont 1986, 188). According to his ethnographic account, some Pramalai Kallar natus are totally exogamous. Others include groups of lineages which have affinal relations with other lineages within the natu, as well as outside it.

Earlier we saw that for the Pudukkottai Kallars alliance does unite lineages, and that it does so at the level of the natu, the basic unit of endogamy. The natu is represented by its preeminent lineage, but the natu is a social unity by virtue of the constitution of a group of exogamous lineages into an affinal whole, which has a social, ritual, political, and territorial expression. This contrast leads to an interesting theoretical conundrum. Most criticisms of Dumont's later work on kinship concern his contention that affinal relatives form a complementary group which, though similar in a structural sense to agnatic descent groups, is of more general importance for the organization of south Indian kinship than agnatic descent. Alliance for Dumont is the fundamental principle of south Indian kinship (Dumont 1957a, 44). But in his ethnographic reconstruction of the Pramalai Kallars, Dumont emphasizes alliance while simultaneously proposing that the lineage is the fundamental social unit of Kallar society: "The unity of the nad as a group is based on agnatic kinship: the inhabitants are members of seven patrilineal lineages descended from a common ancestor" (Dumont 1986, 171); "there is no real unit larger than the lineage" (p. 161).

Since Dumont can find no social basis for the formation of the natu other than as a collection of lineages, he proposes that the natu is the level at which "territory transforms a kinship multiplicity into a political unity" (Dumont 1986, 184). Neither the social nor political influence of territorial principles – both preexisting conceptions of area and the fact of settlement in and control over villages or hamlets or localities – is given any consideration. Territory does not penetrate the system within the natu, for Dumont sees "no territorial subdivisions which would correspond either to the lineages or to the hamlets: the nad is the smallest territorial unit ... the hamlets and the lineages do not correspond at all" (p. 171). The effect of Dumont's argument is to separate kinship as a process of social formation from either political or territorial forces and forms. The political activation of the natu does not, according to Dumont, affect the social organization of the Pramalai Kallar. While territory can thus create political unities, it has no real social value, for society is fundamentally confined to the domains of caste and kinship. In questions of descent and alliance, Dumont finds both territory and politics to be essentially irrelevant. Correct as Dumont may be when he says that the territorial content and political inflection of caste and kinship is limited for the Pramalai Kallars, he then leaps to a general conclusion which is directly contradicted by the example of the Pudukkottai Kallars. Indeed, by excluding territory and politics from any major role in the organization of Kallar society, Dumont makes it possible for his theory of caste to prevail even where it seems least relevant.

This is not to say that Dumont does not introduce ethnographic facts which point to the importance of the political. As we just noted, he discusses the relation of territory to political organization. In addition, when discussing headmen, he notes that the order of precedence among them is based on proximity to the first headman, whose authority was invested by the king of Madurai. Dumont writes that "rank appears to rest on a sort of contagion of this royal consecration through proximity" (Dumont 1986, 169). And yet when all is said and done, "kinship remains the fundamental principle of organization" (p. 184). Kinship is the complementarity of alliance and descent. Caste is the complementarity of purity and pollution. Both power and territory are firmly encompassed by the two (Dumont 1980). The ethnographic study of the Pramalai Kallars thus has served the purpose of demonstrating that if the basic forms of caste society can be identified in an area for a caste which otherwise has been so removed from the cultural center, then Dumont's theory indeed provides the basis for a generalizable sociology of India.

My ethnographic construction of the Kallars in Pudukkottai leads me to challenge Dumont's theory on a number of important points. Territory, for example, plays a major role at every level of social definition. It is so embedded within social and political forms that we cannot say that it merely mediates the political and social domains as Dumont suggests. First, there are many cases of villages corresponding with the particular lineages settled in them. Secondly, as we have seen in different ways with both the AN and VN Kallars, territory could play an important role at the level above the village and below the subcaste. In AN the kuppam was a territorial unit. Importantly, it was a unit that was ranked according to a logic of settlement and political proximity to the king. The importance of territory in Pudukkottai surfaces also in the fact that the ampalams who are honored in subcaste festivals are usually the ampalams of villages, not lineages, except when the villages are settled by single lineages. Finally, among the VN Kallars, the intermediate territorial classification of the natu does not correlate with any kinship content but creates boundaries for both ritual and political purposes. Territory is not restricted in its influence to the macro political level, but intervenes at every level of social organization. Indeed, to extend a phrase of Dumont's, each level of Kallar society has both a territorial and a social content, which are so fused that neither one can be subordinated to the other. Territorial and social forms are expressed by villages, natus, descent groups, and alliance structures, as well as by the temples and headmen which define and assemble each level of the system. To extend Dumont's formulations, we can say that territorial forms become subtly fused with social and political forms in differing ways at every level of the system.

Politics, as we define it here, has to do both with the processes by which authority is constituted at each level of representation and with the linkages of the constituent groups in society to the king (usually through the authoritative figures who represent their social groups). Politics has a territorial dimension, but is not exhausted by territorial forms. In AN, the intervention of the king changed and reconstructed (as well as deconstructed) the internal order of the system, affecting both social and territorial forms. Even in other natus which are less directly influenced by kingship, social organization is only understandable within a framework which is fundamentally political, realized over time (i.e., in history).

It is my argument here that politics plays a powerful role in the social organization of caste and kinship, that politics is fundamental to the process of hierarchalization and the formation of units of identity. Dumont resists the notion that kinship can be politicized. When he does see hierarchical tendencies develop in the domain of kinship he blames them on the ideology of caste, which has to do not with politics but with purity and pollution. Dumont's elevation of alliance as the fundamental principle of south Indian kinship is in large part because alliance mitigates the asymmetrical effects of marriage relations through the generalized exchange of marriage partners within the endogamous group. Hierarchy creeps to the borders of the endogamous group, but only enters in the sense that it can bring about the creation of new endogamous subdivisions. Even though Dumont suggests (1957a; 1957b) the powerful role of political dominance in creating alliances and particular marriage patterns, he explains any such endogamous subdivisions by saying that they arise through bastardy or the differential status of wives in a polygynous marriage. Endogamous groups develop within previous endogamous groups only because of the lower status attached to marriages with women from outside the proper alliance group.

In short, politics occupies a subordinate position in Dumont's general theory, attacked on the one flank by pure kinship, itself invaded by social bastardy and caste hierarchy, and on the other by caste, which elevates the Brahman, and attendant principles of purity and pollution, above the king. Caste, and the hierarchical principle it entails, is fundamental because it is religious, and in Indian social thought, according to Dumont, the religious encompasses the social, the economic, and the political.

Dumont therefore sees caste authority and political authority as fundamentally different. He writes that "the notion of caste, the notion of a caste superior to one's own exhausts all available transcendence. Properly speaking, a people's headman can only be someone of another caste. If the headman is one of their own, then to some degree they are all headmen" (Dumont 1986, 161). This is true in Pudukkottai in that headmen are at one level simply *primi inter pares* in their social group. However, by virtue of their connection to the king, they do "transcend," at some level, their own community. Most importantly, the king himself is at one level simply a Kallar, and not the highest one at that. But by virtue of his kingship, not caste transcendence, he is also the transcendent overlord of the entire kingdom.

Hierarchy in Pudukkottai concerns transcendence in the context of kingship, where the king is both a member of a segmentary lineage system and the overlord of the entire kingdom. What would seem contradictory to Dumont is the paradox upon which the entire caste system rests. Kinship is inflected, at its core, by politics; and politics is nothing more than the curious paradox of a king who encompasses all even as he is one of his own metonyms. In the social and political world of the little kingdom, this meant that the king was an overlord, but one who was nonetheless always embroiled in the strategic concerns of kinship, status hierarchy, protection and warfare, and in the maximization of his own honor and sovereign authority within the little kingdom and in a wider world of other kingdoms and greater overlords.

Part of Dumont's resistance to acknowledging the political inflection of caste and kinship may result from the political marginality of the Pramalai Kallars, a marginality that is not unlike that of the VN Kallars. With both groups, the lack of well-developed affinal boundaries corresponding to discrete territorial units, as well as of a distinct sense of the hierarchy of groups, can perhaps be explained by their incomplete incorporation within the political system of a little kingdom. Everywhere in Tamil Nadu the Kallars had highly developed notions of territory, but subcaste organization achieved its particular level of territorial segmentation and hierarchical articulation in Pudukkottai alone. And only within the royal subcaste of Pudukkottai did Kallars develop the particular forms of territorial bounding and hierarchical marking that we analyzed in the previous chapter. Kingship does make a difference.

Some of Dumont's theoretical problems stem from the fact that he does not pursue an interest in the ethnohistorical reconstruction of the Pramalai Kallars. He is aware of the modern decline of headmanship, and that it no longer expresses itself as fully as it might once have done in the social logic of Pramalai organization. Characteristically acute, he senses a correlation with recent political change: "If authority rests on external sanction, it is to be expected that it cannot maintain itself without formal government recognition" (Dumont 1986, 159). Unfortunately, he does not consider the possibility that colonialism, and the attendant breakdown of the old regime, have much to do with the development of a separation between religion and politics which he has identified and reified into a timeless Indian social theory. A combination of theoretical program, ethnographic "accident," and historical lack of interest have conspired to render Dumont's understanding of the Kallars, however brilliant, limited in fundamental ways.

The extent to which proximity to the political center can affect the social organization of a caste – and indeed the entire caste system – can be seen not only among the Kallars, but also with other castes. Taking Dumont's point that the caste system is a system of relations, we must look at the total system of caste relations in Pudukkottai. We will begin here with the Maravars, then move on to sample some of the other important caste groups of the state. We will see that both social and territorial forms alter as distance from the king increases. Among the Maravars, the lineages, and subdivisions within villages, appear more strongly developed than higher level social and territorial formations, particularly the natu. For other castes, we will note a steady decrease in "order," as defined by the Kallars, and even more particularly in control over, and autonomy with respect to the definition of, this order. If, in short, we look at the caste system as a whole, in a historical context in which there was a king who played a strong role in the local articulation of social order, then we can see even more clearly and trenchantly the implications of our earlier remarks about the political nature of hierarchy and the hierarchical consequences of politics.

## The Maravars

The Maravars were not nearly as important, as numerous, or as involved in the political history of Pudukkottai state as the Kallars. Nonetheless, they were the caste with the greatest claim to dominance in the southern part of the state, largely uninhabited by Kallars. The position of the Maravars was enhanced by the rule of Maravar kings in the two kingdoms of Ramanatapuram and Civakankai just to the south of Pudukkottai.

Maravars and Kallars, along with Akampatiyars, are said to make up the three families: mukkulattar. Despite this classificatory association, these castes did not generally live together. Where one of them has settled and become dominant the others tend not to be found. Maravars share many features of Kallar social organization, having strong lineage and subcaste affiliations. Like the Kallars, the Maravars have always had the reputation of being a fierce group renowned for their military prowess. Many of the Tamil palaiyakkarars were Maravars, and in areas of Maravar political dominance ethnographic surveys reveal remarkable similarities between the two caste groups (Dumont 1957a). A comparison of the Maravars with the Kallars can therefore reveal a great deal about the influence of their respective political histories on their social and cultural organization within a single state system. My brief sketch of the Maravars will compare them to Kallar society as a whole, and highlight certain correlations that can be made at a general level between the political position and social organization of two similar caste groups.

The Maravars settled in the southern region of Pudukkottai, south of the river Vellar, in the area stretching from Ponnamaravati in the extreme southwest to the central part of the southern half of the state. The eastern border of Maravar settlement stretches south from Kottur and Lempalakuti to Konapet and continues beyond the southern borders of the state, intensifying in the Maravar kingdoms of Ramanatapuram and Civakankai.

Like Kallars, Maravars have exogamous lineages called karais which are grouped together in territorially named endogamous subcastes.[3] In one instance, the subcaste comprises a single village, Viraccilai. In other instances, the subcaste ranges in size from three to six major villages, with many smaller hamlets often being enumerated as well. Unlike

---

[3]  Some Maravars said that they had kilai, a matrilineal unit of society noted by Thurston and others. However, none of my Maravar informants had any idea of what a kilai was other than occasionally attaching a name to it and I could find no traces of a residual matrilineal kinship structure.

Kallars, the lineages have no pattapeyars, and the subcastes are not called natus, as they sometimes are elsewhere among Maravars. All Maravars share a comon title: Tevar. The subcaste groups are usually named after the constituent villages, as for example the Maravars of the six villages (*arūr*, the group which includes Ponnamaravati, Cevalur, and Kulipirai), or the Maravars of the three villages (*munnūr*, the group consisting of Lembalakuti, Kottur, and Pilivalam). In addition, all Maravars are divided into those of Konatu or Kanatu. This classification, less relevant for social organization, is usually only invoked in a discussion of the history of settlement in Pudukkottai, when the Maravars assumed the territorial units of the Vellalars under whom they served. Nondominant castes commonly take on the territorial divisions of the local dominant castes. When the Maravars succeeded in wresting local control from the Vellalars they kept the Konatu and Kanatu divisions as macro-classifications, but these classifications have since lost their importance in favor of more local territorial orientations. Some residual use of the classifications remains, as with the name of the goddess (Konattu Nayaki) in one Maravar village in Konatu (Melapanaiyur).

No Maravar villages have been settled by single lineages. The lineages do not have titles per se, but take their names from the names of the first two ancestors of the lineage group. For example, one lineage is called "Kommayyatevan-Piccatevan." The headman of this lineage continues to bear one of these names himself, his eldest son the other. The names thus alternate down the generations. As in multi-lineage Kallar villages, the ampalam who represents the village is the head of the preeminent lineage within the village. Each village has a stone pillar which represents the ampalam. The head village of all Maravar subcastes has a stone platform in the central space of the village. This platform (the *ampalakkal*) supports a number of stone pillars on its perimeter, one for each of the ampalams of the constituent villages. Meetings of the subcaste assembly take place on this platform. The right to the hereditary office of ampalam is passed down to the eldest son. When an ampalam dies, his body is bathed and dressed in the cloth (parivattam) worn by the goddess, the same cloth used to honor the ampalam on the occasion of the annual festival in the goddess temple. Before his corpse is taken to the cremation ground, his successor is brought and made to sit in front of it. The successor distributes a mixture of grain (called a *tāṉiyam*, meaning grain and gift) to the village servants, both as remuneration for the services surrounding the funeral itself, and as a symbol of his position as chief patron. After the new ampalam has been thus installed, the corpse is taken to the cremation grounds.

Most Maravar villages are composed of lineages and classificatory "streets" (teru), there being sometimes two, three, and four such subunits. In some cases, the lineage does not constitute the actual unit of exogamy, as marriage is prohibited between lineages which are members of the same street. In the two adjacent villages of Melapanaiyur and Kulamankalam where there are three streets and eighteen lineages, the streets constitute the units of exogamy. In these two villages, individual lineages do not have separate family deities (kula teyvams, or vittu camis), sharing them instead with other lineages from the same street. Further, some Maravars believe that a lineage can subdivide more readily than do the Kallars. The overarching significance of the street suggests first, the bipartite focus of lineage organization, and second, that territorial forms exert an important influence on social organization at the level of exogamy.

For Kallars, the territorial principle exerts its greatest force at the level of the natu, and only secondarily at the level of the village. It has a greater and more systematic impact on units of endogamy than on units of exogamy. Among Maravars, however, territory exerts its force at the level of the street and the village, and is more important for units of exogamy than those of endogamy, with the single exception of the endogamous village of Viraccilai. Not only are Maravar subcastes named after their constituent villages, the most important temples represent villages rather than natus. Only some of the subcastes have a subcaste temple. Where they do, Maravars are given first honors. The problem with subcaste-cum-territorial (i.e., natu) temples is that if a group does not have acknowledged territorial control, other groups contest for first honors. When a Maravar subcaste looks to no particular temple as its "natu" temple, it is likely that such a contest had either been lost or threatened. In a later chapter we will see that Maravars have recently been competing against the merchant Cettiyar caste for control over a number of temples. In the last century the Cettiyars have acquired great wealth outside Pudukkottai state, particularly in Southeast Asia, investing much of it in disputes over temple control and management. This often pitted them against the Maravars, who because of this powerful and well-endowed threat have had great difficulty maintaining their monopoly over certain large and important temples in southern Pudukkottai.

The way in which territory figures in the social organization of any group is strongly related to the nature and extent of political dominance exercised by the group. The Maravars exert dominance more in the villages in which they have settled than in any generalized localities. Unlike the situation in Kallar natus, Maravar villages (urs) are interspersed with other villages which are controlled by other castes.[4] The naming of subcaste groupings after their constituent villages rather than a general area may have resulted in part from this. Whether as a further result or cause, Maravar villages contain (usually quite a few) powerful lineages, which, whether organized into streets or not, exert a strong centrifugal influence on village organization. The lack of a Maravar king, who like the Tondaiman might have forged a greater unity among his caste and facilitated a more extensive form of dominance over the countryside, correlates with and perhaps explains the relative localization of Maravar social forms at the village level. The recent problems with the Cettiyars have further eroded any macro-territorial structure of ritual dominance in Maravar areas of settlement. Where there were Maravar kings in other parts of the Tamil country, subcastes were far more important in Maravar social organization, as with the Cempinattu Maravars of Ramanatapuram, or the Kontai-yankottai Maravars of western Tirunelveli.

While the Kallars of Pudukkottai had a strong sense of their participation in royal authority and in a political system that transcended the particularities of localized dominance, the Maravars were virtually excluded from any position of importance within the state. There were no Maravar Cervaikarars, no Cervais, no amarakarars. Although only Kallars qualified for the first two positions, there were non-Kallar soldiers (amarakarars), but I was told that Maravars were excluded from serving in this way. Akampatiyars, locally far less important than the Maravars, were palace guards, some of them attaining high positions in the state. Maravars were, on the other hand, given land grants as village and sometimes even locality ampalams, and thus participated in the Tondaiman Raj at the village and locality level. Nonetheless, when discussing the subject of kings and royal authority many of my Maravar informants ignored the Tondaimans. They spoke instead of the Vellalar kings who preceded them, from the Konatu and Kanatu Vellalar chiefs up to the Pallavaraiyar kings of the mid seventeenth century. The copper plate inscriptions and various traditions produced by Maravar informants to document their kaniyatci rights in land and temples had been issued by Vellalar kings. Perhaps because of the tenuousness of this connection, virtually all Maravar lineages and villages have preserved such copper plates; among the Kallars I found very few. When the Karumaravars, said by some to be

---

4   Village in this sense refers to ur rather than kiraman. For a compelling cultural explanation of the difference between the two terms see Daniel 1984.

remnants of the Kanatu Maravars, settled in the southern part of the state, convened a subcaste assembly – they had a subcaste organization with an ampalam in charge – they invited the local Kanatu Vellalar chief to sit in the ampalam's place.

The decline of Vellalar rule had led to Kallar gains which were, in the long run, at the expense of the Maravars who had been the principal contenders for caste dominance in the Pudukkottai region. The deliberate settlement of many Kallar Cervaikarars and amarakarars in and around the Maravar country attests to the Tondaiman's perception of the Maravars as potential rivals. After all, the Pudukkottai Maravars might have decided that their political position would be better advanced by the success of the Ramanatapuram Cetupatis than by the continuing rule of the Tondaimans. This settlement of Kallars is documented in Inam Settlement records and in the honor roles at a number of Maravar temples. For example, in the large Mariyamman temple in Konnaiyur, an important temple for the Maravars of the six villages, the first four honors were given to non-Maravars who had been settled in the region by the Rajas.[5] The local Maravars and their representative leaders only received honors after these four were distributed.

In modern Pudukkottai, more Maravar than Kallar villages have lost their social and religious unity. The apparent decay of social and ritual cohesion in many Maravar urs resembles that of some Kallar natus. Festivals are rarely celebrated; disputes between lineages for dominance in the village and management of the local temple are rampant. Ironically, these disputes provide further evidence that the village was an important unit for Maravars, the locus both of the most strenuous conflict and cultural resilience. Viraccilai is a dramatic case in point. It not only contains all the units of exogamy but constitutes the unit of endogamy. In structural terms it is the same as a Kallar natu. For the last hundred years, at least, there have been serious and sustained quarrels between, and within, lineages over who should be ampalam and who should manage the temple. The Viraccilai Maravars only put up a united front once when they were threatened by newly wealthy Cettiyars who

5    The first honor was given to the palace, the second to the Rajakkal Nayakkanmar, the third to the local Uriyakarar, and fourth to the Amarakarar. The Raja was of course honored first in all state temples; the second category consisted of chiefs of Vatuka (Telegu) castes who had been invited to settle in the state and become Generals in the Raja's army; the third of members of the Akampatiyar caste who were palace guards and servants; and the fourth of military retainers and soldiers, all Kallars.

tried to take over the local Siva temple during the period when most Maravar quarrels focused on the tutelary goddess temple (see Chapter 12).

If the Maravars' relative lack of generalized political dominance was at least partially responsible for their not possessing strong subcaste and territorial institutions, then many of the social structural traits we have just observed must be even more pronounced for other "nondominant" castes. Though the Maravars were not politically dominant, they were not subservient. Indeed, they were perched, rather precariously, just outside the polity of Pudukkottai, powerful big men of the countryside (nattars) on whom the Kallar rulers had to keep a wary eye. We will now survey some of the other castes in Pudukkottai, beginning with the Akampatiyars.

### Akampatiyars

The Akampatiyars are the third of the "family of three," the muk-kulattar. Though less important and dominant in the Pudukkottai countryside than the Maravars, they became central members of the political establishment of Pudukkottai. Indeed, in part because they did not pose the same kind of (potential) political threat as the Maravars they were chosen to protect the king. Because their status was so exclusively tied to their political position, they practically abandoned their local base in favor of their newly acquired one in the central town and palace.

In 1931 there were 11,416 Akampatiyars in Pudukkottai, where they were concentrated in three zones: in villages to the west and south of Kiranur town in the northwest; in villages across the southern band of the state from Kilanilaikkottai to Ponnamaravati; and in Pudukkottai town itself. Each of these zones of settlement correlates with one of the three major subcastes into which the caste is divided.

First, and most important, are the Uriyakarar Akampatiyar. They established close relations with the Raja, to which fact they probably owed their very existence as a subcaste. As we can now recall, Uriyakarar was the title given to all palace guards and servants, all of whom came from this subcaste. Originally they had settled in villages to the west of Kiranur, but after their recruitment to the service of the Pudukkottai Raja as Palace Guards and Servants many of them shifted their residence to Pudukkottai town itself. The fact that a separate subcaste (most probably the residual lineages that never were excluded from the social transformation) continues to live in the villages from which they migrated after their recruitment to palace service strongly suggests that the political connection actually created a new subcaste.[6]

These Uriyakarars guarded the palace, provided escorts for the royal family when on tour, served betel nut to the Raja and his guests, performed sundry services in the palace, and organized the Raja's hunting expeditions and other travels in the state. In the mid nineteenth century a British Political agent described them as "a class of menial servants, who are somewhat lower than the amarakarars and will eat what has been left by others. They are employed now in much the same duty, such as watching the Gates of the Palace ... " One of my better informants, a VN Kallar, described the Uriyakarars as a group of people "who used to wait for the Raja to finish his meals so that they could take his plate or leaf. It was considered a great job." This puja-like transaction was perhaps the mechanism whereby the political connection between the Uriyakarars and the Tondaimans rendered the subcaste separate. The substance of the caste was transformed by their daily contact with the saliva of the king, in perpetual mundane mimesis of divine puja.

In addition, the puja-like nature of the relationship through which they partook of the nature of the king might have been designed to ensure the loyalty of the Uriyakarars in the intimate and dangerous circumstances of the palace. After all, the Uriyakarars were entrusted with the protection of the king's life. A Kallar in this role might have been perceived as a potential rival, and therefore a threat. Another caste that could not harbor royal aspirations – one which was small, politically unimportant and yet not of low status – was chosen. Significantly, the one Uriyakarar who did try to spearhead a revolt against the Raja did so not as a leader of Akampatiyars but by attempting to mobilize the Kallar Cervaikarars. And his lack of success was at least in part because he was an Akampatiyar and not a Kallar.

The other two groups of Akampatiyars were of very little importance in the state. One of these other subcastes was the Kottaipattu Akampatiyars, who lived in villages to the south of Kiranur, the original base of the Uriyakarar Akampatiyars. As mentioned above, they might once have had some relationship to the Akampatiyars who went into royal service, a relationship that was severed because the remaining Kottaipattu group was not similarly favored by royal contact. The last group were the Pillaiperan Akampatiyars, who lived in the southern part of the state.[7]

6   In Pudukkottai town they outnumbered all other caste groups except the Brahmans, who monopolized the administrative services of the state.
7   This group might have been related to the Akampatiyars of Ramanata-

## The service castes of Pudukkottai: dominance and social order

We now turn to the most important client castes, the groups who were often the hereditary servants (atimai) of the Kallars and Maravars.[8] The client castes replicate the social structure of the dominant groups in many respects, though they have less clearly defined forms of territorial unity and endogamy because of their dependent position in society. Some of these groups have no systematic way of marking lineages (pankalis). Even when they are clustered in territorial groupings such as natus, such large-scale units have only limited significance for marriage networks, let alone other social or political purposes. Despite the difficulty in making generalizations of this nature, it is clear that client castes have had minimal control over the articulation of their social order. They often imitated the dominant groups. Rarely initiating new social forms, they had little autonomy from the patron groups that dominated their lives in virtually every domain – political, social, ritual, and economic. The client castes that merit discussion here are the Valaiyars, the Pallars, and the Paraiyars. The position of the Valaiyars is the most anomalous of these, the Pallars and Paraiyars being untouchable groups that were in every way clients and dependants of their respective dominant groups.

puram. These Akampatiyars had a particularly interesting relationship to the Rajas of Ramanatapuram and Civakankai. One group of Akampatiyars provided all the junior wives for the Maravar Rajas. The male offspring of these alliances were prohibited from succeeding to the throne and were enjoined to take Akampatiyar wives. These inferior alliances produced many of the ministers and important court retainers who though royal by birth were disqualified from kingship. Their function was very similiar to that of the Uriyakarar Akampatiyars of Pudukkottai. They were additionally useful in that they lessened the number of rivals for the throne. The famous Marutu brothers who engineered the last of the palaiyakkarar rebellions were sons of this kind of Maravar-Akampatiyar union and chief ministers of the Civakankai Raja. In Ramanatapuram members of this group were called Cervaikarars.

8    We will not concern ourselves here with the other castes in Pudukkottai, however important they are in the total social formation. At other points in this analysis we will deal with some of these castes, for example the Velars (potters, often priests at Aiyanar temples) and the Cettiyars (a merchant caste which became increasingly important in the nineteenth and twentieth centuries because of the wealth they accumulated as moneylenders and colonial agents in Southeast Asia). However, it would be superfluous for the purposes of this book to treat every caste in Pudukkottai, such as certain groups which lived on the periphery of Pudukkottai and were far less significant politically: e.g., the Vallampars of the extreme southeast and the Urali Kavuntars of the extreme west.

## The Valaiyars

Though there are several etymologies for this caste name, the most common and probable root for it comes from *valai*, meaning net. In the late nineteenth and early twentieth centuries British commentators noted that Valaiyars often made their living from hunting and trapping animals, though by then many Valaiyars lived in settled villages and engaged at least part of the time in agricultural labor. Today no Valaiyars actually call themselves by this title, preferring instead such titles as Mutturaiyar, Mutturaja, and Ampalakarar. The statewide Valaiyar population in 1931 was 56,607, with about 26,000 in Tirumayyam Taluk, 19,000 in Alankuti Taluk, and 11,000 in Kolattur Taluk. The most numerous caste in Pudukkottai state, the Valaiyars were, after the Pallars and Paraiyars, the most widely dispersed. However, they were not dominant, nor did they hold extensive land rights, in any locality.

Valaiyars were most often found in villages on the periphery of areas which had been forests in the eighteenth and nineteenth centuries.[9] Where they engaged in agriculture they did so as tenants and as *paṇṇaiyāl*, or agricultural laborers hired on a year to year basis by Kallars, Maravars, Vellalars, Brahmans, and more recently Cettiyars. Most of the villages granted by the Tondaiman kings to Brahmans in the seventeenth and eighteenth centuries had their lands worked by Valaiyars. In caste rank the Valaiyars were often placed below all other castes except Pallars and Paraiyars. Although included in the original list of the eighteen *kuṭimakkaḷ* castes accompanying the Vellalars, they were sometimes referred to as atimai rather than *kuṭimai*. The use of the term atimai indicates that the groups so named were "hereditary servants" of some other group.[10]

Much of the extension of agriculture in Pudukkottai in the seventeenth through the nineteenth century was based on the Kallars' increasing control over Valaiyar labor. Because of their orientation towards the peripheral aspects of peasant life and their continued immersion in the forest the Valaiyars were unable to acquire the

9    See 1931 Census. The largest numbers of Valaiyars were settled in Ponnamaravati and Cenkirai divisions. The former is extensively forested and includes the eastern half of the largest hill in the area, Piranmalai, in the shadow of which many of the Valaiyars lived. Cenkirai division today has the largest reserve forest, a remnant of one of the Raja's most favored hunting areas in the eighteenth and nineteenth centuries.

10   The British usually translated the term to mean slavery. It derives from the root *ati*, which means base, source, foot, thus indicating lowness in the same metaphorical way as does the term sudra in the Dharma Sastras.

protection rights which, with their associated privileges, provided entry into the local world of peasant power. But the Valaiyars never became as fully dominated as the Pallars and Paraiyars, who – never grouped with the kutimakkal – lived within villages as vital components of the internal economies of Kallar and Maravar (inter alia) villages. In contrast, the Valaiyars often lived in their own villages (ur, not to be confused with the untouchable hamlets, or *cēri*), maintaining a certain separateness from the dominant castes. The Valaiyars also kept some control over their own social forms, but they were never accorded any significant rights of possession, land use, or, later in the nineteenth century, title to land. When dominant caste groups expanded, they frequently did so by forcing Valaiyar groups to cultivate new, often previously forested, lands in order to produce surplus grain. Though the Kallars held much of their land on tax-free grants, they always required surpluses of grain for their chiefs and king as well as for the military-cum-grain trade that constituted much of Pudukkottai's mercantile diplomacy. Thus, whereas Pallars and Paraiyars were used as agricultural laborers within dominant caste villages working to produce grain directly for the dominant castes, the Valaiyars worked as pannaiyal laborers and as tenants and sharecroppers on land – often within "their own" villages – which produced much of the grain that sustained the commercial and political economy of the early modern period.

In spite of their low rank, Valaiyars played an important role in the ritual organization of the state. Many Valaiyars acted as the officiating priests in small rural temples to Aiyanar, Karuppar and village goddesses. Like other pujaris they were granted puja maniyams by the king for these services. The king also gave many Valaiyars maniyam lands to beat the forests for the royal hunt, for which service their settlement near forests and their knowledge of wild animals made them the natural choice.

Ethnohistorical fieldwork among the Valaiyars was difficult. Memories of the past were dim and constructions of present day social organization vague. Several informants asserted that Valaiyars were grouped into a set of natus. However, they had scant notions of natus other than their own even though the natus were said not to be endogamous.[11] All of the Valaiyar natus were said to consist of the familiar eighteen villages. These natus rarely had names. The lineages were called karais. In some natus, the karais were said to exist primarily for ritual rather than social purposes. For example, Cittanavacal village

---

[11] In the Pudukkottai manual these natus were said to be endogamous, so perhaps the opening up of marriage restrictions has been rather recent.

had five karais. The first karai's responsibility was to assure the performance of worship at the local Aiyanar temple; the second karai's to provide the sacrificial goat at festivals there; the third karai's was to hold the goat when it was sacrificed; the fourth karai's to skin and cook the sacrificed animal; and the fifth karai's to provide someone to cup his hands to catch the betel spat out by the *cāmiyāṭi* (the Valaiyar who was possessed by Aiyanar during the festival). Whether, as I was told, the ritual organization of the caste around the village festival determined the social relations of agnates and affines, or whether the social relations of the caste organized the ritual, cannot be answered. What must be appreciated, however, is that the social and ritual relations of the caste were represented in the same terms. We have noted before that many groups talk about karais as if they were organized in such a way as to arrange and celebrate the village festival. This case is only slightly more extreme and no doubt results from the caste's perception of its primary significance as residing in its priestly role in ritual.

What is especially intriguing about the ritual role of this caste resides in its special connection to the forest. For the most part, the ritual responsibilities of Valaiyars concerned their priestly duties for protection deities such as Aiyanar and Karuppar (the black god, whose shrine is adjacent to that of Aiyanar's). These gods' location on the periphery of the village often situated them on the boundaries of forest regions, where they protected the lives and crops of the local population against the myriad threats that lurked outside. These threats include wild animals, which the Valaiyars used to control and capture for their subsistence, and a variety of ghosts or spirits (*pēy*) with which the Valaiyars had intimate and prolonged contact during their extended, often nocturnal, forays into the bush. On the principle that the "lords of the forest" were probably the most suitable priests for deities who protected settled civilization from the forests, the Valaiyars' special appropriateness as priests for protection deities has been widely acknowledged. Their low position is structurally reversed only in the ritual domain since the gods who protect the village dwellers from external threats require ritual attention. The Valaiyars never sank as low as untouchables in part because they always maintained a definite, if peripheral, autonomy, and in part because their very marginality endowed them with an important ritual role.[12]

Insofar as the Valaiyars became part of the social, economic, and ritual structure of the state, they did so as agricultural laborers, forest

---

[12] This interpretation was first proposed to me by P. M. Subramanian Iyer of Pudukkottai. Also, see J. Waghorne's discussion of this (1983).

beaters, and priests of protection deities. The incorporation of Valaiyars into the expanding agricultural ecosystem has been as landless laborers working new lands for Kallars, Maravars, and Brahmans; their incorporation into the new socio-economic structure has been as the low caste group perched somewhere between the untouchables and the caste Hindus; and their incorporation into the ritual structure has been as lords of the forest, the priests of protection from the uncertain and threatening elements of the forest over which they once had conspicuous control. However, they never gained any other form of control. Unlike Kallars and Maravars they have been the passive recipients of incorporation, unable to initiate or alter these processes. They never gained the kaniyatci rights, let alone the kingly status, that once provided other outsiders with a way to enter the mainstream of Tamil culture and society.

### Pallars and Paraiyars

The two basic groups generally known today as "untouchables" because of their ritually polluting position in local caste society and their social as well as spatial exclusion from village life are the Pallars and Paraiyars. Both of these groups were classified as atimai, the hereditary servants, of the dominant Kallars and Maravars. The Pallars, many of whom were agricultural laborers, were less numerous and generally considered to be higher in status than Paraiyars in the state. The Paraiyars were employed as village servants (*toṛilāḷi*), though they also performed agricultural labor. In marked contrast to the Valaiyars, Pallars and Paraiyars, despite their spatial exclusion from central residence within villages, were almost always attached to villages dominated by other castes. Their social forms were far more dependent on the dominant castes than were those of the Valaiyars. In 1931 there were 32,822 Paraiyars and 24,921 Pallars.[13]

The Pallars and Paraiyars are divided into endogamous and territorially named and situated subcastes (natus). These natus are none other than the natus of the dominant castes: AN, Kulamankilya Natu, Varappur Natu, etc., for the Kallar country; Kanatu, Konatu for the

---

[13] There were many more Paraiyars than Pallars in Alankuti taluk, and slightly more Pallars than Paraiyars in the other two taluks. This distribution corresponds with the Tamil Nadu statewise distribution as found in Moffatt, where Pudukkottai is in fact just on the border of two areas characterized by the greater settlement of Paraiyars to the north and east and the greater settlement of Pallars to the south and west (Moffatt 1979, 60).

Maravar country; and so on. Although these natus are the units of endogamy, in most cases marriages take place between karais inside single villages. This suggests the limited nature of the natu as a territorial unit except in so far as it creates an identity between the untouchables and the natu of the dominant caste lineage or village under which they serve.[14]

The Pallars call their caste headman the *Kutumpam*. There is one Kutumpam at the village and one at the natu level. Among Paraiyars the title of the headman is *Periyatanakārar* at the level of the natu, and either *Talaiyari* or *Cāmpu* at the village level. These headmen arbitrate the same kinds of minor disputes as do the headmen of other castes. However, the dominant caste headmen asserted their right to intervene in local Pallar or Paraiyar affairs at any level and at any time. The Pallars and Paraiyars claimed that only when their disputes extended beyond their own particular caste would the dominant caste (i.e., village) headman intervene. Nonetheless, since any serious dispute among Pallars and Paraiyars had disruptive implications for the dominant caste, with respect to either the labor they performed in the agricultural domain or to the ritual services they provided for individual dominant caste households and the entire village in temple festivals, such intervention was easily and frequently justified.

The term used by Kallars and other dominant castes for order, control, and restriction (kattuppatu) implied the need for intervention and the appropriation of adjudication rights. The Kallars, for example, prided themselves on the maintenance of strict discipline and conformity to specified codes of conduct within their caste and also within the caste groups under their control. These dominated groups were considered to have no kattuppatu of their own. The appropriation of adjudication rights over dependent groups was an important sign and activity of dominance. As a result of this appropriation, however, any disputes among or between Kallar lineages often brought about disputes among or between the respectively dominated Pallar or Paraiyar lineages. They were often difficult to disentangle. One of the stratagems of dominance was the displacement of conflict. The patrons shifted the unpleasantness of conflict on to a dependent group, thereby avoiding the indignity and messiness of infighting while simultaneously displaying their dominant power over subordinate groups.

[14] In other parts of Tamil Nadu and Tamil Sri Lanka, Pallars were said to be left hand castes, and Paraiyars right hand castes. These were the only castes in Pudukkottai that had any inkling of what I was talking about when I asked about this (for fuller explanation here, see Beck 1972; Pfaffenberger 1982; Moffatt 1979).

With the introduction of legal courts over the last hundred years these Pallar and Paraiyar disputes have increasingly leaked out of the village and into the public view. Many of them are copies of disputes between or among the lineages of the dominant patrons. Most of these disputes center around honors and perquisites relating to kaniyatci and worship. The issue was often which group (a lineage if only Pallars or Paraiyars are present, or a caste if they both are), could walk down a particular street during the festival, or which group had the right to tie the *kāppu*, a necessary part of any village festival. Even when these disputes went to the modern courts, the dominant castes were consulted, since no decision could be arrived at without their participation and concurrence. The mechanisms of dominance have been reproduced within a new domain.

Within villages, Paraiyars and Pallars are divided into exogamous lineages called karais. In some cases, the karais are named after the deities worshipped by families (kula teyvams) in that particular lineage. According to some older informants, from both dominant and subordinate castes, these karais used to be grouped under the dominant caste karais traditionally served by them, in which case they were simply named first karai, second karai, and so on, corresponding to the order of ranking in the dominant caste karais. Here the basis of replication is not simple imitation, but the relations of servitude established and maintained between patrons and clients.

Most Pallar and Paraiyar informants, when asked about the meaning of the term kaniyatci, responded that it meant the right (urimai) to render service to a particular family or a village. In all castes kaniyatci means an original and hereditable right, but in each caste the exact nature of the right differs significantly. Among the service and artisan castes of the village – the barbers, washermen, carpenters, and blacksmiths – kaniyatci means similarly the right to render service (*toṛil*) to the village or to particular families therein. Toril is a term for service used only by untouchables and service-artisan castes; it is not used by Kallars and Maravars. Among Pallars and Paraiyars, kaniyatci rights are called kaniyatci *pāttiyam* (pattiyam means both claim, or right of possession, and connection, affinity, relationship). In one village, the Paraiyars are divided into two groups, one with rights to serve in that village, and the other with rights to serve in the neighboring village. Only if its own group of Paraiyars give their permission can either village employ the services of another group.

The untouchable caste owe an immense and indefinite amount of work to their patrons. In return the patrons have to assure their subsistence, as well as give them special gifts on private and public ritual occasions. The toril or service of the Paraiyars includes cleaning the village streets; beating the drum (*tappu*) outside of a deceased person's home, telling the news (*kētam*) of a death to relatives both inside and outside the village, and burning the corpse; and decorating the village for festivals and households for weddings, as well as beating the drums for and helping in the menial tasks associated with both. Until recently, the untouchables were given a certain share (cuventiram) of the harvest, either by the village as a whole or by the lineages and/or families under whom they served. Although the shares varied, the amount of grain was supposed to be just enough for their subsistence needs. When a death occurs in a harijan family, the miraci patron still has to give rice (*vaikkarici*) and other gifts; and when there is a wedding he has to provide the wedding chain (*tāli*), clothes, and feast. The untouchables can receive honors during temple festivals, but only after all other groups within the village and sometimes in a different place and manner from the other village members.

The Vettiyars were the highest of the Paraiyars. They were responsible for services rendered to the entire village rather than to individual families or lineages. They were given small maniyam lands by the Rajas in addition to their other shares and subsistence payments. The Vettiyar was to assist the village headman, the ampalam or miracidar, by carrying his emblems – including his staff of office – and walking behind him wherever he went. This task explicitly associated the head of the local untouchable group with the honor of the village headman.

When dominant caste informants talked about the ritual services of untouchables the central factor they emphasized was that it was considered an honor to have untouchables serving one and beating the drum on one's behalf during ritual occasions. Or, more to the point since the above services were actually considered perfunctory in the normal course of events, it was a sign of dishonor not to have them do this. To be denied the services of untouchables was to be denied a position of dominance in a village. The performance of a wedding without the emblems of command, authority, and honor provided by the untouchables was like the performance of a royal ritual without the flywhisk and umbrella.

While there was both great exploitation and degradation involved in the relationship between untouchables and other villagers, in particular the dominant caste groups under whom they served, and though their ritual position was the lowest of all groups, the village untouchables were nonetheless seen as indispensable. This is exemplified in a story told by the Paraiyars of Puvaracakuti about why their ancestors had migrated many generations before from another natu. I had asked them why they did not have a local family deity (kulateyvam). They responded by saying:

Our ancestors were doing bonded, or hereditary, service (*āṭimai toril*) in Vakavacal. There was a marriage there and a family asked us to fetch a large number of *tumpaippū* flowers. We did not go to the wedding to beat the drums and do our usual services because we could not procure so many flowers. The ampalam was angry with us. Our talaiyari said to him that it was not our fault. The ampalam then ordered his people to set fire to our homes. We sent the women and children from the village immediately. We then set fire to the homes of the Kallars that night and came running here to Vallanatu. When we ran we covered our foot prints by dragging bunches of thorns behind us. We came to the Tiruvarankulam temple (the natu temple of Vallanatu) where the Puvaracakuti ampalam was sleeping. He offered to take us to his village since there were no untouchables there. When the Vakavacal villagers, who were chasing us, saw us at the temple they came to attack us. But the Puvaracakuti ampalam intervened and told them that they could not do nothing since they had passed out of their natu and entered his own natu. Ever since then we have been living here.

One of the implications of this story (in addition to that regarding the territorial bounding of nattampalam authority) is that when abuse of the untouchables, particularly over the general issue of obedience, went beyond a certain limit, they could sometimes migrate to new areas where they would be accepted and protected as low but indispensable members of the community. There was some conflict among dominant caste groups for their services. Clearly, there were certain implicit, if minimal, rules and constraints binding patrons in their behavior.

On those occasions when the untouchables saw themselves as exploited beyond the usual limits, migration to some other locality was not the only, and never the first, option. In addition to informal expressions of their grievances, untouchable groups were known to boycott their ritual services of sweeping the village, clearing carcasses from the streets and fields, beating drums for weddings and funerals, and even burning the village corpses. The most notable example of this that came to my attention occurred some fifty years ago in the town of Pudukkottai, when the municipality decided to organize its own government crematorium. The untouchables ceased performing all ritual and social services. The public outcry was so great that the town government backed down in a matter of days. Not all of these proto strikes were successful, as the Vakavacal migration story shows. Successful or not they reveal the importance, rendered intelligible within a framework of honor and service, of the ritual tasks of untouchables.

It has been well documented and argued in the ethnographic literature that the ritual tasks of untouchables involved the acceptance of pollution on behalf of the ritually purer caste Hindus. The problem with this is that the emphasis on pollution (and by implication purity) brings about a conflation of one (albeit important) idiom with a total discourse and field of action. The decision of most anthropologists to favor the terms of purity and pollution is a reflex not only of the separation of religion from politics but also of the specification of ritual as being solely about such issues as purity. However, as others have shown and as I have argued, ritual is also about privilege, honor, service, power, and dominance. We need not choose between purity and pollution on the one hand and (in what is the flip side of the Western epistemological coin) power pure and simple on the other.

The ritual nature of untouchable service is further symbolized by a variety of ritual actions which demonstrate the need for the presence and participation of untouchables in village festivals. For example, on the ninth day of the natu festival in Vallanatu the Paraiyars have to touch and pull the ropes (vatam) attached to the temple chariot in order for the festival to proceed.

> It is believed that the chariot will not move unless it is touched first by a harijan. Once, the Raja questioned this preference given to the harijans and he touched the chariot vatam himself [touching the vatam first is often a royal prerogative]. The chariot did not move for eight days. He gave up and asked the harijans to do it and the chariot moved as soon as a harijan touched it. The harijan was given umpalam lands for this. Even today the ayyar (temple gurukkal) gives us pracatam.

Untouchables also usually have the exclusive right to tie the kappu, which has to be done for any major village festival to commence. In addition, harijans are often camiyatis, the people whom the god or goddess possesses during village festivals. Further, a number of state temples have priests who are harijans. As priests, they give pracatam to higher castes, including Brahmans.[15] I was told that when anyone, even a harijan, worshipped that lord as the priest, he became the agent, the representative (kariyakarar), of the god itself. No pollution can accrue from this.

These ritual privileges are neither meant nor thought to contradict the overwhelming social fact that the dominant castes can and have demanded the services of untouchables in a ruthless manner. The inferiority of untouchables is most vividly symbolized by their spatial exclusion from the central ur, or village, and their social and economic

---

[15] The tutelary deity of the family of the Brahman who was my chief informant was the Aiyanar of Perunkalur, where the pucari was a Pallar.

dependence on the inhabitants of the central village. Pallars and Paraiyars live in their own separate ceris, or colonies, where they have their own wells and temples and where their "inferior" and potentially polluting presence is bounded off from the rest of the village. Untouchables have to offer marked forms of deference, ranging from covering the mouth and avoiding eye contact when speaking to higher castes to staying out of high caste houses and away from high caste streets except when performing specified services. In our eyes, and increasingly in those of my younger untouchable informants, the limited ritual entitlements of untouchables are far outweighed by their fundamental exclusion from any major form of privilege within the social, political, economic, and ritual life of the village. Improving tenurial rights and a national political ideology stressing equality and the legitimacy of the social and economic aspirations of the downtrodden are just beginning to have an important impact in Pudukkottai.

But until recently, the subordination of untouchables in the rigid ordering of social life – the kattuppatu – as the obedient servants of the dominant castes has been reflected in the social organization of the untouchable castes themselves and in their social relations with the dominant castes. Their spatial, social, ritual, political, and economic exclusion represents the social fact that they are not seen – nor have they seen themselves – as having the ordered and ordering qualities of civilized life possessed by higher castes. They are as far removed from the ordered center as possible, even further than the Valaiyars. The latter's mediation between the disorder of the forests and the peripheral zones of social settlement has rendered them low and placed them beyond the pale of the normal social hierarchy of local society. Given that the dominant castes strive for the enunciation as well as the enforcement of order, the untouchable groups are, however necessary they may be for the full articulation of this order (being the most important objects of this ordering principle), the most manifest symbols of disorder in the social universe. In so far as the untouchables have had order, this order has been seen by the dominant castes as nothing more than an extension of their own order, their own natus, their own karais, their own village and natu assemblies (see also Pfaffenberger 1982). Where the untouchables have had rights, such as kaniyatci, it was only to live a life of servitude under their dominant caste patrons. To the extent that the untouchables have had rights to any social order at all, they had it through their submission to and dependence on their patrons. In this sense, to use Michael Moffatt's terms, the larger caste system was replicated in the internal caste relations of untouchable groups in Pudukkottai. The dominance of the superior castes was pervasive, including within its scope not only economic and political superordination but total cultural and discursive dominance.[16]

## Authority as a social fact

Political hegemony was actualized through the dominant cultural and social position of the Kallar caste, the royal community in the little kingdom. But political hegemony had to be enforced and implemented. At the village and locality levels, this was often done through the ampalams, or headmen. The ampalam was thus the crucial link between kingship as an abstract institution and the caste system as the everyday local social world of the disparate groups that made up the little kingdom.

Some natu headmen (nattampalams) were considered so powerful that whatever they said would happen. A curse uttered from their lips carried great danger; their blessings were widely sought after. They could muster a crowd of loyal supporters in a matter of minutes. The Antakuti Cervaikarar (a title he had assumed) was one of the most powerful. Reputedly, at his very call 50,000 people immediately mustered. He fed up to 1,000 people every day. All the servant (atimai) castes in the area called him *appā* (father). In addition to working on his lands, they did whatever job he required of them without specific remuneration. If times were hard they were fed and sheltered by him; he always kept large stocks of grain on hand. Feeding was the most appropriate and the most effective way of securing one's authority and the other's dependence. The Raja often sent food to his chief nobles in order to ensure their support of him.

"In the village of Virapatti in VN," a Brahman informant told me,

there was once a village official by the name of Alakayya. He was very harsh and used to beat people for no reason. Ayyacami Panturar, the grandfather of today's ampalam in Kupakuti (in VN), found fault with Alakayya and suspended him. Now Ayyacami was an honest and just person. He never had any desire for other's property. Wherever he went he took his own food so that no one else would have to feed him. He had such a large moustache that two people could hang on each side of it. When he challenged Alakayya the latter became very angry and challenged Ayyacami and said, "What kind of ampalam are you? Will God say that I made a mistake? Will the lizard chirp in the place

[16] If there is a difference in emphasis between what I write here and what Moffatt writes in his important book (1979), it is that relations between dominant and untouchable groups replicate a larger caste structure in the terms of the caste structure as I have defined it here, emphasizing honor, command, and social order more than purity and pollution.

that you choose?" Ayyacami said it would. He put a stick in the center of the tank. Immediately a huge tree lizard jumped from the tree on the bank of the tank, swum to where the pole was, climbed it and chirped three times. Because of ampalams like this, the days were pleasant and happy. There were seasonal rains and good harvests. But nowadays things and people are bad. That is why there has been no rain for the past eleven months.

Such stories were frequently told, mirroring the grander stories of kings and emperors. The ampalams were seen as little kings, both in their own right as representatives of the local communities, and because they were granted their authority and privilege by a greater king from outside the community. Like kings, the ampalams were invested with the responsibility to sustain dharma. If they did this the moral and natural world would be ordered, and the countryside under their jurisdiction would be prosperous.

The ampalams were responsible for the maintenance of peace and the protection of property. If anything was stolen, it was their responsibility to recover it or make good the loss to the unfortunate victim. Like the kavalkarars in other parts of the Tamil country (e.g., Tirunelveli), they used their authority to guarantee the behavior and possessions of the people under their command. I was told many stories about thefts of goods which, when the crime was reported to the ampalam, were recovered within hours. According to another Brahman informant:

The Ponnampalam [of Viraccilai] was the grandfather of the present Ponnampalam. He was a very powerful and influential person, almost like a king. When something was stolen in his area he would recover it in twelve hours if he wished. A cow was stolen from my grandfather when he went to harvest his fields in Melatematipatti. He went to Ponnampalam and told him the problem "Look, under your authority (atikaram) such things are happening." The Ponnampalam told him not to worry, to go home and rest assured that the cow would come back by that evening. Of course it did.

The position of the ampalam as the protector of property and the guarantor of peace was further strengthened by his role in the various assemblies. Disputes over issues as diverse as marriage, adultery, irrigation, boundaries, and village or locality festivals would be settled in these assemblies. Presiding over these assemblies, the ampalams arbitrated the disputes brought before it. The authority of the ampalam was complemented by that of the village or subcaste deity, in whose temple compound the assembly usually met. A special puja was often performed on these occasions. Significantly, the ampalam's role was not so much to punish the offender as to restore communal harmony. The fines for most offences were relatively minor, usually taking the form of a donation to the village temple for the annual festival. Fines were assessed according to the seriousness of the crime and the pecuniary position of the offender. More important than any material transfer, however, was the public contrition of the offender and the restoration of peace and honor between disputants. Entrusted with the regulation and control (kattuppatu) of social action and caste interaction in his area, the ampalam, again mirroring the king, was responsible for maintaining the local order of things.

The ampalam was granted tax free lands called maniyams and umpalams by the king. In one sense, these grants simply confirmed the original and privileged rights of settlement (kaniyatci) appropriated by the head of a lineage or a subcaste. In another sense, however, the grants were honors bestowed by the king upon his representative in a village or locality – grants which both marked and rewarded the privileged recipient of royal favor. In the nineteenth century, these grants were "rationalized" and the inams were specified as remuneration for simple services performed. After this time the official position of ampalam – which had state recognition and for which inam lands were thought to be held – became designated as that of miracidar. The person who had been the ampalam usually continued as the new miracidar, although there were disputes between contestants within families as well as cases where another contestant from a different lineage was awarded the position by the state. Although we have no records of disputes for the eighteenth century, traditional stories suggest that the king had the right to adjudicate disputes and effectively to appoint whomever he desired for the local position. But the king was aware that the local ampalam derived his authority from the local community as well as from his own gift. Doubtless both the hereditary nature of the position as well as major realignments of local power were considered by the king when arbitrating these issues. In a later chapter we will see that while disputes over this position were continuous, significant changes took place both in the specification of local authority and in the criteria involved in the resolution of local disputes.

The authority of the ampalam in the old regime came from a number of different though interdependent sources. The ampalam was the headman of the first lineage of the dominant caste within a village or a natu. As the representative of the community the headman was *primus inter pares*, first among equals rather than first over subordinates. As the representative of the king, however, he transcended the social whole. Signified by maniyam lands, privileges of position and service, and emblems of office, this latter form of authority had the immediate effect of separating the head from his group and incorporating him into a higher sovereignty. The representative quality of the headman, however, made him the medium through which the entire community was incorporated into the sovereignty of the king. Thus in the old regime the ampalam could not be two separate people, one a caste headman and the other a government servant. The two sources of authority were structurally and conceptually interdependent. Only during the colonial regime did the possibility, however rarely enacted, of having the positions of miracidar and ampalam held by different persons arise.

The authority of the ampalam was perhaps most importantly displayed in the temple. There he received first honors on behalf of his community. These honors were seen as marks of prestige and sources of merit for the individual who received them. Like pirutus, they were emblems or badges of office. Thus, particularly once offices became increasingly bureaucratized, temple honors became the most valued perquisites of any office. The first honor for the ampalam also usually meant that the ampalam, like the priest, mediated the distribution of all honors to the local community. The honors to be distributed to the rest of the village were handed over by the priests to the ampalam, and then by the ampalam to the members of the village community in order. The ampalam thus acted as in loco regalis, the fount of honor. During temple festivals the ampalam also displayed the emblems of his authority which had been handed down from his ancestors and sometimes granted by kings. In the next chapter we will explore the relationship of the authority of the ampalam to the temple in greater detail.

### The caste system in Pudukkottai

The "caste system" of Pudukkottai was organized around principles of honor (mariyatai), order/discipline (orunku, kattuppatu), royal status (antastu), rights and shares to puja and associated ritual entitlements (urimai, panku, kaniyatci), and kinship (affinity and alliance, or inam and uravumuraikal). The capacity to define what this "order" was, how it was to be regulated and maintained, and how it correlated with structures of authority, worship, territory, etc., was constituted by proximity to the Raja. This proximity was implied in the term for honor and status, antastu, which took its particular significance from the central position of the king himself.

The positions of Brahmans and untouchables were defined as much in the terms we have emphasized in this study as in terms of purity or pollution, categories which have always been seen to have their highest relevance for these two castes. The highest ranking Brahmans were those whose presence in the kingdom generated the most merit and honor for the king, who emulated well-established norms of kingship in granting land to them. As we saw earlier, grants to Brahmans were important episodes in the major transformation from tribal chief to Hindu king, a transformation which had in large part to do with the increasing honor of the king. Even with reference to Pallars and Paraiyars, concern over purity and pollution played only a partial role in the articulation, by informants of all castes, of social order and disorder, of hierarchy, and of the organization of lineages, villages, natus, and castes.

Therefore, not only was the internal ordering of Kallar lineages and subcastes organized by kingship, but other castes were also profoundly affected by their relative proximity to the king. The caste system as a whole was ordered in relation to the king. Or rather, we should say that it was ordered in relation to kingship, as we have outlined it in terms not only of the person of the king but also the principles of honor, status, and order embodied by the king. Hocart is right when he says that the entire caste system was a sacrificial order, in which the king was the ritual principle (Hocart 1970). The king, who in the classical model was the upholder of dharma, became dharma. The textual prescriptions relevant for his caste and others, and how social order was defined, maintained, and enforced, all became encoded in the activities of the king. Hierarchy, as seen both in temples and in the king's court, was thus literally nothing more than first, proximity to the king, second, the kinship ties and caste relations that were part of this, and third, the honor, offices, land rights and other privileges that constituted and reconstituted this proximity.

The reproduction of caste relations from the top to the bottom of the caste system had to do with brutal and subtle forms of cultural hegemony. Because of the confluence of brutality and subtlety, everything from the degree of autonomy in intra caste relations and the role of territory in enabling and circumscribing social relations to the economic, ritual, and political dependency of subordinate groups became part of a totalistic social formation. This totalization – the combination of religion and politics and the mutually reinforcing complementarities of brutality and belief – ironically renders any single theory seeking to account for the things we call caste problematic at best.

# 9

# *Temples and society*

## Honor and privilege

Once privileges and honors are given, people will live only for them, preferring to starve rather than, for example, being served on anything but a double plantain leaf.

*The Pallavarayar chief, July 1982*

Kaniyatci, one of the fundamental rights in local society, was seen, inter alia, as a right (urimai) to a share (panku) in one's local temple (kovil). Without this right, one did not qualify as a full member of the local community. As we have seen in the last two chapters, temples were often regarded as the primary institution which enabled the formation of communities. These then took on consanguineous, affinal, and territorial forms. The temple was the common ground where each caste had a role, and where the position of each unit of the community was ordered with respect to all the other constituent units. Each social and territorial unit – from the subcaste natu to the village, from the lineage to the family – had a temple which defined its social and ritual being. Temples also situated local society within the larger context of the subcaste/territory and the little kingdom by creating contexts for participation and worship stretching all the way up to the grand state festivals which took place in the tutelary temple of the royal family. Everyone in the state worshipped the family deity of the Tondaimans. The annual Dasara festival during which the kingdom was regenerated by the goddess's empowerment of the king and his emblems was celebrated in this temple, the *Camastānam Kōvil*. Participation in the worship of this temple was an important element in the definition and specification of the little kingdom. The word for temple, kovil, itself means the place of the king (*kō*).

The right to a share in the temple meant, by definition, a right to a share of honors in the temple. The importance of honor, and honors, in temple worship is the key to the sociological significance of temples.

Louis Dumont was the first anthropologist to identify honor (as mutalmai, primacy) as a key component of worship. He notes that hierarchy itself has no word in Tamil, but that the closest word would be mutalmai, for precedence:

This precedence appears in defined situations, as in the distribution of honors (mutalmei [sic]) in a temple. It is a relative concept, and consists of the comparison of ranks. In particular cases, as in the old judicial council presided over by the headman, the entire group orders itself in this way. We designate the order of precedence applied to this totality as hierarchy. The importance of the hierarchical principle is also clear in the fact that the group's own self-definition is almost identical with the proclamation of this order of precedence. (Dumont 1986, 159)

Dumont's realization that temple precedence and kinship/caste rank correspond extremely closely prefigures much of what is to come in this chapter. However, Dumont also holds that temple honors are purely religious, in contrast to kingly honors, which are solely political. "Thus, in order to show that the lineage or locality has highest rank, reference is made either to primacy at a temple (which is in fact due to purely religious factors, cf. III A 1. 5e) or else to a service rendered to the king" (Dumont 1986, 166). I have already argued that these two factors can not be separated.

The political nature of honor, and more generally the socio-cultural significance of temple honors (as mariyatai) in south Indian history and society have been investigated more recently in great detail by Carol Breckenridge and Arjun Appadurai (Appadurai and Breckenridge 1976). They have argued convincingly that temple honors denote far more than the results of a purely religious process. Their work has been instrumental in the identification of the temple as an important domain, of temple honors as a key resource, and of the ritual components of authority and group formation within the temple. My concentration on the social importance of temples and honors owes a great deal to their insights.

Appadurai and Breckenridge have demonstrated that honors, and in particular the exchanges associated with honor in the context of temple worship, played a constitutive role in social relations. Temple honors (mariyatai) are the redistributed leavings of the deity, and in the context of the south Indian temple denote "a whole series of objects, actions and transactions, linking the deity with its servants, worshippers and protectors, whose substance, order and context, provides a public code for the demarcation of status" (Appadurai and Breckenridge 1976, 197). But honor does not simply mark the relationship of deity and devotee, or even the status relations of respective devotees. Rather, the receipt of specific honours, in any given context, renders authoritative the individual's share (*panku*) in the temple conceived as a redistributive process. Such a share would be composed of: the right to offer service (*kaiṅkaryam*) to the deity, either through endowment or through prescribed ritual function; the right to move the resources allocated for the specific ritual event; the right to command the relevant persons involved in the actualization of the given ritual; the right to perform some single part of a complex ritual event; and, finally, the right to worship the deity, by simply witnessing the ritual. (Appadurai and Breckenridge 1976, 198)

Because honors establish authority and provide access to privileged participation in the redistributive process of the temple, the right to receive these honors is considered to be an important, and distinctive, aspect of worship. Honors have come both to denote and to constitute various authoritative positions and offices, as well as rights to perform service to the deity. Breckenridge has further stressed that the temple became an arena in which local leadership was not only accorded but, even more importantly, contested (ibid., 204. See also Breckenridge 1977). Since the sovereign source of honor, the deity, is unable either to arbitrate among claims to honor or to adjudicate conflict about honor, temple honors create a great deal of conflict over issues of rank and authority. This has meant that the temple has always required the protection and occasional intervention of the king.

Endowment is the principal means by which honors are secured. Endowments to temples, whether by kings or far lesser individuals, "permit the entry and incorporation of corporate units into the temple" (Appadurai and Breckenridge 1976, 201). Thus the gifting activity which has created and sustained so many temples in southern India has at its root the goal of entering the temple community, and then increasing one's rank within it and one's relative proximity to the deity. Like the offering of service which initiates a political relationship, the endowment to a temple has a structural logic which unfolds in the redistributional cycle suggested above. The greatest endowers were kings.

We have seen that kings endowed temples with a considerable proportion of their kingdoms' resources, and that the ritual activities of temples were fundamental to sovereignty in southern India. Royal endowments were bestowed to make a particular kingship culturally appropriate, and to bring prosperity to the kingdom. In Appadurai's formulation, however, the king depends on endowments in even more critical respects. As Appadurai claims, "Without endowment, the king would cease to place himself in an active relationship with the redistributive powers of the deity and thus would fail to acquire the honor constitutive of authority" (Appadurai 1981, 71; see also Breckenridge 1978). According to this view, sovereignty is quintessentially procured in temples, where the deity is the paradigmatic sovereign. Further, all endowers are equal at the level at which they are dependent on particular endowments for their status within the temple.

Appadurai's temple-centric view helps to explain why temples have been so crucially important to sovereignty. However, we have seen that the king is in an a priori sense first devotee and first to be honored in any state temple. To see the endowment as the most critical determinant of standing in the temple underemphasizes the position of the king, who is neither structurally nor rhetorically *dependent* on the temple. None of the family histories we examined contain any reference to the dependence of royal authority on temple honors. Royal gifts to temples were as much signs of the king's increasing sovereignty as the means by which this sovereignty was augmented.

Further, the myriad institutions or domains – particular subcastes, territories, villages, lineages, families, etc. – that constitute temple communities are only dependent in limited ways on the kinds of endowments Appadurai and Breckenridge document for their level of participation in their temples. Even though temples may be seen as primary communities, temples were themselves largely contingent on specifiable social and political processes. While these processes took place in and with respect to temples, it is important to note that the view from the temple is always a partial view. Village headmen might have fought more zealously for the temple honors incumbent to their position than for anything else, but no one (of my informants or in my texts) believed that this fight could take place solely in the temple through contests of endowment. Appadurai has himself written about the problem of establishing the boundary of the temple, and I can propose no simple solution to this problem here. In brilliantly redressing the previous tendency of scholars to see temples as nothing more than reflections of other social realities, Appadurai and Breckenridge have put too much stress on the autonomy of temples and temple honors.

Part of the problem is historical. Appadurai and Breckenridge concentrate on large temple complexes in post-medieval and modern urban contexts, when kingship was on the wane and when certain large temples expanded, gradually usurping the cultural centrality of the king and the royal court. A study of a range of smaller temples in their local social and political context is a necessary complement to their work. In what can be reconstructed of old regime Pudukkottai, the temple system cannot be isolated for the social, territorial, and political processes specific to the rural roots of old regime social formations. Kaniyatci at one level did mean the right to receive temple honors, but it also had to do with grants from kings, territorial dominance, control over local labor and the ritual and agricultural services of the eighteen castes, shares in lineage systems, marriage exchanges within subcastes, and ideological agreement about (and ideological control over) the cultural components of subcaste organization and domination. Kaniyatci was also rooted in the political forms established through the granting of protection rights to local chiefs in the period after the fourteenth century.

The kinds of honors that constituted authority in the old regime were those received as shares of worship in local temples as well as those granted as emblems and titles (pirutus) by kings. The authority to arbitrate disputes concerning honor in temples, and the gifts and privileges upon which these temple honors were necessarily predicated, came from the Raja. Indeed, the honors received in temples from deities were at another level privileges accorded by the king. The deity was not so much the paradigmatic sovereign as worship was paradigmatic exchange. To repeat what I have said before, puja was a root metaphor for political relations.

In spite of these caveats, temple honors were seen as a special privilege. I was often told by my informants that the mariyatai in a temple was invaluable. One can buy and sell land but no one can buy the mariyatai of another person; it is not for sale at any price. However, my informants on this subject were themselves frequently engaged in a process of trying to buy honor, not in the market but in government offices and legal courts. In all social groups, disputes erupted most frequently around honors. During my year in the field, I saw more energy and more money invested in disputes over honor than in all other disputes combined. In fact, as an interested foreign scholar, participants often attempted to coopt me in these disputes. Village often fought against village over which one would head the honors roll in the local festival. Lineage headmen invariably intrigued against each other over who was to receive the honor of being head ampalam; similar quarrels took place within lineages. Even among Pallars and Paraiyars, the central subject of dispute was honor: who would have the honor of tying the kappu to start the village festival, or of parading first in a particular street during the festival, and so on. Today these disputes are taken to law courts, which have gradually appropriated the right to arbitrate all such disputes. Victory there correlates more closely to the amount of money spent than to any other single factor. In the colonial and princely period, colonial bureaucrats kept most of these disputes from proceeding to law courts, arbitrating them instead with reference more to social order than "legal" precedent.

Honors (and here I include both royal and temple honors) were important not only in and of themselves, but because they signified, even if they did not autonomously constitute, authority, position, and stature in the community. To be given honors in a particular place and time meant that one held a particular office, position, or status. To be a village ampalam one had to be given honors in the village festival as the village ampalam. Without these honors, one would lose one's office, position, or status. Honors were the perquisites of office at the same time that offices were the perquisites of honor. My informants told me that honor was public (potu). It was something accorded in public, and took its meaning precisely from being given in, and in relation to, a particular public. All my informants concurred that their own standing and prestige in society was more importantly determined by their position in the temple, signified by honors, than by anything else, including the amount of lands they held. Thus they would not part with them for any amount of money; and thus they incurred financial ruin to contest matters of honor. In a sense, of course, honor was all that they had left. As I shall argue in a later chapter, honors attained new, increasingly autonomous, and fetishized meanings after the demise of the old regime. The cultural system of both state and temple was radically revised under colonialism. Like religion itself, the temple was reinvented in an attempt by the colonial state to appear as the protector of all that was good and inviolable in Indian culture and institutions while removing the life-force that had pulsed through them in the old regime.

## The order of honor

Given the importance of temple honors for displaying authority, status, and rank, the roll call of honors at the village festival is an important source for determining how the village community is defined, of which groups it is composed, and how these groups are ranked. In all the anthropological work on ranking[1] only Appadurai and Breckenridge have stressed the general importance of the *mariyātai varicai*, the order in which honors are distributed. But even in their work little attention is paid to the actual order of rank and the potential of honor roll calls to

---

[1] Marriott has provided the most sophisticated and accurate means of calibrating rank in villages according to the exchange of food (Marriott 1968). Puja also involves the exchange of food, and in one sense simply confirms Marriott's model. But puja also provides a formal locus for food transactions in which the exchange of food is specially valorized because of the central position of the deity and the structural integrity of the temple.

provide important evidence about rank within localities, villages, lineages, and subcastes.

The first honor in all state temples belonged to the Raja. I was told that the Raja had this first right everywhere (*Rājāvukku ellāmē pāttiyam*). The Raja's participation in village life is further evidenced in that certain festivals would often not begin until honors were received from the Raja. According to informants belonging to the temple in Narankiappattu, "we only begin the festival after receiving the coconut, fruit, etc., blessed and sent from the Raja. The pujari and one of us will go to the Raja in Tiruchi and we will ask him to give us the mariyatai for commencing the festival. We get it and do the first offerings (arccanai) after getting back to the temple." The Raja was in a similar sense the first devotee in each of the important temples in the state, giving and receiving the first honors in theory if not in practice.

The second honor in most temples was given to Brahmans, if any were present to receive it. Brahmans were subdivided into two and sometimes three categories; learned (srotriya) Brahmans were always given honors before other Brahmans, next came Brahmans who were present and who were engaged in secular (laukika) occupations, and last the temple priest, if Brahman, would receive his honor. While Brahmans ranked very high – they were thought to be *bhudeva*, gods on earth – even the srotriya Brahmans had to follow the king. As we have noted earlier, the conundrum of the relationship between Brahman and king was resolved here; while the Brahman was superior to the king as Kallar, he was inferior to the Kallar as king. The so-called material dependence of Brahmans on kings, which countered against their spiritual dominance, was not upheld in the domain of temple honors, which itself can be seen as neither exclusively spiritual nor exclusively material.

After the Brahmans, the way in which the order of honor was calibrated varied greatly. Some of the factors behind this variance were the stature of the village and the kind of temple. Between the Brahman and the village ampalam there usually came a number of categories for persons in the village or locality who represented the government, thereby symbolizing the participation of the village in a wider political context. For example, in one large Maravar village (Ponnamaravati), after the Brahmans, honors were given to the Rajakkal Nayakkanmar, the Uriyakarar, the Amarakarar, and then the Ampalam. The Rajakkal Nayakkanmar was the descendant of a family of Telegu warriors who were given lands in the state in the late eighteenth century because of their military skill, which had won them an important leadership position in the militia. The Uriyakarar were palace guards; the amarakarars were Kallar soldiers. Both were placed high on the list for military reasons. In

291

Piliyur, the head village of the western moiety of the VN Kallar, the order of the distribution of honors in the goddess temple was as follows: king, Brahmans, "government employees" (the Munsiff and the Karnam), the Cervaikarar, the Rajakkal Nayakkanmar, the Mantakapatitar, and then the Ampalam. Here, the new bureaucratic form of government was represented by the Munsiff (in charge of collecting revenue) and the Karnam (in charge of preparing and maintaining village accounts). After them the vestiges of former kingly rule were still encoded in the honor scheme of the village temple. The "Cervaikarar" (not one of the great Vakuppu Cervaikarars) was the head of one of the families of AN Kallars who had been settled among the VN Kallars to keep an eye on them; the Rajakkal Nayakkanmar was another Telegu warrior who had been given land for his military services; and the Mantakapatitar was the person who had the right to sponsor that particular day's worship.

After the honoring of the persons and categories who represented the larger political and social context of the village, the village ampalam received honors. Of course, the ampalam himself was often the actual giver of all the honors, since in some villages he maintained the list (the mariyatai varicai) and was occasionally given all the honors by the temple pujari to distribute (sometimes before anyone else, sometimes only at the point at which the ampalam was given his own honors). After the ampalam, the heads of the various dominant caste lineages received their honors in the rank order of their karai position. Then the rest of the village was honored. In Piliyur, the karaikarars (heads of Kallar lineages) were followed by lower government officials (the Panchayat V. P. and village teacher and doctor), then by the Cettiyars, the Konars (the cattle herders, sometimes also the sheep herders, or formerly Itaiyars), the village servants ((i) *Paṇṭāram*, priest; (ii) *Mēlakkārar*, pipers; (iii) *Kollaṉ*, blacksmith; (iv) *Taccaṉ*, carpenter; (v) *Tōpi*, washerman), and finally the *Ampaṭṭaṉ* (barber), the Pallar, and the Paraiyar. The last three groups were not given their pracatam on the tray like the others; instead, the Pantaram priest handed their honors directly to them. This list varied from village to village according to the range of castes present. In most villages there was only a single honor for nondominant castes, although in a few cases where such a caste had grown in stature more than one honor was given to the two or three caste headmen. The honors given to the untouchables were structurally differentiated from the other honors, as in the above case where they were not given on a tray, or in other cases where they were not given in the temple. The mariyatai varicai thus revealed not only rank, but internal units of classification, as for example in the separation and ranking of Brahmans, the dominant caste, subordinate castes, and untouchables (see Table 2).

Special participation in a temple festival was achieved through the sponsorship of particular days of the festival. Such sponsorship involved the endowment of a particular piece of land or the annual provision of a sum of money to support the expenses of one day of the festival. Chief among these expenses were the kalanji, the items to be used as respects: bananas, coconuts, betel leaves, rice balls, garlands, etc. Sponsorship of this kind was called mantakappati, literally meaning the lordship (*pati*) of a *maṇṭakam*, or *maṇṭapam* (see Breckenridge 1976). The mantapam was a structure, often found in or near temples, which was specifically designed as a place to which a deity could be brought while

Table 2 *The order of honor (mariyatai varicai)*

A. The list of honors in Piliyur, the chief village of the western division of Vicinki Natu:
  1. Raja
  2. Brahmans
       (i) outside Brahmans
       (ii) Brahmans who live in village
       (iii) Gurukkal who performed puja
  3. Government employees, Munsiff and Karnam
  4. Cervaikarar (head of the local family of AN Kallars)
  5. Nayakar (some local Rajakkals who had been given attavanai umpalam)
  6. Mantakappatitar (the person or group who sponsors that particular day of the festival)
  7. Local Kallars
       (i) Panturar ⎫
           Coratirayar ⎬ the natu miracidars
       (ii) Ur ampalam – the Coratirayar (not actually given a second honor)
       (iii) Karaikarars – heads of each Kallar lineage, excepting those individuals who had already received honors (note, you get your honor at the highest possible place, like the king who gets honor as Raja and not as Tondaiman)
  8. Other village officers: Panchayat Vice President, village doctor, and village teachers
  9. Cettiyar
  10. Konars
  11. Torilalikal: village servants, in the following order:
       (i) Pantaram, priest
       (ii) Melakkarar, pipers
       (iii) Kollan, blacksmith
       (iv) Taccan, carpenter
       (v) Topi, washerman
       (vi) Ampattan, barber
       (vii) Pallar ⎫
       (viii) Paraiyar ⎬ untouchables

The last three were not given practam on a tray.

(*Contd.*)

Table 2 (*Contd.*)

B. The list of honors in Karampakuti, a village in Ampu Natu, and the head village for the Karampakuti kuppam:
   1. Raja (the maniyakarar, i.e. the one given maniyams by the Raja in order to be the intermediary between the Raja and the kuppam, receives this honor; note he qualifies for this not only because of his office, but also because he is an AN Kallar)
   2. Then the Stanikarar calls out to see if there are any other representatives from the other eight kuppams of Ampu Natu.
   3. The Stanikarar (a Coliyar Vellalar, related to the Ampu Natu Kovil stanikarars and with the same local functions)
   4. Tennatiraiyar karai (the first lineage of the Karampakuti kuppam)
   5. Kantiyar karai (the second ranked lineage of the K kuppam)
   6. Maravarayar karai (the third)
   7. Valankontar karai (the fourth)
   8. Pettaiyar (head of the Cettiyar caste)
   9. Konar (the head of the shepherd caste)
   10. Acari
   11. Melakkarar

   Then the Pallars and Paraiyers get respects but they are not called. This is a relatively short list, mostly made up of local lineage heads within the kuppam. There are no Brahmans because this list is for an Aiyanar festival, which means it involves goat sacrifices to Karuppar on the side; the role of the priest is performed not by Brahmans or by Valaiyars or Velars, but by the Stanikarar. Note that the lineages of the dominant caste are not only prior to but structurally equivalent to other whole caste groups.)

C. The list of honors in Ponnamaravati: an important Maravar and Cettiyar village in southwestern Pudukkottai:
   1. Aranmanaiyar (representative of the palace)
   2. Racakkal Nayakkanmar (descendant of military general)
   3. Uriyakarar
   4. Amarakarar
   5. Peralurar
   6. Peria (big) Ampalakarar
   7. Cinna (small) Ampalakarar
   8. Kattan Karuppan Ampalakarar
   9. Kotikkamuttan Ampalam
   10. Ataikkappan Ampalam
   11. Kuppaiyan Ampalam
   12. Periya Konar
   13. Cinna Konar
   14. Kumarappan Ampalam
   15. Ataikkan Ampalam
   16. Ampalam Cevukan Cettiyar
   17. Ampalam Muttu Paraniyappa Cettiyar
   18. Urar (village headman)
   19. Nakarattar (head of Cettiyar community)
   20. Ramati
   21. Periya karuppakkon (store keeper)
   22. Cankili piccan (one who lifts fire)
   23. Kollacari (blacksmith)
   24. Taccacari (carpenter)
   25. Tattaracari (goldsmith)
   26. Velar (potter)
   27. Melam (piper)

   The Paraiyars are given the respects but they are not called out during the distribution.

Table 2 *(Contd.)*

D. The list of honors in Karaiyur: a large village in southwestern Pudukkottai, dominated by Vellalars:

1. Aracankam (representative of the state)
2. Brahmans
3. Caivas
4. Outside Vellalars
5–9. Five local karais of Vellalars
10. Ullur Vellalars
11. Palace accountant
12. Kankani (village head)
13. Cervai (VN Kallar)
14. Amarakarar (Terkketi Kallar)
15. Carapoki
16. Konattu ampalam
17. Katanpatti
18. Mankalipatti
19. Kollars (blacksmith)
20. Taccans (carpenter)
21. Kompu (god bearer)
22. Pucari (priest)
23. Pantaram (priest)
24. Vairavi (temple store keeper)
25. Taci (dancing girl)
26. Melam (piper)
27. Mey Kaval (protector)
28. Dhobi (washerman)
29. Barber
30. Natar
31. Pallar
32. Paraiyan

on procession. In large towns and temple centers, the mantakapati literally meant that the deity was brought to rest in the mantakam of the person sponsoring that day of the festival.

There, the sponsor was allowed to perform a special puja in which he received first honors. In most smaller village temples, the mantakappati meant that the person who sponsored a day of worship was on that day given honors high up on the list, above the local dominant castes. Additionally, in some cases when the deity was taken on procession it was brought outside the house of the host where a special puja was performed.

In the temple festival at Piliyur referred to in the above list, each day of the annual nine day goddess festival was sponsored by one person or group. The order of mantakappatis was as follows:

1. Village Brahmans
2. Nayakar
3. Government employees
4. Cervaikarar

5.    Mudaliar Munsiff
6.    The Raja
7.    Cettiyar
8.    VN Kallars
9.    Village

It was a tremendous privilege to be allowed to sponsor a day of worship during the festival, when the whole community congregated and the deity was charged with maximum powers (I was told that the deity was charged with maximum powers both because of specifically ritual and calendrical reasons and because of the collective worship of many devotees). In all the state temples, the Raja sponsored the sixth day of the festival, when special pujas were performed in his honor. While the list of mantakappatitars usually included the groups and individuals who were already placed high on the list of honors in the ordinary varicai, it was easier to alter the list of mantakappatis than the varicai itself. Newly powerful and wealthy groups who wished to convert their power and money into honor often began by trying to endow a mantakappati.

Honor in temples pertained not only to order and privilege, but service as well. Participation in the temple festival was not limited to the receipt of honors and the sponsorship of a mantakappati. Many services had to be performed in order for the festival to be a success. And, of course, many regular services had to be performed in the temple throughout the year. The Raja gave maniyam lands for these regular services, which included the performance of the puja, dancing in front of the deity (devadasi), sweeping the temple grounds, cooking, and the provision of the objects required in worship. In the Kutumiamalai temple, an important temple about ten miles west of Pudukkottai town where early Pudukkottai kings were reportedly crowned, there were 135 separate *māniyakārars*, that is individuals who were granted some form of maniyam for services to the temple. The number of maniyakarars in the royal temple at Tirukokkarnam came close to 1,000.

That a temple could not exist without the provision of services is made clear by the following story. Some informants in the natu temple in Vallanatu told me that

Long ago, Cinnamannan and Periyamannan were the war ministers (*yutta mantiris*) for the Raja. They were from Vallanatu. They went for the annual festival to the natu temple in Tiruvarankulam. On the way back, Periyamannan was slaughtered by dacoits. Cinnamannan went back to the capital and resigned his post. The Raja asked him what he wanted, and he replied that the first mantakappati, as well as the right to tie the kappu, should be given to his pankalis.

In addition, since he wanted to make sure that this temple in which he had now secured such an honorable position would continue in perpetuity, he asked the Raja to grant maniyams to the following temple servants whose services were necessary in the temple: the head dancer, the panegyrist, the bearer of the fly whisk, the blower of the conch, and the bearer of the torch. The Raja granted these umpalams, as well as other maniyam lands to the priests of the temple. These umpalams were granted only because of this request by Cinnamannan, who thereby acquired the honor of donating the first mantakappati in this our great temple.

This story illustrates the extent to which fame and position were used for gaining honor within temples, and the sense as well that for this honor to mean anything the temple had to be well and perpetually served.

In addition to the regular services of the sort mentioned above, all landholders (*paṭṭadārs*) had to perform service (uriyam) during the festivals of the temples in their localities. This uriyam consisted for the most part of carrying the deity or pulling the chariot. The privilege of landholding also entailed the responsibility of participating in the maintenance of the local temples and their ritual performances. In this extended sense, all land was a maniyam for temple service.

In some places all residents of the temple area had to contribute an annual fee, as a kind of tax, for the expenses incurred in the annual temple festival. This was common both in natu temples and in village temples. At the natu level, taxes were often assessed by the subcaste when they corporately sponsored a mantakappati. In some cases, the tax was assessed on all land holders, or those with titles to land; in other cases, the tax was assessed on households or lineage heads within the dominant caste. In the village temples, however, customary contributions were not usually made in cash but in kind, often in the form of some specified item such as a goat for the sacrifice. In goddess temples, and in shrines to deities such as Aiyanar, who was almost always accompanied by the blood thirsty Karuppar and Munisvaran, there were many animal sacrifices, mostly of goats, sometimes of water buffaloes. (In larger temples, the Raja sometimes gave maniyams to the people responsible for donating animals to the temple.) Each of the dominant caste lineages was responsible for providing one or more goats in many villages, e.g., Kottur. For the ritual feast following the puja the first portion of the sacrificed goat was offered to the deity, with shares then allocated to the taxonomized groups of the villages according to specified shares, with a special portion for the person who slaughtered the goat. The harijans were usually given the innards (*kuṭal*).[2]

[2] See Sahlins (1976) regarding homologies between food and social groups.

## Village festivals and local authority

No two village or natu festivals were exactly the same. Nonetheless, I will briefly outline one of the many village festivals I attended. The importance of this festival can be generalized since it was for the god Aiyanar, an important village deity in the Pudukkottai region and for Kallars and Maravars in particular. A further word about the deity and about the general structure of these festivals (tiruvira) and their implications for understanding village communities is necessary. Although the basic structure of worship surrounding Aiyanar has been well described in Whitehead (1976) and other sources, I will focus here on the social and political components of the ritual, which, I feel, have been unduly neglected.

In Pudukkottai, Aiyanar was often the principal village deity, though there are villages which include Aiyanar temples in which *the* village deity was said to be a goddess. According to most of my informants, the most significant feature of Aiyanar was his role as the protector (*kāvalar*). He was more specifically called the protection deity (kaval teyvam), the protector of the boundaries (*ellai kāvalar*) and the one who protected those who took refuge with him (*aṭaikalankāttān*). The festival for Aiyanar, called the *kutirai eṭuppu*, or the installation of the horse, should precede and inaugurate all other village festivals. Aiyanar gave "permission" for all other festivals to begin, even as the village headmen gave permission for the kutirai etuppu to begin. The festival would begin a month before the main festival day. The head of the potters (*Vēlārs*), the community that made the terracotta offerings and often acted as principal priests for Aiyanar, would take a handful of clay (pitiman) from the village tank. (The other communities that commonly acted as priests for Aiyanar were Valaiyars and Pantarams.) The pitiman was placed in a brass plate and handed to the village ampalam, who then returned it to the Velar, along with the ritual dues (daksina) consisting of some money and betel and areca nut (*vettalai pakku*). The ampalam then announced the date of the festival, which he had determined with the aid of an astrologer and all the lineage and caste headmen when they had all gathered together in the ampalam's house. The ampalam had to make this gift, signifying his permission for the festival to begin, to entitle the Velars to proceed with the preparation of the offerings. The gift was made in part in the form of puja, as the blessed return of a gift that was first offered to the superior being; the gift was also like that made by the ancient yajamana, or sacrificer, who sponsored a Vedic sacrifice and paid all daksinas to the priests. The position of the ampalam, the mukiyastar or most important man in the village, was thus enunciated and displayed at the moment of the festival's inauguration. According to a Velar informant,

we should pray to Aiyanar for protection and prosperity. Just as in other pujas we offer coconut, fruit, camphor, and flowers, in this puja we offer horses, bulls, and elephants, the vehicles (*vākanam*) of Aiyanar, and of his constant companion, Karuppar. Thus we pray for prosperity, victory over the forces of evil and destruction (*tuṣṭam*), for progeny, and for the health of our families, fields, and animals. At times the crops might be destroyed by wild pigs and foxes; Aiyanar can protect the fields. The village offers horses and sometimes elephants as well [made of clay]. [Individuals can also make offerings, which they pay for, usually when they make some vow – *virattam*.] Aiyanar must have these vehicles in order to make his rounds (*cavāri*) and protect the village. Aiyanar is the main deity (*pirātana teyvam*). Karuppar is Aiyanar's main assistant. Aiyanar is like the Raja of the village. Teyvam and Raja are the same. The Raja looks after his people while the teyvam looks after his creations.

At this point I intervened and asked what was the difference between the goddess (amman) and Aiyanar.

Amman protects the people whereas Aiyanar protects the people, village, crops, cattle, everything. We do not have fields in the village. They are outside the village, where wild animals can destroy the crops. Aiyanar protects all that in the interest of the best wishes of the people of the village. That is why he must be near the fields. Amman protects the people of the village (ur) from illness and bad luck. Just like a mother protects her child. That is why she is in the middle of the village. Aiyanar protects the village from all kinds of evil (tustam). He has got all the evil deities, i.e., Periyakaruppar, Cinnakaruppar, Cankili, Kali, Muni, etc. to help him in this. Just like we have watchmen. Aiyanar, the son of Hari and Haran, was sent to the earth to look after the villages.

Most villages above a certain size had a temple, or shrine, to Aiyanar, which was usually situated in a forested area near the boundary of the village, usually to the west of the main settlement. Aiyanar shrines, whether out in the open or housed in structural temples, were also often located on the banks of irrigation tanks, thus suggesting a further correspondence between Aiyanar and the prosperity of the village. Aiyanar temples were conspicuous because the shrines, however large or small, were fronted by terracotta horses which flanked the processional avenue to the temple. Sometimes one or more clay elephants accompanied the horses, which could number thousands, in rows several hundred yards long. The horses and elephants – vehicles of lord Aiyanar – were installed each year in the annual festival when Aiyanar was worshipped, together with Karuppar (whose shrine is next to that of Aiyanar), to whom animal sacrifices were offered. Although Aiyanar was (and remains) an important deity throughout the Tamil country, temples to Aiyanar were particularly ubiquitous in Pudukkottai.

The Aiyanar festival I have chosen to describe was celebrated in the Kallar village of Puvaracakuti, in Vallanatu, about eight miles southeast of Pudukkottai town, in early July 1982.

The festival began at the house of the ampalam. When I arrived the ampalam was bathing and a number of village folk and members of the ampalam's family were busy decorating the front of the ampalam's house, festooning it with mango and coconut leaves. The Paraiyars who had assembled some distance from the house built small fires to tune their drums. Flowers, coconuts, and other items for the puja were brought to the front porch of the house (*tinai*). There were five red ribbons to tie on the horns of the horses and bulls, five towels for the possessed camiyatis and veshtis and towels for the service castes (*vēlai ceyvavōrkōl*) such as the dhobi, barber, and Paraiyars. The ampalam came to the front porch after his bath, and worshipped the images of gods and goddesses hung on the interior walls of the porch.

The emblems of the ampalam were brought out from the vacant house next door, called the *periya vītu* (literally the big house), which was unoccupied because of a quarrel within the ampalam's family between collateral contestants for the position of ampalam. These emblems (virutu) consisted of a spear (*ītti*), a sword (*veṭṭu arivāl*), a cane (*pirampu*), and a club (*taṇṭāyutam*). The emblems symbolized the office and authority (atikaram) of the ampalam, and were said to have been presented many generations before by the Raja. Under a small tiled roof mantapam about twenty yards to the west of the ampalam's house, they were placed next to the pattavan, a sword representing an ancestor of the ampalam's family who was worshipped as the family deity (vittu cami). The emblems and the pattavan were shown the flame (*tīvārātanai* or *ārti*), camphor was burnt and coconuts were broken, the three most common elements of any performance of puja. After this, the emblems were carried by other Kallars in the village, and the ampalam was summoned. The first procession of the day was ready to begin.

The emblems were carried by Kallars. The entire procession was led by Paraiyars beating their drums. Though the ampalam was the central character, attention was increasingly focused on the camiyatis, here five Kallars who were to be possessed by the god. Initially chosen for possessing special spiritual powers, they were the hereditary camiyatis who participated in the festival each year. They walked immediately behind the drum-beating Paraiyars. Not yet in full trance, the camiyatis began to show signs of possession as they walked on to the beat of the drums, their bodies sporadically quivering at the touch of Aiyanar, who was shortly to enter into them. The procession walked straight to the small structural temple to Aiyanar. Adjacent to this shrine were two large icons of Karuppar (Periya Karuppar and Cinna Karuppar), both of which looked terrifying and had large, snake-like moustaches and big swords in their hands. About fifty yards to the east a spear representing Munisvarar constituted a separate, though related shrine. A puja was performed for Aiyanar, and sacred ash (*vipūti*) was distributed to all those present. The people who had come in the procession, led by the ampalam and the camiyatis, then worshiped Karuppar and Muni. The camiyatis then picked up bags of viputi and began walking back to the village, accompanied by the Paraiyars. As they walked through the village, the women of each house came towards them and poured water over their feet to cool them. The camiyatis blessed the women with the ash they carried. We walked through the Kallar section of town, via the ampalam's house, to the Velar settlement on the eastern side of the village. There the procession was welcomed by the playing of the mela talam by the Melakkarars (the pipers) of Tiruvarankulam temple (the natu temple of the village, which was in Vallanatu) and by exploding fire crackers. Six terracotta figures, each about four feet high, were lined up on the Velar street – one elephant, three horses, and two bulls – in the final stages of decoration. They had been whitewashed, painted with colored stripes, and crowned with stalks of flowering paddy and the ribbons from the ampalam's house. The five Kallar camiyatis stood in front of the terracotta figures. A Paraiyar from a nearby village came forward, and carefully dressed the camiyatis in special clothes. The Paraiyar wore a garland made of silver balls, his head was wrapped with a red cloth, his chest was draped with multicolored strands of cloth, a new towel was tied around his waist, and garlands of bells were wrapped around him. His face was painted with vermilion and sandal paste. This Paraiyar was called the *munnōti*, the leader or the one who went first. In a few minutes he became possessed on his own, to the music of the drums and nadaswaram played by the Melakkarars. He began to jump wildly when the incense and camphor smoke was shown to him and he stared fixedly at the sky. He suddenly leapt into the crowd, snatched the ampalam's spear, and began to beat the ground with it. He was jumping and running around and through the crowd, all the while circumambulating the six figures. The ampalam then came up to him, garlanded him and smeared sacred ash on his forehead. After this, the munnoti led the other camiyatis into states of possession. Someone whispered in my ear that the munnoti was the burning lamp which lights other lamps. Full possession was achieved when the munnoti held the camphor up to the camiyatis, one by one.

Now that the camiyatis were fully possessed, the procession was ready to commence. The Paraiyars went first, followed at some distance by the Melakkarars, then by the munnoti and the five camiyatis, then the terracotta offerings, with the elephant in the lead, followed by the smaller offerings of individual villagers. Behind them walked the ampalam, surrounded by many of his kinsmen. As the procession moved around the village, on its way back to the Aiyanar temple, villagers came up to the camiyatis to be blessed, often asking questions about the future which the camiyatis answered. When we reached the temple, the eyes of the terracotta figures were opened with the blood of a cock, sacrificed by the munnoti (who was then given the cock). The terracotta animals were then installed in front of the temple, on the southern edge of the pathway leading directly westward to the temple. A grand puja was held to Aiyanar. The Velar priests offered tamarind rice, broke coconuts, and then showed the light (*tīpa arattanai*), after which they offered ash to the worshippers. Then the pujaris left the Aiyanar shrine, shutting its doors. Aiyanar was said to be vegetarian (*caivar*), and ought not to see the sacrifice to Karuppar.

Moving to Karuppar, the priests performed puja again. The villagers surged forward en masse to obtain some ash. One of the priests laid a stone a few yards in front of the Karuppar temple. The villagers assembled in a circle; finally a goat was brought forward. The goat was black, without blemish. One man held the back of the goat, others came forward and poured water over the goat's head, anxiously attending the sign that the goat accepted its sacrifice. The goat shivered and shook its head, signifying its permission. The fifth camiyati came forward bearing a large sword taken from the Karuppar shrine. With one swift slice he cut off the goat's head. As they intently watched the spilling of blood and the final convulsions of the goat's body, the crowd became increasingly excited and jubilant. The carcass of the goat, which had been donated by the ampalam's family, was now handed over to the Velar priests.

A cloth was laid on the ground for the ampalam to sit on. The Velars brought him the huge bowl of tamarind rice and all the pracatam from the puja: flowers, coconuts, and plantains. Sitting there the ampalam distributed the honors, first to the Kallar lineage heads, then to the Valaiyars, and the artisans. Finally, the village elders took up the ampalam's emblems once again, and beckoned to him to lead the procession back to the village. All returned to his house, where the emblems were returned to their accustomed place in the big house. This concluded, the village Pallars and Paraiyars were given their pracatam in the village square in front of the ampalam's house, along with sufficient rice and a chicken for a feast of their own.

Several aspects of this festival deserve special consideration here, while many others will not be dealt with either because they have been well described earlier or because they are not germane to the limited points I wish to make in this context. First, it was a village festival in the full sense of the term; everyone in the village participated in the festival, Kallars and Paraiyars, men and women. Throughout the festival each caste and social group acted as part of the whole. Each part was gradated in relation to the whole, and each gradation was marked by the nature of participation in the festival (through service) and by the order in which the pracatam was distributed (through honor).

The role of the ampalam was particularly conspicuous. The festival began and ended at his house, the central locus of all village gatherings. There the first ritual action of the festival had taken place a month earlier, when the ampalam returned the pitiman to the head of the Velars. Similarly, the first ritual action of the festival day itself was the puja performed to the ampalam's family deity, adorned with the emblems which represented and encapsulated the family's heritage. Granted by the Raja, and passed from generation to generation within the family, these emblems now symbolized that this festival was sponsored by the village ampalam, a festival at once personal and public, the private puja of the ampalam's family and the public performance of the entire village.

The special significance of Aiyanar for village cults in Tamil Nadu has been commented on before, most trenchantly by Louis Dumont (1959). Dumont is correct to point to Aiyanar as the village deity par excellence, and to suggest that Aiyanar can only be fully understood in terms of his relation to other village deities. But Dumont places too much emphasis on the opposition of purity and impurity in his characterization of Aiyanar's position in the village pantheon. He equates Aiyanar's vegetarianism with purity, and Karuppar's (and the Amman's) carnivorousness with impurity. Considering etymology, diet and ritual position, Dumont deduces that Aiyanar is principally modeled on the Brahman, even though in behavior and legend Aiyanar is more like a king. Dumont is correct in saying that the ambiguity of the blood sacrifice being offered in the Aiyanar temple but not to Aiyanar is the ambiguity of the structural relations of village gods. "More generally, we can suppose that the pantheon tends to become homogeneous, the superior gods adopting the characteristics of the lower and *vice versa*" (Dumont 1959, 85). But Dumont further supposes that because, as he understands it, the Brahman is always superior to the king ("in actuality hierarchy is bicephalous, except that the second head, the king, is not recognized when confronted with the first [the Brahman]") (Dumont 1959, 85–86), the vegetarianism of the higher deities symbolizes their fundamentally Brahmanic nature. In the case of Aiyanar, Dumont views the deity as a combination of Brahman and king, though, as he says, Aiyanar "is above all a Brahman" (Dumont 1959, 86). In my field work I found that while all my informants agreed that Aiyanar is like a king, they could not follow my reasoning when I suggested that Aiyanar is also like a Brahman, although they did grant that his vegetarianism rendered him like a Brahman in one limited respect.

Dumont's sense of the combination of king and Brahman in the structural formulation of Aiyanar, and more generally of the structural relations of village deities, is nothing other than his theory of hierarchy and caste relations.[3] "Aiyanar, then, commands the inferior gods, not because he is one of them, but precisely because he is different from them – such is hierarchy in the caste society" (Dumont 1959, 85). As we noted earlier, hierarchy for Dumont can only derive from difference; thus, for example, the king must be of a different caste from his subjects to transcend them. But Aiyanar, like the Kallar king, is at once the same

[3] For the problems of such an approach, see Fuller (1979, 459–476).

as and different from the others. Aiyanar is a king who protects the village and its environs, combining in himself the powers of kings and Brahmans (and, of course, deities and demons) in order to achieve maximum power. Though the principles relevant to the hierarchical ordering of men cannot fully account for the divine hierarchy, in this instance the homologization of king and Aiyanar is vividly symbolized. If anything, Aiyanar, often depicted as mounted on the royal steed, is above all a king.

Dumont's failure to provide a fully satisfactory analysis of Aiyanar is thus part of his refusal to grant that a king can, in certain contexts, encompass and incorporate the divine, the brahmanic, as well as the social and political constituents of caste solidarity and warrior strength. In Pudukkottai, the king was both the sovereign of his kingdom and *primus inter pares* in a segmentary lineage system, both Raja and Tondaiman, both god and warrior. In the village, where the king was represented by the ampalam, the festival at once elevated the ampalam and his political authority, displayed the ampalam's relation to the king, effected an identity between the latter and the village, and produced, through the celebration of a festival on behalf of a god who so dramatically exemplified the royal function, the conditions under which the village could be victorious against the forces of evil. The position of the ampalam and his royally granted emblems was the central pivot for all ritual activity in the village. This is not to reduce all ritual to society in Durkheimian fashion, but rather to emphasize the important political components of the principal deity and the social forms of worship.

At the same time, many of the meanings of the Aiyanar festival, as is true of all rituals, only emerge when we find that such festivals were the foci of tremendous dispute and conflict within villages (or natus, castes, lineages, etc.). Well after I attended this particular festival, I discovered that two such festivals took place in the same village. The one I attended was hosted by Kallars, the other I later found out about by rival Konars (sheep and cow herders). The statement I made earlier about the festival being a total village event was in fact no longer true. In recent years, the Konars have been asserting their autonomy in the village and protesting their inferior position vis-à-vis the Kallars, who no longer had their royal connections to sustain their local authority. The Konars finally demanded some years ago that they share the honor of distributing pracatam to the villagers. When denied this right, they withdrew from the main festival, setting up their own rival festival. Ritual, as we see here, denoted and sustained not only unity, but also disunity. What was significant was not that ritual always resulted in order and integration, but that even disorder and conflict manifested themselves first, and most conspicuously, in ritual arenas. Ritual crystallized ordinary lived experience by providing a vehicle for significance and display in a way presented by no other domain. We will examine these conflicts, and the altered context for their structure and meaning in the late nineteenth and early twentieth centuries, in a later chapter.

# PART 5

# Colonial mediations: contradictions under the raj

# 10

## *Agrarian rebellion? Last gasp of the old regime*

From late 1853 through the better part of 1854, Pudukkottai was the scene of an agrarian rebellion of sufficient seriousness for British troops to be called into the state. As it turned out, that was all that was needed; the mere presence of the troops checked the potential violence, if not the fury, of the angry "mob." But however muted the "rebellion," it did have serious consequences for the state, in the events associated with it and in the measures taken by the British to assure that the problem never recurred. During the revenue year 1853–54, over half the assessed tax went uncollected; Rs. 146,859 was unpaid out of a total assessment of Rs. 211,226 (MPC, no. 7, 1 August 1854, p. 3339). Armed bands roved throughout the state and an unusually heavy incidence of rural violence was reported; even in towns shopkeepers closed their shops and refused to pay their municipal taxes. During the most critical phase of activity large crowds collected in Pudukkottai town and threatened to cause major disruption before troops arrived.

The rebellion was led principally by Venkannan Cervaikarar, a palace uriyakarar who had been dismissed from service on four separate occasions for reported insubordination. Among his supporters he claimed a wide cross-section of Pudukkottai society, ranging from amarakarars and uriyakarars to miracidars and merchants.

The first notice of trouble came in late 1853 when Parker, the Political Agent, wrote that

large bodies of men irregularly armed, surrounded my carriage (without offering violence) and I ascertained that they were Amergars (kind of Cuttoobady Peons) who were yielding obedience to one Vengane Shervagaren, who has an Enam of 12 valies (60 acres) of land as a kind of sub office of this militia. I sent for this person who came to the Residency bungalow, dressed as an officer of the highest rank, and followed by these armed people to the number of about 200. On being questioned he said that their grievances were their land being measured by a short rod, the extravagance of the Rajah, and his maintaining in his service a number of young men who pandered to his vices. After I had remonstrated with him on the impropriety and illegality of his collecting a large concourse of men with arms in their hands and expressed my willingness to attend the complaints of individual grievances as properly presented, he carried his followers away, but

I ascertained by means of peons that they remained about his lodgings in the town. (MPC, no. 32, 28 March 1854, p. 1644)

During the same visit to Pudukkottai, the Diwan brought to the Political Agent's attention that the administration of justice, the collection of taxes and cesses (kists), and the "ordinary operations of Government" were being obstructed by a large group of "Ameragars and ryots acting under the directions of the above-mentioned person" (ibid.). Reports also came in that Venkannan Cervaikarar was levying contributions from the peasants for the express purpose of supporting a visit to Madras to represent their grievances. The peasants were persuaded to side with the rebellion by promises that their taxes would be reduced by half; as a start they were instructed to withhold all payment of taxes, cesses, and quit-rents to the state until a settlement had been reached. The methods of recruitment often exceeded simple persuasion. The Cirkar was besieged by petitions from Pudukkottai citizens who complained that they were being intimidated to join the rebellion, and physically harassed if they did not.

For instance, one "Soobramoneyan Ambalagaren," a "Merassedar of Anlengoody" village, wrote in a petition (MPC, no. 14, 23 May 1854, p. 2121) that

the Ringleader of the mob sent messages to me with various threats through several persons to attend the meeting ... but I refused to attend it consequently they have resolved upon ill treating me and wife, robbing my house, inserting bones of cattle and margosa leaves in my house, and forbidding people from giving me water and fire and declaring me outcast. With this purpose 500 people armed with sticks and etc. and furnished with horns, drums, and etc. approached my house. I saw them and fled.

A similar plaint was entered by one "Palamalantha Pellay," who in addition to complaining of the above wrote that the washerman was prohibited from serving him. Apart from physical harassment, both complainants were symbolically and effectively excluded from the village community by being ritually polluted and by having their customary services denied them.[1] And this was not all; a number of murders and beatings related to similar intimidation were reported throughout the state.

The rebel group, called variously in the records the "association," the "confederacy," and the "league," was also responsible for putting pressure on shopkeepers and town merchants to join them. They

---

[1] MPC, no. 14, 23 May 1854, p. 2178. Remember that in Chapter 8 we saw that it was a sign of great dishonor to be excluded from the network of social and ritual services.

directed that the lighting of the streets, the payment of taxes on the shops, and the submission of the *Nirkhnāma* (a tariff on trade) all be discontinued. When meetings of the "association" were held, the shopkeepers were ordered to close their shops and attend, and these orders were accompanied by threats and shows of force. Shopkeepers who were questioned by the Cirkar stated that they signed their names on palm leafs (cadjans) as directed by the association and followed their direction in these other matters out of fear, though we must evaluate these depositions as similarly influenced by the legal sanctions available to the Cirkar if the shopkeepers refused to cooperate in its investigations.

Venkannan Cervaikarar and his group had other measures available to them, the use of which suggests the appropriation of royal functions by the rebels. For instance, one "Carpenarayana Amblagaren" of Temmavur and his cousin complained that the rebels transferred their miraci right to a rival in the village who, unlike themselves, had volunteered to join the rebellion:

Venganen Seroovagarun, moreover, transferred the Petitioners' Ambalaum meerasi and its emoluments, over to Lutchoomana Tengondan ... to substantiate which he caused Mootooveeran the curnam of Temmavoor to write out a document, and to do this he got his adherents or gang of people to sign their names, after which he gave the document to the said Lutchmana Tengondan. Venganen Servagaren and others further caused Lutchmana Tengondan's bullocks to be displayed, at the usual ceremony of Matoo Pongole, after the Pagoda bullocks were so displayed with drums and trumpets instead of allowing the Petitioners to do so with their cattle, according to village custom, in order to show their (Petitioners) right to the Meerasy in question, and they also caused the Petitioners to be struck and otherwise ill treated. Regarding all this the monegar made a report to the talook, and Petitioners preferred a complaint at the Talook Police, which has not been enquired into. Venganen Servagaren and his adherents, therefore, again threatened to steal the Petitioners' cattle, set fire to their houses and murder them, should they refuse to join their gang and should they pay the kists to the Rajah. (MPC, no. 14, 23 May 1854, p. 2209)

The miraci right was signified, inter alia, by the honor of having one's bullocks displayed just after the temple bullocks in the yearly harvest festival of *Māṭṭu Poṅkal*. In the process of intimidating important ryots to join with him Venkannan set himself up not only as an opponent of the Raja, but as a Raja himself. He appropriated the right to reassign village honors to his supporters in a direct challenge to the authority of the king. The above petitioners noted in their complaint that Venkannan was a "man anxious to acquire more than usual honors in the country." Even as he arranged for his followers to usurp the emoluments and honors of village rights and offices, he took upon himself another royal

311

prerogative, the honor of settling disputes over village rights and honors. At one point Venkannan even arbitrated a dispute between right and left hand castes, thus boldly displaying his aspirations to kingly authority (ibid., p. 2113).

One of the earliest incidents which Parker connected to the "formation of the Confederacy" was the Raja's intention to measure the inam lands of Kannanur Ramacami Cervaikarar, a Sardar who was alleged to have encroached on government lands. As Parker wrote:

To prevent this he entered into a conspiracy with other Sheroogars and their followers, all interested to oppose a step so likely to be attended with general loss, since there is little doubt that such encroachments are very frequent. They were early joined by Venganen Sheroogaren, a man of popular manners and great address. (MPC, no. 22, 17 October 1854, pp. 102–103)

This group complained about the "oppressions which the bulk of the people suffered from Gopal Naik" (MPC, no. 14, 23 May 1854, p. 2077), the Deputy Sirkele. According to three members of the original "conspiracy," Kannanur Ramacami Cervaikarar, Panunkutipatti Rakunata Cervaikarar, and Murukan Cervaikarar Atapakar, this original complaint was attended to by the Raja, who not only dismissed the Deputy Sirkele but "was pleased to order ... recognition of all claims for succession to lapsed jeevitham enams, even if the claimant be an adopted son of the deceased incumbent ... (and also) ... to remit the taxes levied on mantapams, trees, fish, etc." (ibid.). As partial an observer as Parker was convinced that the fear occasioned by the intent to check the encroachment of the prominent Sardars was the cause of considerable alarm among all the military retainers of the state, and thus operated as a sort of first cause (ibid., p. 2062).

The Kannanur Cervaikarar was one of the principal Vakappu Cervaikarars and an affinal kinsman of the Raja; if he had continued with the "confederacy" the rebellion would have been far more serious. But, having achieved his major goal, he withdrew from the movement. Not all among the confederacy were similarly satisfied by the Raja's pronouncement, most notably Venkannan Cervaikarar. As one of the loyal Cervaikarars put it, "Your Excellency not having approved the attempt of the said Venganen Shervagaren to avail that opportunity to secure to himself certain unusual honors he has formed a league as before" (ibid., p. 2077). Venkannan tried to recruit the temporary disaffection of the Kannanur Sardar for his own plans of rebellion, even though the Sardar had now rejoined the Raja as an ally. In a letter dated February 24, 1854, Venkannan and certain of his "adherents" wrote to Kannanur Ramacami Cervaikarar:

Aware as you are that complaints have been preferred to the Honorable Government and to the Political Agent by the community assembled for the purpose after solemn asseverations between us comprised of ryots, Amaragars, and Ooliagars including yourself against the injustices variously practised by the Cirkar in opposition to the treaty between them and the government and to the Circular orders of 1842, and that enquiries are going on regarding them, yet taking advantage of your being the relative of M. R. R. the Rajah you continue to acquire your livelihood from the Palace and live happy and free from distress, and encouraged by this motive, you have assembled a mob on behalf of the State, and annoy many persons by assaulting them and breaking their heads. We are at a loss to know whether you are inclined to partake the benefit derivable from a just decision which may be passed by Government in this matter. Should we know your views on that head, it would become necessary to have you dealt with according to your desert by bringing your conduct to the notice of Government, and of the assembly held in other districts ... (ibid., pp. 2092–2093)

By rhetorical implication the Sardar was told not only that he was selfish and shortsighted to succumb to the very privilege that was naturally constituted by his close relations to the Raja, but that he must choose which side he was on. He was told that the consequences of siding with the Raja would be violent harassment as well as the rebels' presentation of complaints of violence against him in their negotiations with the government. Though unpersuaded by these threats, the Kannanur Sardar was disturbed by them, a testimony itself to the growing power of Venkannan and his group. In a petition to the Raja in which he enclosed the above-quoted letter he wrote:

One Sannasee Solagan Velayoothacandan, Poomalay Ambalagaren, Lechoomanasolatherayan, Mathoova Taven, and 4 others tempted by Ooleyam Venganem Servagaren, who in contravention to the rules, regulations, and to the public peace, assembled a tumultuous association in Naseran Tope near the cusbah of the Kavinad Talook, as well as in the town of Poodoocottah, armed with offensive weapons, have on the 24th February addressed me a letter disclosing their intention that I and others should join the mob and implying punishment in event of our refusal by bringing the same to the notice of the Government and to a certain company similarly assembled in certain other districts and fearing that this illegal communication would render them liable to great punishment, fraudulently added words to charge me and others with having ill-treated certain persons connected with the mob and despatched the same by Trichinopoly post ... As they moreover desire us to combine with the mob and frighten to put us to great inconvenience in the event of our disobeying their orders, I solicit that punishment should be inflicted on them as they deserve. (ibid., p. 2067)

Similar correspondence was exchanged between Venkannan's "mob" on the one side and the Raja on the other with six other principal Sardars: Ramacami Rankia Tevar of Katayapatti, Muttu Vira Ampalakaran of Munacantai, Ramacami Kaliya Raya of Marutampatti, the Cervaikarar of Nankupatti, Pimomanna Velar of Antakkulam, and Alakappan Cervaikarar of Pakkuti. Venkannan thus attempted to recruit the entire top tier of the nobility of the state. But each Cervaikarar remained loyal to the Raja, in spite of the annoyance many of them felt about their neglect at the hands of the Raja, who among other things seemed to have turned his back on his AN subcaste. In addition, if we believe Parker we must assume that the Cervaikarars were concerned about the intentions of government to measure their lands.

If most of the principal Sardars remained loyal, what group constituted the rebellion? One potential source of discontent and civil disobedience of which Venkannan took advantage was the landholders who performed festival service to the state temples. During the Cittirai festival of 1854 (March/April) Venkannan Cervaikarar was able to dissuade some of the Tirukkokarnam uriyakarars from pulling the temple cart, a refusal which constituted both a denial of the Cirkar's right over amani lands (this uriyam was often attached to amani tenure) and more generally an affront to the Raja to whom the principal honors of the Tirukkokarnam festival accrued.

But the real source of the disaffection of 1854 lay with the "military auxiliaries," the amarakarars and the palace uriyakarars, as Parker correctly pointed out in his final report. Their position in Pudukkottai society had become increasingly insecure well before the Inam Settlement of 1888 because of the changing structure of political relations. While Pudukkottai had attained its privileged position as a Princely State because of its military prowess, the military "retainers" had now become obsolete and unnecessary. In the next few pages we shall examine the structure and nature of their participation in this rebellion.

Venkannan drew up and circulated two lists of grievances, if not to reflect, certainly to create, two major constituencies. One was for the military retainers, the other for "merasdars, inhabitants, and merchants." The first list demanded that lands which had been usurped be restored, that inam lands be continued hereditarily, that all quit-rents be abolished on inam land, that the old longer measuring rod be used as opposed to a newly introduced putatively short rod, and that other taxes affecting waste and garden lands be abolished. The second list more or less followed the first, with various additions designed to appeal to a broader constituency, including tax boons to shopkeepers, the institution of tax remissions during bad seasons, regulations for the duties of village washermen, the revival of a particular honor for village miracidars – the tying of a "doputty" or cloth on the miracidar by each respective division – and finally, the request that official business be conducted in Tamil or English rather than in Marathi as had been the case due to the predominance of Maratha Brahmans in Pudukkottai administration.

The intended constituency of a movement of this sort and its original base are not necessarily the same. Parker noted that the first petitions came from amarakarars who denounced the favorites of the Raja and generally complained about their neglect in the state. At this point there was no mention of the short measuring rod; only later did it become one of the rallying cries of the movement. When this issue was added to the confederacy's agenda, according to Parker (who must have been inclined to discredit the movement at least in areas that would reflect badly on British concerns), "the ryots were either intimidated by threats or gained over by the immense advantages that were to accrue to all by establishing a longer land measure and procuring all the advantages enjoyed by the Government ryots as well as those peculiar to them- selves" (MCP, no. 22, 17 October 1854, p. 103). Letters and petitions were written and depositions taken which, as we have already seen, do suggest a certain degree of intimidation. Further, whether the claim that a new short rod was being used was legitimate or not the confederacy clearly gained supporters from the general paranoia stemming from the Raja's threat to resume "encroached" lands.

But the principal leadership was not made up of these retainers. Venkannan made alliances with a number of important persons in the state who had their own reasons to be unhappy with the Raja, including Krishna Pannikontar (MCP, no. 14, 23 May 1854, p. 2062), a brother- in-law of the Raja who was his firm enemy (having lost his jagir and a pension of Rs. 1,000 a year during the reign of the late Raja and was at this time still nursing his wounds), and one "Tunneaver Sholay Alagan" (MCP, no. 22, 17 October 1854, p. 103), a leading member of the Vicinki Natu Kallars with whom a general alliance was made by Venkannan Cervaikarar (MCP, no. 14, 23 May 1854, p. 2068). The VN Kallars were the largest of all the Kallar subcastes within Pudukkottai, and as we have seen their relations with the royal Kallars were not always entirely cordial. Even among the VN Kallars Sholay Alagan was singled out as being very fierce. According to Parker, "This man and his relations are a terror to all the inhabitants – nearly all the deponents before me, even those who complain of the Rajah, begged to be protected from this man, fear of whom they said had compelled them to resist the Cirkar" (MPC, no. 22, 17 October 1854, pp. 103–104).

After these initial contacts and alliances were made, members of the "league" sent notices to all the ryots not to pay kists or attend to police summons and warrants, and those who disobeyed were reportedly fined or beaten. In many places the league appropriated police functions altogether, collecting regular charges and meting out punishment (ibid., p. 104). At this stage, early January of 1854, the above mentioned lists of grievances were first compiled and submitted, though for this I must accept Parker's word. Parker's theory was that:

It was necessary to justify what had been done, and a careful comparison was therefore made between the system of this territory and the Company's districts and every point in which the former is less liberal than the latter is set forth as an innovation, while the fact of the teerwah being much lighter is concealed. The list is swelled out by complaints relating to individual cases for which redress could have been procured in the ordinary manner... (ibid.)

Parker supported his contentions by quoting from extensive reports made by the Sirkele which demonstrated that revenue policy and practice had not changed at all in the recent past. This not only refuted the charges of innovation but cast suspicion on the legitimacy of the discontent. Of course, it was clearly in the best interests of the Sirkele (the early title of the Diwan) to defend his record of agrarian administration.

What Parker conceded as a legitimate source for discontent (a view that was encouraged by the Sirkele) was the profligacy and extravagance of the Raja, which had already caused the British considerable unhappiness: in the conclusion to his final report he wrote that:

It seems clear that it is the personal conduct of the Tondiman, his reckless extravagance and his profligacy with the countenance and support he gives to low and disreputable parasites and favourites and the influence they exercise over him which have alienated the affection and respect of the people, and of the respectable old retainers of the family, and led to the disturbances under notice. (ibid., p. 215)

Parker further wrote that:

The indulgence of his passions and an extravagant fondness for dress and display, subjects him to the grossest extortion. Temptations are continually thrown in his way by people chiefly from Trichinopoly, who, when he has committed acts of which he is ashamed, threaten to expose him and make their own terms for silence. His hereditary respect for the Government and their Agent has been thus made to turn to his prejudice. His gifts to the flatterers around him were in money, cloths, and jewels on the occasion of marriages and festivals. (ibid., pp. 106–107)

The story of the Raja's debts is as long as the list of creditors, the story of his sins based on insubstantiated rumor; neither can be told here. I shall simply say that this reasoning appealed to the British for reasons that hand nothing in particular to do with the rebellion in Pudukkottai. Indeed, most British observers saw indebtedness and mismanagement as heinous sins, and were more than ready to accept as true charges of this nature to explain any problem connected with "native" rule. I need only invoke here the authority of a subsequent Political Agent to substantiate my summary claim of the inadequacy of this reasoning. Some twenty years later (and those were twenty years of extravagance and indebtedness) J. B. Pennington wrote, in his distinctive oxymoronic style, about the very same Raja Ramachandra:

No doubt he is inexcusably weak and extravagant; but what can be expected of a Rajah whose only associates are narrow-minded, jealous wives, and intriguing parasites? If a really just estimate of the extent to which he is *personally* responsible for all his follies could by any possibility be formed, I am inclined to think that many others would be found to be more guilty than the Rajah himself even in the matter of continually-recurring debts. It may be added that a state of indebtedness appears to be a characteristic of the family, perhaps a mark of dignity. The Rajah's grandfather died 70,000 pagodas in debt, and universally respected. (MPGO, no. 703, 15 October 1875)

Like so much British commentary, Pennington was right, but for the wrong reasons. Conspicuous consumption and extravagant display were indeed important components of kingship. As I was told by an informant about the king who ruled after Ramachandra, "He was every inch a king; he gave so many gifts that had he not left the state when he did he would have died a pauper." There could be no higher compliment.

However, if indebtedness constituted a problem for Ramachandra, this was because the recipients of the advantages of the Raja's indebtedness were Cettiyars, and the group of hangers-on at court included, as Parker had mentioned, many people from out of state. In addition to the courtiers from Trichinopoly were affinal relations through the Raja's second wife, who was the daughter of the Zamindar of Gantarvakkottai in nearby Tanjavur District. The royal subcaste was largely ignored, symbolized vividly by the Raja's treatment of his first wife, an AN Kallar, who was never allowed in court and not even permitted to arrange the various necessary ritual functions for her daughters.

Although in his post-rebellion recommendations Parker opposed the granting of additional privileges to the state's nobility, "for it would appear very inexpedient that the privileges of an insubordinate class should be extended at a time when their services are no longer useful" (MPC, no. 22, 17 October 1854, p. 121), he did realize that something had to be done to ameliorate a threat which though abated for the moment "may occasion future trouble" (ibid., p. 120). Parker therefore wrote that: 'the Sirdars ought to be treated by the Rajah with respect. I have urged him to consider how much more the occasional reception of some of them at his Durbar, by which they would be gratified, would conduce to its respectability, than the extravagance by which he now endeavours to render it imposing' (ibid., p. 121).

We will see in the next chapter how these concerns continued into the 1880s and then were encoded into the Inam Settlement. But here Parker glimpsed only a part of the problem, as did the settlement officers years later. First, Parker felt that all the problems causing discontent could be alleviated by honors and ceremony, however abstracted the latter had become from the contemporary exigencies of political authority and power in a state increasingly ruled by British precedent and Brahman bureaucrats. On the one hand Parker and the Madras government wished to see the total demise of this system of military relations: Parker never understood "why so small a state should have so large a body of militia" (MPC, no. 32, 28 March 1854, p. 1649) in the first place, and the government requested that an inquiry be instituted to see whether the force "could not be abolished altogether" (MPC, no. 24, 17 October 1854, p. 221). On the other hand Parker recommended that the system be buttressed by respects and honors bestowed by the Raja in the Durbar to the principal Sardars. Secondly, Parker assumed that the hierarchical relations among groups that composed the old military "elite" could be maintained simply by attending to the needs of those at the top and ignoring the middle level members of the old military elite.

But as we have seen in structural terms the latters' position in the new colonial regime was already precarious. They had been given no part in the ritual and ceremony of the princely state, and after 1803 the militia had been called up but once. Instead, the amarakarars of the nineteenth century performed nonmilitary services such as the guarding and monitoring of grain associated with the amani system. The number of amarakarars had shrunk by almost half during the first half of the century, and no doubt their impending demise was already very clear. Perhaps they also reacted against the new form of land measurement and revenue assessment already being proposed because they feared it would make even their now provisional role in agrarian life obsolete, not to mention leading to the loss of their privileged tenures.

While the Raja had no intention of resuming military inams or totally ignoring the head Sardars, he too was aware that the lines of authority had shifted from the internal structure of political relations I have described to a newly defined form of princely politics. Parker was correct in his observation that Raja Ramachandra pandered to a court which had lost touch with the political realities of the little kingdom of the eighteenth century, for as Parker should have been aware these realities had changed. While the Raja continued to give great sums of money to temples and charities, he also, as mentioned above, squandered many of his resources by supporting the extended family of his second wife, who in marked contrast to his first, and soon ostracized wife, was not connected by any kinship relations to the head Cervaikarar families of the state.

While the Sardars were uneasy, they were not ready to do more than complain to the Raja. When their complaints were heard, they quickly lined back up behind him. After all, their very position was constituted by their relationship to the person of the Raja. It was the old "military group" below the Sardars, those who had neither conspicuous honors nor kin relations to the Raja, and no longer any of the infrastructural benefits of the old regime with its shared power and its political mobility, who were potentially disaffected and dangerous. It was therefore no surprise that Venkannan and his group were able to gather supporters, even if some of them had been intimidated to join actively in the rebellion.

Given this background, Venkannan's leadership falls into clearer perspective. His ancestor was listed as the second most prominent palace uriyakarar in 1802. Like his ancestors, Venkannan was an officer in the palace guard, although we know little about his precise position and duties. Parker complimented him for his "popular manners and great address," but thought for the most part that the uriyakarars were even lower than the amarakarars (MPC, no. 14, 23 May 1854, p. 2323). However low the group, Venkannan himself was a superior member. Indeed, he could hardly have been classed as a "menial servant" since he held sixty acres, which was considerably more than the holdings of most other inamdars, though less than those of the major Sardars. In addition, he must have been a figure of some importance in the Palace to be reinstated time and again after being dismissed from service for insubordination, as happened in 1825, 1828, 1829, and 1840. Though his importance is further attested by the Raja's wedding gift of Rs. 220 to him, official opinion of him never seems to have been very high. In 1841, Soyeraba Naik, the Sirkele, wrote that: "Being improperly desirous to have much respect, he never went to the Cirkar and stood there as all other Shervagars do in order to effect anything from the Cirkar ... " (ibid., pp. 2324–2325).

The Sirkele went on to explain Venkannan's official position:

As to his claim to the title of Sirdar, I beg to say that it is unusual to mention in Cirkar accounts the rank or office of persons who hold it, but the Venganen Shervagar himself and his father and grandfather being enlisted only as Ooligars he has no claim to the title of "Sirdar." The Shervagar, his father and grandfather, continued to do low and common services for His late Excellency and his predecessors as other Ooligars did. As some Ooligars were placed under him that he may command them as the other 13 Shervagars do, he as well as others are called as Shervagars, but are not entered so in Cirkar accounts. (ibid., p. 2326)

Venkannan's position was an intermediate one; though a Uriyakarar he commanded a group of palace retainers; though called Cervaikarar he had not the official rank of a Sardar. Venkannan constantly tried to take advantage of the ambiguity of his position and claim the rank of a Sardar, which led to frequent criticism of him for being too desirous of unearned honors. So it was, perhaps, that his "insubordination" particularly incensed Gopal Naik, the Deputy Sirkele in 1853, who wrote that: "Nothing could be more disgraceful to this state than to allow, with impunity, such a disloyal and ungrateful person as Venganen Shairvagaren to create disturbance and to misbehave himself, without submitting to the authority of the Cirkar" (MPC, no. 33, 28 March 1854). Given that the initial petitions of the rebel association singled out Gopal Naik as the architect of the Cirkar's policy of curbing the encroachments of Sardars, Gopal Naik's special venom for Venkannan becomes clear.

Official opinion was not alone in reacting negatively to Venkannan's aspirations in the matter of respects and status. For example, a petition drawn up by "Ragoonatha Servaikaran," a resident of "Pinnagoodiputty" and Sardar over a hundred men in the military service of the Raja, states that: "The above-mentioned Venganen Servagaren who is a vagrant and most anxious to acquire unusual honors, availing himself of the present confusion occasioned by the mob, requested the Maharajah to bestow these honors on him" (MPC, no. 18, 23 May 1854, p. 2198). Venkannan's ambivalent position – which in this particular case resulted in the Maharaja's refusal to bestow the requested honors – led not only to official dismissal, but also to concern and suspicion among many in the old political elite. As we have already noted, the old guard maintained a structure of privilege, which however static at least gave them a substantial stake in the new regime. Venkannan had not been allowed to participate fully in this privilege, and his exclusion from official title was symptomatic of a larger exclusion from the possibility of privilege in the new regime.

The rebellion was thus headed by a notorious individual who, in contravention of both official and local opinion, fashioned himself as a major military chieftain, a principal Sardar, and in some respects even as a king. Ironically, many of his actions during the rebellion reveal far more about the culturally appropriate activities of kingship than those the Tondaiman king engaged in at the time; as we saw Venkannan adjudicated disputes, assigned offices and honors, undertook police duties, instructed peasants about their revenue duties and political loyalties, and rewarded his followers with gifts and honors. Yet Venkannan was unsuccessful because his attempts to become "king" – to stage a palace revolution as he no doubt desired – were ridiculed and dismissed by those who could not follow the lead of a lowly uriyakarar, an unroyal Akampatiyar. His main followers were amarakarars and uriyakarars, from the middle and lower ranks of the rural military retainers who had already lost much of what they had. They therefore joined together for their last hurrah, to signal their discontent with a historical fate which no longer reserved an honorable or significant place for them. Amarakarars had become lowly revenue servants, guarding village granaries and assuring the safe transport of grain from village to court. Although the amarakarars could not yet have had any inkling of the Inam Settlement which was to dissolve even this form of service relationship to the state, the records of the settlement strongly suggest the increasing fragmentation and frequent lapse of their holdings as well as the extent to which they were shunted about from one place to the next with no particular claim to the consideration of either state or Cervaikarar.

Even as the rebellion never constituted a real and lasting threat to civil order – British troops needed to do little more than appear on the scene in August 1854 to quell a number of incipient riots – Venkannan Cervaikarar was not the man to lead a successful revolt of the very amarakarars who might have followed one of the head Cervaikarars in what could have been a far more serious revolt. Despite their dissatisfaction with the behavior of their king, the principal Sardars found themselves conspicuously supporting him rather than yielding to Venkannan's threats for complicity. The structure of political relations had not yet fully excluded the Sardars who could still be honored at the Durbar and whose local position had to all appearances not been as substantially undermined as that of their subordinates.

Indeed, the Cervaikarars even benefited from the rebellion they helped to quell. After the rebellion the British developed a heightened appreciation of the precarious nature of the Sardars' position, and recommended that the Raja be more concerned about affording them respects in future. In so doing, the British perpetuated one of the fundamental cornerstones of early colonial policy. While the old regime was systematically though slowly dismantled, the British attempted to maintain the facade of its forms, buttressing them with honors and ceremonies which no longer signified a referential world of position and power that extended through what were now differentiated spheres of action and disarticulated structures of political relations. But the contradictions of early colonial rule continued to mount. The dispensation of honors to the elite, even if rigorously continued, could not in the long run ameliorate the effects of a series of actual and anticipated structural changes in the political economy of the state, whether or not these changes might lead to more revolt.

Even though the rebellion fizzled out almost as quickly as it began, it reflected the tensions and peculiar contradictions of the colonial situation in southern India. Resumption was less a literal fact in 1854 than it was a metaphor for the decline of the old rural elite. The rallying cry of the short rod had a powerful effect on those who realized that the changes in the political economy made local privilege and land tenure precarious. Bureaucrats – both the British who provided directives and precedents and the Brahmans who kept records in a language only they could understand – were in control. The gift had ceased to constitute the state, honors had ceased to signify the structure of local level social and political relations, kinship had been reconstructed as an autonomous category, and military rights and services had been replaced by revenue duties and would soon be rationalized in the form of proprietary rights and bureaucratic offices. But all this was taking place in what still seemed to be a little kingdom; there was a king and his nobles, and the rituals and emblems that at one time had regenerated the political authority of the king and thus provided the basis for the construction of political relations and the hierarchical sharing of power were now being propped up specifically to avoid disorder and disaffection. While it is hardly ironic that the leader of a movement protesting the changes of a colonial regime had as his principal goal the accumulation of personal honor and his inclusion as a Sardar (if not his attainment of kingship itself), neither should it surprise us that these aspirations were held by a man who had been frozen in a position far lower than that he felt he might otherwise be able to achieve. Such was the nature of the colonial situation.

The rebellion – or rather "non-rebellion" – ended as quickly as it had begun. The "ringleaders" were imprisoned but no major punishment was meted out to those who had participated in the assemblies and activities of the confederacy beyond the few and easily identifiable leaders. Instead, the British resolved to investigate any potential sources of discontent in an attempt to ensure no further recurrence of disorder. As we have already seen, this investigation yielded the principal conclusion that the extravagance and indebtedness of the Raja were responsible, if not directly for the rebellion, at least for creating a climate of uncertainty and dissatisfaction. Typically, the British blamed one remnant of the old regime for the troublesome consequences of dismantling other components of that same regime. But at the same time they used the rebellion to further consolidate their control over Pudukkottai. The finances of the state were temporarily put under the Political Agent's control shortly after the outbreak of rebellion. Once the rebellion was quelled the British took upon themselves the right to control the selection of Sirkele or Diwan and to maintain direct correspondence with him about the affairs of the state. As we will see in Chapter 13, these changes set the stage for the curious drama that took place in Pudukkottai in the late nineteenth and early twentieth centuries.

# 11

## *The colonization of the political order: land settlements, political intervention, and structural change*

In attempting to study the old regime through the blinkers of nineteenth-century records, and to analyze contemporary ethnographic data with the retrospective concerns of an ethnohistorian, we confront colonialism at every turn. In the remainder of this book I will be examining colonialism and its contradictory mediations. I will show that the changes of the nineteenth and twentieth centuries have often been particularly difficult to chart because many of the things we assume to constitute Indian "tradition" are in curious ways the products rather than the predecessors of colonialism.

In this chapter I will look at the Inam Settlement itself. The nineteenth-century records that provide much of the data for the redistributive nature of the pre-colonial political system are difficult to use for two related reasons. First, in reading these records we must reconstruct and recombine the integral relations of certain "subjects" just as they are being separated and reordered in new taxonomies. Second, we realize that much of what we wish to analyze has already disappeared from the sedimented survivals at our disposal. Not only, that is, do we have to try to put certain things back together, a task sometimes not dissimilar from that confronted by all the king's horses and all the king's men who were called to attend Humpty Dumpty, we have also to make distinctions and differentiations between and among things that have been soldered together in new forms by new technologies of power. Fortunately, I do not read these records in a vacuum, but with the interpretive framework provided by my reading of many earlier records and ethnohistorical texts, as well as by my subsequent ethnographic fieldwork. In this chapter, however, I will turn my attention to the new technologies of power themselves, both because of what they reveal about the older forms and because of the need to scrutinize the contradictory character of colonial change. We will see that the Inam Settlement was in part a colonial attempt to buttress the forms of an old regime that, as we saw in the last chapter, no longer had any substance.

## The Inam Settlement

When in 1801 Stephen R. Lushington, the Collector of Poligar Peshkash in the southern part of the Tamil country, looked into the affairs of six southern palaiyakkarar estates which had been sequestered for their role in the "poligar wars," he was distressed to find not only a disorderly state of record keeping but the lack of any records whatsoever relating to almost one-half of the lands of the state. According to Lushington, these lands had been appropriated to "Tendal service" and the private cultivation of the palaiyakkarars. *Tendal* (from *tantal*) meant the head or commander of a body of men. The lands had in fact been granted as jivitam to local military chiefs by the palaiyakkarars, and Lushington noted that "after the Poligar had assigned them [the lands] in Jeevidum they were alienated from his interference."[1]

Lushington felt that these lands should be measured and assessed as fully entitled revenue-producing tracts. Indeed, the Collector believed that this massive "alienation" – the British term for all transfers of land rights – had at least in part the purpose of reducing the amount of tribute that could be exacted from the palaiyakkarars: a deceptive decentralization of the palaiyam's revenue resources. Lushington felt that he had made

the most complete refutation of the shameless pretexts upon which the Poligars of these countries withheld their tributes, and though their means of paying it were much diminished by the alienation of a great part of their countries into the hands of military dependents yet as they were always competent to resume such improvident transfers, this consideration affords no palliation of their failure.

We have seen that transfers were improvident only with respect to British intentions for assessing revenue; they had been the basis of the military and political systems of the palaiyams. However improvident they were, in Lushington's view the land, though alienated, was rightfully resumable, as it was simple compensation for services rendered. The land could be resumed, he argued, either if the services for which it was granted were not performed properly or if the services were no longer required.

The alienated land in question in these six palaiyams was only the tip of an iceberg. Throughout India, and in particular in many areas in southern and western India, large amounts of land had been alienated for many different reasons, some "military," some "religious," some having to do with the local infrastructure of village communities. Inam

[1] *Collector's Report Regarding the Tinnevelly Poligars and Sequestered Pollams, 1799–1800* (Tinnevelly: Printed at the Collectorate Press, 1916).

was the single term the British chose to characterize these lands, all of which they saw as fundamentally the same because they were removed from the state's revenue rolls. Like many other terms used for land in the eighteenth century, inam was of Persian origin. It was introduced into the Tamil country by the Tanjavur Marathas and the Nawab of Arcot. The British made it part of their reified lexicon of "land systems." As a part of this lexicon, inam came to substitute for many different terms; it was defined in a new way, and became a code for a particular classificational scheme designed with explicit instrumental goals. These goals struck a balance between maximizing revenue and minimizing disruption. Inam further became a part of colonial political theory. It had not only to do with the definition of land, but with the specification of the rights of the colonial state.

Inam was a classificatory gloss for a great many terms that described the sharing of rights to land and other things by the sovereign with one or a group of his subjects. Some of these terms were maniyam, umpalam, jivitam, uriyam, lavanam, rokkakutikai, brahmadeyam, devadayam, etc. (see Appendix). These terms differ not only in describing different kinds of land rights (and other rights) given for different kinds of reasons, but also in that some terms related to the lists in which the rights were recorded, some described the type of grant, and some emphasized the honor of the grant, indeed of the relationship constituted by the grant. None of these terms concerned land alone, but referred as well to titles, offices, and honors that were entailed along with the land rights given in the grant, as well as understandings about how these various rights might be shared. These rights were all rights to privileges, privileges which had as their source the sovereignty of the king, and whose structure revealed the basic elaboration of political relations within the little kingdom.

The British assumed that most inams were illegitimate, if not the result of downright deception, usurped through illegal means during the chaotic and decadent years of the eighteenth century, when the decline of political order made it necessary for the East India Company to take extraordinary political measures to protect their right to trade. As Munro wrote in 1807:

These enaums are in many villages, thirty or forty per cent of the revenue, but in others, not more than two or three per cent. In general, all above five per cent may be regarded as unauthorized. The frequent changes of government, and the loss or rather concealment of accounts, have during a long course of years, facilitated the fraudulent extension of these enaums, at the expense of the cirkar. (Firminger 1918, 273)

Given British assumptions about the Indian state, all inams, and not just those over a certain minimum, were at "the expense of the cirkar." Munro, however, did not wish to upset social relations in the countryside by immediately resuming them all. Instead, he combined his experience in the field with his sense of expediency and necessity to determine the average number of acceptable inams.

Munro formed his notions of average in part on the basis of his experience in the Baramahal and the Ceded Districts which had, in the few years previous to Munro's arrival on the scene, undergone major changes. The situation in these areas, as the accounts in Munro's Fifth Report give ample and often dramatic testimony, had to do specifically with the attempts by Tipu Sultan to destroy the local palaiyakkarars and implement a rigorous and extractive revenue policy. As a part of this policy, Tipu resumed a number of inams, although he neither resumed them all nor refrained from making a number of grants of inam land himself (Hasan 1971). Had Munro worked in areas such as Pudukkottai, he would have faced a very different landscape.

When the Madras Presidency Inam Settlement Commission was set up in 1859, its officers were just as concerned as Munro had been to determine which inams were "legitimate." According to the Inam Commission's charter, "Very many of the existing inams, where they have the semblance of authentic origin, were given by parties who had no right at all to alienate revenue in perpetuity, such as renters, petty zamindars, poligars, etc." (CPRIS, 21). In other words, all inams granted by those whom the British did not define as proper kings – a highly variable definition in itself – were illegitimate. While the British never saw the palaiyakkarars as proper kings, at the beginning of the nineteenth century they had conceded them an important political status as a result of the strong following they commanded in their respective localities. At that time the British considered it crucial to settle the military inams that constituted the basis for the palaiyakkarar's threat to order, although most other inams, particularly those held by local magnates such as miracidars and "religious" persons and institutions, were left untouched. The British had been fighting too long and too hard not to wish to monopolize the means of force. They justified their increase of the peshkash of the southern zamindaries from the amount paid to the Company after the 1792 treaty in which the Nawab gave the Company rights of revenue collection to that stipulated in the deeds of Permanent Settlement in 1803 by arguing that the enhanced amount represented the commutation of military service, unnecessary now that the British were providing protection and maintaining order. This justification was based on the assumption that military inams had been alienated on a quid pro quo basis for military service, however shaky the grounds for this assumption: "None of the sunnuds produced by the Zamindars... specify the number of troops to be furnished by them, but of the obligation of military service, no doubt can exist either under the terms of the Sunnuds, or by the actual service of the troops of the Poligars with the Company's armies" (PRTVK, 33).

However they justified it, the British saw the dismantling of zamindari armies as conducive to peace and revenue, as well as providing the zamindars with a splendid opportunity to reclaim their "military peons from the pursuits of an unprofitable profession" and use them instead for "the improvement of agriculture." The zamindars themselves would be released "from the expence and anxiety of military service." On the basis of this purported "expence" and "anxiety" the commutation was in most cases fixed at two to three times the amount of the former peshkash! (PRTVK, 21).

By the middle of the nineteenth century any residual regard for these local rulers had evaporated, and their claim to local authority could be ignored. All inams not settled under the terms of the 1803 agreement were seen as fair game by the British, who calculated that the value of all inams in Madras Presidency was Rs. 1,05,00,000 (10 million), or "upwards of a million sterling of annual revenue." The government went on to observe that, "even this represents only the value ostensibly held, and keeps altogether out of sight the additional extent of land obtained and held, by encroachment in excess of that professedly claimed" (CPRIS, 17).

The British justified their own pecuniary interests by explaining that the enfranchisement of inam lands would have untold benefits:

The institution of private property lies at the foundation of human society, and the progress of improvement is generally commensurate with the respect in which the rights of property are held by the Government and the community. In this instance, an enormous mass of property, situated in every part of British India, has been kept for a long period in a state of unsettlement. Its precariousness, under the various and uncertain conditions of resumption, has been so much, that for many years it has had the character of property only in the lowest and most qualified sense. (CPRIS, 50)

In addition to justifying the imposition of taxes, this statement reveals a completely new set of ideas about the significance of landholding under colonialism. The bottom line was that the British were replacing the "various and uncertain conditions of resumption" with *certain* conditions: the holding of land was now conditional on the payment of revenue.

The British were aware that the benefits of "property" might not necessarily be readily appreciated. In particular, they knew that the holders of inams would oppose any immediate settlement of inams: "the fact that these inams are found in every village, and always owned in great part by the office bearers and other most influential members of the community... affords the means of forming some idea of the very powerful body leagued together to prevent or baffle investigation" (CPRIS, 17). It took the British half a century to get to the point where they felt willing and able to undertake the settlement of inams. Robert Frykenberg has argued that the British were fully aware of the potential opposition, and that they deliberately left many inams alone in what he has felicitously termed the "silent settlement" in order to win over these "influential members of the community" (Frykenberg 1977b).

Yet suggestions that any genuinely serious trouble would result from the enfranchisement of inams were discounted. For example, when a disturbance broke out in the district of Cuddapah in 1846 after certain orders had been made affecting the status of military inams, those involved in an initial investigation suggested a correlation between the proposal that inams should be registered and the revolt that ensued (CPRIS, 12). On the basis of evidence that only those who gave allegiance to a particular palaiyakkarar had revolted, a subsequent investigation instead concluded that the cause of the revolt was feudal, based on the residual regard held by subjects for their "ancient family leaders" rather than on anything connected with the inams themselves. The possibility that the inams – their status and the honors and perquisites attached to them – were perceived as being directly linked to the status of the palaiyakkarar and to the nature of his followers' relationship to him never occurred to the British.

The Inam Settlement officers based their operations in large part on the theory that in traditional India all land was "owned" by the king. Their conclusion was, therefore, that all inams were inherently resumable by the king (substitute here the colonial state). At the same time, some British writers were forced to admit that: "There can be little doubt that the whole of these grants, which appear to have been made by the Rajas of the country and their Ministers, for an endless variety of reasons, to institutions and individuals, were all intended by the grantors to be permanent" (CPRIS, 252).

The officers invoked a theory of history to suggest that this normative intention was rarely sustained across generations:

But as this mark of favour, a grant in land or grain, was of such frequent occurrence with the native powers, it must in a few generations have exhausted the resources of a country, had there been no check to its progress. The occurrence of political revolutions by cancelling all the acts of the last dynasty was one remedy, but even these were not of sufficient frequency, and when the wants of the Government required, it is probable that there was not much scruple on the part of the reigning Raja in resuming the whole or part of any grant made by his predecessors. (CPRIS)

However logical the British theory of resumption, there is little historical evidence to suggest that resumption was an important function of the precolonial state. The very word resumption seems inappropriate for rights which all acknowledged to be the king's rights anyway. Inam lands acquired special value because the king's rights were redirected to another person or institution, thereby sharing sovereignty and establishing a royal relationship. While the disloyalty of a chieftain would no doubt have occasioned war between the Raja and his chief (the cessation of the gift relationship, in Mauss's terms), without disloyalty there could and would be no resumption of land.

This is not to say that the military followers of a fallen king remained unchanged; they would have followed their chief in migrating elsewhere. The British were correct to say that political revolutions changed things. But the British denied that they had brought about a political revolution, and maintained that they had no desire to change radically the political alignments of the countryside. Only the chiefs and the kings at the top of each local system were to be displaced. Where possible, at least in the early years of British colonial rule, these chiefs were invited to stay on as zamindars to become the local gentry. This gentry was to behave like the gentry in England. Although they were given the right to do so – property being property – they were not supposed to continue giving gifts, alienating land and revenue. They were instead supposed to start maximizing production and profit rather than the honors and political relationships upon which the success of old regime states had depended.

That the "gentry" did not abruptly adopt the new political logic is another story (Dirks 1986, Price 1979). Their failure to change their political behavior can be attributed in part to the same reason that accounted for the distinctive position of gifts in the old regime. In the old regime, inams, as gifts, became associated with the person who gave the gift and took on meaning from the fact that they were given by that person (and in the case of dynastic lines this personal relationship was passed on). As such, inams were to be given, only taken away when they were to be given again. The permanent resumption of inams entailed the creation of a new political system.

The British saw the resumption of inams as an indispensable

activity of their own political establishment, even when, as in the case of the Princely State of Pudukkottai, or in permanently settled zamindaries, they did not stand to benefit directly by such resumption. In Pudukkottai, the ambiguous nature of indirect rule made the role of the British slightly more complicated. But by the 1880s the British had transferred so many of the king's powers to the chief minister, or Diwan, who was seen to represent the state and was directly answerable to the British Political Agent, that in effect the British had only a little less control over internal policy than in the Presidency, though they were usually more reticent to exercise it. The 1888 Inam Settlement in Pudukkottai not only followed the Madras model, but it was initiated and carried out at the urging of the Presidency Government. In his administration report for 1881–82, the Diwan, announcing his intention to undertake the settlement, wrote:

The Government of Madras in reviewing the last Administration Report have remarked that, "The total acreage under Inam (311,054) greatly exceeds the acreage (228,860) at present paying revenue to the Rajah," and add, "The Government have frequently advised that this difference should receive the serious attention of the Pudukkottai authorities, not with any view to confiscatory measures, but in order to enfranchise on suitable quit rents the antiquated service tenements, and generally to bring the others under some such settlement as was effected by the Madras Inam Department."

The alienation of such a major portion of Pudukkottai's potentially revenue-paying lands was seen as a problem only by the British, whose preoccupation with revenue was so great as even to exceed their self-interest. Because Pudukkottai paid no tribute to the Raj, they had nothing directly to gain from carrying out the settlement.

Under the provisions of the Inam Settlement Commission, the particular rules for settlement were directly correlated with the theoretical presumptions about the resumability of inams. The classificatory logic of the Commission was basically instrumental; the commissioners were less concerned with adhering to any native political theory behind inams than they were with molding tenurial relations to their own political theory, and more specifically with devising expeditious procedures to attain that end. The first concern of the commissioners was to determine whether or not a particular inam entailed a service requirement, and after that whether or not the service could be defined as useful and necessary. Inams which were primarily for "religious" purposes were considered to have the sanction of heritability, a privilege that was otherwise ordinarily to be disallowed. As the Commission put it: "Inams for charitable and religious objects stand on different grounds as these are already permanent alienations for the support of the institution or for service therein... They will continue uninterruptedly, so long as these objects are fulfilled" (CPRIS, 78). Clearly, this was an area in which the British wished neither to interfere nor to suggest that they were in any way undermining traditional institutions. In fact, the admission that many grants had been intended to be permanent was now reformulated as justification for the special treatment of "religious" inams. This was not simple calculated mischievousness on the part of the British. They were concerned about revenue, but they were also keen to sort out what seemed to be a messy overlap between "sacred" and "secular" domains of activity. In the process, the government appropriated to itself the right to determine whether or not religious objects were being met, and indeed to define the domain of the "religious" itself. This was important, for as we have seen there was often no clear cut distinction between many village services inams and other "religious" inams.

Even so, there were times when the British admitted their confusion in sorting out inam "tenures." Most frequently the British attributed their confusion to the administrative incompetence of former regimes, or the corrupt motives ascribed to the granting of most inams in the first place. Whatever the particular reason assigned, we confront here a general colonial tendency – born out of the combined force of deliberate policy and cultural difference – to substantialize titles and categories by taking them out of context and fixing static meanings on what had been highly fluid relationships. For example, maniyam had been a generalized term which was used, *inter alia*, to specify certain grants by kings, including grants to Brahmans and temples as well as grants to village headmen (who were often called maniyakarars). A term meaning honor and privilege, maniyam had no specific connection to land *qua* land until the nineteenth century. But under the colonial regime, maniyams in particular and inams in general were viewed as simple types of land tenure which could be differentiated and enfranchised according to the twin matrices of service/nonservice and religious/secular.

The British used a nineteenth-century form of modernization theory to justify the colonial assumption of rule and administration in India. These justifications depended upon a systematic conceptualization of the pre-British past and a set of goals that motivated and also limited all colonial innovations. The British first invoked and then developed a quasi-feudal theory in India to justify transferring sovereignty to themselves. Feudalism explained the messiness of land tenure. But then the feudal transfer of authority yielded to a new logic of political economy. For land tenure for the British was not (and under the colonial regime could not be) about relationships, but about revenue. Nonetheless, the British were extremely reluctant to permit the full and uncontrolled operation of a free market in land, preferring to keep "agriculturalists" of the right castes on the land, agricultural laborers in their dependent positions, merchants in their markets, and Rajas and nobles in their ceremonial processions. Ideally, the political economy of colonialism was to be unregulated. In fact it required active regulation in many more areas than had been anticipated. For colonialism subverted the fundamental structures of the old regime at the very moment it put on the appearance that nothing had changed, indeed, that nothing could ever change again. Colonialism attempted to freeze social and political relations, while it simultaneously displaced the political dynamics of the old regime upon which social and political relations had previously been predicated. Under colonialism politics was replaced with the cultural economics of empire. This cultural economy was inherently contradictory.

These contradictions characterized the structures of intervention under colonialism, even in Pudukkottai, where colonialism was mediated by indirect rule. Under the inam settlement, religious grants were separated from nonreligious grants, service was proclaimed to be central to the structure of landholding, kinship was divorced from political relations and from landholding, honors were made into autonomous markers of old regime inheritances and colonial favors, and the system as a whole was ordered and then placed within the colonial deep freeze. But the temperatures never got low enough to prevent transformations. The disorder that resulted provides the tension for the narratives that follow here. We begin with the story of the settlement of the Cervaikarar nobles, move from this to the plight of the royal Jagirdars, and end the chapter with a discussion of the other settlements, the logic of enfranchisement, and the overarching framework of colonial rule.

## The settlement of the Cervaikarars

The inams that had been granted to Cervaikarars were classified by the Inam Settlement Officers as "light service inams," defined as "land granted for the performance of some light service in the palace occasionally or for services which are seldom rendered." While these inams were considered to have a higher standing than those which required more onerous services, they were not classified with subsistence or maintenance inams, where the fact of service was deemed irrelevant and the terms of settlement were more generous. Cervaikarar inams were treated under Rule 13 of the rules for settlement, which stipulated that the lands would be enfranchised for a quit-rent equal to three-eighths or five-eighths of the full assessment depending on whether or not the inamdar had competent heirs.

Because of this classification, the British thought it necessary to specify the services that were to have been performed as the condition attached to the inam, even though there were no sanads to prove that the inams were contingent upon service. The British set out to determine not only the original services which had occasioned the grant but also those that continued to be performed in the nineteenth century. In the cases concerning Cervaikarars the settlement officers found the first determination easy to make, for all the Cervaikarars were anxious to announce that their ancestors performed military services for the Pudukkottai Rajas. But for the Cervaikarars these services were not distinct from their "relationship" to the Raja, most concretely their kinship ties. The settlement officers, who on the other hand were keen to make this distinction, asked their questions in such a way as to elicit particular responses. For example, in one entry "the inamdar said that the inam was granted for these military services and on account of their marital relationship (pantuttuvam) with the royal family (raja paramparai), but most probably, in response to further questions, in reward for the military services rendered by his forefathers... From the evidence it was clear that the inamdar's forefathers had rendered military service ninety years ago, and the inam was granted only as a reward for these services..."(PFR, no. 1698). The word "only" was key. The settlement officers excluded the kinship connection from their classificational scheme.

The services performed after the demise of the military system were not so evident. The compulsion to identify a continuing service in order to invoke Rule 13 led to the claim that the inamdar had been obliged to visit the palace on specific days according to the orders of the Raja, long after military service ceased. The settlement officers defined the attendance of Cervaikarars at state festivals such as Dasara or royal marriages as service obligations. According to one entry in the Inam register:

The inamdar says that he attends the important functions at the palace on account of his relationship (pantuttuvam) at the invitation of the palace people but would never pay casual visits to the palace. He does not *have* to attend the Dasara. He says that he has not attended the sanad *cavari* [an assembly in which sanads are given and proclaimed, as for example the sanad given to princes by

Lord Canning allowing them to adopt sons to keep their lines reigning in 1834] and the like for the last fifteen years but has attended the Governor's camp. (PFR, no. 823)

The Cervaikarar rejected the classification of the settlement officers, insisting that he attended palace functions "on account of his pan-tuttuvam." This term meant bond in an unmarked sense but strongly implied a kinship connection, in this case one of affinal alliance. The Cervaikarar further insisted that he was under no compulsion to attend the Dasara festival, participation in which would have been construed as an honor in most other contexts. The resistance to the questions posed by the settlement officers extended even to the terminology employed by both parties. The settlement officers called attendance at the Dasara festival a service, cevakam or uriyam. But the word the Cervaikarar used for "service" was neither of these, but rather ottacai, which we saw earlier to mean aid, help, assistance, or attendance, as at the wedding of a kinsman. The Cervaikarar claimed that his relationship with the Raja was simultaneously defined by kinship and by the actions performed by the Cervaikarar's family on behalf of the Raja's ancestors on the battlefields of old. This correlation of military service and kinship is reinforced in the semantic and pragmatic closeness of "attendance" and "kinship obligation" in the word ottacai.

But kin relations did not fit the new bureaucratic model in which offices, roles, and service obligations were seen as rigidly and rationally structured. The settlement officers had to insist that attendance at important palace functions was a service, of the same sort as sweeping village streets or providing flowers for temple worship (PFR, no. 1698). Kinship relations explained why the Cervaikarars attended "social occasions" such as marriages in the palace but not "political occasions" such as royal Durbars. As noted in another registry, the nature of a Cervaikarar's service was that "he would visit the palace for Darbars, during the Governor's camp, and on important occasions according to the wishes of the Raja. Being a relative (*pantuvam*) of the royal family it was his custom also to attend the marriages at the palace" (PFR, no. 1698). Thus kinship was separated off from the world of politics, service, and landholding, and made into an isolated social fact.

The demise of the military component in the relationship between Raja and Cervaikarars and the introduction of bureaucratic imperatives led to an increased emphasis by the settlements on the service nature of ceremonial activities accompanied by a total rejection of the significance of kinship. In the case of one Cervaikarar, there was some discussion in the records about whether an actual affinal relationship existed between the Cervaikarar and the Raja. Ultimately, however, this was of little concern to the settlement officers:

Even if the inamdar's details pertaining to this relationship are taken to be true I do not think it necessary to trace the actual relationship since it is not going to be useful to us. It seems that his forefathers were granted the inam in reward for their military services as in the cases of the other high Cervaikarars and not for their maintenance as claimed by the inamdar. Had it been granted for maintenance what would be the necessity for military service... it is clear that it is a service grant and not a maintenance grant. (PFR, no. 1718)

Here the underlying assumptions about classification as they affected the treatment of Cervai holdings (*lāvanams*) are clearly stated. If services were performed, then the grant must have been for those services; if kinship relations were the reason for the grant, then there should be no other relationship between grantor and grantee. It never seems to have occurred to the settlement officers (or did it?) that there might be some integral relationship between the selection and capability of these Cervaikarars to perform "military services" and their kinship and caste relations to the royal family.

The cynical interpretation of the settlement officers was that the Cervaikarars were emphasizing their kinship connections and the absence of required services in order to obtain the classification of "lands granted for subsistence without any condition of service whatever" which would have entailed enfranchisement with a quit-rent of one-fourth the regular assessment rather than three-eighths, as was the case for "light service inams" (RSI). No doubt this was true on some level; otherwise it is hard to explain why the Cervaikarar went to such lengths to insist that he was under no obligation to attend Dasara, normally a source of great honor, even when we take into consideration the contests over rank and honor that kept Cervaikarars away from such ceremonial occasions for years at a time. But there remains an important difference between the classificational categories of the settlement officers and the Cervaikarars. The Cervaikarars maintained some residual sense of the polyvalent nature of their connection to the Raja. Given their position at the top of the structure of privilege in the state, it was absurd to label them as inamdars in the same category as most others, just as it was absurd to say that they offered the kind of service classified as uriyam, and to insist that their kinship connection to the Raja had no political relevance. The Cervaikarars had had a special relationship with the Raja defined in terms of their former military position in the kingdom, in terms of the supporters and retainers under them, in terms of the emblems which they possessed, and in terms of their affinal relations with the Raja. While a kinship connection was not a sufficient explanation of their privileged position, the old political relationship was one that did in fact consist more of "attendance" at the Raja's battles and of kin relationship than of "service" pure and simple.

While bureaucratic reification was separating kinship from politics, the Cervaikarars were becoming more interested in honors than they had been before. Detached as they were from any infrastructural base, honors became all the more salient and negotiable as markers of status and relationship. In most of the registry entries, the Cervaikarars claimed more pirutus than the settlement officers could find supporting evidence for in earlier "land" records. These claims were usually denied. The settlement officers themselves were not initially interested in what emblems were or were not displayed during ritual occasions. Rather, they were concerned that claims for honors led to claims for land: Taking a safe approach, the settlement officers evaluated claims both for lands and for honors on the grounds of whether there was adequate record of these grants in the past.

However, the settlement officers often found themselves having to make decisions about how many honors were necessary to sustain the residual ritual-political system in the nineteenth century, and were thus drawn into the adjudication of disputes over honors. Like the Prime Minister of the state, the Diwan, the settlement officers appropriated the arbitrating function of the king. Although this function was merely an unintended outgrowth of a concern to maximize revenue and efficiency, no question concerning honor was simple. At times the settlement officers admitted to concern about the implications of their decisions on the political system itself and on occasion they realized that they had to prop the honor of the Cervaikarars.

The settlement of enfranchising the inam jivitams according to the inam rules has been made to enable the inamdars to continue to live a respectable life and visit the palace with their pirutu honors on important occasions; but now it is found that it cannot be done without a hitch. So far the ultimate right over the lands has been with Government and the lands could not be alienated by mortgage on any account; hence the inam lands remained in their original state as when they were granted by Government. The inamdars could live on the income from those lands and were able to visit the palace at the order of Government. But when the lands are being enfranchised they are liable to be mortgaged and can be taken over by others by way of repayment of a debt or under any other commitment. When the inamdars lose their lands this way they are not only left stranded without any means for their subsistence but the main aim of the Government in having the Cervaikarars visit the palace with their pirutus on important occasions is also lost. Therefore I think that the best way to accomplish our purpose with due consideration for the inamdars is to keep the minimum lands required for subsistence unenfranchised and enfranchise the remaining lands alone. (PFR, 691)

The decision to leave certain inams unenfranchised was made specifically to freeze the system, to ensure that any further change, whether the unlicensed maximization of honor or the trading of honor for money, could not happen.

In so doing, the settlement officers simply furthered a process that had begun with the colonization of the old regime in the beginning of the nineteenth century. Honor, land, and service had previously been integrally linked. The settlement officers' job was to rationalize the landholding system, reduce the waste of land allocated to frivolous non-revenue producing pursuits, bureaucratize necessary political, social, and ritual services and abolish all others. At the same time, they had to preserve for posterity, and for reasons of security, the ceremonial relations of the Cervaikarars with the state.

This process was nowhere more vividly demonstrated than in the decision to allow the Kannanur Cervaikarar, who had been absolutely crucial to Tondaiman ascendancy in the late seventeenth and early eighteenth centuries, to succeed only to enough land to maintain a specified number of emblems but not to the rest of his land because of the lack of direct succession in the family.

As for pirutus, these belong to the Cervai holding. They were successively enjoyed by the eldest member of the Cervai family along with the Cervai lavanam lands and were stopped when the Cervai lavanam lands were resumed. But these pirutus and the due respect specially granted to the Cervaikarars in reward for their military services have been continued to be held by the inamdars so that they could honorably attend the important functions at the palace accompanied by their emblems. Because of this the special honors and pirutus have never been changed by the Cirkar. Hence it seems to be a good thing to continue these pirutus to this family of the Kannanur Cervaikarar since they have been the most distinguished of all Cervaikarars. Moreover, unless these pirutus are granted to him there will be no Cervaikarar of this family who can honorably visit the palace on important occasions accompanied by the family's pirutus. Therefore, the pirutus can all be continued in the name of this inamdar who belongs to that family. (PFR, 691)

But the intentions of the settlement officers were not fully realized. By 1934 the Kannanur Cervaikarar was no longer listed as a Sardar, being grouped instead with the lower Kurikarars (R. Dis., no. 375, 1934, PDRO). He was listed as having only three pirutus: a horse, an umbrella, and a page boy. The uneven and incomplete nature of change in the nineteenth century was such that the loss of full lands and privileges, in spite of the best efforts of the settlement officers, led to a loss in the prestige of the family. Ironically, in spite of all of the supports of a colonial situation, when honors were abstracted and detached from their full set of significations they developed into what the British first mistook them for: mere trifles (see also Breckenridge 1978).

Paradoxically, however trifling honors became in the long term, the immediate effect of setting them free from their social and political context was to give them an added currency and value. They became fetishized as commodities which could now be pursued with the single-mindedness of capitalist acquisition, though not in a modern market. The commodity fetishism of honor under a peculiar colonial system in which honors were detached from their previous significations and yet endowed with the task of saving the appearance of the old regime will be an important focus in the remainder of this book.

With this in mind, let us look at the quarrel between Annacami Pallavarayar and his cousin, Poram, one of the greatest of the Vakuppu Cervaikarars. At the time of the settlement Annacami, who had been granted twenty-eight al jivitams in his name for his maintenance since he had refused to remain under the direct support of his cousin, advanced the arguments that his claims to his father's jivitams were equal to his cousin's. He contended that the jivitams were partible. The settlement officers responded by enunciating the principle of primogeniture:

Generally, these inam grants of jivitam are registered as lavanas under the head of one Cervai forming a group. In each generation the Cervai lavanam is registered in the name of the eldest son with all his pirutus under him in order to avoid the holding of lavana jivitams in separate parts which would eventually proliferate to such an extent that it would destroy the position of the Cervaikarar. So it has been the custom for the Cervaikarar to enjoy the pirutus holding the lavanam in his name without making it partible. (PFR, no. 2026)

The settlement officers went on to observe that in the cases of other Cervaikarars the number of jivitams and a precise list of pirutus were included in the lavanam registers for members of the Cervai families other than the principal Cervaikarar; they also observed that they could only conceive of the applicability of notions of equal partibility in cases of lesser chiefs such as the Kurikarars (which of course means they would become even lesser all the sooner). But honors were more often thought to be impartible, the property of office and not the perquisite of maintenance. In this particular case the compromise solution proposed that the Cervai holding itself be continued impartible but that the other two categories of the inam, the *irrattakāṇi* (meaning the right of blood, usually referring to the death of some ancestor) umpalam and the umpalam for the support of the women in the family be divided equally between the two claimants. This compromise was based on the notion that these latter inams were granted for the "subsistence" of the family and were not part of the Cervai inam granted in reward for military services which constituted the basis for the status of Cervaikarar.

This resolution did not end the dispute between the two cousins. In 1901 the older cousin, Poram Pallavarayar, submitted a petition to the Diwan in which he complained that Annacami had, in an unauthorized manner, used the insignias of his family during the Governor's visit in 1899 (R. 1774/c – 1901, 2 December 1901, PDRO). Upon investigation the Diwan learned that some junior member of the families of Sardars who had separate holdings in their names had also used insignias at that Darbar. The Diwan found this situation highly problematic, as he wrote to the Raja (in English):

All the jivitams have now been enfranchised and there are now no lavanams, and it seems to me to be high time that Your Highness issues commands about the use of these insignias in future. I believe that hitherto the Senior member alone of a Sirdar's family was entitled to use their insignias to betoken his rank and that, if some Junior member also were allowed to use them it should be regarded as a mark of royal favor shown in recognition of some sort of individual meritorious service. If every member of a Sirdar's family who happens to enjoy any portion of the lands which once formed the emoluments of the Sirdar's office should be allowed to use insignias the special honor attaching to the use of insignias will in a short time vanish.

The Diwan went on to entreat the Raja to make some decision on the matter, since "such insignia should, after all, be enjoyed only by those whom Your Highness may specially authorise by name."

While the latter entreaty specified the key point, that honors had always signified a particular relation with an overlord, this late-nineteenth-century dispute revealed the changed significance of the entire domain of honor. By this time the shifting political universe no longer provided a clear set of contextual and interrelated indices as a basis for adjudication. In any case, the centrality of the Raja was so diminished that old regime forms could barely stick even as veneer. The Raja of Pudukkottai had been so long and so far removed from such questions that he had no interest in them and so made no decision. Annacami continued to get away with the use of the insignias he claimed; by 1934 he was officially recognized as having as many pirutus as his cousin. Ironically he took over the position among the top seven Cervaikarars that had previously been held by the formerly great

Kannanur Cervaikarar, who had by this time sunk to the level of Kurikarar (R. Dis. no. 375, 1934, PDRO).

Transformations thus continued under the colonial situation, taking place through institutional processes that were set up to minimize change, indeed to arrest the dynamic nature of old regime society. Symbols that had been a crucial part of the old regime economy of signs were set adrift in a sea which the Raja no longer controlled. New forms of property transformed nobles into landholders and ceremonial figures. As a result, the British were increasingly implicated in new and often unanticipated forms of intervention, arbitration, and regulation. Some of these issues come into clearer relief in the next section on Jagirdars, the collateral relations of the Raja.

## The jagirs

Approximately one-third of all inam land was alienated in the form of three jagirs or estates, two for collateral branches of the royal family and one for pin money for the royal women. Vijaya Rakunata Raya Tondaiman granted the two jagirs to his brothers when he ascended the throne in 1730 after a violent succession dispute between himself and his uncle, the former king's younger brother, that came in the wake of a history of collateral division and rivalry. The creation of the jagirs, the Cinnaranmanai (small palace) and the Melaranmanai (the western palace), can thus be seen as an attempt to neutralize two potential rivals to the throne. Collateral relations were characterized by two conjoining yet conflicting principles: the first the solidarity of brothers, represented by the undivided family, and the second the potential for serious fraternal rivalry, represented by the divided family.

One of the basic questions concerning Jagirdars to arise in the nineteenth century, as in the case of the Cervaikarars, had to do with whether these jagirs were granted for "services" or for reasons of "kinship." Obviously kinship had more to do with these grants than it did with the Cervaikarars; both of the Raja's brothers had been granted these lands, and there were no non-collaterals in this group. And yet, because of the ideological inflections of descent in a society where there was no primogeniture, the very closeness of the collateral circle led to special problems. These problems had to do with the extraordinarily permeable "boundary" which marked off the center from the first circle of collateral relations.

The nineteenth century opened up a number of new arenas for the realization of collateral conflict even as the demilitarization of political action and the adjudication of succession by the British rendered fraternal competition less explosive. Most quarrelsome of all was the Melaranmanai Jagirdar of the second half of the nineteenth century, by his own spelling M. R. R. Ratha Kristna Tondaiman Sahib. He filed case after case contesting his subordinate relation to the Raja. Each of these cases reveals both the structural problems of that relationship and the altered position of the Raja himself.

Each jagir contained a structure of alienation which paralleled the state at large, including service inams in the villages and uriyakarars and amarkarars in the service of the palace. Although the Jagirdars appear to have had considerable autonomy in the eighteenth century, in the early nineteenth century they were explicitly prohibited from alienating their land (MPGO 24 October 1864, no. 296). At the same time the state interfered in the local concerns of their inams and inamdars in a number of instances. For example, when in 1857 one Gopalan Cervaikarar complained to the Cirkar that the Jagirdar had taken away his jivitam villages for no discernible reason, the Cirkar responded by taking the villages under attachment (R. 10 – 1863, PDRO). The Jagirdar complained in turn that it had for a long time been in his power to resume the jivitam and umpalam lands in cases where the inamdars behaved "improperly" towards him and that this particular resumption had been "in pursuance of this long-standing custom." The Political Agent refused to intervene in this particular case, though he made it clear that the Jagirdar and the Cirkar had both behaved improperly, thereby making clear the ascendency of his own arbitrative function.

The effective appropriation of the right of arbitration by the Political Agent, albeit in the name of the Cirkar, had far reaching implications for subsequent disputes. This was particularly true for disputes between the Jagirdar and the Raja, who had formerly been the sole arbiter and therefore never a disputant, unless there was outright rebellion. While the subsequent cases reveal certain structures which had been a vital part of the political world of the eighteenth century, the disputes themselves are artifacts of colonial rule.

In many of his complaints against the Raja, the Melaranmanai Jagirdar based his claim on his descent, which he said gave him an equal right to the throne and thus equal rights with the Raja. This was clearest in disputes over honors. In one case, the Jagirdar wrote:[2]

At the time of the separation from the State of the aforesaid Jaghires, the original owners thereof had and exercised as a hereditary privilege, several of the marks of honor then used by the Ruling Rajah...I am a member of the

---

[2] Quoted in *The History of the Western Palace Jaghire, Pudukota State, Madras Presidency* (Trichinopoly: St Joseph's College Press, n.d.).

family to which His Excellency belongs and the matter whose disposal is required is one which concerns me not as a subject but as a descendant and member of the royal family.

The Raja responded to such challenges by complaining that the Jagirdar used "insignias which were never bestowed upon him by me and which would be highly improper in him to use against my express concurrence" (R. 10–1863 [letter no. 24, 22 October 1863], PDRO). In short, the Raja reserved to himself his customary position as the fount of all honor. But the appropriation of the right of arbitration by the Cirkar, and the contemporaneous separation of the Raja from the state, undermined this position and led to a vastly altered kingship in Pudukkottai.

A serious dispute over honors arose between Raja Ramachandra and the Jagirdar in 1863. In a letter written to the Political Agent, the Raja complained:

I have learnt from reliable sources that Radhakristna Tondiman a Jaghiredar of this territory has on the 20th Inst. caused his sword to be borne by his men to his palace thro the public streets of the town accompanied by Chamars and Chourees, etc., insignias which were never bestowed upon him by me and which would be highly improper in him to use against my express concurrence... I hope you will perceive that the act in question is one really opposed to the custom and derogatory to the honor of the State and that the Jaghiredar cannot with any degree of propriety put forward any claim to any Birids or marks of distinction. (ibid)

The Raja enclosed two documents to prove his contention. The first was a translation of a Tamil memo from the late Political Agent, John Blackburne, to the Sirkele (Prime Minister) and Fouzdar (Treasurer) of Pudukkottai dated June 17, 1842:

Having been told that it is the intention of Raj Gopaul to solemnize a marriage which is now to take place in his palace with an ostentation derogatory to the honor of the Samasthanam, I request you to inform him that if he acts anything derogatory to the honor of the Samasthanam, his Jagheer shall be taken under zuft [attachment].

The second was a letter sent to the late Deputy Sirkele by the father of the Jagirdar dated October 21, 1852:

His Excellency knows that I behaved in all respects agreeably to the Maha Rajah's will. I beg you will inform the Maha Raja Sahib that I shall be much indebted to him, if he would be pleased to cause a pair of Thibetian Cow's Tails I am long asking for to be given me tomorrow, being the grand feast of Dusra, and to continue them to my son R. Radhakrishna Tondiman, if the Maha Rajah Sahib would think it proper to do so upon my son's behaving agreeable to the will of the Maha Rajah Sabih, and that he has no claim whatever to them, if His Excellency does not bestow them upon him.

The Raja's case was strongly supported by the Sirkele, who wrote that the fact that insignia could only be used with the "express concurrence of the ruling prince... is so indisputable that I need hardly make any comment upon it." But it was precisely the need for the express (or for that matter implicit) concurrence of the Raja in these situations that was increasingly challenged as the nineteenth century unfolded.

The Jagirdar responded by arguing that since he was a member of the royal family "he was not bound to execute documents for the purpose of using the Birudoos," and further that precedent established the rights of his family. As such his use of previously sanctioned insignias was "not liable to new sanction from the Maharajah." He did not seem to mind (or to notice) the apparent contradiction between these two arguments, the adoption of one negating the force of the other. What seemed more relevant to him was that he had stated the first on a number of other occasions, and that the second one appealed to British legal notions of precedent. On the grounds of precedent he claimed that he had made no "breach of custom." This argument directly opposed the assertion of the Raja and the Sirkele, that custom was not established by precedent but had to do with the vesting of ultimate arbitrating authority on all matters of honor with the Raja. While the Jagirdar lost this particular dispute, the force of his argument for the British was proved in another dispute four years later.

In 1867 the Raja complained about the use of certain musical instruments by the Jagirdar in a marriage ceremony (R. 13–1867, PDRO). In his petition to the Political Agent the Raja provided his explanation for the perceived importance of honors:

I need not dwell upon the tenacity with which the distinctions of caste and national privileges of rank and dignity are held by the natives of India; as from your long residence in India, and knowledge of the social character of its people, you are too well acquainted with them. You are doubtlessly aware that there are certain insignias of royalty peculiar to the dignity of this State, as well as in other Native States, which if assumed by others not entitled to them is deemed a direct insult derogatory to the Authority and Dignity of the Head of the State, such as the use of certain decorations, bands or instruments of music, etc., which when assumed is productive of the greatest annoyance exhibiting thereby an open defiance to the authority of the Head of State... Viewing the objection I raise to their use intrinsically it may indeed seem absurd, but you are aware how jealously it is necessary to guard the *merest trifles*... among the natives. (Italics mine)

The Political Agent responded by requesting the Sirkele to investigate precedent in the use of musical instruments. Upon receiving a rather ambiguous response he determined that there was no reason to sustain the Raja's objection. And so, a complaint based on the "merest trifles" turned out to have rather more than a trifling effect on the authority of the Raja, who was here ruled to be as governed by precedent as he maintained precedent had previously been governed by him.

In 1878 the question of the status of insignia was again raised in connection with the private debts of the Jagirdar.[3] In that year some of the emblems of the Jagirdar, including one pair of silver sticks, one embroidered umbrella, and some chowries and camarams, were attached and carried to court as collateral for his debts. As a result of the Jagirdar's petition to have them returned, the government decided that these insignia were not the private property of the Jagirdar but rather the property of the Jagir, and ordered them to be returned to the palace. This judgement followed the precedent of a decision concerning the palace itself, which after being attached for debts had been returned to the Jagirdar on the same grounds. But while these cases worked to the immediate advantage of the Jagirdar, they set a precedent which was to have disastrous consequences for him in just two years when in 1881 the jagir was resumed.

This incident brought the relations between the Jagirdar and the Cirkar to a head. The ostensible reason for the resumption was that in previous years the father of the Jagirdar had alienated virtually all of the assets of the jagir to a host of creditors who subsequently recovered far more than the original loans. The Jagirdar brought this to the attention of the Diwan because he wanted to recover the mortgaged assets for himself. The Cirkar responded that resumption by the state was the only way to accomplish this recovery, and proposed that the Jagirdar be given an annual pension for his support.

The creditors (many of whom were also the creditors of the Raja) vigorously protested the resumption. In a petition to the British Political Agent they wrote:

It is a well known fact that this Jagheer is not, like the rest of Jagheers and grants in the State, one granted for any military or other service rendered or to be rendered by the Jagheerdar's family; but is an hereditary estate unconditionally granted for the support and maintenance of a branch of the reigning family, in consideration of forfeiting its rights to the throne. This is strongly evidenced by the single circumstance that, in the case of other Jagheers and grants they are

---

[3] See letter from Political Agent to Jaghiredar, dated May 8, 1878, quoted in *The History of the Western Palace Jaghire.*

attached by the State on the death of the holder and subsequently made over to his heir by a fresh order, whereas such has never been the case with the Mala Aramany Jagheer since its original grant up to the present time, although it has passed through several generations during the period. (MPGO 17 March 1883, no. 233)

Here we see this curious distinction between "military service" and "kinship" raised again, though with a slight difference. After reviewing the situation the Political Agent decided that, whereas the jagir had been granted for military service in the eighteenth century, in the next century it had become the "hereditary appanage of one branch of the ruling family of Pudukkottai" (MPGO 12 January 1881, no. 25). The Political Agent therefore concluded that while because of its origins in military service the jagir could legally be resumed at any time, its subsequently acquired function of maintenance would have to be continued by substituting the inam with a money pension suitable to the position of the family. The creditors had no outstanding claims since their loans had been amply repaid; in any case the Jagirdar had no rights of alienation.

The Jagirdar contested the decision of the Political Agent by claiming that "the Western Palace has an origin almost contemporaneous with that of the Ruling Family itself. This fact is particularly noteworthy for it clearly shows that the Jaghire has an independent origin which is a powerful argument in favor of its continuance." He further argued that only four of his villages were granted specifically for military service and could therefore be resumed. He did not contest the decision about the status of the alienations; on the contrary he cited Blackburne, in a case concerning his great grandfather, that:[4] "the holders of service tenures have no property in the land and cannot alienate a foot of it for any purpose... to permit the alienation for any purpose or advantage of the temporary holder would be a breach of the law and custom". Again, he did not seem aware that in using this quote as evidence on his behalf he negated his previous claim that his was not a "service tenure."

The Jagirdar revealed the principal reason for the vehemence of his protest against resumption in a letter to the Sirkele written in February of 1881:[5]

I request you to have the kindness of mentioning in your report that the present arrangements should not affect the long standing tenure of my being a Jaghiredar, that the honors and privileges pertaining to my position should

---

[4] Quoted in *The History of the Western Palace Jaghire*, p. 7.
[5] Ibid., p. 25.

continue to me according to the mamool, and further that the interests of the minor sons in the Jaghire should not in any way be jeopardized.

The Jagirdar here gave voice to his apprehension, founded on previous rulings, that the honors and appurtenances of the Jagir would disappear upon resumption. He feared the consequences of being pensioned off for his and his family's position in society. As it turned out, the Jagirdar was allowed to keep some of the very emblems that had been returned to him only a few years earlier because they were not considered his private property. But in spite of the fact that the Jagirdar was to be maintained in a position of some honor, his fears had substantive grounds.

These fears found little sympathy with the Diwan, Seshaiah Sastri, who made the final decision in favor of total resumption and a pension, additionally proposing a schedule of expenditure to ensure the proper allocation of this pension. As he wrote:

A life of sensual pleasures, improvidence, extravagance, and consequent indebtedness are the curse of the Kuller aristocracy. The present Jaghiredar of the Western Palace is no better or worse than many of his class or of his ancestors. He, like most others, has been from a long time, and is still saddled with the burdens of supporting an illegitimate family (consisting of a woman and two boys for the present) and children, whose comparatively flourishing condition is a conclusive proof of their enjoying a greater share of his regards than his legitimate family and children. (MPGO 14 May 1881, no. 261)

Because of these concerns, far more pejoratively phrased here than in British documents concerning this family, Sastri believed that "Nothing but constant supervision and check in all pecuniary matters can keep persons of this class within the limits of propriety." He intended to exercise this supervision by devising a detailed budget which would ensure the "proper" support of the Jagirdar's "legitimate" family.

Predictably, the Jagirdar was outraged at this further involvement of the state in his affairs, now at the level of the politics of the zenana.[6] He protested first of all that there was nothing illegitimate about his multiple marriage; the British themselves confirmed that "on several former occasions, more than one bride, and as many as seven, were simultaneously affianced to the Rajahs and their brothers of the Tondiman family" (MPGO 25 February 1881, no. 106). Of deeper concern was the affront to his position and honor that this interference in his domestic affairs constituted, ominously foreshadowing the extent to which the provision that the Jagirdar would continue to be accorded

[6] Ibid., p. 145.

the "usual ceremonial honors" after resumption was an empty promise (MPGO 14 May 1881, no. 261).

Nothing concerning the household schedule of expenses was unrelated to the Jagirdar's honor. As a miniaturized Raja, he supported many of the same activities as the Raja on a smaller scale. When the Jagirdar learned that resumption was inevitable he requested an annual pension of Rs. 30,000, of which over Rs. 1,000 was for annual feasts such as those at the Dasara festival, the Jagirdar's birthday, and other similiar ritual occasions, and almost Rs. 6,000 was for household staff and servants, including pujaris, Brahman preceptors, zenana guards, Brahman and non-Brahman cooks, attendants called Cervaikarars, four insignia bearers and thirteen palanquin bearers, a hariyakarar, a teacher, and a physician. Though the Diwan decided that the total request was extravagant, recommending that only Rs. 15,000 be allocated as pension, he cut only trivial amounts from the request cited above, while more than halving the table money and pocket expenses asked for. The Diwan was concerned that the office of Jagirdar maintain a semblance of its customary honor and position, although he had no love for this particular Jagirdar, whose private as opposed to public expenses he reduced to a bare minimum.[7]

The Diwan's recommendations were accepted by the then British Political Agent. Five years later a new Political Agent listened to the Jagirdar's constant complaints about the nature and level of interference occasioned by the schedule and its management. The Agent decided that the Diwan had been rather too zealous in his interference in the Jagirdar's expenditure of his pension. He suggested a number of palliative measures, from providing the amount of hay and grain required by the Jagirdar in kind rather than at the fluctuating market rate, to allowing the Jagirdar to choose a fellow Kallar as the manager of his estate rather than a Brahman, as the Diwan had stipulated. A Brahman himself, Sir Seshaiah Sastri's disdain for Kallars was intense as the above quote shows (MPGO 7 July 1886, no. 663). Despite these recommendations the spate of petitions penned by the Jagirdar did not decrease measurably; in 1888 the schedule system was abolished altogether.

In spite of the concern of the Diwan and the Political Agent that the Jagirdar maintain his position and its accompanying honors, his fears that the resumption of his jagir would of necessity entail a lowering of his honorable position in society were confirmed when the Diwan resumed his kattalai, or endowment, in the state temple at Tirukokkarnam in 1888 (MPGO 17 May 1890, no. 239). The ancestors of the Jagirdar had

[7] See letter no. 342, Pudukkottai Sirkele's Office, 28 July 1881.

set apart certain jagir villages to support several kattalais, of which this was the most important because Tirukokkarnam was the state temple which housed the tutelary deity of the Tondaiman family, the Goddess Brihatampal. The yield from the village lands which had been alienated for this kattalai amounted to Rs. 4,050 per annum. After 1881 this endowment was administered by the Diwan. In 1882 the kattalai was deemed an exception, and the Jagirdar was allowed to manage it. However, the kattalai was resumed in 1888 when the schedule system was abolished. As usual, the Jagirdar complained bitterly. The response from the Political Agent came as follows:

You claim the right of managing the kutlei on the ground that it has always been managed by your family. The Dewan Regent admits that your family have always managed the kutlei but contends that such management, as well as the management of several other kutleis, managed until lately by your family but now resumed, was merely an incident of your late Jaghire tenure, and that any right, that you may have had to the management ceased, when your Jaghire was resumed. The management of these kutleis was hereditary in your family; but so was the Jaghire, and as the State has resumed the latter, so has it power to resume the former. (ibid.)

Here we see the British neatly separating the rights of an individual or family line from those of an office, which in this case they saw as constituted principally by a form of land tenure. Since they defined this tenure as based on service, it was resumable by the state; consequently all honors and appurtenances attendant on that office could equally be resumed. The notion that the ritual activities of the Jagirdar were an important component of his "political" position was ignored by the British, because they perceived the religious realm as non-political, and because they no longer accorded the old political hierarchy in Puduk-kottai any real political function. The Princely State was ceremonial in a new sense which was neither fully ritual nor political.

This new formulation by the Government thus postulated an absolute distinction not only between person and office, but also between "private" and "public" religious activity. This was further underscored when the Jagirdar was told that he would have to conduct his customary *Paṟani kāvaṭi* ceremonies (the pilgrimage to the temple at Parani to undertake certain vows to the god Murukan) using his own money rather than collecting, as he had before, a stipend for this purpose from state Devasthanam funds. The Diwan claimed that these religious activities were no longer affairs of state but were now "purely personal."[8]

[8] Quoted in *A History of the Western Palace Jaghire*, pp. 277, 278.

The separation of person from office had serious consequences for the Raja as well. This can be seen in a case concerning the Manovarti Jagir, which was granted by Raja Vijaya Raghunatha Tondaiman sometime between 1789 and 1807 (MPGO 20 October 1898, no.742). Four villages were designated for the support of the Raja's three wives, one for each and the fourth for all three together. The jagir was passed down to the wives of succeeding kings, the usufructuary rights being based on position rather than heredity. Succeeding Rajas added villages to the jagir, until in 1840 the jagir amounted to twenty-five villages. When subsequently the Raja resumed nine of those villages, he paid Rs. 6,000 in state funds as compensation each year.

Several years after his accession to the throne in 1894 Martanda Bhairava Tondaiman petitioned to resume the jagir on the grounds that he was unmarried and, as an adopted successor, had no "royal" women to support. The brief written on his behalf by E. Norton contained a very interesting claim:

The Manovirti jaghire was created at a period and under conditions when the reigning power pardonably assumed that the whole State was the private property of the Raja for the time being, over which he had absolute power of disposition, unfettered by the modern political theories which tend to holding a king the trustee of his people. It needed an express proclamation in 1820 by Major Blackburne, forbidding any further alienation by the Raja of State property, to place a limit on extravagant pretensions. But the old system acted hard and so late as 1827 the ruling Raja endowed his daughter with a territorial marriage portion sliced out of the dominions of the State. (ibid.)

Norton makes explicit one component of the transformation from the old to the colonial regime. Interestingly, he held that what was new about "modern political theories" was not that the king was held to be the trustee of the people but rather that he was held to be the trustee of their property and of the property of the state. Norton's argument was that up through the first third of the nineteenth century there was no theoretical distinction between the Raja and the state. From this premise he proceeded to claim that as long as that theory had operated the land which had thus been alienated could properly be resumed by the Raja. He added as additional proof for the Raja's right of resumption the government's own theory of the reversionary status of inams: "The grants of Manovirty, like the Ombalams or lands held either for continuing service or by the families of persons formerly rendering service, have always been held to be resumable at the will of the ruling sovereign." But again, the success of this argument hinged on the continuing identification of the Raja and the state, an argument which had been systematically refuted in the provisions of the Inam Settlement itself.

The Political Agent, R. H. Shipley, responded by saying that the only valid grounds for the Raja's case would be if he could prove that the jagir was his private property, a proof which would be impossible to sustain (ibid). As for the Raja's right of resumption, he noted first that the Raja could no longer be said to have full enough powers "to perform an act of State of this nature," and second, that the vital distinction between the Raja and the state meant that even if the Raja could perform such an act the jagir would be included in state lands. Shipley elaborated on this point, perhaps the most crucial one regarding British administrative intervention in the princely states:

Mr. Norton ignores the distinction between the Raja as ruler and the Raja in his private capacity. This distinction is vital, and I submit that the fallacy involved in ignoring it is fatal to His Highness' case. I did not, of course, expect His Highness' counsel to dwell upon the distinction. I might even conceal my surprise at his not mentioning it, if only to refute it. But I was not prepared to find him actually quoting with approval an official pronouncement which emphasizes it. I refer to the Government Order quoted at the top of page 4 of the opinion: "The only person who can interfere with the donee ... is the donor, the Raja or State ... " "The Raja or State" – this collocation proves that the words as used in this connection are synonymous – not in the sense of the famous L'etat, C'est moi, but rather as L'etat, C'est le Roi. It is no doubt true that, in the olden days, the Raja looked upon his State as his private property: "To have and to hold, or to sell for gold, or pour in a mistress' lap." But as early as 1820 alienations of State lands were prohibited by proclamation ... I need, perhaps, some time about 1840 to finally dispose of this argument. For, those nine villages on resumption did not become the private property of the Raja, they were reincorporated with the State. (ibid.)

Shipley did not quibble with Norton as to the state of affairs prior to 1820; he summarily noted that whatever may have been the case earlier, the past was not going to influence the new regime. As for the jagir, he advocated its continuance so as to provide a fund for expenses in connection with the births and marriages of the grandchildren of the late Raja, and of their children: "The Government is aware how little love is lost between the members of the Tondiman family," so that "there should continue to be a fund from which the Political Agent can impartially sanction payments on account of such events." Not content with separating the Raja from the state, the British became the (Princely) State itself, and proceeded to manage the private affairs of Jagirdars and Rajas.

## Enfranchisement and the settlement of land

This chapter has dealt with the rules for the Inam Settlement and the ways in which particular inams had either been enfranchised according to those rules or, on occasion, left unenfranchised. The intention of all the settlements proposed and then undertaken by the Government was to dissolve, to the fullest extent possible, the relationship between landholding and social relations. The enfranchisement of inam land meant that a title would be given and a tax assessed; the title could then be bought and sold subject only to the constraints of a proprietary market. The Pudukkottai Settlement Office is full of title deeds granted at this period to newly enfranchised landholders, whose experience of "property" in the British sense of the word began in 1888. This settlement gave the Pudukkottai government an additional and permanent land revenue of about Rs. 150,000 a year from inam lands which had formerly provided little or no revenue at all. The British saw enfranchisement as a benefit which could be shared by these former inamdars and present pattadars. Their land now acquired "value" by the creation of a market in land in which they could participate.

The bureaucratic objective of total settlement could not always be achieved. Not all inams could be enfranchised for the full tax. Variable quit-rents were assessed depending on the nature and distinction of the inam and on whether or not it would continue in the family of the original inamdars. In addition, not all inams could be enfranchised. Some services, particularly those deemed religious, continued to be remunerated by unenfranchised lands. Other lands, such as units of jivitams supporting the honors of Cervaikarars, were also left unenfranchised, to assure their continued usage for the stated purpose. Thus the Inam Settlement was in many respects only a partial settlement. There were to be two more settlements in the twentieth century before the initial objectives of the first settlement were finally completed in 1955.[9]

The other major settlement of the late nineteenth century was the Amani Settlement, or the settlement of lands which had been farmed on the amani, or share, system (Ayyar 1938, 346–350). Inaugurated in 1879, a decade before the Inam Settlement, this settlement was intended to establish secure proprietary titles to land for cultivators who had previously had to negotiate the right to farm a piece of land and to retain four-ninths of its produce every year. In fulfilling this intention, it created a problem the old share system did not have, namely, how to

---

[9] Report on the Settlement of Pudukkottai Inams Under Act (XXII) of 1955, by the special officer (Inam Settlement, Pudukkottai – vol. 1). Typescript PSO.

survive Pudukkottai's considerable seasonal fluctuations? As in the case of the Inam Settlement, one of the fundamental objectives of the Amani Settlement was to secure a steady revenue base for the state government. The architects of the settlement felt that this objective could only be achieved if there were no remissions. Only a few years after being given proper title to their land, many of the cultivators who were supposed to benefit from the Amani Settlement found themselves either close to or caught in the fatal web of bankruptcy. Attempts to ameliorate this situation led to a reevaluation of the assessed rates for amani lands, and the occasional granting of remissions in spite of the stated policy insisting that they should never be necessary (MPGO 23 April 1887, no. 324; Garu 1909).

The full implementation of bureaucratic rationalization with regard to temple management was also incomplete and riddled with continuing problems. In 1897, the Pudukkottai state government incorporated state-managed Devasthanam and "charity" revenues with state lands, and established a fixed budget for the maintenance expenses of these institutions.[10] The rationale for amalgamation again followed the lead of Madras Presidency, this time of its establishment of the Hindu Religious and Charitable Endowments Board (Mudaliar 1976). The new mode of state support for temples meant, according to the government, that the "pagoda services will be permanently ensured without the chance of fluctuation," and that the "pagodas will be supported permanently relieved of the inconvenience and difficulties of collection of revenue assigned for the purpose" (RDC 1931). However, the rationalization (I use this term in the Weberian sense) of temple support caused unexpected problems, such as the insufficiency of fixed allotments when there was inflation of prices, which necessitated a continuing administrative relationship between the state and the temples. The assumption of this relationship necessarily brought questions of temple respects and honors to the attention of the state, which had to reinstitutionalize modes of dispute arbitration after the traditional authority of the Raja had begun to erode with the separation of person and office. The bureaucratization of the state in the late nineteenth century was almost inevitably conjoined with the decline in the importance and authority of the Raja, and brought on contradictions when the state consequently appropriated, in various forms, old regime royal functions.

---

[10]  MPGO, no. 356, 22 May 1897. The allocations fixed were Rs. 71,774 for temples inside the state, Rs. 10,774 for temples outside the state, Rs. 10,607 for cattirams, and Rs. 25,000 for Dasara and other state festivals.

The encroachment of bureaucratic rationalization can be seen in the recommendations of the State Devasthanam Committee on the question of temple honors; the Committee suggested that "a record of the existing practice in each temple should be prepared and maintained in each temple as of Patrams and Parivattams [temple honors] so that the Government may have the benefit of what in law is called pre-appointed evidence" (ibid.). The precedent of law was to replace the precedence of the Raja, and the structure of political relations was to be reconstituted in a bureaucratic mode in which the Raja was a mere figurehead. Ironically, all the proposals of the state meant to make temple affairs self-regulating had the opposite effect; the history of the close relations between the temple and the king was destined to be repeated, only this time with the state standing in for the king.[11]

The changes of the nineteenth century involved the replacement of this relational political system with a bureaucratic one in which offices, roles, and precedents became preeminent. The Raja was separated from the state, state dignitaries found themselves temporary occupants of newly created offices, the honors constitutive of office and person became detached from their infrastructural base, inam land was classified and introduced into an independent proprietary market, kinship was redefined as an autonomous domain, service was linked to a classificational system designed to justify and facilitate the resumption of alienated land, and temples were put under centralized bureaucratic management. All of these changes were partial, often leading to contradictions. In studying them we can develop a better picture of the old regime as well as of the peculiar character of the colonial regime.

## Colonial contradictions

My invocation of Weber to discuss bureaucratic rationalization under colonialism fails to capture the complexity and the contradictions of the introduction of property and bureaucracy in nineteenth-century India. Colonialism did not usher in modern institutions and ideologies, instead curiously blending its own forms with those of the old regime. The British did not dismantle any more than they felt they had to of the old regime, as when they left unenfranchised those inams which supported "necessary"services or the appropriate honors of Cervaikarars. The Jagirs were resumed but immense effort went into the management of the Jagirdar's family. The government wished to preserve the dignity of

---

[11] For a detailed and incisive analysis of this historical development in Madras Presidency, see Appadurai 1981.

the Jagirdar, and yet at every point had to control the problems that developed from the frozen world and schedules of the Jagir's legacy.

In a recent important paper David Washbrook has proposed that the reason the British did not in fact introduce a free market in land and property in nineteenth-century India was that such a system would have led to uncontrollable chaos, and would not have facilitated the kind of peace and order devoutly desired by colonial administrators (Washbrook 1981). Indeed, the British attempted to maintain peace and order both by controlling the operation of the market, and by carefully fusing the rhetoric of a modern political economy – seen above in the statement about the benefits the introduction of property was sure to bring with it – with the appearance of an old regime only moderately altered from its eighteenth-century form. Some of the initial success of this latter venture rested in the representation of the eighteenth century as politically decadent but socially stable; some had to do with the colonial economy of symbols that the British instituted and managed. The Princely State, even more than the zamindaries, was such a symbol, represented as a full blooded survival of the old regime. True, its 8,000 military tenures had immediately been converted to the management of the collection of grain and revenue. But the Cervaikarars were interfered with only in certain ways, and many of the structures of the old regime remained, at least in principle, in place.

Not until the Inam Settlement, the Amani Settlement, and the resumption of the Jagirs did the colonial stage of the old regime play begin to be dismantled, betraying the cardboard of which it was made. Nevertheless, the end of the nineteenth century saw no abatement of attention to form and staging. The Jagirdar – and as we shall soon see the Raja – was not abandoned to contest his debts with Cettiyar creditors in the law courts. Instead, like the Raja, the Jagirdar was declared exempt from the civil courts. Valuable land was left unenfranchised in order to maintain the honors and emblems of Cervaikarars whose only identifiable function was to attend one or two festivals a year, festivals which themselves drained much administrative time and effort because of disputes among courtiers about order and rank. Though the political dynamic of the old regime was finally shown for what it was, an emptiness at the center of the stage, the stage itself and the actors on it had to be propped up by the efforts of powerful stagehands and puppeteers. If ever there was a theatre state in south India, this was it.

Nowhere were the contradictions of the colonial situation more apparent than in the domain of honor. Honors had previously been integrally linked to a whole set of interrelated processes. Honor had to do with one's servants and retainers, endowments, rights (kaniyatci) within villages, temple honors, caste standing, relations to and grants of privilege from the Raja, heroism and maintenance of royal codes for conduct, office and responsibilities, and also the services one performed and the proximity one was permitted to kings, deities, and superior beings in general. Like the goods exchanged by the Maoris, which according to Mauss were thought to contain and confer the life force (*hau*) of their producers, honors took on part of the person of the king (donor) and then became part of the person of the subject (donee), thereby establishing a substantial bond. These honors were also vitally connected to rights to land and to political privileges which made up the political "system" of the old regime.

But under the colonial regime honors were suddenly cut off from this total system. Like commodities under capitalism, honors became fetishized things which no longer reflected an integrated set of social relations. Michael Taussig, anthropologizing the famous insight of Marx, has written that "Fetishism denotes the attribution of life, autonomy, power, and even dominance to otherwise inanimate objects and presupposes the draining of these qualities from the human actors who bestow the attribution. Thus, in the case of commodity fetishism, social relationships are dismembered and appear to dissolve into relationships between mere things" (Taussig 1983, 31–32). But unlike commodities under capitalism, honors were never introduced into a market. Rather, honors were taken out of their social and political context only to be regulated by colonial administrators for the purpose of saving the appearances of the old regime, in order ultimately to commoditize both kings and subjects under colonial prerogatives. Value thus never became located in the mystifications of market exchange, but rather in the peculiar judgements of bureaucrats and lawyers. While the market could theoretically have freed certain subject groups from the dominant structures of the old regime, colonialism tried to keep everything as it was, without its former dynamism and reciprocity. The success of colonial forms had in part to do with the residual traces of the old regime found in the emotions and sentiments aroused by honors, and in part to do with the fact that in spite of this fetishism honors, adrift without their moorings, alone often did become trifling. The Kannanur Cervaikarar was allowed honor but not land, and could not maintain his place among Cervaikarars even under the colonial regime. And the Jagirdar of the Western palace could keep his silver sticks but no longer use them in the temple festivals in which he had lost the wherewithal to march and worship after the resumption of his jagir.

Washbrook has argued elsewhere that the privatization of property was not the only reason for a decline in the incentives for investment in local resources and infrastructures (Washbrook 1984). He has maintained that as honors and local position could no longer be secured through the integrated relation of community benefaction and patronage, local magnates began to invest instead in the new economic opportunities afforded by colonial trade. This sudden shortfall was not made up by colonial public works, which were lamentably inadequate. The dismemberment of the old regime thus did far more than provide local dramas in which Cervaikarars and Jagirdars fought legal battles to buoy up their declining perquisites. But the two narratives (Washbrook's and mine) are in fact part of the same larger story, in which the full extent of infrastructural decline was not immediately betrayed. The parts survived, but not the architechtonic relations which had rendered the parts into the whole.

Ultimately, colonialism must be seen as a hegemonic structure, which articulated its own particular impact and influence through a variety of institutional and ideological forms. These forms were, for example, the very notion of an Inam Settlement, the creation of new bureaucratic offices and procedures, the establishment of new bureaucratic offices and responsibilities of village miracidars, local tahsildars, Diwans and Political Residents, and District Collectors, members of the Board of Revenue, and judges. Law and property, and a whole set of discursive formations predicated on the free and autonomous functioning of these modern ideas and institutions, were set up to appropriate the political function. They were represented as autonomous, as fundamentally non-political. But this autonomy from political concern and process was as much a myth as the taming of wild elephants by some eponymous ancestor. Like all myths, it gained its power and authority through ritual and effective domination. Regulation itself was made to seem as if it was enacted in order to render regulation obsolete.

Colonial hegemony took a variety of indirect forms. In nineteenth-century India, hegemony worked through the successes of colonial contradictions. Because, for example, honors became so genuinely sought after and fetishized, because property had certain real if often evanescent advantages, because law provided a discourse and an institutional arena of such seemingly independent power and drama, many actors in the system were distracted from the fundamental transformations brought about by the demise of the old regime. The "Poligar wars" were ultimately won not on the battlefield but in law courts, in the offices of Diwans and Political Residents, and in correspondence books. The charade was remarkably effective.

# 12

## *Temples and conflict: the changing context of worship*

Mine honour is my life, both grow in one;
Take honour from me, and my life is done;
Then, dear my liege, mine honour let me try;
In that I live, and for that will I die.
Shakespeare, *Richard II*, I.i

The centrality of temples in Pudukkottai's history is perhaps nowhere more evident than in the conflicts that developed over issues related to temples. These issues involved rights and privileges concerning worship, honors, festivals, temple management, and service in temples. In this chapter I will give examples of some of these disputes, demonstrating the kinds of structural cleavages and ideological issues that were crystallized and activated by dispute and conflict in and over temples. In examining these cases, it is impossible to ignore the fact that the petitions, counter-petitions, evaluations, and judgements were generated in a particular bureaucratic context, far different from previous contexts in which these disputes, themselves vital components of the old regime political system, were resolved directly by the Raja, the Cervaikarar, the nattampalam, or the ampalam, depending on the level and nature of conflict.

We have seen that disputes of this type were omnipresent and often crucial in the old regime. For example, the great war between the Konatu and Kanatu Vellalars began largely as a dispute over temple honors. Beyond assuming that these disputes, when they did not lead to war, were resolved by the relevant political authorities, as they were in the early nineteenth century (Ayyar 1938, 421–437), we have scant information about the specific nature of dispute arbitration, nor do we have any way to assess the frequency of disputes in temples. Whether the extraordinary number of disputes in the late nineteenth and early twentieth centuries was the result of the breakdown of the old regime, or simply represented the continuance of previous patterns, may be impossible ever to know with certainty.

### The bureaucratization of temples

Disputes that concerned temples were not only about temples. We have stressed that temples were far more than just places of worship.

They were fundamental social institutions in which issues of rank, honor, and authority had repurcussions for every other aspect of social and political life. As we have seen, the way in which lineages, subcastes, and castes were both constructed as groups and ranked (internally and externally) often had to do with issues that concerned temples. Because disputes over rank, honor, and authority usually took place in temples, the growing bureaucratization of temples in the late nineteenth century had profound implications for the way in which these disputes arose and were settled from that time forward, and hence for the entire logic by which the social system was constructed. They were not channeled into newly developed legal institutions, unlike other disputes which were instantly classified into civil and criminal domains of jurisprudence. In Pudukkottai, because the state managed the temples, disputes in temples were handled by the Diwan Peishkar, who as second in command to the Diwan was in charge of the Revenue Department, which later included the Devasthanam Department. Thus the state, *qua* state, continued to play a crucial, though altered, role in the construction of society and its relation to temples.

In analyzing the material before us here, we once again confront the problem of indirect rule. Were the predominantly Brahman bureaucrats who manufactured official discourse spokesmen for the British Raj, for the Princely State, or for themselves? How was their discourse constructed and valorized? Remember that almost all of the innovations discussed in this book, from the land settlements to the bureaucratization of temples, followed the specific lead, sometimes direction, of British administration. British rule might have been indirect, but its tentacles were powerful and far-reaching. This was particularly true in the small and, after 1854, compromised state of Pudukkottai.

The principal administrative mediation for indirect rule by the second half of the nineteenth century was not the Raja himself but rather a number of powerful Brahman bureaucrats. As the bureaucracy expanded enormously with the land settlements from 1878 on, increasing numbers of Brahmans, most of them the descendants of srotriya Brahmans living in the state, were recruited to state service, replacing in some cases the Maratha Brahmans who had dominated the earlier though smaller local administration. Under the new administration these new "srotriya" (now turned laukika, or worldly) bureaucrats began wielding British directives, introducing in the process certain definitions and assumptions about questions as various as "caste" character and "religious" conduct. Much of what we will see in this chapter is the result of a symbiosis between Britons and Brahmans which had begun with the establishment of canons of Hindu law much earlier.

While the Brahmans took more than they gave, Brahman bureaucrats clearly emerged as significant voices in many of the issues that developed during the period of bureaucratic expansion. In Pudukkottai, srotriya Brahmans who had previously been honored but largely isolated (non-Brahmans having generally had contact with only that inferior class of Brahmans who conducted puja in the higher temples) now wielded greater influence over the political and therefore social life of the state. In addition to implementing new land settlements, for the first time bureaucrats meddled with long established and customary activities, for example proscribing the remarriage of non-Brahman widows in temples once they became managed by the state (R.C. Dis No. D–R–18359/43, 14–2–44; RD No. 6909/1944, 6–8–44).

The term "colonial" does not therefore mean something exclusively British, but rather signifies a form of hegemony that embodied a dialectical process of transformation and refinement. This process escalated in the late nineteenth century, when the domains of intervention expanded immeasurably. In this chapter we will examine those domains that were brought under the compass of "colonial" rule through the establishment of the Devasthanam Department in 1897.

As late as 1885 154 villages out of a total of 1584 in the state were still held by temples and cattirams, the so-called religious and charitable institutions. Until 1879, when amani was abolished and money rents were instituted, these lands were administered independently by these institutions, which collected their share of the melvaram produce of the land in kind under the share (amani) system. In 1897 the state government took over these lands which had originally been gifted by the former Rajas of Pudukkottai, each temple and cattiram being allotted cash grants from the state revenues. At this time the Devasthanam Department was created to administer these lands and temples, and placed under the jurisdiction of the Diwan Peishkar (the assistant Diwan). Most of the records concerning temple disputes that I found date from this year, since from thence forward record keeping became far more centralized than before, when temple accountants and Taluk level Revenue Inspectors and Tahsildars had had a greater share in the management of temple affairs.

While the original intention of the bureaucratic rationalization of temple management under the Devasthanam Department was to regularize landholding throughout the state and assure that temples were well managed and adequately funded, the problems of the Devasthanam Department reflected the complexity of the social location of temples in Pudukkottai's history. First, the steady inflation of prices after 1897 meant that cash allotments did not keep pace with the value of the lands and usufruct originally gifted as temple endowments. Second, the creation of new intermediaries provided many new opportunities for "corruption," "intrigue," and conflict. Third, the drafters of the new bureaucratic regime did not anticipate the difficulties of arbitrating disputes over temple management and honors. In a file assembled in 1923, the question of the extent to which the Devasthanam Department should intervene in temples which had been handed over for private management gave rise to the following consideration by the Diwan of the issues involved (R. No. 8175 of 1923, dt. 18–5–25):

> With reference to the query whether it would not be sufficient, in respect of temples handed over for private management, if the sirkar reserves the right of interference only in cases where there is actual misappropriation or fraud, I consider that such a right may not be quite sufficient always. Temples are national or local institutions which play an important part in the social life of village communities. Right of worship with incidental privileges connected therewith is sometimes more important than the money or cash endowments allotted for the temple. I consider that the sirkar should have a right to question the act of the trustee and set right any of his actions if they infringe the fundamental elementary rights or social privileges of a citizen.

The Diwan identified the key problematic in resolving disputes in temples; temples were "public" institutions and disputes in temples involved the most significant of "public" issues in the social life of villages. The newly constructed (colonial) category of "public" connoted both the visible expressions of religiosity and the social relations enacted in temples. "Public" also meant the trust now to be administered by the state, which would undertake to protect the "private" (a term defined in complementary opposition to public) and "elementary" rights of state citizens and maintain the public dignities that were so crucially contested in "religious institutions." The private protruded into the public through disorder, which was always the concern of the state. The bureaucratic discourse of the nineteenth century constructed honors themselves as a particular form of "public" commodity. However continuous some of the concerns with honor might have been, honor no longer meant the same thing as it had in the old regime.

The residual – and in some respects growing – concerns over honor and the contradictions of their bureaucratic commoditization often caused simple questions of management and corruption to pale before the more hotly contested issues of "rights" and "privileges." Despite bureaucratic imperatives to deal with these issues, the Diwan Peishkar often complained that far too much of the time of government officials was taken up by inquiries into cases of disputes regarding respects, as honors were often called in contemporary documents. Such cases generated immense numbers of petitions and documents, while being delicate and difficult to solve. Appointed in 1925 to look into the management of temples by the state, the Devasthanam Committee was aware of the problem but supported the Diwan's point that disputes over respects were important and necessarily the province of the Devasthanam Department. The Report of this Committee concluded that:

The temples are all Sirkar temples and the Sirkar have allowed certain respects to certain persons on certain considerations and the regulation of these respects is a matter which vitally concerns the grantor and the grantees, namely the Sirkar and the recipients of the respects. We do not see how the government can try to shift the responsibility on other shoulders. Respects or honours shown in temples in the midst of a large gathering are the cherished possessions of those who have been receiving them. We can very readily pardon their frailty in being keen about these respects, if frailty it is, when we realise that even those who are vastly learned and profess to discard all distinctions between man and man, nay, even between man and beast, are very fastidious on matters affecting their dignity. We do not think it right on the part of the Diwan Peishkar to have considered the time spent by Government officials in inquiring into disputes regarding respects as time wasted. It is time legitimately spent we should consider.

My argument that disputes over temple honors were of crucial significance, both for the participants and for the state, which saw itself as inheriting the perquisites and the responsibilities of the Raja, is nothing more than an elaboration of the remarks of the administrators and leading citizens of the state. Temples were national or local institutions of great importance, rights and privileges in which were often more highly valued than items of potential pecuniary gain. Honors in temples were cherished possessions of even the most modernized citizens of Pudukkottai, clearly including the drafters of the above report. The Diwan was thus loath to trivialize and dismiss the importance of continuing to play a role in these disputes. For these reasons, the files I am about to analyze were maintained at the central government office and preserved for the purpose of enforcing the decisions of the state and for providing precedent for future decisions. The use of precedent for the first time in bureaucratic decision making regarding temples does not mean that all of the structural dynamics of the disputes were necessarily new as well.

### The structure of conflict

Disputes concerning temples fall into three major kinds; we will look at examples, some in more detail than others, of each. First, there are disputes within the dominant caste, sometimes within lineages and sometimes between them; second, disputes between traditionally dominant castes (nattars) and newly rising merchants (nagarattars); and third, disputes between dominant castes and service castes. A cautionary note should be inserted here. In the disputes that reached the Diwan Peishkar's files, the contestants always included members of the dominant caste. This was because only when disputes involved as participants the very people who otherwise resolved them at the village level were they taken elsewhere, higher in the system, for arbitration. When the many similar kinds of disputes which occurred within and among other castes could not be resolved by the contestants themselves, the village or locality assembly, headed by the chief of the dominant caste, would in all but a few cases adjudicate them.

### Dominant caste disputes

In 1926 there was a major dispute in a VN Kallar village in which there were two lineages, the Vallataracus and the Tenkontans (R.D. No. 4213 of 1926, dt. 1–8–27). In the late nineteenth century the heads of the two lineages had both been miracidars, their miraci rights including trusteeship of the village temple. The two had been chosen because they were the hereditary ampalams of the two lineages of the dominant Kallar caste. The head lineage, the Vallataracus, were given first honors. When the Tenkontar miracidar died in the early twentieth century, the Sirkar decided not to continue miraci rights for his son, judging him to be irresponsible and the rights unnecessary. This judgement was particularly convenient because there was a succession dispute between brothers. Nonetheless, the eldest son, Daksinamurti Tenkontar, continued to act as head of his lineage and received honors in the temple in the same position as his father had. He claimed that these honors were not given on the basis of the conferment of government miraci rights but because these two were the traditional ampalams of the village.

In the 1920s Ponnucami Tenkontar, Daksinamurti's second cousin, who had moved to Tanjavur and become wealthy, came back to the village "in a motor car" and began to invest some of his money in the village temple. As a result of these financial contributions, the Diwan Peishkar appointed Ponnucami as a second trustee, granting him respects as such. According to the Deputy Peishkar:

The Tahsildar recommended the appointment of the counter-petitioner Ponnucami Thengondan as joint trustee to the Tiruvilappadi maniyam lands in as much as he was found to be greatly helping the trustee Rengasami Vallatharasu in the conduct of the temple festivals etc., in a grand scale. This was also supported by the Vadamalai nattambalam, Annasami Narangian of Themmavur who is the head of all the villagers comprising Vadamalai Nadu including Koppampatti [the village in question]. It was also found that the petitioner Dakshinamurthi Thengondan was not a desirable man for the place ... The reports of the police authority also speak to the fact that he is connected with some cattle theft in the village. Nothing has been proved against the counter petitioner [Ponnucami]. He appears to be a rich man quite able to improve the temple affairs to the required extent.

The Diwan Peishkar went on to say that since both contestants were pankalis, numbers of the same lineage, they both had "equal claim and share in the Thengondan karai." He justified his grant of honors to the newly appointed trustee on the grounds that honors were granted because of Sirkar office (i.e. miraci rights), not because of the village member's position as the hereditary caste or lineage headman. As he put it, "The temple being a Sircar one, the Sircar are at liberty to order the grant of respects to the trustees as a mark of honor and recognition even though there be no precedent in the institution." He did not disallow the giving of honors to caste or lineage headmen, but insisted they come after those given to government officials.

The effect of this decision was that the new trustee received temple honors before the son of the previous miracidar, who, very disturbed, immediately petitioned against the order:

One Ponnusami Thengondan who lives at Tanjore and who has no hold in the state came upon the scene a few days back. His only qualification is that he has got some money and travels in a motor car. He has lent money to villagers and Rengasami Vallatharasu is heavily indebted to him. The said Thengondan took a fancy to get some hold in the said temple and with the assistance of the said Vallatharasu and Annasami Narangian began to put in a series of petitions to the authorities for being appointed as a joint trustee of the temple. Things move slowly in the official world; and yet the petitions presented by Ponnusami were disposed of with lightening [sic] rapidity – the above Thengondan being able to secure the good-will of the Revenue Inspector as the latter's actions will clearly show his partiality to the former ... Justice, equality, and fair play will lead to the only one conclusion that the petitioner should be given a share in the lands instead of an outsider whose only qualification is that he hankers after honours and respects to which he is not entitled in the least degree.

Whether or not Ponnucami was as disreputable a fellow as the Diwan Peishkar made out, the petitioner clearly had a point. Ponnucami had come upon the scene with a lot of money and had been able to use that money to become the new trustee. The Diwan overruled the Diwan Peishkar and took the petitioner's side. He found that since Daksina-murti had been representing his karai in the temple by arranging for the performance of services (uriyam) by members of his lineage, he should continue to receive honors on behalf of his lineage. The Diwan was also canny enough to realize that, his objective so easily secured, there was no guarantee the new trustee would continue to give money to the temple since he had made no permanent endowment. The Diwan therefore wrote that he had "no objection to reconsider this order provided the counter petitioner is prepared to make substantial contribution towards the improvement of the temple and provided also he does not claim respects prior to those who have been getting them according to mamool [custom]." Here the Diwan suggested in no uncertain terms that a permanent endowment would be a necessary prerequisite for any extraordinary governmental recognition. Honors were thus quite explicitly given a price, though less a free market price than one carefully constructed by the bureaucratic authorities. But the more important bureaucratic construction was the separation of honors into two kinds, those granted to government officers and others granted to the heads of traditional kinship groups. Indeed, the constitution of a kin universe uninflected by political decisions concerning representation, leadership, and relations between local groups and the state was implemented largely through many similar decisions in parallel bureaucratic contexts.

There were many cases where the superimposition of a new system of governmental offices over the older structure of village authority (itself politically constituted), in which caste and lineage position perfectly matched the village "office," made for even greater difficulties. In most cases, however, the new miracidars, and trustees, were none other than the hereditary ampalams, and so the contradictions of the new system did not surface immediately. However, even where authority in the village had not begun to fragment because of the intervention of state bureaucrats, there were occasional disputes. For example, in Temmavur, the head village of the Vatamalai VN Kallars, the nattampalam, who was also miracidar and trustee of the temple, caused a furor when he decided his glory would be enhanced if he were given two separate honors, one as nattampalam and one as Sirkar miracidar (R – 3292 of 1934, dt. 28–9–35). This claim so infuriated the heads of the other lineages (the karaikarars) that they thereupon accused the nattampalam of mismanaging temple accounts. Arguing that if the honors were separate the position should also be separately defined, they challenged the nattampalam's claim to serve as miracidar. Ironically, they appropriated his discourse to reverse his claim.

When the hereditary ampalam or nattampalam was not awarded the office of miracidar disputes were inevitable. For example (R. 8207 of 1939) in one dispute the Sirkar miracidars protested against the nattampalam's continuing to receive first honors since he had not been made a miracidar. They argued that the position of nattampalam, unlike that of miracidar, was not an "office" with special duties attached to it; therefore they should be awarded first honors. In another dispute (3336 of 1939), the hereditary ampalams who were not made miracidars complained that despite the time-honored custom of continuing first respects to ampalams, the Sirkar officials had procured a ruling to supersede them just in the last year. As they wrote: "Such kalanchi honours are being given to the members of the same family in this village, and other villages, whether the mirasdarship was continued in the family or no." In addition to their case, the petitioners provided a number of other examples, such as that of a Muslim, Mohamed Rowther Ampalam, who had been given the "Hindu temple kalanchi honours ... even though he is not a member of the Hindu community and not a miras. Such honours are given to him because the honours are hereditary." In yet another case (RD No. 3598 of 1943, dt. 16–4–44) the creation of two new miracidars from two hamlets adjoining a major village led to a dispute of precedence in honors not among the miracidars – everyone conceded the precedence of the ampalam / miracidar from the main village – but between the inhabitants of the villages and the two new miracidars. The villagers felt that the act of government served to lower their position in the total structure of village hierarchy, in effect subverting the complete dominance of the main village over the two subsidiary hamlets. In a similar instance, the creation of a second miracidar from the same lineage as that of the first miracidar led to unhappiness on the part of other lineage heads who felt slighted at having to wait for the Paraiyars to beat the drums in front of two houses from that lineage rather than one before coming to invite them to the festival (2718 of 1934).

The government took no consistent line as these questions came before the Devasthanam Department. Despite their predisposition to defend their right to decide such questions and to grant precedence to their own officials, they often followed precedent in the form of mamul, or custom, whether it favored the hereditary ampalam or the Sirkar official. In some cases they favored the newly created miracidars (R. 3598 of 1943 and R. 2718 of 1934); in others they attempted compromises in the form of rotational schedules among competing ampalams and miracidars (3336 of 1939); and in others they supported the local nattampalam on the grounds that tradition clearly sanctioned such a measure (R. 8207 of 1939). While on one level it may seem odd that the Diwan's office never set down any strict bureaucratic guidelines regulating the resolution of such disputes, they saw the necessity of judging each case in its particular context. When they did try, rather late in the game, to collect data that would provide evidence for a codification of procedures, they gave up in despair. There was nothing systematic about the practice of precedence, and thus they realized that any attempt to codify it would open up an immense can of worms (3598 of 1943).

In theory, miraci rights were granted to new claimants to further the interests of the Princely State by securing the services of the most loyal, honest and industrious members of the village elite to represent it in the delicate and difficult matters of managing village and temple affairs. But given that the "hereditary" leaders almost invariably had more power and influence in their localities than any one else, the Diwan was reluctant to replace them. When a new claimant was given the miraci post, it was invariably someone from the same lineage as the ampalam, someone who had distinguished himself in the eyes of the revenue officials as being extraordinarily able to take over the village headman's duties. Undoubtedly there were many cases like that of Ponnucami Tenkontar, who gained distinction by spending money and displaying wealth in conspicuous ways. Whatever the particular reasons for which new claimants were given miraci posts, this displacement of "traditional" leaders by newly appointed officials led to the continuation of conflict. The interests of the bureaucratic state were thus frustrated by the continuing strength of kin ties and organizational structures in the localities, however altered these local relations might have become since the demise of the old regime.

The creation of the post of miracidar was not the sole cause of conflict. Rather, it tended to exacerbate conflict that was already present. Wherever an effective challenger for the post of miracidar emerged, he was sure to have been quarreling with the ampalam prior to the Devasthanam Department's new-found interest in the dispute. Many files reveal longstanding disputes between lineages within dominant castes. The village of Viraccilai has experienced trouble between the dominant lineage and the other nine lineages for at least the last seventy years (R. 1135 of 1923, dt. 2/12/33). There, as in most cases of interlineage conflict, the challenger within the first lineage tried to mobilize support not only within his lineage but within the other lineages in his attempt to become the nattampalam.

In other cases, groups of lineages struggled against each other in seemingly perpetual conflict. For example, there were two settlements of Kallars in Antakkulam, one consisting of four lineages and the other of seven (RD. No. 9783 of 1941, dt. 28–10–41). On several occasions between 1917 and 1941 the former complained that they were being excluded from any participation in their own village temple. In response, the latter claimed that this was the village temple of their own settlement; consequently the four lineages from the other settlement had no kaniyatci in this temple. Basing his decision on a 1905 document which stated that there were seven kaniyatci lineages in the temple, the State Administrator concluded that the larger group's complaint was justified. The 1905 document nowhere considered the nature of the relationship between these two groups of lineages, whether for example the group of four divided off from the seven or whether they were trying to usurp the standing and honors of a group with which they had no prior relation.

Perhaps the most extraordinary, most longlived, and most expensive dispute that I came across was the following quarrel between two villages. According to informants from both villages, Melapanaiyur and Kulamankalam, these two villages were originally one, though there was some disagreement as to which of the two was the original center of settlement. The dominant caste of both villages was a group of Maravars which many years ago had split off from the Maravars of the six villages (the group which had settled further to the west), forming an endogamous unit together with a small number of hamlets containing migrants from the main place of settlement. There are as many stories about the origins of the dispute as there are informants. In one of the most popular versions, long ago the people of the two villages found a wooden box floating in a river. They disagreed as to who should take the contents of the box. When they opened it, they found an idol, and they decided that it should be shared by them all. Accordingly, the idol was used for festivals in both villages. However, this provoked a further dispute, which was resolved by making different idols for each village, though both villages were to share the common idol in the big festival of the year, held in alternating years in each village. During one such festival, the idol disappeared, and each village blamed the other for its disappearance.

On the most general level, this story reveals that the greatest difficulties and disputes were usually centered around ritual issues. More specifically, it reveals that the two villages must have begun quarreling with each other well before this particular episode, which begins not with harmony but with the dispute over who should take the box. The dispute probably originated in a quarrel between the two primary lineages in the village, resulting in the formation of two villages where there had been one. To this day the people of the two villages think of their subcaste organization in terms that do not immediately separate the villages. The Panaiyur-Kulamankalam Maravars are said to have eighteen small karais (*cirunkarais*) which are combined together in nine large karais (*perunkarais*). These in turn are classified into three streets (terus), east, north, and south, two of which are present in each village. Though this is not the only Maravar village in which the lineages were organized into residential streets, it is the only Maravar subcaste in which the streets continued to have an exogamous function, at least until relatively recently. Six of the karais settled in Melapanaiyur, the other twelve in Kulamankalam. Marriages were regularly contracted between lineages in both two villages, even during periods of particularly heated conflict between them.

The principal focus of the dispute has been honors; which village should be called first for honors in the Konattu Amman temple in Melapanaiyur and in the Malaiya temple (dedicated to Murukan, son of Siva) which, though located a short distance to the east of Kulamankalam, is within its borders as a revenue village. According to some informants, the people of Kulamankalam gave first honors to Melapanaiyur in their temple and expected to be treated in like fashion as honored guests when they went to the temple in Melapanaiyur. While this dispute has assumed various manifestations over time, the issue being fought today in the courts of law is still over which village should have precedence. My fieldwork in these two villages provided me with my first glimpse of the degree to which disputes over honor could mobilize popular support. In both villages I was told that mariyatai was more important than anything else; it was invaluable, and could not be sold for any amount of money, unlike land. That honor was once part of the same bundle of rights as land has been forgotten. In the last five years (before 1982), more than Rs. 60,000 was collected to fund the legal battle.

No conversation in either of the villages could go for long without reference to the dispute. The terms used in talking about the dispute resonated with the taxonomic structure and grammar of the Devasthanam files. Honor was important because it was public (the Tamil term used was *potu*, which instead of being opposed to private means something rather more like genus in relation to species), not because it was part of an integrated structure of local power. It had been commoditized in a new construct of public domain in which the new institutional source of authority, after the amalgamation of the state with the Indian Union in 1948, was the law.

Despite my efforts to stay neutral I was, in the end, undone by the dispute. Each side saw my access to the state archives as potentially useful to itself; even more important, each side decided that my book would announce in rather dramatic (and incontrovertible) fashion the victor. My work in these two villages became appropriated by the dispute in one final incident. Unbeknownst to each other and to me the headmen of both villages, who had not met for years, unfortunately chose the same moment to visit my house. The dead silence that accompanied their meeting followed it as well; clearly I was to be told nothing further and to be trusted no more. This tale of two villages must therefore end here.

### Nattars vs. Nagarattars

One of the most visible of the major changes in the social life of Pudukkottai in the nineteenth century was the gradual accumulation of new and immense wealth, bringing increasing power and status in its wake, by the chief merchant caste of the region, the Cettiyars. The eighteenth- and nineteenth-century term for merchants was the same as that in medieval inscriptions: nagarattars, literally the honorable people of the city, the nagara. There had always been a marked difference between the merchants of the cities and the peasants of the countryside, the dominant groups of which were called – another term persisting from medieval times – the nattars.

While the nattars continued their traditional dominance over subordinate castes in the countryside by virtue of their control over political influence, office, and landholding, they were slow and uncertain entrants into the new commercialized economy that was gradually opening up. In Pudukkottai, commercialization seems to have affected local social life only marginally; this was true for the merchants as well. The Cettiyars did not make their money in Pudukkottai, but in Ceylon, Malaya, and Burma, as agents for British firms, middlemen for local investment, as well as in their traditional role as money lenders. Armed with huge sums of money made overseas, the Cettiyar men returned to their native villages where they had always maintained their home base, kept their women, celebrated their marriages, and in general continued their tightly knit social and religious life. There they built large and impressive houses, importing tons of Burmese teak and rare Ceylonese satin wood to support and decorate these new palatial structures. The Cettiyars also tried to buy land, which became increasingly possible because of the new market in land created by the settlements of the latter half of the century. In particular, the Cettiyars cornered the market on brahmadeyas, buying whole Brahman villages after the Inam Settlement of 1888. The Cettiyars were particularly interested in buying these lands because they were among the most fertile, came in large packages, and had very low tax assessments through the provisions of the Inam Settlement. The Brahmans sold these lands because their holdings had fragmented with each new generation, more and more of them having mortgaged their lands already for cash in what became an escalating move to the towns and cities, where they could obtain education and then government employment as office workers and bureaucrats.

The Cettiyars also invested their money in temples. Here they ran into major resistance. For the Cettiyars invested in temples not only out of religious fervor, but to secure higher honors in important regional temples, if possible displacing or at least superseding the regnant nattars. Not that religious fervor was unimportant; the Cettiyars, like other groups of Indian merchants, saw a direct relationship between their temple worship and business success. In one case, for example, some Cettiyars who had allowed their own management of the Sundaram temple to lapse to the government petitioned for a second chance to manage the temple saying that (see RD No. 859/H of 1927 dt. 4–3–27; RD No. 8480 of 1923 dt. 10/2/29):

Owing perhaps to influx of new ideas and to the undue development of self at the expense of other mental qualities among the members of the community, the temples and their properties ceased to engage the dominating attention of the members of the community. In proportion as their interest in such communal matters continued to flag, the petitioners believe that their prosperity and numerical strength began also to decline.

The serious questions raised by the petition were the usual ones as to the capability and resources of a particular group to resume the management of a temple from the state on the basis of the group's long association with the temple.

More often, the Cettiyars used their new-found wealth to invest in key regional temples important to locally dominant nattars which were physically in need of repair and restoration (tiruppani). In the large Siva temple in Rankiem (see R. no. 654/c and R. 3103/c of 7–3–15 and 12–12–15 respectively), after the local Nagarattars invested about Rs. 13,000 in tiruppani works, they petitioned that they were willing to spend even more on such works providing that the management of the temple be vested with them. According to the Diwan Peishkar, "they added that the ooliemdars should be continued to do ooliem as before, that fuel should be supplied from Muttankadu as usual and that six of them should be given mariyatai next to the Sircar styling them as trustees or Dharmakarta." The traditional nattar managers of the temple, Maravars, who had been the dominant group in Rankiem for centuries, objected violently to this proposal. Again we turn to the Diwan Peishkar's report:

The chief of the objectors are [the nattars] which appears to be headed by Muttu Raman Ampalam. Their contention is that they enjoy mariyatai next to the

Sircar from a long time, that the temple was built by their ancestors, that there were lands granted to them for the management of this temple and that they were subsequently resumed and the paditharam fixed was disproportionate to the lands resumed. They urge that the Chetties or Nagarathars as they are called were actuated by this petition for the management with the vicious intention of depriving the petitioners from enjoying their mamul [i.e. customary] respects next to the Sircar.

The Diwan Peishkar tried without success to presuade the Cettiyars to abandon their intention of securing first respects. He felt that their "ardent desire is a little bit tainted by their desire to have also an open mariyatai thus making their charity to have the taint of *rājavalam* (gross material desire) instead of the superior *cātmīkam* (peaceful, subtle, sweet spirituality)." In spite of the objections of the Nattars, the management of the temple was handed over to the Nagarattars a year later, in 1916. As usual, this decision only occasioned further contention. A case regarding this dispute was filed in the Madras High Court as recently as 1958.

A similar dispute took place in Maravar dominated Viraccilai (see RD No. 2204/c of 1914, dt. 25 – 9 – 1914). While the Maravars were fighting amongst themselves over the local goddess temple, the Siva temple was falling into increasing ruin. In 1912, the Cettiyars of Viraccilai petitioned the government for management of the temple, saying that they would invest up to Rs. 100,000 in restoration work if they were awarded the management rights. A few years earlier the management of the Siva temple in nearby Kulipirai had been given to the local Cettiyars; this was cited as precedent by the Cettiyars of Viraccilai. One of their petitions said: "We beg to assure your honor that we in offering our services to renovate and maintain the temple at a cost of a lakh of rupees, are not actuated with any motive of self-gain or aggrandisement but by our sense of duty which every Hindu is bound to do and we Nattukkottai Chetties consider it paramount to prevent an ancient temple collapse." The Cettiyars also made it clear that they were not prepared to show any honors to the local nattars.

The villagers who were consulted by the Diwan Peishkar's office said that they had no objection to entrusting the renovation of the temple to the Nagarattars providing that "the mariyatai that is now shown to the ten *karaikaḷ* should continue to be so done in future," and that "the temple be managed by the Sircar only." After making personal inquiries in Viraccilai, the Diwan Peishkar reported that:

The nattars in this place though not rich (even to a one hundredth of the nagarattars) wield considerable amount of influence and it will be the worse folly to hand over the temple to the chettis without the nattars' consent and cooperation, from the point of view of general administration and future peace of the place. With all the money the chettis may possess, the villagers from the lowest Panchama to the biggest Nattan would respect the head of the Nattan and not the chetti. Wealth will be secondary when brutal power raises. Even in respect of sentiment, I am of opinion that they are entitled to certain amount of consideration as the mariyatai has been enjoyed from time immemorial.

The Diwan Peishkar noted that after the customary first three honors (to His Highness and family or any next representative official; Rajus and Nayakas; Velupatti Cervaikarars) the next ten honors were given to the ten karaikarars, or Maravar lineage heads; after the Maravars the Nagarattars received their honors. He went on:

It is not clear when these *mariyātaikaḷ* [honors] were granted and many of them have copper plates about them dating several centuries back. It is no wonder that these people though overpowered in wealth by the chetties (who have sprung up in their midst) not having yet lost their influence, are trying to keep up their old traditions connected with the temple and their village. Even if their claims should be overruled by a Sircar mandate of the transfer of the temple to the chetties against their will, the frequent recrudescence of the feelings of the deprivation of their rights will be a fruitful source of trouble for several decades...I took each side separately and discussed with them their own weakness and merits and the Nattars would withdraw their condition of Sircar management but as for mariyatai item 1 they are obstinate.

The Nattars further insisted that the ancient titles of the lineages be recited at the time honors were given. In turn, the Cettiyars were adamant at each point, in the end turning down a proposal agreed to by the Nattars that they only receive two honors each year before the Nagarattars, the ten lineages consenting to take turns in groups of two.

The assertions of my informants that mariyatai is invaluable are echoed throughout the pages of these and similar files. Mariyatai is the sticking point, the one issue around which negotiations break down. Mariyatai was also the primary motive behind the Cettiyars' immense monetary investment in the temples of southern Pudukkottai. This was because mariyatai was not restricted to the act of worship but still signified residual forms of representing authority and status in the local community. To translate their wealth into status, even, as the Diwan Peishkar's words imply, into "brutal power," the Cettiyars had to usurp the position of the Nattars in the local temples. In one sense, therefore, the struggle between the old and new regimes took place in old regime form, in temples over honors. In attempting to resolve this struggle, the Pudukkottai government was doomed to inconsistency, trying as it did to balance two contradictory imperatives, investment in temples and the need to maintain local peace and order. In areas where the Maravars were not well organized or politically very powerful, the state tended to support the Cettiyars. But in villages such as Viraccilai, where the headman of the Maravars, while not a man of great wealth, was one of the most influential people in the southern Pudukkottai countryside well into the twentieth century, it sided with the Nattars, as had the kings of old. But the reasons for the decision were new. Not least important in this respect was the emergence of a new category of "religion" to correspond to a new public domain of temple, often situated in their physical rather than their social components. As we shall see in the next section, other "constructions" of religion were emerging at the same time in the files of the Devasthanam Office.

## Patrons vs. clients

This section will consider two typical disputes which took place between headmen of the dominant caste and their clients from subordinate castes over their respective privileges and responsibilities in temples during festivals. Both of these examples concern festivals in Aiyanar temples. In Chapter 9 we saw that the kutirai etuppu, or the installation of the horses at the Aiyanar temple, was in many places the most important village festival, for it inaugurated the festival season and required the participation of the village in ways that reflected and displayed the hierarchical relations of the constituent units of the village with the ampalam at the center of all these relations. That the centrality of the ampalam was not always accepted in the twentieth century will be apprehended from these two cases. The new bureaucratic context in which these disputes were arbitrated presented new sources of argumentation to clients who could now confront their patrons without facing the prospect of having to flee their homes and take up employment elsewhere under new patrons.

In both cases, the dispute was between the Kallar headman of Tiruvappur and the Velar pujaris, or priests, who fashioned the clay horses in their capacity as potters and installed them in the temple in their capacity as priests. The Velars had to obtain permission from the village headman to begin making the horses for the festival. They would present a handful of clay they had collected from the bottom of the village tank and present it to the ampalam, who would then give it back to them. According to my informants, who included both dominant caste headmen and Velar priests, this ritual signified the necessity for the village headman to endow the commencement of this all-important village festival with his approval, or permission. Our earlier discussion demonstrated the ampalam's central role in this festival: he was the host for the festival which began and ended at his house, his emblems were as importantly involved in the procession as were the horses themselves, and he received the first honors, which he then distributed to the other members of the village at the conclusion of the puja. The ampalam represented the totality of the village in a rite which celebrated and regenerated the village itself.

In the early 1920s in Tiruvappur, a village close to Pudukkottai town and made up mostly of Kallars, weavers, and service castes, the Velars petitioned that they were under no compunction to give or receive the pitiman from the village headman (RD. No. 1587 of 1923, dt. 30 – 3 – 25). They insisted that since the headman had not been given maniyam lands in which the terms of the maniyam grant specified that he should give pitiman as part of his responsibility for assuring the successful conduct of the festival, there was no other authoritative basis for the claim that pitiman be given only by the headman. The dominant Kallars were divided into six karais, each of which was led by a *nāṭṭāmai*. The head of all these karais was called the *Nāṭṭār*. He in turn petitioned the government that the performance of the festival without his permission, granted through the pitiman, was an infringement of his hereditary right, as proved by the fact that his family had been granted maniyam lands with the specific injunction to conduct the ordinary pujas and other festivals in the Aiyanar temples of Tiruvappur. Both petitions employed the same bureaucratic logic, insisting that the granting of inam lands was the key to the specific services and privileges to be rendered and claimed by the inam holders.

For the Diwan Peishkar, the resolution of this case rested first on the proper interpretation of the significance of the grant of pitiman. His inquiries led him to decide that the grant of pitiman signified far more than the intended cooperation of the nattars. "If it signifies mere cooperation without the slightest tinge of authority or idea of special privilege the villagers would not have objected to the continuance of the system. On the other hand, the grant of pitiman is considered to be a grant of permission by the nattars to conduct the kutirai etuppu. Both the nattars and the carpenters view it in this light and it is why the former are unwilling to lose the privilege and the latter anxious to discontinue the system." He then had to decide whether this privilege could be sustained under the bureaucratic terms of service implied by the wording of the inam grant, which was vague enough to accommodate both interpretations put forward in the petition and counter petition. The Diwan Peishkar investigated customs in other Aiyanar temples to determine precedent only to find that each case differed, hardly the stuff of precedent. To further complicate matters, the Diwan Peishkar felt that he had to determine whether the dispute concerned the hereditary privileges of the headmen as Nattars or as Miracidars, i.e., more recently appointed state functionaries.

The (Brahmanical) Diwan Peishkar was also troubled by his belief that religion was an individual concern, and that all devotees should be able to commission the Velars to make horses for them without the intervention of the Nattar. Such control over the individual vows of others seemed to him to be "revolting to a devotee's sense of honour and reason." The Diwan Peishkar recommended that the Nattars be allowed to commission the installation of horses on their own behalf, but not on behalf of others. The separation of the individual rights of Nattars from their right to commission horses on behalf of the entire village only made sense in terms of a newly formulated bureaucratic conception of religion, since the individual vows of devotees would have been encompassed by the social fact that the festival was a village festival. The Diwan Peishkar's recommendation struck at the core of the Nattars' objections, since they saw their privilege as an enactment of their authoritative position in the village temple and indeed in the village at large.

As it turned out, the Diwan was less zealous than the Diwan Peishkar to upset the local structure of authoritative relations in Tiruvappur. He recommended that the Nattars continue to be vested with the right to give the pitiman. He did, however, insist that the Nattars had to signify their permission by giving back the pitiman immediately and routinely, thus heading off the mischievous possibility that they might abuse their right, a sacred trust. "Authority" was defended in name but the right to exercise real authority was reserved by the bureaucratic establishment itself.

Tiruvappur had been the scene of many similar disputes at least as early as 1885. At one point the local Paraiyars asserted themselves against the ampalam by refusing to beat drums outside the Mariyamman temple; the Sirkar intervened, forcing them to resubmit themselves to the authority of the Kallar headman. In another dispute between the Velar priests and the ampalam in a different Aiyanar temple, the state again supported the latter against the Velars (R. 299/c of 1913, dt. $4-2-13$). In this temple, the usual practice had been for twenty-six sheep to be sacrificed outside of the temple at the various street intersections forming the boundary line of Aiyanar's sphere of influence. One of the special privileges claimed by the ampalam in this festival was the right to carry the scythe used for the ritual slaughter and present it to the Velars who performed the sacrifice. The ampalam was to be accorded fifteen of the sacrificed sheep, as well as a share of $\frac{15}{26}$ per cent if any more sheep were sacrificed (which the ampalam would then distribute among the Kallar community).

The Velars began sacrificing sheep inside the temple to lessen the share accorded to the ampalam. They also refused to concede the ampalam's right to carry and present them with the sacrificial scythe. On one occasion they even refused to give him pracatam from the temple. While the files do not tell us what grievances led them to these actions they do contain a report of the contentions and grievances of the ampalams, which were considered favorably by the Diwan and Diwan Peishkar, who sustained the rights they claimed. Tiruvappur may have been the scene of this exceptional vertical conflict because it was the suburb of Pudukkottai where many of the laborers of Pudukkottai lived. I found very few other examples of similar disputes between dominant and service castes reaching the files of the Diwan Peishkar's office, no doubt because most such disputes were summarily dealt with at the local level, either through official or unofficial channels. Again, it is impossible to know whether (and if so what percentage of them and to what extent) these disputes were caused by the changing conditions of the nineteenth century. We can only be sure that the disputes, whenever and however they occurred, altered in tone and content after the implementation of the new bureaucratic procedures whereby the Diwan Peishkar's office became responsible for handling these disputes.

## Service in temples

The final stage of the bureaucratization of temples occurred with respect to the traditional obligations of all landholders (pattadars) in the state to render service (uriyam) to temples. According to the 1925 Report of the Devasthanam Committee "ooliem or service to temples and to the Sovereign is one that is attached to the land and the liability follows ownership of land." Major uriyams entailed an obligation on the part of each pattadar to send one person to drag the temple car in the large temples that had annual car festivals. Minor uriyams entailed an obligation to send people to carry the processional deities during monthly and annual festivals in the temples, to send kids, coconuts, festoons, and other items necessary for temple festivals. Two other types of uriyam also obtained for some landholders: the need to beat the forests for the Raja's hunt, and the obligation to assist in the routine as well as emergency maintenance of tanks and other irrigation works. Unfortunately, I was able to find out very little about the operation of this system before the nineteenth century. It is likely that each landholder, which for the most part meant the shareholders in dominant

377

caste groups, sent one of his clients to perform these various duties. A; the various land settlements of the nineteenth century dramatically changed the nature of landholding, providing deeds of ownership to minor inam holders and holders of small plots of previously share (amani) lands, the responsibility to provide services to temples became increasingly dispersed, and increasingly difficult for landholders who were themselves the only cultivators for their plots of land.

The first complaints about the compulsory uriyam services came no from small landholders, however, but from non-Hindu pattadars, firs Christians and then Muslims. Whereas in the nineteenth century those non-Hindus who owned any land sent people to perform temple services without complaint, and for that matter received temple honors where they had these local privileges, the Jesuit missionaries of the early twentieth century became concerned about the continued participation of their converts in Hindu institutions. Rev. Father Castet wrote repeatedly to the Diwan Peishkar complaining about the incidence of Hindu duties on Christian landholders (see for example RD No. 2213/c of 1914, dt. 27–9–14). As a result of his intervention, as well as of the newly developing bureaucratic reading that religion was more an individual than a social matter, non-Hindu pattadars were excused from personal responsibility to render temple services in 1913. Instead, they were asked to pay a fee to be used to engage a substitute for them. The logic behind this was articulated in the Devasthanam Report: "Ooliam or service to temples and to the Sovereign is one that is attached to the land and the liability follows ownership of the land and the non-Hindu should not grudge doing the service which is a liability attaching to the ownership of the land he has purchased. The religious sentiment will revolt only if a non-Hindu is asked to render personal service to Hindu Gods. He ought to have no objection to contributing to the cost of engaging a substitute."

The chorus of complaints over uriyam was soon swelled by Hindus, though again not from the quarter one would have expected, that is from the poorer pattadars who had recently acquired rights of landownership made available by recent social, economic, and administrative change. Instead, the complainants were principally miracidars, AN Kallars, Brahmans, and Cettiyars who had purchased Brahman lands. It soon became evident that in the past the responsibilities of uriyam had not been organized by a bureaucratic system; so the Diwan Peishkar's office decided that the only way to make judgements was, wherever possible, to hold that anyone who held land must, without exception, perform uriyam.

But why did complaints come from the privileged classes of Pudukkottai, for whom the performance of the service could hardly have been a major burden? What seems likely is that the major landholders had previously sent their atimai laborers on behalf of the village rather than having to arrange for someone to represent them personally. The privileged classes objected to the new assertion that they personally perform service, perhaps to the related implication that under the new code all landowners were equal in the eyes of the law, and finally to the changing economic situation in which they no longer had full command over all subordinate castes – the ones who would have been sent on their behalf – in villages where they were dominant. Whereas in the past the performance of temple services had signified their local power and dominance, the new system of uriyam obligations displayed their growing loss of power and dominance.

Most importantly, as usual the Diwan Peishkar's office could not avoid making a few exemptions. Each privileged group now viewed such exemptions as a privilege which they could use in their struggle to maintain, if not to increase, their position in the status hierarchy of the state. For example, when a few relatives of the royal family were exempted from uriyam service, many other AN Kallars applied to the Diwan Peishkar for similar exemptions on the grounds that all AN Kallars were rajapantu, relatives of the royal family. The new bureaucrats responded by organizing and publishing a list of those relatives who were deemed close enough to the royal family to merit exemption (R – 5368 of 1937, dt. 5 – 1 – 38). Far from stifling the matter, it opened the flood gates of petitioning.

Alarmed by this deluge of petitions claiming exemptions, the predominantly Brahman bureaucrats misinterpreted what was in fact a new status game as a disturbing decrease in religiosity. They wrote in the Devasthanam Report:

There were perhaps days when people considered service to God as an act conferring a great merit on them. To bear the vehicles of Gods in procession, to hold umbrellas over them, to carry torches in front of them, to whirl chamarams by their sides and to carry all other marks of Sovereignty over both temporal and spiritual realms, people might have vied with one another. They are recognized in didactic Puranas as virtuous deeds. Man's ideas of morality have undergone a thorough change.

They forgot what the longsuffering readers of this book have not been allowed to, that only fifty years before, their predecessors were arbitrating disputes among the state's subjects about rights to perform the very actions that the same subjects were now so anxious to avoid. As long as service provided a hierarchical index of position within the little kingdom, it was sought after. Now, through the bureaucratic changes in the Princely State, exemption from service provided this same hierarchical index, and things turned upside down.

The bureaucrats responded by trying to curtail exemptions, replacing the service requirement with an additional tax on landholdings to be used to hire the necessary laborers for temple services. This plan began with the assessment of a fine for those landholders who did not perform their duties. The growing list of persons defaulting from service led to the creation of ad hoc mechanisms to assess and collect fines. In 1930 an order was promulgated to the effect that a levy of one anna per Rupee of land revenue be paid by each pattadar for temple service. However, the conversion of the service requirement to a cess met with stiff opposition, to the utter bewilderment of the bureaucrats. In the Legislative Council Session held in early 1931, all the non-official members voted for the abolition of the cess. Members of the Council and a deputation of ryots went directly to the Darbar with their objections. "The Hindu representatives of the ryots contended that they regarded the service not only as a religious duty but as a privilege, and did not wish it to be replaced by the payment of a cess" (Ayyar 1938, 468). Six months later, the government decided to abolish the cess; instead fines would be assessed for non-performance, though they would not be applicable to non-Hindus. Some of the officers of government noted that they would rather have kept the cess in order to be consistent in their aim of rationalizing landholding, but the force of protest proved too strong. Once again, systematic bureaucratic resolution of issues relating to old regime vestiges proved to be difficult. As it turned out, collecting fines for the non-performance of uriyam took up a great deal of the bureaucracy's time during the next years.[1]

## Conclusion

In the nineteenth and twentieth centuries temples continued to play a central role in the social life of Pudukkottai. As has been well documented for larger temples in Madras Presidency (Appadurai 1981), during this period many of the same concerns and aspirations of earlier centuries continued to motivate worshipful activity and conflict over

---

[1] See RD. No. 653/c of 1920, dt. 4–10–20; R. 5368 of 1937, dt. 5–1–38; RD No. 11871 of 1937, dt. 4–6–38; RD. No. 10685 of 1937, dt. 4–1–39; RD. No. 11425 of 1937, dt. 27–4–38; R. No. 387 of 1923, dt. 19–7–23; R. No. 387 of 1923, dt. 19–7–23; RD. No. 754 of 1919, dt. 22–9–19; RD No. 3597 of 1933, dt. 7–4–35.

worship in temples. At the same time, the changing bureaucratic nature of the colonial state (and by implication, though later and to a lesser extent, of the Princely State) rendered the procedures by which disputes were adjudicated, and finally the sociological bearings and cultural significance of disputes, radically different. New institutional procedures and new ideas were generated by colonial changes in the Presidency at large and by the dismantling of the old regime.

Appadurai sees change in the colonial period as revolving around four major points. First, under British rule temples inevitably relinquished the critical importance they had had under Hindu kings. Second, the British attempted with increasing success to appropriate the local management of temples through systematic bureaucratic procedures and institutions. Third, the executive and judiciary components of temple administration were separated. Finally, the generalizing tendency of British colonial intervention led to a "growing cycle of interactions, which resolved little but provoked much new conflict" (p. 215). Perhaps the most important structural component of all of these changes had to do with the reification of customary usages into codified laws, destroying the "context-sensitivity" of the old regime (p. 69). In spite of Pudukkottai's status as a Princely State ruled by a Hindu monarch, we have seen the same widening gyre of intervention there.

In Pudukkottai, we have also seen that intervention led to serious changes not just in the way in which a growing number of disputes were handled but also in the definitions and discourses that constituted disputes in the first place. The resumption of temple lands and their replacement by cash allocations involved the state more directly with temple management than ever before. These changes were conjoined with newly developing administrative ideas and associated discourses about a public domain and about religion. Ironically, the attempted introduction of Western notions of state and religion caused unanticipated transformations while simultaneously serving to facilitate the process of colonial and bureaucratic control.

The discourse of the bureaucratic regime achieved its hegemony because both winners and losers, both "traditional" leaders and "new" entrants, both British officers and Brahman bureaucrats, found themselves using the new forms of discourse. The contestants in all of the disputes we have examined agreed about more than they disagreed. For example, they concurred that there were separate rather than single honors for government servants and "traditional" headmen, that inam grants constituted the terms of service in bureaucratic rather than relational form, and that temples now reflected bureaucratic rather than royal realities. While the stakes in the political process seemed to stay the same, the means by which these stakes were fought over and the terms in which they were defined changed dramatically. The bureaucratic regime achieved its hegemony whether it won or lost, whether it achieved full control over the local miracidars or had to yield, as it did on most occasions, to the local loyalties and power of individuals who did not hold their position solely because of state recognition. Even when the state maintained local positions of authority, the state appropriated to itself the right to appoint local officials in ways that abstracted the world of kin relations from politics and held the two domains apart.

The Brahman bureaucrats of Pudukkottai also appropriated, and disseminated, new forms of discourse concerning religion. In particular, they developed a sense of the autonomy of religious practice from the full set of social, political, and cultural referents that had always contextualized religion in the old regime and which, paradoxically, continued to provide some of the ideational and operational impetus to religious practice during the period under discussion. They viewed religion on the one hand as an individual concern, as inherently egalitarian and without social implications apart from the need to preserve the integrity of this private domain, and on the other as a public concern, especially inasmuch as it provided an arena for the display of dignities and official position. The inherent contradictions of this taxonomy emerged in virtually every dispute over honor.

Contradictions were also revealed when the bureaucrats tried to defend the sacredness of their trust by setting an implicit price for the management of a temple. They did this to satisfy their own concern to use any available means to preserve and maintain the physical structures of temples, often in direct contravention of measures which would best maintain the order and balance of the social structure of temples. Similar contradictions came to the fore when the bureaucrats chided the landholders of the state for what they perceived to be a decrease in religiosity in their complaints about uriyam service. In the end, the decisions of bureaucrats about the public domain of their administrative concerns were motivated by their growing conviction about the private nature of religious devotion and belief. This conflation of public and private domains, however, was based upon their separate definition in sharp contrast to their fundamental unity in the old regime.

Nonetheless, the old regime was by no means obliterated in the transformation to a new colonial order. The bureaucracy, for example, continued to take disputes over honors seriously, since the men who inhabited the new file-cluttered offices of power were themselves hardly exempt from the quest for dignity and status. Despite their repeated attempts to order and codify disputes over honor the bureaucrats found themselves unable to set up any fully satisfactory system. Bureaucratic innovations, such as the issuance of exemptions from the performance of temple services, became appropriated by old forms of status hierarchy and grew rapidly unrecognizable as rationalized bureaucratic activity. As we have seen in other contexts, we have witnessed not a movement from a traditional to a modern world, but a shift in forms and structures of meaningful activity which often looked, both to observers and participants, fundamentally the same.

But the changes in forms and structures, though gradual and partial, were changes nevertheless. The "cultural systems" of state and temple were radically and irrevocably altered. The Raja no longer arbitrated disputes, and was no longer at the center of the political relationships that had once determined hierarchies of status and authority. Codified terms of service began to supersede, if not fully displace, the older politics. Through the cultural forms embodied in the new system of bureaucratic relationships the practice, and, perhaps even more important-ly, the discourse of authority changed dramatically. In addition, the increasing challenge offered by the merchants to the old regime elites in the southern part of Pudukkottai reflected even as it contributed to the general demise of the old regime. While commercialized activity had always been accorded an important role in social relations, it now took on a new relationship to the political forms which determined status, hierarchy, and authority throughout the state. Money could now be used to buy honors in the rural bases of old regime political power.

That money could buy honor, at least when the bureaucracy determined that the material benefits outweighed the social and political costs, had less to do with the presence of money than with the transformation of the logic of political life. The elevation of religion to an autonomous status, and the interpretation of temples as physical rather than socio-cultural structures, led to the commercialization of worship. Gold garnered as the spoils of war by great kings who then endowed temples to celebrate and augment their kingship was different from the gold earned through trade and investment by merchants who then used it to purchase management rights. Although the merchants were emulating kingly behavior, they could now look forward to a future in which they could be kings and merchants at the same time. This, too, heralded the end of the old regime. But while honors never became commoditized in a market sense, it was through the very concerns of maintaining "religious" institutions in Pudukkottai that temples and honors ultimately, if provisionally, did become colonial commodities after all.

# 13

## The theatre state: princely politics in colonial south India

subjected thus,
How can you say to me, I am a king?
Shakespeare, *Richard II*, III. ii

Not until the advent of colonialism would the stage be finally set for India's "theatre state," to borrow somewhat impiously Clifford Geertz's felicitous phrase. For under British rule little kings in India were constructed as colonial objects[1] and given special colonial scripts. They were maintained, altered, and managed as part of a systematic, if awkwardly developing, set of colonial purposes and understandings. It was initially seen as dangerous, perhaps impossible, to remove the feudal layer of lords ruling over much of the Indian countryside in the late eighteenth and early nineteenth centuries. As the dangers waned, permanent settlements with local lords yielded to settlements with cultivators, annexations increased, and efforts to control those lords who had been appropriated by British rule intensified. Colonized lords – whether as talukdars, zamindars, or even more saliently as princes in the one-third of India under indirect rule – were progressively constructed as edifices not only of loyalty and subservience, but of a newly created and gentrified managerial elite: a tribute, and a support, to British rule.

When these efforts failed, as they generally did, the British increasingly tried to intervene in the forms and operations of management itself. But, at the very moment they came closest to achieving one component of their objectives, the complete separation of kings from their states, they scented new dangers and withdrew to the creative muddle of indirect rule. However absurd and often impossible to manage, indirect rule proved to be one of the fundamental cornerstones of colonial control. In this chapter I will show how the success of British efforts to gentrify the Rajas of Pudukkottai led to an unforeseen and profoundly disturbing (if farcical) end: the de facto abdication of a Raja and the only sedition case in the record books of the Princely State.

[1] The creation of India as an "object" under colonialism has been discussed by Cohn (1970; 1986) and Metcalf (1984).

## The background and formulation of indirect rule

Political relations between Pudukkottai and the British government officially began, as with the other southern palaiyams, with the treaty of 1801, in which all the administrative powers of the Nawab of Arcot were transferred to the British (Aitchison 1930, 10:72–76). At this point, even with the continuing ambiguity in their attitude to the formal locus of sovereignty, the British interpreted the administrative rights accruing to them from the transfer of power as being far more inclusive than they might have thirty years before. The report of a Select Committee dated April 3, 1771 (S. R. Aiyar 1916, 256) had made the case that Pudukkottai was independent both of Tanjavur and the Nawab; thirty years later the Nawab became the source of the sovereign rights accorded to the British.

When the final transfer of power occurred in 1801 because of the "discovery" of the Nawab's disloyalty, the British needed to interpret the Nawab's power rather broadly in order to justify their own assumption of political control over large areas of southern India. A general feudal theory was invoked in order to construe all political entities that had any kind of "subordinate" dealings with the Nawab as now subordinate to the East India Company. Nonetheless, in part because no treaty was ever formally drawn up with Pudukkottai, the transfer of authority did not clarify the relationship between Pudukkottai and the British. In 1803 the first Political Agent for Pudukkottai, William Blackburne, wrote that the gifts and honors exchanged between the Tondaimans and the Nawab had been made because of "extortion" and thus were devoid of political significance, an admission that hardly sustained the feudal theory that justified his own position (Ayyar 1938, 285). While Blackburne was in fact merely supporting Pudukkottai's tribute-free status, the steady loyalty of Pudukkottai to the East India Company never necessitated any clear definition of its subordinate position. Only after the passage of half a century, after the rebellion of 1853–54 and the Raja's incorrigible indebtedness and inattention to managerial concerns had raised the issue of what should be done with Pudukkottai, did British bureaucrats find themselves having to consider what could be done under the terms of political relationship and precedent.

The dominant view, echoing the much earlier sentiments of Lushington, was expressed by T. Pycroft (MPP, no. 58, 26 September 1863):

his ancestor was "no more than a Poligar chief of a superior description." He and his predecessors had solicited and obtained insignia and titles of honor from the ancient kings of the Carnatic, the Nabob Mahomed Ali and the British Government, and had paid large nuzzers to the Nabob.

In the same exchange, E. Maltby concurred, sketching out some of the implications of this view:

> though a quasi independent Prince, the Tondiman is in reality a dependent chief, whose minor and subordinate position apparently rendered it unnecessary for the Government to enter into any formal Treaty with him. He was completely subservient to and a Tributary of the Nabobs of the Carnatic without whose assent no new Rajah was recognized.

Yet another correspondent noted that he saw no precedent for any interference "with ... the management of his territory." In spite of this kind of dissent, itself echoing the statements made by Blackburne in a different time and context, the general official view was that of Pycroft and Maltby. The Pudukkottai kings were seen as "completely subservient."

Clearly, the development of an official discourse had less to do with Indian political relations than with British colonial interests and theory. We have seen repeatedly that while gifts and exchanges were central to the articulation of political relations, these relations were never absolute or fixed. Perhaps we should therefore not be surprised that the Pudukkottai Rajas (and their state chroniclers) saw no contradiction between claiming their independence from the Nawab, citing the nonpayment of tribute as evidence, while at the same time boasting about the honors they were given by the Nawab (Ayyar 1940, 818–820). Up until 1804 the locus of sovereign relations as recorded in the copper plate inscriptions of the Tondaimans was still the virtually defunct kingship of Vijayanagar.[2]

It is even less surprising that the first exchange of letters between the Tondaimans and the British after the 1801 treaty concerned a request by the Tondaiman that the Company bestow certain honors on him. Blackburne relayed the request to the Board of Revenue (MPP, 5 July 1803):

> There was another point which he [the Tondaiman] proposed to state, not as a claim, in any respect, but merely as a suggestion for the favourable consideration of His Lordship. The Emperor or other great and Powerful Princes were accustomed to bestow particular Titles and Ensigns of Distinction on the most deserving of their dependents. The ensigns of distinction, which he was authorized to use, had been granted to His Ancestors by the ancient kings of the Carnatic – and, in one instance by the Nabob Mahomed Ally Cawn, who had

---

[2] See the copper plate inscriptions in the Pudukkottai State Museum.

386

authorized him to add Rajah Behauder to his name. Any additions to these titles, or ensigns, of Distinction, which his Lordship might do him the Honor to confer upon him he should receive with the highest respect and gratitude. At my request, Tondiman particularly instanced the title of Maharajah; and permission to have a white umbrella and gold chubdar sticks, carried before him.

The Board decided to grant him the honors, but, interestingly, not the title, which to them suggested a rather more enhanced status than they were prepared to acknowledge. They also granted him a fort and the district of "Keelanily," which the Raja of Tanjore had confiscated some years before. They insisted that in return the Tondaiman present them with one elephant a year "as a mark of homage for the tenure." The Tondaiman was pleased with the grant, but very distressed about the elephant, which he saw as destroying his tribute-free status. The Tondaimans avoided giving the elephants, until in 1836 the requirement was formally excused (MPC, vol. 248, 21 June 1836). The honors were a different story. Those he accepted with ceremony and respect. As Blackburne reports (MPP, 10 August 1803):

Tondiman, attended by all his principal Sirdars, and a considerable part of his Military Force, met me on the road, at the distance of two miles from the place of His Abode, – he received the Governor's letter with demonstrations of the highest respect, and placed it upon his head, – he then held it up to the View of all the People, while the troops saluted and cannons were fired.

But even as such gifts had not unambiguously defined the political relationship of Pudukkottai with the Nawab before, this gift did not allay British doubts about the extent and nature of their authority over this Princely State.

The British had problems in defining the exact nature of their relations with the Princely States throughout India, as the many treatises and debates about their status in the late nineteenth and early twentieth centuries amply demonstrate (Lee-Warner 1920; Tupper 1893). Despite the relative insignificance of Pudukkottai, the British had particular difficulty in understanding this relationship because of the absence of any formal treaty or sanad. From 1853 to 1918[3] virtually every British record about Pudukkottai contained an attempt to define its political status; some of this correspondence has already been excerpted. This issue first occasioned serious concern after the 1853–54 rebellion, and the explanation that the rebellion was principally caused by the indebtedness and mismanagement of Raja Ramachandra gave license

[3] As late as 1918 a long report was written on this subject. See MPGO, no. 236/A/Secret (Under Secretary's Safe), 24 August 1918, TNA.

for even more active concern. When, in 1863, the Raja dismissed the Sirkele (Diwan) appointed by the government, the British after much debate concurred that there was no justification for "describing the Tondiman as an independent Prince" (MPGO, no. 291, 26 September 1863). After recounting the history of the Tondaiman's "dependence" on the Nawab, one Government Order proclaimed:

although no tribute has been paid, the Sovereignty of the British Government has been repeatedly acknowledged; and it is clearly within the power, as it is the duty, of the Madras Government to take any precautions that may be necessary to prevent mis-government and anarchy, such as compelled it in 1853, to place the control of the finances under a minister appointed with its concurrence; and in the following year to restore the Rajah's authority by the presence of British troops.

As clearly as this formulation expressed the powers and the duties of the British government, it stopped well short of accepting the suggestions of some that the administration of the state be assumed and the Raja made a pensioner. Nonetheless, the Collector was enjoined

to impress upon the Rajah that, if he persists in his present profligate course of expenditure and continues to neglect his judicial duties and to disregard the advice and remonstrances of the Political Agent, the Government will have no alternative but to take the administration of the country out of his hands in pursuance of the warnings which have repeatedly been given him.

As before, the warning – this time to remove the Raja entirely from the affairs and responsibilities of state and simply grant him a pension for his maintenance – did not have the desired effect. The Raja neither abated his expenditure nor assumed his prescribed role as manager and judicial steward of the state. Nor, however, did the government take further steps to assume the administration, revealing the same reticence to follow through with their threats that they displayed in the context of the Permanent Settlement with zamindars, whom the British bailed out time after time rather than auctioning their estates as they threatened (Dirks 1986). The British took their strongest punitive action in the same ambiguous domain that inaugurated official relations between the British and Pudukkottai: honor. In 1859 they withdrew the title of "His Excellency" granted to the Tondaiman Rajas in 1830, revoking it when the Raja incurred an additional five and a half lakhs of rupees of debts after the severe warnings following Parker's investigation of the rebellion in 1854.

While this act was vigorously protested by the Raja, it too had little effect. Despite the absence of any measurable improvement in his behavior the title was restored in 1870 (MPP, no. 16, 15 July 1870) as a special favor upon the visit of the Duke of Edinburgh to Madras, though it was subsequently pointed out to the Raja that this conferment was "provisional" on his good behavior (MPP, no. 39, 18 December 1873). In 1884, and again without any measurable change in his behavior, the government conferred on him the title of His Highness and a hereditary salute of eleven guns (MPGOs, nos. 475, 476, 487, 6 May 1886), though a year later it was announced that this did not indicate an increase in rank (as the Raja had taken it) but was rather done so that "the title of 'Excellency' might be reserved for the Viceroy and Government" (MPGOs, nos. 877, 878, 10 December 1885). Despite Raja Ramachandra's flagrant violation of British codes of leadership (and in spite of all the reservations the Government had in connection with their various conferrals of titles and honors) the Raja's reign looked if anything more dignified by British honors at its conclusion than when it began. The colonial logic of political relations had more to do with the necessity of preserving the appearance of Princely States and zamindari estates than with the rhetorical justifications that for the British brought them into being in the first place. The rhetoric of the Permanent Settlement and of accommodation with Princes had always been couched in the terms of classical political economy, always abandoned when push came to shove. The importance of the rhetoric, though it points to genuine cultural and socio-economic clashes, hardly justifies the unrealistic debates about the illusory rationality of colonial lords and the chimera of state/estate management in nineteenth-century India.

## The play's the thing

The British let out a noticeable sigh of relief when Raja Ramachandra died in 1886, and was succeeded by his eleven-year-old adopted grandson, Martanda Bhairava Tondaiman. Part of the relief was because now the Diwan, Sir Seshiah Sastri (previously the Diwan of Travancore), whom the British held in high esteem, could and did assume even more extensive powers as the Diwan-Regent during Martanda's minority, when he completed the extensive revenue and administrative reforms he had earlier begun. Despite the satisfaction universally expressed by the British about Sastri's tenure as Regent and Diwan, the historical record leaves little doubt that he bankrupted the state with an ambitious building program that was far more representative of his own aspirations for honor than it was of the needs of state citizens. His amani settlement, as we noted in an earlier chapter, created the context for the exploitation of the very amani cultivators whose woes he had documented in piteous detail only to justify their more systematic exploitation and his own developing reputation as the bureaucrat par excellence. In retrospect the indebtedness of the Raja seemed almost innocuous.

The British were also relieved when they contemplated the future under the new Raja, a minor whom the Diwan had chosen over two elder brothers, perhaps reflecting the government's desire for more influence over the Raja. They probably wanted as much of the new Raja's youth as possible to train him to become a proper Raja. Further, given his youth and his adoption from outside the main family, he had so far been unexposed to the intrigue of the zenana. The government resolved to carefully oversee the education of the minor Raja, in 1887 appointing Mr Crossley, a graduate of Cambridge, as his English tutor with explicit instructions to ensure the inculcation of British ideas and values (Ayyar 1940, 873). Travel was an important component of this new education, paramount importance being attached to exposing the young Raja to wider vistas and perspectives so he would not become engulfed in the narrow and byzantine preoccupations of court life in the state. The young Raja was taken on grand tours of northern India and Europe to accomplish these objectives.

While he was thus occupied, the government resolved to build the Raja a new palace outside the town. The old palace occupied the town center, constituting the matrix for municipal structure and geography. The streets were named after the points of the compass, taking their reference from the old palace. Surrounded by imposing crenelated fort/compound walls with large open spaces for assemblies and displays, the structures within were themselves unimpressive from the outside. But their modest facades gave no idea of the intricate world within. The rambling internal structures were not laid out according to a master plan but appeared to be haphazard, organic growths, chance accretions, focused as much on the zenana as the durbar hall. Involuted and inward, they reflected more the ramified kinship structure of the royal family than any clearly lit vision of sovereignty. In contrast, the new palace was to be altogether different and more accessible to the British and their conceptions of rule. Designed by European architects, the new palace was to present an impressive façade, with the internal rooms built for formal entertaining rather than for the convenience of an extended Kallar family. Unlike the honeycombed old palace with its myriad small rooms and separate buildings, the new palace was a single free-standing monument, with only two bedrooms. It was to be built on classical Indo-Saracenic lines on spacious grounds outside the town, close to the tutelary temple of the royal family, but even closer to the large brick residence of the British Political Agent.

The progress of his able and eager student so pleased Crossley that the British viewed Martanda's accession to the throne in 1894 with a mixture of complacency and optimism. But it soon became apparent that the very qualities so assiduously instilled in him by Crossley were to make his rule highly troublesome. In 1897 (MPGO, no. 523, 6 August 1897) a British report tells us that "the Raja is more a coloured European gentleman, with entirely European tastes, than a Native Prince." But instead of rejoicing the report went on to reveal the problems with what had at first been construed as the success of their careful policy: the Raja was "an absentee chief and unduly addicted to amusements." Between his installation in November 1894 and the writing of this note in August 1897, the Raja spent a total of eight weeks in the state, returning principally for festivals and shooting expeditions. These were the very occasions which, in spite of all the talk about the need for management, the British privileged more than any others, regarding festivals as the basis of feudal rule and shooting as the most exquisite perquisite of their connection with the Princes. While it was noted that this particular Prince had kept himself "remarkably free from intrigue," the regrettable explanation was that he did not spend enough time in Pudukkottai to get involved in much of anything.

Martanda's absenteeism was in part caused by a series of trips to Europe, where his fondness for things European developed beyond matters of general taste to his choice of a wife. In 1914 he astounded the British by announcing his decision to marry a European (MPGO, 22 May 1914). Their first response was to encourage a marriage with a Europeanized North Indian girl, while prohibiting outright a marriage with a non-Indian (MRR, box 903). As it became increasingly clear that the Raja was adamant about a European bride, the British began discreet inquiries as to the repercussions. L. A. Vibert, the Political Agent at the time, wrote that since the Raja had already totally disregarded all his caste obligations as well as his ritual role as head of state in temple ceremonies there would be little change in this regard (ibid.): "He is the Head of State ... as the disciple or votary of Sri Brihadamba; and the question has apparently already been raised whether a non-orthodox Hindu can continue as head of the State, but H. H. is understood to have a legal opinion in his favor."

Moving to the question of caste custom, Vibert noted that "technically it would be less than a marriage from the orthodox point of view, but while this would theoretically make the lady's position somewhat equivocal, she would probably never realize the fact and HH would not look at it of course in this light." The question of the status of a son from such a marriage was considerably more delicate:

Plainly the legal position of these children of an irregular marriage will be in the last degree doubtful, and that any of them can succeed as heir I should say, as a legal point, inadmissable. This is also local opinion. We may therefore take it that at H. H.'s death the question of succession will come up in an aggravated form and the idea of his being succeeded by one of these children will be resisted and disliked. Indeed, one informant even talks of armed rebellion as a possibility.

These concerns and objections notwithstanding, the British were unable to prevent Martanda from marrying, on August 10, 1915, an Australian woman by the name of Molly Fink. Eleven months later she gave birth to a son (Ayyar 1940, 892–894).

The Raja and his new wife resided in Pudukkottai for six months from November 1915 to April 1916, but then left for Australia, not to return for any extended period of time. The marriage had only disposed the Raja further away from thoughts of management and rule, and the royal couple's stay in Pudukkottai had hardly been eased by apparent – or perhaps conveniently alleged – attempts to poison poor Molly with extract of leaves of oleander during their stay at the palace (MRR, box 903). Ironically, by the time the splendid new palace was ready for triumphant occupation by a couple who would have readily appreciated the immense improvement over the previous palace, the Raja and his wife were permanently out of town. By 1920 matters took a turn for the worse. The Raja made clear his wish to abdicate his throne in favor of a pension, adopting the very position which for quite different reasons many British administrators had recommended for his predecessor only fifty years before.

When the British finally got what they wanted it turned out not to be such a good idea. For one thing, by 1920 the political climate had changed dramatically, what with the noncooperation movement throughout India and the growing political activity of the Congress in the south. As mentioned in a memo of November 24, 1920 (ibid., R/2 temp. no. 903/438 (1)):

The most marked feature of the State of Puthukottah till now has been its loyalty to the Ruling House ... But should his [the Rajah's] absence be continued it is not to be expected that the Darbar as at present constituted or even with increased powers will be able to exercise the same authority as the Ruler himself ... The question therefore is does not the State at this juncture require the presence of His Highness? Is it safe to allow the bond between him and his people on which the happiness and safety of the State has depended to be entirely broken? If this is broken what guarantee have we that any other arrangement will be loyally accepted by the people? And finally once even an elementary consciousness of their "rights" has awakened in the minds of the people is it not a factor in the situation which no wise ruler can afford to ignore?

What had in the nineteenth century been more vaguely stated as the need to protect the "native aristocracy" became now a matter of urgency for the Empire because of the anxiety about the growth of nationalist and anti-British sentiment.

The investigation of the probable effects of the Raja's abdication turned up nothing of an encouraging nature. Sydney Burn, Superintendent of the State, wrote in June of 1921 (ibid., see letter from Burn, June 2, 1921):

The marriage itself was a shock. No one could say that they liked it; they could not be expected to like it. But they were willing to accept the fact, as they are willing to accept whatever HH does, in the hope that now at last HH would be able and willing to settle down amongst them ... What will be the effect upon them of a sudden announcement that HH is never coming back? It is not hard to see that they will be deeply disappointed and sorely hurt. The offer of a Regency will appear a mere mockery of their grief. They do not want a Regent. They want a Ruler whom they have known and loved from his birth. No regent can take his place.

The next concern was over the effect of an announcement that twenty-five lakhs of rupees were to be withdrawn from the State Treasury to support the Raja after his abdication; Burn anticipated nothing but trouble. He was aware that the people in Pudukkottai might balk and squarely place the responsibility for supporting a Raja whose taste for things European the British had so carefully cultivated back on the British government. Ironically, the perceived threat to public order meant, as Burn recognized, that the British might have to assume financial responsibility for maintaining the Raja in his European life (ibid.). In the end a compromise was reached whereby twenty lakhs from the state surplus fund and 1.60 lakhs from the marriage fund were given to the Raja as a final settlement in 1922 (Ayyar 1940, 899). In the last of the Raja's official proclamations dated October 23, 1922, Martanda announced his intention to live permanently out of the state. He delegated the administration of the state to his brother, the former Diwan who was now to become Diwan Regent, empowering him to exercise the "full powers of His Highness the Raja" (State Gazette of November 1, 1922; also see Administration Report of the State for Fasli 1332).

The final settlement was not an actual abdication. Abdication was unthinkable, both according to informants and the notions of kingship communicated in legal discourse of the time. Some informants said that there could be no new king as long as the old king was alive. In the Pudukkottai Law Reports concerning a case in which the status of the Raja had to be determined in order to establish the grounds for a sedition trial, the state's vakil (lawyer) had written that (PLR, Sessions Appeal No. 14 of 1927):

His Highness the Raja of this State, although he has decided to reside permanently out of India as announced in his Proclamation ... has not abdicated the throne but continues to be the Sovereign Ruler of this State having arranged for the administration of the State by a Deputy to whom he has delegated his full powers of administration.

But even this minimal statement became a source of contention. The vakil for the appellant argued that by adopting this course, "His Highness the Raja has refused to perform his regal functions by withdrawing himself out of the State and is therefore not entitled to the allegiance of the subjects of this State." The appellant's vakil quoted from a footnote in Halsbury's Laws of England to the effect that the refusal of the king to perform "regal functions, by withdrawing himself out of the realm or otherwise, is abhorrent to the spirit of the constitution, and would probably be regarded by Parliament as a breach of the contract between the Crown and people as in the case of James II."

The state vakil countered this by arguing that "The above is not an authoritative statement of a legal principle, but is only a mere opinion hazarded by the writer. It is not put forward as a principle of universal application but is based on the peculiar nature of the British constitution in which the powers of the Sovereign are limited by his contract with the Parliament and the people, and as such it would not serve as a useful guide in determining the rights of the Ruler of this State who is not fettered by any such limitations." In any case it would have been impossible to provide precedents for abdication in Hindu kingship, since the concept was unknown. Throughout the legal brief, the state lawyers steadfastly maintained not only that the authority of the Raja was uncompromised by contracts, but that it was indistinguishable in any sense whatsoever from the person of the king. As they put it, "The Sovereign is superior to all his subjects and is the fountain head of law and order." Even more dramatically, they insisted that "according to the Hindu ideas of sovereignty, his powers are absolute and unlimited and akin to those of God, the King being looked upon as a representative of God on earth and even an avatar of God Vishnu himself." Divine kingship was alive and well as late as 1927, receiving institutional sustenance at least from the legal structure of Pudukkottai.

Although Martanda had irrevocably turned his back on the state (though not on its money, and as rumor has it on the state jewels), preferring the gambling halls of Monte Carlo and the drawing rooms of London and Paris, his sovereignty, unfettered by any conditions, was to be unquestioned. But it was questioned, as Burn had anticipated and as the above legal case reveals. In 1926 and 1927 two articles in the local Tamil newspaper *Janamitiran* strongly criticized the Raja and led to an extraordinary sedition case. During the same decade that saw Gandhi and the nationalist movement subdued by British laws of sedition (the same Section 124 – A of the Indian Penal Code was used both in this case and in the famous case against Gandhi in 1922; here it was adjusted to apply to the Pudukkottai king mutatis mutandis) a Brahman editor in Pudukkottai was tried and sentenced to rigorous imprisonment. The editor's act of sedition was to criticize the Raja for neglecting his state and leaving the Hindu fold.

The first seditious article, an excerpt from a speech given by the President of the Pudukkottai People's Conference which had met in December of 1926, began thus: "Many praise the Maharajah as an extremely good man. You must form an estimate of him from his deeds," such as his taking twenty lakhs of Rupees out of the state for his personal use in return for which he did nothing for the state. The short, at times cryptic article ended by decrying the deplorable state of the kingdom, connecting the serious problems of famine and poverty with the Raja's absence and appropriation of funds: "The Kingdom is Desolate. Tears of blood shed by the poor are running. There is famine everywhere. People are emigrating from the country for their livelihood. All round there is scarcity. There are no handicrafts. How long are the people to suffer in this way?" As the state's vakil said, "One could well conceive of such a speech having been directed against King Louis XVI of France during the French Revolution by one of the revolutionist and not by a loyal subject towards his Sovereign." Such is the nature of the seditious.

The second article was written by the accused as an editorial in his paper concerning the question of succession. The article began with a statement that the Raja was no longer, strictly speaking, a Hindu. His marriage with a non-Hindu and his extended residence in a foreign country had made him a *patitan* (translated in the record as apostate but in fact more like outcaste). The article then asked a question in the form of an incomplete conditional: "If the Maharaja himself be not a

Hindu..." The obvious implication was that the Maharaja was no longer fit to carry his title, let alone the state's trust. He had abdicated his authority if not his crown. This was further suggested in a subsequent sentence: "As for the Ruler of the State he is not one who could pay any regard for the permanent future well-being of the State by reason of his excessive affection for his son." Although technically the article left much unsaid, the authors' opinions came through clearly: that the son was even less a Hindu than his father; that any thought of proposing the succession of this son to the kingship of the state was absolutely opposed to the interests, indeed the entire conception, of the state; and that the Maharaja had abandoned all concern for the state which had made him what he was.

Irony follows upon irony. The first awareness of the rights of citizens in Pudukkottai emerged out of a royal context whose external form the British had preserved precisely because it was supposed to have retained a feudal hold on the consciousness of its citizens. The complaints that led to the restlessness the British had anticipated were based in part on British complicity in the detraditionalization of Hindu kingship. It was British success in wresting young Martanda away from the seething intrigue of zenana and state that led to his premature retirement, indeed total withdrawal, from that peculiar artifact known as the Princely State.

When the Raja died in 1928 the potential crisis was averted by deciding to confer succession on Rajkumar Rajagopala Tondaiman, a direct descendant of the Melaranmanai Jagirdar who had earlier proved so quarrelsome and resistant to the bureaucratic attempt to separate him from the source of his honors and control over his own domain. In a curious way the old regime triumphed once again for a brief moment at a time when the days of British empire on the subcontinent were already numbered (Ayyar 1940, 905). The new Raja was invested with full powers on January 14, 1944, only a short time before Independence in 1947 and the amalgamation of the state into the Indian Union in 1948. The new prince turned out to be a model ruler, though this was too late for both the old and the colonial regime. But, to reflect back on the history of Pudukkottai since the death of Raja Ramachandra in 1886, the British had for the most part what they had often argued in favor of (and then just as often had to find ways to manage): a state without a ruler, first because of the minority, absenteeism, and final withdrawal of Martanda, and later because of the minority of his successor.

The Raja was reconstructed – and ultimately deconstructed – as an object of colonialism. But when the British achieved the total separation of the Raja from the state, and in the process appropriated the total enunciative function that had once been the Raja's, they realized that this too was not what they had in mind. What they really wanted, of course, was a fiction: a mummified simulacrum much like the displays in museums of natural history.[4] That they did not get what they wanted is a tribute to the old regime. That it turned out not to make a fundamental difference either to the success or finally to the failure of British rule is a testimony to the hegemonic flexibility of the colonial regime. The fiction of the preservation of the old regime worked rather well, after all. The very failures that so distressed the British provided dynamic structures to replace those that had been frozen with permanent settlements and princely states. The "intrigue" and "corruption" so bemoaned by bureaucrats and historians provided the drama – the engagement that renders fiction real – for what otherwise would have been an inert and lifeless stage.

[4] The museum aspect of the Princely State is revealed in many of the files surrounding the establishment of the Tondaiman prince in the late nineteenth and early twentieth centuries. Perhaps the clearest example of this can be found in the files of the "Dignity Establishment," which record the full list, pay, and responsibilities of the myriad retainers kept on in the princely court to carry the fly whisks, sceptres, and other insignia of the King (PDRO). See Waghorne (1983).

# PART 6

# Conclusion

# 14

## *Ethnohistory and the Indian state*

A great many works have prepared the way for this book. Several have provided particularly important models for what has been written here. Perhaps Clifford Geertz (1980) states more clearly than any one else the problem of studying the Indic state – although in its particularly minute as well as byzantine Balinese form – from the perspectives of much comparative sociology and Western political theory. Geertz writes that Bali, where the state was articulated by the doctrine of the exemplary center, was a "theatre state," where the drama was ritual, and ritual was power:

It was a theatre-state in which the kings and princes were impresarios, the priests, the directors, the peasantry, the supporting cast, stage crew, and audience. The stupendous cremations, teeth-filings, temple dedications, the pilgrimages and blood sacrifices, mobilizing hundreds, even thousands of people and great quantities of wealth, were not means to political ends, they were ends themselves, they were what the state was for. Court ceremonialism was the driving force of state politics. Mass ritual was not a device to shore up the state; the state was a device for the enactment of mass ritual. To govern was not so much to choose as to perform. Ceremony was not form but substance. Power served pomp, not pomp power. (Geertz 1980, 13)

But despite his redefinition of the basis of state power, Geertz still sees significant tensions between the unifying force of the theatre state and the decentralizing tendencies of all the other dominant forces – from clans and lineages to temples and irrigation societies – that made up Balinese social structure.

nineteenth century Balinese politics can be seen as stretched taut between two opposing forces; the centripetal one of state ritual and the centrifugal one of state structure. On the one hand there was the unifying effect of mass ceremonial under the leadership of this or that lord; on the other there was the intrinsically dispersive, segmental character of the polity considered as a *concrete social institution*, a *power system*, composed as it was of dozens of independent, semi-independent, and quarter-independent rulers. (Italics mine. Geertz 1980, 18–19)

But can we isolate concrete social institutions or power systems from their cultural and symbolic expressions; and in what sense does such an analytic isolation allow us to characterize something as "intrinsically dispersive"? We are left to wonder what Geertz really means by power. Does power serve pomp, or, as the second quote suggests, does pomp merely counteract power?

Although Geertz gives a resounding call to battle against the kind of comparative political assumptions that masquerade as hard minded analysis and empirical precision, he does not deliver on all of the promises and claims that he makes. Not only is the ritual basis of the Balinese state insufficiently explored – the central ritual text turns out to be the incredulous report by a man named Helms of a royal cremation – but the choice of thespian metaphors makes Bali, with all the anthropological romance of the island, seem even more special a case than is perhaps justified. Nonetheless, Geertz provides examples of the kind of analysis required to understand the interpenetration of the state and society, and argues persuasively that ethnographic and historical study must be combined. Geertz's synthesis of title group stratification, Chinese-box kinship, temple congregations, irrigation societies, and other local social institutions in terms of their political forms and functions suggests (even if it does not fully reveal) the immense contribution historical perspective and explanation can make to anthropology. And in spite of the fact that I take the name "theatre state" in vain to underscore the farcical turn of little kingdoms under colonial rule, I happily acknowledge that Geertz formulates what could be a theoretical preamble to this book when he writes that:

The confinement of interpretive analysis in most of contemporary anthropology to the supposedly more "symbolic" aspect of culture is a mere prejudice, born out of the notion, also a gift of the nineteenth century, that "symbolic" opposes to "real" as fanciful to sober, figurative to literal, obscure to plain, aesthetic to practical, mystical to mundane, and decorative to substantial. To construe the expressions of the theatre state, to apprehend them as theory, this prejudice, along with the allied one that the dramaturgy of power is external to its workings, must be put aside. The real is as imagined as the imaginary. (Geertz 1980, 135–136)

As Geertz so rightly insists, the symbolic aspects of power are not, as the saying goes, "merely" symbolic. However, Geertz himself sometimes seems to be suggesting that power, certainly state power, is "only" symbolic. As a consequence, he raises more questions than he answers about the problems of liberating interpretive analysis for the purposes of ethnohistorical investigation.

The work of Stanley Tambiah is in some respects more helpful in delineating the particular kinds of pitfalls attendant upon concern with rituals and cosmological mentalities in the analysis of state power. In his careful and – in his own terms – cosmological analysis of the traditional kingdoms of Southeast Asia, Tambiah develops the idea of a set of "pulsating galactic polities" (Tambiah 1976, 1977). He sketches the way in which cultural models following the mandala pattern provide a recurring design at various levels, but emphasizes that this recurring design is always "the reflection of the multifaceted polyvalence built into the dominant indigenous concepts" (1977, 91). As he says, "the cultural model and the pragmatic parameters are in concordance and buttress one another, and cannot be disaggregated" (ibid.). Given these caveats, Tambiah tries to relate both the representation and actualization of the cultural model to his own analytic categories, thereby surmounting the difficulties of Western theoretical constructions by bracketing them out of his analysis, at least at certain key moments. When Tambiah constructs Thai concepts, he goes on to note that "if their meanings are mapped onto a western conceptual grid of 'levels,' we shall have to say that they are, in varying degrees of overlap, at once cosmological, territorial, politico-economic, administrative, and so on" (1977, 73). By bracketing out Western analytic constructions, however, Tambiah does not mean to ignore them. Rather, he recognizes his role as both translator and analyst, and thus tacks back and forth in an effort to demonstrate that the "key concepts do resonate with the polyvalent implications that we attribute to these levels." What results is less elegant than Geertz's analysis, but more revealing too in its depiction of the analytical process.

The only work that provides similar inspiration for students of India is Burton Stein's *Peasant state and society in medieval south India* (1980). Stein uses the model of the segmentary state developed by Aidan Southall in his work on East Africa (1956). Southall developed his theory to characterize the Alur State, which neither fitted the requirements of the unitary state nor conformed in structure to African societies which have been classified as stateless, or acephalous (Fortes and Evans-Pritchard 1940). The "segmentary state" was proposed as an intermediary category between these two ideal-typical poles. Stein was attracted to the segmentary state hypothesis because it provides an alternative to the terms "centralized," "bureaucratized," or "feudal," which he felt had been widely and wrongly applied in the Indian context.

Stein uses the "segmentary state" as an immensely powerful deconstructive tool and as a way to explicate the structure of locality organization in medieval Cola times. And he does not follow the model blindly, for he is brilliantly clear about the particularities of the south Indian historical experience. However, the model itself facilitates neither the detailed analysis of change or variation in the Indian state nor a complete appreciation of the cultural as well as socio-political mechanisms that were involved in the distribution and exercise of political authority throughout Indian society. Perhaps even more critically, Stein's use of the model reproduces the separation of "real" from "ritual" sovereignty, postulating a state that is fundamentally based on ceremony. Stein is correct to locate agrarian management in locally based "ethnic-territorial" units, and he provides many of the signposts that have made this study possible. But he too sees local society largely as autonomous from the state, and the state itself appears to be weaker than its impressive durability and penetration otherwise suggest.

In this book I have proposed the need for a totalizing analysis, one which in the Indian case is sensitive to the complex interweaving of ritual-symbolic forms with the so-called actual mechanisms of state power. I have shown that the shared sovereignty of overlord, king, chief, and headman was enacted and displayed through gifts and offerings: through privileges, honors, emblems, "material" resources, women, service, and kinship. Indeed, kinship, caste, territorial organization, temple worship, and the growth of protection networks and local chiefship were all variably but powerfully inflected by a discourse of order, control, dominance, and power; this discourse was in turn expressed through, and in, these gifts, offerings, and related political and social processes. I have further shown that the social relations which made up Indian society, far from being "essentialist" structures, were permeated by "political" inflections, meanings, and imperatives. Caste, as it is still portrayed in much current anthropological literature, is a colonial construction, reminiscent only in some ways of the social forms that preceded colonial intervention. Dumont's insistence on the "religious" foundations of hierarchy reflects both post-colonial Orientalist classificatory structures and the depoliticization of Indian society under colonial rule. Thus I have argued that the study of "caste" must be historical.

The death of the old regime came not with the swift slice of the guillotine, but with the slow and blunted chops of colonial contradictions. Colonial hegemony succeeded in part by disguising its own intervention, creating masks that continue to deceive. So I have argued that ethnohistorical perspectives, methods, and concerns are necessary to reconstruct the pre-colonial dynamics of Indian state and society. Ethnohistory can thereby facilitate tasks that have been divided into "historical," "anthropological," and "literary" domains. To study caste, the state, or their textual representations is to study three avataras of the same thing. And colonialism too must be studied, for it is a critical component in the history of mediations and reconstructions.

The key concern in ethnohistory is to represent the complexity, polyvalence, and reflexivity of the past. In order to do this successfully, we must reconstruct our analytic tropes as we use them. As I stated in the introduction, neither "history" nor "anthropology" can be taken as bodies of knowledge to be received and then blithely used. Ethnohistory must risk subversion by its own objects of study. Nonetheless, since I believe that ethnohistory must concern itself with power (whether exerted by analytic techniques or by the forces of the past themselves), the constituted object must never be permitted to speak (or to appear to speak) only for itself; it speaks with "interests" and in situations that must be identified and decoded.

Using textual, ethnographic, colonial, inscriptional, and administrative records I have attempted to present a picture of a relatively small south Indian state which differs from medieval or early modern Western states in certain key respects, as well as from many previous characterizations of non-Western states, big and little. I have for the most part steered clear of such comparative questions as whether the Indian state was weak or strong, not because I am against comparison (all cultural description entails comparison) but rather because I have primarily sought to construct anew the relevancies of Indian state formation. And, far from finding Pudukkottai atypical – an example, however illustrative, of a marginal vestige – I have suggested that its political and social relations reveal modal forms for India in the old regime. I have also proposed that comparative sociology as a general set of preoccupations and analytic conventions must be reanimated by a critical sense of its cultural relativity: in this instance stemming fundamentally from its historical implication in and epistemological derivation from colonialism. However, I do not make a critique of comparative "sociology" to throw it aside, but precisely because it cannot be thrown aside. It is our received history; and it provides our salient categories of discourse about India, about social forms, and about ourselves.

When I first went to the field I had a marvellous informant who came to my verandah each evening with a wonderful story and important new facts. I avidly set up my tape recorder to capture all of his wisdom. It was only after a week or so of nightly sessions that I realized I had heard it, or rather read it, all before. My informant was memorizing portions of the State Manual and then reproducing, sometimes verbatim, whole sections on the history and ethnology of Pudukkottai. I realized then and there that a brief tour of fieldwork was inadequate, indeed that, to paraphrase Pope, a little fieldwork could be a dangerous thing. I subsequently learned that all anthropologists have similar stories; some have found their own ethnographies used as sources for their informants' answers. What I only realized years later, after I was finally able to conduct extensive fieldwork, was that my immediate embarrassment about being misled was based not only on my initial ignorance but on my misplaced empiricism. For I had until then clung to notions of authenticity that turned out to be as spurious as the originality of my first informant's tales. I trust now that I have learned the real lesson. Ethnohistory does not, necessarily, permit us to recover the past as it really was. However, ethnohistory can reveal a complex sense of the historical production and social dimensions of thought and practice. Thus I hope that I have found ways in which we scholars have in the past been misled; but I realize that I have also suggested that the reconstruction of the social and cultural dynamics of the past is always a fragile operation, and must be done over, and over, again.

# Land and privilege: inams in Pudukkottai

Much of our information about the disposition of inams in Pudukkottai comes from the records of the 1888 Inam Settlement. The terms and operations of this settlement were based largely upon those devised by the Inam Settlement Commission in Madras Presidency which had carried out the settlement and enfranchisement of inams in the Presidency in the 1860s (CPRIS). This earlier settlement was the outgrowth of concerns and policies which the British had articulated from the first days of their administration over Madras, namely to abolish all "feudal" forms of agrarian relations, introducing instead proper rights of property. While these concerns and policies were made explicit (as we saw in some detail in Chapter 11), we must keep in mind that the grouping together of all inams in a single category was itself a vital if not verbalized component of the Inam Settlement. In other words, much of our very data is the artifact of a scheme that was designed to eliminate the different kinds and forms of land, privilege, and political relationship that are the subject of much of this book.

The classification of inams in Pudukkottai varied until 1880, by which time there was general agreement between local officials and British agents on basic classes and definitions. The term "inam" was defined in the *Rules for the Settlement of Inams* as meaning "whole villages or small holdings exempt wholly or partially from land-tax" (RSI 1888). As we have noted before, the one common denominator of the variously labelled grants of land concerned their revenue status. Since the structure of much of the data that follows derives from the taxonomies of the settlement, we must lay them out briefly. In the settlement rules, nine categories of inam were listed: (1) "Devadayam," (2) "Chatrums," (3) "Jaghires," (4) "Brahmadeyam," (5) "Oombalam," (6) "Rokkakuthigai," (7) "Amaram," (8) "Ooliems," and (9) "Sundry Inams."

Devadayam lands were divided into two classes: first, lands attached to temples (or mosques) which were under direct state management, and second, lands granted to minor temples which were held by persons who performed worship (puja) or who managed the temples. Lands granted for chatrums (cattirams, or feeding houses for pilgrims and specifically Brahmans), often more generally classified as dharmadayam, were separated into the same two classes. The third category, "Jaghires," was excluded from the 1888 Settlement, though by then the forty-four villages of the Western Palace Jagir (Mel Aranmanai Jagir) had already been assumed by the state. Brahmadeyams were also divided in two: "lands granted hereditarily to Brahmans for subsistence" and "similar lands granted for the performance of some specific service (*vritti*)."

Oombalams (umpalam) were lands held "for actual service rendered or by families of men formerly in service"; rokkakuthigai (*rokkakuttikai*) were lands held "in lieu of a certain amount of salary"; amarams were lands held "for military service by men, who are in the remnants of the old militia of the country"; ooliems (uriyam) were lands held "for service not strictly military, but in connection with the guarding of the Palaces and escorting members of the Royal Family when they go out"; and sundry inams "comprised grants of land for the support of Ooranies or Drinking water ponds or water-pundals and the like" (Ad. Rep. 1881–82). These last five categories, which were said in the Inam rules to be "so mixed up together that it is difficult to draw a distinct line of difference between each" (RSI), were classified according to the nature of the service performed. These groups were functionally defined but instrumentally conceived; each classification was correlated with a particular rule for settlement and enfranchisement. Enfranchisement meant that a title was given in exchange for an agreement that a specified quit-rent would be paid. The amount of the quit-rent was determined both by the functional group of the inam and by whether or not there was a competent heir.

Religious inams were in general considered to be irrevocable. Grants to temples and cattirams were to continue as long as the institutions continued to exist, and gifts to Brahmans were in perpetuity "since the Shastras say that to continue a gift made by another is twice as meritorious as to make a gift himself, and he, who takes away what is given by another, loses even the merit of his own gift" (Ad. Rep. 1881–82; RSI). Service inams connected with religious institutions were to continue as long as the service was properly performed; and no judgement about the necessity of the service would be made if the object of service was deemed religious or charitable. Jagirs and umpalams were "all along considered resumable at the will of the ruling sovereign, though the obligation of service may not be so strict in their case." Finally, the rokkakuttikai, amaram, uriyam, and "sundry" inams were "held under an obligation of service and are equally resumable at the will of the sovereign, no kind of hereditary claims in their case being theoretically admissable." In these cases, the service could be declared unnecessary as well as improperly performed, and cancelled for either reason.

When each inam was actually classified on a village by village basis, a number of extra terms and one additional differentiation were used. For example, the term rokkakuttikai, meaning a kind of "military tenure," was used to subsume Cippanti Ijara inams, which were functionally specified as "in lieu of salary." This latter category was usually used for lands granted to military personnel such as cavalry "Jemedars," "Subadars," and to others serving in the Palace. In addition, umpalams were divided into two categories, kuti and attavanai. The former were said to have been granted for particular services performed locally, the latter for "subsistence" to eminent members of the state.

Thus by 1888 the terms of our discourse have been so long caught up in dialectical interaction between the precolonial system and a developing set of colonial assumptions and taxonomies that it is difficult to reconstruct the relationships of the pre-British period with total purity and accuracy. In interpreting the data provided by the Pudukkottai Inam Settlement, we must not merely be wary of mistaking British classificational theory for pre-British political relations. We must also take the structural changes of the nineteenth century into account. The pacification of Tamil Nadu in the nineteenth century and the creation of a British revenue state brought about major changes at each level of the political system. Political position was no longer determined by military prowess and success but by political relations with the new British overlords. These relations were defined by British notions of precedence, history, and loyalty, and by adherence to British standards of stability, management, and gentry-like behavior. Thus the military system which had played such an important role in Pudukkottai's rise to prominence in the eighteenth century not only became obsolete but was in the nineteenth century considered by the British to be both dangerous and wasteful.

Even so, Pudukkottai's status as a Princely State meant that it was the only Tamil kingdom in which the militia was not completely dismantled. However, it was gradually converted to the uses of a colonized economy. Amarakarars, the former soldiers of the state, were assigned the duties of watching over the harvest and protecting the state's share of grain while it was being transported to and stored in the state godowns (storage houses), tasks made necessary by the amani (share) system of revenue collection on non-inam lands. The military commanders maintained their privileged position in society by virtue of their special relationships to the Raja and to their own retainers as well as their extensive landholding rights, even though these relations and rights became totally abstracted from the original military context. That the changed basis of relations was not realized without anxiety and protest was demonstrated most saliently in 1854, as we saw in Chapter 10. Fortunately, for the purposes of understanding the nature of the eighteenth-century military system, the military inamdars maintained their old titles, and at least until 1854 their old identities. Although the fierce soldiers of old had become village revenue servants and pampered though powerless nobles, we can reconstruct the origins of their inam grants and discern the basic features of eighteenth-century political relations from the entries in the Inam Settlement records.

In spite of all the caveats above, the sources I found in the record offices of Pudukkottai are impressive in the nature and extent of information they provide about local level social and political relations. The principal records for the study of inams are those of the Inam Settlement Faisal Registry. These registers, hand-written in Tamil during the years of the Inam Settlement in the late 1880s, contain an entry for each inam in the state, numbering over 13,000. The entries list particulars about the nature and history of the inam, the extent settled and the excess measured, its classification and the consequent rate and amount of quit-rent assessed on it. The histories of the inams were based on the statements and records filed by the inamdars and on an examination of the pre-settlement records by the settlement officers. There was in addition a village by village ("villagewar") index of inams in which the number and types of inams for each village were listed. From these records, I was able to construct the distribution maps found in this book. I also found and used excerpts from volumes entitled

*Yuttakurippu* dating back to the late eighteenth century in the Settlement Office; these were literally "notes on war" and contained accounts of the names of wars, the number of men furnished by the Rajas, the names of commanders, and their respective assignments and contributions with respect to eighteenth-century military efforts. In addition, I used volumes called *Amara Lavana Pativu*, which had been discarded in a back room of the Government Office buildings. These volumes contained listings of the orders of government sanctioning the transfer of registries of amaram inams on the death of the registered holders. I supplemented the records of the Palace and the Settlement Office with records from the Darbar Office, which housed periodic reports, endorsements on petitions, correspondence of the Diwan, and after 1856 yearly administrative reports submitted by the Diwan to the British Political Agent who was assigned to Pudukkottai. Unfortunately, the clerical scribblings of a century or more ago, even when inscribed on paper that survived the ravages of time, neglect, white ants, rodents, and the tropical cycle of intense dry heat and monsoon damp, were often illegible even to the trained eyes of modern day Settlement Office clerks. But enough survived to paint the picture presented in this book.

There is often no direct proof that inams were given by kings. Nonetheless, even British officers who were reluctant to grant the legitimacy of inams accepted the fact that "these grants ... appear to have been made by the Rajas of the country and their Ministers, for an endless variety of reasons" (CPRIS, 252). As I have argued, we can view these as the products of anarchy and decay only if we accept the political doctrines of early British colonial sociology, which saw the palaiyakkarars themselves as illegitimate. If instead, the eighteenth century is seen as a period when the decentralization of the political world was part of a vital expansion of new, often previously peripheral, political centers and initiatives, then the charge that inams were simply a sign of political weakness holds little or no weight. While the extensive granting of inams would not have been conducive to the development of the kind of state desired by the British in India (and created by the Xing rulers in China), these grants were fundamental to the old regime political system operated by local little kings.

The granting of inams reflected social realities even as it constituted them. Local grants had to be based on consensus while simultaneously creating it. The king's role in the giving of grants was at some times active and at others passive, to the extent of simply giving permission for others to do what they proposed. (The word for permission is *uttaravu*: it also means an order; thus permission in this sense is given by a superior to an inferior and entails more than simple concurrence.) The full range of potential involvement and noninvolvement obtained in the case of inams. But in cultural terms the king was always involved, however distantly. He was the center of the redistributive transactional system.

An interesting point that emerged from an interview I had with the descendant of one of the Pudukkottai Cervaikarars concerned the nature of the participation of village communities in grants which would effect them. This Cervaikarar told me that the granting of inam lands always involved two things: first, the giving of the gift by the Raja; and secondly (and simultaneously) the allowing of, or acquiescence in, it by the village. This second statement was phrased as *inām vitu*: i.e., the inam was allowed to happen, which is not the same as giving permission in the sense of uttaravu. This formulation suggests consensus from below. When I questioned the Cervaikarar about the possibility of the Raja and the village failing to reach an agreement I could not get the Cervaikarar to grasp what I was talking about. While this does not prove that consensus was achieved in every instance (and I have many records of instances of failures for the late nineteenth and early twentieth centuries), it does suggest that the assumption of consensus was an implicit aspect of the granting of an inam.

Inams were given and approved of by kings, often "little kings" as I have defined them. The inam represented the redistribution of the king's right to the first share of the produce of the land, and was symbolic – in this metonymic sense – of the favor of the king, showered down on the subjects of the kingdom much as Kattapomman showered prosperity on his realm. In this sense the little kingdom was a redistributive process in which the relations developed and maintained by the gifting of inam land constituted the essential structure of that process. As decentralized and segmentary as the little kingdom might appear, the king was the symbolic center of this system of redistribution, which, even as it allotted rights to local power configurations, underscored the moral pre-eminence of the king and the king's rights.

Inams – the concretized favors of the king – represented a structure of privilege. Privilege in Pudukkottai was a special dispensation from the king to one or a group of his subjects. This dispensation had manifold implications for the social relations of the subjects concerned in any given transaction. A detailed exploration of each type of inam is necessary to show the particular ways in which this redistributive process constituted a structure of privilege, or to put it differently, the ways in which these favors of the king created and represented privilege.

## The structure of landholding

Whereas Thomas Munro had found in the Ceded Districts further north in the Andhra country that from two or three to up to thirty or forty per cent of the revenue had been written off as inam, in Pudukkottai we find that a far greater percentage of land, and by implication of "potential revenue," had been alienated. Given the steady process of encroachment by village magnates, in the Pudukkottai data from 1888 some figures may be higher than they would have been a century before, but for the most part the structural changes of the colonial period lessened the numbers and amounts of inams. This was most true of military inams, which, though they had not been settled, had not been renewed on a regular basis upon the death of the inamdar after the first years of the nineteenth century.

First, we see in Table 3 that between 1856 and 1882 more than two-thirds of the cultivated land in the state was inam. The drop in 1882 was caused by the resumption of one of the jagirs. Excluding jagirs, we find that just under two-thirds of the cultivated land was alienated. Although on one level jagirs must be

Table 3 *Per cent inam of total cultivated land*

| | Per cent inam of cultivated land – including jagir | Per cent inam of cultivated land – excluding jagir |
|---|---|---|
| 1266/1856 | 71 | |
| 1272/1862 | 67 | |
| 1278/1868 | 69 | |
| 1284/1874 | 73 | 63 |
| 1288/1878 | 75 | 66 |
| 1292/1882 | 67 | 59 |

Table 4 *Amounts and percentages of cultivated land: 1874, 1878, 1882*

| | Fasli 1284/1874 | | Fasli 1288/1878 | | Fasli 1292/1882 | |
|---|---|---|---|---|---|---|
| | acres | per cent | acres | per cent | acres | per cent |
| Devasthanam (temples) | 95,627 | 22 | 95,637 | 23 | 97,565 | 23 |
| Cattiram (charities) | 9,583 | 2 | 9,592 | 2 | 9,580 | 2 |
| Carvamaniyam and Shrotriem (Brahmans) | 44,899 | 10 | 44,899 | 11 | 46,337 | 11 |
| Lands in lieu of salary (military) | 8,126 | 2 | 7,949 | 2 | 7,877 | 2 |
| Amaram (military) | 22,517 | 5 | 22,132 | 5 | 21,548 | 5 |
| Uriyakarar (palace servants) | 8,361 | 2 | 8,310 | 2 | 8,201 | 2 |
| Umpalam (village servants) | 11,747 | 3 | 11,573 | 3 | 11,585 | 3 |
| Jagirs | 109,910 | 25 | 109,910 | 26 | 82,465 | |
| Sundry inam | 2,114 | 0.5 | 2,114 | 1 | 2,154 | 1 |
| Money rents | 38,802 | 9 | 29,028 | 7 | 38,816 | 8 |
| Amani under cultivation (share) | 79,546 | 18 | 74,231 | 18 | 100,225 | 25 |
| Total cultivated lands | 431,232 | | 415,377 | | 430,406 | |
| Amani lands uncultivated | 103,337 | | 124,255 | | 113,225 | |

considered as inam land, namely, as land alienated from the revenue rolls, on another level we must bracket jagirs out of our analysis of the relative distribution of inams since they contained within them inams which paralleled the structure of alienation in the state at large. Although I do not have an exact accounting of the percentages of alienated acreage within jagirs, we can see that if we take the inams within jagirs rather than the jagirs as inams an accurate estimation of the amount of "alienated" land in the state as a whole would fall roughly at around two-thirds of the total cultivated land.

Table 4 shows us the acreage amounts and percentages of different categories of all cultivated land in the state for 1874, 1878, and 1882. In 1874, 25 per cent of all cultivated land was in the jagirs; 22 per cent had been given to temples; 10 per cent to Brahmans, and 5 per cent to amarakarars. We must remember that by 1874 the amarakarars had been reduced to less than half their number in 1800, so that the percentages for this, and other similar categories, are under represented.

In 1874, 27 per cent of all land was assessed for revenue. Only half of this amount, or 9 per cent of the total, was assessed on a money rent. The level of monetization was clearly very low in the countryside, where the Government collected two-thirds of all revenue in grain. The table further reveals that more of the lands classified as share (amani) were uncultivated than cultivated. Whether this indicates a lack of potential cultivators, or the unfavorable nature of the terms and/or land is difficult to know. According to the extensive reports made by a late-nineteenth-century Diwan, Sir Seshaiya Sastri, the problem lay in the nature of the amani lease, whose unfavorable terms created intolerable conditions. But his report is not fully believable. The 1879 settlement of amani lands conducted by Sastri led to heavy assessments on the land which funded Sastri's massive and ambitious building program in Pudukkottai town. After an

Table 5 *Percentage of total inam: distribution of acreage*

| Category of inam | Fasli 1284/1874 per cent | Fasli 1288/1878 per cent | Fasli 1292/1882 per cent |
|---|---|---|---|
| Devasthanam (temples) | 31 | 31 | 34 |
| Cattiram (charities) | 3 | 3 | 3 |
| Carvamaniyam and Shrotriem (Brahmans) | 14 | 14 | 17 |
| Amaram (military) | 7 | 7 | 7 |
| Uriyakarar (palace servants) | 3 | 3 | 3 |
| Umpalam (village servants) | 3 | 4 | 4 |
| Jagir | 35 | 35 | 29 |
| Sundry | 0.6 | 0.6 | 0.7 |

Table 6 *Excluding jagirs, percentage of different categories of land of total inam land and of total cultivated land*

| Category of inam | Fasli 1284/1874 | | Fasli 1288/1878 | | Fasli 1292/1882 | |
|---|---|---|---|---|---|---|
| | per cent of total inam | per cent of total cultivated land | per cent of total inam | per cent of total cultivated land | per cent of total inam | per cent of total cultivated land |
| Devasthanam (temples) | 47 | 31 | 47 | 31 | 47 | 28 |
| Cattiram (charities) | 5 | 3 | 5 | 3 | 5 | 3 |
| Carvamaniyam and Shrotriem (Brahmans) | 22 | 14 | 22 | 15 | 23 | 14 |
| Amaram (military) | 11 | 7 | 11 | 7 | 10 | 6 |
| Uriyakarar (palace servants) | 4 | 3 | 4 | 3 | 4 | 2 |
| Umpalam (village servants) | 6 | 4 | 6 | 4 | 6 | 3 |
| Sundry | 1 | 0.6 | 1 | 0.6 | 1 | 0.6 |
| Lands in lieu of salary | 4 | 3 | 4 | 3 | 4 | 2 |
| Cultivated Cirkar (government) lands | — | 38 | — | 34 | — | 41 |

extensive inquiry in the early twentieth century the assessment rates were radically lowered.

Table 5 shows us what percentage of total inam land belongs to each inam category. In 1874 the jagirs made up 35 per cent of total inam acreage. A staggering amount of land was thus bestowed upon the two collateral branches of the royal family, along with a smaller portion allocated as pin money for the royal women.

In Table 6 jagirs have been excluded. We can now see that 47 per cent of non-jagir alienated acreage was for temples, 22 per cent for Brahmans, 11 per cent for amarakarars, 6 per cent for village servants, 5 per cent for charities, and 4 per cent each for (1) lands granted to eminent state persons and families of military commanders "in lieu of salary" and (2) for palace uriyakarars. Excluding jagirs, therefore, the greatest amount of land was allocated first to temples, and next to Brahmans. Again, however, we must keep in mind that the numbers for "military retainers" were far lower in 1874 than they had been in the late eighteenth century.

Table 7, which shows the percentage of wetland to dryland (*nunja* to *punjai*) in the different categories of land offers dramatic evidence that inam land was neither waste nor inferior land. In 1853, 50 per cent of all inam land was irrigated by tanks or canals, whereas only 32 per cent of all land assessed in the state was irrigated. This later figure excludes the amani land that had been left uncultivated, only 17 per cent of which was irrigated. Table 7 also provides an answer to our earlier question about amani; the disproportionately vast amount of uncultivated amani can be at least in part explained by the fact that the percentage of irrigated land was lower for this category than for any other in any given year. The greatest amount of wetland was in inams given to uranikarars, or those who were responsible for the maintenance of tanks, canals, and other irrigation works; often these inamdars were also village officers such as miracidars. Interestingly, land given for the support of individuals, ranging from palace uriyakarars and amarakarars to Brahmans and village servants, came next, with percentages of wetland in the forties. Land given to temples and charities was relatively dry, only one-third being irrigable. Jagirs had the lowest percentage of wet lands. Lands which were taxed or given on share were considerably drier than inam lands, but much of the dry land was not farmed, so that, for example, share land under cultivation had only a slightly lower percentage of wetland than all inam land given to individuals.

Tables 8 and 9 record data from the village ("villagewar") inam index, and show percentages of individual inams and not of acreage. The data here include inams within the one jagir that remained unresumed in 1888. If we exclude the jagir, we see that 23 per cent of inams were for Brahmans, 20 per cent for temples, 19 per cent for village servants, 18 per cent for amarakarars, 9 per cent for palace uriyakarars, 6 per cent for rokkakkuttikai, and 3 per cent for attavanai, with only 1 per cent for charities. This gives a rather different perspective on the nature of political participation implied by inams, for in individual terms amarakarars made up a large percentage of inam holdings. The average size of inam holdings for temples was much larger than for individuals.

Table 7 *Percentage of wetland in different types of inams*

| | Fasli 1263 (1853) | Fasli 1263 (1853) | Fasli 1284 (1874) | Fasli 1284 (1874) | Fasli 1288 (1878) | Fasli 1288 (1878) | Fasli 1292 (1882) | Fasli 1292 (1882) |
|---|---|---|---|---|---|---|---|---|
| Devasthanam (temples) | | | 33 | | 33 | | 33 | |
| Cattiram (charities) | | | 34 | | 34 | | 34 | |
| Carvamaniyam (Brahmans) | | | 41 | | 41 | | 41 | |
| Lands in lieu of salary | | | 44 | | 44 | | 44 | |
| Amaram (military) | | | 46 | | 46 | | 46 | |
| Uriyakarar (palace servants) | | | 49 | | 49 | | 49 | |
| Umpalam (village servants) | | | 41 | | 42 | | 42 | |
| Jagir | | | 24 | | 24 | | 22 | |
| Urani (water works) | | | 61 | | 61 | | 60 | |

| | | | | | | | |
|---|---|---|---|---|---|---|---|
| Total | 50 | | 33 | 38 | 33 | 38 | 33 | 38 |
| Lands under money rent | | | 31 | | 36 | | 40 | |
| Amani under cultivation | | | 40 | | 38 | | 38 | |
| TOTAL | 32 | | 37 | | 37 | | 39 | |
| Amani uncultivated | 17 | 25 | 14 | 26 | 17 | 26 | 13 | 28 |

Table 8 *1888 villagewar inam index (number and types of inams in each village)*

| Category of inam | Pudukkottai (w/o Jagir) | | Cinnaranmanai Jagir | | Pudukkottai and Jagir | |
|---|---|---|---|---|---|---|
| | Number | % of total | Number | % of total | Number | % of total |
| Amaram<br>(military) | 2,222 | 18 | 413 | 26 | 2,635 | 19 |
| Uriyam<br>(palace service) | 1,171 | 9 | 114 | 7 | 1,285 | 9 |
| Kuti umpalam<br>(village service) | 2,327 | 19 | 442 | 28 | 2,769 | 20 |
| Rokkakuttikai<br>(military and other) | 787 | 6 | 98 | 6 | 885 | 6 |
| Attavanai<br>(military and other) | 393 | 3 | 99 | 6 | 492 | 4 |
| Brahmadeyam<br>(Brahmans) | 2,889 | 23 | 231 | 15 | 3,120 | 22 |
| Devadayam<br>(temples) | 2,526 | 20 | 160 | 11 | 2,686 | 19 |
| Dharmadayam<br>(charities) | 151 | 1 | 13 | 1 | 164 | 1 |
| Total | 12,466 | 99 | 1,570 | 100 | 14,036 | 100 |

## Table 9 *1888 villagewar inam index (by taluk, excluding jagir)*

| Category of inam | Tirumayyam | | Kolattur | | Alankuti | |
|---|---|---|---|---|---|---|
| | Number | % of total | Number | % of total | Number | % of total |
| Amaram (military) | 1.064 | 21 | 951 | 19 | 207 | 9 |
| Uriyam (palace service) | 348 | 7 | 595 | 12 | 228 | 10 |
| Kutiumpalam (village service) | 1,002 | 19 | 895 | 18 | 430 | 19 |
| Rokkakuttikai (military and other) | 336 | 7 | 316 | 6 | 135 | 6 |
| Attavanai (military and other) | 113 | 2 | 156 | 3 | 124 | 6 |
| Brahmadeyam (Brahmans) | 1,327 | 26 | 937 | 18 | 625 | 28 |
| Devadayam (temples) | 891 | 17 | 1,185 | 23 | 450 | 20 |
| Dharmadayam (charities) | 79 | 2 | 51 | 1 | 21 | 1 |
| Total | 5,160 | 101 | 5,086 | 100 | 2,220 | 99 |

Brahman holdings were certainly no larger than amarakarar holdings, and perhaps even smaller. The statistics for the jagir show a relatively higher incidence of inams for amarakarars and village servants and a far lower incidence of inams for temples and Brahmans. The Jagirdars did not, or were not permitted to, set themselves up as little kings in every respect.

Table 9 breaks the distribution of inams down by taluks (see Map 2). There was a slightly higher percentage of amarakarars in Tirumayyam than in Kulattur, and interestingly a much lower percentage in Alankuti. As we noted before, though many of the Kallar natus were in Alankuti it contained none of the lands given to Cervaikarars, who as members of AN actually came from this region. Other percentage comparisons are roughly equal, with Tirumayyam, formerly Pantiyan rather than Cola territory, coming last in lands granted for temples. The distribution of different categories of inam for each taluk can be vividly seen in the first three pie charts (see Figs. 1–3).

Six pie charts (see Figs 5–10), constructed by a computer program which took account of each inam in each village, depict the distribution of different types of inams in different portions of the state, broken down into smaller units than the larger administrative taluks (see Fig. 4). Region 9 is the central southern area of the state around Tirumayyam; region 15 is the area in and around Pudukkottai town; region 14 is the area due west of Pudukkottai, falling on both sides of the river Vellar; region 16 is due east of Pudukkottai, all of it north of the river;

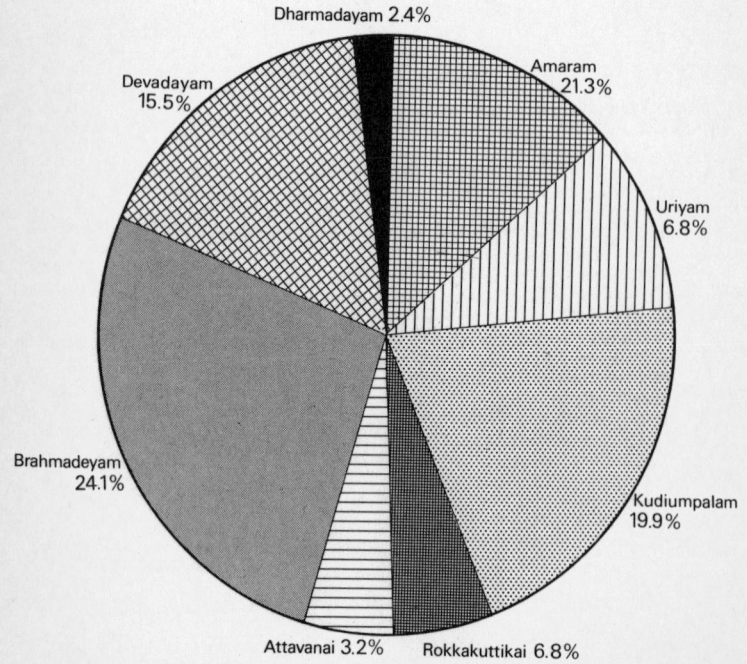

Figure 1  Alankuti Taluk

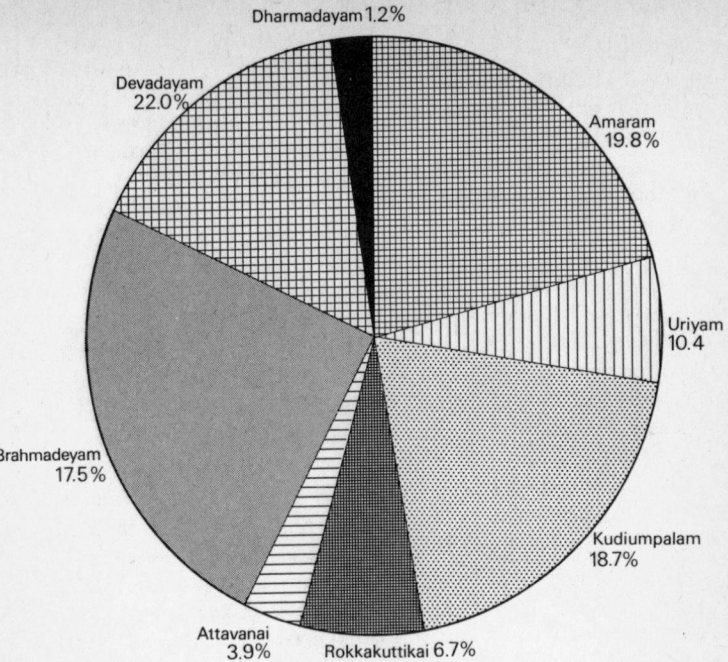

Figure 2  Tirumayyam Taluk

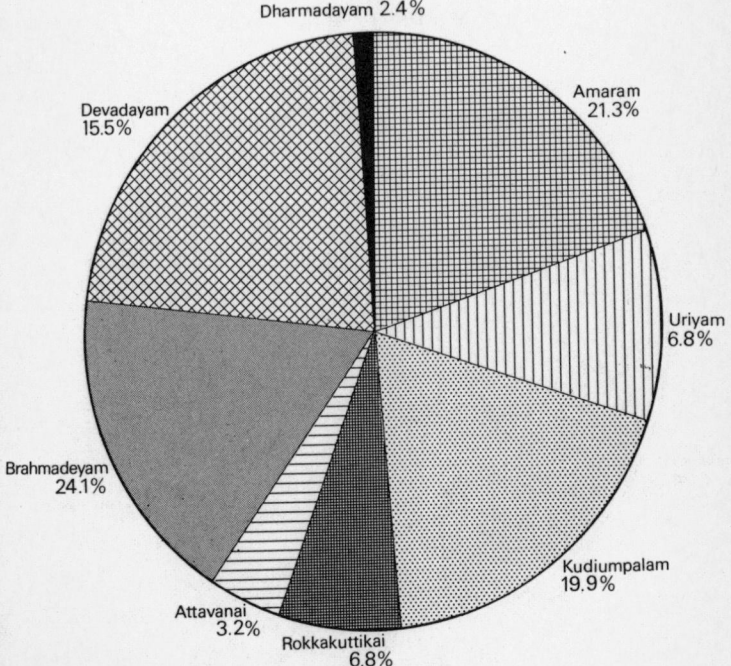

Figure 3  Kulattur Taluk

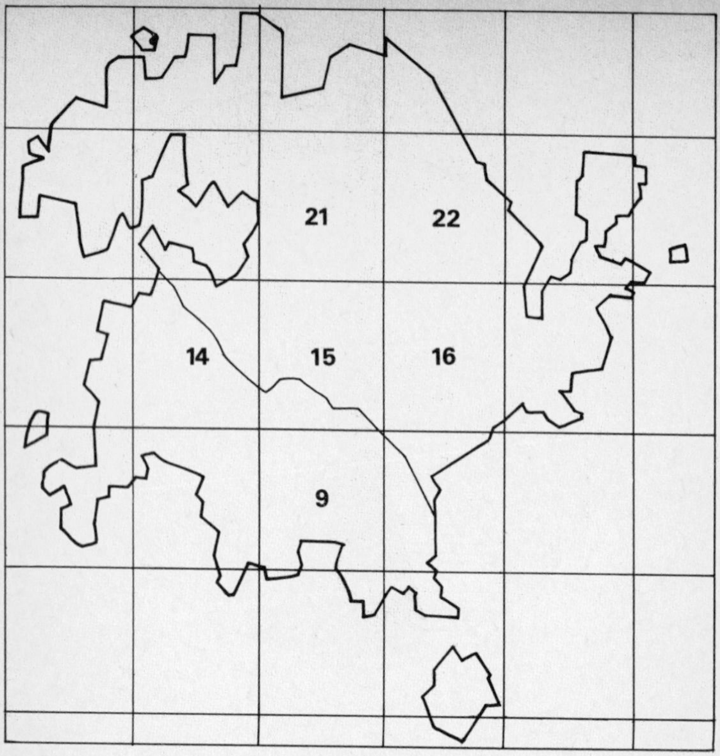

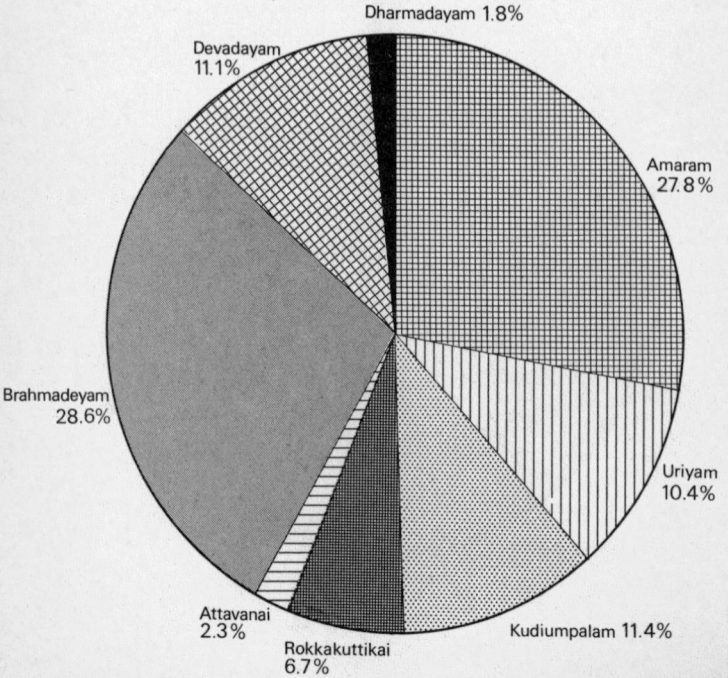

Figure 4 Key to regions for distribution pie charts

Figure 5 Region 9

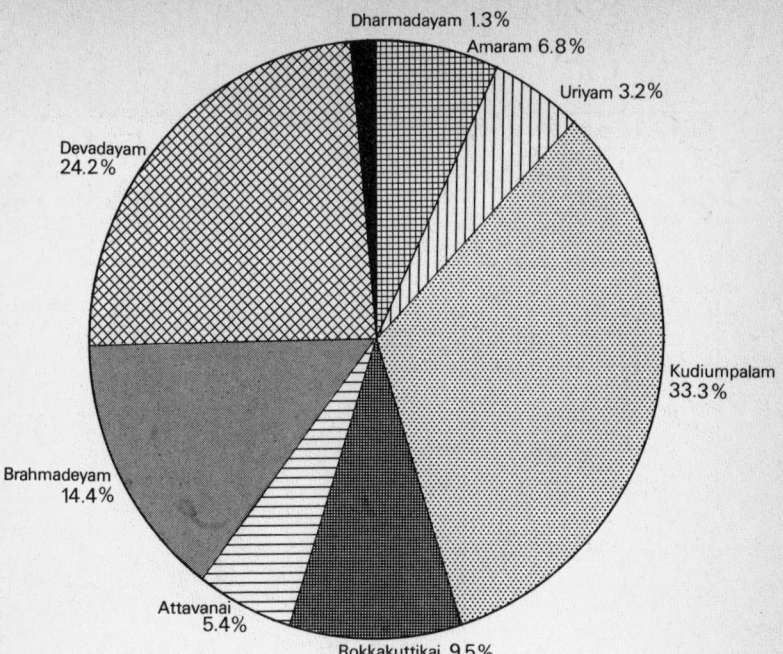

Figure 6 Region 14

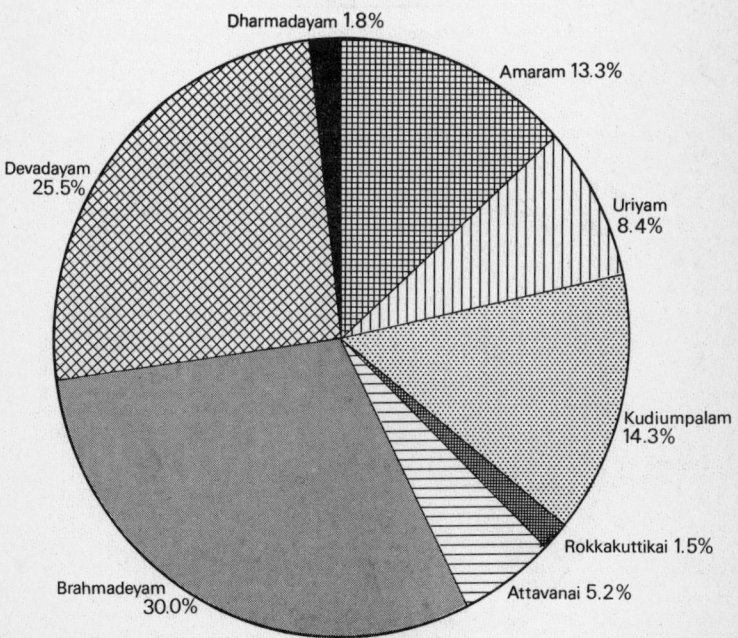

Figure 7 Region 15

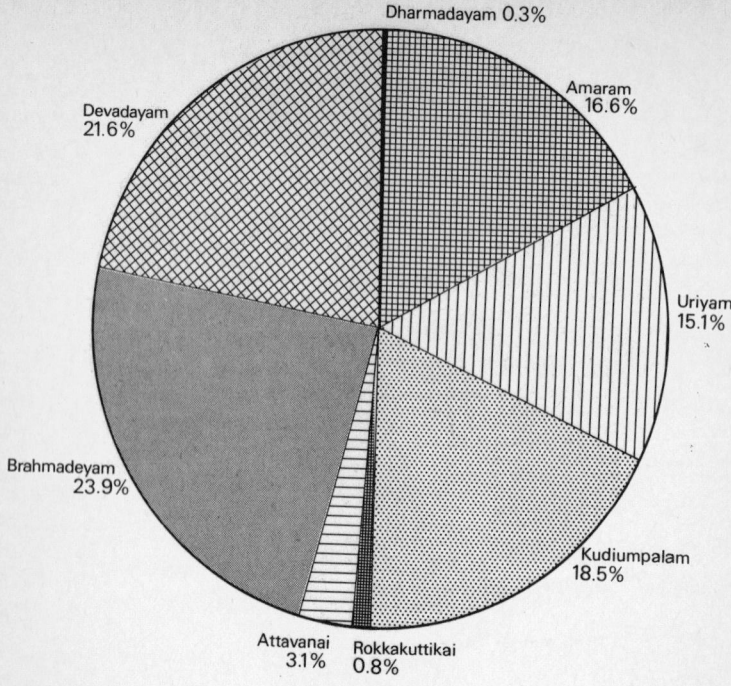

Figure 8  Region 16

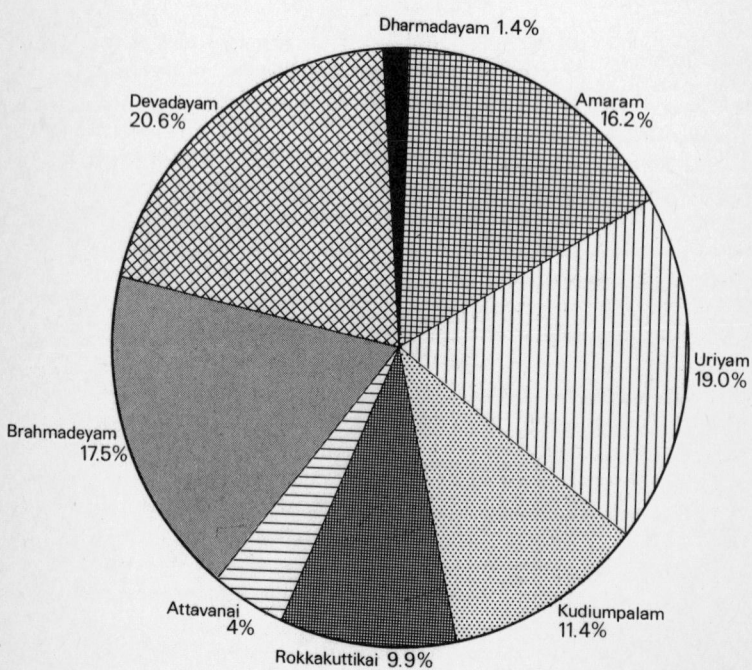

Figure 9  Region 21

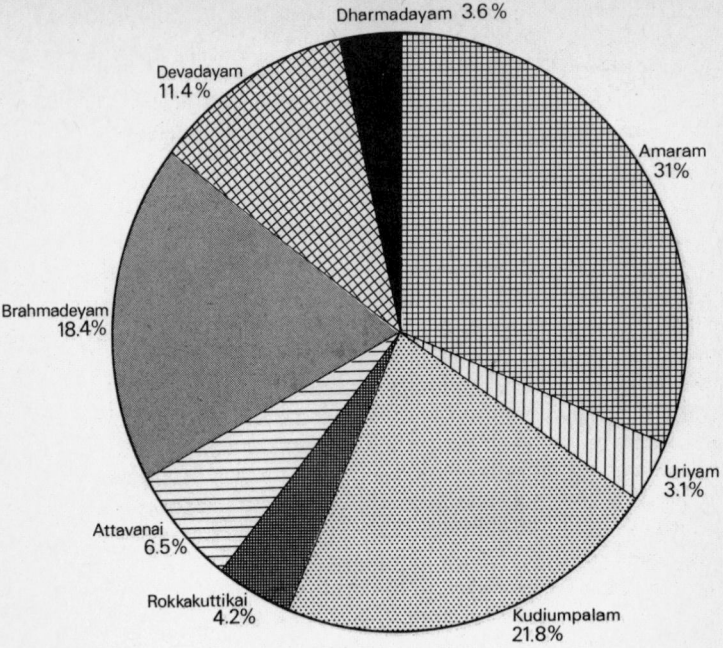

Figure 10  Region 22

region 21 is due north of Pudukkottai, the area around Kulattur town; and region 22 is the northern part of Alankuti taluk, due east of region 21.

Amarakarars figure with greatest relative frequency in regions 9 and 22, and with least relative frequency in regions 14 and 15. This correlates with the absolute numbers of amarakarars as seen in Map 8. The reason for this is clearly military. Concentrations of amarakarars correlate with two factors, (1) the positioning of Cervaikarars and (2) the three strategic zones confronting Ramnad, Tiruccirappalli, and Tanjavur. Village service inams occur relatively evenly throughout the state, as Map 14 also verifies; if they are at all concentrated, it is along the river Vellar, where one would expect to find the largest populations because of the accessibility of irrigation water. Attempted correlations between different types of inams and population are mildly positive but do not in fact suggest that village service inams were any more likely to fall in areas of highest population density than any other type of inam. Brahmadeyams occur with greatest relative frequency in regions 9, 15, and 16, where they are concentrated along the river Vellar (see Map 15). Lands granted to temples occur with greatest frequency in regions 14, 15, 16, and 21. Map 16 shows a concentration of devadayam lands in the western half of the state. This area was not only closer to major temple centers in Tiruccirappalli and Madurai, but was part of Konatu, that part of the state which had fallen under the compass of Cola temple endowment. Brahmadeyams did not last as long as temples, and they reflect a historical geography more in line with recent political history than do temples.

In the text I have already dealt at great length with the structure of "military inams." In this appendix I will present details about the other kinds of inams, in particular village service inams and inams that were granted to Brahmans, temples, and charities.

## Village service and the structure of privilege

Inam lands granted to village servants and officers were variously called umpalam, kuti umpalam, and maniyam. At its simplest level, maniyam, like umpalam, meant land which was granted tax-free; but as we noted earlier it also denoted that the grant was an honorable one. The full range of culturally necessary services in the village community was supported by inam lands and by cuventirams, or specified shares of the village harvest, which averaged between 10 and 12 per cent of grain production in Pudukkottai.

In the Inam records, inams specifying some form of "village service" were categorized as *kutiumpalam*. Kutiumpalam means land granted for the livelihood of those who served the village, or kuti (which means a small group of people related by territorial and/or kinship ties as well as a village or hamlet). Recipients of kutiumpalams included village carpenters, potters, blacksmiths, barbers, washermen, town criers and drum beaters, sweepers, and those charged with the maintenance and operation of irrigational facilities, among others. Village servants and artisans were also given inam grants to provide pots or other necessary articles or services to village temples, and sometimes to provide their trade articles or services to members of the village community. The term kutiumpalam was also used for land grants to village officers such as miracidars (village elders or headmen who acted as revenue officials from the nineteenth century on) and karnams (accountants). Map 14 shows the distribution of kutiumpalams throughout the state; not surprisingly their relative frequency is higher and their distribution more even than that of other inams.

Miracidars had an important role in organizing village rights and responsibilities, though their control over other village servants and artisans was in some instances mediated by the state. In one particular case that took place in 1836 a group of miracidars, though they claimed this right as their own, had to apply to the government to substitute one village artisan for another, implementing their wishes only after receiving the government's permission. After approving the dismissal of a carpenter deemed disobedient by the miracidars, the government, acting upon representations made by the carpenter, later reconsidered its decision and ordered his reappointment (MPC, 4 October 1836).

As we have seen, village service inams were also granted to village servants and artisans for certain agricultural services and other services more directly related to the ritual activities of the village community. Since both these kinds of service were seen as contributing to the prosperity of the village community, they were, in Hocart's terms, "ritual services." One of the most prestigious, and remunerative, of these village services was that surrounding the maintenance

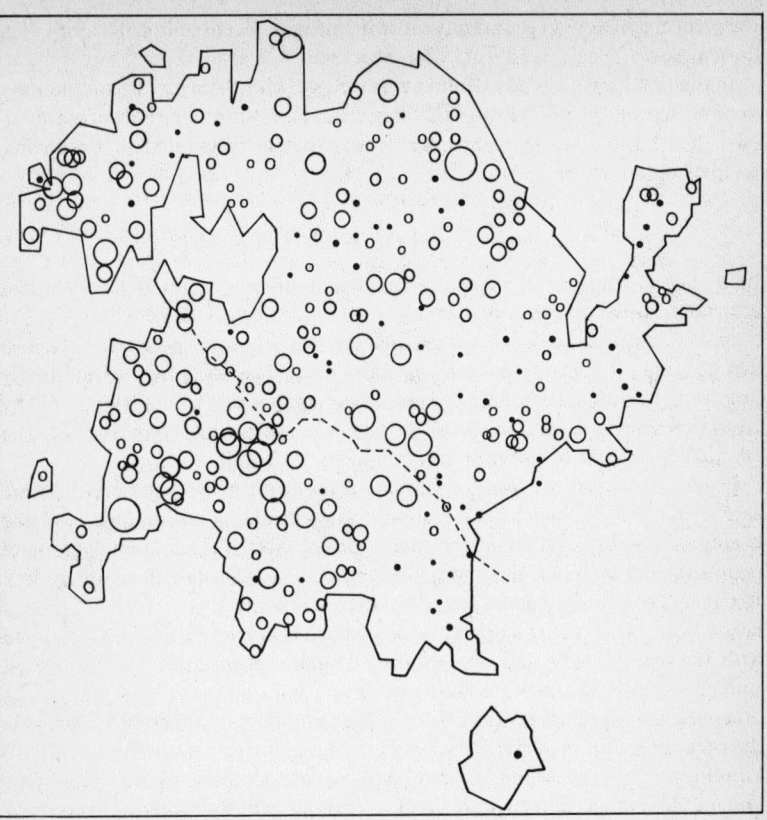

Map 14 Kutiumpalam inams

and operation of local irrigational facilities, such as tanks, canals, and sluices, for which urani maniyams were granted (PFR, no. 3652). This was particularly important in Pudukkottai, where agriculture was so dependent on tank irrigation. Holders of urani maniyams had the highest percentage of wet land of any category of inams at roughly 60 per cent (see Table 7). This is not surprising, the most obvious connection being the proximity of the lands given them to their place of work. But there might be a more potent explanation, already alluded to. Many holders of these maniyams possessed other inams as well, particularly inams associated with village officialdom such as miraci. Miracidars had the power to arrange matters so that they were awarded good wet-land inams. In any case among their "responsibilities" was that of determining the irrigation "murai," the mode of sharing available water within the village. We might also recall that early local headmen, both as protectors themselves or as nattars contracting with araiyars for protection, had to arrange for the maintenance and protection of vital village infrastructures (see Chapter 5).

Grants to village servants for specified "ritual services" were also given to barbers and washermen. In one village an inam was granted to the barber for serving it as a barber and for decorating mud horses in the local Aiyanar temple on festival occasions (CFR, no. 108). Elsewhere, a washerman received an inam for decorating the temple chariot and for supplying torn cloth for torches during the two major processions in the months of Cittirai and Atipuram (PFR, no. 3663). Inams also supported *veṭṭimai* service, namely that of the head (vettiyar) of the Paraiyar caste. He was responsible for organizing all the village services which only the Paraiyars could perform, from beating drums for funerals to removing dead carcasses. His own duties often included those of the town crier (PFR, no. 3659).

Village service inams were also granted to local artisans. There were inams for potters who provided pots for ordinary use and for ritual occasions in the village, local temples, cattirams, and jagir palaces (PFR, no. 4824a; CFR, nos. 164, 137, 151); for carpenters for services to villages and temples, for example the service of fitting out temple chariots for festivals (CFR, nos. 163, 157); and similar inams for blacksmiths (CFR, no. 153). Some inams were exclusively for village service, some for temple service; frequently service to both was specified. Inams called *arttamāniyam* (*artta* means half) were most often either shared equally by two different artisans or held by one artisan for two separate services (CFR, nos. 156, 165).

Another group of village service inams was exclusively for services (uriyam) to local temples. In one case, an inam for *kūttāti* service was shared by three pankalis (coparceners) who respectively played the *mattalam* (tambourine), the *tavil* (a large hand-held drum), and danced the *kūttu* (a kind of folk dance drama) during the two yearly festivals (PFR, no. 5057). A similar inam was granted for the dancing and acting in a particular drama (*līla*) on the closing days of festivals in two local Aiyanar temples (CFR, no. 134). Inams were granted for other services to temples; for example, one *caṅku* (conch) umpalam entailed guarding the temple, blowing the conch, making flower garlands and sweeping the temple floor (CFR, no. 119). Various inams were given for bearing temple deities during processions, dragging temple chariots, putting up sheds and bearing torches during festivals, as well as for cleaning vessels and performing other "menial" tasks in temples (CFR, nos. 152, 154, 155, 159, 161, 162).

Inams called maniyams were also given to pucaris for ritual services in temples. Some of the major copper plate inscriptions record grants by Tondaiman rulers to such temple servants; for example, one plate records the grant of land along with the *makamai* (certain dues given to temples) "for the conduct of puja and festivals to the Lord Kokarnesa and his consort Brihatampal in the Tirukokkarnam temple" (copper plate no. 27, PSM). For less important temples, the king gave small inams for specified ritual services and for the provision of materials necessary for performing them. One inamdar told the Inam Commission that in return for one of his grants he purchased a mud pot every Tuesday, filled it with water, burned incense and camphor, and performed puja with plantain offerings; in addition he offered a goat and ponkal (sweet rice) on four festival days of the year. This particular inamdar also held a *caṅku* maniyam and a *nanatavaṉa* maniyam (inams for blowing the conch and for tending a flower garden) (PFR, no. 4447B).

The Inam Commission reported that another inamdar performed (PFR, no. 5262) "pujas two times a day in the temple with one measure of rice, one-eighth measure of oil and other articles such as camphor, incense, turmeric, perfumes, betel and nuts worth 0.1.0 anna for each puja. He incurs an extra expenditure on festival days such as one-half a Rupee on Dipavali, one Rupee on Civanrattiri, and three-fourths of a Rupee on Navarattiri."

Thus even small locality temples were linked to the king through the inam. These local temples organized the ritual systems of villages, often constituting some of their fundamental cultural coordinates as well: they demarcated boundaries, centers, the relationships of social groups within the village, defining and internally ranking lineages, subcastes, and castes.

Though the exact nature of these relationships in eighteenth-century Puduk-kottai is difficult to determine from our materials, we can appreciate the extent to which village services supported by inam land, as well as by shares (cuventirams) provided by the village community, articulated the structural form of relation-ships within villages as well as between the village and the state. In order to examine further some aspects of these relationships we will now turn to what the British classified as "religious" inams, in marked contrast to the inams we have just considered. "Religious inams" were grants to Brahmans, temples, and charities. While no clear boundary separates many devadayam grants from the maniyam grants mentioned above, the former usually concerned the larger temples in the state, to which the Pudukkottai Raja granted more conspicuous and direct gifts than he did to smaller village temples.

### Grants to temples, Brahmans and charities

From at least the eighth century one of the fundamental requirements of Indic kingship was that the king be a munificent provider of fertile lands to the following: to Brahmans who would study and chant the Vedas, perform sacrifices and provide ritual services for the kings upon which the prosperity of the king and his kingdom depended; to temples which were the centers of worship (puja) and performed major festivals such as Dasara; and to cattirams which provided sustenance for itinerant Brahmans and pilgrims. The merit (punyam) of the king who made the grant could be shared by all those who continued and protected the gift, the duty that was enjoined upon all subsequent kings.

Inam lands held by Brahmans were called carvamaniyam (meaning with full honors, or completely free of tax); *curōttiriyam* (often spelled shrotriem); arttamaniyam (land granted with half of the tax assessment forgiven); *pattavirtti* (often spelled bhattavirthi; *virtti* derives from the Sanskrit *vritti*, which means mode of life, devotion to or occupation with, or to get or procure a maintenance for (Monier-Williams 1979, 1010) and *paṭṭaṉ* means a learned man, or Brahman, and thus this term means something like occupation with learning and the maintenance for such activity); and *cāturpākam* (also spelled chaturbhagam, in

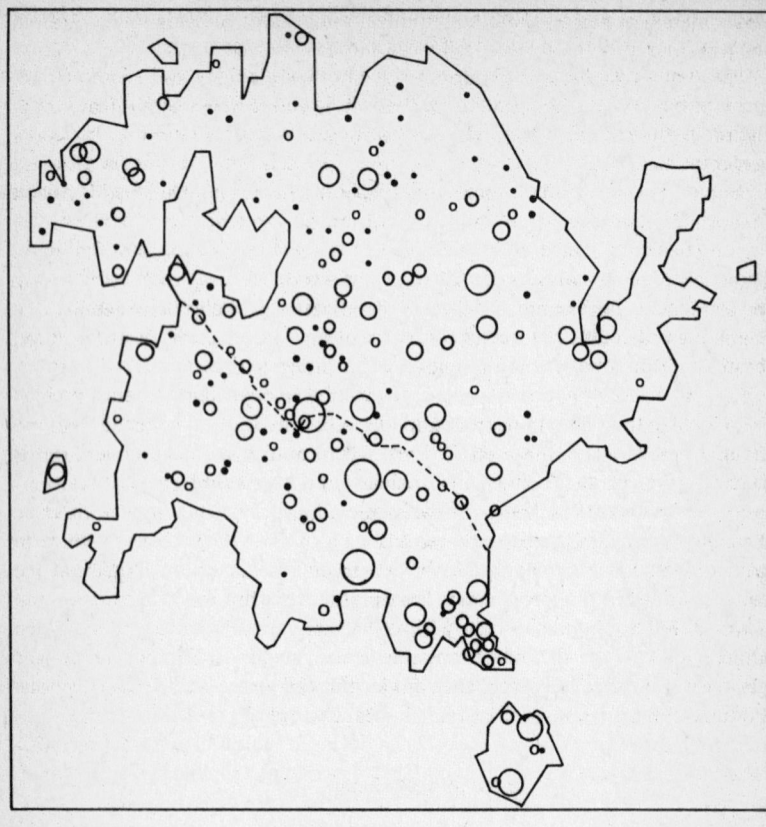

Map 15  Brahmadeyam inams

which *cātur* means a quarter and *pākam* means part, the term thus meaning that
the land is assessed only at a quarter of its value, or that only a quarter of the
usual tax has been forgiven). The most special of these were the curottiriyam
grants to learned Brahmans for their maintenance.

Shortly before the Inam Settlement there were fifty-six whole villages covering
about 44,899 acres classified as Brahmadeyam. Brahmadeyam rights usually
included the usufruct of waste land (*purampoku*), forests, minerals, etc. within
the boundaries of the lands. Map 15 shows the distribution of these grants
indicating that while there were Brahmans throughout the state, they were
concentrated along the river Vellar, and near some of the major temple center
(see for example Ludden's estimations about the settlement of Brahmans in
Tirunelveli District in his 1978 thesis). Lands granted to Brahmans were likely to
be closer to the state's only major river and to the center of villages, to be better
watered by tanks, of higher classification in terms of the quality of the soil, and
relatively secure and productive. Learned Brahmans, usually highly distinguished Vedic scholars, were enticed to Pudukkottai by an initial royal gift of

between twenty and forty acres per family. This largess was especially attractive because they were beginning to suffer the effects of increasing population on their wetland holdings along the river Kaveri. The fixed plots granted to an ancestor generations earlier in the nearby districts of Tanjavur and Tiruccirappalli were becoming untenably small as they were subdivided with each succeeding generation.

Some of these grants were engraved on copper plates (copper plates, nos. 30, 31, Pudukkottai State Museum); others were written orders on palm leaves, many of which were preserved in the Darbar Office. Brahmadeyam grants were almost always considered to be irrevocable and hereditary, except when the bona fides of the initial grant or of the succession were questioned, this being the only culturally acceptable form of revocation. As with miraci lands, brahmadeyam land was initially granted in shares to specified families. These shares were often divided into percentages of shares as increasing numbers of pankalis (shareholders) succeeded to the estate as well as when shares were bought and sold (PFR, no. 8602). Even where proper succession could not be certified, the enfranchisement of brahmadeyam inams under the terms of the settlement only entailed a quit-rent of one-eighth the full assessment, and many Brahman inamdars, particularly those who looked to the towns and cities for education and employment, actively welcomed, if only temporarily, the entry of their holdings into a proprietary land market (this information comes from Thiru P. M. Subramanian Iyer, Retired Head Clerk, Pudukkottai Settlement Office). There were also non-brahmadeyam inams for Brahmans. These were given for some specific reason, such as teaching the Vedas (vedavirtti). One such Pudukkottai inam consisted of 1,424 kulies of wet land granted for the teaching of the Ṛg and Yajur Vedas. Like others of its kind, this inam was not necessarily hereditary, that is, it was not automatically passed patrilineally but was meant to be passed on from one learned Brahman to another (PFR, no. 12025).

Just as the set of services necessary for the daily functioning of temples was provided for by discrete endowments in the form of inams, so was the institution of the temple itself supported by inam. Devadayam lands which were principally held by temples were divided into two classes (RSI): those under the direct management of the state and those under the management of private individuals. The latter, as we have already seen, consisted of small parcels of land and other endowments held directly by priests for maintaining local temples, performing ritual functions, and supporting calendrical festivals. The former class was further subdivided into two categories: the first, called *ulturai* inams, consisted of inam lands held by temple servants in Devastanam villages, and the second category was that of inams reregistered in the name of a temple or of a temple's deity. Fifty-six state temples were included in this latter category, one hundred and twenty-two villages having been granted for their maintenance. There were also endowments (kattalai) for eleven important Tamil temples outside the state (*pararāshtram kōvils*) supporting specified ceremonies. These Tondaiman Kattalais had been instituted, for example, in Citamparam, Madurai, Tiruvayaru, and the shrine in Nerur which was the site of the *cammāti* of the Tondaiman's tutelary guru, Cataciva.

431

In 1881 136 Devasthanam villages were set apart for the support of temples. Twenty-one villages, one in Alankuti taluk, and ten each in Tirumayyam and Kulattur taluks, were alienated for purposes of supporting the Camasthanam temple in Tirukokkarnam, which had a total yearly revenue of Rs. 17,317 in 1888 (these statistics are from a "list of the major religious and charitable endowments under the direct management for which villages were endowed by the rulers" found among the records of the Pudukkottai Inam Settlement). Another fifty-five temples had already been granted 102 villages for their support, with a total value estimated at Rs. 48,238 per annum. Twenty-two villages, with a combined estimated value of Rs. 9,159, were granted to support Tondaiman Kattalais. There were also a variety of other endowments for smaller temples. Map 16 provides a rough idea of the distribution of lands granted to support temple establishments throughout the state.

The second category of "religious and charitable" inams was that for Dharma dayam, gifts for the performance of dharma, usually for cattirams which

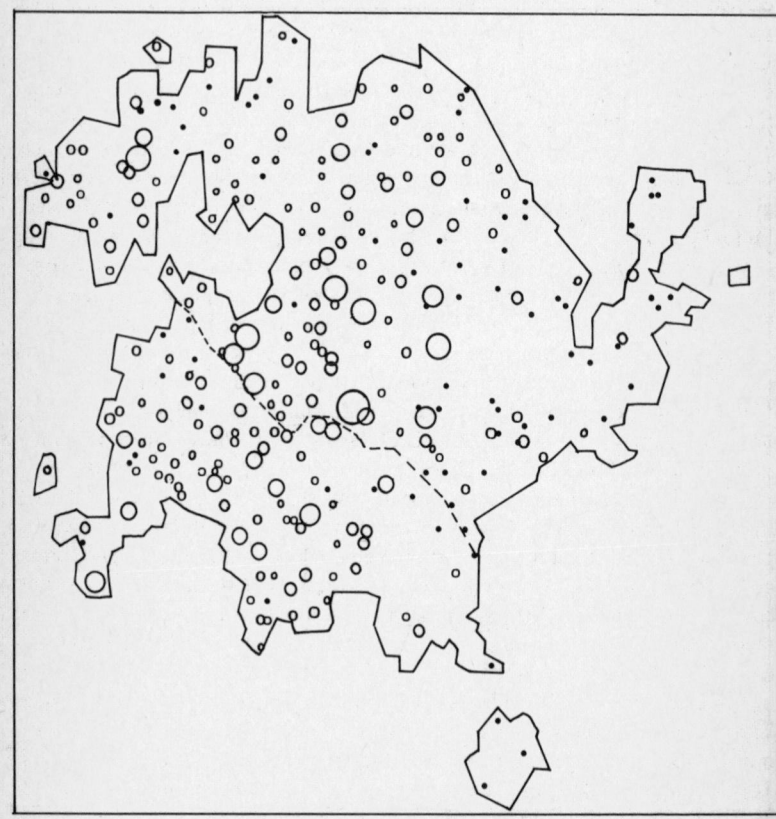

Map 16 Devadayam inams

provided food and drink for itinerant pilgrims and Brahmans. Several major copper plates record grants from a Raja, Vijaya Rakunata Tondaiman Bahadur (1789–1807), to individuals for the establishment and maintenance of cattirams (copper plates, nos. 24, 25, 26, 29, PSM). The inscriptions, which begin with panegyrical prefaces (prasastis) to the Vijayanagara sovereigns, include grants of land in different villages, dues such as makamai, and other endowments, such as oil from the *vāniyas* (oil pressers), vessels, cows, sheep, and specified rights to irrigational facilities. Like the brahmadeyam grants, these gifts were meant to last for ever (copper plate no. 25, PSM):

Until the moon and the sun cease to exist, they are ordered to perform this charity. People can further this charity by their words, by their labor, and by charitable acts [such as adding further endowments]; those who do these things will enjoy the merit of a bath in the holy Ganges, as indeed they will reap the benefit of establishing innumerable Siva linkas at Ramesvaram. Let no one cause harm to this charity ...

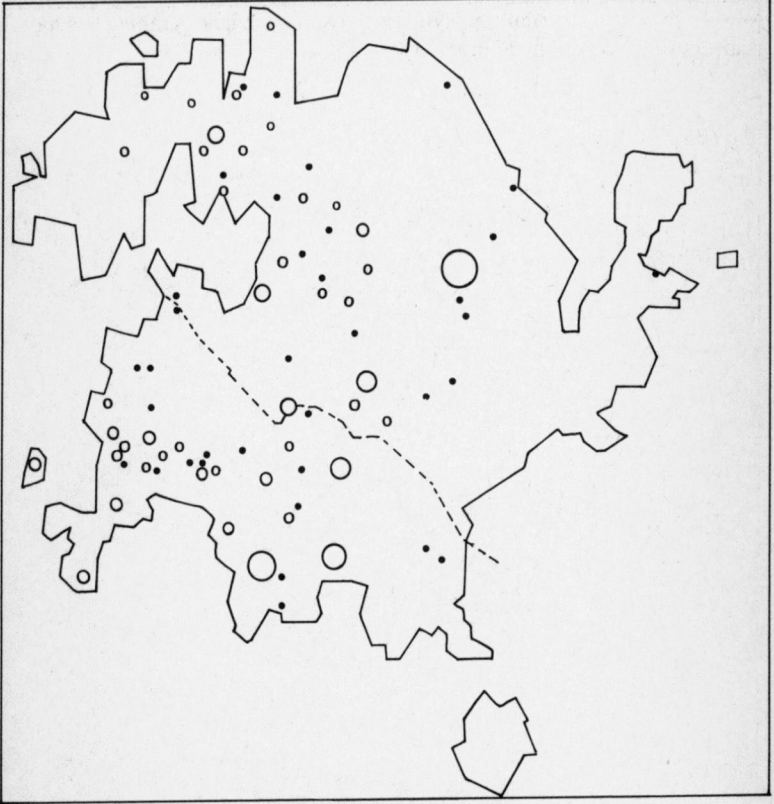

Map 17 Dharmadayam inams

An example of one of the smaller charities which dotted the Pudukkottai countryside is found in the testimony to the Inam Commission (PFR, no. 4819) concerning the "watershed" (*tannīr pantal*) carvamaniyam of Naraciman Ayyankar, who said that "he shared half of his grant with another Pantaram, and that while he gave pure water and buttermilk to thirsty people every day for three months, the Pantaram gave food prepared from rice and lentils to those who desired it."

At the end of the nineteenth century there were ten major and quite a few minor cattirams for which lands had been granted. These cattirams were often located near major temples which were pilgrimage sites, such as the temple in Tirukokkarnam. They were spread out along the main roads leading into Pudukkottai from Tanjavur, Tiruccirappalli, and Madurai, as well as on the road which branched off towards Ramesvaram, one of the major pilgrimage sites in the south. The ten major state-managed cattirams had twelve villages granted to them, eight in Kulattur taluk and two each in Alankuti and Tirumayyam, with a combined value of Rs. 7,283 p.a. Six other villages had been alienated for the support of Hindu sectarian matams and Islamic mosques. Map 17 shows the distribution of dharmadayam inam lands granted to support charities of all descriptions in the state.

# References

Aitchison, C. U. 1930. *A collection of treaties, engagements, and sanads*, 10 vols. Calcutta: Government Press.

Aiyar, R. Sathyanatha. 1924. *History of the Nayaks of Madura*. London: Oxford University Press.

Aiyar, S. Radhakrishna. 1916. *History of the Pudukkottai state*. Pudukkottai: Sri Brihadamba State Press.

*Alakāpuri Zamīntār Vamcāvaḷi*. Madras: GOML, D. 3685.

Appadurai, Arjun. 1974. Right and left hand castes in south India. *The Indian Economic and Social History Review* 11(2–3): 216–260.

 1976. Worship and conflict in south India. Ph.D. thesis, University of Chicago.

 1977. Kings, sects and temples in south India. *The Indian Economic and Social History Review* 14(1): 47–73.

 1981. *Worship and conflict under colonial rule: a south Indian case*. Cambridge: Cambridge University Press.

 1983. The puzzling status of Brahman temple priests in Hindu India. *South Asian Anthropologist* 4(1): 43–52.

Appadurai, Arjun, and Carol Breckenridge. 1976. The south Indian temple: authority, honour and redistribution. *Contributions to Indian Sociology* n.s. 10(2): 187–211.

*Āvuṭaiyārpuram Pāḷaiyakkārar Mallarāca Vamcāvaḷi*. Madras: GOML, D.3685.

Ayyar, K. R. Venkatarama. 1940. *A manual of the Pudukkottai state*, vol. 2, part 1. Pudukkottai: The Sri Brihadamba State Press.

 1944. *A manual of the Pudukkottai state*, vol. 2, part 2. Pudukkottai: The Sri Brihadamba State Press.

 ed. 1938. *A manual of the Pudukkottai state*, vol. 1. Pudukkottai: The Sri Brihadamba State Press.

Babb, Lawrence. 1975. *The divine hierarchy: popular Hinduism in central India*. New York: Columbia University Press.

Baden-Powell, B. H. 1892. *Land systems of British India*, 3 vols. Oxford: Clarendon Press.

Baliga, B. S. 1960. Early land revenue systems in Madras. *Studies in Madras administration*. Madras: at the Government Press.

Barnett, Richard B. 1980. *North India between empires: Awadh, the Mughals, and the British 1720–1801*. Berkeley: University of California Press.

Barnett, Stephen A. 1970. The structural position of a south Indian caste:

Kontaikkaṭṭi Vēḷāḷars in Tamil Nadu. Ph.D. thesis, University of Chicago.

Barth, Fredrik, 1959. *Political leadership among Swat Pathans*. London: The Athlone Press.

Bayley, W. H. and W. Hudleston, eds. 1862. *Papers in Mirasi right: selected from the records of the government and published by permission*. Madras.

Bayly, C. A. 1983. *Rulers, townsmen and bazaars: north Indian society in the age of British expansion, 1770–1870*. Cambridge: Cambridge University Press.

Bayly, Susan. 1984. Hindu kingship and the origins of community: religion, state and society in Kerala, 1750–1850. *Modern Asian Studies* **18**(2), 177–214.

Beaglehole, T. H. 1966. *Thomas Munro and the development of administrative policy in Madras: 1792–1818*. Cambridge: Cambridge University Press.

Beck, Brenda E. F. 1972. *Peasant society in Konku: a study of right and left subcastes in south India*. Vancouver: University of British Columbia Press.

1982. *The three twins: the telling of a south Indian folk epic*. Bloomington: Indiana University Press.

*The Bellary Gazetteer*. 1904. Madras: Government Press.

Béteille, André. 1971. *Caste, class, and power: changing patterns of stratification in a Tanjore village*. Berkeley: University of California Press.

Bharati, Swami Shuddananda. 1942. *Alvar saints*. Ramachandrapuram, Trichy District: Anpu Nilayam Publishers.

Blackburne, Stuart H. 1978. The Kallars: a Tamil "criminal tribe" reconsidered. *South Asia*, n.s. **1**.

Bourdieu, Pierre. 1982. *Outline of a theory of practice*, translated by Richard Nice. Cambridge University Press.

Braudel, Fernand. 1982. *The wheels of commerce: civilization and capitalism, 15th-18th century*. New York: Harper and Row.

Breckenridge, Carol. 1976. The Sri Minaksi Sundaresvarar temple: worship and endowments in south India, 1833–1925. Ph.D. thesis, University of Wisconsin.

1977. Risking incorporation: worship in a south Indian temple. Mimeo.

1978. From protector to litigant – changing relations between Hindu temples and the Rājā of Ramnad. *South Indian temples*, ed. B. Stein. New Delhi: Vikas Publishing House.

1984. Social storage and the extension of agriculture in south India, 1350–1750. Mimeo.

Burgess, James. 1886. *Tamil and Sanskrit inscriptions*. Madras: At the Government Press.

Burrow, T., and M. B. Emeneau. 1961. *A Dravidian etymological dictionary*. London: Oxford University Press.

Caldwell, R. 1881. *A political and general history of the district of Tinnevelly in the presidency of Madras from the earliest period to its cession to the English government in A.D. 1801*. Madras: At the Government Press.

*Census and Dehazada of the Province of Tirunelvelie*, Revenue Department Sundrie, no. 39. Tamil Nadu Archives (TNA).

# References

Chandrasekharan, T. 1954. *Sivagangai-c-Carittira-k-kummi and Ammanai.* Madras: Government Press.

Clifford, James. 1983. On ethnographic authority. *Representations.* **1**(2): 118–146.

Cohn, Bernard S. 1962. Political systems in eighteenth century India: the Banaras region. *Journal of the American Oriental Society,* **82**: 312–320.

1963. Comments on papers on land tenure. *The Indian Economic and Social History Review* **1**(2).

1968. Ethnohistory. *International encyclopedia of the social sciences,* ed. D. L. Sills. Vol. 6. New York: Macmillan.

1970. The census, social structure and objectification in south Asia. Paper read at the Second European Conference on Modern South Asia, Elsinore, Denmark, June 1970.

1977. African models and Indian histories. *Realm and region in traditional India,* ed. R. G. Fox. Durham: Duke University Press.

1980. History and anthropology: the state of play. *Comparative Studies in Society and History* **22** (April): 198–221.

1981. History and Anthropology: towards a rapprochement? *Journal of Interdisciplinary History* **12**(2): 227–252.

1983. Representing authority in Victorian India. *The invention of tradition,* ed. Eric Hobsbawm and Terence Ranger. Cambridge: Cambridge University Press.

1986. The command of language and the language of command. *Subaltern Studies IV,* ed. R. Guha. New Delhi: Oxford University Press.

*Collector's report regarding the Tinnevelly Poligars and sequestered Pollams, 1799–1801.* 1916. ASO-D, no. 339. Tinnevelly: The Collectorate Press. Tamil Nadu Archives.

Conlon, F. 1977. *A caste in a changing world: the Chitrapur Saraswat Brahmans, 1700–1935.* Berkeley: University of California Press.

Daniel, E. Valentine. 1984. *Fluid signs: Being a person the Tamil Way.* Berkeley: University of California Press.

Davis, Natalie. 1981. The possibilities of the past. *The Journal of Interdisciplinary History* **12**(2): 267–276.

Derrett, J. Duncan M. 1977. J. H. Nelson: A forgotten administrator-historian of India. *Essays in classical and modern Hindu law,* ed. J. D. M. Derrett, 3 vols. Leiden: E. J. Brill.

Dirks, Nicholas B. 1974. Brahmans in South Indian history. Mimeo.

1976. Political authority and structural change in early south Indian history. *The Indian Economic and Social History Review* **13**(2): 125–157.

1979. The structure and meaning of political relations in a South Indian little kingdom. *Contributions to Indian Sociology* n.s. **13**(2): 169–204.

1981. Little kingdoms of south India: political authority and social relations in the southern Tamil countryside. Ph.D. thesis, University of Chicago.

1982. The pasts of a *Pālaiyakārar*: the ethnohistory of a south Indian little king. *Journal of Asian Studies* **41**(4): 655–683.

1984. Ritual kingship and civilization: the political dynamic of cultural change in medieval south Indian history. Paper prepared for conference, The Historical Experience of Change and Processes of Reconstruction of Selected Axial Age Civilizations, Jerusalem, January 1984.

1985. Terminology and taxonomy; discourse and domination: from old regime to colonial regime in south India. *Studies of South India: an anthology of recent research and scholarship*, ed. Robert Frykenberg and Pauline Kolenda. Madras: New Era Publications.

1986. From little king to landlord: property, law, and the gift under the Madras permanent settlement. *Comparative Studies in Society and History*, **28**(2): 307–333.

Dreyfus, H. and Rabinow, P. 1983. *Michel Foucault: beyond structuralism and hermeneutics*. Chicago: University of Chicago Press.

Dumont, Louis. 1957a. *Hierarchy and marriage alliance in south Indian kinship*. Occasional Papers of the Royal Anthropological Institute **12**. London.

1975b. *Une sous-caste de l'Inde du sud*. Paris: Mouton & Co. Translated into English as *A South Indian Subcaste*. Delhi: Oxford University Press, 1986.

1958. Hocart on caste-religion and power. *Contributions to Indian Sociology* **2**(2): 45–63.

1959. A structural definition of a folk-deity. *Contributions to Indian Sociology* **3**: 75–87.

1962. The conception of kingship in ancient India. *Contributions to Indian Sociology* **6**. Reprinted in Dumont 1980.

1964. Distribution of some Maravar sub-castes. *Anthropology on the march: recent studies of Indian beliefs, attitudes and social institutions*, edited by Bala Ratram. Madras: The Book Centre.

1980. *Homo hierarchicus: the caste system and its implications*. Chicago: University of Chicago Press.

Ellis, F. W. 1814. A reply to the first seventeen questions stated in a letter from the secretary to government in the revenue department, dated the 2nd of August 1814, relative to the Mirasi right. *Three treatises on Mirasi right*, ed. C. P. Brown. V 4898, IOL.

*Emakkalāpuram Zamīntārutaiya Vamcāvalikkanakku*. Madras: GOML.

*Ērayiram Pannai Citampara Vanniyan Vamcāvali*. Madras: GOML, D. 3577.

Errington, S. 1979. Style in the meanings of the past. *The Journal of Asian Studies* **38**(2): 231–244.

Fabricius, J. P. 1972. *Tamil and English dictionary*. Tranquebar: Evangelical Lutheran Mission Publishing House.

Finley, M. I. 1965. Myth, memory, and history. *History and Theory* **5**: 281–302.

Firminger, W. K., ed. 1918. *The fifth report from the select committee on the affairs of the east India company, 1812*, vol. 3. Calcutta: R. Cambray & Co.

Fortes, M., and E. E. Evans-Pritchard, eds. 1940. *African political systems*. London: Oxford University Press.

Fox, Richard G. 1971. *Kin, clan, Raja, and rule: state–hinterland relations in preindustrial India*. Berkeley: University of California Press.

ed. 1977. *Realm and region in traditional India*. Durham: Duke University Press.

# References

Frykenberg, Robert E. 1977a. Company Circari in the Carnatic, c. 1799–1859: the inner logic of political systems in India. *Realm and region in traditional India,* ed. Richard G. Fox. Durham: Duke University Press.

    1977b. The silent settlement in South India, 1793–1853: an analysis of the role of Inams in the rise of the Indian imperial system. *Land tenure and peasant in south Asia,* ed. Robert Frykenberg. New Delhi: Orient Longman.

Frykenberg, R. E., and N. Mukherjee. 1969. The Ryotwari system and social organization in the Madras presidency. *Land control and social structure in Indian history,* ed. Robert Frykenberg. Madison: University of Wisconsin Press.

Fuller, C. J. 1977. British India or traditional India? An anthropological problem. *Ethnos* **3–4**: 95–121.

    1979. Gods, priests and purity: on the relation between Hinduism and the caste system. *Man,* n.s. **14**: 459–476.

Geertz, Clifford. 1980. *Negara: the theatre state in nineteenth-century Bali.* Princeton: Princeton University Press.

Fullerton, William. 1787. *A view of the English interests in India and an account of the military operations in the Southern part of the peninsula during the campaigns of 1782, 1783, and 1784.* London: T. Cadell in the Strand.

Ganapathi Pillai, W. E. 1890. *Ettaiyapuram past and present.* Madras.

Garu, P. Venkataramanuja Chetty. 1909. *Revenue settlement scheme for Pudukkottai,* 19 December 1909, PDRO.

Geertz, Clifford. 1980. *Negara: the theatre state in nineteenth-century Bali.* Princeton: Princeton University Press.

Gordon, Stewart. 1977. The slow conquest: administrative integration of Malwa into the Maratha empire, 1720–1760. *Modern Asian Studies* **11**(1): 1–40.

    1978. Legitimacy and loyalty in some successor states of the eighteenth century. *Kingship and authority,* ed. J. F. Richards. Madison: University of Wisconsin Publications Series.

Gough, Kathleen. 1981. *Rural society in southeast India.* Cambridge: Cambridge University Press.

Granda, Peter. 1984. Property rights and land control in Tamil Nadu: 1350–1600. Ph.D. thesis, University of Michigan.

Greenough, Paul. 1982. *Prosperity and misery in modern Bengal: the famine of 1943–44.* New York: Oxford University Press.

Guha, Ranajit. 1963. *A rule of property for Bengal: an essay on the idea of the permanent settlement.* Paris: Mouton.

Gunasekara, Alex. 1978. Rajakariya or the duty to the king in the Kandyan kingdom of Sri Lanka. *The concept of duty in south Asia,* ed. W. D. O'Flaherty and J. D. M. Derrett New Delhi: Vikas.

Hardgrave, R. 1969. *The Nadars of Tamilnad: the political culture of a community in change.* Berkeley: University of California Press.

Hasan, Mohibbul. 1971. *History of Tipu Sultan.* Calcutta: The World Press Private Ltd.

Heesterman, J. C. 1978. The conundrum of the king's authority. *Kingship and authority in South Asia*, ed. J. F. Richards. Madison: University of Wisconsin Publications Series.

Hickey, W. 1874. *The Tanjore Mahratta principality in Southern India*. Madras.

Hill, S. C. 1914. *Yusuf Khan, the rebel commandant*. London: Longmans.

*The History of the Western Palace Jaghire, Pudukota State, Madras Presidency* n.d. Trichinopoly: St Joseph's College Press.

Hocart, Arthur M. 1927. *Kingship*. London: Oxford University Press.

1950. *Caste: a comparative study*. London: Methuen and Co.

1968. *Caste: a comparative study*. New York: Russell and Russell. Reprinted in 1968.

1970. *Kings and councillors: an essay in the comparative anatomy of human society*. Chicago: The University of Chicago Press.

Inden, Ronald. 1976. *Marriage and rank in Bengali culture: a history of caste and clan in middle-period Bengal*. Berkeley: University of California Press.

1977. The ceremony of the great gift (Mahadana): structure and historical context in Indian ritual and society. Mimeo.

1978a. Ritual, authority and cyclic time in Hindu kingship. *Kingship and authority in south Asia*, ed. J. F. Richards. Madison: University of Wisconsin Publication Series.

1978b. Cultural-symbolic constitutions in ancient India. Mimeo.

1980. Lordship and caste in Hindu discourse. Mimeo.

1983. Orientalism and India. Paper presented to South Asian Anthropologists Group at LSE, London.

Inden, Ronald, and McKim Marriott. 1974. Caste systems. *Encyclopaedia Britannica* 1.

Inden, Ronald, and Ralph Nicholas. 1977. *Kinship in Bengali culture*. Chicago: The University of Chicago Press.

*An inquiry into the policy of making conquests for the Mahometans in India with the British arms*. 1779. London.

Iyer, P. M. Subramaniam. 1977. *Detailed list of several categories of Inams in the Pudukkottai state*, compiled from 1888 Faisal Registers, P.S.O., May 1977.

Jeffrey, Robin, ed. 1978. *People, princes and paramount power: society and politics in Indian princely states*. Delhi: Oxford University Press.

Kadhirvel, S. 1970. History of the Maravas, 1700–1801. Ph.D. thesis, University of Madras, 1970.

1977. *A history of the Maravas, 1700–1802*. Madurai: Madurai Publishing House.

Kanakasabhai, V. 1965. *The Tamils eighteen hundred years ago*. Tinnevelly: The South India Saiva Siddhanta Works Publishing Society.

Kane, P. V. 1974. *History of Dharmaśāstra*. Poona: Bhandarkar Oriental Research Institute.

Karuttaranku, Nattuppura Iyal. 1977. *Proceedings of Conference on Folksongs*, Ulakattamiraraycci Niruvanam, March 26–27.

Kearns, Rev. J. F., ed. 1873. *Some accounts of the Panjalamcourchy Polegar and the state of Tinnevelly previous to Major Bannerman's expedition in 1798*, *compiled from the records of government*. Palamcottah: Printed by order of Government at the Church Mission Press.

Kessinger, Tom G. 1974. *Vilyatpur 1848–1968: social and economic change in a north Indian village*. Berkeley: The University of California Press.

Krishnaswami Pillai, A. 1964. *The Tamil country under Vijayanagara* (Annamalai Historical Series, no. 20). Annamalainagar: Annamalai University.

Kumar, Dharma. 1965. *Land and caste in south India*. Cambridge: Cambridge University Press.

Leach, E. R. 1961. *Pul Eliya: a village in Ceylon*. Cambridge: Cambridge University Press.

Lee-Warner, Sir William. 1920. *The native states of India*. London: Macmillan.

Leonard, K. 1978. *Social history of an Indian caste: the Kayasths of Hyderabad*. Berkeley: University of California Press.

———. 1979. The great firm theory of Mughal decline. *Comparative Studies in Society and History* **21**(2): 151–167.

Letter from Board of Revenue to Collector Lushington, 4 September 1799, in *Correspondence between Mr. S. R. Lushington, Collector of Ramnad and Poligar Peshcush and the Board of Revenue and the Special Commission on the Permanent Settlement of the Southern Pollams and of Ramnad and Shevagungah Zemindaries in the District of Madura*. Madura: Collectorate Press, n.d., ASO (D)304, TNA.

Lévi-Strauss, Claude. 1967. *Structural anthropology*, trans. Claire Jacobson and Brooke Grundfest Schoepf. Garden City, NY: Doubleday.

Lingat, R. 1973. *The classical law of India*. Berkeley: University of California Press.

Ludden, David E. 1978a. Agrarian organization in Tinnevelly district: 800–1900 A.D. Ph.D. thesis, University of Pennsylvania.

———. 1978b. Mirasidars and government in nineteenth century Tinnevelly district. Mimeo.

———. 1985. *Peasant history in south India*. Princeton: Princeton University Press.

Mahalingam, T. V. 1975. *Administration and social life under Vijayanagar*, part II. Madras: University of Madras Press.

———. ed. 1972. *Mackenzie manuscripts*, vol. 1. Madras: University of Madras.

———. ed. 1976. *Mackenzie manuscripts*, vol. 2. Madras: University of Madras.

Maine, Henry. 1890. *Village communities in the east and west*. London: John Murray.

*Maravar Cāti Vilakkam*. Madras: GOML, R. 370a.

Marriott, McKim. 1965. *Caste ranking and community structure in five regions of India and Pakistan*. Poona: Deccan College Postgraduate Research Institute.

———. 1968. Caste ranking and food transactions, a matrix analysis. *Structure and change in Indian society*, edited by Milton Singer and Bernard S. Cohn. Chicago: Aldine.

Marriott, McKim, and Ronald Inden. 1977. Toward an ethnosociology of caste systems. *The new wind: changing identities in South Asia*, ed. Ken David. The Hague and Paris: Mouton.

Marx, Karl. 1972. The British rule in India. *On colonialism: articles from the New York Tribune and other writings*. New York: International Publishers.

1974. *Capital*. Moscow: Progress Publishers.

*Maturaikkalampakam*. 1968. Madras: Saiva Siddhanta Karakam.

Mauss, M. 1967. *The gift: forms and functions of exchange in archaic societies*, trans. Ian Cunnison. New York: Norton.

McGilvray, Dennis B. 1982. Mukkuvar Vannimai: Tamil caste and Matriclan ideology in Batticaloa, Sri Lanka. *Caste ideology and interaction*, ed. Dennis B. McGilvray. Cambridge: Cambridge University Press.

Medick, Hans. 1985. Missionaries in the row boat? Ethnological ways of knowing as a challenge to social history. Mimeo.

Metcalf, Thomas. 1979. Rural society and British rule in nineteenth century India. *The Journal of Asian Studies* **39**(1): 111–119.

1984. Architecture and the representation of empire: India 1860–1910. *Representations* **6**: 37–64.

Mill, J. 1820. *The history of British India*. London.

Mintz, Sidney. 1985. *Sweetness and power: the place of sugar in modern history*. New York: Viking.

Moffatt, Michael. 1979. *An untouchable community in South India: structure and consensus*. Princeton University Press.

Monier-Williams, M. 1979. *A Sanskrit–English dictionary*. Delhi: Motilal Banarsidass.

Mudaliar, Chandra. 1976. *State and religious endowments in Madras*. Madras: University of Madras.

Mudaliyar, P. K. Gnanasundara. 1940. *Note on the permanent settlement*. Madras: Government Press.

Mukherjee, N. 1972. *The Ryotwari system in Madras: 1792–1827*. Calcutta: Firma K. L. Mukhopadhyay.

Murton, Brian. 1973. Key people in the countryside: decision makers in interior Tamil Nadu in the late eighteenth century. *The Indian Economic and Social History Review* **10**(2): 157–180.

Naidoo, T. Rungasamy, ed. 1874. *Translations, copies and extracts of the several letters in which the services of the ancestors of His Excellency the Maharajah of Poodoocottah are particularly acknowledged and approved by the governors and other public officers of the Honorable East India company and the Nabobs of the Carnatic*. Puducotta: The Sree Brehadamba Press.

*Nātuvakkuricci Pālaiyakkāran Vamcāvali*. Madras: GOML, D. 3586.

Neale, Walter C. 1969. Land is to rule. *Land control and social structure in Indian history*, ed. R. E. Frykenberg. Madison: University of Wisconsin Press.

Nelson, J. H. 1868. *The Madura country*. Madras: The Asylum Press.

Obeyesekere, Gananath. 1967. *Land tenure in village Ceylon: a sociological and historical study*. Cambridge: Cambridge University Press.

O'Flaherty, Wendy D. 1984. The aura of renunciation. *Times Literary Supplement* no. 4 (November 23): 260.

Orme, Robert. 1803. *A history of the military transactions of the British nation in Indostan from the year 1659*. London: John Nourse.

Ortner, Sherry. 1984. Theory and anthropology since the sixties. *Comparative Studies in Society and History* **26**: 126–166.

Pantārattār, T. V. Catāciva. 1966. *Pāṇṭiya Varalāru*. Madras.

Pate, H. R. 1917. *Gazetteer of the Tinnevelly District*. Vol. I. Madras: Government Press.

Perlin, Frank. 1978. Of white whale and countrymen in the eighteenth century Maratha Deccan: extended class relations, rights and the problem of rural autonomy under the old regime. *The Journal of Peasant Studies* **5**(2): 172–237.

———. 1983. Proto-industrialization and pre-colonial south Asia. *Past and Present*, no. 98: 30–95.

Pfaffenberger, Bryan. 1982. *Caste in Tamil culture: the religious foundations of Sudra domination in Tamil Sri Lanka*. South Asian Studies #7, Syracuse University.

Polanyi, Karl. 1957. *The great transformation*. Boston: Beacon Press.

Price, P. 1979a. Rajadharma in Ramnad, land litigation, and largess. *Contributions to Indian Sociology* n.s. **13**(2): 207–240.

———. 1979b. Resources and rule in Zamindari south India, 1802–1903, Sivagangai and Ramnad as kingdoms under the Raj. Ph.D. thesis, University of Wisconsin.

Rabinow, Paul. 1977. *Reflections on fieldwork in Morocco*. Berkeley: University of California Press.

Rajayyan, K. 1971. *South Indian rebellion: the first war of independence*. Mysore: Rao and Raghavan.

———. 1974. *Rise and fall of the Poligars of Tamilnadu*. Madras: The University of Madras Press.

Ramanujan, A. K. 1973. *Speaking of Śiva*. Baltimore: Penguin Books.

Ramasamy, A. 1972. *Tamil Nadu district gazetteers, Ramanathapuram*. Madras: Government Press.

Richards, J. F. 1976. *Mughal administration in Golconda*. Oxford: Oxford University Press.

Rosaldo, Renato. 1980. *Ilongot headhunting, 1883–1974: a study in society and history*. Stanford: Stanford University Press.

Rudolph, L., and S. Rudolph. 1967. *The modernity of tradition: political development in India*. Chicago: University of Chicago Press.

Sahlins, M. 1972. *Stone age economics*. Chicago: Aldine.

———. 1976. *Culture and practical reason*. Chicago: University of Chicago Press.

———. 1985. *Islands of history*. Chicago: University of Chicago Press.

Said, Edward W. 1979. *Orientalism*. New York: Vintage.

Sastri, K. A. Nilakanta. 1955. *The Cōlas*. Madras: University of Madras Press.

———. 1966. *A history of south India*. Madras: Oxford University Press.

———. 1975. *The Colas*. Madras: The University of Madras.

Schneider, David M. 1968. *American kinship: a cultural account*. Englewood Cliffs, New Jersey: Prentice-Hall.

Scott, James. 1976. *The moral economy of the peasant: rebellion and subsistence in southeast Asia*. New Haven: Yale University Press.

Sewell, R. 1970. *A forgotten empire*. New Delhi: India Book House.

Sewell, W. 1981. *Work and revolution in France*. Cambridge: Cambridge University Press.

Shulman, David. 1980. On South Indian bandits and kings. *Indian Economic and Social History Review* **17**(3): 283–306.

Siddigi, N. A. 1968. *Land revenue administration under the Mughals, 1700–1750*. Delhi: Oxford University Press.

Siegal, J. 1979. *Shadow and sound: the historical thought of a Sumatran people*. Chicago: University of Chicago Press.

Sircar, D. C. 1966. *Indian epigraphical glossary*. Delhi: Motilal Banarsidass.

Southall, Aidan. 1956. *Alur society: a study in processes and types of domination*. Cambridge: W. Heffer.

Spencer, G. W. 1976. The politics of plunder: the Cholas in eleventh century Ceylon. *The Journal of Asian Studies* **35**: 405–419.

Srinivasachari, C. S. 1943. *A history of Gingee and its rulers*. Annamalainagar: Annamalai University.

Srinivasan, C. K. 1944. *Maratha rule in the Carnatic*. Annamalainagar: Annamalai University.

Stein, Burton. 1960. The economic function of a Medieval south Indian temple. *The Journal of Asian Studies* **19**(2): 163–176.

1968. Brahman and peasant in early south Indian history. *The Adyar Library Bulletin*. (Dr V. Raghavan Felicitation Volume), **31–32**: 229–269.

1969. Integration of the agrarian system of south India. *Land control and structure in Indian history*, ed. R. E. Frykenberg. Madison: University of Wisconsin Press.

1975. The state and the agrarian order in medieval south India: a historiographical critique. *Essays on south India*, ed. Burton Stein. Honolulu: The University of Hawaii Press.

1977. The segmentary state in south Indian history. *Realm and region in traditional India*, ed. R. G. Fox. Durham: Duke University Press.

1980. *Peasant state and society in medieval south India*. Delhi: Oxford University Press.

1981. Munro Sahib: an element of the political structure of early nineteenth century south India. Mimeo.

1982. South India: some general considerations of the region and its early history; the south; and the far south. *The Cambridge economic history of India*, Vol. 1, ed. T. Raychaudhuri and I. Habib. Cambridge: Cambridge University Press: 14–42, 203–213, 452–457.

1984. State formation and economy reconsidered. Mimeo.

Stern, Henri. 1977. Power in traditional India: territory, caste and kinship in Rajasthan. *Realm and region in traditional India*, ed. R. G. Fox. Durham: Duke University Press.

Stocking, George W., Jr. 1983. The ethnographer's magic: fieldwork in British anthropology from Tylor to Malinowski. *Observers observed: essays on ethnographic fieldwork*, edited by George W. Stocking, Jr. Madison: University of Wisconsin Press.

Stokes, Eric. 1978. *The peasant and the Raj: studies in agrarian society and peasant rebellion in colonial India.* Cambridge: Cambridge University Press.

Sturtevant, William C. 1966. Anthropology, history, and ethnohistory. *Ethnohistory* **13**:1–51.

Tambiah, Stanley J. 1976. *World conqueror and world renouncer: a study of Buddhism and polity in Thailand against a historical background.* Cambridge: Cambridge University Press.

——— 1977. The galactic polity: the structure of traditional kingdoms in southeast Asia. *Anthropology and the climate of opinion*, ed. M. Freed. Annls of the New York Academy of Sciences 293.

Taussig, Michael T. 1983. *The devil and commodity fetishism in South America.* Chapel Hill: The University of North Carolina Press.

Taylor, Rev. W. 1835. *Oriental historical manuscripts in the Tamil language.* Madras.

——— 1858. *A catalogue raisonée of oriental manuscripts in the Library of the (late) college, Ft. St. George.* Madras.

Thurston, Edgar. 1909. *Castes and tribes of southern India*, 7 vols. Madras: Government Press.

*Tiravankakalampakam.* 1957. Madras: S. Rajam Publishers.

Trautmann, Thomas R. 1981. *Dravidian kinship.* Cambridge: Cambridge University Press.

Tupper, C. L. 1893. *Our Indian protectorate.* London.

Turnbull. 1817. *Geographical and statistical memoir of Tinnevelly.* Palamcottah.

*Ūttumalai Pālaiyapaṭu Vamcāvali.* Madras: GOML, D.3583.

Vanamamalai, Na, ed. 1971. *Vīrapāṇṭiya-k-Kaṭṭapommu kataip-Pāṭal.* Madurai: Madurai Palkalaikkarakam.

——— ed. 1972. *Kancakipu Cantai.* Maturai: Maturai Palkalaikkarakam.

Vansina, J. 1961. *Oral tradition: a study in historical methodology.* Chicago: Aldine.

*Vencata Swara Yettiapah Naicker vs. Alagoo Mootoo Servagarer*, Tinnevelly Court Records, Bundle 62, TNA.

Vriddhagirisan, V. 1942. *The Nayaks of Tanjore.* Annamalainagar: Annamalai University.

Waghorne, Joanne Punzo. 1983. *The naked and the dressed: sacral kingship on the borders of orthodox India.* Mimeo.

Wallerstein, Immanuel. 1980. *The modern world system II: mercantilism and the consolidation of the European world economy, 1600–1750.* New York: Academic Press.

Washbrook, David. 1981. Law, state and agrarian society in colonial India. *Modern Asian Studies* **15**(3): 649–721.

——— 1984. Colonialism, underdevelopment, and the making of a backward economy: the case of south India, 1770–1870. Presented to a Humanities seminar at Caltech, April 30, 1984.

## References

Weber, Max. 1958. *The religion of India*. Translated and edited by Hans H. Gerth and Don Martindale. New York: The Free Press.

White, H. 1973. *Metahistory: the historical imagination in nineteenth-century Europe*. Baltimore: The Johns Hopkins University Press.

Whitehead, Henry. 1921. *The village gods of south India*. Delhi: Sumit Publications. Reprinted in 1976.

Wilks, Mark. 1810–1817. *Historical sketches of the south of India*, 3 vols. London: Longman, Hurst, Rees, and Orme.

Wilson, H. H. 1828. *The Mackenzie collection: a descriptive catalogue of the oriental and other articles illustrative of the literature, history, statistics and antiquities of the south of India*. Calcutta; republished 1882: Madras: Higginbotham.

Winslow, Miron. 1862. *A comprehensive Tamil and English dictionary of High and Low Tamil*. Madras.

Winstedt, Sir Richard. 1969. *A history of classical Malay literature*. Kuala Lumpur: Oxford University Press.

Yule, H., and A. C. Burnell. 1968. *Hobson-Jobson*. Delhi: Munshiram Manoharlal Reprints.

Zvelebil, K. 1975. *Tamil literature*. Leiden/Köln: E. J. Brill.

# Records and abbreviations

*The Baramahal Records* (BR). The ancient records of Salem District, Madras 1906–1920. Section V.

*Chronological List of Inscriptions of the Pudukkottai State* (CLIPS). 1929. Pudukkottai: Sri Brihadamba State Press.

*A Collection of Papers Relating to the Inam Settlement of Madras Presidency* (CPRIS). 1906. Selections from the Records of the Madras Government, New (Revenue) Series, no. 1. Madras: Printed at the Government Press.

*Cinnaranmanai Faisal Register* (CFR).

*Epigraphia Indica* (EI). 1892. Delhi/Calcutta: Archaeological Survey of India.

*Inscriptions (Texts) of the Pudukkottai State* (IPS). 1929. Pudukkottai: Sri Brihadamba State Press.

*Madras Journal of Science and Literature* (MJSL).

*Madras Military Consultations* (MMC).

*Madras Political Consultations* (MPC).

*Madras Political Government Order* (MPGO).

*Madras Political Proceedings* (MPP).

*Madras Residency Records* (MRR). IOL.

*Papers Relating to the Treaty with the Nawab of Arcot and the Zamindaries of Venkatagiri, Kalahasti, etc. 1802–1872* (PRTVK), ASOD–40, TNA.

*Proceedings of the Court of Wards* (PCW).

*Pudukkottai Faisal Register* (PFR).

*The Pudukkottai Law Reports* (PLR). Select decisions of the Chief Court, Pudukkottai, and of the Second Appeal Court. 1926. Vol. XIV. Pudukkottai: The Sri Brihadamba State Press.

Pudukkottai Settlement Office (PSO). 1909. *Revenue Settlement Scheme for Pudukkottai* (RSSP), typewritten report, December 19.

*Report on the Administration of Pudukkottai for the Year, 1881–82* (Ad. Rep.). Pudukkottai Darbar Record Office (PDRO).

*Report of the Devasthanam Committee, Pudukkottai State, 1925* (RDC). 1931. Pudukkottai: Sri Brihadamba State Press.

*Revenue Consultations of the Madras Council* (RCMC).

*Rules for the Settlement of Inams* (RSI). 1888. Pudukkottai: Published in the State Gazette Extraordinary, September 7.

*Selections from Old Records: Papers Relating to the Poligar Wars* (PRPW), ASO(D) 338. TNA.

*Selections from Old Records: Papers Relating to Zamindaries, Mittahs, etc., Tinnevelly District, Board Received* (SORBR). 1934. Madras: Government Press.

*Selections from Old Records: Papers Relating to Zamindaries, Mittahs, etc. Tinnevelly District, Board Sent* (SORBS). 1934. Madras: Government Press.

*South Indian Inscriptions* (SII). 1961. Archaeological Survey of India, Madras.

*Tamil Lexicon* (TL). 1936. Madras: University of Madras.

*Tinnevelly Collectorate Records* (TCR).

# Archives and record offices

GOML Government Oriental Manuscript Library. Madras, University of Madras.
TNA Tamil Nadu State Archives. Madras.
PDRO Pudukkottai Darbar Record Office.
PSO Pudukkottai Settlement Office.
PSM Pudukkottai State Museum.
IOL India Office Library (and Record Office). London.

# INDEX

agamas, 38

agency (kariyam), 45–48, 98–101, 278, 282

agraharam (see also Brahmans), 91, 92, 97

Aitchison, C., 21

Aiyanar, 121, 207, 224, 253, 269n., 271, 297–304, 374–376, 428

Aiyar, R. Sathyanatha, 43n., 45–46, 49

Aiyar, S. Radhakrishna, 30, 43, 45–46, 49, 144, 146, 148, 156, 161–164, 166, 203, 250, 385

Akampatiyars, 118, 160, 173, 262, 267–269, 321

al jivitam, 170–171, 176, 180–181, 191, 251, 325–326, 337, 339, 342, 352

Alankuti, 143, 420–421, 425, 432, 434

amani: 117, 314, 318, 352, 360, 378, 412–413, 415, 417; settlement, 352–353, 360, 389

amarakarar, 118, 168–171, 175, 180–181, 183–189, 194, 266, 291, 309, 312, 314–315, 318–319, 321, 409, 412, 415, 420, 425

amaram, 124, 169–171, 408, 410, 412, 414, 416, 418–425

amildar, 26n.

Ammacattiram, 166

ampalam, 118, 207, 211, 213, 236, 252–256, 258, 263, 265, 277, 280–283, 290–291, 298–304, 358, 365–366, 374–377, 381, 426–427

Ampu kovil, 221, 230–235, 237

Ampu Natu (see also Kallars), 143, 157, 164, 175n., 206

ancestor deities, 207, 221

Antakkulam, 162, 178, 181, 314, 367

antastu, 225, 239, 242, 283

Appadurai, A., 7n., 79n., 134, 212n., 245, 286–288, 290, 354n., 380–381

aracu ancu, 226–227, 229

araiyar, 34, 144–147, 148–155, 157–158, 427

Arantanki, 152

Arcot (see also Nawab), 98

assemblies: locality assemblies (natu, periyanatu), 14, 30, 32–34, 153; communal assemblies (kuttam), 210, 231, 235–236, 279, 281, 363; king's assembly, 225

Atalaiyur Natalvan, 150

atimai, 127, 140, 269–270, 273–280, 379

attavanai, 178, 187, 408, 415, 418–425

authenticity, 406

Avur, 163

Ayyar, K. R. V., 113, 115, 134, 140, 142, 144, 146, 152, 157, 160, 175, 352, 358, 380, 386, 390, 393, 396

Babb, L., 38n.

Baden-Powell, B. H. 118–119

ballads: general, 20, 60–61; Kattapomman ballad, 62–70, 91

Bana, 88, 152

bandits (highway robbers), 5, 74, 78, 84–86, 94–96, 129, 203–205, 240, 242

Baramahal, 327

Barnett, R., 9n.

Barnett, S., 247

Bayley, W. H., 125

Bayly, C., 9n., 54

Bayly, S., 9n.

Beaglehole, T. H., 24

Beck, B., 62, 79, 139, 247, 274

bhakti, 75, 80, 82–85, 95

Bharati, S., 83

Blackburne, J., 343, 346

Blackburne, S., 74

Blackburne, W., 169, 185, 385

blood, 214, 239, 302, 339–340

Bouchet, 163

Bourdieu, P., 12, 133

brahmadeya (see Brahman settlements)

Brahmans: general, 4, 8, 10, 28, 71, 74, 81, 91; gifts to Brahmans, 38–39, 91–92, 94, 103, 129–130, 429–434; Brahman settlements (brahmadeya), 29–31, 91, 94, 103, 120, 141, 149n., 152, 154, 165, 249, 326, 370, 378, 407, 412, 418–425, 429–434; in

450

# Index

# Index

455

# Index

Srirankam, 84, 158

Stanikar (temple manager), 231–232, 235, 294

state (*see also* kingship): theories of state, 3–5, 7, 9, 11, 135–138, 290, 381–383, 401–404, 408, 410, 429

Stein, B., 9n., 24, 27, 30, 32–34, 43, 51, 54, 71, 78–79, 125, 148, 153, 247, 403–404

Stocking, G., 12

Stokes, E., 22, 135–136

subcaste, 14, 72n., 206–208, 213–215, 217–218, 222, 231, 239–246, 252, 264–268, 288, 359, 429; deity, 210

Tambiah, S. J., 402–403

tandal, 325

Tanjavur, 32–33, 49–50, 98, 112, 116, 159, 163–165, 205, 247, 267, 269, 273, 297, 317, 326, 385, 387, 425, 431, 434

Taussig, M., 356

Tawney, R. H., 13

tax-free grants (*see* inams)

Taylor, W., 49–51, 90, 97n.

Tekkatur, 142

Tekkatur manuscript, 139–140, 152

Temmavur, 212, 363–365

temples: general, 14, 29–32, 38, 43, 51, 83–85, 94, 103, 129, 134; in Pudukkottai, 121–123, 128, 145, 148, 152, 196, 207, 210–213, 223, 264, 283, 285–305, 353–354, 407, 412–413, 415, 418–420, 425, 428–434; under colonialism, 358–383; trustees, 206, 230, 371; Kallar temples, 207, 211–213, 218, 221–222, 229–230, 239, 242, 254–256

Ten Teru, 217, 220, 222–230, 235–239

Terketti Kallars, 213

territory, 33, 165, 206, 214–215, 221–222, 249, 255–261, 264–265, 277, 283, 285, 289, 426

text, textuality, textualization (*see also* family histories, ballads), 6–7, 11, 15–16, 56–61, 65, 75–80, 94–96, 106–107, 156n., 405

theatre state, 8, 355, 384, 401

Thomas, K., 11

Thurston, E., 156, 173, 262

Tinnan, 80–82, 84

Tipu Sultan (*see* Mysore Sultans)

Tiruccirappalli, 22, 27, 50, 112, 157–158, 160, 425, 431, 434

Tirukokkarnam, 166, 314, 348–349, 428, 432, 434

Tirumalai Nayakar, 24, 46, 49, 102, 105–106

Tirumalai Tondaiman, 166

Tirumankai Alvar, 83

Tirumayyam, 163–164, 178, 420–421, 432, 434

Tirunelveli, 19, 22, 24, 27–28, 33, 45, 50, 60, 65, 71, 74, 76, 89, 115–116, 160, 163, 173

tirupatam rite, 41, 82, 84

tiruppani, 83, 371

Tirupati, 89, 116, 203, 220

Tiruppuvalaikkuti, 146

Tiravankakalampakam, 87

Tiruvilaiyatal Puranam, 75n.

titles, 65, 86, 93, 98–99, 129–130, 150–151, 158, 164, 173, 191, 196, 244, 326, 388–389

Tondaiman, Radhakrishna (Melaranmanai Jagirdar), 342–349

Tondaiman (Pudukkottai king): 16, 20, 50, 91, 111–112, 116, 122, 130, 147, 152, 156–199, 227n., 237, 248, 250, 265, 285, 309, 316–317, 320–321, 340, 344, 351, 358, 384–397, 429, 431; royal lineage, 224, 226, 228–230, 235–236, 238, 242–246

Tondaiman vamcavali, 77, 156–168

Tontaimantalam, 32, 90, 139, 159n.

toril (*see also* service), 273, 275, 277

Trautmann, T., 10

Travancore, 98

tulabhara, 37

tulapurusadana, 37

Tupper, C., 387

Turnbull, W., 204

Turner, V., 11

Umayanti tank, 148

umpalam (also oompalam and kudiumpalam), 181, 191, 252–253, 340, 342, 407–408, 412, 415, 418–429

untouchables, 127, 272–280, 292, 297

Urali Kavuntars, 269n.

urani maniyam, 119, 415–416, 427

Uriyakarar, 118, 189–192, 266–268, 291, 294, 309, 312, 314, 319–321, 412–416

uriyam (ooliem), 179, 191, 297, 326, 335–336, 364, 371, 377–380, 407–408, 418–425, 428

uttaravu, 410

Uttumalai, 60, 71–97

Vaisnavite, 84, 89, 159

Vaittikovil, 166

Vaittur, 152

# Index

Valaiyars, 33, 112, 127, 141, 174, 205–206, 224, 269–273, 279, 294, 298

Vallampars, 118

vamcavalis (*see* family histories)

Vanamamalai, N., 62

Vanatiraiyar, 142, 152

Vansina, J., 56

Varappur Natu, 208, 213–214

Vata Teru, 217, 220, 222–231, 235

Vatukas, 50, 53, 60, 76, 92, 174, 204, 266

Vedic instruction, 196, 429, 431

Vedic sacrifice, 28, 30, 38

Velars, 269n., 298, 300–303, 374–377

Vellaikurricci, 97

Vellalars: general, 33–34, 71, 90, 253; in Pudukkottai, 115, 130, 139–143, 145, 148–149, 205, 223–224, 247–248, 263, 265, 295; Kavalar, 140, 142; in Ampu Natu, 230–236

Vellar river, 111–112, 148, 149n., 160, 164, 425

Venkannan Cervaikarar, 190, 208–322

Venkateswarar, 89

Vetars, 33, 90, 140

Vettiyar, 127, 276, 428

Vibert, L. A., 391

Vicalur, 147

Vicinki Natu (*see also* Kallars), 143, 206, 249–256

Vijaya Rakunata Raya Tondaiman, 166, 195, 341

Vijayanagara: general, 33–52, 60, 76, 89; Talikota, 35, 43, 45; ritual, 35–43; relations with Nayakas, 43–52, 98–106; relations with Tondaimans, 116, 141, 151–152, 154, 158–159, 167, 198–199, 386–433

village: general, 121, 153, 207, 415, 418–419, 428; assemblies, 126, 153, 210; headmen and officers (see also ampalam, miracidar), 31, 117–119, 128, 130, 141, 206–207, 292–295, 365, 367, 374–377, 426; servants and artisans, 31, 44, 117, 121, 127–129, 140, 269–280, 292–295, 300, 310, 315, 374–377, 415, 418–420, 425–429; deities, 207, 210, 221, 264, 297–298, 304; organization, 213, 215, 217–218, 222, 254, 259, 263–265, 278–279, 285, 288, 368–369, 429

Viraccilai, 147, 165, 262, 264, 266, 367, 372, 374

Viralimalai, 165

Viralur, 166

Virasaivism, 82

virutu (*see* emblems)

Visnu, 28, 30, 36, 75n., 83, 89, 91

Visvanatha Nayaka, 45–46, 96, 98–106, 152

vritti (*see* service), 407, 429

Waghorne, J., 272n., 397n.

warrior rule, 43–52

Washbrook, D., 9n., 23, 54, 355–357

Weber, M. 3–4, 353, 354

Wheatley, W. C., 97n.

Whitehead, H., 298

Wilks, M. 194

Wilson, H. H., 76, 90

Winslow, M., 215

Winstedt, R., 56

worship (*see* puja)

Yusuf Khan (Khan Sahib), 21, 92, 193

zamindars, 23, 26–27, 77, 95–96, 239, 317, 327–328, 330, 355, 384, 388–389

Zvelebil, K., 83